Dale Baxter
488 - 2477

# DATABASE PROCESSING

## FUNDAMENTALS·DESIGN·IMPLEMENTATION

# DATABASE PROCESSING

## FUNDAMENTALS·DESIGN·IMPLEMENTATION

**THIRD EDITION**

DAVID M. KROENKE

KATHLEEN A. DOLAN

MACMILLAN PUBLISHING COMPANY
NEW YORK
COLLIER MACMILLAN PUBLISHERS
LONDON

Macmillan Publishing Company
866 Third Avenue, New York, New York 10022

Collier Macmillan Canada, Inc.

**Library of Congress Cataloging-in-Publication Data**

Kroenke, David.
    Database processing: fundamentals, design, implementation / David
    M. Kroenke and Kathleen Dolan.—3rd ed.
        p.    cm.
    Bibliography: p.
    Includes index.
    ISBN 0-02-366871-7
    1. Data base management.    I. Dolan, Kathleen A., 1950–
II. Title.
QA76.9.D3K76 1988
005.74—dc19        87-29372

Printing: 4 5 6 7 8      Year: 9 0 1 2 3 4 5 6 7 8

# Contents

**PART III  USING A DATABASE**　　　　　　　　　　　　　　　　　　　　　**217**

PART VI DISTRIBUTED DATABASE PROCESSING                                    571

Chapter 15    **Fundamentals of Distributed Database Processing 573**

# Preface

Although no particular event marks the birth of database processing, the first database applications were implemented in the day-to-day business world during the years 1968–1970. In the twenty years that have passed since then, the use of database applications has spread tremendously.

In the final analysis, such growth occurred because this technology trades computer resources for human resources. Database processing makes more demands on hardware while it makes fewer demands on people. Database processing substantially increases the productivity of both systems developers and systems users. Since 1968, we have seen a steady increase in the cost of personnel and a dramatic reduction in the cost of hardware. Consequently, companies have sought ways of exchanging computer power for human resources, and many have turned to database processing for just that purpose.

Today, database processing is fast becoming the rule for the development of new computer applications. The advantages so far offset the disadvantages that it has become difficult to justify not using this technology. Unquestionably, today's graduates will encounter database processing in the course of their careers, and knowledge of the subject has therefore become essential.

## THE EVOLUTION OF DATABASE TECHNOLOGY

The development of database technology and its use have progressed in the last twenty years through the efforts of the blind leading the blind. Perhaps it is always that way with new technology. We know we have progressed because we can use this technology to produce effective information systems far more quickly and reliably than we could some years ago. It has been an odd progression, however, because we seem to have backed into this improved position. Twenty years ago we didn't know what we were doing, but we were blessed, in a way, because we didn't know that we didn't know what we were doing. We compensated for our ignorance with gusto, élan, delayed schedules, and projects that exceeded their budgets. Gradually we have learned many of the worst mistakes that we can make and ways of avoiding them much of the time.

We have also learned how to employ the computer to facilitate database development. In fact, the history of database processing can be summarized as the process of moving from a primary focus on the needs of the computer to a primary focus on the needs of people. Each step along this transition created a gap. We filled the gaps with software. For example, in 1971, we were writing re-entrant assembler language code. If it ever worked, the users got whatever was produced. They compensated as well as they could. Today, general-purpose software fulfills the function of the assembler language code and another ten layers or so of software have brought us to the point of automated program generators and graphical database definition tools. We can expect this trend to continue.

The editions of this text reflect this general trend. This edition is far more concerned with the mental set of users than were earlier editions. The evolution of DBMS products has freed us from a need to focus so much on the needs of hardware and software and enabled us to focus more and more on the needs of users. The layers of software that have been thrown in the gaps save us from many of the nitty-gritty technical tasks that had to be performed in the past.

This is not to say that we can ignore hardware and software entirely. It is a question of shades of gray. We still need to be concerned with performance. We still need to be concerned with control over concurrent processing. We still need to know how to express logical designs in terms of the structures available with a particular product. Although the relational model continues to gain prominence, the hierarchical and network data models will be with us for some time to come. Thus, you will find many sections of this text focused on interfaces with the DBMS.

Concern for the needs of the end user is most clearly exemplified in the use of *objects* to provide a framework for database development.

## OBJECT-ORIENTED DATABASE PROCESSING

As stated, this text differs substantially from previous editions. The material has been brought up-to-date, and more material on microcomputer databases and distributed processing has been included. The greatest difference, however, is in orientation. The text presents database technology from the standpoint of objects. *Object structures provide a unifying conceptual theme that greatly simplifies the teaching and learning of database technology.* You can gain a sense of the usefulness of this orientation by reading Chapters 4, 6, and 8.

In brief, the goal of a database is to support applications that the end user finds natural and easy to use. In this sense, ease of use does not refer to keystroke sequences or other human factors, but rather to the logical coherence of the application. The structure a user sees on the computer screen or the printed report needs to resemble a structure in the user's mind. If a user expects an invoice to show invoice data, followed by customer data, followed by line-item data, followed by invoice totals, then all materializations (forms and reports, for instance) must reflect that view. To make this possible, the stored form of the invoice in the database must also reflect that view.

An *object* is a stored data representation of an entity of concern to the user. Examples are INVOICEs, CUSTOMERs, EMPLOYEEs, and ASSETs. Unfortunately, most objects do not conveniently fit into a single file or relation. Object representation usually requires several relations. The invoice, for example, includes data from three relations: INV, CUSTOMER, and LINE-ITEM. Furthermore, objects often overlap. The SALESPERSON object, for example, may include data from the INV relation as well as EMPLOYEE and other relations. Thus, the INVOICE and SALESPERSON objects overlap in that they both include INV data. This means, among other consequences, that changes to INV data must be compatible with the constraints of both of these objects.

The use of objects tremendously simplifies the development of databases and database applications. During requirements definition, the development team works backwards from forms and reports to determine underlying object structures. The use of objects focuses the requirements activity on the specification of the structures that have meaning to the user. Additionally, object definitions are entirely compatible with existing tools, such as dataflow diagrams, as illustrated in Chapter 4.

Once the underlying objects have been identified, they are readily converted into logical database designs. In Chapter 6 we show four fundamental types of objects and provide transformation rules for converting them into relational designs, which can then be converted into hierarchical or network designs, as shown in Chapters 12 and 13.

Additionally, object definitions facilitate the development of database applications, as shown in Chapter 8. The structure of the object determines the structure of forms, reports, and, as implied by M. A. Jackson in 1975, the structure of transaction programs. Object boundaries define boundaries for logical transactions or logical units of work in concurrent processing applications. They also provide a framework for developing referential integrity rules.

## OVERVIEW OF THIS TEXT

The object orientation does not mean, however, that this text is narrowly focused. Our aim is to provide a broad introduction to database technology using objects as a unifying framework. This text considers database design and implementation in the context of both microcomputers and main-frames. It includes material on the relational model (especially as this model pertains to database design), as well as on the hierarchical and network models. The goal is to provide a balanced presentation of the database technology that today's graduate is likely to encounter in his or her career.

The first part concerns fundamental concepts. In Chapter 1 we introduce database processing and discuss its nature, advantages, and disadvantages. Chapter 2 describes database applications. This chapter has two major goals. First, because databases exist to support applications, this chapter presents the end goal of the database development effort. This chapter shows the student what we want to produce. Thus, it shows the top of the mountain before we descend into the trees. Second, in almost all cases, application requirements drive database requirements. Thus, to be able to develop databases, we must first understand database applications.

Chapter 3, the last chapter on fundamentals, discusses the components and functions of database management systems. This chapter is important not only because it shows the student what we have to work with, but also because it describes what a DBMS *ought* to be. This chapter will help students understand that what is sometimes marketed as a DBMS is a far cry from what a DBMS needs to be.

The second part addresses database design. Chapter 4 describes database and database application requirements. An understanding of the development and specification of requirements is crucial because these requirements determine the database design. Chapter 4 introduces the concept of *objects,* which we believe greatly simplifies the teaching, learning, and utilization of database technology. Because this concept will be used throughout this text, students need to understand Chapter 4 thoroughly.

Chapter 5 concerns relation definition and normalization. In this text, we use the relational model in two ways. In Chapter 5, we show how this model can be used as a design tool. We use it to express logical (or DBMS-independent) designs. Later, in Chapters 9 and 11, we consider the relational model in a different light—as the basis for a category of DBMS products.

Chapter 6 concludes the design part with a discussion of logical database design. This chapter describes the transformation of the fundamental object types into logical database designs. Thus, Chapter 5 looks at the design of *relations,* and Chapter 6 examines the design of *databases.*

The utilization of databases is the subject of Part 3. Chapter 7 considers database administration. This chapter includes management procedures required of the database administrator as well as the control procedures required of the DBMS. These include the management of concurrent processing, security, and backup and recovery. Chapter 8 addresses the design and development of database applications. Form and report design is discussed in the context of database objects. This chapter also discusses the application's role in the implementation of data constraints.

The next two parts consider database implementation. Chapters 9–11 focus on the implementation of end-user databases, and Chapters 12–14 examine the implementation of organizational databases.

Chapter 9 discusses the end user's interface with the relational model. The essentials of relational algebra are described, and SQL is presented in detail. Chapter 10 considers microcomputer databases and defines three fundamental types: those that stand alone, those that extract data from mainframes; and those that connect to each other via local area networks. Finally, Chapter 11 presents a case example of an end-user database that is implemented with DB2, IBM's mainframe product for end-user processing.

Chapter 12 introduces organizational databases and defines transaction processing. It sets out a sample transaction-oriented database design that is used for this and the next two chapters. Chapter 12 also presents the essential concepts of DL/I, a hierarchical data model that has seen wide use in industry as the basis of IMS. Chapter 13 presents the network model and defines the fundamental concepts of the CODASYL DBTG. Finally, Chapter 14 presents an implementation of the sample database using IDMS/ R, a DBMS based (originally, at least) on the DBTG model.

Chapter 15 introduces the subject of distributed database processing. It builds on concepts from Chapters 7 and 10. This chapter defines distributed database processing, discusses the components and functions of a distributed DBMS (DDBMS), and describes four major goals for the DDBMS. Finally, distributed concurrency control and failure processing are considered in some detail.

Two appendices are also included that carry over material from earlier editions. Appendix A describes input/output processing, and Appendix B summarizes data structures.

## LEARNING ENHANCEMENTS IN THIS TEXT

Teaching and learning database processing can be difficult tasks. Several features of the third edition will help instructors and students use the text effectively:

- Outlines at the beginning of each chapter indicate the general plan for the chapter.
- Clear, realistic examples from both the student's world and the business world occur throughout the text.
- Thorough summaries at the end of each chapter provide a convenient review.
- End-of-chapter questions are divided into two groups that test students' understanding of the chapter and challenge them to use what they've learned.
- A glossary defines all important terms in one place.
- The design and pedagogical use of color facilitates understanding.

## SUPPLEMENTARY MATERIALS

In addition to this text, the publisher has developed a number of supplementary materials. John Windsor and J. Wayne Spence of North Texas State University have developed a casebook to accompany this text. Additionally, SRA has contracted with Microrim Inc. to provide a student version of R:Base System V to adopters of the casebook. For the instructor, SRA offers an Instructor's Guide, which includes overhead transparency masters, and an extensive text bank booklet.

## ACKNOWLEDGMENTS

The authors wish to thank the reviewers and others who have provided insightful comments throughout the development of this text. They are Roy Ageloff, University of Rhode Island; Bob Brobst, University of Texas at Arlington; Thomas L. Brown, East Texas State University; Caroline N. Curtis, Lorain County Community College; Steve Guynes, North Texas State University; Herman P. Hoplin, Syracuse University; Thom Luce, Ohio University; Scott C. McIntyre, University of Colorado, Colorado Springs; Marilyn Moore, Indiana University Northwest; Christopher W. Pidgeon, Hughes Aircraft Company; John Windsor, North Texas State University; and Peggy Dent Wingo, Richland College. Thanks especially to Caroline for assistance in developing the Eastcoast State University Lab example in Chapters 2 and 3.

Thanks as well to Roger Dobratz and Donald Nilson, both independent consultants in Seattle, for their insight into the use of objects for databases and database applications design.

Finally, we wish to thank our editors, Michael Carrigg and Mary Konstant, of Science Research Associates. They both have been most helpful (as well as exceedingly patient) throughout the development of this manuscript. Thanks also to SRA's development and production departments for the excellent design and timely production.

We are particularly grateful to editor Kevin Neely at SRA, whose tireless efforts brought the production together in record time.

# PART I

# FUNDAMENTAL
# CONCEPTS

In Part 1 you will be introduced to database processing. After considering
the role of information in business, you will discover how database processing can facilitate the creation of timely and accurate information. In Chapter
1 you will study basic database concepts; you will learn how to distinguish
a database system from a file processing system. In Chapter 2 you will learn
the components of a database application in the context of a university microcomputer lab. In Chapter 3 you will look behind the user interface to study
the components of a database management system—the complex software
that makes database processing possible.

# Introduction

**D**atabase processing is one of the most important courses in the information systems curriculum. There are several reasons for this.

First, databases can store large volumes of corporate operational data. Such databases become the heart of many transaction processing applications, such as order entry, inventory control, and general ledger accounting. Due to the advantages of database systems over file processing systems, many companies have converted (or are converting) their older file processing systems to database systems.

Second, databases can be queried on an ad hoc basis, making them the foundation for decision-support systems (DSS). Data stored in a database can be readily accessed and processed. Consequently, users can get answers to their questions much faster if the data is stored in a database than they would if it were stored in files. Further, database query languages allow users to be more self-sufficient. Users often obtain answers to their questions without the assistance of an information systems professional.

Third, databases can be implemented on computers of all sizes, making them feasible for almost any business or organization. Thus, the likelihood that you will employ database processing during your information systems or business career is almost certain.

But perhaps the most fundamental reason for studying database technology is that it facilitates the production of *information*. Before proceeding any further, we must understand what information is and why we need it.

## THE NEED FOR INFORMATION

The word *information* comes from the Latin word *informare,* which means "to build form" or "to give structure." Information systems build structures from data by processing it to reveal patterns, trends, and tendencies. These patterns, trends, and so forth are the information that users need in order to perform their jobs. If we did not derive information from the huge volumes of facts we store in our computers (the data), then users would be overwhelmed with details, floundering about to find the knowledge they need. They would drown in a sea of facts.

People strive to make order in their world. Think about the first time you endured the add/drop process during class registration (or the first time you went to an airport, or the first time you did anything new). If your college is like most, the room was large, hot, noisy, and chaotic. People were moving all around you and you didn't know quite what to do. Probably your anxiety level was high as you tried to make any meaning out of the scene before you. Unconsciously, you gathered data through sight and sound, related this data to prior knowledge (such as knowing how people line up and wait their turns or take numbers and wait to be called), compared this new data to your goal (dropping a course, for example), and decided on a course of action (to get into the line marked "DROP COURSE").

The key element in this scenario is the processing of your perceptions. As you gathered data by examining the room, you built patterns and structures in your mind and tried to relate them to structures you already had. You looked for clues in people's behavior. You might have asked somebody for help. If so, your plea was a request for information. You wanted someone who had already processed the scene and built patterns and structures to tell you what they were.

As you gained information about the add/drop process, your uncertainty decreased. When you entered the room, you did not even know in which direction to turn. Once you knew which line to join, you became more sure of yourself. Information reduced your uncertainty.

Computer systems provide a similar function for users. One of the main reasons for information systems is to reduce the user's uncertainty. Let's consider that statement in the context of a business problem.

### An Illustration

Suppose you work for a nationwide record club as the marketing manager in charge of re-released albums of 1960s rock music. Near the end of your fiscal year, you have $50,000 remaining in your promotion budget. You need to decide how to spend that money so that you maximize your sales per promotional dollar. In order to make that decision, you need information.

You have at your disposal many facts, such as the record club's list of all record sales over the past year. Somewhere in that mountain of data there are probably patterns that will help reduce your uncertainty about how to most effectively spend the $50,000. The task you face is to find those patterns.

Figure 1–1a is a partial list of your company's record sales. For each sale it shows the member's name and membership number as well as data

**Figure 1–1**
Developing information

| Customer Number | Customer Name | Album Number | Album Name | Product Code | Amount | Date |
|---|---|---|---|---|---|---|
| 100 | McDonald | 301 | Smooth Stuff | 30 | 1 | 11/30/86 |
| 410 | Arnold | 822 | Rock Stuff | 45 | 1 | 11/04/86 |
| 680 | Edling | 615 | Classical Stuff | 65 | 2 | 12/10/86 |
| 700 | Mellott | 987 | Country Stuff | 70 | 1 | 11/25/86 |
| 550 | Janner | 543 | Oldies Vol. 1 | 30 | 1 | 12/05/86 |
| 360 | King | 833 | Rock Stuff Vol. 2 | 45 | 1 | 11/27/86 |
| 220 | Deeks | 301 | Smooth Stuff | 30 | 1 | 12/08/86 |
| 890 | Manion | 763 | Hard Rock | 45 | 1 | 12/10/86 |

a.  List of record purchases

| Customer Number | Customer Name | Album Number | Album Name | Product Code | Amount | Date |
|---|---|---|---|---|---|---|
| 360 | King | 833 | Rock Stuff Vol. 2 | 45 | 1 | 11/27/86 |
| 410 | Arnold | 822 | Rock Stuff | 45 | 1 | 11/04/86 |
| 890 | Manion | 763 | Hard Rock | 45 | 1 | 12/10/86 |

b.  List of rock record purchases

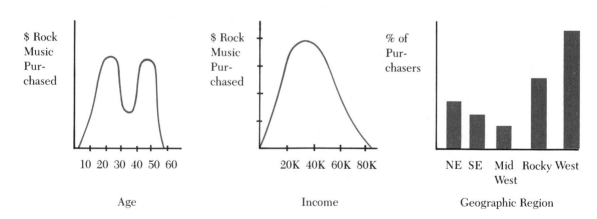

c.  Characteristics of active members

about the record purchased. This is pure data—facts and figures. It is unlikely that this list will enable you to develop an effective promotion campaign because you cannot see any structures or patterns.

Suppose you eliminated from the list all but rock music purchases. Notice that you can do this because rock music is classified as Product Code 45. Then suppose you sorted the list by Customer Number so you could see which customers were most active. The result of these operations is shown in Figure 1–1b.

You have gained information from these operations. You have eliminated clutter (record purchases you are not interested in), and you have organized the remaining data to reveal a pattern (how many rock music purchases were made by each member). However, you still do not have the solution to your problem—namely, how to effectively spend the $50,000. For this you need access to even more data.

Your record club maintains a list of characteristics of purchasers that it has developed through questionnaires and telephone interviews with members. You decide somehow (we'll discuss how in the next section) to combine this customer profile data with the sales data, sort the resulting data by total sales, and finally print the characteristics of customers who have purchased more than $100.00 worth of rock music in the past year. Among other characteristics, you print graphs of the ages, incomes, and geographic regions of the active members (see Figure 1–1c). The result of these operations is information—information that will help you to design a promotion campaign aimed at the segment of the population most likely to purchase rock music from you. Now you have some ideas on how to spend the remaining $50,000 in your budget.

Since this is not a marketing textbook, we will not consider this problem any further. The point here is that in order to reduce your uncertainty you needed information. You acquired that information by processing data in such a way that you identified patterns related to the problem you needed to solve. As promised, the information you found reduced your uncertainty.

In this example we did not specify how the lists of purchases and member profiles were actually stored. They could be in manual files. Imagine how difficult and error-prone it would be for clerks to read receipts for all record sales (there could be thousands of them), copy the information for rock music sales only, then manually sort the selected records and match them with customer profile data (also stored on paper). Obviously, computer technology is needed to perform this process in a timely manner. Remember, it needs to be done before the end of the fiscal year.

Two approaches to this problem could be taken: one based on file processing and the other based on database processing. In the next section we will consider file processing systems. Following that we will consider database processing systems.

## FILE PROCESSING SYSTEMS

Even the earliest business computer systems were used to process business records and produce information. They were generally faster and more accurate than equivalent manual systems. These systems stored groups of records in separate files, and so they were called *file processing systems*. Figure 1–2, for example, shows two file processing systems that might be

**Figure 1–2**
File processing
systems

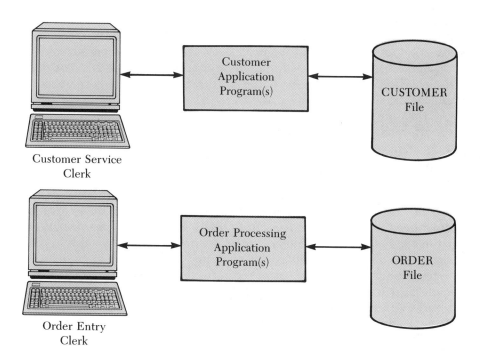

used by the record club. One system processes customer data, and the other one processes order data.

Although file processing systems are a great improvement over manual systems, they do have the following limitations:

- Data is separated and isolated.
- Data is often duplicated.
- Application programs are dependent on file formats.
- It is difficult to represent complex objects using file processing systems.

*Data is separate and isolated.* Recall that as the marketing manager you needed to relate sales data to customer data. For the system in Figure 1–2, this will be difficult. Somehow you need to extract data from both the CUSTOMER and ORDER files and combine it into a single file for processing. To do this, computer programmers determine which parts of each of the files are needed. Then they determine how the files are related to one another, and finally they coordinate the processing of the files so the correct data is extracted. This data is then used to produce the information. Imagine the problems of extracting data from ten or fifteen files instead of just two!

*Data is often duplicated.* In the record club example, a member's name, address, and membership number are stored in both files. Although this duplicate data wastes a small amount of file space, that is not the most serious problem with duplicate data. The major problem concerns *data integrity*. A collection of data has integrity if the data is logically consistent. This means, in part, that duplicated data items agree with one another. Poor data integrity often develops in file processing systems. If a member were to change his or her name or address, then all files containing that data need to be updated. The danger lies in the risk that all files might not be updated, causing discrepancies between the files.

Data integrity problems are serious. If data items differ, inconsistent results will be produced. A report from one application might disagree with a report from another application. At least one of them will be incorrect, but who can tell which one? When this occurs, the credibility of the stored data comes into question.

*Application programs are dependent on file formats.* In file processing systems, the physical formats of files and records are entered in the application programs that process the files. In COBOL, for example, file formats are written in the DATA DIVISION. The problem with this arrangement is that changes in file formats result in program updates.

For example, if the Customer record were modified to expand the ZIP Code field from five to nine digits, all programs that use the Customer record need to be modified, even if they do not use the ZIP Code field. There might be twenty programs that process the CUSTOMER file. A change like this one means that a programmer needs to identify all the affected programs, then modify and retest them. This is both time-consuming and error-prone. It is also very frustrating to have to modify programs that do not even use the field whose format changed.

*It is difficult to represent complex objects using file processing systems.* This last weakness of file processing systems may seem a bit theoretical, but it is an important shortcoming. The records in a file represent something the user needs to keep track of. In this text, we call such a thing an *object*. For example, in Figure 1–2, CUSTOMER records represent customers and ORDER records represent orders. Customers and orders are objects in the user's business world. In the record club example, each object is readily represented with a separate file. More complicated objects are not so readily represented, however.

Suppose we needed to store the representation of a customer invoice. As illustrated in Figure 1–3a, invoices have a fixed-length heading and a variable-length body. The number of lines printed on the invoice depends on the number of purchases the record club member made. Thus, the invoice is a variable-length object. Such objects are difficult to represent with files. One approach is shown in Figure 1–3b. Notice that the file contains two types of records interleaved with one another. This arrangement is difficult to process in application programs. Other objects in the business world are even more difficult to represent in file processing systems.

**Figure 1–3**
Using files to store complicated objects

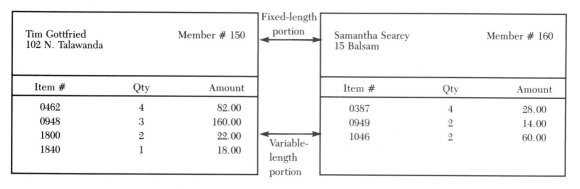

a. Member invoices

| 150 | M | Tim Gottfried | | 102 N. Talawanda | . . . |
| 150 | P | 0462 4 82.00 | 0948 3 160.00 | 1800 2 22.00 | |
| 150 | P | 1840 1   18.00 | | | |
| 160 | M | Samantha Searcy | | 15 Balsam | . . . |
| 160 | P | 0387 4 28.00 | 0949 2   14.00 | 1046 2 60.00 | |

b. CUSTOMER file with Master and Purchase records

## DATABASE PROCESSING SYSTEMS

Database technology was developed, in large measure, to overcome the limitations of file processing systems. To understand how this is accomplished, consider the database version of the record club's system illustrated in Figure 1–4. A new component, the database management system (DBMS), has been added. The DBMS is a program (or a set of programs) that allows stored data to be integrated, reduces data duplication, ensures data integrity, eliminates program dependency on file formats, and allows even complicated objects to be easily represented and retrieved. In short, a DBMS is the program that processes the database.

Notice the difference between the file processing system in Figure 1–2 and the database system in Figure 1–4. File processing programs actually access files of stored data. In contrast, database processing programs call the DBMS to access the stored data. This difference is significant because it makes the application programmer much less concerned with the ways

**Figure 1—4**

Customer and order processing using a database

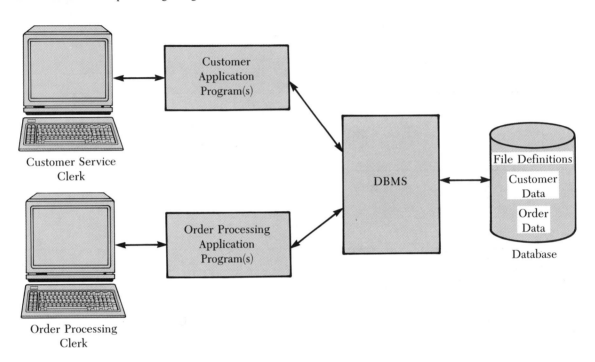

data is physically stored, freeing him or her to concentrate on producing information for the user.

In a database system, all application data is stored in a single repository called the *database*. An application program can ask the DBMS to access customer data, order data, or both. If both are needed, the application programmer needs only to specify how the data is to be combined and the DBMS will perform the necessary operations to combine it. Thus, the programmer is not responsible for the difficult programming needed to coordinate the file processing system in Figure 1–2.

With database processing, duplicate data is minimal. For example, in the record club's database, the member number, name, and address need to be stored only once. Whenever they are needed, the DBMS can retrieve them. And if they are ever modified, only one update will have to be performed. Because data is stored in only one place, data integrity problems seldom occur; there is no opportunity for discrepancies between multiple copies of the same data item.

Database processing eliminates the dependency of programs on file formats. All file formats are stored in the database itself (along with the data—an interesting and powerful arrangement), and they are accessed by the DBMS, not by application programs. Application programs need only include a definition (the length and data type) of each of the data items they need from the database. Unlike file processing programs, database processing programs do not require file and record formats. All of those details are handled by the DBMS. This is called *program/data independence.*

With program/data independence, the changes made to the physical format of stored data have a minimal impact on application programs. Those details are used by the DBMS to update its list of physical record and file formats. For the most part, application programs are unaware that any changes have taken place. It also means that whenever data items are added to, changed, or deleted from the database, only the programs that use those particular data items need to be modified. For applications containing dozens of programs, this can represent considerable time savings.

Finally, as you will learn throughout this course, database technology makes it possible to represent, in a straightforward fashion, the objects found in the user's world. An invoice, for example, can be represented by a combination of data extracted from two record types. As illustrated in Figure 1–5, one record type provides data needed for the fixed-length portion of the invoice, and the second record type supplies data on purchases. There can be a different number of sales records for each member. When an invoice needs to be printed or displayed on a computer screen, the DBMS constructs it by combining the correct data from the two record types.

### The Definition of Database

A *database* is a self-describing collection of integrated records. It is important that you understand each phrase in this definition, especially because the term *database* has been given many different meanings. Although *database* is sometimes used to refer to everything from a collection of index cards to the volumes of data governments collect about their citizens, we will be more precise.

**A Database Is Self-describing.**    A database is self-describing in that it contains, in addition to application data, a description of its own structure. This description is called the *data dictionary* (or the *data directory*, or *metadata*, meaning data about data). The data dictionary makes program/data independence possible.

In this sense, a database is similar to your college's library. A library is a self-describing collection of books. In addition to books, the library contains a card catalog describing the books in the library. In the same way, the data dictionary (which is part of the database, just as the card catalog is part of the library) contains descriptions of the data contained in the database.

Why is this self-describing characteristic of a database so important? For one thing, we can always determine the structure and contents of the database by examining the database itself. We do not need to guess what is there, nor do we need to maintain external documentation of file and record formats (as is done in file processing systems). Second, if we change

## Figure 1–5
Representing invoices with two types of records

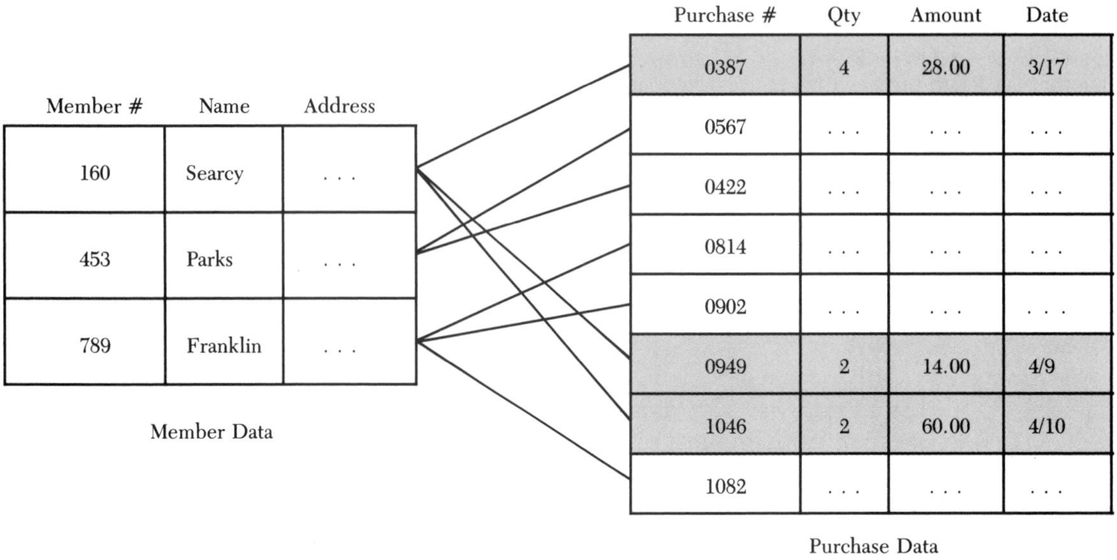

| Member # | Name | Address |
|---|---|---|
| 160 | Searcy | . . . |
| 453 | Parks | . . . |
| 789 | Franklin | . . . |

Member Data

| Purchase # | Qty | Amount | Date |
|---|---|---|---|
| 0387 | 4 | 28.00 | 3/17 |
| 0567 | . . . | . . . | . . . |
| 0422 | . . . | . . . | . . . |
| 0814 | . . . | . . . | . . . |
| 0902 | . . . | . . . | . . . |
| 0949 | 2 | 14.00 | 4/9 |
| 1046 | 2 | 60.00 | 4/10 |
| 1082 | . . . | . . . | . . . |

Purchase Data

a.  Storing invoice data in two record types

| Samantha Searcy<br>15 Balsam | | Member # 160 |
|---|---|---|
| Item # | Qty | Amount |
| 0387 | 4 | 28.00 |
| 0949 | 2 | 14.00 |
| 1046 | 2 | 60.00 |

b.  Constructed invoice

the structure of the data in the database (such as adding a new data item to an existing record), we simply enter that change in the data dictionary. Few, if any, programs will need to be changed.

If you are familiar with COBOL, you know that the structure of the data for file processing programs is described in the DATA DIVISION. Compared to database processing, this practice is inefficient. It's like putting a copy of your library's card catalog in the home or office of every library user. What happens when the library buys a new book? The card catalog needs to be changed in dozens or hundreds of places!

You may have learned in your COBOL or other programming courses that the modern practice is to store the structure of files in a copy library and to extract the file structure from the library at the time of compilation. A similar strategy is used with databases. The structure of the database is extracted from the database and loaded into the program prior to its compilation.

**A Database Is a Collection of Integrated Records.**   You probably know the following hierarchy of data structures: bits are aggregated into bytes or characters, characters are aggregated into fields, fields are aggregated into records, and records are aggregated into files (see Figure 1–6a). It is tempting to say that files are aggregated into databases. Although this statement is true, it does not go far enough.

A database is more than a collection of files. A database includes not only files, but also a data dictionary and a description of the relationships among the records in the files. These relationship descriptions are stored and recalled during database processing (see Figure 1–6b). For example, consider the record club with CUSTOMER and ORDER files. At various times, we may need to know the orders placed by a particular customer or the customer who placed a particular order. A database is able to store these relationships. Thus, a database is a collection of *integrated* records.

In order to represent relationships, the DBMS will probably need to store some additional system data. This data, described in Appendix B, is sometimes called *overhead data*. Overhead data consists of linked lists, indexes, and similar data. Thus, there are three fundamental parts of a database: the application data, the data dictionary, and overhead data.

### The Database as a Model of an Organization

A database contains representations of facts about an organization that can be manipulated to produce information. Each item of data is a tiny measurement of the organization's status at some point in time. The names and addresses of employees, the names and quantities of parts in inventory, and amounts of cash, receivables, and payables are measurements of the status of the company. The collection of all these measurements is a model, or a representation, of the company. You have probably seen physical models

---

**Figure 1–6**

Hierarchy of data
elements

bits } bytes or characters } fields } records } files

a. Hierarchy of data elements in file processing

bits } bytes or characters } fields } records } files

data
dictionary
(database
structure    } database
descriptions)

overhead
data
(relationships)

b. Hierarchy of data elements in database processing

of buildings, boats, and other objects. A database is a data model of an organization.

Data models vary in their completeness. Some are simple and crude. A list of customers and the amounts they owe is a very rough and approximate model of a retail store. A more detailed model would include product, inventory, and accounting data. A very detailed model would include even more data.

**Figure 1–7**
Transactions keep the data model current

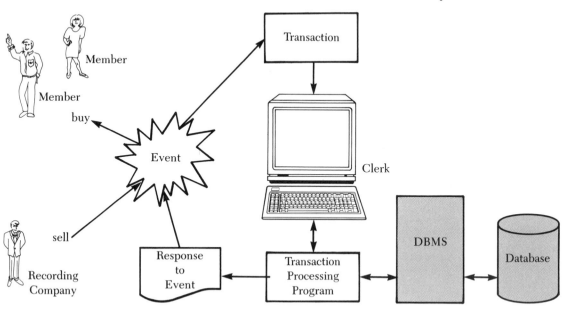

The degree of detail that should be incorporated into a data model depends on the information desired. Clearly, the more information that is needed, the finer the level of detail will be. Deciding which data and how much data to store in the database are key design questions we will address.

Businesses change. People come and go. Products are introduced and phased out. Money is earned and spent. As these changes occur, the data model must be altered. If not, the model will become out-of-date and be an inaccurate representation of the company.

*Transactions* are representations of events. By applying transactions to the database we can keep the data model current. Consider Figure 1–7, which summarizes this activity. Events that change the status of the company occur in the business world. For example, customers buy and return goods, shipments arrive, and so forth. When an event occurs, a business record, called a *transaction*, is made. Some examples of transactions are customer invoices, credit slips, and deposit records. Transactions are representations, or models, of events.

When events that change aspects of the business modeled by the database occur, then transactions for the events must be processed against the database. To do this, someone (a data entry clerk, a salesperson, or a teller, for example) activates a transaction processing program and enters the transaction data. The program then calls on the DBMS to alter the database. Transaction processing programs usually generate displayed or printed responses such as order confirmations or receipts.

## Database Applications

Since a database is a model of an organization, the processing of the database should correspond to the processing of the organization. Except for very small organizations, business activity is divided into functions. The record club, for example, includes these functional areas:

- Member Service
- Order Processing
- Purchasing
- Collections

Each of the business functions has its own information requirements. Member Service needs information about members and orders. Order Processing needs information about members, orders, and inventory. Purchasing needs information about orders and inventory. Collections needs information about members and their accounts.

Figure 1–8 shows the categories of data required for a database to support the record club's information needs. Observe that no functional area needs all of the data. Different portions are used by different functional areas. Also note that some of the data is shared by two or more functional areas. Member data, for example, is needed by Member Service, Order Processing, and Collections.

In a file processing system, each functional area would probably maintain its own file of Member records, resulting in terrible data duplication problems. Also, it is likely that all copies of the MEMBER file would not be maintained precisely the same way, and so the data would likely soon disagree, causing other problems. In a database system, all the areas share the same centralized data. It is precisely because centralized data can serve many functional areas that databases are so popular.

A *database application* is a business computer system that processes a portion of a database in order to meet the information needs of a business group, department, or functional area. In a sense, an application provides a window into the database for a particular user group.

We will discuss the components of a database application in detail in the next chapter. For now, think of an application as a collection of computer screens, printed reports, and transaction processing programs that access the part of a database needed to solve problems for a user group.

Database processing systems are usually very large; after all, they support the needs of many diverse user groups. Therefore, we divide database processing into separate applications. The reasons we do this are listed in Figure 1–9.

First, recall that a business is usually divided into separate functional areas. Thus, the computer screens, reports, and transaction processing programs for the Order Processing area are probably different from the computer screens, reports, and transaction processing programs for the Collections area. When we develop applications, we incorporate the interfaces

**Figure 1–8**
Categories of data by
functional area

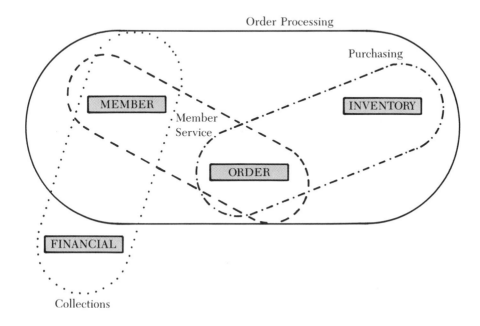

**Figure 1–9**
Reasons for dividing
database processing
into applications

• Application conforms to business's functional area

• Control access to database

• Limit scope of development

(screens and reports) needed by one group into a cohesive package. Thus, for example, order entry clerks would see a computer screen format that was meaningful to them, while collections agents would see the style of computer screen they could best read and understand.

Second, database data is one of an organization's most valuable assets. It is undesirable to allow every user to access every portion of the database.

Loan processing clerks in a bank, for example, should not be permitted to change savings account balances. Breaking database processing into applications provides improved control over access to the data.

Finally, it is easier and less risky for developers to build applications one by one than to try to build them all at once. Dividing processing into applications limits the scope of development to a series of smaller projects as opposed to one large project.

## Kinds of Database Systems

Database systems are made up of five components: hardware, DBMS software and application programs, the database itself, procedures, and people. One way to classify database systems is according to the number of users and the number of applications they support (see Figure 1–10). This classification will affect each of the five components of the system.

For example, in a single-user database system, only one user at a time processes the database. In contrast, multi-user database systems are processed concurrently by many users. The hardware in a multi-user system is much more extensive than that of a single-user system. Similarly, when databases are processed concurrently, special precautions need to be taken to prevent one user's processing from interfering with another's. Thus, the DBMS software and user procedures for a single-user system are different from those of a multi-user one. (We will study the problems of multi-user systems in Chapters 7 and 15.)

Database systems can also support one or many applications. The record club database in Figure 1–9 is a multi-application database. Some database systems support only a single application. A microcomputer user, for example, might have a customer database that is used only to prepare customer bills.

**Figure 1–10**
Kinds of database systems

|  | Single-User | Multi-User |
|---|---|---|
| Single-Application | Common on Microcomputers | Micros with LANs<br>Minicomputers |
| Multi-Application | Generally Occur on Microcomputers | Common on Mainframes, Minis, and<br>Micros, with LANs also possible |

Combining these two dimensions, there are four basic types of database systems. Single-user, single-application databases are most frequently found on microcomputers. Multi-user, single-application databases are found on microcomputers connected via local area networks (LANs) and also on minicomputers. Multi-user, single-application databases often are used by software vendors who develop packages for specific uses called *vertical markets*. Such a vendor might incorporate a database into a general ledger accounting package, for example. If so, the database generated would serve only that particular application.

Single-user, multi-application database systems are generally found on microcomputers. Finally, multi-user, multi-application databases are generally found in larger companies on mainframe computers.

Database systems can migrate from one category to another. For example, a single-user, single-application database system can be extended to support multiple users. Even more commonly, a second application can be added to a single-application database system. During such migrations, developers try to implement the second application without negatively impacting the first one. For example, sometimes the presence of a second application will degrade the performance of the first.

## A SHORT HISTORY OF DATABASE PROCESSING

Database technology can seem complex and complicated. In part this is because database terminology is inconsistent. Similar concepts have different names (for example, *object* and *entity* are synonyms in some contexts), and the same names often refer to different concepts (for example, the term *object* has different meanings depending on the context). This situation exists because database technology did not originate from a single source. In fact the technology has developed within three different contexts: the organizational context, the end-user context, and the distributed database context. To understand this subject you need to learn the evolution of database processing technology within each of these contexts.

### The Organizational Context

The initial application of database technology was to resolve the problems with file processing systems we examined earlier. In the mid-1960s, major corporations were producing data at phenomenal rates in file processing systems. The data was becoming difficult to manage, and new systems were becoming increasingly difficult to develop. Further, management wanted to be able to relate the data in one file processing system to that in another.

The limitations of file processing prevented easy integration of data, as we have seen. Database technology held out the promise of a solution to these problems, and large companies began to develop multi-application, multi-user databases. Within these databases companies centralized their operational data, such as orders, inventory, and accounting data. The applications were primarily transaction processors.

But the technology was new, and early database applications were difficult to develop. There were many failures. Even applications that were successfully developed were slow and unreliable; computer hardware was not fast enough to quickly handle the volume of transactions, developers had not yet discovered more efficient ways to store and retrieve data, and because programmers were still new at accessing databases, sometimes their programs did not work correctly.

Companies found another important disadvantage of database processing: vulnerability. If a file processing system fails, only that particular application is out of commission. But if the database system fails, all of the dependent applications are out of commission.

The early days of database development were learning experiences. Hardware and software engineers learned how to build systems powerful enough to support many concurrent users and fast enough to keep up with the daily workload of transactions. New ways of controlling, protecting, and backing up the database were developed. Standard procedures for database processing evolved, and programmers learned how to write more efficient and more maintainable code.

Thus, by the mid-1970s, effective multi-user, multi-application databases had been developed and were in use in many organizations, efficiently and reliably processing daily operational data. With many of the early problems resolved, management turned its attention to developing new uses for this huge pool of corporate data.

Managers knew that somehow all of that data could provide information for both tactical (short-term) and strategic (long-term) decision making, if only users could access it directly and not have to wait weeks or months for programmers to "get the information out of the computer."

Unfortunately, most of the applications had to be developed in procedural languages such as COBOL and PL/I, and users did not have the time or resources to become professional programmers. Besides, users were interested only in getting the answers to their questions, not in learning COBOL or how to navigate through a database to extract just the right items of data. It seemed that users and computers were existing in two different worlds. And yet, all that data was there, waiting to be put to even more good uses. This situation set the stage for the second context of database development, the end-user context.

### The End-User Context

In 1970, a mathematician named E. F. Codd published a landmark paper in which he applied concepts from a branch of mathematics called relational algebra to the problem of storing large amounts of data. This paper started a movement within the database community that within a few years led to the definition of the *relational database model*. This model is a particular way of stucturing and processing a database, and we will discuss it thoroughly in Chapters 5 and 9.

**The Relational Model.** The beauty of the relational model is that data is stored, at least conceptually, in a way the user can understand and access directly. Unlike the earlier database models, the relational model made it possible for users to get answers to some of their questions without requiring the assistance of MIS professionals. Thus, the relational database model introduced a new context: the end-user context. Let us briefly examine the relational model.

Recall that we store in databases not only data but also relationships among data. Figure 1–11, for example, shows sample student and completed course data. In addition to the data, there is also a relationship between students and courses: each student has completed certain courses. In order for the DBMS to construct a transcript, it must be able to represent this relationship.

DBMS products vary in the way that they represent relationships. Early DBMS products stored the relationships only in overhead data. These data structures were hidden from the user. In order to process such a database, some knowledge of the overhead data is needed: programmers and other MIS professionals understood these hidden data structures and knew how to use them to navigate through the database. The typical end-user, however, did not know what they were and really did not want to find out. Users simply relied on information systems professionals to write programs to get their information. This always took time.

The relational model changed this situation. One of the keystones of the relational model (there are several, as you will learn in Chapters 5 and 9) is that relationships must be stored in the data. In Figure 1–11 the relationship between students and courses is stored *in* the Student-ID field found in the Course record. We can retrieve a Course record and, by examining its contents, determine which student took that course. We can also process the data in the other direction: given a student's ID number, a relational DBMS will be able to determine which courses that student has completed. All the user needs to do is to specify which records to process (for example, all the Course records for student 100 or the names of all the students who completed course BD100). The DBMS will figure out how to navigate through the database.

The relational model encountered a good deal of resistance at the start. Relational database systems require more computer resources, and as a result they were much slower than systems based on earlier database models. Although they were easier to use, the slow response time was often unacceptable. To some extent, relational DBMS products were impractical until the 1980s, when faster computer hardware was developed and the price/ performance ratio of computers fell dramatically.

**Figure 1–11**

Relationship stored as data

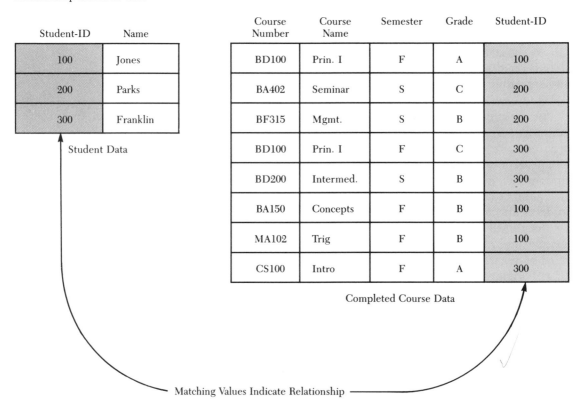

Student Data

| Course Number | Course Name | Semester | Grade | Student-ID |
|---|---|---|---|---|
| BD100 | Prin. I | F | A | 100 |
| BA402 | Seminar | S | C | 200 |
| BF315 | Mgmt. | S | B | 200 |
| BD100 | Prin. I | F | C | 300 |
| BD200 | Intermed. | S | B | 300 |
| BA150 | Concepts | F | B | 100 |
| MA102 | Trig | F | B | 100 |
| CS100 | Intro | F | A | 300 |

Completed Course Data

Matching Values Indicate Relationship

Also, the relational model seemed foreign to many programmers. They were accustomed to writing programs in which they processed data one record at a time. But relational DBMSs most naturally process data an entire file at a time. Programmers needed to learn a new way to view data.

Finally, relational systems were supposed to enable a lay person to process a database with limited assistance from an MIS professional. While there is no doubt that relational processing more closely resembles the user's world than processing databases based on other models, relational DBMS products are still foreign to many users. Despite the problems, the relational model has become very popular.

Relational database management systems can be used for most applications, including transaction processing of operational data. But one application type has found the relational model to be particularly useful, namely decision-support systems (DSSs). Decision support applications typically address unstructured problems and involve much ad hoc, or unpredictable, processing. As one executive put it, "I know I'm doing DSS when I don't know the second question to ask until I see the answer to the first question." DSS users are typically higher-level managers (or assistants to such people) who are willing and able to learn relational DBMS tools to accomplish their goals. Because the products based on the relational model are generally easy to use, relational databases are often the heart of DSSs.

At about the same time relational DBMSs were becoming widely used in decision-support systems, making access to the corporate database easier for users, the microcomputer explosion occurred, making computer power even more available. The combination of microcomputers and the relational model presented some tremendous opportunities in end-user database processing.

**Microcomputer DBMSs.** In 1979, a small company called Ashton-Tate introduced a microcomputer product called dBASE II (pronounced "d base two") and called it a relational DBMS. In a promotional move, over 100,000 copies of the product were distributed to purchasers of the then-new Osborne microcomputers. Many of the people who purchased these computers began to develop microcomputer applications using dBASE. Sales of dBASE increased dramatically, and Ashton-Tate became one of the major corporations in the microcomputer industry.

The success of this product confused and confounded the subject of database processing. The problem was that by the definition prevalent in the late 1970s, dBASE was neither a DBMS nor was it relational, though it was marketed as both. In fact, it was a programming language with generalized file processing (not database processing) capabilities. The systems that are developed with dBASE appear much more like those in Figure 1–2 than the ones in Figure 1–4. Today there are over a million users of dBASE, most of whom think they are using a relational DBMS, and perhaps several thousand professors of information systems who, quite correctly, know that dBASE is not a relational DBMS.

The point is that the terms *database management system* and *relational database* are often used loosely in the microcomputer world. In this course you will learn how to tell a DBMS from a file management system and how relational DBMSs differ from nonrelational ones. It is important that you realize that much of what we will be discussing as database technology bears little resemblance to what are sometimes called "relational DBMS" products in the microcomputer market.

Not all microcomputer DBMS products are subject to the above criticism. In fact, in Part 4 we will consider the usefulness of microcomputer DBMS products in end-user database processing.

On a very positive note, microcomputer DBMS products have dramatically improved user interfaces. The true microcomputer DBMS products are easier to use by orders of magnitude than most minicomputer and mainframe DBMS products. Micro vendors understand that typical micro users are not MIS professionals and will not put up with the inconvenience that professional MIS users have endured. Further, micro DBMS products operate on dedicated computers. Consequently, more computer power can be dedicated to processing the user interface.

Finally, many (not all) microcomputer DBMS products are based on the relational model, a model that by its nature is more familiar to the end-user. By and large, micro DBMS products are user-friendly. These advances have in turn positively affected products used on larger computers.

In summary, joining the relational model and the microcomputer has bolstered the development of end-user database processing. Certainly users can employ DBMS products on larger systems as well. In fact, we will study such a mainframe product, IBM's DB2, in Chapter 11. But it is safe to say that the ease of use of microcomputer DBMSs and the availability of micro-computer hardware have made end-user database processing an important aspect of business.

## The Distributed Database Context

Organizational database systems were supposed to solve the problems of file processing and allow more integrated processing of operational data. End-user database systems brought database technology even closer to the user by allowing direct access to the corporate data. Distributed databases are an attempt to allow even more flexibility in terms of data access and processing; however, distributed databases pose many problems not yet solved.

Distributed database systems evolved out of a need for users to have even more access to corporate data. In essence, various user groups download, or copy, portions of the corporate database onto their own computer storage equipment, then process it as if it were their own private database. Thus microcomputers, minicomputers, and mainframes all access the same pool of data.

Among the more pressing problems with this arrangement are those of security and control. Ensuring that users actually are entitled to access the database is a difficult task because there could be hundreds of concurrent users.

Coordinating and synchronizing the data is also very difficult. If one user group downloads and updates part of the database and then transmits the changed data back to the mainframe, how does the system prevent another user from attempting to use the version of the data it finds on the mainframe in the meantime? Imagine this problem involving dozens of files and hundreds of users employing scores of pieces of computer equipment.

In fact, as you will learn in Chapter 15, the concept of a distributed database actually blurs the definition of a database. It is supposedly a centralized, controlled collection of data and relationships. But if we fragment it and copy it onto many different computers, we have altered the original database concept.

Whereas the transition from organizational to end-user database processing was a relatively easy one, the difficulties facing database designers and engineers of distributed DBMSs are monumental. You will learn what they are, and the current attempts to overcome them, later in this course.

### Comparing the Three Contexts

There are differences among database systems that have developed within the three contexts. We have noted some of them during this discussion.

Although it is important that you recognize the differences, it is equally important that you see the similarities. There is a body of knowledge common to all three contexts, and if you understand that common knowledge, you will go a long way toward understanding applications and products in all three categories.

You should be warned, however, that in this area of study, terminology is a problem because it has not yet been standardized. Concepts common to all three contexts might have different names, and different concepts might be given the same name in different contexts. We will point out these conflicts throughout the text.

This text is organized to teach you the common body of knowledge first (Chapters 2–8). Following those chapters, we will discuss each of the three contexts and illustrate typical applications for which each was developed.

## SUMMARY

The study of database processing is important to you for several reasons: databases are widely used in industry for transaction processing; databases are the heart of decision-support systems, allowing ad hoc processing of data; and databases can be implemented on computers of all sizes, increasing the chances that every business person and information systems professional will encounter them.

Database technology facilitates the production of information. The fundamental purpose of all information systems is to reduce uncertainty.

File processing systems store data in separate files with each file containing a different type of data. File processing systems have several limitations: it is difficult to combine data stored in separate files; data is often duplicated among files, leading to data integrity problems; application programs are dependent on file formats and other physical data descriptions, inviting maintenance problems when such formats change; and it is difficult to represent objects from the user's environment using files.

To overcome these limitations, database processing systems were developed. In the database environment, the database management system

(DBMS) is the interface between application programs and the database. Only the DBMS is affected by changes to the physical formats of stored data. And if data items are changed, added, or deleted, few application programs will require maintenance. Objects from the user's environment can be represented in a straightforward way using database technology.

A database is a self-describing collection of integrated records. It is self-describing because it contains a description of itself in a data dictionary. The data dictionary is also known as a data directory, or meta-data. A database is a collection of integrated records because relationships among records are stored in the database. This arrangement enables the DBMS to construct even complicated objects by combining data according to the stored relationships. Relationships are often stored in overhead data. Thus, the three parts of a database are the application data, the data dictionary, and the overhead data.

A database is a data model of an organization. The degree of detail incorporated in the model depends on the information users need to derive. Transaction processing keeps the data in the database current so that the database is always an accurate model of the company.

Many users can be serviced by one database system. A database application is a business computer system that processes a portion of the database to meet the information needs of a particular business group. Database processing is divided into applications to conform to the functional areas of the business, to control access to the data, and to limit development to a series of small projects rather than one large one.

Database systems can be classified by the number of users and the number of applications they support. Each type of system affects the type of hardware, the programs, the amount of data, and the procedures followed by the users in the system.

The technology surrounding database processing has developed within three different contexts: the organizational context, the end-user context, and the distributed context. The earliest database applications focused on transaction processing of operational data for large organizations. After such systems were well established in business, managers turned to database data for information they needed in decision making. This led to the end-user context.

Because the relational database model is based on data structures familiar to the user, it opened the door to end-user database processing. At the same time, microcomputers made computer power even more accessible to larger numbers of people. Before long, the relational model was implemented on microcomputers. There are also mainframe and microcomputer DBMS products that end-users can employ, but the microcomputer fueled the development of user-friendly database software.

The third context of database technology is distributed database processing. Distributed database processing involves users at separate locations importing data from other sources, such as the corporate database, building their own "private" database that they process with their own computer equipment, and then transmitting the new data back to its original sources. The idea of distributed database processing is blurring the definition of a database as a centralized collection of integrated records. There are many as yet unsolved problems with distributed database processing. It is a relatively new database application, and we have much to learn.

---

QUESTIONS **GROUP I**

1.1 What is the purpose of an information system? Give three examples not used in the chapter.

1.2 List four disadvantages of file processing systems and give an example of each.

1.3 Explain how a DBMS overcomes each of the disadvantages of file processing.

1.4 Define database management system. Define database. What is the relationship between them?

1.5 What is a data dictionary?

1.6 What is the function of overhead data?

1.7 What are the three fundamental parts of a database?

1.8 What is transaction processing?

1.9 Define database application.

1.10 List three reasons for dividing database processing activity into separate applications.

1.11 Describe the four types of database systems.

1.12 What were some of the weaknesses of early organizational database applications?

1.13 How did organizational database processing lead to end-user database processing?

1.14 What were some of the reasons for resistance to the relational model?

1.15 How did the relational model contribute to end-user database processing?

1.16 How have microcomputer DBMSs contributed to end-user database processing?

1.17 How have microcomputer DBMS products affected end-user database processing on mainframe computers?

1.18 Describe two problems introduced by distributed database processing.

---

QUESTIONS **GROUP II**

1.19 Should a database course be required for an information systems major? Give reasons to support your answer. (It might be interesting to save your reasons and review them at the end of the course.)

1.20 List some objects from a user's environment. Identify those that are easy to represent as one record in a file and those that are complicated.

**1.21**   Interview a salesperson at a local computer store. Ask for information on microcomputer database management systems. Does the store distinguish between file management systems and database management systems? If so, what are the differences? Determine if the store distinguishes between relational and nonrelational DBMSs. If so, what are the differences?

# Database Applications

- Eastcoast State University Computer Lab
- Database Application System Components
- Database Application Functional Components
- Summary

**A**lthough people develop databases to generate information, they do not actually access databases directly. Rather, users access database *applications*, which in turn access and process the database.

To understand database applications and how they are developed, you need to learn answers to three fundamental questions. First, what is a database application? You need to know the components of applications and how they interact to produce information. Next, what is the role of the DBMS? As you will see, the DBMS provides a set of tools for developing, processing, and administering the database. You need to know what those tools are and how they can be used. Finally, how are database applications developed? You need to learn a process for building database applications. There are many such processes, and we will consider one in this text that has been used successfully in many organizations.

In this chapter we will address the first question: What is a database application? In Chapter 3 we will address the role of the DBMS and the application development process. Throughout this discussion, we will use the term *common-database applications*. It refers to all of the applications that process the same (or common) database. We will begin by introducing a case example.

## EASTCOAST STATE UNIVERSITY COMPUTER LAB

The Information Systems Department at Eastcoast State University operates a microcomputer lab. This lab contains twenty-five computing stations. Each station has a microcomputer with a video display device. Some stations have printers and others have both printers and plotters. The computers are all of the same basic type but they vary by amount of memory, disk types and sizes, and specialized options (for example, some have speech synthesizers, others include communications modems).

Each computer is equipped with an operating system as well as standard university software, such as word processing, spreadsheet, and database management products. Special-purpose software, such as some graphics products, is also available, but this software must be checked out on an as-needed basis.

To use the lab, a student presents his or her student activity card to the lab attendant posted at the entrance to the lab. The attendant (a student employee) verifies that the student is enrolled in a class that uses the lab and schedules time for the student. The lab attendant also checks out special-purpose software to students who require it.

Despite the fact that a lab attendant is scheduled to control access to the lab whenever it is open (from 8:00 A.M. until midnight), several months ago a microcomputer disappeared. No one knew if the computer was misplaced, inadvertently taken to another lab on campus, or stolen. Unfortunately, through a variety of procedural and filing errors, no one was able to produce the computer's serial number and little action could be taken to recover the computer.

When the loss was discovered, the department chairperson decided that some action needed to be taken to obtain greater control over the equipment. The chairperson asked a graduate assistant, Samantha Green, to look into the existing system and devise a better way to keep track of the equipment.

## An Information System for the Lab

Before enrolling in graduate school, Samantha had worked for five years as a programmer and systems analyst. She was no stranger to projects like this. When she accepted the job, she knew to look beyond the immediate problem regarding the missing computer. Consequently, she decided to interview the chairperson, the department faculty, and students who worked as attendants in the lab. Samantha also spent some time in the lab observing how the system worked.

As a result of her investigations, Samantha discovered three fundamental information system problems. First, the lab needed to keep better records of equipment and to verify the presence of the equipment against those records. Second, Samantha discovered problems in the scheduling of equipment and the checkout of special-purpose software. In fact, on several occasions, the same computer was scheduled to two people at the same time! At other times, the equipment was poorly utilized. Third, the procedures for checking out special-purpose software were lax and informal, and several of the lab assistants suspected that, contrary to policy, software had been removed from the lab overnight and over weekends. No software was actually missing, but several assistants suspected that illegal copies of software might have been made.

As Samantha discussed these problems with the professor who managed the lab, she realized that there was a need for several different lab usage reports. Samantha knew that if a computer application were used to schedule the lab, then the data generated by the application could be used to produce these reports.

## Database Applications for the Lab

In Chapter 3 we will discuss the process by which database applications are developed. At this point, we will jump ahead to the results of Samantha's work so we can illustrate the nature of database applications.

Samantha discovered that there were four functional areas in the lab: scheduling, inventory, software checkout, and usage analysis. Accordingly, she decided that the lab needed four separate applications: SCHEDULING, INVENTORY, CHECKOUT, and USAGE ANALYSIS. The SCHEDULING application is used to make student appointments as follows: a student presents his or her activity card to the lab assistant. The assistant checks student data and class rosters to make sure the student is enrolled in a class that is authorized to use the lab and then asks the student if he or she has any special computer equipment requirements (large memory, hard disk, and so forth). Finally the lab attendant checks appointment records for an available machine (Figure 2–1). The SCHEDULING application requires access to data about students, class rosters, appointments, and computers. The data requirements for all four applications are summarized in Figure 2–2.

The INVENTORY application is used to keep track of the lab equipment. This application stores and maintains data about each computer in the lab as well as all of the peripheral equipment attached to each computer.

To improve control over software, Samantha decided to develop a CHECKOUT application. This application records the use of special-purpose software in the lab by appointment. In this way, the lab personnel can determine who has used which software. Should software disappear, lab personnel can determine from their records who used it most recently.

The USAGE application produces reports that show lab use by class, student, and computer. Figure 2–3 shows examples of two reports produced by this application, the CLASS USAGE report (Figure 2–3a) and the STUDENT SUMMARY report (Figure 2–3b). The first report summarizes use by class. This report is produced on a regular basis for the department chairperson and the professor who manages the lab. The second report shows lab usage for each student. This report is printed only when an instructor requests it. Some of the professors wanted this capability so they could determine how much effort had been put forth by their students. The data required for the USAGE application is listed in Figure 2–2.

When you examine the data requirements in Figure 2–2, you will see that the four applications share much common data. Samantha observed

**Figure 2—1**

Processes in the SCHEDULING application

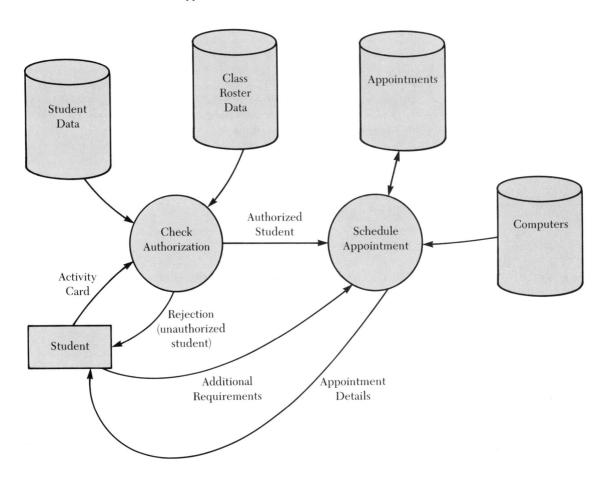

this too. On the basis of the amount of overlap in data, as well as other considerations, she decided to build a database to support these four applications. She also determined that each of the applications could be performed at different times, so there was no need for concurrent access to the data. Only one user would access the system at any time. She decided that the database system could be implemented on a microcomputer in the lab. Using the terms from Chapter 1, Samantha decided to develop a multi-application, single-user database system.

We will now turn to a discussion of the components of a database application. We will illustrate this discussion with the SCHEDULING application from Eastcoast University's lab.

**Figure 2–2**
Summary of application data requirements at Eastcoast Lab

| Data | Scheduling | Inventory | Checkout | Usage Analysis |
|---|---|---|---|---|
| Student | ✓ | | | ✓ |
| Class Roster | ✓ | | | ✓ |
| Computer | ✓ | ✓ | | |
| Appointment | ✓ | | ✓ | ✓ |
| Peripheral Equipment | | ✓ | | |
| Software | | | ✓ | ✓ |
| Software Use | | | ✓ | ✓ |
| Class | | | | ✓ |

## DATABASE APPLICATION SYSTEM COMPONENTS

A database application is a business computer system. As such, it has five system components: hardware, programs, data, procedures, and people. We will consider each of these in turn.

### Hardware

Computer hardware is required to run the DBMS, application, and other programs. Database applications do not generally require any specialized hardware, but they often require more hardware than file processing systems do. Database systems can be installed on computers of all sizes, from microcomputers to very large mainframes. Depending on its capabilities, a DBMS can occupy from 256,000 to 1 million bytes or more of main memory.

**Figure 2—3**
Sample reports

```
                        Eastcoast Lab
                     Class Usage Report


   Class Name        Section Number        Instructor        Total Student Hours


     BD 120                 1                James                 37.4
     BD 120                 2                Parks                114.7
     BF 100                 1                Washington            81.3
```

a. Format of Class Usage report

```
                     Student Summary Report

   Student Name               Student ID            Total Lab Hours
   Mary Jackson                 12345                    17.3


                        Software Used                Total Hours
                           Lotus                          9.4
                           R:base                         7.8
                           Other                           .1

                        Class Enrolled               Total Hours
                           BD 120                         4.5
                           BF 200                        12.8
```

b. Format of Student Summary report

Additionally, the DBMS requires CPU time to execute its large number of instructions. If you compare a file processing application to a comparable database application, you will most likely find the database application takes from 15 to 50 percent more CPU time. Thus, faster computer hardware may be necessary for a database system.

Furthermore, because the database system's overhead data can double or even triple the data storage requirements, more peripheral storage, such as disks, may be required than for a comparable file processing application (ignoring storage space savings due to reduced data duplication).

The hardware of the Eastcoast Lab database is a state-of-the-art microcomputer with 1 million bytes of main storage and a 100-million-byte hard disk. This configuration can comfortably support a single-user, multi-application database system. More hardware might be required if the database system had to support multiple concurrent users.

In general, all common-database applications share some hardware. For example, the applications can all be implemented on exactly the same hardware (as is the case at the Eastcoast Lab illustrated in Figure 2–4a). At the other extreme, the applications might share only the disk on which the database is stored (see Figure 2–4b). This occurs in a distributed processing environment and on a local area network (LAN). In this case, each application has its own CPU and obtains data from the database by means of a communications line. (Actually, the DBMS at one work station accesses the database and transmits data to and from the other workstations in the network.)

Several companies have developed special purpose computers called *database machines*. These computers, which are dedicated to the task of processing the database, are designed to provide exceptionally fast performance when processing very large databases. Database machines have not enjoyed much acceptance in the market.

## Programs

A variety of programs is needed to support database applications. At the very least, an application requires a database management system and an operating system. In addition, all but the simplest applications require one or more *application programs*. Further, if the database is shared concurrently, a communications control program (CCP) is needed. On local area networks and minicomputers, the CCP is built into the operating system. On mainframes, however, the CCP is a separate program. Figure 2–5 shows the relationship of these programs. Note that the DBMS can be accessed both by batch application programs and by online users via the CCP.

In almost all applications, only the application programs are written by the developer (usually a programmer or user). The CCP, the DBMS, and the operating system are supplied by vendors. Usually the operating system is supplied by the hardware vendor, and in many cases, the DBMS and the

**Figure 2—4**

Alternative arrangements for common-database applications

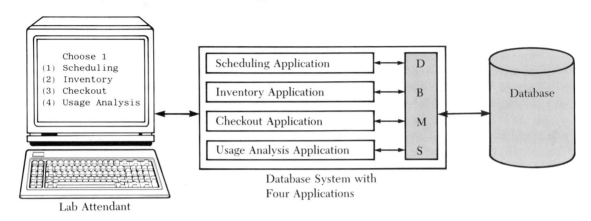

a. Eastcoast's common-database applications implemented on one computer

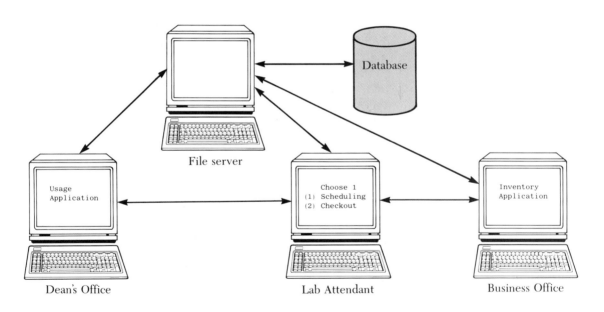

b. Using a local area network (LAN)

CCP are provided as well. It is also common, however, for the DBMS and the CCP to be obtained from independent software vendors.

Application programs fall into two major types. The first category includes applications that are written in a standard programming language such as COBOL or Pascal. These programs access the DBMS through subroutine calls.

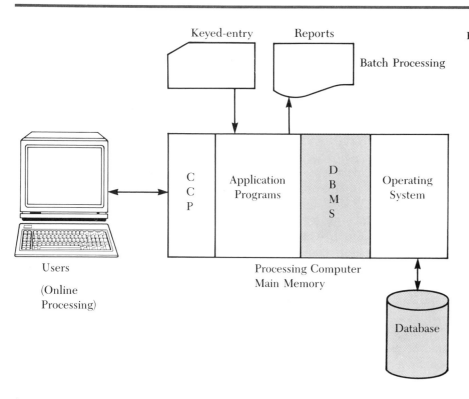

**Figure 2–5**
Programs involved in typical database processing

A second type of application program consists of programs that are written in the DBMS product's own language. Most such languages came into existence through the back door. That is, the initial version of the DBMS included an interactive query/update language that users began to employ. As users became more proficient in this language, they began to do more complex tasks requiring longer sequences of instructions. DBMS vendors provided methods for storing sequences of query/update commands, and soon these stored commands took on the complexity and capability of application programs. The use of such DBMS-unique languages is particularly common on microcomputers.

## Data

As you would expect, the data component of a database application is the database itself. As described in Chapter 1, the database contains source data, meta-data in the data dictionary, and overhead data. Source data is the facts stored in the database, such as account numbers, names, and dates. The data dictionary describes the structure of the database. Overhead data is used for lists, indexes, and other data structures that represent record relationships.

In most cases, different applications process different, but overlapping, subsets of the database. This situation is illustrated for the lab in Figure 2–2.

Some new terminology will facilitate the discussion of database data. The structure of the entire database is called the *schema*, or the *conceptual view*. Thus, the structure of all of the data types shown in Figure 2–2 comprises the Lab Database Schema, or the Lab Database Conceptual View. That portion of the database structure that is processed by a particular application is called a *subschema*, or *application view*. A subschema is also known as a *logical view*. For example, the COMPUTER and PERIPHERAL-EQUIPMENT data types together comprise the INVENTORY subschema, or the INVENTORY application view (see Figure 2–2).

Application programs are aware only of data that is in their view. This fact has both advantages and disadvantages. The advantage is that data can be protected from unauthorized access. The user of the INVENTORY sub-schema, for example, is unable to access SOFTWARE data. In fact, that user probably does not even know such data exists.

The disadvantage concerns conflicts over shared data between programs or users of overlapping subschemas. At the Eastcoast Lab, if a user who is accessing the database via the INVENTORY application view deletes a COMPUTER record, this action may cause problems for programs or users that access other application views that include CUSTOMER records. For example, the user of the SCHEDULING application view may have made an appointment for the computer that was subsequently deleted by the user of the INVENTORY application.

The potential conflicts among application views must be identified and then prevented. Database system developers prevent conflicts from occurring by carefully defining the database schema and subschemas; by using facilities available in the DBMS product that address the problems of concurrent processing (see Chapter 7); and by writing application programs that can detect and resolve problems. For example, Samantha might decide that an application may not delete a COMPUTER record if there are any appointments scheduled for that computer. This is called an interrecord constraint. Enforcement of this constraint might require an application program. Some DBMSs enforce such constraints, although on a limited basis. We will discuss this issue further in subsequent chapters.

Some DBMS products store a fourth type of data in the database. *Application meta-data* is data about constructs (such as reports and screens) used by particular applications. For example, some DBMS products include a report generation subsystem that users employ to define report formats. Report formats include the report name, names of column headings, names of data items that appear in the report, control breaks, report variable definitions, and so forth. Once the report format is defined and stored, it can be referenced by an application. Such a structure is called *application meta-data* because it pertains to a particular application, not to the database as a whole.

## Procedures

The fourth system component of a database application is procedures. Both users and the operations staff need documented procedures describing how to run the system. Users need to know how to sign on to the system, how to enter data and commands, how to operate the computer or terminal, and how to employ the system to perform the tasks they need to accomplish.

Consider the Eastcoast Lab, for example. The Lab is staffed each day by an average of six assistants. The assistants need standardized procedures for processing the database. If every assistant had his or her own way of scheduling a computer, the database would soon become a mess.

Programs and procedures are different ways of doing something. We can get something done by having a person do it (a procedure) or by having a computer do it (a program). Consider the procedure for scheduling an appointment at the Eastcoast Lab. A manual system might require the assistant first to validate the student ID by checking the student list. Then, in a separate query to ensure the student is enrolled in an appropriate class, the assistant would check the class roster. Finally, in a third operation, the assistant would find an available time slot and actually schedule an appointment.

Alternatively, all of these procedures can be designed into the scheduling application program. In this case, the program will ask for the student ID and class and then will verify this data without further interaction with the assistant. If these data values are appropriate, then the program can automatically find and display on the screen a number of available appointment slots. The assistant need only select one to schedule an appointment. The same process is followed in both cases, but in the manual system the assistant performed all of them, while in the database application the program performed most of them.

Either of these alternatives can be appropriate. The point is for you to recognize that many procedures can be programmed into application programs. Alternatively, procedures can be documented and manually implemented.

In addition to procedures for normal operation, procedures for backup and recovery operations are also needed. When a database system fails, both users and operations personnel need procedures describing what to do. Such procedures are especially important for multi-user database systems because many people depend on the database. Users need to know what manual procedures to follow during the failure, what data to save, and what to do with business transactions that cannot be processed during the failure. When the system is returned to operation, users need to know what to do to resume processing. For example, how can a user tell how much work needs to be redone? Also, how much of the data gathered manually during the failure needs to be input before new transactions can be processed? All these issues need to be considered in developing user recovery procedures. We will consider these issues in Chapter 7.

Similar procedures are required for computer operations. When the database system fails, operations personnel need to know what to do. What action should be taken to identify the source of the problem and to correct it? What must be done to minimize damage to the database? Who should be called? Once the problem is corrected, how should the database be restored? These actions need to be carefully thought out and documented during the design and implementation of the system. Waiting until the error occurs is very dangerous.

Business is a dynamic activity, and business needs will change. For a database system, however, changes must be made very carefully. A change made to benefit one user may be detrimental to users in seemingly unrelated departments. Consequently, changes to the database need to be made with a communitywide view. Procedures must be defined and documented to control change to the database.

## People

People are the final systems component of a database application. *Clientele* are the people for whom the system is developed. The clientele of an airline reservation system are the airline passengers. The clientele of a payroll system are employees. Students are the clientele at Eastcoast's computer lab. Since clientele do not usually have an active role in database system development or use, we will not generally be concerned with them.

*Users* employ the system to satisfy a business need. The users of an airline reservation system include ticket agents and travel agents. The users of a payroll system include payroll administrators, clerks, and business managers. The users of Eastcoast's system are the lab attendants.

*Operations personnel* run the computer and associated equipment. Typically, the operations department includes computer operators, data control personnel, and data entry people.

*Systems development personnel* design and implement the database and its applications. They determine requirements, specify alternatives, design the five components of the system, and implement the system. Systems development personnel include systems analysts, application programmers, and systems programmers (those people who support and maintain the operating system, the CCP, the DBMS, and other similar systems support programs).

The final category of people involved in database applications consists of the *database administration (DBA) personnel*. A database may be a shared resource. As such, its design and use must be managed with a view toward all users (sometimes called the *user community*). The functions of the DBA staff are to protect the database and to resolve conflicts among users. The DBA should be a representative of the community as a whole, not of any particular user or group of users. In this role, the DBA must arbitrate the processing rights and responsibilities of each user. We will discuss the position of DBA in Chapter 7.

The personnel involved in database applications vary widely. At the Eastcoast University Lab, the personnel include Samantha (the system developer), the lab attendants, and the professor who supervises the lab. The lab attendants are both the users and the operators. The managing professor serves informally as the DBA, with the help of several of the more knowledgeable lab assistants.

Now consider the database personnel working in a large bank. Here, there are hundreds of users, dozens of operations personnel, and a formal database administration staff. The bank has a Management Information Systems Department that includes professional systems developers to build and maintain the system.

The discussions in this book are oriented primarily toward systems development people who might work in any of the widely varying database environments. However, it is important for development people to know the roles and needs of users, operations, and DBA. Therefore, a discussion of the needs of these people will be included when appropriate. The five system components of a database application are summarized in Figure 2–6.

**Figure 2–6**

Summary of database
application system
components

*Hardware*
- Possibly faster CPU and larger main memory than for file processing applications
- More online storage for data dictionary and overhead data

*Programs*
- Operating system, DBMS, possibly CCP, and application programs

*Data*
- Source data, data dictionary, and overhead data; possibly application meta-data

*Procedures*
- Required for users, operators, systems development, and DBA personnel
- Procedures for normal processing, and for backup and recovery

*People*
- Clientele
- Users
- Operations personnel
- Systems Development personnel
- Database administration (DBA)

## DATABASE APPLICATION FUNCTIONAL COMPONENTS

In the previous section, we discussed the *system components* of a database application. These components are important when considering the application as a *system* solution to a business problem. They are important to all business computing systems, whether or not they involve a database. They are usually studied in detail in systems analysis and design courses.

Database applications have another set of components that relate directly to the technology that you will learn in this class. These components provide three functions of a database application: a mechanism for updating the data, a mechanism for displaying the data, and a mechanism for controlling processing. We will consider each in turn.

### Mechanisms for Updating Data

A database application must provide a mechanism for updating data. *Updating* means entering, deleting, and editing (or changing) database data. The word *mechanism* may seem strange in this context. We use such a general term because a wide variety of methods are used.

Consider Figure 2–7, which shows several typical methods for updating APPOINTMENT data in the Eastcoast Lab database. In Figure 2–7a, the user enters data using a load utility program that is part of the DBMS. This is a primitive database update method. The user is prompted with only the name of the data item—a load utility does not indicate the format or length of the data to be entered. If the user enters erroneous data, she will get only the most rudimentary error messages, such as "INVALID DATA. TRY AGAIN."

Figure 2–7b shows the same data being entered by means of a form. Like the simple prompting above, this form was generated by a DBMS utility. This data entry form provides slightly better prompt text and also indicates the length of the data item to be entered. Error messages will still be limited (depending on the DBMS product being used).

A third updating mechanism is shown in Figure 2–7c. Here, the APPOINTMENT data is displayed in tabular format. The user can scroll up and down the APPOINTMENT data, adding or deleting lines and changing data by simply moving the cursor to the correct data item and keying the change. This format is not supported by all DBMSs, but when it is, the form generation and processing are done automatically by the DBMS. The form in Figure 2–7c, for example, would be generated and processed by a command such as "BROWSE APPOINTMENT DATA WHERE APP-DATE EQ 12/11/88." Error messages for this facility are somewhat better than for the previous examples, but since they are generated by the DBMS, they must be generic.

A fourth method for updating data is to use an interactive query/update command language. In this mode, the user accesses a DBMS query/update

**Figure 2—7**
Update mechanisms

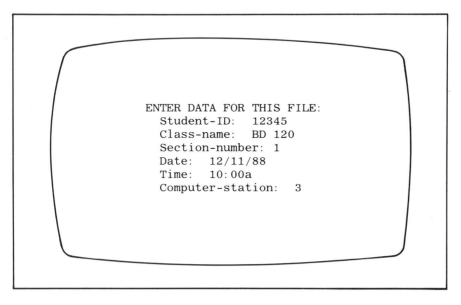

a.  Entering data via a load utility

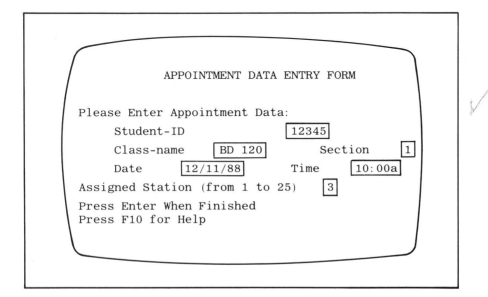

b.  Entering data with a form

**Figure 2–7**
(*continued*)

| Date | Time | Station | Student-ID | Class-name | Section-number |
|------|------|---------|------------|------------|----------------|
| 12/11/88 | 8:00a | 1 | 12345 | BD 120 | 1 |
| 12/11/88 | 8:00a | 2 | 44728 | BD 120 | 2 |
| 12/11/88 | 8:00a | 3 | none | — | — |
| 12/11/88 | 8:00a | 4 | 86241 | BF 100 | 1 |
| 12/11/88 | 8:00a | 6 | 44513 | BD 120 | 1 |
| 12/11/88 | 8:00a | 7 | 88751 | BD 120 | 2 |
| 12/11/88 | 8:00a | 9 | 62143 | BD 120 | 1 |
| 12/11/88 | 8:00a | 11 | 33349 | BF 100 | 1 |
| 12/11/88 | 8:00a | 14 | 83290 | BD 120 | 3 |
| 12/11/88 | 8:00a | 15 | 17144 | BD 120 | 3 |

c. Entering editing data in tabular format

program (the particulars depend on the DBMS product) and then issues a command to make the desired changes. In Figure 2–7d, the lab assistant is removing all future appointments for a particular student since he successfully completed all of his projects and needs no more lab time.

Updates like this are quite dangerous. The user is given great power, power which, when used correctly, can rapidly accomplish the task at hand, but when used incorrectly, can cause serious problems. In Figure 2–7d, for example, imagine what would happen if the lab assistant accidentally typed < instead of =. Appointments for quite a few students would be incorrectly deleted. Updating a database via interactive languages, if used at all, must be used carefully.

A fifth update mechanism allows the user to input a mass of data, such as an external file produced by another system or stored on another computer. Sometimes this process is called *importing* data. Figure 2–7e shows a sample command to import data.

**Figure 2−7**
(*continued*)

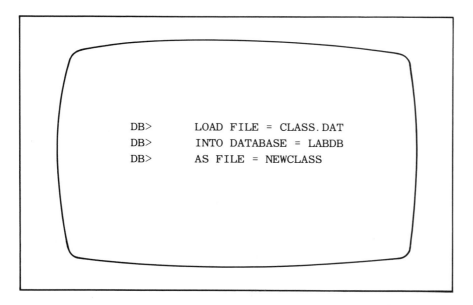

```
DB>      UPDATE APPOINTMENT
DB>      SET STUDENT-ID TO NULL
DB>      WHERE STUDENT-ID = 88751
DB>      AND DATE > 12/11/88
```
System        User-input update command
Prompt

d.  Updating data with an update language

```
DB>      LOAD FILE = CLASS.DAT
DB>      INTO DATABASE = LABDB
DB>      AS FILE = NEWCLASS
```

e.  Example of mass data input

None of the updating mechanisms in Figure 2–7 involve application programming. All of them are accomplished by using features of the DBMS product. Many of these features can be employed by users without any assistance from a professional systems developer.

The advantage of this approach is that users can often get the systems developed faster than if they waited for someone to write a program. But using utilities to update data also has drawbacks. Error messages will be generic and often unhelpful. Processing is limited to features anticipated by the designer of the DBMS. Help text, if it exists at all, will be generic and of limited use. To overcome these problems, nearly all DBMS products provide an interface between the DBMS and a standard programming language (such as COBOL), or between the DBMS and the DBMS's own programming language, or both. Application programs can be much richer and more complex than utilities, as you will see.

Figure 2–8 shows two examples of application programs performing database updates. In Figure 2–8a, the program displays a screen and leads the user through the update process. The program first displays a form heading (APPOINTMENT SCHEDULING, date, and time) and prompts the user for the student number (Please enter Student-ID). The program then looks up that student ID number in a file, displays the data (This is the ID for Mary Jackson) and asks if the correct student has been identified

**Figure 2–8**

Application programs performing database updates

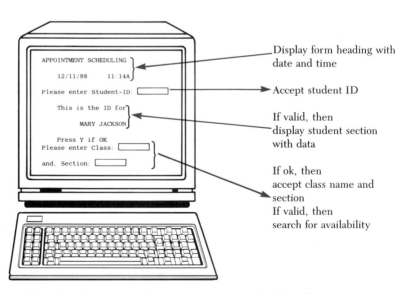

a. Example of a program that processes a transaction via a form

**Figure 2—8**
(*continued*)

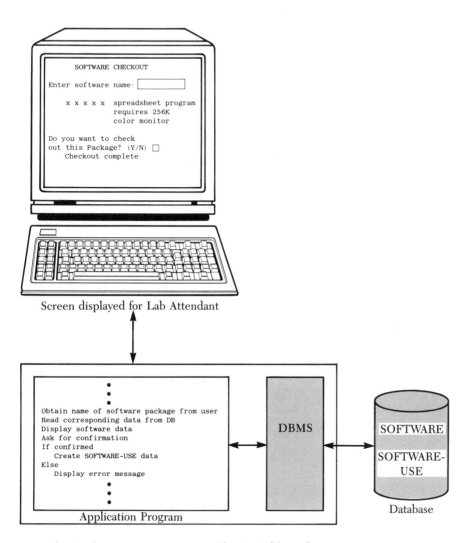

SOFTWARE CHECKOUT

Enter software name:

    x x x x x  spreadsheet program
                requires 256K
                color monitor

Do you want to check
out this Package? (Y/N)
    Checkout complete

Screen displayed for Lab Attendant

Obtain name of software package from user
Read corresponding data from DB
Display software data
Ask for confirmation
If confirmed
   Create SOFTWARE-USE data
Else
   Display error message

Application Program

DBMS

SOFTWARE

SOFTWARE-
USE

Database

b. Application program creating data invisible to the user

(Press Y if OK). If so, processing continues. Otherwise, an error message explains the next step. The error message is not shown in the figure.

If the user indicates that the student has been correctly identified, the program then asks for and looks up class data (Please enter Class, Section). Following that (but not shown in Figure 2–8a), the program would display a list of available appointment times and the user would select one. Eventually the program would set an appointment for the student and would update the appropriate database data. As you can see, processing is tailored to the requirements of this particular situation. The person writing this program would need to design its logic just like any other program he would write. Although program design is not a topic in this course, the techniques you have learned in other courses should be applied to database processing programs as well.

A second way in which application programs update data is shown in Figure 2–8b. In this case, the data being updated, SOFTWARE-USE, is invisible to the user. As you can tell from the figure, the user merely enters the name of a software package and then indicates whether or not it should be checked out. The data being updated, SOFTWARE-USE, is not referenced by the user—it is invisible to her. In order to update this hidden data, an application program *must* be used. No current DBMS product has utilities powerful enough to support this kind of processing.

As you can see, there are many different ways of updating data in a database. The problem for the application developer is to select the method that will meet the needs of the user at the least cost. Built-in DBMS utilities, because they do not need to be developed, are usually cheaper than application programs. However, they are also more generic (thus, less helpful to the user) and sometimes more dangerous. Update mechanisms are summarized in Figure 2–9.

## Mechanisms for Displaying Data

Database applications provide three ways of displaying data: in reports, as responses to queries, and exported in bulk to another system.

---

**Figure 2–9**

Summary of update mechanisms

> *Without Programming*
> - DBMS load utility
> - DBMS default data entry form
> - DBMS-supplied tabular form
> - Query/update language
> - Mass data input via command
>
> *With Programming*
> - Form generated and processed by application program
> - Application program updating database directly

**Reports.**   A report is an extraction of data from the database. Reports can be printed on paper, displayed on computer screens, and issued to other output devices. Some reports are prepared on a regular, recurring basis, others are prepared when exceptional conditions are detected, and still others are prepared only on demand.

Reports are similar to update forms. Reports, however, only display data, whereas forms allow the user to read, update, and delete data. It might be helpful to think of a report as a "display-only form."

Reports, like forms, can be generated either by facilities built into the DBMS product or by application programs. Many DBMS products include a default report format that is automatically defined for every file in the database. Figure 2–10a shows a sample default report format for the APPOINTMENT file in the lab database. This report is not attractive or elaborate. It is simple, but it requires no development time because the DBMS includes the report format automatically.

Figure 2–10b shows a more sophisticated report that was developed using a DBMS report writing utility. It is more attractive, and it has more meaningful column headings. Additionally, this report breaks out appointments by hour and totals the machine usage over each hourly period. The production of this report required knowledge of the DBMS report generation facility, but it did not require any programming. Consequently, it could have been produced by someone who had only a few hours of instruction and was not a professional programmer.

A much more complex report can be produced by an application program. With the power and flexibility of programming, a report can be tailored exactly to the user's most demanding requirements. The disadvantage of writing programs to produce reports is that it takes significantly longer to develop a report with an application program than it does with the report generator feature of a DBMS. Further, its development would require the services of a professional programmer.

It is important to distinguish between a report and the medium of a report. The same report can be displayed on a computer screen, paper, microfiche, or some other medium. Changing the medium does not change the report. Similarly, there is a difference between report content and report format. Report content is the information in a report. The report format is the design of the report, including details like column headers, blank lines, and page numbers. Such details are meta-data about the report. You might think of a report as the materialization of information in a format that is meaningful to the user.

**Query Response.**   The second major type of display facility in a database application is the response to a request made with a database query language. While there are many query languages (seemingly as many as there are DBMS products), one language, SQL (pronounced "S-Q-L"), is quite popular and in August of 1986 became a national standard. We will discuss this language at length in Chapter 9.

**Figure 2—10**

Sample reports

```
                    Listing of APPOINTMENT Data

   Date      Time    Station   Student-ID   Class-name   Section-number

 12/11/88   8:00a      1        12345        BD 120           1
 12/11/88   8:00a      2        44728        BD 120           2
 12/11/88   8:00a      3          —            —              —
 12/11/88   8:00a      4        86241        BF 100           1
 12/11/88   8:00a      6        44513        BD 120           1
 12/11/88   8:00a      7        88751        BD 120           2
 12/11/88   8:00a      9        62143        BD 120           1
 12/11/88   8:00a     11        33349        BF 100           1
 12/11/88   8:00a     14        83290        BD 120           3
 12/11/88   8:00a     15        17144        BD 120           3
```

a. DBMS-supplied default report format

For now, consider two SQL examples. To list all of the appointments for student #12345, an SQL user would type:

```
SELECT      *
FROM        APPOINTMENT
WHERE       STU-NUMBER EQ 12345
```

The result of this query would be a list of all of the data items in APPOINTMENT for the indicated student.

A more sophisticated query is to list all of the software packages ever used by a particular student. The following SQL statements would do this for student #12345:

```
SELECT UNIQUE SFT-NAME
FROM APPOINTMENT, SOFTWARE.USE
  WHERE      STU-NUMBER EQ 12345
  AND        APPOINTMENT.STU-NUMBER EQ SOFTWARE-USE.STU-NUMBER
  AND        APPOINTMENT.APT-DATE EQ SOFTWARE-USE.APT-DATE
  AND        APPOINTMENT.APT-TIME EQ SOFTWARE-USE.APT-TIME
```

**Figure 2–10**
(*continued*)

```
                        HOURLY LAB USE REPORT
                          December 11, 1988
          ----------------------------------------------------------

UTILIZATION FROM 8:00 AM TO 8:59 AM
          Station         Student-ID        Class Name        Section
             1              12345            BD 120              1
             2              44728            BD 120              2
             3              none               —                 —
             4              86241            BF 100              1
             6              44513            BD 120              1
             7              88751            BD 120              2
             9              62143            BD 120              1
            11              33349            BF 100              1
            14              83290            BD 120              3
            15              17144            BD 120              3
TOTAL USE FROM 8:00 AM TO 8:59 AM IS 22 HOURS
          ----------------------------------------------------------

UTILIZATION FROM 9:00 AM TO 9:59 AM
          Station         Student-ID        Class Name        Section
             1              89847            BF 100              1
             2              21182            BF 100              1
             3              30002            BD 120              2
             ⋮
            25              46312            BD 120              3
TOTAL USE FROM 9:00 AM TO 9:59 AM IS 25 HOURS
          ----------------------------------------------------------
```

b. Report prepared with DBMS report utility

The result of this query is a list of all the software packages ever used by student 12345 for any class and during any appointment. Do not be alarmed if you do not understand this query. For now, just realize that query languages are one important mechanism for displaying data from the database.

**File Export.**   A final way in which applications can display data is to *export* files. This is similar to importing a mass of data, except the application is generating rather than receiving the file. For example an application might

**Figure 2–11**

Application display
mechanisms

```
Reports
    • Default
    • Developed by utility report generator
    • Generated by application program

Query
    • SQL
    • Other query languages

Export
    • Generating a file for another system
```

export to a word processing package the names and addresses of all customers who have purchased something in the past six months.

Display mechanisms are summarized in Figure 2–11.

### Mechanisms for Control

A database is a valuable resource. In a sense, an application is a doorway to this resource. As such, the application must implement control policies established by management. These restrictions control who accesses the database and what they do once they have accessed it.

There are several principles and techniques for controlling access to the database. First, users should not be able to access data that they do not need. This means that an application view should contain only data relevant to the application purpose. Someone working on a checking account application, for example, should not be able to access loan data.

Second, the DBMS should provide some means for controlling access to the application itself. Passwords and account numbers are often used to ensure that people do not use applications they are not authorized to use.

Third, employees should not be taught how to use applications that they have no need to use. Ignorance can be an effective control. However, it is not dependable.

Once a user has accessed a database application, processing the database must be controlled. Such controls are primarily intended to reduce the likelihood of inadvertent errors, such as deleting data instead of changing it.

*Menus* are one form of application processing control. Figure 2–12 shows a two-level menu structure used by the Eastcoast Lab. In Menu 1, the user is given the options of processing Student, Class, or Class-roster data. If

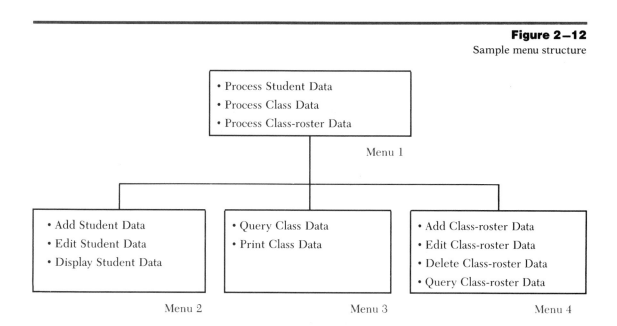

**Figure 2—12**
Sample menu structure

the user chooses Process Student Data, then Menu 2 is displayed, and so forth. Observe that Menus 2, 3, and 4 provide different processing options. The user can Add, Edit, and Display Student data, but can only Query or Print Class data. The structure of the menu and the options allowed provide one important means of application processing control.

Application programs provide another form of processing control. For example, suppose the user selects Add Student Data from Menu 2 of Figure 2–12 and further suppose that the application is constructed so that this option invokes an application program. The application program can contain further controls. It could, for example, confirm that the user truly wants to add a new student and did not invoke this program by mistake. It could check the time of day or the day of the month to determine if adding students is allowed at this time. After the user enters data, the program could ensure that the student whose data is supposed to be added is not already in the database. Many other controls could be incorporated into the application program.

Another form of processing control is to reduce the command set available to the user. With some DBMS products, certain commands can be enabled and disabled on a user-by-user basis. For example, some users can be given access to the MODIFY command and others may not. Also, some vendors provide different versions of their products. In particular, some microcomputer vendors provide a feature that allows developers to produce run-time versions of their systems. Programs are initially developed in source code, languages that people can understand. Before they can be executed, though, programs are translated into machine code, understandable only by the computer. A run-time version of an application is the machine code

**Figure 2–13**

Summary of application control mechanisms

> • Limit database views to required data
>
> • Limit access to application via passwords and account numbers
>
> • Teach applications to users only as they are needed
>
> • Restrict processing via menus
>
> • Limit processing through design of application program
>
> • Restrict allowable command set

translation, which can be employed but not read, understood, or modified by the average user. Run-time versions of an application are therefore more secure.

Mechanisms for application control are quite important. Figure 2–13 summarizes the forms of control described here. We will discuss this topic further in Chapters 4 and 7.

## SUMMARY

Database applications are developed so that users in different functional areas can get information from a common database without interfering with one another. A database application is a business computer system. As such, it has five components: hardware, programs, data, procedures, and people.

More computer equipment (such as memory or storage devices) is often required for database systems than for file processing systems. Common-database applications generally share some hardware. They might share the computer itself, or they might share only the disk on which the database is stored.

Database applications include several types of programs, such as the operating system, the DBMS, a communications control program, and application programs written to solve specific user problems. Application programs can be written in a language specific to the DBMS product, or they can be written in a standard language like COBOL.

Database data consists of the source data, the data dictionary, and overhead data. The structure of the entire database is called the schema. The portion of a database that is visible to an application is called a subschema, or application view. Most applications do not have access to the entire database. This arrangement helps protect database data from unauthorized access. It can also cause problems, though, because users may attempt to perform some database function that they do not realize might interfere with another user sharing the same data. Database system designers must design applications to avoid this.

Some DBMS products store report and form formats. This data, called *application meta-data*, is stored in the database.

Users and computer operators need procedures to tell them how to operate the system under normal conditions and what to do if the system crashes. Procedures that guide users through normal processing are often built into application programs. The program prompts the user through each step of the process.

Many groups of people are involved in a database application. Clientele are the people who will ultimately benefit from the system, though they do not interface with it. Users employ the application to perform their jobs. Computer operators run the computer equipment. Systems development personnel design and build database applications. The database administrator (DBA) protects the database and resolves conflicts among users.

Database applications include three functional components: mechanisms for updating database data, mechanisms for displaying data, and mechanisms for controlling access to and processing database data.

Database updates include adding new records, deleting unwanted ones, and modifying records. DBMSs provide a wide spectrum of facilities to update data. One category of approaches is generic utilities; they require no program development effort but are not very sophisticated. However, users can often employ them without the assistance of systems development personnel. The other category employs programs written by professional developers. Such programs can be tailored to meet stringent user requirements but take longer to develop, and therefore are more expensive.

DBMS applications include facilities for outputting database data. They are called mechanisms for displaying data, although the term *display* here includes printed reports, computer display screens, and machine-readable computer files. Reports, like forms, can be generated by DBMS utilities or by application programs. The latter is more expensive but can accommodate complicated requirements.

The second mechanism for displaying data is in response to a database query. In this case, the user formats and enters a query command identifying the data that should be extracted from the database. The DBMS locates the specified data, and formats and displays it on the computer screen. The query language SQL is a popular one.

The final mechanism for displaying data is by exporting files to another computer system. This data is in machine-readable format, unlike the previous categories, which were designed for use by people.

DBMS applications include mechanisms for controlling access to data and controlling database processing. Menus restrict the user's access and processing options and are often an effective means of control. Application programs can be designed to impose even more control on user processing because they can contain more complex and sophisticated validation and authorization routines. Also, some DBMS products allow the DBA to restrict the command set available to each user. Thus, some users would be allowed more extensive processing rights than other users.

In Chapter 3 we will examine the DBMS and the role it plays in developing database applications.

---

**GROUP I**          QUESTIONS

2.1   Why did Samantha Green decide to develop four applications for the university's computer lab? What factors influenced her?

2.2   Why did Samantha decide to develop a single-user, multi-application database system? Is there really only one user?

2.3   What type of data is common to the SCHEDULING application and the CHECKOUT application in Eastcoast's database system? What data is shared by the INVENTORY and CHECKOUT applications?

2.4   Could Eastcoast's problems have been solved with a file processing system? What problems would that approach present that can be overcome with a database system?

2.5   What are the five components of a database application? Give examples of each using the Eastcoast Lab as an illustration.

2.6   What special hardware is required by database applications?

2.7   Do professional programmers develop database application programs? Do users? Do you suppose most users want to learn how to write COBOL or Pascal programs to access a database? How do you suppose this has influenced the development of DBMS features?

2.8   What are four types of data in a database application? How are they related?

2.9   What is a subschema, or application view? How can views be used to control access to a database?

2.10  What are procedures? List four events for which the lab attendants at Eastcoast would require procedures. Do you suppose Samantha would develop these procedures? If not, who would?

2.11  Describe three techniques for updating database data. What are the advantages and disadvantages of the techniques you listed?

2.12  What technique must be used if data invisible to the user needs to be updated?

2.13  Describe three techniques that are used to display data in a database.

2.14  Why is it necessary to control access to and processing of a database?

2.15  Describe three controls you would incorporate into the Eastcoast Lab's database system.

2.16  Besides the lab attendants, who might other users of the lab database system be? Should all users have equal access to the database system? Should students? How would you prevent students from accessing the lab database?

QUESTIONS AND EXERCISES                                             **GROUP II**

**2.17**  Interview the manager of a small business that uses a database management system. Describe the applications installed in the system. For any two
applications, identify the five system components.

**2.18**  Interview the DBA of a local company. Find out if users develop any of
their own applications in that company. If so, what tools do they use? If
not, who develops applications? What tools do they use?

**2.19**  Design the logic for an application program that would delete a piece of
computer equipment from Eastcoast Lab's database. Keep in mind that
appointments might be scheduled for it. Also keep in mind that a "white-
collar thief" might want to delete such a record in order to cover up a theft.
What procedures would you put in place to keep this from happening?

# Database Management Systems: Toolkits for Application Development

- The DBMS
- Generic DBMS Functions
- The Subsystems of a DBMS
- The Application Development Process
- Summary

In this chapter we will examine the DBMS tools that system developers employ to build applications. These tools allow developers to quickly design screens, reports, and other interfaces, and even to build prototypes for user review. Database system development, as mentioned in Chapter 2, is often accomplished one application at a time.

In the simplest terms, an *application* is the collection of menus, forms, reports, and programs that satisfies the needs of a functional business unit. Consequently, the menus, screens, reports, and programs in one application are usually closely related. You might think of a database application as a subsystem that is employed by one user group. Let us consider an illustration from Eastcoast State University's Computer Lab.

When a lab attendant loads the Micro Lab Database System, the first screen he sees is the main menu (Figure 3–1). Let us suppose that a student wishes to schedule an appointment for computer time, so the lab attendant selects option 1 from the main menu. The next screen displayed for the user is the Scheduling Application menu that is illustrated in Figure 3–2.

**Figure 3–1**

Main menu for Micro
Lab Database System

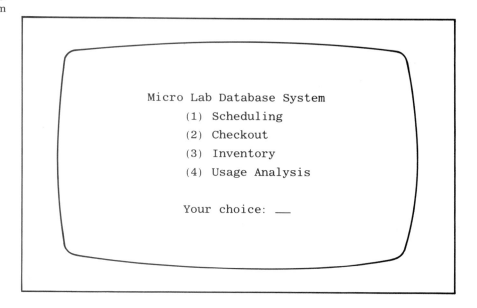

**Figure 3–2**

Scheduling applica-
tion menu

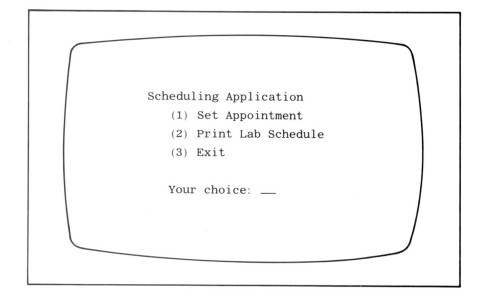

**Figure 3-3**

Portion of an appoint-
ment scheduling form

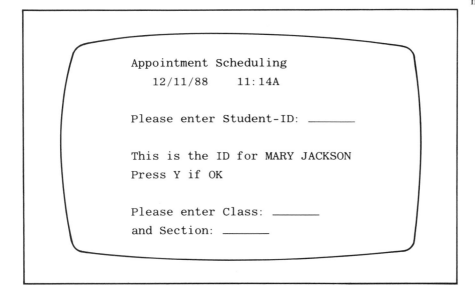

```
    Appointment Scheduling
        12/11/88    11:14A


    Please enter Student-ID: _____


    This is the ID for MARY JACKSON
    Press Y if OK


    Please enter Class: _____
    and Section: _____
```

The lab attendant selects option 1 to schedule an appointment. The third screen presented to the user is the form you saw in Figure 2–8a. It is reproduced in Figure 3–3 for your convenience. The lab attendant completes the form, one entry at a time. If he should make an error, an appropriate error message will appear at the bottom of the screen. As the attendant enters data, the transaction processing program uses it to formulate requests for the DBMS—sometimes to find matching data in the database, such as a student's name, and sometimes to update the database with new data, such as a newly scheduled appointment.

This form is actually the user's interface to the transaction processing program. It is the vehicle for input to and output from the program. Remember that a transaction is the record of an event that occurs in the business world. A transaction processing program requires input to keep database data current with the real world. In order to schedule an appointment, then, a lab attendant employs two menus, one form, and a transaction processing program.

Now let us suppose that every three hours the lab attendant prints a lab schedule to be posted outside the lab. He selects from the Scheduling Application menu option 2, Print Lab Schedule. This activates a report writing program. After responding to a few prompts (such as "Enter the date and time periods to be printed:") and readying the printer, the lab attendant waits for the program to produce the Lab Schedule report. The report is an output interface to the application—it is visible to the user, while the program that produces it is not.

You can see that the SCHEDULING application consists of the menus, forms, reports, and programs needed to perform scheduling and related functions. The SCHEDULING application is one of four related applications in the computer lab database system.

The database developer, Samantha Green, needed to carefully define, design, build, and implement all of the system components (hardware, programs, data, procedures, and people) for each of these common-database applications. To do this effectively, she employed many development tools available in the DBMS product chosen for Eastcoast. In this chapter we will examine features of DBMS products with a special emphasis on those features that are used for system development—the system development tools. Then we will examine the process of developing database applications.

## THE DBMS

Since an application is a business computer system, then in a sense a DBMS is a toolkit that helps system developers to design and implement the system and users to employ it. A DBMS provides a set of functions and utilities. Some DBMS vendors provide more tools than others. Some tools are easier than others to use or they provide better performance. In this section, we will describe a generic set of functions and tools that are incorporated into almost every DBMS product. When we discuss implementation in the later chapters, we will be more specific about DBMS products.

A DBMS is a set of programs that are used to define, process, and administer the database and its applications. Notice several implications of this statement. First, a DBMS is *software*. Second, this software is *used* by people or programs that need to interface with the database. Finally, some DBMS programs are used to *define* and *build* both the *database* and database *applications,* other DBMS programs *process data* in the database, and still other DBMS programs *provide administrative facilities.*

A system developer such as Samantha uses the *definition* features of the DBMS to establish the structure of the database, such as the formats of files and data items, and to define constraints governing the data values and processing of the database data. The system developer also defines data entry forms and other vehicles for loading, reading, and updating the database. She also defines database applications that users can employ to process the database. Once these aspects of the system are defined, data can be loaded into the database.

With data now in the database, users can employ the applications to store, retrieve, and update it. The programs in these applications access the *processing* features of the DBMS. Concurrently, other DBMS programs *administer* the database.

## GENERIC DBMS FUNCTIONS

Figure 3–4 lists generic DBMS functions. First, as stated, the DBMS stores, retrieves, and updates user data. The manner in which the data is processed depends on characteristics of the database application accessing the DBMS. For example, data might be retrieved and then printed in a report, displayed on a computer screen, or transmitted to another computer.

As the DBMS stores and updates source data on behalf of the application, it must also maintain the appropriate overhead data. If, for example, a database includes customer records and the DBMS keeps an index of customer numbers, then the index must be changed whenever new customers are added or deleted. Various types of overhead data are discussed in Appendix B.

The next DBMS function is to store, retrieve, and update the meta-data stored in the data dictionary. Remember that the data dictionary contains descriptions of database files and record formats, cross-references among data items, files, records, and programs, and much other data about the structure of the database. This data is particularly useful to the database administrator. It can also be accessed by users who need to know the physical formats of data items of interest to them. Some data dictionaries are *active*. This means that, except for retrieval, which is frequently done by users or the DBA, much of the updating of meta-data is done by the DBMS itself. We will discuss data dictionaries in the next section.

A third function of the DBMS is to enforce integrity rules and constraints. Earlier we mentioned that the developer can define content rules and processing constraints on the database. Once they are established, it is the responsibility of the DBMS to enforce them.

Some constraints are easy to enforce. For example, suppose no appointment for the computer lab can be scheduled between midnight and 7:00

---

**Figure 3–4**

Functions of a generic
DBMS product

- Store, retrieve, and update user data (maintain overhead data) OVERHEAD
- Store, retrieve, and update meta-data
- Enforce integrity rules and constraints          SPACE
- Enforce security constraints SECURITY
- Provide coordination and control facilities for multi-user processing SHARING
- Provide facilities for backup and recovery   CRASH RECOVERY

A.M. It is possible to define a rule such that the value of a data item called Appointment-time must be between 7:00 A.M. and 11:45 P.M. The rule becomes part of the database. It is then up to the DBMS to enforce the rule by rejecting as an error any appointment time not within the allowable range.

Integrity rules are sometimes more difficult to enforce. For example, one of the constraints imposed by the lab is that only active students enrolled in a class that is authorized to use the lab can schedule appointments. This means that the Student-ID on an Appointment record added to the database must match one of the Student-IDs on the STUDENT file and that the student must be enrolled in one of the classes on the CLASS file. The DBMS should be responsible for ensuring that both conditions are satisfied before adding to the database an appointment for any student. However, most current DBMS products are unable to enforce this kind of a constraint. Instead, an application program must be written to do it.

A final example illustrates a different type of problem. Each appointment, of course, involves a computer and a student. Suppose a student drops out of the class that allowed her access to the computer lab. In this case, the lab attendant must remove her record from the STUDENT file. If appointments are scheduled for this student, then simply removing the Student record will destroy the integrity of the two files (STUDENTs and APPOINTMENTs) because one or more Appointment records will be for a student no longer on file. The integrity rule that Appointment records must be for authorized students only must be enforced not only when records are added, but also when data is changed or deleted from the database. Ideally, the DBMS enforces such a rule. Many DBMS products are as yet unable to enforce such a constraint, however, and programs must be written to handle it.

The fourth function of a DBMS is closely allied with the third. The DBMS must enforce security rules and constraints. To maintain order and protect the database, companies that use databases need to ensure that only authorized people can perform authorized database functions at authorized times. The DBMS provides facilities to define user authorization (for example, each user might be assigned a password recorded in the database), and processing rights (for example, User #123 might be allowed to read the appointment data, but not to update it; User #456 might be allowed to set appointments, but not to delete computer equipment). Once these security constraints are entered into the system, it is up to the DBMS to enforce them.

The next DBMS function pertains to concurrent applications. When two programs attempt to process the same record at the same instant, conflict can occur. If both programs simply want to read the data, then there is no problem. But if one or both of the programs want to change the data, then precautions must be taken to ensure that while one program is updating the data, the other program cannot update it. The DBMS includes features such as *locks* that control concurrent access to data. While one application uses a record, a lock is placed on it that prevents all other applications from accessing that record. When the lock is released, other applications can access it again. Techniques besides locks are also employed by the DBMS to maintain order in concurrent applications. We will address this topic more fully in Chapters 7 and 15.

Finally, the DBMS provides facilities for backup and recovery. Unfortunately, in spite of everyone's best efforts, equipment can fail, programs can contain bugs, and users can make mistakes. When any of these occur, the organization must have a means for correcting the database. Sometimes this means the database must be reloaded from a backup copy, and all transactions that have been processed since the backup was done must be reapplied. In other cases, an error is corrected by backing out of the database the effects of one or more transactions. In any case, the DBMS must provide facilities for making backup copies, for logging all transactions, and for reestablishing the database to an earlier version when necessary.

We will now consider the subsystems of a typical DBMS product.

## THE SUBSYSTEMS OF A DBMS

Figure 3–5 shows the subsystems of a DBMS. As you might imagine, a DBMS is a large and complex program. For example, the code for one microcomputer database management system, R:BASE System V, is over 4 million bytes. Recalling all of the functions a DBMS must perform, it should be no surprise that it is so large, much larger than the application programs it serves. Let's consider each of the subsystems shown in Figure 3–5.

### The DBMS Engine

The DBMS engine is the heart of the DBMS. This subsystem receives *logical I/O requests* from other subsystems and translates those requests into reads from or writes to database files. Logical I/O requests are expressed in terms of data contents, or logical position, rather than as physical storage locations. Two examples of logical I/O requests are

```
READ CUSTOMER 123
CHANGE Credit-limit IN CUSTOMER 123 TO 5000.
```

The DBMS engine determines the location of the requested data using data in the data dictionary, then issues a corresponding *physical I/O request* to the operating system. The operating system in turn executes the I/O commands. Physical I/O requests are usually expressed in terms of the storage location of the requested data, such as

```
READ BLOCK 714 FROM FILE DBMS3.DAT INTO MEMORY LOCATION 22458.
```

**Figure 3–5**

Functional compo-
nents of a DBMS

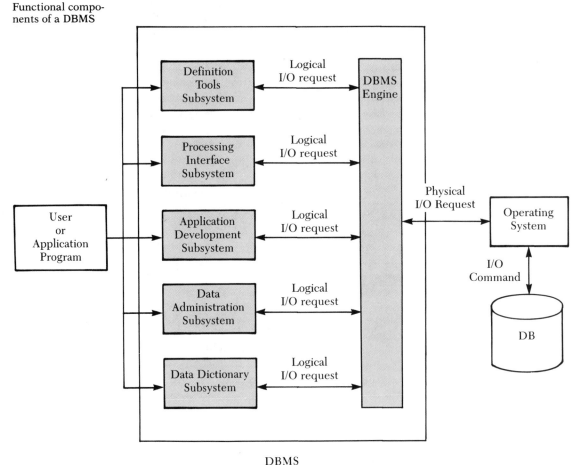

DBMS

To appreciate the complexity of the DBMS engine, consider the following illustration. Suppose the DBMS engine receives the request

```
CHANGE Credit-limit IN CUSTOMER 123 TO 5000.
```

To process this command, the engine must accomplish the following tasks:

1. Determine the physical file location of the data dictionary (meta-
   data) for Customer records.
2. Read the meta-data.
3. Using the meta-data, determine the location of overhead data that
   pertains to Customer records.
4. Read the overhead data for Customer 123's record.
5. Using overhead data, determine the operating system file and block
   address of Customer 123's record.

**Figure 3—6**
Structure of a block
of database data

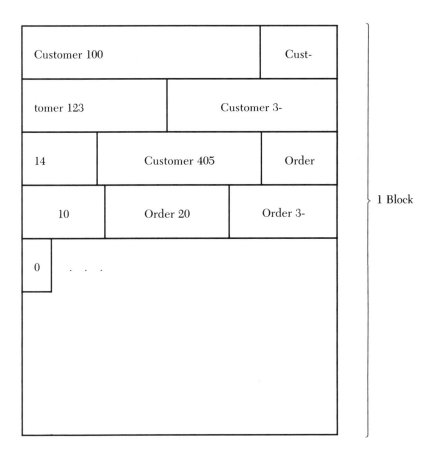

6. Read the block containing Customer 123's data.
7. Using meta-data, determine the location of Customer 123's record within the block just read and the location of Credit-limit within the record (see Figure 3–6).
8. Change the value of Credit-limit.
9. Mark this block for rewriting to the file (or rewrite it now).
10. Check meta-data for overhead data that may need to be changed in light of the data change.
11. For each related index or other overhead structure, read, change, and replace overhead data as appropriate.

This is an impressive list of tasks to accomplish for a relatively simple change. There are complications, too. Before data can be read, there must be space in memory. The DBMS keeps a large buffer (section of memory) just for this purpose. But if that buffer is full, data in the buffer must be removed or overlaid. Thus, the DBMS engine must perform *memory management* by managing buffers, keeping track of available memory locations, and so forth.

The DBMS engine also performs *disk management*. When data is added to the database, the DBMS engine must find available space in a disk file and allocate it. When records are deleted, the DBMS engine must remove the data (or mark it as deleted) and then somehow make available the newly freed space. As all of this activity is taking place, the DBMS engine constantly *maintains both the overhead data and the meta-data stored in the data dictionary*. The functions of the DBMS engine are listed in Figure 3–7.

### The Definition Tools Subsystem

Examine Figure 3–5 again. Notice that the other five subsystems in a DBMS interface with either a user or an application program. These subsystems call on the DBMS engine for services.

The first subsystem, the Definition Tools Subsystem, consists of tools and utilities for defining and changing the database structure. The user employs this subsystem to create the structure of the database. This structure includes the files, fields, relationships, constraints, overhead data structures, and other components of the database. Recall that the word *schema* refers to the complete logical view of the database. The Definition Tools Subsystem is used to define the schema.

As stated in Chapter 2, for security and control reasons, it is undesirable to allow a program or user to have access to the entire schema. During design, the subset of the database that each program and user needs is identified. This *subschema*, or *application view*, is also defined using the Definition Tools Subsystem.

Nothing remains the same. Business needs change, people learn more about the tasks they wish to accomplish, and decisions are made that necessitate storing more data in the database. As these changes occur, the struc-

**Figure 3–7**
Functions of the
DBMS engine

- Map logical I/O requests into physical I/O activity
- Manage memory space
- Manage disk space
- Maintain overhead and meta-data structures

**Figure 3—8**
Functions of the
Definition Tools
Subsystem

- Build schema structure
- Build subschema structure
- Change schema structure
- Chang subschema structure

ture of the database may need to be altered. New files become necessary. New data items must be added to existing files. Overhead data structures must be added, or they become obsolete and need to be removed. All of these changes are accomplished using the Definition Tools Subsystem. The functions of the Definition Tools Subsystem are summarized in Figure 3–8.

## The Processing Interface Subsystem

The Processing Interface Subsystem allows users and programs to access the database system. Users can make direct queries against the database by means of an interactive query language such as SQL (see Chapter 9). Users can learn a useful subset of such languages in a short period of time. Such languages allow users to extract data from the database and display it on the computer screen. For example, if a lab attendant wanted to quickly see all of the appointments scheduled for May 11, she might enter

```
SELECT *
FROM APPOINTMENT
WHERE APPTDATE = "05/11"
```

No programming is needed. An application does not have to be developed that includes menu options for this "report," nor does any report or form need to be designed. The DBMS product simply displays the extracted data in columns on the computer screen. The Processing Interface Subsystem of the DBMS product interpreted the SQL statement and then made the I/O request of the DBMS engine. When data was extracted, it was passed to the Processing Interface Subsystem, which formatted and displayed the results.

Besides languages such as SQL, there are other, more graphic user interfaces. One such product is called Query by Example, or QBE. Using QBE, a user indicates what data is to be extracted from the database by completing entries in a template displayed on the screen. An example of a

**Figure 3—9**

QBE example

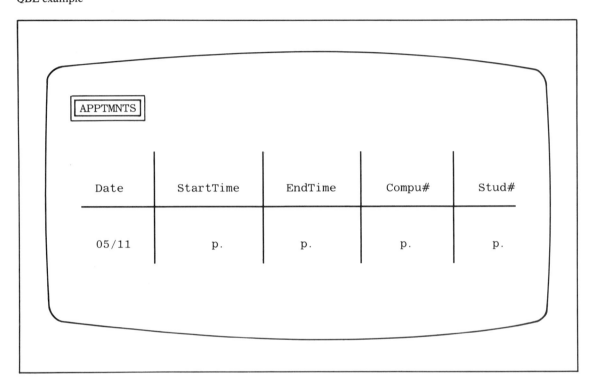

QBE request to do the same function as the SQL example above appears in Figure 3–9. The Processing Interface Subsystem for the DBMS must be designed to interpret QBE requests.

The disadvantage of interfaces such as query languages or graphic interfaces is that users need to learn the syntax of the language or interface. Depending on the product, this can be difficult and confusing. In an effort to make users more self-sufficient, some vendors have developed another type of user interface, called *natural language*. A natural language interface allows users to express their queries in standard English (or other human language) sentences. As you might expect, the nature of natural languages makes interpretation difficult. English sentences can be structured many ways, and they are often ambiguous. The Processing Interface Subsystem needs to decide how to interpret a query expressed in a natural language. If a request is ambiguous, then the interpreter might extract the wrong data.

For example, suppose a user entered this query:

```
Show all of the employees who earn more than the average sal-
ary in California.
```

This sentence has several meanings, two of which are: show all the employees in California who make more than the companywide average, or show all the employees in the company who make more than the average California employee. A natural language interpreter needs to either (1) recognize the ambiguity and ask the user for clarification, or (2) guess which interpretation is the "right" one and answer that question. Of course, it might not be the question the user had intended to ask. Natural language interfaces are still being developed and improved. They are not as widely used as more structured (and therefore less ambiguous) languages such as SQL.

In addition to accepting requests directly from a user, the Processing Interface Subsystem also includes interfaces for third-generation programming languages, such as COBOL and PL/I. In the simplest case, the DBMS product includes a program library of DBMS routines. The programmer calls the appropriate routine for DBMS service. An example is

```
CALL DBMS-READ (file, field-name, field-value, buffer, status)
```

where the parameters indicate the name of the file to be read, the name of the key field, the value of the key field, an address to place the record in, and a status flag to indicate normal or error conditions. The command would obviously need to be expressed in proper host language syntax.

Writing call statements like this one can be complex and tricky. It is easy to make programming errors. To make the programmer's job easier, some DBMS vendors provide special DBMS commands for the application programmer to use in place of call statements. These commands, which are simpler and easier to use than the equivalent programming statements, replace the call statements in the host program. An example is

```
SELECT Customer-name INTO .cname FROM CUSTOMER
WHERE Customer-ID = .id
```

In this example, .cname and .id represent program variables. This command obtains the name of the customer whose Customer-ID equals the value of the variable .id and places it in the variable .cname.

Statements such as this are not part of any standard programming language, so the language compilers do not recognize them. Therefore, the application program is first translated by a pre-compiler (provided by the DBMS vendor). The pre-compiler replaces the database commands with standard programming language statements. Thus, for example, the SELECT command above would be replaced with the equivalent external program call.

The procedure for a COBOL program is illustrated in Figure 3–10. In this example, the application programmer identifies the database needed by means of an INVOKE command: INVOKE SUBSCHEMA ALPHA. INVOKE is not a COBOL instruction, so the pre-compiler must translate it into COBOL instructions before the COBOL compiler reads the program.

**Figure 3–10**

Illustration of use of pre-compiler

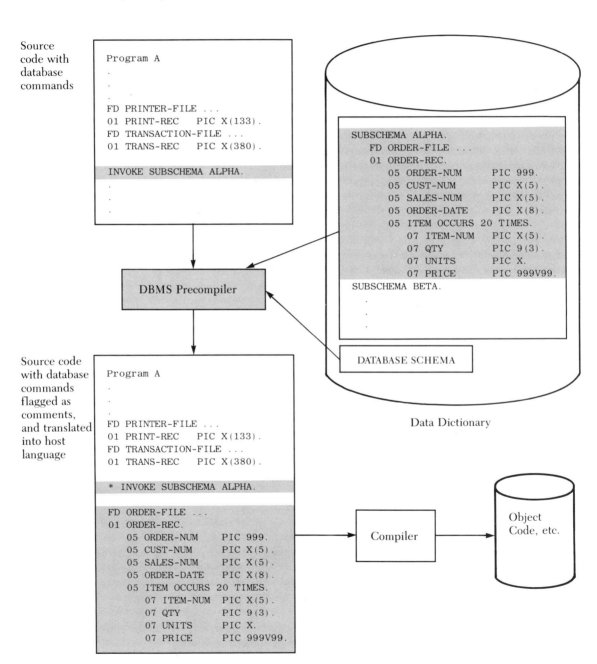

The pre-compiler locates the subschema, ALPHA, in the data dictionary and inserts the appropriate COBOL description in the DATA DIVISION. Other DBMS instructions in the program are likewise replaced with the equivalent COBOL code. After pre-compilation, the COBOL compiler can be used. The particulars of pre-compilation are unimportant at this point. You simply need to realize that the Processing Interface Subsystem enables programmers to include database access commands in their host-language programs by providing pre-compilation when needed.

In addition to the three standard database system interfaces we have seen—SQL, natural language, and interfaces to third-generation host languages—users can also perform database accesses through the DBMS manufacturer's own language. Products such as Ashton-Tate's dBASE and MicroRIM's R:BASE include programming languages that were developed as part of the DBMS (or DBMS-like) products. These are called *DBMS-specific* programming languages, because they pertain to only one DBMS.

## The Application Development Tools Subsystem

The next subsystem in Figure 3–5 concerns application development. This subsystem contains tools for developing application components such as forms, reports, and menus. It may also include program code generators. Sometimes these tools are sold separately from the DBMS, and at other times they are integrated with it.

Consider the development of a data display form. Suppose you want to define a form that has data from both CUSTOMER and INVOICE records. A form includes both constants, such as the form title, column headers, and prompts, and variables, such as the customer's name and address and the invoice number and line items. Defining the form is relatively easy when using a forms generator, which is part of the Application Development Subsystem. Forms generators employ several techniques for constructing a form, but one typical way is to present the user with a blank screen on which she can "paint" the form just the way she wants it to look. Thus a forms generator employs a what-you-see-is-what-you-get (known as WYSIWYG) approach to screen design.

The user positions the cursor and enters constants precisely where they will appear on the form. She also indicates the positions of variable data. This might be done by placing the cursor at the appropriate screen position and then pressing a function key, such as F3. This tells the forms generator that a variable will appear here. The user enters the name of the variable. Because the forms generator can access the data dictionary, it can rapidly determine the length of the field and automatically allocate enough space on the form to accommodate the field. (Most forms generators allow the user to override the field length. Sometimes a user needs to display only the first several characters in a field.)

After positioning all of the constants and variables, the user can store the format of this form as part of the application meta-data. Thereafter, the

DBMS can retrieve it whenever it is needed in an application. The form format can also be retrieved so the user can modify it.

The Application Development Subsystem includes similar tools for developing menus, reports, and application programs. In each case, the subsystem uses the meta-data stored in the data dictionary to speed up the development process and to reduce the likelihood of errors. And it stores the results for future reference.

### The Data Administration Subsystem

Databases need care and maintenance. They need to be backed up, and occasionally they need to be recovered. As time passes, obsolete data will need to be archived or purged from the database. Requirements will change, and the structure of the database or the applications will need to be adjusted accordingly. All of these functions are handled by the Data Administration Subsystem. The Data Administration Subsystem is a collection of utility programs that perform maintenance functions on the database itself. Its functions are more likely to be used by the computer operations staff or by the DBA than by users or application programmers.

### The Data Dictionary Subsystem

The last DBMS subsystem shown in Figure 3–5 is the Data Dictionary Subsystem, which provides query and report functions on the database meta-data. This subsystem is employed most often by the DBA. The data dictionary is a gold mine of information needed for administering the database. Because it contains complete descriptions of the database structure and all the relationships among programs and data, and because it can be queried using the same commands as users employ for source data, its value to the DBA is inestimable.

For example, suppose the format or length of a data item needs to be changed. By querying the data dictionary, the DBA can determine which records contain the data item, the forms, reports, and programs that use the data item, security considerations regarding the data item, and so forth. This information helps the DBA to determine the extent of work needed to implement such a change and how making such a change will affect the rest of the database system. Knowing this, the DBA is able to approve the change (or not), to allocate people and other resources to implement it, and to notify all those individuals who will be affected by the change, such as data entry clerks and users.

Database administration will be considered in detail in Chapter 7. This is an important function, and one that is often neglected until the problems of poor data administration manifest themselves. Realize that a DBMS product should provide tools to support this function.

# THE APPLICATION DEVELOPMENT PROCESS

So far you have been introduced to applications (in Chapter 2) and the tools available for developing them (in the previous section). In this section we are going to examine the process of developing database applications. This is an overview of a very complex process. Your systems analysis and design course treats the subject in much more depth.

Developing a database system requires the same steps as developing any business computer system. It is generally more complex, though, because database systems frequently involve multiple applications, each with many users, all processing concurrently. Nonetheless, the process involved is the same.

Although there are many ways of defining the systems development process, we will describe a process in this chapter that captures the essence of most development methodologies. Although some people might differ with the terminology described here, most would agree with the fundamental phases. Developing a database application involves hundreds of discrete steps. These steps can be summarized in the five general phases shown in Figure 3–11.

## The Definition Phase

The first phase of an application development project is to define what the project is to do. The project may be to modify an existing application, it may be to develop a comprehensive set of applications around a common database, or it may be something else. The goal of this phase is to find out what is to be done.

The first task is to form a team of people to work on the project. The members of this team may vary over time. The team might consist of only one person, as it did for the Eastcoast Lab database system, or it might include dozens of people.

Once the team has been formed, it must define the problem to be solved. The team members need to agree among themselves what is to be done. Problem definition often sounds easier than it is. A problem is a perceived difference between what is and what ought to be. Since a problem is a perception, different people will have different understandings of it. The team members must bring their collective experiences to bear on the situation to define both what is and what ought to be. At the Eastcoast Lab, Samantha's experience enabled her to view the problem as more than just the disappearance of a microcomputer. She looked both more deeply and more broadly to define the problem.

The third task of the definition phase is to establish the scope of the project. Users, understandably, want to have systems that perform numerous functions for them. Unfortunately, system developers are often unable

**Figure 3–11**

Summary of database and application development

*Definition Phase*
- Form project team
- Define the problem
- Establish scope
- Assess feasibility

*Requirement Phase*
- Interview users
- Determine data requirements
- Determine update, display, and control mechanisms

*Evaluation*
- Select system architecture
- Reassess feasibility and possibly defer requirements
- Set priorities

*Design*
- Develop database design
  - Files
  - Data items
  - Relationships
- Develop application design
  - Determine views
  - Specify update, display, and control mechanisms
  - Design program logic

*Implement*
- Construct database
- Build applications
- Install database and applications

to put all the features the users want into the first release of a new system. Thus, when the team determines the scope of the system, it may be limiting development to certain functions or even certain users.

At Eastcoast, Samantha defined the scope to include scheduling, usage reporting, and software checkout as well as inventory control. She expanded the scope from the problem set out by the department chairperson. And although Samantha knew that the Computer Science Department operated a similar lab, she did not expand the scope of her project that far.

The final task of the definition phase is to assess feasibility. There are three kinds of feasibility: cost, technical, and schedule. Can the problem be solved with a cost-effective system? It makes no sense to solve a $100 problem with a $100,000 information system. The team needs to make a rough estimate of the rate of return on the money invested to see if the solution is cost feasible.

Technical feasibility pertains to whether a computer-based system can solve the problem. If Samantha implements the lab database system and computers and software continue to disappear, then perhaps she has developed an elegant solution to the wrong problem. Maybe a thief has gotten a key to the lab and is sneaking in at night to steal equipment. Changing the locks on the door would then be a better solution than Samantha's approach.

The solution to another problem (unrelated to Eastcoast's Lab) might require a near-perfect machine translation from English to Russian. If so, the problem is technically infeasible since such machines do not yet exist.

Scheduling is the third aspect of project feasibility. Can the application be developed in time? If the application is required to file tax forms this April and if it cannot be developed until next September, then the project is schedule infeasible.

In summary, the definition phase includes preliminary activities. The goal is to get organized, to determine what is to be done, and, insofar as possible, to determine if it makes sense to proceed. Depending on the project, the definition phase should take somewhere between one hour and one month.

At the end of this phase, as is true for the other four phases as well, the team should report to its sponsor (probably a company manager). The sponsor deserves to be informed of progress and needs the opportunity to make corrections as the team proceeds or to cancel the project.

## The Requirements Phase

The purpose of the requirements phase is to determine, as specifically as possible, what the new system must do. During the definition phase, the team will have determined the general goals of the system. For example, during the definition step, Samantha concluded that the new system would support the four applications—inventory, scheduling, checkout, and usage analysis. She also felt that they would probably be common-database applications. However, the output from the definition phase is insufficient to design and implement the database and applications. More detail is needed.

The ultimate authority on application requirements is the users. In fact, a development team should include some users. Often, users are unable to articulate their needs to the development team. It's not that users are not intelligent—it's simply that the terminology and concepts that computer people use are often alien to the user community. Also, many users are not aware of all the things a system *can* do for them, so they can't ask for such features. As one user put it, "I can't tell you what I want, but I'll know it when I see it." This user was not being difficult; recognition is far easier than recollection. Imagine a restaurant without menus—customers must recall and describe exactly what they want.

A development team needs to bring to bear its knowledge, experience, and intuition to help the users describe their needs. The team may develop *prototypes* of forms, reports, and menus and show them to the users. A prototype is a quickly developed mock-up of the real thing—a working model. Prototyping is possible because DBMS tools allow a developer to very quickly (and therefore inexpensively) show the user what a screen might look like, or what a report might contain, or how one menu might chain to another one. If users have the opportunity to help specify their interfaces during the early stages of system development, then the system is much more likely to meet their real needs. Prototypes can provide a context for dialogue between users and the development team.

By examining the system outputs and by investigating the user's business functions in depth, the team can determine what data must be captured and stored in the database. In the next chapter we will study this important step of specifying database requirements.

The output of the requirements phase is a statement of requirements. This statement can take a variety of forms. It can be a verbal description, a collection of dataflow diagrams and other schematics, one or more prototypical systems, or all of these. The requirements document needs to be reviewed and approved both by the users and the sponsor of the project.

At the Eastcoast Lab, Samantha produced an informal requirements document. After she had interviewed the chairperson, the lab manager, and several lab attendants, she used one of the lab's microcomputer DBMS products to build a prototype of each application. This included all the menus plus one or two forms and reports for each application. This skeletal system gave lab attendants an opportunity to try out the system before it was actually built. Samantha, like any developer, listened to the users' criticisms of the prototype and made some adjustments to it. When they were satisfied with the prototype, Samantha began the next phase: evaluation of alternatives.

## Evaluation

The third phase of systems development is evaluation. It consists of three tasks. First, alternative application system architectures are identified. Second, the feasibility of the application is reassessed now that the requirements are known in more detail and the basic alternative solutions have been specified. Finally, all user requirements are reevaluated within the context of each possible solution. If all requirements cannot be accommodated during this project, then priorities must be set and some requirements deferred to future projects. With this data available, the users and the project sponsor can select the alternative solution they feel is the best one.

These three tasks are not necessarily performed in sequence. Sometimes a particular approach can be feasible only if one or several of the most demanding or troublesome requirements can be deferred. Thus, in some instances, requirements are first ranked by priority, and then possible solutions are proposed.

Often, several solutions can satisfy the requirements. For example, at Eastcoast Lab, a file processing system *could* support the four applications Samantha identified. But lab attendants would be unable to post appointments so quickly, and usage reports would probably be produced only overnight, when the computer was not being used for the other programs. Also, Samantha considered implementing the system on the lab's local area network (LAN), which would allow the lab attendant to schedule appointments at the same time that, for example, a professor was printing some usage reports. This approach would be more costly and would be more difficult to develop. Consequently, Samantha recommended neither a file processing system nor a LAN-based system to solve the lab's problems. Samantha decided to develop a single-user, multiple-application database system on the microcomputer at the lab assistants' station.

## Design

The goal of the design phase is to develop a blueprint for the database and its applications. During this phase the development team establishes the database schema, the application subschemas, formats for forms, reports, and menus, the logic for transaction processing programs, and so forth. The team also selects mechanisms for update, display, and control (Chapter 2).

In many cases, system development means adding a new application to an existing database system. For example, a year after Eastcoast State University implemented the four applications that Samantha developed, it decided to add a PURCHASING application to the system. This new application required alterations to the schema of the lab database. It also meant that new forms, reports, menus, and transaction processing programs had to be developed. In this case, during the design phase the team needed to design changes to the database and to the other application components.

The output of the design phase consists of several documents. An example of database design documents for Eastcoast's system can be seen in Figure 3–12. First is the database design, consisting of a description of the files in the database, the data items within each file, and the name and both logical and physical descriptions of every data item (Figure 3–12b). The relationships among the files must also be specified (Figure 3–12a). You will learn the process of database design in Chapter 6.

Once the database has been designed, the development team can design each application. Remember that an application is the collection of menus, forms, reports, and programs that addresses the needs of a group of users. The techniques you have learned in other courses for screen design, report

## Figure 3–12

Example of logical database design documents for Eastcoast Lab

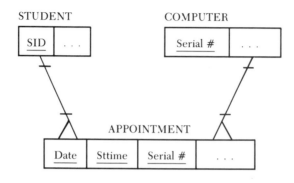

a. Relation diagram

| STUDENT | | | COMPUTER | | | APPOINTMENT | | |
|---|---|---|---|---|---|---|---|---|
| Item | Length | Type | Item | Length | Type | Item | Length | Type |
| SID | 4 | A/N | Serial # | 6 | A/N | Date | 8 | date |
| Name | 20 | A/N | Location | 2 | A/N | Sttime | 4 | time |
| | | | Memory | 8 | A/N | Endtime | 4 | time |
| | | | Storage | 15 | A/N | Serial # | 6 | A/N |
| | | | Monitor | 1 | N | SID | 4 | A/N |

b. Relation definitions

design, and program design are employed here. In addition, the team defines the database subschema, or application view, for each application.

Several techniques for expressing database and application design can be used. The diagram in Figure 3–12a is a modification of a graphic called an *entity-relationship*, or E-R, diagram. Database files can be described in tables, such as the ones in Figure 3–12, or more formally in data dictionary format. Report and screen formats can be illustrated on grid paper or can be computer-produced prototypes. Transaction processing program logic can be illustrated with pseudocode, flowcharts, structure charts, and other tools. The particular methods used depend on the size and complexity of the project, the needs of the users, the preferences of the developers, and the facilities available in the DBMS product being employed.

All design documents should be subjected to a thorough review before implementation begins. This is the last opportunity the team has to find errors before building the system. After this phase, errors become much more costly and difficult to repair. Such reviews are absolutely vital to the success of any project when the cost of a mistake in implementation is high.

Samantha was working on a relatively small project. She had designed the system by herself and asked another graduate student to review it with her. Even though it was informal, the review was worthwhile because the other student found two flaws in the design. This project was not critical, nor would the cost of fixing errors after implementation have been high— Samantha, after all, was working at *very* reduced rates. If these factors had not pertained, a more formal design document and review would have been necessary.

## Implementation

The final phase of the development process is implementation. The details of implementation greatly depend on the particular DBMS product to be used. This situation is similar to that for programming: once an algorithm has been developed and expressed in pseudocode, the implementation of that algorithm depends on the programming language to be used.

The primary task of implementation is to construct the system according to the design. The definition facilities of the DBMS are used to define the schema and subschemas. Developers use the features of the application development subsystem to build forms, reports, and menus and also to build transaction processing programs. Other programs may need to be written in a standard programming language and linked to the DBMS via the processing interface.

Each component of each application needs to be tested. The amount and type of testing depend on the nature of the system and how the components were developed. We will discuss this issue further in the implementation chapters of this text.

Installation is the last stage of the development. If it has not yet been done, then users need to be trained on the new system. Sometimes user training is done in parallel with the design phase. User and operator procedures are documented during this final stage and data is loaded into the database.

When implementing a new system, a company must decide whether to abandon the old system (if there was one in place) and adopt the new one all at once or to run two systems *in parallel*. Immediately abandoning the old system in favor of the new one can be dangerous because the new system may contain as yet undetected errors. On the other hand, running the new system in parallel with the old one can be more expensive because two complete systems must be operated with the same data at the same time and their results need to be compared. However, this approach is less risky. With parallel implementation, the old system is not abandoned until the organization is convinced that the new system is at least as good.

This section has presented a brief overview of a process for developing database systems. In the next chapter we will focus on one critical step in this process: how to develop database requirements.

## SUMMARY

An application is a collection of menus, reports, forms, and programs that addresses the needs of a user group. A database management system provides tools to system developers for designing and implementing applications for users who need to employ the system. A DBMS is a set of programs that provides facilities to define, process, and administer the database and its applications.

Major components of the DBMS are the DBMS engine, the Definition Tools Subsystem, the Processing Interface Subsystem, the Application Development Subsystem, the Data Administration Subsystem, and the Data Dictionary Subsystem.

The DBMS engine services I/O requests for the other subsystems. It also maintains overhead data and the meta-data in the data dictionary. The Definition Tools Subsystem is used to establish and maintain the structure of the database, including the schema and subschemas. Defining a database means establishing its structure. The Processing Interface Subsystem supports update/query languages and provides an interface to the DBMS for programs written in standard languages, such as COBOL. The Application Development Tools Subsystem enables system developers to quickly and easily develop forms, reports, menus, and some transaction processing programs. The Data Administration Subsystem provides facilities for backup, recovery, archiving, purging, and other database maintenance functions. The Data Dictionary Subsystem allows the DBA to query the meta-data in the data dictionary. The information there is invaluable to the DBA, who is responsible for managing additions to and modifications of the database and applications.

The database system development process has five phases. During the definition phase, the project team is formed, the problem is defined, and feasibility is assessed.

During the requirements phase, the team determines what data needs to be stored in the database and what business functions the system must satisfy.

The third phase is called the evaluation phase. During this phase the general designs of several alternative solutions are studied and the feasibility of each is assessed. Requirements might be ranked by priority and some might even be deferred until later projects. One solution is selected from the alternatives offered.

During the fourth phase, the database and all components of each application are designed. Database design includes descriptions of files, data items, and file relationships. Application design includes specifying application views (subschemas) and the update, display, and control mechanisms to be employed. All user interfaces, such as reports and forms, are designed during this phase.

The final phase is implementation. Activities in this phase include constructing the database, building the applications, and installing the database and applications in the user's environment.

---

## QUESTIONS

**GROUP I**

**3.1** Each application in the Eastcoast Lab database system is itself a business computer system that has five components. Describe the five components for the USAGE ANALYSIS application.

**3.2** Explain each of the DBMS functions listed in Figure 3–4.

**3.3** What is the difference between integrity constraints and security constraints?

**3.4** Give an example of an integrity constraint and a security constraint.

**3.5** Some integrity rules cannot be enforced by the DBMS. How can they be enforced?

**3.6** Describe the function(s) of each of the subsystems in a DBMS.

**3.7** Why is it important that a DBMS include an interface to a standard programming language?

**3.8** What is the function of a pre-compiler?

**3.9** Why are natural languages not yet used as widely as more structured query languages? What are the potential problems of natural language queries?

**3.10** What is the advantage of integrating application development tools with the DBMS?

**3.11** Why is access to the data dictionary important to the DBA? Should users have access to the data dictionary? What are the advantages and disadvantages of allowing users to access the data dictionary?

**3.12** Describe the five phases of database system development.

**3.13** How does the development process for a database system differ from the development process for any other business computer system?

**3.14** Why is the requirements definition phase vital to the database system development process?

**3.15** Should users be involved in the requirements definition phase of system development? What are the advantages of user involvement? What are the costs to the user?

**3.16** Under what circumstances might users *not* be involved in the requirements definition phase of system development?

**3.17** If you were Samantha Green, which users at Eastcoast State would you involve in the system development process? What difficulties might you encounter in trying to work with student lab attendants during this crucial phase?

**3.18** What is prototyping? When during the database system development process would prototyping yield the greatest results? Why?

**3.19** When should reviews be done? What is the benefit of a formal review? What is the cost of a review?

**3.20** Should the database system development tools discussed in this chapter be one aspect of comparison shopping when selecting a DBMS? Besides system development tools, what other DBMS characteristics would you compare before choosing a DBMS?

---

**GROUP II**    QUESTIONS AND EXERCISES

**3.21** Investigate a database product for a mainframe computer. Some possibilities are IDMS (Cullinet), DB2 and SQL/DS (IBM), and ORACLE. There are dozens more to choose from. Find out what application development tools are included with the DBMS. Talk to a user of the product. Are the development tools easy to use? Besides the features described in this chapter, what other development features are provided? Is there a data dictionary subsystem? If so, how is it accessed? Is access restricted to the DBA (and other authorized personnel), or can anyone access it?

**3.22** Using a microcomputer database product such as R:BASE, build a prototype for any one of the applications for the Eastcoast Computer Lab. Would you be able to do the same thing in COBOL? Would it take you longer to build a prototype using COBOL (or PL/I, or Pascal)?

**3.23** Using a mini- or mainframe DBMS (such as ORACLE, IMS, DB2, or SQL/DS), build a prototype for any one application for the Eastcoast Computer Lab. How difficult was it to build such a prototype? Would it have been easier, harder, or about the same to build a prototype using COBOL?

# PART    II

# DATABASE
# DESIGN

In Part 2 you will learn the database design process. Chapter 4 presents an object-oriented approach toward *identifying database system requirements*. Then, in Chapter 5, you will learn how to *design database records* that not only will support the requirements you identified in the previous stage, but also will be robust enough to facilitate modifications to the database data. This process is called *normalization*. Finally, in Chapter 6 you will learn how to design *databases*, which are, in part, groups of database records. The designs considered here are *logical*; they are independent of any DBMS product. Later, in Parts 4 and 5, you will learn how to implement these designs using particular DBMS products. Like the material in Part 1, the topics covered in Part 2 are fundamental to the remainder of this text.

# Specifying Database Requirements

In this chapter we will discuss a process for developing and documenting database application requirements. These requirements are important because they are the blueprint for database design and implementation activities. We need to know what the user needs from a system before we can build it.

Many books have been written about systems development and the process of identifying and documenting system requirements. We will not attempt to discuss all the possible techniques, procedures, and tools available. Rather, we will describe a procedure and a set of tools that have been used effectively for building many database applications. Naturally, since this is a book about database processing, this discussion will have a distinct database bias. We will focus on database structure, objects in the database, the functional components of database applications, and the like. Requirements definition that pertains to hardware, programs, procedures, and people will not be covered in this text.

The material presented in this chapter has evolved over the last ten to fifteen years. In particular, the discussion of objects and their relationship to database structures has evolved from work by Chen on the Entity-Relationship Model, by Codd on RM/T, and by Hammer and McCleod on the Semantic Data Model. After you read this chapter, you may wish to consult the Bibliography for works by these authors to obtain more information on these topics.

## REQUIREMENTS DEFINITION

Suppose you need to develop a database system, as Samantha Green did for the Eastcoast State University Computer Lab. How would you proceed? How would you know how many applications were needed? How would you design them? What reports, forms, menus, and transaction processing programs would you build? After you were done, how would you know whether or not you had done a good job? In order to answer these questions, you must first know what the system is supposed to do for the users. Identifying the objectives of the system is called *requirements definition*.

### Goals for the Requirements Phase

Fundamentally, defining the requirements for a database and its applications involves two major goals. First, you must identify the objects the user needs to track and define their structure. An *object* is the representation of an entity in the user's work environment, such as a customer, salesperson, or inventory item. The database will contain objects, or, more precisely, the database will contain instances of objects. An *instance of an object* is a representation of one particular entity. For example, an order entry database includes instances of an object called INVOICE. These instances are representations of actual invoices that exist in the business. You must identify objects and their structures to be able to determine what data must be stored in the database.

Second, you must determine the functional components of each application that will use the database. Each application includes update, display, and control mechanisms. These components provide the means by which the user keeps the database current and obtains information from it. In this chapter we will discuss means by which you can achieve these two goals.

### Determining User Requirements

To learn what objects are important to the user and to identify the manner in which those objects need to be processed, you must talk to the people who will use the applications. User involvement is critical throughout systems development, but it is most crucial during the requirements definition phase. Without a clear goal in mind, the development team will almost certainly build an inadequate, disappointing system. Thus, you must carefully interview the users to discover their needs and expectations. Depending on the application and the organization, you might need to interview the operations and database administration personnel as well. In many cases, DBA personnel are development team members.

Besides interviewing, other fact-finding techniques are also used, such as questionnaires, group discussions, and observation of users performing their jobs. Direct contact with users is very important and effective, however, and user interviews supply most of the answers to the team's questions.

Since this is not a text on systems development, a comprehensive discussion of interviewing techniques would be inappropriate. However, there are several important points about interviewing users that relate directly to the development of database applications. First, the word *database* is dangerously general. When users hear it, they may expect the system to do far more than it actually will. Consequently, the mere fact that you are interviewing a user about the possibility of developing a database application might establish a level of expectation greater than you can achieve. It is important from the outset that you discuss with the user the scope and general goals of the project. Not only will such boundary setting keep user expectations realistic, but it may also increase user cooperation and confidence. Furthermore, if users believe that a new system is going to eliminate their jobs, then they may choose not to cooperate with you. After all, they will feel they have a vested interest in the failure of your proposed system. Explaining the scope of the system to users may put some of their fears to rest and make them more cooperative.

Second, as one experienced management consultant put it, "Information users are children in a candy store. They want everything" [Druker]. You can expect that the answer to any question that begins "Would you like . . . ?" will be YES! Putting questions in that form is an invitation to serious problems. It would be better to spend some time with the user discussing his or her basic needs. Once those have been identified and documented, you might offer some other options the user has not considered. Frequently, users are not aware of what a system *can* do for them. Your experience will help you to offer reasonable and helpful options to the user.

Third, for multi-application and multi-user database systems, users need to realize that the system serves a community. The goal of the development project is to build applications that best satisfy the needs of the entire user community. At times this may mean that the needs of one user or group conflict with those of another because both cannot be fully accommodated. In this case, the requirements of one user may have to be deferred in favor of the needs of another user. A great deal of diplomacy is required to keep all users cooperating. This aspect of database system development often falls to the DBA (see Chapter 7). The interview process is a good time to introduce the users to the notion that the database system must serve the greater good.

Finally, keep in mind during the interview process that users interface with database *applications*, not with the database itself. Users see the system only in terms of screens, menus, and reports, not stored data. Thus, when users express requirements, they are probably requirements for an application interface. Translating *application* requirements into *database* requirements is the responsibility of the development team. Thus, users are more likely to respond effectively to questions such as "Does this sample report have all the data you need?" than to questions such as "Do you need separate files for COMPLETED and UNCOMPLETED ORDERS?"

## DATABASE OBJECTS

The purpose of a database application is to enable the end user to acquire the information he or she needs to know about things that are important in the work environment. The dual goals of the requirements phase are to determine what those *things* are and to specify the *update*, *display*, and *control mechanisms* for processing them. We mentioned earlier that representations of entities users want to keep track of are called *objects*. Now we will be more specific in our definition of an object:

> An object is a *named collection of properties* that *sufficiently describes an entity* in the user's work environment.

An object has a *name* that distinguishes it from other objects. The name of the object corresponds to the name of the entities it represents. Thus, if there is an entity in the user's work environment called a student, the database will contain a corresponding object called STUDENT. In this text we will write object names in capital letters.

An object is a *collection of properties*. Each property represents a characteristic of the corresponding entity that is important to one or more users of a database application. For instance, suppose that an application needs to track student name, home address, height, date of birth, campus address, and declared major. Each of these characteristics is represented with an object property for STUDENT.

Further, this collection of properties is a *sufficient description* of a real-world entity. Any entity has an infinite set of characteristics. In addition to the characteristics we mentioned before, a student also has a shoe size, hair color, rank in high school graduating class, part-time job history, favorite rock musician, number of eyelashes, and so forth. Obviously, not every characteristic of an entity needs to be represented in the database. Remember that our goal is to satisfy the information needs of the users. Thus, the description is sufficient if the properties meet, or can be manipulated to meet, the information needs of the users.

Finally, an *entity* is something a user perceives as an independent unit, meaning it can stand on its own. For example, INVOICE, an object, stands on its own. The parts of an invoice called line-items do not stand on their own—they are merely parts of an object.

It is important for you to distinguish among entities, entity instances, objects, and object instances. An entity is a class of things that exist in the business world. Entities are perceptions and may or may not be physical. Credits, for example, could be an entity, but they do not have a physical form. An entity instance is an occurrence of an entity, such as a particular credit. An object is a structure that represents an entity; an object instance is a particular object. CREDIT is a general structure; CREDIT# 10045 is a particular object instance.

## Object Characteristics

Both objects and object instances have names. The name of the object is the name of the entity it represents. Example object names are CUSTOMER, INVOICE, STUDENT, PROFESSOR, PAYMENT, DEPARTMENT, SHIP-MENT, TREATMENT, and so forth. In a database, an object has one and only one name.

Object instance names are the names of particular customers, invoices, students, etc. ABC Plumbing, Kansas Flax, and Parks Printing are names of customers—they are the names of instances of CUSTOMER objects. The name of an object instance is a value of one of the properties of the object. The name of a DEPARTMENT instance, for example, is one value of the property Department-number. Object instances sometimes have alternative names. The name could be a value of either Department-number or Depart-ment-name.

Object instance names may or may not be unique, depending on how the user perceives the object. For example, a small business might not be concerned with non-unique customer names—having two John Smiths might be perfectly acceptable. If there ever is a need to distinguish one from the other, the user says, I can simply examine the whole record to select the appropriate one. In other cases, unique names are essential. For example, a user would need to distinguish each invoice from every other one and might therefore assign a unique invoice number to each form.

Figure 4–1 is an example of an *object diagram* for the DEPARTMENT object. An object diagram helps the development team to summarize its knowledge of an object and to present it visually and unambiguously. The name of the object appears beneath the box. Inside the box is a list of all the properties of the object. Some of the properties are written in lowercase letters, while others are in uppercase letters and are enclosed in small boxes. Some of the properties have the letters MV next to them. Let's examine this figure and learn how to interpret it. Later you will learn how to develop object diagrams.

The DEPARTMENT object includes nine properties. Each property represents an important characteristic of a department in this university, such as the name of the department (Name), the name of the department chair (Chairperson), and information about all the faculty members in the department ($PROFESSOR_{MV}$). The first six properties listed in the figure are called non-object properties. The last three, which are capitalized and enclosed in boxes, are called object properties. An *object property* is a characteristic of the entity that is actually another object. Thus, there will be other object diagrams for COLLEGE, PROFESSOR, and STUDENT. The COLLEGE object

**Figure 4–1**
DEPARTMENT object
diagram

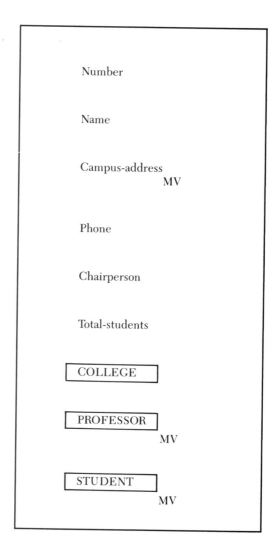

DEPARTMENT

will contain properties of the college to which this department belongs, the PROFESSOR object will contain properties of the faculty members who teach in this department, and the STUDENT object will contain properties of the students who have declared this department as their major. The object diagram describes objects in the user's world and their relationships to one another. Thus, one object can "contain" other objects—in fact, this is very common. Users often see objects that way.

**Figure 4—2**
DEPARTMENT object
instance

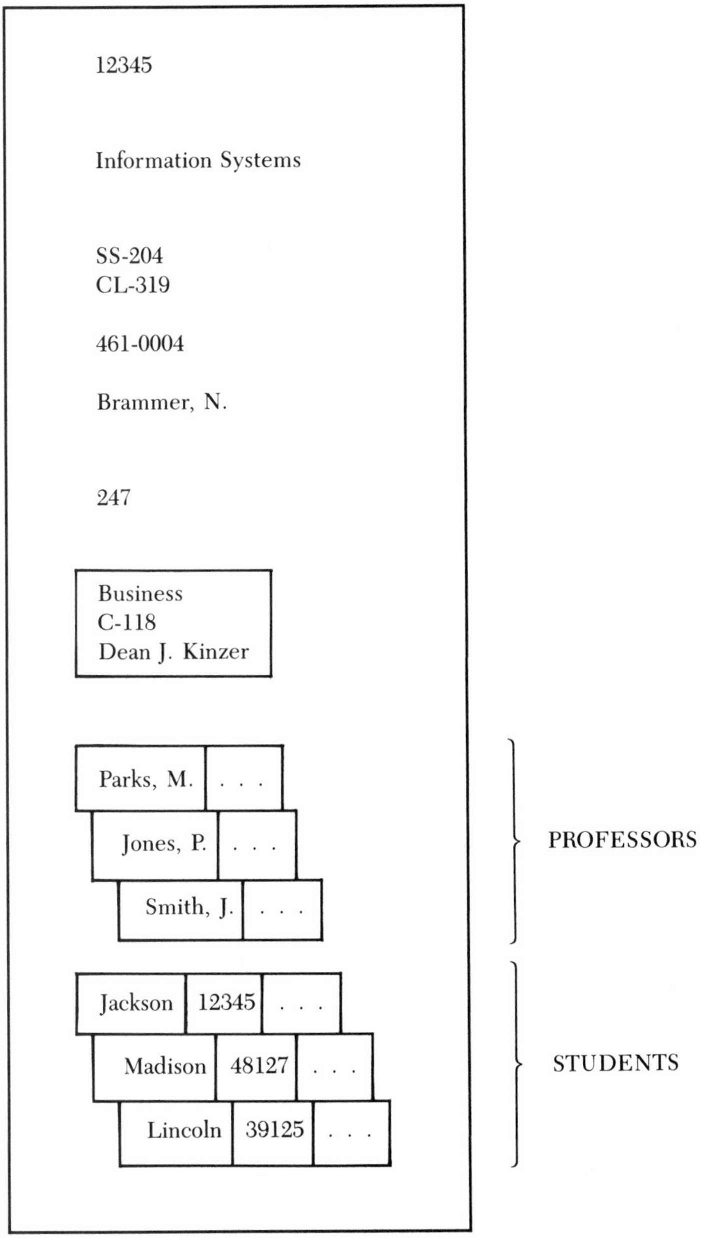

12345

Information Systems

SS-204
CL-319

461-0004

Brammer, N.

247

Business
C-118
Dean J. Kinzer

| Parks, M. | . . . |
| Jones, P. | . . . |
| Smith, J. | . . . |

PROFESSORS

| Jackson | 12345 | . . . |
| Madison | 48127 | . . . |
| Lincoln | 39125 | . . . |

STUDENTS

Some properties are allowed to have at most a single value, while others are allowed to have multiple values. For example, a department instance is allowed to have only one value for Number, Name, Chairperson, Total-students, and COLLEGE. However, any department could have more than one value for Campus-address, PROFESSOR, and STUDENT. Campus-address is allowed multiple values because some departments are located in two or more buildings. PROFESSOR and STUDENT are allowed multiple values because there can be many professors and many student majors in each department. MV means multivalued.

Notice that whether a property is single- or multiple-valued has nothing to do with whether it is an object or non-object property. Non-object properties can be single-valued or multiple-valued, and object properties also can be single-valued or multiple-valued. Examples of each appear in Figure 4–1.

The object diagram for DEPARTMENT shown in Figure 4–1 is a format, or general structure, that can be used for any department. An instance of the DEPARTMENT object is shown in Figure 4–2. This figure shows each property's *value* for the Information Systems Department. Observe that there are two values for Campus-address because the Information Systems Department has two locations on campus. Other departments might have only one value or several more values for this property.

Further, there are multiple values for the PROFESSOR and STUDENT object properties. Each PROFESSOR instance is a complete object. It has all the properties of PROFESSOR. To keep this diagram simple, all but the name of the person has been omitted from the sketch. The ellipsis (. . .) indicates that other properties are not shown. Remember that the object diagram is a picture of the user's perception of an object in the work environment. Thus, in the user's mind, the DEPARTMENT object includes all of the PROFESSOR properties as well. Similar comments pertain to the STUDENT object property. Each instance of STUDENT represents a complete STUDENT object. Again, the ellipsis represents properties omitted from this diagram for simplicity.

## Property Domains

The *domain* of a property is the set of all possible values the property can have. The description of a non-object property domain is different from that of an object property domain. The domain of a non-object property consists of both a physical and a semantic description. The *physical description* indicates the type of data (for example, numeric versus string), the length of the property, and other restrictions or constraints (such as that the first character must be alphabetic or that the value must not exceed 9999.99). The *semantic description* describes the function or purpose of the property. It distinguishes this property from other properties that might have the same physical description. For example, the domain of Department-name might be defined as "the set of strings of up to seven characters that represent names of departments at Eastcoast State University." The phrase "strings of up to seven characters" is the physical description of the domain. The phrase "that represent names of departments at Eastcoast State University" is the semantic description. The semantic description differentiates strings of seven characters that represent names of departments from similar strings that represent, say, names of courses or buildings or some other property.

The domain of an object property is a set of object instances. In Figure 4–1, for example, the domain of the PROFESSOR object property is the set of all PROFESSOR object instances. In some cases, the domain of an object property will be only a subset of the object. For example, the PROFESSOR object might include these properties: Name, Address, Marital-status, Date-of-birth, Education-history, Current-salary, Medical-history, Blood-type, Dependents, and Religious-preference. However, only some of those properties are perceived by the user as being carried to the DEPARTMENT object, such as Name, Address, Education-history, and Current-salary. This is not uncommon. In fact, carrying only a subset of all the data about one object to another one is the basis for establishing views of an object. We will discuss views in the next section.

When you identify objects, you need to specify both the properties and the property domains. Typically, the object properties and domain names are listed with the object definition. Domain definitions are separate from object definitions. This helps reduce duplicate domain definitions because one domain may be used by many properties. For example, the same domain definition can be used for Scheduled-review-date and Date-of-last-review properties. You will study examples of this later in this chapter. Skip ahead to Figure 4–16 if you just can't wait.

## Object Views

Users access objects through applications. An application may or may not require access to all of the object's properties. For example, in Figure 4–3, three applications view the DEPARTMENT object. Some properties of DEPARTMENT (its Name, for example) are seen by all three applications. Other properties are seen by just one or two of these applications. For example, STUDENT is seen only by Application1, while COLLEGE is seen only by Application2. The portion of an object that is visible to a particular application is called a *view*.

Since an application's view may not encompass all the properties of an object, the development team must consider the views of all applications in order to completely describe the object. Remember that during requirements definition the team is trying to determine what data must be stored to satisfy *all* users' needs. In the process, the team works with various users, each of whom offers his or her view of an object. The team then develops a composite picture of the object by putting together all the views. This final picture becomes the object diagram.

**Figure 4–3**

Three application views of DEPARTMENT object

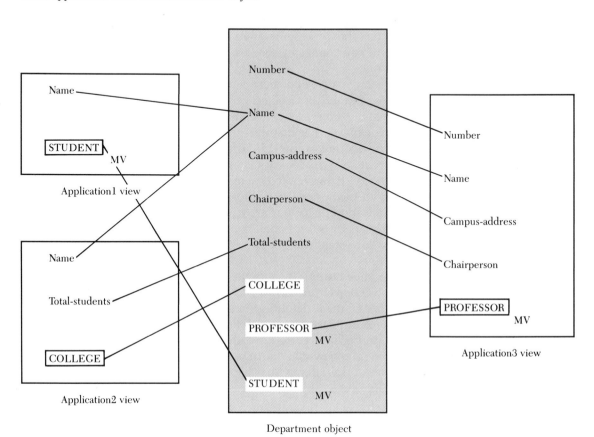

Department object

The definition of objects and views of objects is iterative. The team discusses data needs with each user, putting together several views of an object. Then the team combines the views to build a composite picture. Now the team reviews user needs again, in light of the object definition. Adjustments often need to be made. Users might also adjust their requirements when they become aware of what data might be available. Object definition is not a straight-line process. There is considerable reiteration of the definition of views and the definition of objects.

### A Process for Identifying Objects

One of the goals of the requirements phase is to identify and describe objects to be represented in the database. There are two ways of accomplishing this. One approach is to examine the application outputs—reports and screen displays—and work backwards to derive the object structure indirectly. This approach is based on the theory that if you know what must come out of the system, you can determine what must go in. For example, to derive the structure of a DEPARTMENT object, we could first gather all of the reports, forms, and other views of DEPARTMENT. From them we could define a DEPARTMENT object that would enable those reports, forms, and views to be constructed.

A second method for identifying and describing objects is to ask the user what objects he or she wants to keep track of and then to imagine, from the nature of the objects and the application, which properties need to be stored in the database. This approach requires knowledge and experience in the application domain and is risky. There is a significant chance that the imaginations of even skilled database system designers will be insufficient and that important properties or objects will be left out.

Probably the best approach is a combination of the two. We begin by examining reports, forms, and other views to determine an initial set of objects and properties. Then we consider the preliminary structures in light of the semantics of the applications and revise them accordingly. We can then use the revised object diagrams to suggest to the user new reports, forms, and views. This process can be repeated until all users agree that the system will be able to produce the information they need.

For a completely new application there will be no reports, forms, or views to examine. In this case, the developers have no choice but to begin by discussing with users what "things" are important to them. With this data, developers can begin to develop object diagrams that can then be embellished as more details about the new system become evident. Often developers use prototypes to help users through this process. As mentioned earlier, a prototype is a mock-up that represents the real thing—a screen, report, menu, or some other structure. We will discuss the use of prototypes later in this chapter.

## OBJECTS FOR THE UNIVERSITY ADMINISTRATION DATABASE

In this section we will illustrate the process for object definition with examples drawn from a case study. Suppose a university wanted to keep track of department, faculty, and student major data. Without getting into the details of the applications, suppose that the system needs to produce five reports (Figures 4–4, 4–6, 4–8, 4–10, and 4–12). Our goal is to examine these reports and determine what objects and properties need to be stored in the University Database to produce them. The approach we are taking is based primarily on studying what the system outputs are in order to figure out what the inputs will have to be.

### The COLLEGE Object

Consider the first report in Figure 4–4. What objects does this report seem to be about? This is a report about a college—specifically, the College of Business. Because this is an instance of a report, we can be sure that there will be similar reports about other colleges, such as the College of Arts and Sciences, the College of Medicine, and so forth. The fact that a user wants a report about colleges tells us that a college is an object.

Examining the report, we find that there is data specific to the college, such as the name, telephone number, and office of the Dean, and there are also facts about each of the departments within the college. This *suggests* that the database might contain COLLEGE and DEPARTMENT objects, with DEPARTMENT contained within COLLEGEs. We describe our preliminary findings in the diagram in Figure 4–5. Notice that we have omitted from the object diagram all but the non-object property Name and any object properties, such as DEPARTMENT. A complete object diagram includes all properties, of course.

In the report in Figure 4–4, department data repeats underneath college data. Such repeating groups are often a signal that the repeating group is data about another object. *However, this is not always the case.* The repeating group could also be COLLEGE data that happens to have several values. As a guideline, when you see a repeating group in a form or report, consider the possibility that this repeating group *may* represent another object.

---

**Figure 4–4**
COLLEGE listing

```
                          College of Business
                        Mary B. Jefferson, Dean
           232-1101                                        SS-101
      -----------------------------------------------------------------

      Department              Chairperson         Phone     Total Majors

      Accounting              Seymour P. Jackson   232-1841      318
      Finance                 Linda R. Smith       232-1414      211
      Information Systems      Nathaniel D. Brammer 232-4146      247
      Management              Christine A. Tuttle   236-1732      184
      Production              Jack T. Barnes        236-1914       98
```

**Figure 4—5**
Preliminary
COLLEGE and DEPARTMENT
object diagrams

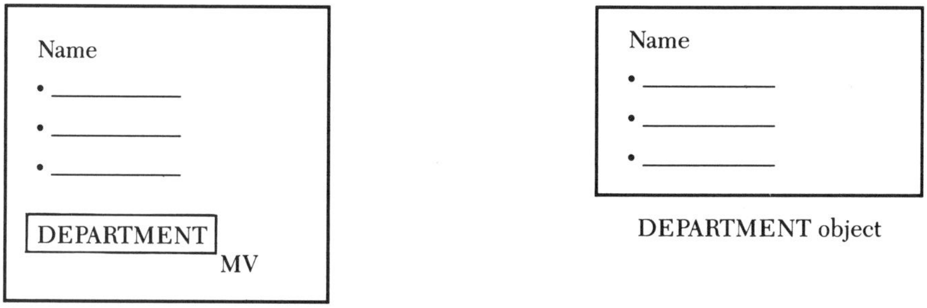

COLLEGE object

DEPARTMENT object

## The DEPARTMENT Object

Now examine the report in Figure 4–6. It is a report about a department, specifically the Information Systems Department. Within the report is data about the faculty members who teach in the department. Like the report above, this one suggests that DEPARTMENT is an object (there is a report about it) and that PROFESSOR might be an object contained within DEPARTMENT. This suggests the adjusted DEPARTMENT object diagram in Figure 4–7.

Notice that we have not included the COLLEGE object as a property of DEPARTMENT. There is no college data in the report in Figure 4–6, so as far as we can tell from this report, there is no reason to place the COLLEGE object within DEPARTMENT. Other reports may provide a reason. Be aware that whenever one object is contained in another, there is always the possibility that the second object may also be contained in the first. In this case, since COLLEGE contains a DEPARTMENT property, it is prudent to investigate whether DEPARTMENT contains a corresponding COLLEGE property.

The structure of the DEPARTMENT/MAJOR report in Figure 4–8 is similar to that of the DEPARTMENT/FACULTY report in Figure 4–6. This report is also about a department, reinforcing the notion that department is an object. But this report lists data about students who major in the department, implying that student is also an object within department. Thus, the DEPARTMENT object needs to contain the STUDENT object as well as the PROFESSOR object. This is shown in Figure 4–9. The reports in Figures 4–4 and 4–6 present two different views of the DEPARTMENT object. This is similar to the situation shown in Figure 4–3.

**Figure 4—6**
DEPARTMENT/FACULTY listing

```
                    DEPARTMENT and FACULTY Report

        Information Systems                     SS-204
        College of Business                     CL-319
        Nathaniel D. Brammer, Chairperson       232-4146
    ------------------------------------------------------------

           Faculty                   Office              Phone
        Jones, Paul D.              SS-219            232-7713
        Parks, Mary B.              CL-308            236-5791
        Smith, James C.             SS-207            232-9112



    ------------------------------------------------------------
```

**Figure 4—7**
Adjusted DEPARTMENT
object diagram

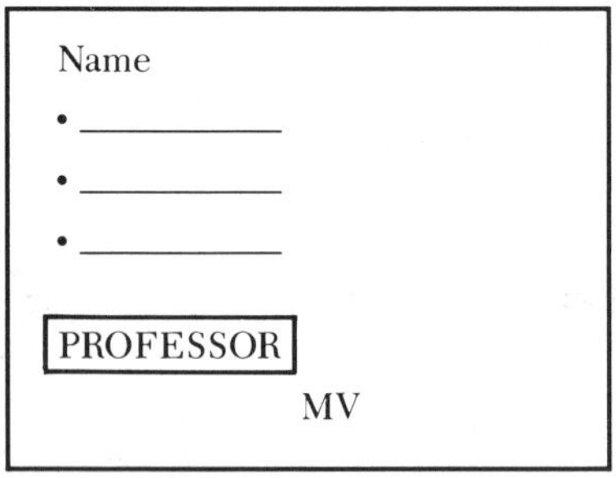

DEPARTMENT object

**Figure 4–8**
DEPARTMENT/MAJOR listing

```
                    DEPARTMENT and MAJOR Report

        Information Systems                    SS-204
        College of Business                    CL-319
        Nathaniel D. Brammer, Chairperson      232-4146
------------------------------------------------------------------
            Major              Student-ID          Address
    Jackson, Robin R.            12345             DL-984
    Lincoln, Fred J.            48127             DL-841
    Madison, Janice A.          39125             DA-1141



------------------------------------------------------------------
```

**Figure 4–9**
Further adjustment
to **DEPARTMENT**
object diagram

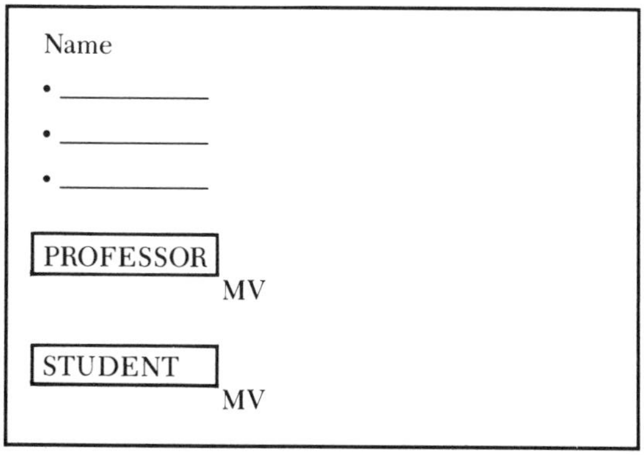

Name
• _____
• _____
• _____

PROFESSOR
MV

STUDENT
MV

DEPARTMENT object

### The STUDENT Object

Figure 4–10 shows an example of the acceptance letter that the university sends to its incoming students. This is a report about a student. Data items that need to be stored in the database are shaded in this example. In addition to data about a student, the letter also contains data about the student's major DEPARTMENT and the student's PROFESSOR advisor. A sketch of a STUDENT object that would support this report is shown in Figure 4–11. In this object diagram, both DEPARTMENT and ADVISOR are single-valued. A student at this university has at most one major department and one advisor.

---

**Figure 4–10**
Acceptance letter

Mr. Fred Parks
124 Elm Street
Los Angeles, CA 98002

Dear Fred Parks :

You have been admitted as a BIOLOGY major to Eastcoast State University starting the Fall Semester, 1988. The office of the BIOLOGY department is located at SC-213 . The department phone number is 232-4101 .

Your advisor is Dr. James . Please schedule an appointment with your advisor as soon as you arrive on campus. Your advisor's office and phone are SC-105 and 232-7220 .

Congratulations and welcome to Eastcoast State University.

Sincerely,

James J. Saen
President

JJS/rkp

**Figure 4–11**
STUDENT object
diagram

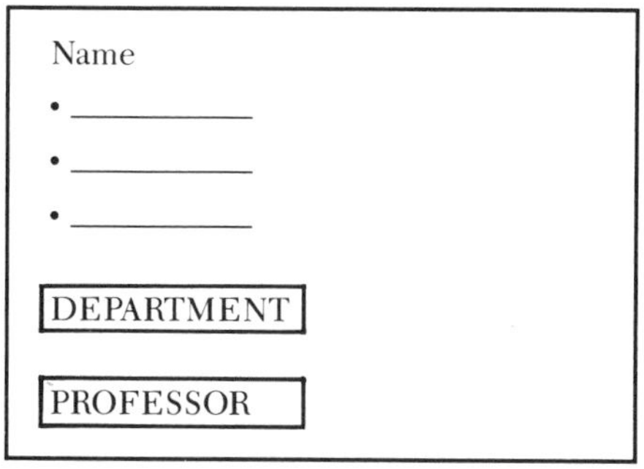

STUDENT object

Figures 4–9 and 4–11 illustrate the situation in which two objects contain each other. STUDENT contains DEPARTMENT and DEPARTMENT contains STUDENT. Although this situation at first may seem unrealistic, it makes sense from the users' perspectives. When one user envisions a DEPARTMENT, he sees the STUDENT as a subset of the DEPARTMENT (a department has student majors in it). At the same time, another user views a STUDENT, seeing the DEPARTMENT as a property of STUDENT (this student has declared her major in a particular department). The database needs to support these different perspectives. Thus, defining objects this way will make the jobs of database design, application design, and implementation much easier.

## The TEACHING-STAFF Object

The final report is the university's faculty directory, shown in Figure 4–12. This report lists faculty names sorted in alphabetical order, their offices, and telephone numbers. Though it appears to be a very simple report, the faculty directory presents a very subtle problem. What is this a report about? What is the underlying object? It is tempting to say the underlying object is PROFESSOR. However, PROFESSOR is not the underlying object.

Is a directory a report about *a* professor? No. A directory is a report about a *group of professors*. It is actually a report about the university's teaching staff. Thus, the underlying object here is TEACHING-STAFF.

The words *sorted alphabetically* are an important clue. Sorting implies a group because there must be several members to sort. Thus, whenever a report is sorted by something, the underlying object is probably a collection of the things that are being sorted. Accordingly, the underlying object for the report in Figure 4–12 is TEACHING-STAFF.

**Figure 4–12**
Listing for faculty
directory

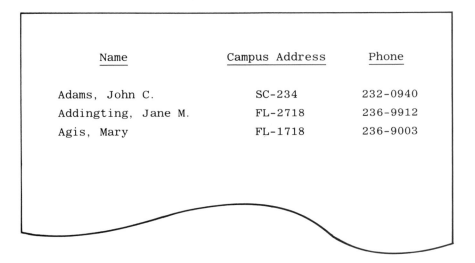

| Name | Campus Address | Phone |
| --- | --- | --- |
| Adams, John C. | SC-234 | 232-0940 |
| Addingting, Jane M. | FL-2718 | 236-9912 |
| Agis, Mary | FL-1718 | 236-9003 |

The object diagram for TEACHING-STAFF appears in Figure 4–13. TEACHING-STAFF has two properties: PROFESSOR, which is a multiple-valued object property, and Date.

### Validating Object Definitions

One technique to help you identify objects is to consider what constitutes an *instance* of a report. Imagine that a computer run has been made and that a stack of continuous form paper is sitting on your desk. Suppose the stack is a group of acceptance letters like the one shown in Figure 4–10. Where will you tear the paper? Put more formally, what constitutes a complete report? Obviously, one acceptance letter is an instance of the report. You will tear the paper after each letter and send each one to an accepted student. This paper tearing is a physical manifestation of the fact that the underlying object is a single STUDENT.

Now consider the faculty directory. If the stack of paper on your desk is a printout of the directory, you would not tear it at all. The instance of the report is the entire stack of paper. To have copies of the directory printed and bound, you would ship the entire stack of paper to the printer as is. This is evidence that the underlying object of the directory is TEACHING-STAFF.

Thinking about reports in this way can help you conceptualize objects. Think about the COLLEGE report shown in Figure 4–4. If this report were produced on continuous form paper, where would you separate it? To answer

**Figure 4–13**
TEACHING-STAFF
object diagram

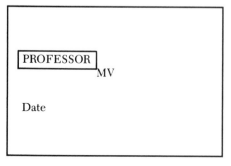

TEACHING-STAFF  object

this question, you may need to dig deeper into user requirements. You might need to know who the users of this report are before you can be sure what the underlying objects are. There are two possibilities. If the dean of each college receives the section of the report for his college, then the underlying object is COLLEGE, defined as we did in Figure 4–5.

However, if the entire report goes to the university president's office, then the report is really about the university—an object that contains a multivalued COLLEGE object property. Upon discovering this, we would need to return to the object diagrams and add one for UNIVERSITY.

The most important point from all of this is that the only way to correctly identify objects is to consider the vantage point of the user. Thinking about which portions of a printout would go to whom is just another way of considering the user's perspective of objects. Of course, you must work closely with the user throughout the requirements definition phase.

## The PROFESSOR Object

The objects shown in Figures 4–5, 4–9, 4–11, and 4–13 contain enough data to produce the necessary reports. However, we have omitted one final detail. We have not yet defined a PROFESSOR object, though we have treated PROFESSOR as an object property of DEPARTMENT, STUDENT, and TEACHING-STAFF. We have *guessed* that PROFESSOR is an object, but there is no report about professors. If there were, for example, a payroll check printed for each professor, then that report would be evidence that professor is an object.

In the absence of such hard evidence, we must ask a key question: Do the users of this system have a reason to view faculty as independent objects or do they see professors only as subordinate properties of other objects?

**Figure 4–14**

Alternative object
diagrams for Univer-
sity Administration
Database (no PRO-
FESSOR object)

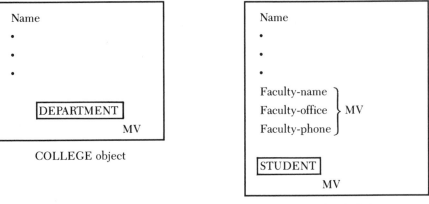

COLLEGE object

DEPARTMENT object

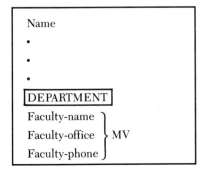

STUDENT object

TEACHING-STAFF object

The question is not whether professors are separate from the other objects. Obviously, they are. A teacher and a department are not the same thing. The question here is whether the users of this system need to see them separately.

Based on the five reports we just studied, there is no reason to define professor as a separate object. If we are confident that these five reports constitute a complete requirements specification, then we do not need to define a PROFESSOR object. In this case, the set of object diagrams that describe the data requirements for this system appears in Figure 4–14. We

**Figure 4–15**
Object diagrams for
University Adminis-
tration Database
(with PROFESSOR
object)

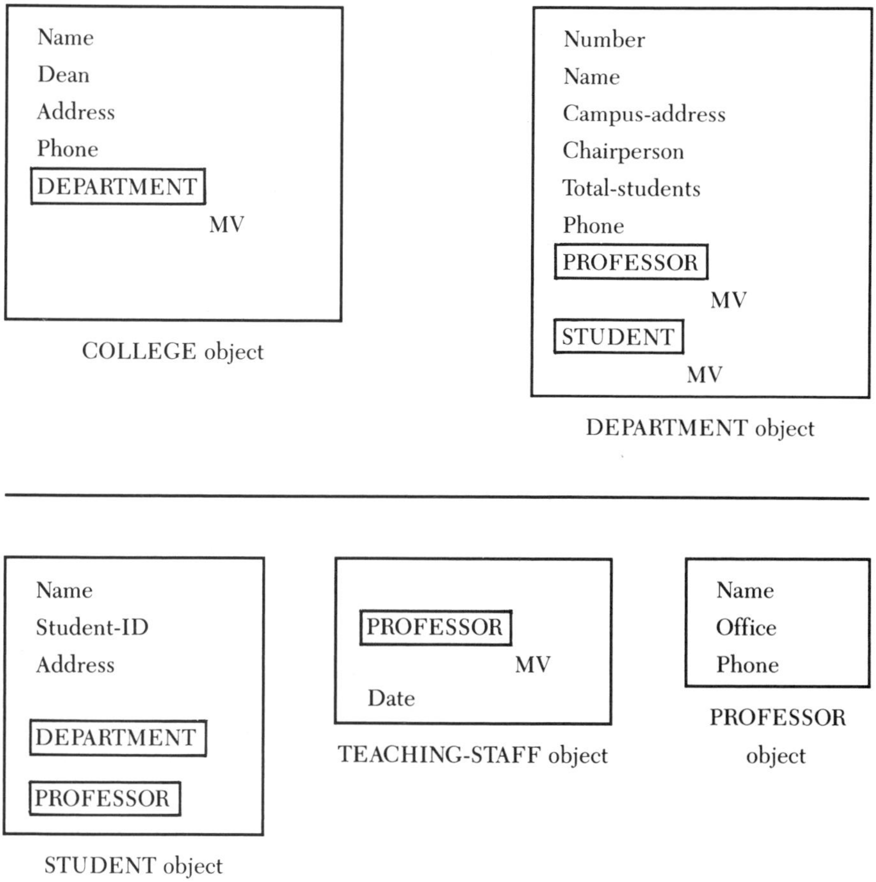

COLLEGE object

DEPARTMENT object

STUDENT object

TEACHING-STAFF object

PROFESSOR object

have replaced the object property PROFESSOR with a set of data items—
Faculty-name, Faculty-office, Faculty-phone—which appear in the
DEPARTMENT, STUDENT, and TEACHING-STAFF objects.

However, it is far more likely that eventually some user will need to
view professor as an object. In this case, the object diagrams in Figure 4–15
would be appropriate. The final authority, of course, is the user. But skilled
database designers sometimes need to call on their experience and instincts
to supplement the information given by the user. We will assume that professor is actually an object and that the diagrams in Figure 4–15 are correct.

### Object Specification

Figure 4–15 shows completed object diagrams for the University Database. The purpose of these diagrams is to show graphically the properties of each object and to indicate the relationships among objects—that is, which objects contain which other objects. Object diagrams give the overall picture of object relationships.

Figure 4–16 presents the complete object specifications for the University Database. This specification is made up of two parts: object definitions and domain definitions. An object definition lists all the properties of an object and indicates the domain from which values for each property can be drawn. Domain definitions specify formats, lengths, and special restrictions on the values of each domain. We will examine the entire object specification document in this section. Object specifications are sufficiently detailed that, once they are completed and approved, they can be used for database design.

Although there is no formal syntax for object specifications, we have adopted some standards for use in this text. Other designers may present their specifications differently. Under each object name we list all of the properties for that object. We separate the name of each property from its domain with a semicolon (;). If the domain is another object, and if only some of the properties of the object are to be carried to the object being specified, then we use the keyword SUBSET and enclose the appropriate properties of the foreign object within brackets ([ ]). (A *foreign object* is the object from which the properties are being drawn. For example, in Figure 4–16a DEPARTMENT is foreign to COLLEGE.)

A domain definition describes the set of values from which an instance of a property may be drawn. As described earlier in this chapter, it consists of both a physical and a semantic description. In some cases, the physical description includes restrictions on the allowable values. For example, Campus-phones (Figure 4–16b) is a domain whose description includes a mask—or restriction—that specifies that the first two digits must be 23 and that the third digit must be either a 2 or a 6. Total-student-count is an example of a domain that is specified by a formula. It is computed as the count of STUDENT objects in DEPARTMENT. Such domains, called *computed values*, occur frequently in financial applications when a balance is computed as the sum of values from the local object, or even from a foreign object.

Other items in this figure are self-explanatory. This format is one of many acceptable formats for specifying objects. The particular format used is not as important as being sure to clearly and unambiguously set out the structure and content of objects and to define the property domains.

## SPECIFYING APPLICATIONS AND THEIR FUNCTIONAL COMPONENTS

So far we have described a process for defining database object requirements. Now we need to discuss a process for specifying database applica-

Object Definitions

COLLEGE OBJECT

Name; College-names
Dean; Faculty-names
Address; Campus-addresses
Phone; Campus-phones
DEPARTMENT; DEPARTMENT object; MV; SUBSET [Name, Chairperson, Phone, Total-students]

DEPARTMENT OBJECT

Number; Dept-numbers
Name; Dept-names
Campus-address; Campus-addresses; MV
Chairperson; Faculty-names
Total-students; Total-student-count
Phone; Campus-phones
PROFESSOR; PROFESSOR object; MV
STUDENT; STUDENT object; MV

STUDENT OBJECT

Name; Student-names
Student-ID; Student-IDs
Address; Campus-addresses
DEPARTMENT; DEPARTMENT object; SUBSET [Name, Campus-address, Phone]
PROFESSOR; PROFESSOR object; SUBSET [Name, Office, Phone]

TEACHING-STAFF OBJECT

University-name; U-names
PROFESSOR; PROFESSOR object; MV

PROFESSOR OBJECT

Name; Professor-names
Office; Campus-addresses
Phone; Campus-phones

a. Object definitions

tion requirements. In order to do this, we need to identify each application and then define the update, display, and control mechanisms for each one.

In the example in the last section, we did not actually identify any applications. Rather, we defined the objects to be stored in the database without stating which applications would process them. Now, to complete the requirements specification, we must decide how many applications there will be and the function of each. It may turn out that only one application is necessary, in which case we will develop a single-application database system. On the other hand, users may need many different applications.

**Figure 4–16**

(*continued*)

---

Domain Definitions

Campus-addresses:
>    Text 6, mask BB-NNN,
>        where BB is building code, NNN is room number
>    Official campus mailing addresses

Campus-phones:
>    Text 8, mask 23X-NNNN,
>        where X is either 2 or 6, NNNN is any four digits
>    Number of a telephone in the university's exchange

College-names:
>    Text 25
>    Names of colleges at Eastcoast State University

Dept-names:
>    Text 20
>    Official university department name

Dept-numbers:
>    Numeric 5
>    Unique number of a university department

Faculty-names:
>    Text 40: Mask:
>            First-name Text 15
>            Initial Text 2
>            Last-name Text 23
>    Names of full- and part-time professors at Eastcoast State University

Student-names:
>    Text 40; Mask:
>            First-name Text 15
>            Initial Text 2
>            Last-name Text 23
>    Names of students who have been accepted to the university

Student-IDs:
>    Numeric 5
>    Unique and permanent student number

Total-student-count
>    Numeric 999; computed as count of STUDENT objects in DEPARTMENT
>    Number of students who have declared a major in a department

U-names
>    Text 30
>    Official university names

b. Domain definitions

It should be apparent by now that during requirements definition we rely heavily on user input. User involvement is crucial when trying to identify applications. The user is in the best position to tell the development team what an application should *do* for her. Knowing this, the team can build the application to meet that defined goal.

We will focus on the functions of an application because they will lead us to a definition of the update, display, and control mechanisms we will use for each application.

There are many ways to identify applications within a system. In some cases, the scope of each application is obvious. Some businesses compartmentalize their activities in such a way that the organizational structure can dictate the definition of applications. At a bookstore, for example, there might be SALES, INVENTORY, PURCHASING, and RECEIVING applications. It may be that no other division of functions is sensible. If so, the applications and their scope would be known even before any objects were defined. There is no requirement during system development that object definition precede application definition; in fact, database system developers often work on both aspects of system requirements at the same time.

## Dataflow Diagrams

If it is not clear that applications will mirror the organizational structure of a business, then the team must use another approach to study the business functions and address subsets of them with different applications. One widely used tool for studying business functions is the *dataflow diagram*. We use dataflow diagrams to determine how the organization creates, edits, deletes, and displays objects. We must also understand who is authorized to do what to which data.

Since this is a book about database processing and not about system development, we will not teach you how to develop dataflow diagrams. If you have not learned them already, you most likely will study them in a systems analysis and design course. We will, however, present one dataflow diagram and show how it can be used to define each application, its scope, and its functional components.

Figure 4–17 shows a dataflow diagram for the University Administration Database System. This is the final product of the team's work—many other versions of this dataflow diagram were drawn and revised before this one was approved by the development team and the users.

Circles in a dataflow diagram represent processes (and sometimes the people or programs that perform them) within the scope of the applications. Rectangles represent processes or people that are external to the system, but that interface with it. Most often circles represent system users and rectangles represent the system clientele.

**Figure 4–17**

University administration dataflow diagram

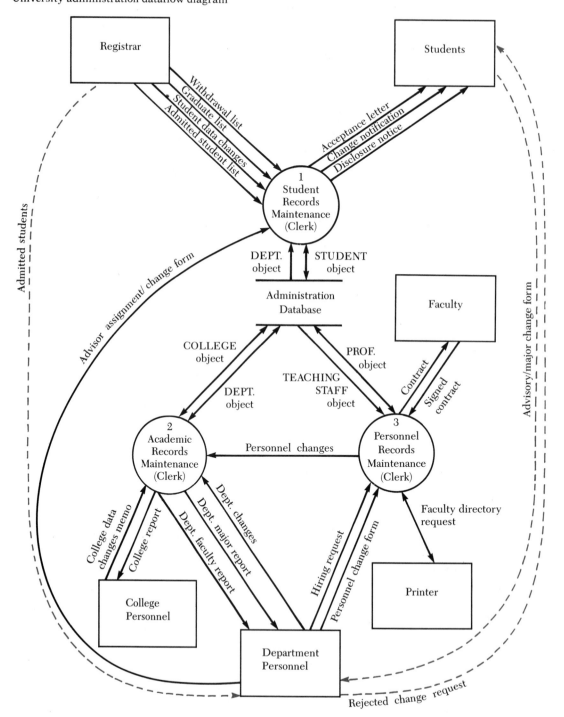

Arrows represent data flowing from one process (either internal or external) to another. The labels on the arrows identify the data being passed. The medium used to transport data from one process to another can include paper documents, reports, keyboard input, screen displays, and others. A dataflow diagram does not indicate the medium.

Files of stored data (which includes the database) are shown as two parallel horizontal lines. Note that dataflow diagrams do not usually show any interaction between external processes (represented by rectangles), but we have included dataflows (dashed lines) on the diagram in Figure 4–17 to support our discussion of the university's operations. They would have to be removed to make this document strictly correct.

Now turn to Figure 4–17 so we can trace the various activities this dataflow diagram portrays. The registrar (an external entity) sends a list of admitted students to each department. Each list contains the names of students who will major in that field. The department personnel assign an advisor to each student and then forward the list to the student records clerk in the university's administrative offices. The student records clerk enters the new student data, creating instances of the STUDENT object.

Acceptance letters are then printed and mailed. Periodically, students request a change of advisor or major. To do this, the student submits a change form to the department. If department personnel approve the change, the form is forwarded to the student records clerk in administration. The clerk modifies the appropriate STUDENT object and mails a change notification to the student. If the change is not approved, the department marks the request disapproved and sends it back to the student.

At the end of every semester, the registrar sends both a list of graduates and a list of students who have withdrawn to administration. The student records clerk removes from the database STUDENT objects for graduated and withdrawn students.

College personnel provide data about changes in college data (a new dean, for example). When necessary, personnel from the college forward to the academic records clerk in administration a memo describing the change. The clerk then modifies the appropriate COLLEGE object.

Department personnel also interact with the academic records clerk in administration. The department sends notification of changes in departmental data (new chairperson, for example) to that clerk. The academic records clerk also processes the opening and closing of departments. Finally, the academic records clerk prepares both the DEPARTMENT-MAJOR and DEPARTMENT-FACULTY reports and sends them to the department.

Department personnel forward both hiring requests and personnel change forms to the personnel records clerk in administration. In the case of a new professor, the clerk fills out a contract using data supplied by the department and sends the contract to the prospective professor. When the signed contract is returned, the personnel records clerk creates an instance of a PROFESSOR object. In the case of a change or termination, the clerk uses the form to make changes to the appropriate PROFESSOR object. Once a semester, the personnel records clerk prepares the faculty directory, which is sent to the printer, where directories are printed and bound.

The dataflow diagram in Figure 4–17 clearly shows three business functions: student records processing, academic records processing, and personnel records processing. Each function is performed by a different user (there are three clerks) and accomplishes a related subset of record-keeping activities for the administration. From this, it makes sense to develop three separate applications: STUDENT-RECORDS, ACADEMIC-RECORDS, and PROFESSOR-PERSONNEL. We will consider the functional components for each of these in the next section.

The processing in Figure 4–17 fell quite naturally into three pieces, with each piece processing a different object in the database. This happens frequently, but not always. Sometimes, several different applications process the same object. Other times, the definition of applications will not be so clear. A guideline used by many skilled system developers is to consider the application user: Who will actually be sitting at the terminal? An application should make available to a specific user the functions he or she needs. For example, an order entry clerk at a mail-order company needs to access different functions than does a customer service representative at the same company. Some of their processing might overlap (for instance, both might need to query stock-on-hand amounts). But applications are designed with the user in mind, not the processing that will be done. For this situation it would be sensible to develop an ORDER ENTRY application and a CUSTOMER SERVICE application.

### Determining Functional Components

Figure 4–18 summarizes a process for developing application requirements. The first part of this process is to identify the applications by drawing dataflow diagrams of the business operation. We did this in the previous section. The dataflow diagrams will also reveal who processes which objects. We can use this knowledge in the next step, determining the functional components of each application.

Let us examine this process. First, for each application, we must identify the objects and object views it requires. Then, for each object view, we need to determine the update, display, and control mechanisms. At this point, the goal is to determine requirements: Who needs to do what to which data? It is not yet our goal to design programs to satisfy user needs. At this point, we focus on *what* must be done, not *how* we will do it.

Consider this process for the STUDENT-RECORDS application.

### The STUDENT-RECORDS Application

According to Figure 4–17, the student records clerk reads the DEPARTMENT object and both reads and writes the STUDENT object. (Dataflow arrows coming out of a file indicate a read process, while dataflow arrows

**Figure 4—18**
Summary of process for determining functional application requirements

I. Identify applications
  A. Construct dataflow diagrams of business activity
    1. Identify internal and external processes
    2. Identify dataflows and actions on objects
  B. Collect subsets of activities to be accomplished by one user or user group. Each subset will be addressed by an application.
II. Determine functional components for each application
  A. Identify objects processed and views of those objects
  B. Determine mechanisms for each view
    1. Determine update mechanisms
      a. Input sources
      b. Processing requirements
      c. Forms
    2. Determine display mechanisms
      a. Reports—who, when, medium
      b. Queries—who, how, when
      c. Other outputs
    3. Determine control mechanisms
      a. Ways in which access must be limited
      b. Processing restrictions
      c. Control coordination with other applications
    4. Volumes and frequencies of activities

going into a file indicate a write, or update, function.) During the requirements interview the development team learned that the student records clerk was responsible for all aspects of student record-keeping. This meant that this user's application needed to create, edit, and delete instances of STUDENT objects. The only reason the clerk needed to read the DEPARTMENT object was to verify faculty names. Sometimes the penmanship on an advisor assignment/change form was so poor that the clerk needed to access the DEPARTMENT object to decipher a name. PROFESSOR is not an input object because unlike DEPARTMENT, PROFESSOR occurs only as a sub-element of STUDENT. PROFESSOR data is never accessed in its own right.

**STUDENT-RECORDS Update Mechanisms.**  The clerk created STUDENT objects using data from two sources. At the start of every semester, the clerk received a list of newly admitted students from the registrar. The list contained all STUDENT data except the advisor's name, phone, and office. The advisor data was supplied from the department using the advisor assignment form. When the clerk received the list of newly admitted students, he or she added all of the data except advisor. Then, when the clerk received the advisor data from the department, he or she completed the STUDENT object and printed the acceptance letter.

The data for changes to STUDENT objects was obtained from the same two sources. Changes to student data, such as name or address, were received from the registrar. Advisor changes came from the departments.

Finally, the clerk received lists of graduated and withdrawn students at the end of every semester. These were used to remove STUDENT data.

The development team considered the processing requirements of the student records clerk and decided that two forms were necessary. (Keep in mind that the word *form* means a computer screen in which data is entered and displayed.) The forms are shown in Figure 4–19. The first form (Figure 4–19a) is used for adding and editing student data. This data might come from the admitted student list, student data changes from the registrar, or an advisor assignment/change form from department personnel.

We have used notation in these figures to indicate which variables are entered by the user (UI) and which values will be taken from the database (DB). Thus, in Figure 4–19a, the user will input the name of a department (Dept-name) and the application is to look up the corresponding Dept-office and Dept-phone values in the database. These will then be presented on the screen.

When the form is used to edit STUDENT data, changes can be made to any property of student, to the department name, and to the advisor's name. Changes may *not* be made to other DEPARTMENT or PROFESSOR data. If changes to these objects need to be made, they will be done by other applications.

The form in Figure 4–19b is used to remove instances of STUDENT objects from the database. To use this form, the clerk simply enters the ID of the student to be removed. The application responds with identifying student data and asks if this is the correct record to delete. If the clerk responds YES, then the object is deleted. Otherwise the clerk is asked to enter the correct Student-ID. Update mechanisms for the STUDENT application are summarized in Figure 4–20.

**STUDENT-RECORDS Display Mechanisms.**    The STUDENT application requires three printed reports and two screen displays. The three reports are sent to students. The first report is the ACCEPTANCE LETTER that was shown in Figure 4–10. Another is a CHANGE NOTIFICATION FORM. This form is sent to the student whenever changes are made to the student's record. Among these would be name or address changes and changes in major or advisor. Finally, the university has a policy that any student can request a report of data kept about him or her. This report is called a DISCLOSURE NOTICE and is sent to the student on request.

The two screen displays are produced when the clerk makes a query on STUDENT or DEPARTMENT objects. In order to query a student, the clerk wants to be able to key in either the Student-ID or Student-name and have all of the student data presented. The clerk realizes that Student-name may not be unique. Therefore, the application must display data for all students with a non-unique name.

**Figure 4—19**
Forms for STUDENT-RECORDS application

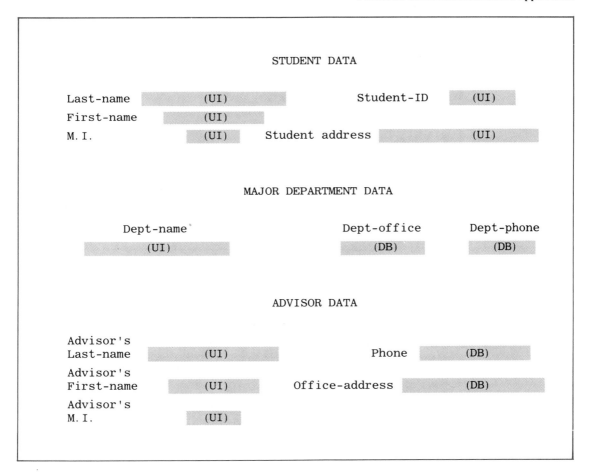

UI = user input

DB = value taken from database

a. Form for adding and editing STUDENT data

The DEPARTMENT/PROFESSOR LIST is necessary when the clerk cannot read the writing of an advisor's name. In these cases, the clerk wants to be able to retrieve the DEPARTMENT record to decipher the name of the advisor. Display requirements for the STUDENT application are summarized in Figure 4–21.

**STUDENT-RECORDS Control Mechanisms.** There are a variety of important control mechanisms needed by the STUDENT application. First,

**Figure 4–19**

(*continued*)

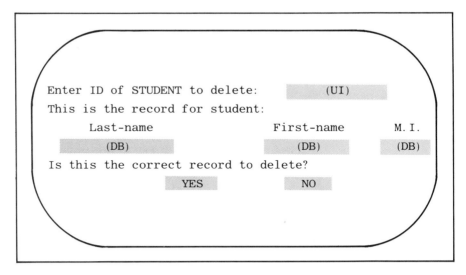

b. Form for deleting STUDENT data

only the student records clerk and his or her supervisor are authorized to access STUDENT data. This policy is important since the university has both an ethical and a legal responsibility to protect the confidentiality of student data. To implement this control, the STUDENT-RECORDS application must be protected by passwords.

Second, since STUDENT object data originates from two sources, there is a need for processing controls to ensure that every admitted student is assigned an advisor. This means that periodically the clerk must query the database for STUDENT objects that have not been assigned an advisor. If any are found, the clerk must determine if the department has had sufficient time to respond to the request for an advisor. If so, then the clerk needs to remind the department personnel to assign an advisor.

This control will require a report that shows, by department, which STUDENT objects have not yet been assigned an advisor. This control also means that the date that STUDENT data is entered must be stored in the object so that the clerk can tell how long the department has had to assign an advisor. We will not show these changes here, but you will have an opportunity to make them in the exercises at the end of this chapter (Question 4.23).

The processing of STUDENT data has an important control weakness. One person makes all data changes. If this were a financial application involving employee pay rates or customer balances, then this situation would be unacceptable. There would have to be at least two individuals involved to provide a balance in duties and authorities.

**Figure 4—20**
Summary of STUDENT update mechanisms

STUDENT Update Mechanisms

I.   Add new STUDENT data
    A.   Inputs
       • List of admitted students—from registrar
    B.   Outputs
       • New STUDENT object instance in database
       • Confirmation message on screen
    C.   Processing notes
       • Advisor data may be unavailable
       • Ultimately want to import this data in mass
    D.   Volume
       • 800 students, fall; 150 students, spring
    E.   Frequency
       • Twice per year

II.  Add advisor data to STUDENT
    A.   Inputs
       • STUDENT object instance from database
       • Name of advisor from department
       • DEPARTMENT object from database
    B.   Outputs
       • Modified object instance to database
       • Confirmation message on screen
       • Acceptance letter
       • Change notice
    C.   Processing notes
       • This function adds advisor data to new students
       • Processing clerk needs option to read DEPARTMENT object during processing
       • PROFESSOR office and phone are not keyed by clerk—this data is taken from the database
    D.   Volume
       • 800 students, spring; 150 students, fall
    E.   Frequency
       • Add twice per year
       • Edit weekly

III. Edit non-advisor data in STUDENT
    A.   Inputs
       • STUDENT object instance from database (including PROFESSOR properties)
       • STUDENT change data from registrar
       • DEPARTMENT object form database
    B.   Outputs
       • Modified object instance to database
       • Confirmation message on screen
       • Change notice to student

(*continued on next page*)

**Figure 4—20**
(*continued*)

    C.  Processing notes
- This function changes non-advisor STUDENT data
- Processing clerk needs option to read DEPARTMENT object during processing

    D.  Volume
- 1500 at start of each semester
- After semester start 15 per week on average

    E.  Frequency
- Twice per year for large batch; otherwise, weekly

IV.  Edit advisor data in STUDENT

    A.  Inputs
- STUDENT object instance from database (including PROFESSOR properties)
- Advisor change from department
- DEPARTMENT object from database

    B.  Outputs
- Modified object instance to database
- Confirmation message on screen
- Change notice to student

    C.  Processing notes
- This function changes advisor assignments
- Processing clerk needs option to read DEPARTMENT object during processing
- PROFESSOR office and phone are not keyed by clerk—this data is taken from the database

    D.  Volume
- 10 students per week

    E.  Frequency
- Weekly

V.  Delete STUDENT Data

    A.  Inputs
- List of students to delete—from registrar
- STUDENT objects in database

    B.  Outputs
- Confirmation notice on screen

    C.  Processing notes
- Backups of STUDENT data should be made prior to processing a batch of deletion requests

    D.  Volume
- 100, fall; 850, spring

    E.  Frequency
- Twice per year

It is unlikely that anything could be gained or lost by surreptitiously changing a student's middle initial or address. Thus, stricter controls are probably unnecessary because the user can tolerate this weakness in the system. However, if these were student grade records, an altogether different approach to security and control would need to be taken. For this application, the clerk's supervisor must periodically spot check student data for accuracy. If the clerk's activities are careless or error-prone, the univer-

**Figure 4—21**
Summary of STUDENT display mechanisms

STUDENT Display Mechanisms

I.  Query on STUDENT
    A.  Output description
       • Form showing all data for a student
    B.  Source data
       • STUDENT object
       • Student name or ID keyed by clerk
    C.  Processing notes
       • Used by student registration clerk
    D.  Volume
       • 25 per week
    E.  Frequency
       • Daily

II.  Acceptance letter
    A.  Output description
       • Word-processed letter mailed to student
    B.  Source data
       • STUDENT object
       • Student name or ID keyed by clerk
    C.  Processing notes
       • Sent to student when STUDENT data is complete
    D.  Volume
       • Fall, 800; spring 150
    D.  Frequency
       • Twice per year

III.  Change notification
    A.  Output description
       • Word-processed letter describing changes made to STUDENT data; only changed data are shown
    B.  Source data
       • STUDENT object
       • Student name or ID and changes keyed by clerk
    C.  Processing notes
       • Letter is sent whenever a change is made to STUDENT
    D.  Volume
       • 1500 at start of each semester
       • 25 per week after that
    E.  Frequency
       • Large batch at start of fall and spring semesters
       • Weekly after that

IV.  Disclosure notice
    A.  Output description
       • Report showing all STUDENT data

*(continued on next page)*

**Figure 4–21**

*(continued)*

> B.  Source data
> > • STUDENT object
> > • Student name or ID keyed by clerk
> C.  Processing notes
> > • This report is sent to student on demand
> D.  Volume
> > • 50 per year
> E.  Frequency
> > • Daily as requested
>
> V.  DEPARTMENT/PROFESSOR list
> > A.  Output description
> > > • Form listing names of all faculty in a department
> > B.  Source data
> > > • DEPARTMENT object
> > > • Department name keyed by clerk
> > C.  Processing notes
> > > • This form is requested by clerk when identity of assigned advisor is illegible
> > D.  Volume
> > > • 50 per day
> > E.  Frequency
> > > • In accordance with processing of advisor data

sity's STUDENT data could become a source of embarrassment and frustration. Processing controls are summarized in Figure 4–22.

### Functional Components for ACADEMIC-RECORDS and PROFESSOR-PERSONNEL Applications

The functional components of both the ACADEMIC-RECORDS and PROFESSOR-PERSONNEL applications also need to be specified. The process is similar to the one we just followed for the STUDENT application and we will not document it here. Each of these applications has update, display, and control requirements that need to be set out.

### Inter-application Requirements

When applications share a common database, there are usually requirements concerning coordination of processing among the applications. In the university administration example, the academic records clerk produces DEPARTMENT/MAJOR reports for all department chairpersons. Each report lists all of a department's majors and advisors AND CANNOT BE PRODUCED UNTIL ALL STUDENT DATA HAS BEEN ENTERED. Thus, before the academic records clerk produces this report, he or she must check with the student records clerk to determine if all of the STUDENT data has been entered. Similarly, the student records clerk sometimes reads faculty names from the DEPARTMENT object. Unless the personnel records clerk has

**Figure 4–22**
Summary of STUDENT control mechanisms

---

STUDENT Control Mechanisms

I.  Provide password system to ensure that only the student records clerk and the student records supervisor can access STUDENT data

II.  Set up procedures with appropriate reports to ensure that every student is assigned an advisor

III.  Define procedures, forms, and reports for supervisor to make periodic spot checks on accuracy of STUDENT data

---

entered all new faculty data and assigned professors to departments, the data retrieved by the student records clerk will be inaccurate. Thus, before STUDENT data can be reliably entered, all PROFESSOR data must have been entered. On the other hand, the faculty directory should not be printed until the department has updated all office and telephone assignments.

Similar inter-application requirements pertain to deletions. Personnel cannot delete a professor until that person's advisees have been reassigned to another professor. A department cannot be deleted until all of its majors and faculty have been assigned to another department.

All such inter-application requirements need to be identified and documented, even though they may not relate directly to the database or the programs that process it. These requirements will most likely be implemented through manual procedures.

## OPERATIONS, DATABASE ADMINISTRATION, AND ENVIRONMENTAL REQUIREMENTS

In addition to requirements that relate directly to the structure and processing of database objects, there are likely to be requirements for the support of applications, including operational, administrative, and environmental requirements and constraints. For example, a system dealing with highly sensitive data might be required to be run by professional computer operators in a secure computer room. Another system might require that users operate the system themselves.

Beyond the question of who will operate the applications lies another question: *What* are the operations requirements? Must the system be operational during certain periods of the day? For example, an online bank teller system must be available during banking hours. Must the system *not* be operational during certain periods of the day? For example, at Eastcoast State University, the microcomputer lab system was not to be available while the lab was shut down. Other operational requirements include how backup activities will be accomplished and how recovery will be done.

There may also be database administration requirements addressing such questions as: How will the database be managed? How will change take place? If there are problems between the applications, how will they be resolved? How will the growth of the database be managed? We will discuss the role of the database administrator in Chapter 7.

In a larger context, this database resides in a university that presumably already has information systems. Does this database need to conform to established standards? Will data be imported from another system to be used in this one? Will this system export data in bulk to another system? If so, what are the requirements for such transfers?

There may also be requirements for the environment of this application. Perhaps the database will have to reside in a particular computer. Maybe the processing computer must be physically located within a certain distance of an office or a work group. Perhaps the university has already installed a DBMS and a local area network, and this system must use those products. Perhaps the database development team is familiar with only certain hardware and programs, or the university allows only certain hardware and programs, so these products must be used.

There are often many other system requirements. We will not discuss them any further because such topics are better suited for a course on systems analysis and design. However, you should keep in mind that when you develop a database system you must consider the entire system, not just the stored data component.

## THE REQUIREMENTS REVIEW

We stated at the start of this chapter that requirements are the blueprint from which the database and its applications are designed and implemented. If the requirements are correct, then developers have a good chance of building effective applications. If the requirements are incorrect, there is little likelihood of successful application development. Thus, an accurate statement of requirements is essential.

To be sure that the team fully understands the system requirements, it must review what it has learned with the users. Users can evaluate both the accuracy and the completeness of the requirements statement. For a requirements review to be effective, the requirements must be documented in such a way that users can understand them.

### Requirements Documentation

Requirements documentation serves two purposes. First, it states to the users the development team's understanding of the needs for the database and its applications. Second, the requirements documentation defines the goal of the entire development project—it is a model of what is to be constructed. During design and implementation, the development team will

**Figure 4—23**
Summary of contents of requirements documentation

1. **Object Descriptions.** A description of objects similar to that shown in Figures 4-15 and 4-16. The description should include objects, properties, and domains.

2. **Dataflow Diagrams.** One or more diagrams depicting organizational flow of processing. Every object should appear at least once in these diagrams.

3. **Functional Component Descriptions.** Descriptions of functional components like those shown in Figure 4-20 plus sample forms, reports, and queries.

4. **Miscellaneous Requirements.** A statement of the inter-application requirements, operational requirements, and database administration requirements.

5. **Prototypes.** Prototypes of forms, reports, menus, and transaction processing programs as appropriate.

repeatedly refer to the requirements documentation. The requirements documentation must be written with both of these purposes in mind.

Figure 4–23 summarizes the contents of the requirements document. As you can see, this documentation states the results of the work that we have described so far in this chapter.

Requirements documentation is often expressed in narratives, diagrams, and tables. Some database system developers use their DBMS to store and maintain their requirements documentation. Relationships among objects, domains, forms, reports, and so forth can be stored in a database, and developers then retrieve information about the requirements using database commands. This is sometimes called a requirements data dictionary application. It is a very useful application of database technology during the system development process.

Some parts of the requirements document might be prototypes of reports, forms, menus, and even transaction processing programs. Prototypes are useful when users have difficulty visualizing a screen or progressing from one menu to another. Often users need to see a sample report or process a simulated transaction before they can comment on the accuracy of requirements.

## The User Review

The final stage of the requirements phase is for users (and others, as appropriate) to review the requirements documentation and identify incorrect, partial, or missing requirements. The nature and length of the review depend on the project. In some situations the users simply review the forms and reports for completeness and appropriate format. In other cases, the user review is more comprehensive. The review can be as brief as one or two hours and be completed by a single individual, or it may take as much as a week or more and be conducted by a team of representative users.

If any deficiencies are found during the review, the development team reworks the requirements to eliminate errors. This step may involve repeating interviews, interviewing new users, or simply rethinking the requirements statement. Another user review is scheduled, and the documents are once again judged for completeness and accuracy. This iterative process continues until the requirements document is approved by the user. The culmination of the requirements definition phase is a set of documented and approved requirements for the database and its applications.

## THE EVALUATION PHASE

As described in Chapter 2, the development process has five stages. After the second stage, requirements definition, there are three more steps: evaluation, design, and implementation. We will not be concerned with the evaluation phase beyond the description in Chapter 2. A full description of this phase belongs more appropriately in a systems analysis and design text.

In the next two chapters we discuss database design. We will begin by describing a process by which we can decide how to construct database records. Then we will show how to transform object specifications into database designs.

## SUMMARY

There are two major goals when defining requirements for a database and its applications. The first is to identify and define the objects that the users want to track. The second is to identify the applications and determine their update, display, and control mechanisms. The requirements are determined by interviewing users, studying existing systems, observing employees on the job, and talking with operations and database administration personnel.

An object is a named collection of properties that sufficiently describes an entity in the users' work environment. An object is a structure, or format, while an object instance is the representation of a particular entity. Both objects and object instances have names. The name of an object is the name of the entity it represents. The name of an instance is a value of one or more properties of the object.

Properties can be object or non-object. Object properties represent other objects. Non-object properties represent descriptive characteristics. Properties can be single- or multiple-valued. The domain of a property is the set of all possible values the property can have. For a non-object property, the domain is a physical and semantic description. For an object property, the domain is a set of object instances.

Users access objects via applications. The portion of an object that is visible to an application is called a view. Views may contain some or all of an object.

The best way to identify and describe objects is to work backwards from the application outputs and derive object structure. A risky alternative is to ask the user what the contents of the database should be and then to imagine which properties need to be stored in the database. Although this second approach is dangerous, it is sometimes unavoidable. The risk can be reduced by building prototypes of forms, reports, and menus for the user to review.

Object diagrams illustrate the relationship among object types. Object specifications describe the objects, object properties, object domains, and domain definitions.

A dataflow diagram portrays the business functions and their data interfaces. Dataflow diagrams can be used to identify applications and the data they use. Four symbols are used in a dataflow diagram. Internal system processes are shown in circles, while external processes are shown in rectangles. Data interfaces are illustrated with named arrows, and stored data, including the database, is shown between parallel horizontal lines.

A summary of the process to follow when developing database applications is as follows: First, dataflow diagrams are used to identify the scope of applications. Next, the objects and object views are specified. Finally, the update, display, and control mechanisms requirements are determined for each application.

Applications usually have inter-application requirements that concern the interaction of two or more separate applications. Other sources of requirements concern operations, database administration, and the application environment.

Once requirements have been identified, they must be documented and reviewed. Requirements documentation can include narratives, diagrams, tables, and prototypes. After the requirements documentation has been completed, it must be reviewed by users. If any omissions or errors are found, then the development team must correct them and resubmit the document for another review. The requirements document must be approved by the user before it can be used as input to the rest of the system development project.

## QUESTIONS                                                                          **GROUP I**

**4.1**   Name and describe the two major goals of the requirements phase.

**4.2**   Name and describe the three functional components of a database application.

**4.3**   Why is the term *database* apt to confuse or mislead users?

**4.4**   Explain the phrase "database applications serve a community."

**4.5**   Users interface with the database application, not with the database.

Explain why this is important to keep in mind during requirements interviews.

**4.6**    Define the term *object*.

**4.7**    Explain the meaning of the words *sufficiently describe* in the definition of object.

**4.8**    What is an entity? How does an entity differ from an object?

**4.9**    Explain the difference between an object and an object instance.

**4.10**    How many names does an object have? How many names does an object instance have?

**4.11**    Name and describe two types of properties.

**4.12**    Does the fact that a property has multiple values mean that it must be an object property?

**4.13**    Draw an object diagram for a student dormitory object. Assume the dorm contains the object property STUDENT.

**4.14**    Define the term *domain*. What is the domain of a non-object property? What is the domain of an object property?

**4.15**    Define a possible domain for the STUDENT property in question 4.13. Define a possible domain for the non-object property Dorm-name in the object defined in question 4.13.

**4.16**    Give an example of two objects that contain each other. Do not use the examples in this text.

**4.17**    Give an example of two applications that would have two different views of the dormitory object.

**4.18**    Redraw the object diagram in Figure 4–9 assuming that DEPARTMENT objects also include an object called EQUIPMENT.

**4.19**    Draw an object diagram for the EQUIPMENT object. Assume this object represents computer equipment and has only non-object properties.

**4.20**    Repeat question 4.19 but assume EQUIPMENT has an object property called PERIPHERAL.

**4.21**    Modify the DEPARTMENT object definition in Figure 4–16 in accordance with your answer to question 4.18.

**4.22**    Show the modifications to Figure 4–16 necessary to add an EQUIPMENT object with an object property called PERIPHERAL. Also assume EQUIP-MENT has non-object properties of Serial-number, Description, and Location. Assume PERIPHERAL has non-object properties of Serial-number, Description, Type, and Capacity. Include the necessary additions to the domain definitions.

**4.23**    Modify Figures 4–15 and 4–16 to include the date on which STUDENT data was entered into the database (this data is needed for a control report listing students who have not yet been assigned an advisor).

**4.24**    Explain the meanings of the circle, rectangle, named arrow, and parallel line symbols in a dataflow diagram.

**4.25**    Explain how to identify the scope of applications.

**4.26**    The text identified a control weakness in STUDENT-RECORD processing. To fix this weakness, a new report is required and the STUDENT property must be changed. Define the structure of the report (similar to those in Figures 4–4 and 4–6) and modify the description of STUDENT to eliminate the control weakness.

**4.27**    Give an example of an inter-application requirement.

QUESTIONS AND EXERCISES

**4.28** Suppose you are gathering information for the University Administration Database System. Identify two pieces of information you need from the registrar and a department chairperson. What questions would you ask to obtain the information? Assume you are working with Samantha Green on the microcomputer lab database project described in Chapter 2.

**4.29** Draw object diagrams for STUDENT, APPOINTMENT, and COMPUTER objects.

**4.30** Develop the object definitions and domain definitions for the objects in Question 4.29.

**4.31** Draw a dataflow diagram (only one internal process) for the SCHEDULING application.

# Relation Definition and Normalization

---

- Approaches to Relation Design
- Normalization
- First through Fifth Normal Forms
- Domain/Key Normal Form
- Rules for Composing Relations
- A Note on Constraints
- Summary

---

**A**fter specifying the requirements for the database and its applications (Chapter 4), you begin the process of logical database design. A carefully designed database is the foundation for a system that users and programmers can easily access and that can accept insertions and deletions while remaining error-free. Proper database design is critical to the system development process. Without some guidelines, however, database design can be difficult. Fortunately, others who have gone before you have found solutions to many of the problems you might encounter. This chapter and Chapter 6 present some proven techniques that will reduce the difficulty of developing the database design.

## APPROACHES TO RELATION DESIGN

Several approaches to organizing and manipulating database data, called *data models*, have evolved in the past twenty years. One important development has been the *relational* database model. The relational model is based on the concept that data is organized and stored in two-dimensional tables called *relations*. You can think of a relation as a file, and of each row in the relation as a record. Just as a record is a collection of data items, a row is made up of many attributes. Although the terms are different, the concepts are similar.

We will say more about relations and relational terminology shortly. But for now you need to realize that the purpose of this chapter is to learn the characteristics of a well-designed relation (file). Based on the user's requirements, we need to decide which attributes (or data items) should be collected together and stored in the same relation. This is one aspect of logical database design. In Chapter 6 we will study the other aspect of database design, namely designing a database from *groups* of relations by identifying and storing the relationships among them. Together these chapters cover the logical database design process.

In this chapter we will approach relation design from two perspectives. The first (and larger) part of the chapter examines various relation structures, points out their design weaknesses and flaws (called *anomalies*), and shows how to eliminate them (a process called *normalization*). After mastering that material, you will be able to critically review a relation, identify problems, and make improvements. This is the *analytical* approach to relation design; given a relation, you will be able to analyze and improve it.

The second part of the chapter, entitled "Rules for Composing Relations," takes a *synthetic* approach to design. In that section you will learn how to construct a relation out of attributes. Using this approach, you examine a group of attributes, identify relationships among them, and then decide the best way to combine them into relations. Because there are only three basic types of attribute relationships, there is a known set of ways to combine them into relations. Knowing these "rules" will help you through the seemingly befuddling process of synthesizing, or building, relations.

One approach is not exclusive of the other. On the contrary; a database designer is likely to *synthesize* an initial design from knowledge of the various attributes that must be stored and then *analyze* the design looking for anomalies. Thus both approaches are necessary in the logical database design process.

## Terminology

The topic of normalization is a major part of this chapter. It grew out of a subset of database technology based on the *relational data model.* (We will study the relational data model in Part 4 and other data models in Part 5.) Normalization, however, is an important aspect of database design regardless of the data model you use for implementation. Thus, the relational model is important for design even if a different model is used for implementation. Consequently, you need to become familiar with relational terminology.

As mentioned earlier, the relational database model is based on the concept that data is stored (at least conceptually) in two-dimensional tables called *relations*. Each row in the table represents a record. Each column represents a field. The entire table is roughly equivalent to a file. A row is called a *tuple* (rhymes with *couple*). A column is called an *attribute*.

Certain restrictions are imposed on relations. First, attributes are single-valued; neither repeating groups nor arrays are allowed. Second, entries in any column are all of the same kind. For example, one column may contain employee numbers, and another may contain employee names.

**Figure 5-1**
EMPLOYEE relation

|  | Attribute1<br>Name | Attribute2<br>Age | Attribute3<br>Sex | Attribute4<br>Employee-number |
|---|---|---|---|---|
| Tuple 1 | ANDERSON | 21 | F | 010110 |
| Tuple 2 | DECKER | 22 | M | 010100 |
| . | GLOVER | 22 | M | 101000 |
| . | JACKSON | 21 | F | 201100 |
| . | MOORE | 19 | M | 111100 |
| . | NAKATA | 20 | F | 111101 |
| Tuple 7 | SMITH | 19 | M | 111111 |

Further, each attribute has a unique name, and attribute positions are insignificant. Finally, no two tuples in a relation may be identical, and the order of the tuples is also insignificant. Figure 5–1 shows a sample relation.

Notice that this relation (table) has seven tuples (rows) that are made up of four attributes (columns). If we were to rearrange the order of the attributes (say, by placing Employee-number at the far left) or reorder the tuples (perhaps in ascending sequence on Age), then we would have an equivalent relation.

Figure 5–1 shows one occurrence of a relation. The generalized format, EMPLOYEE (Name, Age, Sex, Employee-number), is called the *relation structure* and is what most people mean when they use the term *relation*.

The terms *relation, tuple,* and *attribute* come from the field of mathematics and are alien to most people. You might find the terms *file, record,* and *field* more comfortable. Users, on the other hand, might prefer the terms *table, row,* and *column* when referring to the structure of stored data. In keeping with industry usage, we will use the terms *relation, row,* and *attribute* when discussing logical database design. *Tuple,* although technically correct and consistent with the other terms, is an awkward word and is seldom used in industry. Figure 5–2 summarizes relational terminology.

## NORMALIZATION

*Normalization* is the process of gathering data items (or properties) into relations. Object diagrams make the normalization process easy because they represent groups of related properties. The goal of logical database design is to represent objects in the database using relations that (1) provide the data needed to construct user objects and (2) are robust enough to allow

**Figure 5-2**

Relational
terminology

| Relational Model | Programmer | User |
|:---:|:---:|:---:|
| Relation | File | Table |
| Tuple (Row) | Record | Row |
| Attribute | Field | Column |

rows to be inserted, deleted, and modified without resulting in inconsistencies or errors in the stored data.

The considerable theoretical work on the nature of a well-designed relation is called normalization because one of the pioneers of database technology, E. F. Codd, defined a variety of *normal forms* that relations (or files) could take. As we examine each of the normal forms later in this chapter, you will see that each one represents an improvement over the previous ones. We will present the results of theorems that are of use and significance to the database practitioner.

We will begin our study of normalization with a discussion of modification anomalies. Then we will examine relationships among attributes. These relationships help determine which attributes (or data items) belong together in the same relation. Following that discussion we will present each of the normal forms.

## Modification Anomalies

Not all relational definitions (that is, table or record definitions) are alike. Obviously, a design that satisfies user needs is better than one that does not, but that does not mean that any relation is a well-structured one. Changing the data in some relations can have undesirable consequences, called *modification anomalies*. As you will see, anomalies can be eliminated by changing the structure of the relation. Usually relations without modification anomalies are preferred.

Consider the ACTIVITY relation in Figure 5–3. As you can see, the attributes are SID (student identifier), Activity, and Fee. The meaning of a row is that a student engages in the named activity for the specified fee. This relation can be used to illustrate what we mean by *modification anomalies*.

Suppose that each activity has a fixed fee that is the same for all students. Using the data in Figure 5–3, if we delete the tuple for student 100, we lose not only the fact that student 100 is a skier, but also the fact that skiing costs $200. This is called a *deletion anomaly*. In deleting the facts about

**Figure 5-3**
ACTIVITY relation

ACTIVITY (SID, Activity, Fee)
Key: SID
*Sample Data*

| SID | Activity | Fee |
|-----|----------|-----|
| 100 | SKIING | 200 |
| 150 | SWIMMING | 50 |
| 175 | SQUASH | 50 |
| 200 | SWIMMING | 50 |

one entity (that student 100 is a skier), we inadvertently deleted facts about another entity (that skiing costs $200). We lose facts about two entities with one deletion.

The same relation can be used to illustrate an *insertion anomaly.* Suppose we want to store the fact that scuba diving costs $175. We cannot enter this data into the ACTIVITY relation until a student takes up scuba. This restriction seems silly. Why should we have to wait until someone takes the activity before we can record its price? This restriction is called an *insertion anomaly* because we cannot insert a fact about one entity until we have an additional fact about another entity.

The relation in Figure 5–3 *can* be used for some user applications, but it obviously has problems. We can eliminate both the deletion and insertion anomalies by dividing the ACTIVITY relation into two relations, each dealing with a different theme. For example, we can put the SID and Activity attributes into one relation (we will call the new relation STU-ACT for Student-Activity), and we can put the Activity and Fee attributes into a relation called ACT-COST (for Activity-Cost). Figure 5–4 shows the same sample data stored in these two new relations.

Now if we delete student 100 from STU-ACT, we do not lose the fact that skiing costs $200. Further, we can add scuba and its fee to the ACT-COST relation even before anyone enrolls. Thus the deletion and insertion anomalies have been eliminated.

Separating the one relation into two relations has a disadvantage, however. Suppose a student tries to sign up for a nonexistent activity. For instance, suppose student 250 wants to enroll in racquetball. We can insert this new row in STU-ACT (the row would contain 250, RACQUETBALL), but should we? Should a student be allowed to enroll in an activity that is not in the relation ACT-COST? Put another way, must the database system somehow prevent STUDENT rows from being added if the value of the activity is not

**Figure 5-4**
Division of ACTIVITY
into two relations

STU-ACT (SID, Activity)
Key: SID

ACT-COST (Activity, Fee)
Key: Activity

| SID | Activity |
|------|----------|
| 100 | SKIING |
| 150 | SWIMMING |
| 175 | SQUASH |
| 200 | SWIMMING |

| Activity | Fee |
|----------|-----|
| SKIING | 200 |
| SWIMMING | 50 |
| SQUASH | 50 |

in the ACT-COST table? This constraint is called an *inter-relation constraint*. Some DBMS products enforce inter-relation constraints. Other products require special routines to be written by application programmers to enforce the constraint.

Suppose the user specifies that activities can exist before any student enrolls in them but that no student may enroll in an activity that does not have a fee assigned to it (that is, an activity that is not in the ACT-COST table). We can state this constraint in any of several acceptable formats:

- Activity in STU-ACT is a subset of Activity in ACT- COST, or
- STU-ACT [Activity] is a subset of ACT-COST [Activity], or
- STU-ACT [Activity] ⊂ ACT-COST [Activity]

In the above notation, the brackets [ ] denote attributes that are extracted from a relation. This notation simply means that the values in the Activity attribute of STU-ACT must exist in the Activity attribute of ACT-COST. It also means that before we allow an activity to be entered into STU-ACT, we must check to ensure that it is already present in ACT-COST. Whether this is done by the DBMS or by a special programmer-written subroutine depends on the DBMS product.

Think about what we just did. We identified two modification anomalies in a relation. We eliminated them by splitting the relation into two separate relations, each dealing with a different theme. In the process, we discovered a constraint governing the allowable values of one of the attributes in the two new relations. We have actually extracted an implicit rule from the original relation (because an activity always had a fee associated with it, a student always signed up for valid activities) and made it explicit in the new relations. Identifying and eliminating modification anomalies is the essence of the normalization process.

## Classes of Relations

Relations can be classified by the types of modification anomalies to which they are vulnerable. In the 1970s relational theorists chipped away at these types. Someone would find an anomaly, classify it, and think of a way to prevent it. Each time this happened, the criteria for designing relations improved. The classes of relations and techniques for preventing anomalies are called *normal forms*. Depending on its structure, a relation might be in first normal form, second normal form, or some other normal form.

E. F. Codd, in his landmark 1970 paper, defined first, second, and third normal forms (1NF, 2NF, 3NF). Later, Boyce-Codd normal form (BCNF) was postulated, and then fourth and fifth normal forms were defined. As shown in Figure 5–5, each of these normal forms contains the other. Thus, a relation that is in second normal form is also in first normal form. A relation in 5NF (fifth normal form) is also in 4NF, BCNF, 3NF, 2NF, and 1NF.

These normal forms were helpful, but they had a serious limitation. No theorist was able to guarantee that any of these forms would eliminate all anomalies. In fact, each form would eliminate only certain ones. This situation changed, however, in 1981 when R. Fagin defined a new normal form called domain/key normal form (DK/NF). In an important paper [39], Fagin showed that a relation in domain/key normal form is free of all modification anomalies, regardless of their type.

Until DK/NF was identified, it was necessary for relational database designers to continue looking for more and more anomalies and more and more normal forms. Fagin's proof, however, greatly simplified the situation. If we can put a relation in DK/NF, then we are guaranteed it will have no anomalies, period. The trick is to know how to put relations in DK/NF.

The next section surveys normal forms. You should strive to gain an intuitive understanding of 1, 2, 3, BC, 4, and 5 normal forms. From a

**Figure 5-5**
Relationship of
normal forms

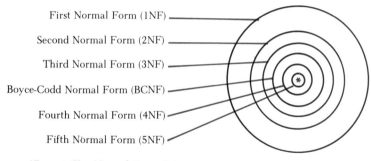

First Normal Form (1NF)

Second Normal Form (2NF)

Third Normal Form (3NF)

Boyce-Codd Normal Form (BCNF)

Fourth Normal Form (4NF)

Fifth Normal Form (5NF)

*Domain/Key Normal Form (DK/NF)

practitioner's standpoint, however, the most important normal form is domain/key. You need to understand it and the implications of domain/key form thoroughly. Domain/key normal form will become the primary design goal when constructing record definitions.

### Relationships among Attributes

All relations, as we have defined them, are in *first normal form*. Thus, the relation in Figure 5–3 is in first normal form. As we have seen, relations in first normal form can be used but they may have modification anomalies. As mentioned, we can eliminate these anomalies by changing the format of the relation—often by splitting it into two or more relations. When we do this, the new relations are in some other normal form—just which one depends on the anomalies we have eliminated, as well as the ones to which the relations are still vulnerable.

To understand this process of normalization, you must first understand two important terms concerning the relationships among attributes in a relation. (This is an example of how terminology in database technology can be confusing. A *relation* is a table. It is not to be confused with a *relationship*, which is an association between two attributes, or two rows.) The terms you need to learn are *functional dependency* and *key*.

### Functional Dependencies

A *functional dependency* is a relationship between attributes. Suppose that given the value of one attribute, we can obtain (or look up) the value of another attribute. For example, if we know the value of Customer-account-number, we can obtain the value of Customer-balance. We say that Customer-balance is *functionally dependent* on Customer-account-number. In more general terms, attribute $Y$ is functionally dependent on attribute $X$ if the value of $X$ determines the value of $Y$. Or, stated differently, if we know the value of $X$, then we can obtain the value of $Y$.

Equations can represent functional dependencies. For example, if we know the price of an item, and if we know the number of items purchased, then we can calculate the total price for that item as follows:

$$\text{Total-price} = \text{Item-price} \times \text{Number-of-items}$$

In this case, we would say that Total-price is functionally dependent on Item-price and Number-of-items.

The functional dependencies between attributes in a relation do not involve equations. For example, suppose that every student, identified with SID, has one and only one major. Given the value of a SID, we can obtain that student's major. Thus, Major is functionally dependent on SID. Or consider that every microcomputer in Eastcoast State University's lab has one and only one size of main memory. Then Size-of-main-memory is functionally dependent on Computer-serial-number. Unlike an equation, such functional dependencies cannot be worked out using arithmetic. Instead, they have to be *listed* in relations in the database.

Functional dependencies are written using the following notation:

$$SID \rightarrow Major$$

$$Computer\text{-}serial\text{-}number \rightarrow Size\text{-}of\text{-}main\text{-}memory$$

$$(Item\text{-}price, Number\text{-}of\text{-}items) \rightarrow Total\text{-}price$$

The first expression can be read "SID functionally determines Major," or "SID determines Major," or "Major is dependent on SID." Attributes on the left-hand side of the arrow are called *determinants*.

A functional dependency is a relationship of attribute values. If SID determines Major, then a particular value of SID will be paired with only *one* value of Major. Conversely, a value of Major may be paired with *one or more* different values of SID. For example, suppose that the student whose SID is 123 majors in accounting. Then any time SID and Major are found in the same relation, SID 123 will always be paired with the Major ACCOUNTING. However, the opposite is not true. The Major ACCOUNTING may be paired with many values of SID (many students may major in accounting). Consequently, we can say that the relationship of SID to Major is many-to-one (sometimes written $N$:1). In general, we can say that if $A$ determines $B$, then the relationship of the values of $A$ to $B$ is $N$:1.

Functional dependencies can involve groups of attributes. Suppose that the relation in Figure 5–3 were expanded to include an attribute to distinguish activities taken for course credit from those taken for fun: ACTIVITY (SID, Credit-status, Activity, Fee). The school's policy might be to determine an activity fee by the activity itself *and* the credit status. Thus, the combination (Credit-status, Activity) determines Fee.

In general, if $X \rightarrow (Y, Z)$, then $X \rightarrow Y$ and $X \rightarrow Z$. But if $(X, Y) \rightarrow Z$, then it is not necessarily true that $X \rightarrow Z$ or $Y \rightarrow Z$.

## Keys

A *key* is a group of one or more attributes that uniquely identifies a row. Every relation has at least one key. Sometimes the key is one attribute. If a student were allowed to participate in only one activity at a time, then the SID attribute in the ACTIVITY relation in Figure 5–3 would be the key field. Any value of SID would appear at most once in the table. Sometimes a group of attributes taken together comprises a key. For example, if students were allowed to enroll in many activities at once, then it would be possible for one value of SID to appear more than once in the table. SID would not uniquely identify the row then. However, the combination (SID, Activity) would be unique. Therefore, it could be the key for the relation.

In general, a key is an attribute or group of attributes that functionally determines the non-key attributes. Thus, if a student were allowed to participate in at most one activity at a time, then SID would functionally deter-

---

**Figure 5·6**
Relation with a two-
attribute key

ACTIVITIES (SID, Activity, Fee)
Key: (SID, Activity)

| SID | Activity | Fee |
|-----|----------|-----|
| 100 | SKIING | 200 |
| 100 | GOLF | 65 |
| 150 | SWIMMING | 50 |
| 175 | SQUASH | 50 |
| 175 | SWIMMING | 50 |
| 200 | SWIMMING | 50 |
| 200 | GOLF | 65 |

mine Activity and SID would functionally determine Fee. (Given the value of a SID, we could look up the student's activity and fee charged for it.) Thus, SID would be the key.

Now suppose students are allowed to participate in more than one activity. This policy is represented by the relation ACTIVITIES, shown in Figure 5–6. In this relation, SID is *not* a key because it does not functionally determine the other attributes. SID cannot determine the value of Activity because students can enroll in several activities. Student 100, for example, has enrolled in both skiing and golf. In this relation, no individual attribute is a key. The key must be a combination of two or more attributes.

Consider a combination of two attributes. The possibilities are (SID, Activity), (SID, Fee), and (Activity, Fee). Is any one of these combinations a key? If so, it must functionally determine the third attribute.

To help us decide, we must consider the user's world. For this application, what makes sense? We cannot simply depend on sample data like that in Figure 5–6 to make the decision because the data there is only one example. We must determine what will be true for all instances of this relation.

Considered in this frame, does the combination (SID, Fee) functionally determine Activity? No. It might for one instance of data, but it won't for all. Student 100 could engage in two different activities, both costing $200. This would mean that the combination (100, $200) generates two different values of Activity. This violates the requirement for a functional dependency that the relationship be N:1.

Can the combination (Activity, Fee) be a key? Does the combination (SKIING, $200) uniquely determine a SID? No, many students can ski. What about (SID, Activity)? Does a combination of values for SID and Activity appear only once in the table? Yes. A particular SID can appear more than once and a particular Activity can appear more than once. But any combination of SID and Activity can appear at the most one time. Thus, (SID, Activity) uniquely determines Fee. Consequently, (SID, Activity) is the key for this relation.

It is very important to understand that we must consider the underlying application when determining if functional dependencies exist. We cannot depend on one or two sample rows to provide us with the answer. Rather, we have to refer to the requirements and to the environment in which the application will be used. We must determine what makes sense in that environment.

## Functional Dependencies, Keys, and Uniqueness

Many students confuse the concepts of functional dependencies, keys, and uniqueness. First, a functional dependency implies nothing about uniqueness in a relation. If *A* determines *B*, then the values of *A* may or may not be unique within a relation. For example, even if SID determines Major, the relation may contain one or more occurrences of a particular SID value. For example, the SID value 123 may occur in one or several rows. If student 123 is an accounting major, and if SID functionally determines Major, then the functional dependency says that wherever SID and Major occur together, the value 123 must be paired with the value ACCOUNTING. Thus, one value of a determinant may appear several times within a relation.

The fact that SID determines Major does not imply that values of Major are unique, either. Clearly, there can be many majors, and they can be paired with many different values of SID as well.

Unlike the determinants of functional dependencies, keys are always unique. A key functionally determines the entire row. If the value of the key were duplicated, then the entire row would be duplicated. But this is not allowed because by definition, rows in a relation must be unique. Thus, when we say an attribute (or combination) is a key, we know it will be unique. If (SID, Activity) is a key, then, for example, the combination (100, SKIING) will occur only once in a relation.

To test your understanding of these concepts, see if you can explain why in the ACTIVITY relation in Figure 5–3, SID is both a determinant and a key, but Activity is a determinant and not a key. (Keep in mind that the relation in Figure 5–3 supports the school's policy that a student may participate in at most one activity at a time.)

These concepts may seem confusing. Work through them several times with examples, if you need to. A thorough understanding of functional dependencies, keys, and uniqueness will make both normalization and record relationships (in the next chapter) easier to grasp.

# FIRST THROUGH FIFTH NORMAL FORMS

We mentioned earlier that any relation is, by definition, in first normal form. That is because a relation, by definition, has no repeating groups in it—that is the characteristic of the first normal form. Unfortunately, as we have seen, relations in first normal form can have modification anomalies. In this section we will examine each type of anomaly discovered and the normal form developed to eliminate it.

## Second Normal Form

As we saw earlier, the ACTIVITIES relation in Figure 5–6 has modification anomalies. If we delete the tuple for student 175, we lose the fact that squash costs $50. Also, we cannot enter an activity until a student signs up for it. Thus, the relation suffers from both deletion and insertion anomalies.

The problem with this relation is that it has a dependency involving only part of the key. The key is the combination (SID, Activity), but the relation contains a dependency, Activity → Fee. The determinant of this dependency (Activity) is only part of the key (SID, Activity). The modification anomalies could be eliminated if the non-key attribute, Fee, were dependent on all of the key, not just part of it—but it is not. Therefore, we must separate the relation into two smaller ones. This situation leads to the definition of second normal form: *A relation is in second normal form if all non-key attributes are dependent on all of the key*. Observe that this definition pertains to relations that have composite keys (keys made up of two or more attributes). If the key is a single attribute, then the relation is automatically in second normal form.

ACTIVITIES can be decomposed to form two relations in second normal form. The relations are the same as those in Figure 5–4, namely STU-ACT and ACT-COST. These relations are in second normal form because they both have single-attribute keys.

## Third Normal Form

Relations in second normal form also have anomalies. Consider the HOUSING relation in Figure 5–7a. The key is SID, and the functional dependencies are SID → Building and Building → Fee (much like SID → Activity and Activity → Fee in Figure 5–3). These dependencies arise because a student lives in only one building and each building charges only one fee. Everyone living in Randolph Hall, for example, pays $1200 per quarter.

Since SID determines Building and since Building determines Fee, then, transitively, SID → Fee. Thus, SID, a single attribute, is the key and the relation must therefore be in second normal form (the key is a single attribute). In spite of this, however, it has anomalies.

What happens if we delete the second row shown in Figure 5–7a? We lose not only the fact that student 150 lives in Ingersoll Hall, but also the

**Figure 5-7**

Elimination of transitive dependency

HOUSING (SID, Building, Fee)
Key: SID
Functional
dependencies:  Building → Fee
                SID → Building → Fee

| SID | Building | Fee |
|-----|----------|------|
| 100 | RANDOLPH | 1200 |
| 150 | INGERSOLL | 1100 |
| 200 | RANDOLPH | 1200 |
| 250 | PITKIN | 1100 |
| 300 | RANDOLPH | 1200 |

a.  Relation with transitive dependency

STU-HOUSING (SID, Building)      BLDG-FEE (Building, Fee)
Key: SID                         Key: Building

| SID | Building |
|-----|----------|
| 100 | RANDOLPH |
| 150 | INGERSOLL |
| 200 | RANDOLPH |
| 250 | PITKIN |
| 300 | RANDOLPH |

| Building | Fee |
|----------|------|
| RANDOLPH | 1200 |
| INGERSOLL | 1100 |
| PITKIN | 1100 |

b.  Relations eliminating the transitive dependency

fact that it costs $1100 to live there. This is a deletion anomaly. Further, how can we record the fact that the fee for Carrigg Hall is $1500? We can't until a student decides to move in. This is an insertion anomaly.

To eliminate the anomalies from a relation in second normal form, the transitive dependency must be removed. This leads to a definition of third normal form: *A relation is in third normal form if it is in second normal form and has no transitive dependencies.*

The HOUSING relation can be divided into two relations in third normal form. The relations STU-HOUSING (SID, Building) and BLDG-FEE (Building, Fee) in Figure 5–7b are examples.

The ACTIVITY relation in Figure 5–3 also has a transitive dependency. In ACTIVITY, SID determines Activity and Activity determines Fee. Therefore, ACTIVITY is not in third normal form. Decomposing ACTIVITY into the relations STU-ACT (SID, Activity) and ACT-COST (Activity, Fee) eliminates the anomalies.

## Boyce-Codd Normal Form

Unfortunately, even relations in third normal form can have anomalies. Consider the ADVISOR relation in Figure 5–8a. Suppose the requirements underlying this relation are that a student (SID) can have one or more majors (Major), a major can have several faculty members (Fname) as advisors, and a faculty member (Fname) advises in only one major area.

Since students can have several majors, SID does not determine Major. Further, since students can have several advisors, SID does not determine Fname either. Thus, SID cannot be a key.

The combination (SID, Major) determines Fname and the combination (SID, Fname) determines Major. Hence, either of the combinations can be a key. Two or more attributes or attribute collections that can be a key are called *candidate keys*. Whichever of the candidates is selected to be *the* key is called the *primary key*.

In addition to the candidate keys, there is another functional dependency that may not be that obvious: Fname determines Major. (Any faculty member advises in only one major. Therefore, given the Fname we can determine the Major.) Thus Fname is a determinant.

ADVISOR is in first normal form by definition. It is in second normal form since any non-key attributes are dependent on the entire key (no matter which composite key we select). Further, it is in third normal form because it has no transitive dependencies. In spite of all this, however, it has modification anomalies.

Suppose student 300 drops out of school. If we delete student 300's tuple, we lose the fact that Perls advises in psychology. This is a deletion anomaly. Similarly, how can we store the fact that Keynes advises in economics? We cannot until a student majors in economics. This is an insertion anomaly.

Situations like this lead to the definition of Boyce-Codd normal form (BCNF): *A relation is in BCNF if every determinant is a candidate key.* ADVISOR is not in BCNF since it has a determinant, Fname, that is not a candidate key.

As with the other examples, ADVISOR can be decomposed into two relations having no anomalies (see Figure 5–8b). For example, the relations STU-ADV (SID, Fname) and ADV-SUBJ (Fname, Subject) have no anomalies.

Relations in BCNF have no anomalies regarding functional dependencies, and this seemed to put the issue of modification anomalies to rest. However, it was soon discovered that anomalies can arise from situations other than functional dependencies.

**Figure 5-8**
Boyce-Codd normal
form

ADVISOR (SID, Major, Fname)

Key (primary): (SID, Major)
Key (candidate): (SID, Fname)

Functional
dependencies: Fname → Major

| SID | Major | Fname |
|-----|-------|-------|
| 100 | MATH | CAUCHY |
| 150 | PSYCHOLOGY | JUNG |
| 200 | MATH | RIEMANN |
| 250 | MATH | CAUCHY |
| 300 | PSYCHOLOGY | PERLS |
| 300 | MATH | RIEMANN |

a. Relation in third normal form but not in BC normal form

STU-ADV (SID, Fname)          ADV-SUBJ (Fname, Subject)
Key: SID, Fname               Key: Fname

| SID | Fname |
|-----|-------|
| 100 | CAUCHY |
| 150 | JUNG |
| 200 | RIEMANN |
| 250 | CAUCHY |
| 300 | PERLS |
| 300 | RIEMANN |

| Fname | Subject |
|-------|---------|
| CAUCHY | MATH |
| JUNG | PSYCHOLOGY |
| RIEMANN | MATH |
| PERLS | PSYCHOLOGY |

b. Relations in Boyce-Codd normal form

## Fourth Normal Form

Consider the STUDENT relation in Figure 5–9. It shows the relationship of students, majors, and activities. Suppose that students can enroll in several different majors and participate in several different activities. Since this is so, the only key is the combination of attributes (SID, Major, Activity).

**Figure 5-9**

Relation with multi-valued dependencies

STUDENT (SID, Major, Activity)
Key: (SID, Major, Activity)

Multivalued
dependencies:   SID →→ Major
                SID →→ Activity

| SID | Major | Activity |
|-----|-------|----------|
| 100 | MUSIC | SWIMMING |
| 100 | ACCOUNTING | SWIMMING |
| 100 | MUSIC | TENNIS |
| 100 | ACCOUNTING | TENNIS |
| 150 | MATH | JOGGING |

Student 100 majors in music and accounting. She also participates in swimming and tennis. Student 150 majors only in math and participates in jogging.

What is the relationship between SID and Major? It is not a functional dependency, because students have several majors. In a functional dependency, the determinant is paired with only one value of an attribute. The same statement is true of the relationship between SID and Activity. The attribute dependency we see here is called a *multivalued dependency*. Multivalued dependencies lead to update anomalies. Let's see why.

First, note the data redundancy in Figure 5–9. Student 100 has four rows. Each one shows one of her majors paired with one of her activities. If the data were stored any other way (say we had only two rows: one for music and swimming and one for accounting and tennis), then the implications would be misleading. It would *appear* that student 100 swam only when she was a music major, and played tennis only as an accounting major. That interpretation is illogical! Her majors and her activities are completely independent of one another. So in this relation, we store all the combinations of majors and activities. But data redundancy is not the important problem with multivalued dependencies.

Suppose that student 100 decides to sign up for skiing, so we add the row [100, MUSIC, SKIING] (see Figure 5–10a). This implies that she skis as a music major, but not as an accounting major. This problem was described in the previous paragraph. In order to keep the data consistent, we must add one row for each of her majors paired with skiing. Thus we must also add the row [100, ACCOUNTING, SKIING] (see Figure 5–10b). This is an

**Figure 5-10**
STUDENT relations
with insertion
anomalies

STUDENT (SID, Major, Activity)
Key: (SID, Major, Activity)

| SID | Major | Activity |
|-----|-------|----------|
| 100 | MUSIC | SKIING |
| 100 | MUSIC | SWIMMING |
| 100 | ACCOUNTING | SWIMMING |
| 100 | MUSIC | TENNIS |
| 100 | ACCOUNTING | TENNIS |
| 150 | MATH | JOGGING |

a. Insertion of a single tuple

| SID | Major | Activity |
|-----|-------|----------|
| 100 | MUSIC | SKIING |
| 100 | ACCOUNTING | SKIING |
| 100 | MUSIC | SWIMMING |
| 100 | ACCOUNTING | SWIMMING |
| 100 | MUSIC | TENNIS |
| 100 | ACCOUNTING | TENNIS |
| 150 | MATH | JOGGING |

b. Insertion of two tuples

update anomaly—far too much updating needs to be done to apply a simple
change to the data.

In general, a multivalued dependency exists when there are at least
three attributes in a relation, at least one of them is multivalued, and the
values of two attributes depend only on the other attribute. In other words,
in a relation $R (A, B, C)$ a multivalued dependency exists if (1) $A$ leads to
multiple values of $B$, and/or (2) $A$ leads to multiple values of $C$, and (3) $B$
and $C$ are independent of each other. As we saw in the previous example,

SID leads to multiple values of Major and multiple values of Activity, but Major and Activity are independent of one another.

Refer again to Figure 5–9. Notice how multivalued dependencies are written: SID $\rightarrow\rightarrow$ Major, and SID $\rightarrow\rightarrow$ Activity. This is read "SID multidetermines Major, and SID multidetermines Activity." This relation is in BCNF (2NF because it is all key, 3NF because it has no transitive dependencies, and BCNF because it has no non-key determinants). However, as we have seen, it has anomalies. If a student adds a major, then we must enter a row for the new major paired with each of the student's activities. The same holds true if a student enrolls in a new activity.

If a student drops a major, we need to delete each of his rows containing that major. If he participates in four activities, then there will be four rows containing the major he has dropped, and each of them must be deleted.

In order to eliminate these anomalies, we must eliminate the multivalued dependency. We do this by building two relations, each one storing data on one of the multivalued attributes. The resulting relations do not have anomalies. They are STU-MAJOR (SID, Major) and STU-ACT (SID, Activity). See Figure 5–11. We will consider multivalued dependencies again, later in this chapter (page 160).

This observation leads to the definition of fourth normal form: *A relation is in fourth normal form if it is in BCNF and has no multivalued dependencies.* (We have simplified the definition of fourth normal form.)

## Fifth Normal Form

Fifth normal form concerns dependencies that are rather obscure. It has to do with relations that can be divided into subrelations, as we have been doing, but then cannot be reconstructed. The condition under which this situation arises has no clear, intuitive meaning. We do not know what the

**Figure 5-11**
Elimination of multi-valued dependency

STU-MAJOR (SID, Major)
Key: (SID, Major)

| SID | Major |
|-----|-------|
| 100 | MUSIC |
| 100 | ACCOUNTING |
| 150 | MATH |

STU-ACT (SID, Activity)
Key: (SID, Activity)

| SID | Activity |
|-----|----------|
| 100 | SKIING |
| 100 | SWIMMING |
| 100 | TENNIS |
| 150 | JOGGING |

consequences of such dependencies are, or even if they have any practical consequences.

Each of the normal forms we have discussed was identified by researchers who found anomalies with some relations that were in a lower normal form. For example, noticing modification anomalies with relations in third normal form led to the definition of Boyce-Codd normal form. But although each normal form solved some of the problems that had been identified with the previous one, no one could know what problems had not yet been identified. With each step, progress was made toward a well-structured database definition, but no one could guarantee that no more anomalies would be found. In the next section we will study a normal form that guarantees there will be no anomalies of any type. Once we put relations into that form, we know that even the obscure anomalies associated with fifth normal form cannot occur.

# DOMAIN/KEY NORMAL FORM

In 1981, R. Fagin published an important paper in which he defined *domain/key normal form (DK/NF)*. He showed that a relation in domain/key normal form has no modification anomalies and, further, that a relation having no modification anomalies must be in domain/key normal form. This finding establishes a boundary on the definition of normal forms. No higher normal form will be needed, at least for the purpose of eliminating modification anomalies.

Equally important, DK/NF involves only the concepts of key and domain. These concepts are fundamental and close to the hearts of database practitioners. They are readily supported by DBMS products (or could be, at least). In a sense, Fagin's work formalized and justified what many practitioners believed intuitively but were unable to express precisely.

## Definition

The DK/NF concept is quite simple: *A relation is in DK/NF if every constraint on the relation is a logical consequence of the definition of keys and domains.* Let us consider the important terms in this definition: *constraint, key,* and *domain.*

*Constraint* in this definition is a broad term. Fagin defines a constraint as any rule on static values of attributes that is precise enough that we can evaluate whether or not it is true. Thus edit rules, intra- and inter-relation constraints, functional dependencies, and multivalued dependencies are examples of constraints as Fagin has defined them. Fagin expressly excludes constraints having to do with *changes* in data values. For example, the rule "Salesperson salary in the current period can never be less than salary in the prior period" is excluded from Fagin's definition of constraint. Except for such constraints on changes in data values (or *time-dependent constraints*), Fagin's definition of constraint is very broad.

As defined in the last section, a *key* is the unique identifier of a row.

The third significant term in the definition of DK/NF is *domain*. In Chapter 2, we said that a domain is a description of the allowed values of an attribute. It has two parts: a physical description and a semantic, or logical, description. The physical description is the set of values the attribute can have and the logical description is the meaning of the attribute. Fagin's proof refers only to the physical part.

Informally, a relation is in domain/key normal form if enforcing key and domain restrictions causes all of the constraints to be met. Further, since relations in domain/key normal form cannot have modification anomalies, the DBMS can prohibit them by enforcing key and domain restrictions.

Now for the bad news: There is as yet no formal way of converting a relation to DK/NF, nor is it even known which relations can be converted to DK/NF. Finding, or designing, DK/NF relations is more of an art than a science.

Despite this, DK/NF can be exceedingly useful for database design. DK/NF is a design objective. We wish to define our relations such that constraints are logical consequences of domains and keys. For many designs, this objective can be accomplished. Where it cannot be accomplished, the constraints must be built into application programs that process the database. We will see more of this later in this chapter and in Chapter 8. To illustrate DK/NF we will use three examples.

### Domain/Key Normal Form Example 1

Consider the STUDENT relation in Figure 5–12. It contains SID, student grade-level, the building in which the student lives, and the student's fee

---

**Figure 5-12**
DK/NF Example 1

STUDENT (SID, Grade-level, Building, Fee)

Key: SID

Constraints:      Building $\rightarrow$ Fee
                  SID must not begin with digit 1

for living in that building. Since SID functionally determines the other three attributes, SID is a key. Assume we also know, from an examination of the requirements, that Building → Fee and that SIDs must not begin with 1.

If we can find a way to express these constraints as logical consequences of domain and key definitions, then we can be certain, by Fagin's theorem, that there will be no modification anomalies. For this example it will be easy.

To enforce the constraint that student numbers not begin with 1, we simply define the domain for student numbers to incorporate this constraint (see Figure 5–13). Enforcing the domain restriction guarantees that this constraint will be met.

Next, we need to make the functional dependency Building → Fee a logical consequence of keys. If Building were a key attribute, then Building → Fee would be a logical consequence of a key. Therefore, we face the question of how we can make Building a key. It cannot be a key in STUDENT because more than one student lives in the same building. It could be a key of its own relation, however. Thus we define the relation BLDG-FEE, with Building and Fee as its attributes. Building is the key of this relation. Having defined this new relation, we can remove Fee from STUDENT. The domain definitions and relation definitions for this example appear in Figure 5–13.

---

**Figure 5-13**
Domain/key definition of Example 1

Domain Definitions

    SID       IN   CDDD, where C is decimal digit not = 1; D = decimal digit
    Grade-level IN   {'FR', 'SO', 'JR', 'SN', 'GR' }
    Building  IN   CHAR(4)
    Fee       IN   DEC(4)

Relation and Key Definitions

    STUDENT (SID, Grade-level, Building)
    Key: SID

    BLDG-FEE
    (Building, Fee)
    Key: Building

This is the same result we obtained when converting a relation from 2NF to 3NF to remove transitive dependencies. In this case, however, the process was simpler and the result more robust. It was simpler because we did not need to know that we were eliminating a transitive dependency. We simply needed to search for creative ways to make all the constraints logical consequences of domain and key definitions. The result was more robust because, when converting the relation to 3NF, we knew only that it had fewer anomalies than when it was in 2NF. By converting the relation to DK/NF, we know that the relations have no modification anomalies whatsoever.

### Domain/Key Normal Form Example 2

The next example involves the relation described in Figure 5–14. It is more complicated than the previous one. The PROFESSOR relation contains data about professors, the classes they teach, and the students they advise. FID (for Faculty ID) and Fname uniquely identify a professor. SID uniquely identifies a student, but Sname does not necessarily identify a SID. Professors can teach several classes and advise several students. A student, however, is advised by only one professor. FIDs start with a 1; SIDs must not start with a 1.

These statements can be expressed more precisely by the functional and multivalued dependencies shown in Figure 5–14. FID and Fname functionally determine each other (in essence, they are equivalent). FID and Fname multidetermine Class and SID. SID functionally determines FID and Fname. SID determines Sname.

**Figure 5-14**
DK/NF Example 2

```
PROFESSOR (FID, Fname, Class, SID, Sname)
Key: (FID, Class, SID)
Constraints:        FID→Fname
                    Fname→FID
                    FID→→Class | SID
                    Fname→→Class | SID
                    SID→FID
                    SID→Fname
                    SID→Sname
                    FID must start with 1; SID must not start with 1
```

In more complex examples such as this one, it is helpful to consider DK/NF from another light. The essence of DK/NF is that every relation must have a single theme. Just as you learned in English composition that every paragraph should have only one theme, so too every relation should have a single theme.

Considered from this perspective, there are three themes in PROFESSOR. One is that FIDs and Fnames are the same. Another concerns the classes that a professor teaches. The third concerns the identification number, name, and advisor of a given student.

Figure 5–15 shows three relations that reflect these themes. The FACULTY relation represents the equivalence of FID and Fname. FID is the key, and Fname is an alternate key. This terminology means both attributes are unique in the relation. Because both are keys, the functional dependencies FID → Fname and Fname → FID are logical consequences of keys.

---

**Figure 5-15**
Domain/key definition of Example 2

Domain Definitions

| | | |
|---|---|---|
| FID | IN | CDDD, C = 1; D = decimal digit |
| Fname | IN | CHAR(30) |
| Class | IN | CHAR(10) |
| SID | IN | CDDD, C is decimal digit, not = 1; |
| | | D = decimal digit |
| Sname | IN | CHAR(30) |

Relation and Key Definitions

FACTULTY (FID, Fname)
Key (primary):   FID
Key (candidate): Fname

PREPARATION (Fname, Class)
Key: Fname, Class
STUDENT (SID, Sname, Fname)
Key: SID

The PREPARATION relation contains the correspondence of faculty and classes. It shows the classes a professor is prepared to teach. The key is the combination (Fname, Class). Both attributes are required in the key because a professor may teach several classes. Finally, STUDENT represents the student and advisor names for a particular SID. Observe that each of these relations has a single theme.

These relations express all of the constraints of Figure 5–14 as a logical consequence of domains and key definitions. These relations are therefore in DK/NF.

Note that the separation of the PREPARATION theme from the STUDENT theme has eliminated the multivalued dependencies. When we examined fourth normal form, we learned that to eliminate multivalued dependencies, we needed to separate a relation into two relations, each with one of the dependencies. Our approach here is to break a relation with several themes into several relations, each with one theme. In doing that, we eliminated a multivalued dependency. In fact, we arrived at the solution using either approach.

### Domain/Key Normal Form Example 3

The next example shows a situation that was not addressed by any of the other normal forms but that occurs frequently in practice. Specifically, this relation has a constraint among data values within a row that is neither a functional dependency nor a multivalued dependency.

Consider the constraints in the relation STU-ADVISOR in Figure 5–16. This relation contains information about a student and his or her advisor. SID determines Sname, FID, Fname, and Grad-faculty-status and is there-

**Figure 5-16**
DK/NF Example 3

STU-ADVISOR (SID, Sname, FID, FName, Grad-faculty-status)

Key: SID

Constraints:  FID → Fname
              Fname → FID
              FID and Fname → Grad-faculty-status
              Only graduate faculty can advise graduate students
              FID begins with 1
              SID must not begin with 1
              SID of graduate student begins with 9
              Grad-faculty-status $= \begin{cases} 0 \text{ for undergraduate faculty} \\ 1 \text{ for graduate faculty} \end{cases}$

fore the key. FID and Fname identify a unique faculty member and are equivalent to one another, as in Example 2. Both FID and Fname determine Grad-faculty-status. Finally, the new constraint is that only members of the graduate faculty are allowed to advise graduate students.

Domain restrictions are that SID must not begin with a 1, SID must begin with a 9 for graduate students, FID must begin with a 1, and Grad-faculty-status is 0 for non-graduate faculty and 1 for graduate faculty.

With these domain definitions, the constraint that graduate students must be advised by graduate faculty can be expressed as a constraint on attribute values. Specifically, if the SID starts with 9, then the value of Grad-faculty-status must be 1.

To put this relation in DK/NF we proceed as in Example 2. What are the basic themes of this relation? There is one about faculty personnel that relates FID, Fname, and Grad-faculty-status. Since FID and Fname determine Grad-faculty-status, either of these attributes can be the key and this relation is in DK/NF (see Figure 5–17).

---

**Figure 5-17**

Domain/key definition of Example 3

---

Domain Definitions

| | | |
|---|---|---|
| FID | IN | CDDD, where C = 1; D = decimal digit |
| Fname | IN | CHAR (30) |
| Grad-faculty-status | IN | [0, 1] |
| GSID | IN | CDDD, where C = 9; D = decimal digit; graduate student |
| UGSID | IN | CDDD, WHERE C ≠ 1 and C ≠ 9; D = decimal digit; undergraduate student |
| Sname | IN | CHAR (30) |

Additional Domain Definitions

| | | |
|---|---|---|
| Gfname | IN | {Fname of FACULTY, where Grad-faculty-status = 1} |

Relations and Key Definitions

FACULTY (FID, Fname, Grad-faculty-status)
Key: FID or Fname

G-ADV (GSID, Sname, Gfname)
Key: GSID

UG-ADV (UGSID, Sname, Fname)
Key: UGSID

**Figure 5-18**

Summary of normal
forms

| Form | Defining Characteristic |
|------|------------------------|
| 1NF | Any relation |
| 2NF | All non-key attributes are dependent on all of the keys. |
| 3NF | There are no transitive dependencies. |
| BCNF | Every determinant is a candidate key. |
| 4NF | There are no multivalued dependencies. |
| 5NF | Not described in this discussion. |
| DK/NF | All constraints on relations are logical consequences of domains and keys. |

Now consider data about students and advisors. Although it may first appear that there is only one theme, that of advising, the constraint that only graduate faculty can advise graduate students implies otherwise. Actually, there are two themes: graduate advising and undergraduate advising. Thus, in Figure 5–17, there is a G-ADV relation for graduate students and a UG-ADV relation for undergraduates. Observe the domain definitions. GSID starts with a 9, Gfname is the Fname of a FACULTY tuple with Grad-faculty-status equal to 1, and UGSID must not begin with 1 or 9.

All the constraints described in Figure 5–16 are implied by key and domain definitions in Figure 5–17. These relations are therefore in DK/NF and have no modification anomalies.

Before continuing, you may wish to review the definitions of the normal forms. Figure 5–18 summarizes the forms we discussed.

## RULES FOR COMPOSING RELATIONS

Keep in mind that we are trying to determine the best way to group attributes into relations. The resulting relations should satisfy two criteria: (1) they should contain data needed to construct user objects and (2) they should not have modification anomalies.

As we have just seen, some combinations of attributes are effective and other combinations are not. We now know that combinations resulting in relations in domain/key normal form are desired. We must then focus on how such DK/NF relations can be constructed. Although there is no algorithm for building such relations, there are design guidelines you can follow. We call them *rules for composing relations,* and in describing them, we focus on relationships between pairs of attributes.

Two attributes, say *A* and *B*, can be related in three basic ways:

1. They determine each other:

   $A \rightarrow B$ and $B \rightarrow A$.

   This is a one-to-one attribute relationship.

2. One determines the other:

   $A \rightarrow B$, but $B \nrightarrow A$.

   This is a many-to-one attribute relationship.

3. They are functionally unrelated:

   $A \nrightarrow B$ and $B \nrightarrow A$.

   This is a many-to-many attribute relationship.

We will consider each of these in turn.

### The One-to-One Attribute Relationship

If *A* determines *B* and *B* determines *A*, then the values of the attributes will have a *one-to-one relationship*. Here's why: We know that if *A* determines *B*, then the relationship from *A* to *B* is many-to-one. It is also true, however, that if *B* determines *A*, then the relationship from *B* to *A* must be many-to-one. The only way both of these statements can be true at the same time is for the relationship to be one-to-one.

This situation is illustrated by FID and Fname in Examples 2 and 3 in the previous section on domain/key normal form. Each of these attributes uniquely identifies a faculty person. Consequently, one value of FID corresponds to exactly one value of Fname, and vice versa.

Three equivalent statements can be drawn from the example of FID and Fname:

- If two attributes functionally determine each other, then the relationship of their data values is one-to-one.
- If two attributes uniquely identify the same object, then the relationship of their data values is one-to-one.
- If two attributes have a one-to-one relationship, then they functionally determine each other.

Attributes that have a one-to-one relationship must occur together in at least one relation. Other attributes that are functionally determined by these may also reside in this same relation. (An attribute that is functionally determined by one of them will be functionally determined by the other as well.) Consider FACULTY (FID, Fname, Grad-faculty-status) in Example 3 in the previous section. FID and Fname determine each other. Grad-faculty-status can also occur in this relation because it is determined by FID and Fname.

Attributes that are not functionally determined by these attributes may not occur in a relation with them. Consider relations FACULTY and PREPARATION in Example 2. Here, FID and Fname may both occur in FACULTY, but Class (from PREPARATION) may not. There can be multiple values of Class for a faculty member, so Class is not dependent on FID or Fname. If we added Class to the FACULTY relation, then the key of FACULTY would need to be either (FID, Class) or (Fname, Class). In this case, however, FACULTY would not be in DK/NF because the dependencies between FID and Fname would not be logically implied by either of the possible keys. These statements are summarized in the first column of Figure 5–19. Record definition rules are listed in Figure 5–20.

Attributes that have a one-to-one relationship must exist together in at least one relation in order to establish their equivalence. The fact that FID of 198, for example, refers to Professor Heart must be stored in some relation. It is generally undesirable to have them occur together in more than one relation, however, because this causes a needless data duplication. Often, one or both of the two attributes will occur in other relations. Fname, for example, occurs in both PREPARATION and STUDENT in Example 2. Although it would be possible to place Fname in PREPARATION and FID in STUDENT, this is generally bad practice. When attributes are paired in this way, one of them should be selected to represent the pair in all other relations. Fname was selected in Example 2.

## The Many-to-One Attribute Relationship

If attribute $A$ determines $B$, but $B$ does not determine $A$, then the relationship among their data values is *many-to-one*. In the advisor relationship in Example 2, SID determines FID. Many students (SID) are advised by a faculty member (FID), but each student is advised by only one faculty member. Thus, this is a many-to-one relationship.

**Figure 5-19**
Summary of three types of attribute relationship

| | Type of Attribute Relationship | | |
| --- | --- | --- | --- |
| | One-to-One | Many-to-One | Many-to-Many |
| Relation Definition* | $R(A,B)$ | $S(C,D)$ | $T(E,F)$ |
| Dependencies | $A \rightarrow B$ <br> $B \rightarrow A$ | $C \rightarrow D$ <br> $D \nrightarrow C$ | $E \nrightarrow F$ <br> $F \nrightarrow E$ |
| Key | Either $A$ or $B$ | $C$ | $(E,F)$ |
| Rule for Adding Another Attribute | Either $A$ or $B \rightarrow C$ | $C \rightarrow E$ | $(E,F) \rightarrow G$ |

*The letters used in these relation definitions match those used in Figure 5-20.

**Figure 5-20**

Summary of rules for
constructing relations

*Concerning One-to-One Relationships*
- Attributes that have a one-to-one relationship must occur together in at least one relation. Call the relation $R$ and the attributes $A$ and $B$.
- Either $A$ or $B$ must be the key of $R$.
- An attribute can be added to $R$ if it is functionally determined by $A$ or $B$.
- An attribute that is not functionally determined by $A$ or $B$ cannot be added to $R$.
- $A$ and $B$ must occur together in $R$, but should not occur together in other relations.
- Either $A$ or $B$ should be consistently used to represent the pair in relations other than $R$.

*Concerning Many-to-One Relationships*
- Attributes that have a many-to-one relationship can exist in a relation together. Assume $C$ determines $D$ in relation $S$.
- $C$ must be the key of $S$.
- An attribute can be added to $S$ if it is determined by $C$.
- An attribute that is not determined by $C$ cannot be added to $S$.

*Concerning Many-to-Many Relationships*
- Attributes that have a many-to-many relationship can exist in a relation together. Assume two such attributes, $E$ and $F$, reside together in relation $T$.
- The key of $T$ must be $(E,F)$
- An attribute can be added to $T$ if it is determined by the combination $(E,F)$.
- An attribute may not be added to $T$ if it is not determined by the combination $(E,F)$.
- If adding a new attribute, $G$, expands the key to $(E,F,G)$, then the theme of the relation has been changed. Either $G$ does not belong in $T$ or the name of $T$ must be changed to reflect the new theme.

For a relation to be in DK/NF, all functional dependencies must be implied by keys. Thus, in DK/NF, every determinant must be a key. If $A$, $B$, and $C$ are in the same relation, and if $A$ determines $B$, then $A$ must be the key (meaning it also determines $C$). If $(A, B)$ determines $C$, then $(A, B)$ must be the key. No other functional dependency, such as $A$ determines $B$, is allowed.

You can apply these statements to database design in the following way: When constructing a relation, if $A$ determines $B$, then the only other attributes you can add to the relation must also be determined by $A$. For example, suppose you have put SID and Building together in a relation called STUDENT. You may add any other attribute determined by SID, such as Sname, to this relation. But if the attribute Fee is determined by Building, then you may not add it to this relation. Fee can be added only if SID → Fee. These statements are summarized in the center column of Figure 5–19.

## The Many-to-Many Attribute Relationship

If $A$ does not determine $B$ and $B$ does not determine $A$, then the relationship among their data values is *many-to-many*. In Example 2, Fname and Class have a many-to-many relationship. A professor teaches many classes and a class is taught by many professors.

In a many-to-many relationship, both attributes must be a key of the relation. For instance, the key of PREPARATION in Example 2 is the combination (Fname, Class).

When constructing relations that have multiple attributes as keys, you can add new attributes that are functionally dependent on all of the key. Number-of-times-taught is functionally dependent on both (Fname, Class) and could be added to the relation. Faculty-office, however, could not be added since it would be dependent only on Fname, not on Class. If Faculty-office needs to be stored in the database, it must be added to a relation about faculty, not to the relation about preparations.

Sometimes adding a new attribute changes the key. For example, suppose we add Classroom-number to PREPARATION. If we do this, (Fname, Class) is no longer the key because a particular teacher can teach a particular class in more than one room. The key becomes (Fname, Class, Classroom-number). BE AWARE THAT WHEN THIS HAPPENS, YOU HAVE CHANGED THE UNDERLYING *THEME* OF THE RELATION.

Changing the theme may or may not be appropriate. If Classroom-number belongs in the relation, then the theme does need to be changed. In that case, PREPARATION is the wrong relation name. WHERE-TAUGHT or some similar name would be more accurate. On the other hand, depending on user requirements, PREPARATION may be completely appropriate as it is. If so, then Classroom-number, if it belongs in the database at all, should be located in a different relation—perhaps SECTION-NUMBER, or CLASS-SECTION, or some similar relation.

### Multivalued Dependencies, Iteration Two

The discussion about many-to-many attribute value relationships may make the concept of multivalued dependencies easier to understand. The problem with the relation STUDENT (SID, Major, Activity) in Figure 5–9 is that it has two *different* many-to-many relationships. One is between SID and Major and the other is between SID and Activity. Clearly a student's majors have nothing to do with the student's activities. Putting both of these many-to-many relationships in the same relation, however, makes it appear as if there is some association.

Major and activity are independent. There would be no problem if a student had only one of each. Then, SID would functionally determine Major and Activity and the relation would be in DK/NF. In this case, the relationships from Major to SID and Activity to SID would both be many-to-one.

Another way of perceiving the difficulty is to examine the key, (SID, Major, Activity). Since STUDENT has many-to-many relationships, all of the attributes have to be in the key. Now, what theme does this key represent? We might say that it represents the combination of the studies and activities of a student. But this is not one thing; it is plural. One row of this relation describes only part of the combination. We need all of the rows about a particular student to get the whole picture. In general, a row should have all the data about one instance of the theme of the relation. A row of CUSTOMER, for example, should have all the data we want about a particular customer.

Consider PREPARATION in Example 2 in the section on domain/key normal form. The key is (Fname, Class). The underlying theme is the fact that a particular professor taught a particular class. We need only one row of the relation to get all of the information we have about the combination of that professor and that class. (The relation might include Course-date, Text-used, and Number-of-meetings attributes.) Looking at more rows will not generate any more information about it.

As you know, the solution to the multivalued dependency problem is to break the relation into two relations, each having a single theme. STU-MAJOR shows the combination of a student and a major. Everything we know about the combination is in a single row. We will not gain more information about that combination by examining more rows.

## A NOTE ON CONSTRAINTS

A database design, as described in Chapter 2, consists of definitions of data items (what we have called *attributes* in this chapter), records, and relationships among records. The definition of each of these includes a section describing constraints. We have been discussing such constraints throughout this chapter, although we have not been explicit about it.

In fact, a data item (attribute) constraint and what we have called a *domain* in this chapter are the same. When we say that UGSID must not begin with 1 or 9, we are stating a data item constraint. Thus, the definitions of domains will provide the material for the constraint section of data item definitions. You will see this when we bring all of the design material together in Chapter 6.

Additionally, a key is a record (relation) constraint. The statement that an attribute is a key is equivalent to stating that it must be unique in the relation. Another way of explaining domain/key normal form is that if a relation is in domain/key normal form, then the only non-domain constraints will be uniqueness constraints. No other constraints will be allowed (or necessary). Thus, the identification of key attributes will provide the material for the constraint section of record definitions.

Finally, there are constraints about relationships. In fact, an inter-relation constraint is a relationship constraint. The statement that Fname in PREPARATION is a subset of Fname in FACULTY is a relationship constraint. Thus, inter-relation constraints will provide the material for relationship constraints.

You will see how all of these concepts interplay in later chapters when we illustrate specific DBMS products. For now, just be aware that normalization provides all of the material for record definitions and much of the material for constraints.

## SUMMARY

In this chapter we presented the first aspect of logical database design, focusing on the characteristics of a good relation. We began by analyzing sample relations, identifying design flaws, and learning how to eliminate them. This is called normalizing a relation.

Normalization is a process by which attributes are grouped together to form a well-structured relation. Normalization arose in the context of the relational model but is applicable to the design of all types of database. A relation is a two-dimensional table that has single-valued entries. Entries in a given column are all of the same kind, columns have a unique name, and the order of columns is immaterial. Columns are called *attributes*. No two rows of a table are identical and the order of rows in the table is also immaterial. Rows are called *tuples*. Sometimes the terms *table* or *file* are substituted for *relation*, the terms *column* or *field* are substituted for *attribute*, and the terms *row* or *record* are substituted for *tuple*.

Some relations, although they contain usable data, suffer from undesirable consequences, called *modification anomalies*, when updated. A deletion anomaly occurs when the deletion of a row loses information about two or more entities. An insertion anomaly occurs when the relational structure forces the addition of facts about two entities at the same time. Anomalies can be removed by restructuring the relations. Usually this is done by splitting the relation into two or more relations.

There are many types of modification anomaly. Relations can be classified by the types of anomaly that they eliminate. These classifications are called *normal forms*.

A *functional dependency* is a relationship between attributes. $Y$ is functionally dependent on $X$ if the value of $X$ determines the value of $Y$. A *determinant* is a group of one or more attributes on the left side of a functional dependency. For example, if $X \rightarrow Y$, then $X$ is the determinant. A *key* is a group of one or more attributes that uniquely identifies a tuple. Every relation has at least one key. Since every row is unique, in the most extreme case, the key is the collection of all the attributes in the relation. Although a key is always unique, the determinant in a functional dependency need not be unique in the relation.

Every relation, as we have defined it, is in first normal form. A relation is in second normal form if all non-key attributes are dependent on all of the key. A relation is in third normal form if it is in second normal form and has no transitive dependencies. A relation is in Boyce-Codd normal form if every determinant is a candidate key. A relation is in fourth normal form if it is in Boyce-Codd normal form and has no multivalued dependencies. The definition of fifth normal form is semantically obscure, and we did not go into detail about it.

A relation is in domain/key normal form if every constraint on the relation is a logical consequence of the definition of domains and keys. A *constraint* is any rule on static values of attributes whose truth can be evaluated. As we have defined them, *domains* have both a physical and a semantic part. In the context of domain/key normal form, however, domain refers only to the physical description. An informal way of expressing domain/key normal form is to say that every relation must have only a single theme. For example, it might be about PROFESSORs or about STUDENTs but not about both PROFESSORs and STUDENTs at the same time.

Relation design can also be approached synthetically using the relationship among attributes. If two attributes functionally determine each other, then they have a one-to-one relationship. If one attribute functionally determines the other, but not the reverse, then the attributes have a one-to-many relationship. If neither attribute determines the other, then they have a many-to-many relationship. These facts can be used to construct relations.

## QUESTIONS                                                                    **GROUP I**

**5.1** What is a deletion anomaly? Give an example.

**5.2** What is an insertion anomaly? Give an example.

**5.3** Explain the relationship of 1, 2, 3, BC, 4, 5, and D/K normal forms.

**5.4** Define *functional dependency*. Give an example of two attributes that have a functional dependency. Give an example of two attributes that do not have a functional dependency.

**5.5** If SID functionally determines Activity, does this mean that only one value of SID can exist in the relation? Why or why not?

**5.6** Define *determinant*.

**5.7** Give an example of a relation that has a functional dependency in which the determinant has two or more attributes.

**5.8** Define *key*.

**5.9** If SID is a key of a relation, is it a determinant? Can there be more than one occurrence of a given value of SID in the relation?

**5.10** Define *second normal form*. Give an example of a relation in 1NF but not in 2NF. Transform the relation into relations in 2NF.

**5.11** Define *third normal form*. Give an example of a relation in 2NF but not 3NF. Transform the relation into relations in 3NF.

**5.12** Define *BCNF*. Give an example of a relation in 3NF but not BCNF. Transform the relation into relations in BCNF.

**5.13** Define *multivalued dependency*. Give an example.

**5.14** Why must multivalued dependencies exist in pairs?

**5.15** Define *fourth normal form*. Give an example of a relation in BCNF but not in 4NF. Transform the relation into relations in 4NF.

**5.16** Define *domain/key normal form*. Why is it important?

**5.17** Transform the following relation into DK/NF. Make appropriate assumptions about functional dependencies and domains. State your assumptions.

HARDWARE (Manufacturer, Model, Memory-size, Site-number, City, State, ZIP)

**5.18** Transform the following relation into DK/NF. Make appropriate assumptions about functional dependencies and domains. State your assumptions.

INVOICE (Number, Customer-name, Customer-number, Customer-address, Item-number, Item-price, Item-quantity, Salesperson-number, Tax-district-of-sale, Tax, Total-due)

**5.19** Perform the same task as in 5.18, but add the attribute Customer-tax-status (0 if nonexempt, 1 if exempt). Also, add the constraint that there will be no tax if Customer-tax-status = 1.

---

**GROUP II**     QUESTIONS AND EXERCISES

**5.20** Using the following relation definition and sample data, answer the questions.

COMP-SFTWR (Cnumber, Pkg-name, Memory)

Where Cnumber is computer serial number
Pkg-name is name of software package installed on that computer
Memory is memory requirements for that package

| Cnumber | Pkg-name | Memory |
|---------|----------|--------|
| 100A | Write-away | 640K |
| 100A | Graph-pak | 512K |
| 100B | Graph-pak | 512K |
| 200A | Write-away | 640K |
| 200B | Write-away | 640K |
| 200C | Melodies | 128K |
| 200C | Graph-pak | 512K |
| 200D | Melodies | 128K |

COMP-SFTWR Relation

Which of the following statements is/are true?
**a.** Cnumber → Pkg-name
**b.** Cnumber → Memory
**c.** (Cnumber, Pkg-name) → Memory
**d.** Pkg-name → Memory
**e.** Memory → Cnumber
**f.** Memory → (Cnumber, Pkg-name)

Answer these questions:
**g.** What is the key of COMP-SFTWR?
**h.** Are all non-key attributes (if any) dependent on all of the key?
**i.** In what normal form is COMP-SFTWR?
**j.** Describe two modification anomalies from which COMP-SFTWR suffers.
**k.** Is Cnumber a determinant?
**l.** Is Pkg-name a determinant?

**m.** Is (Cnumber, Pkg-name) a determinant?

**n.** Is Memory a determinant?

**o.** Does this relation contain a transitive dependency? If so, what is it?

**p.** Redesign this relation to eliminate the modification anomalies.

**5.21** Using the following relation definition and sample data, answer the questions.

ST-USAGE (SID, Cnumber, Class, Sname, Total-hrs)

Where SID is student ID
      Cnumber is computer serial number
      Class is class in which student is enrolled, authorizing student to use lab
      Sname is student name
      Total-hrs is lab hours used by student this marking period

| SID | Cnumber | Class | Sname | Total-hrs |
|-----|---------|-------|-------|-----------|
| 123 | 100A | BASIC | Smith, J. | 12 |
| 123 | 100A | Pascal | Smith, J. | 12 |
| 123 | 200B | BASIC | Smith, J. | 12 |
| 123 | 200B | Pascal | Smith, J. | 12 |
| 456 | 100A | COBOL | Jones, M. | 26 |
| 456 | 200A | COBOL | Jones, M. | 26 |
| 456 | 200D | COBOL | Jones, M. | 26 |

ST-USAGE Relation

Which of the following statements is/are true?

**a.** SID → Cnumber

**b.** SID →→ Cnumber

**c.** SID → Class

**d.** SID →→ Class

**e.** SID → Sname

**f.** SID → Total-hrs

**g.** (SID, Cnumber) → Total-hrs

**h.** (SID Sname) → Class

**i.** Cnumber → Class

**j.** Class → Cnumber

Answer these questions:

**k.** List all of the determinants.

**l.** Does this relation contain a transitive dependency? If so, what is it?

**m.** Does this relation contain a multivalued dependency? If so, what are the unrelated attributes?

**n.** Describe a deletion anomaly from which this relation suffers.

**o.** How many themes are there in this relation?

**p.** Redesign this relation to eliminate the modification anomalies. How many relations did you use? How many themes are there in each of your new relations?

**5.22**   Consider the following relation, key, and domain definitions:

*Domain Definitions*

| | | |
|---|---|---|
| SID | IN | DEC(4) |
| Sname | IN | CHAR(20) |
| Cnumber | IN | CHAR(6) |
| Location | IN | CHAR(2) |
| Memory | IN | CHAR(8) |
| Date | IN | YYMMDD |
| Time | IN | HHMM where HH is between 00 and 23, MM is between 00 and 59 |

*Relation Definitions*
STUDENT (SID, Sname)
Key: SID
Constraints: SID → Sname

COMPUTER (Cnumber, Location, Memory)
Key: Cnumber
Constraints: Cnumber → Location
            Cnumber → Memory

APPOINTMENT (Date, Time, Cnumber, SID)
Key: (Date, Time, Cnumber)
Constraints: (Date, Time, Cnumber) → SID

Modify the above definitions to add this constraint: A student may not sign up for more than one appointment at a time.

# Logical Database Design

- Binary Relationships
- Trees and Networks
- Object Types
- Guidelines for Logical Database Design
- Sample Objects
- Summary

In Chapter 4 we discussed database requirements. In that discussion, we used object diagrams to document the structure of objects. We said then that object diagrams would be used during the database design phase of system development. We will return to them in this chapter.

In Chapter 5 we examined normalization, a technique for determining which attributes should be stored in a relation. We also discovered that normalization can be used to critically review relations to determine if they are vulnerable to any modification anomalies. If they are, then normalization helps us to eliminate the anomalies, resulting in a better design.

In this chapter we will draw these concepts together to perform *logical database design*. During logical database design, the stage that follows requirements definition, a project team produces the blueprint for the database structure. The output from this phase consists of a set of relation diagrams, relation definitions, domain definitions, and a list of constraints. These documents are then used to develop the physical database design. Physical database design adapts the logical design to meet the requirements of the particular DBMS to be used. Thus a logical design is generic, whereas a physical design is DBMS product-specific. We will discuss physical database design in Parts 4 and 5.

This chapter opens with a discussion of the three basic binary relationships used to link records in different relations. Using those simple binary relationships, we can build more complex structures called *trees* and *networks*. Next you will learn how to identify five fundamental object types based on information found in the object diagrams. In the last section, you will learn how to transform object diagrams into groups of relations.

## BINARY RELATIONSHIPS

In Chapter 2 you learned that a database is a collection of data records and record relationships. In this section we will discuss the fundamental ways in which records in one relation can be associated with records in other relations. (Note that we will use the terms *relation* and *record*. In the strictest sense, *tuple* should be used with *relation*. In truth, *tuple* is an awkward word and is seldom used in industry.)

When you look at a set of object diagrams, you can see that the variety of object structures is virtually unlimited. For example, a STUDENT object could contain or be contained in CLASS, PROFESSOR, MAJOR, GRADE, and other objects. A CUSTOMER object might contain INVOICEs, which in turn could hold data from products in INVENTORY. An EMPLOYEE object might have DEDUCTIONs, SKILLs, and a JOB-HISTORY. There is an infinite number of such possibilities.

Yet, in spite of the variety and complexity of such object structures, almost all of them are constructed from a few simple relationships. Just as in chemistry, where an immense number of molecules can be constructed from fewer than a dozen elements, so, too, in database processing, most object structures can be constructed from three types of binary relationship.

A *binary relationship* is a relationship that involves only two *record types*. For example, in Figure 6–1 there is a COLLEGE object and a DEPT object. As you can tell from the object diagrams, DEPT is contained in COLLEGE and COLLEGE is contained in DEPT.

The equivalent relation diagram also appears in Figure 6–1. In this chapter you will learn the process of converting object diagrams into relational structures as depicted in Figure 6–1. Notice that there is one relation for COLLEGE and one for DEPT. (There is not always a one-to-one correspondence between an object and a relation. Sometimes more than one relation is needed to represent an object.) Each of the relations contains records. The forked line connecting the two relations indicates that there may be a link, or a relationship, between a record in the COLLEGE relation and one or more records in the DEPT relation. Thus, this is called a binary relationship, because it involves only two record types: COLLEGE and DEPARTMENT.

In Figure 6–2a, the relationship between professors and students is a binary relationship. This relationship, called ADVISEE, shows which professors advise which students. Observe that all instances of the relationship (shown by the lines) involve only two records.

Two or more binary relationships can be used to build more complicated structures. In Figure 6–2b, there are two binary relationships. One, ADVISEE, shows the relationship between professors and students. The second, EVALUATION, shows the relationship between students and grades. Observe that in both cases, the relationship involves only two records at a time.

In contrast, Figure 6–3a shows an example of a non-binary, triplet relationship. In this case, the relationship is defined by an instance of a

**Figure 6–1**
Transforming objects into relations and a relationship

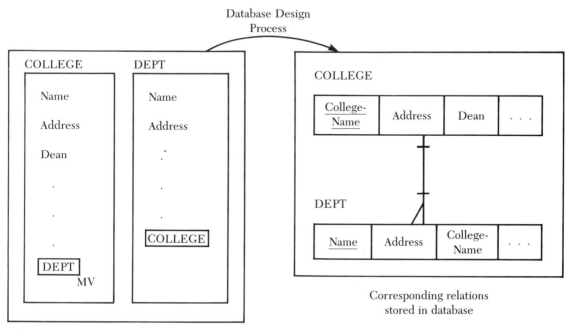

Database Design
Process

Objects as viewed by user

Corresponding relations
stored in database

mother, a father, and a child. Each instance of the relationship involves all three records. Compare Figure 6–3a to Figure 6–2b. Three records were also involved in Figure 6–2b, but each relationship involved only two at a time. In Figure 6–3a, each instance of the relationship involves three records at a time.

Triplet and other higher-order relationships can be decomposed into binary relationships, as illustrated in Figure 6–3b. In this figure, each child participates in two binary relationships, FATHER and MOTHER. Each instance of each of these relationships involves only two records at a time.

Binary relationships are the main building blocks for constructing objects. Said another way, object structures can be decomposed into records and binary relationships between them. There are three types of binary relationship: one-to-one, one-to-many, and many-to-many. We will consider each of these in turn.

## One-to-One Relationships

The simplest form of binary relationship is a one-to-one (1:1) record relationship. For this form, a record of one type is related to no more than one record of another type. For example, suppose each employee were allowed to park one car in the company lot (see Figure 6–4). Notice in Figure 6–4a

**Figure 6–2**
Binary relationships

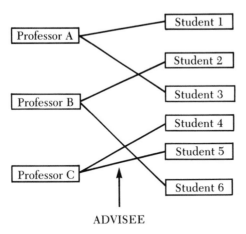

a. ADVISEE relationship

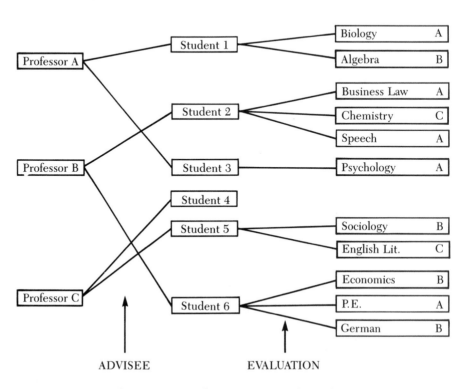

b. ADVISEE and EVALUATION relationships

**Figure 6–3**
Representations of
FAMILY relationship

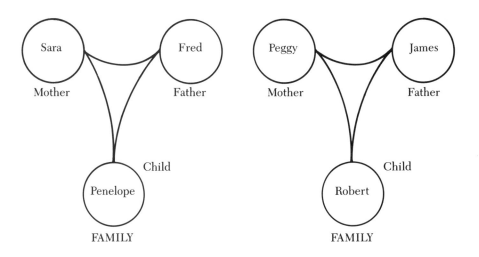

a. Instances of a triplet relationship

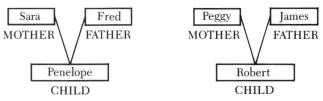

b. Instances of two binary relationships

that each EMPLOYEE record corresponds to one AUTO record, and each
AUTO record corresponds to one EMPLOYEE record.

Figure 6–4b shows a shorthand notation for representing this relationship. Each rectangle represents a relation, or record type, and the line represents the relationship between EMPLOYEE and AUTO records. In this
case, the line has no "fork" on either end (as it did in Figure 6–1). Thus,
the diagram can be read, "An EMPLOYEE record is related to at most one
AUTO record, and an AUTO record is related to at most one EMPLOYEE
record."

The notation used in Figure 6–4b does not indicate if every employee
*must* have a car, or if every auto *must* belong to an employee. Suppose that
it is optional for an employee to have an auto, but that every auto must
belong to an employee. We can add those details to the diagram as shown
in Figure 6–4c. The circle near AUTO indicates that an employee *may* have

### Figure 6–4

One-to-one
relationships

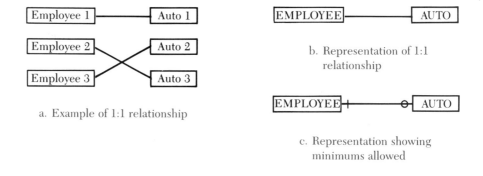

b. Representation of 1:1
relationship

a. Example of 1:1 relationship

c. Representation showing
minimums allowed

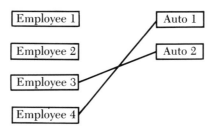

d. Instance of mandatory-to-optional 1:1 relationship

a car, and the bar at the other end indicates that every AUTO record *must* be connected to an EMPLOYEE record. Figure 6–4d illustrates an instance of the relationship defined in Figure 6–4c. Two employees do not have cars, but each car is assigned to an employee.

Figure 6–5 shows another 1:1 relationship. A PROFESSOR record must be related to one OFFICE record, while an OFFICE record may be related to one PROFESSOR record. Specifying the relationship in this way means that:

- Every professor must be assigned exactly one office
- No office may be assigned to more than one professor
- Some offices may be unassigned

A third 1:1 relationship is shown in Figure 6–6. Here, each EMPLOYEE has a JOB-EVALUATION and each JOB-EVALUATION corresponds to a particular employee. The relationship is mandatory in both directions. When the relationship is 1:1 and is mandatory in both directions, there is a strong

**Figure 6–5**
Optional-mandatory
1:1 relationship

likelihood that the records are describing different aspects of the same object. If so, in most cases they should be combined into one record. Learn to regard such 1:1 mandatory relationships with suspicion.

The separation of two records that define the same object can sometimes be justified for operational reasons. For example, one reason that a database designer might want to separate EMPLOYEE data from JOB-EVAL-UATION data is that JOB-EVALUATION data is lengthy and used far less frequently than other employee data. If so, better performance might be achieved by separating the two. A second reason for separating the two records could be security. If the DBMS does not support security at the data-item level, the JOB-EVALUATION data may need to be separated to prevent unauthorized users from accessing it.

Do not conclude from this discussion that all 1:1 mandatory relationships are inappropriate. Only those that appear to describe different aspects of the same object are questionable. For example, a 1:1 mandatory relationship between EMPLOYEE and AUTO would be quite appropriate because each record defines a different entity.

**Identifying 1:1 Relationships.** One-to-one relationships between objects will result in one-to-one record relationships. An object relationship is one-to-one if Object A contains Object B as a single-valued object property, and either Object B contains Object A as a single-valued object property or Object B does not contain Object A.

For example, Figure 6–7a shows the 1:1 relationship between EMPLOYEE and AUTO described in Figure 6–4. Each object contains the other as an object property.

In contrast, Figure 6–7b shows a 1:1 TEACHER/ASSISTANT relationship. Each assistant works for exactly one teacher and each teacher has no more than one assistant. Note that the first object contains the second, but that the second does not contain the first. How could this happen?

When constructing the object diagrams, the development team working on this project found a report about an assistant that included data about the teacher the assistant worked for. So it developed an ASSISTANT object diagram containing TEACHER. However, there was no teacher report or form that included data about an assistant. Therefore, the team developed the TEACHER object diagram without an ASSISTANT object property. Thus, Object A contains Object B, but Object B does not contain Object A. This is still a 1:1 relationship. If an assistant is related to a teacher, then the

**Figure 6-6**

Mandatory-manda-
tory 1:1 relationship

teacher is related to the assistant, like it or not. ASSISTANT is simply not shown as part of TEACHER.

**Representing 1:1 Relationships.**   To represent a 1:1 relationship, make the key of one relation an attribute of the other relation. (Remember that a *key* uniquely defines each record in a relation.) For example, consider the EMPLOYEE/AUTO relationship. As shown in Figure 6-8, each object is represented by a relation. The key of AUTO is Serial# and the key of EMPLOYEE is Employee#. To make the connection between an employee and an automobile, we either place the Serial# in the EMPLOYEE relation (Figure 6-8a), or we place the Employee# in the AUTO relation (Figure 6-8b). A key from one relation that becomes an attribute in another relation is called a *foreign key.* Notice that we have underlined the key of each relation.

Because we are representing a 1:1 relationship, it does not matter which approach we use. We could make the key of each relation an attribute of the other one (as in Figure 6-8c), but this would be redundant.

Now consider the 1:1 relationship between EMPLOYEE and JOB-EVAL-UATION shown in Figure 6-6. Because these relations describe different aspects of the same entity (an employee), the key of the relations is the same—probably Employee-ID. Since the keys are the same, the key of each relation is already an attribute of the other relation, so the relationship is automatically established.

**One-to-Many Relationships**

The second type of binary relationship is one-to-many (1:N). In a 1:N relationship, a record of one type is related to potentially many records of another type. Figure 6-9a shows a one-to-many relationship between professors and students. In this relationship, a professor is related to many students as ADVISEES.

Notation for representing a 1:N relationship is shown in Figure 6-9b. The "fork" at the STUDENT end of the relationship line means that there are potentially many students for each PROFESSOR. No fork at the other end means each student can be advised by at most one professor. As in Figure 6-4c, the circle means that the relationship from PROFESSOR to STUDENT is optional—that is, a professor need not have any advisees. The bar across the line at the other end means that a STUDENT record must correspond to a PROFESSOR record.

**Figure 6—7**
Object diagrams
showing 1:1
relationship

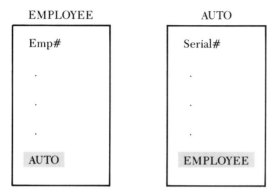

a. Each object contains the other

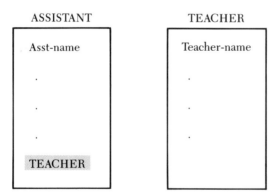

b. Only one object contains the other

The terms *parent* and *child* are sometimes applied to records in 1:*N* relationships. The parent record is on the *one* side of the relationship and the child record is on the *many* side. Thus, in the example in Figure 6–9, PROFESSOR is the parent record and STUDENT is the child record.

Figure 6–10 shows two other one-to-many relationships. In Figure 6–10a, a DORMITORY record corresponds to many STUDENT records, but a STUDENT record corresponds to only one DORMITORY record. Further, a dormitory does not have to have any students assigned to it, nor is a student required to live in a dormitory.

**Figure 6—8**

Representaion of 1:1
relationships

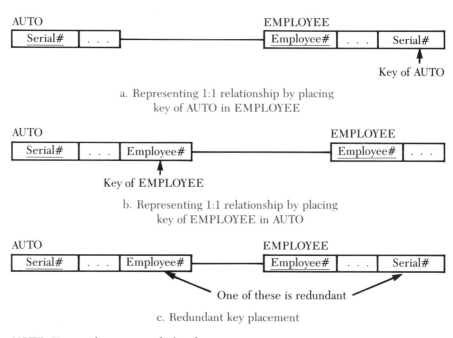

a. Representing 1:1 relationship by placing
key of AUTO in EMPLOYEE

b. Representing 1:1 relationship by placing
key of EMPLOYEE in AUTO

c. Redundant key placement

NOTE: Key attributes are underlined.

In Figure 6–10b, an INVOICE contains many LINE-ITEM records and a particular LINE-ITEM corresponds to only one INVOICE. Moreover, an INVOICE must have at least one LINE-ITEM and every LINE-ITEM must correspond to an INVOICE.

**Identifying 1:N Relationships.**     As with 1:1 relationships, 1:N relationships can be identified by examining the object diagrams. The object diagram from which the structure in Figure 6–9b was derived appears in Figure 6–11a. PROFESSOR contains multivalued STUDENT. Therefore, there is a one-to-many relationship between PROFESSOR and STUDENT.

In Figure 6–11b, only one of the objects (STUDENT) is contained in the other. Despite the fact that no user view included DORMITORY as a property of STUDENT, there is still a one-to-many relationship between the two objects. There is no such thing as a zero-to-many relationship.

**Representing 1:N Relationships.**     The representation of 1:N relationships is simple and straightforward. The key of the parent relation must be stored as an attribute of the child relation. Thus to represent the ADVISEE rela-

**Figure 6–9**
One-to-many (1:*N*)
relationship

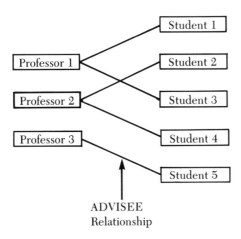

a. Instances of ADVISEE (1:*N*) relationship

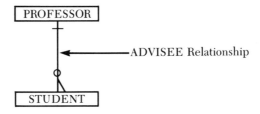

b. Generic structure of ADVISEE (1:*N*) relationship

tionship of Figure 6–9, we need to place the key of PROFESSOR, say Prof-name, in the STUDENT relation (Figure 6–12). Notice that with Prof-name stored as a foreign key in STUDENT, we can always determine a student's advisor. Furthermore, we can also determine all of the students advised by a particular faculty member by searching for the student records containing that professor's name.

Contrast this situation to representing 1:1 relationships. In both cases, we store the key of one relation as a foreign key in the second relation. In a 1:1 relationship it does not matter which key is moved to the second relation. In a 1:*N* relationship, however, it does matter. The key of the parent relation must be placed in the child relation.

To understand this more fully, see what happens when you try to put the key of the child into the parent relation. Since attributes in a relation

**Figure 6–10**

Optional-optional and
mandatory-mandatory
1:*N* relationships

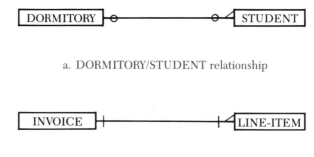

a. DORMITORY/STUDENT relationship

b. INVOICE/LINE-ITEM relationship

can have only a single value, there will be room in a professor's record for only one student. Consequently, such a structure cannot be used to represent the "many" side of the 1:*N* relationship. Again, to represent a 1:*N* relationship, place the key of the parent relation in the child relation.

## Many-to-Many Relationships

The third and final type of binary relationship is many-to-many (*M:N*). In an *M:N* relationship, a record of one type corresponds to many records of the second type *and* a record of the second type corresponds to many records of the first type.

Figure 6–13a illustrates the many-to-many relationship between students and classes. A STUDENT record can correspond to many CLASS records and a CLASS record can correspond to many STUDENT records. The notation for this relationship is shown in Figure 6–13b. The fork at both ends of the relationship line indicates the many-to-many relationship. Notice in this case that both participants in the relationship are optional—that is, a student does not need to be enrolled in a class and a class does not need to have any students.

**Identifying *M:N* Relationships.**    Many-to-many relationships, like 1:1 and 1:*N* relationships, can be identified by examining the object diagrams. The object diagrams from which the diagram in Figure 6–13b was derived are shown in Figure 6–14. In these diagrams, each object appears as a multi-valued object property of the other object.

**Representing *M:N* Relationships.**    Many-to-many relationships cannot be directly represented in relations as one-to-one and one-to-many relation-

**Figure 6—11**
Object diagrams
showing 1:N
relationships

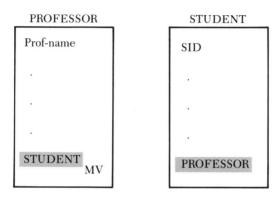

a. Each object contains the other

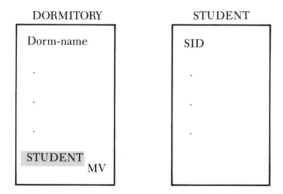

b. Only one object contains the other

ships are. To understand why this is so, suppose we try to use the same strategy we did for 1:1 and 1:N relationships, inserting the key of one relation as a foreign key in the other relation. For example, let's put the key of STUDENT (SID) in CLASS. Because repeating fields are not allowed in a relation, we have room in the first CLASS record to store only one SID. What do we do with the second student enrolled in that class?

The same problem will occur if we try to put the key of CLASS (Class#) in STUDENT. We can readily store the identifier of the first class in which a student is enrolled, but we have no place to store the identifier of the second and subsequent classes.

### Figure 6–12
Representation of 1:*N*
relationship

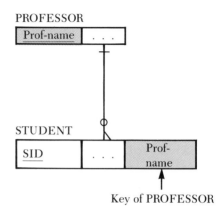

Key of PROFESSOR

### Figure 6–13
Many-to-many (*M:N*)
relationship

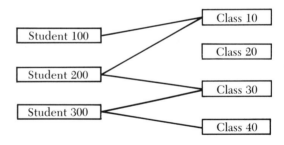

a. Instance of STUDENT/CLASS relationship

b. Generic structure of STUDENT-CLASS
relationship

**Figure 6—14**

Object diagrams
showing many-to-
many relationship

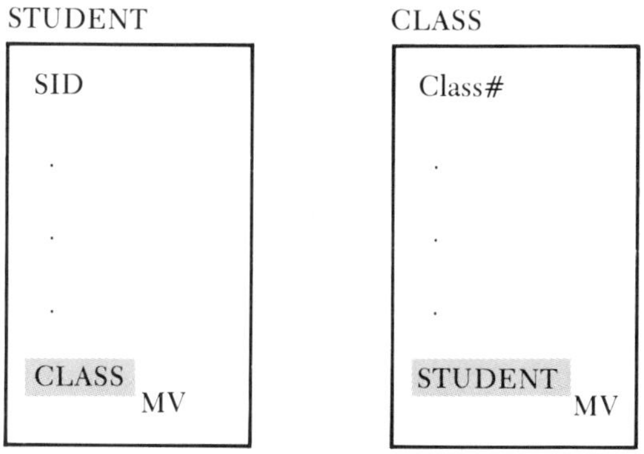

STUDENT

CLASS

| STUDENT | | CLASS | |
|---|---|---|---|
| SID | | Class# | |
| . | | . | |
| . | | . | |
| . | | . | |
| CLASS | MV | STUDENT | MV |

**Figure 6—15**

Inadequate attempt
to represent $M{:}N$
relationship

| SID | Other STUDENT Data |
|---|---|
| 100 | . . . |
| 200 | . . . |
| 300 | . . . |

STUDENT

| Class# | Class-time | Other CLASS Data | SID |
|---|---|---|---|
| 10 | 10:00 MWF | . . . | 100 |
| 10 | 10:00 MWF | . . . | 200 |
| 30 | 3:00 TH | . . . | 200 |
| 30 | 3:00 TH | . . . | 300 |
| 40 | 8:00 MWF | . . . | 300 |

CLASS

Figure 6–15 shows a third incorrect strategy. In this case we have stored a row in the CLASS relation for each STUDENT who is enrolled in one class. Thus there are two records for class 10 and two for class 30. The problem with this scheme is that we duplicate the class data. This will probably result in modification anomalies, because many records will need to be changed if, say, class 10's schedule is modified. Also, consider the insertion and deletion anomalies. How can we schedule a new class until a student has enrolled? And what will happen if student 300 drops out of class 40? This strategy is obviously unworkable.

The solution to this dilemma is to create a third relation that shows the correspondence of students and classes. This third relation is sometimes called an *intersection relation* because it represents the intersection (or over-lapping) of a particular student record with a particular class record. There is one row in the intersection relation for each line between STUDENT and CLASS in Figure 6–13a. Figure 6–16 shows an instance of the intersection relation, STU-CLASS, for the STUDENT/CLASS relationship.

The relation diagrams for the STUDENT/CLASS relationship appear in Figure 6–17. Notice that the relationship from CLASS to STU-CLASS is 1:$N$ and that the relationship from STUDENT to STU-CLASS is also 1:$N$. In essence, we have decomposed the $M$:$N$ relationship into two 1:$N$ relationships.

The key of STU-CLASS is the combination of the keys of both of its parents, (SID, Class#). The key for an intersection relation is always the combination of parent keys.

### Summary of the Three Types of Binary Relationships

The three types of binary relationships are one-to-one (1:1), one-to-many (1:$N$), and many-to-many ($M$:$N$). To represent a 1:1 relationship, we place

**Figure 6–16**

Using intersection relation to represent $M$:$N$ relationship

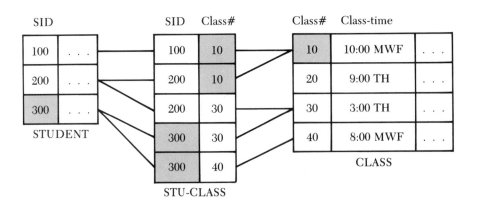

**Figure 6—17**
Generic structure of
*M:N* relationship

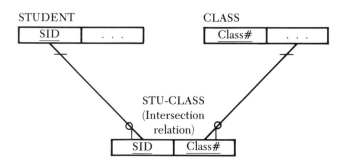

the key of *either* relation in the other relation. To represent a 1:*N* relationship, we place the key of the parent in the child. To represent an *M:N* relationship, we create a third relation, called an intersection relation. Each record in an intersection relation contains the keys of each of the related records in the other two relations. The key of the intersection relation is the combination of the keys of its parents.

## TREES AND NETWORKS

The binary relationships you have just learned can be combined into a variety of larger structures. Two common structures are *trees* and *networks*.

### Trees

A *tree* is a collection of records that have only one-to-many relationships. Figure 6–18 shows an example of a tree (sometimes also called a *hierarchy*). According to standard terminology, the records are called *nodes*, and the relationships between the records are called *branches*. The node at the top of the tree is called the *root* (what a metaphor—roots of real trees are normally at the bottom!). In Figure 6–18a, node 1 is the root of the tree. Every node of a tree, except the root, has a *parent*, which is the node immediately above it. Thus, node 2 is the parent of node 5, node 4 is the parent of node 8, and so on. Trees are distinguished from other record relationships because every node of a tree has exactly one parent, except the root, which has no parent.

The descendants of a node are called *children*. In general, there is no limitation on the number of children a node may have. Node 2 has two children: nodes 5 and 6. Node 3 has no children. And node 4 has three

**Figure 6–18**

Tree relationships

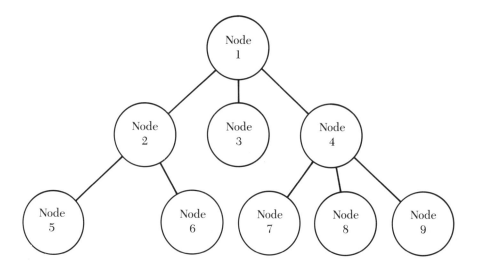

a. Generalized tree structure

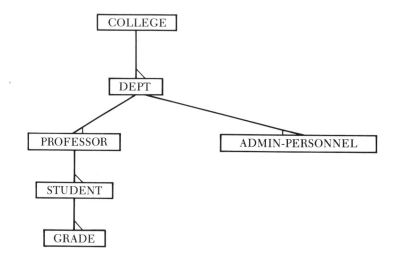

b. Tree of record relationships

children: nodes 7, 8, and 9. Nodes that have the same parent are called *twins* or *siblings*.

Figure 6–18b illustrates a tree. In this example, you can see several one-to-many relationships among records in a university system. Colleges consist of many departments, which in turn have many professors and many administrative employees. Finally, professors advise many students, who have received many grades. There are six different record types in this structure, and all of the relationships are 1:N.

In summary, a tree, or hierarchy, is a collection of records organized so that all relationships are 1:N. All records have exactly one parent except the root, which has no parent. Hierarchies occur frequently in business, especially in manufacturing applications.

## Simple Networks

A *simple network* is also a collection of records and one-to-many relationships among records. In a simple network, however, a record may have more than one parent, as long as the parents are different types of records. For example, in the simple network shown in Figure 6–19, each STUDENT record has two parents—an ADVISOR record and a MAJOR record. This would not be a simple network if the parents of STUDENT records were of the same type, say both ADVISOR records. Further, the data structure in Figure 6–19 is not a tree because STUDENT records have more than one parent.

Figure 6–20 shows the general structure of this simple network. Notice that all relationships are one-to-many but that STUDENT has two parents. In this figure, the parent records are on top and the children records are beneath the parents. This arrangement is convenient but not essential. You

**Figure 6–19**
Occurrence of simple network

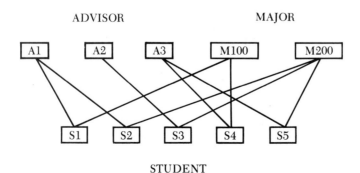

ADVISOR        MAJOR

STUDENT

**Figure 6–20**

General structure of a
simple network

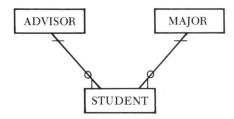

may also see simple networks depicted with parents beside or below the
children. You can identify simple networks in such arrangements by the
fact that a single record type participates as a child in two (or more) one-
to-many relationships.

### Complex Networks

A *complex network* is a collection of records and relationships in which at
least one of the relationships is many-to-many. The complex network in
Figure 6–21a illustrates the relationships among invoices, line-items, parts,
and suppliers. Two of the three relationships are 1:*N* and the third is *M:N*.
Since there is at least one many-to-many relationship, this structure is called
a complex network.

As mentioned in the previous section, *M:N* relationships have no direct
representation in the relational model. Consequently, before this structure
could be stored in relational form, we need to define an intersection relation.
We have done this in Figure 6–21b. Notice that PART-SUPPLIER is the
intersection relation.

## OBJECT TYPES

In this section you will learn the techniques for transforming objects into
relations. As stated in Chapter 2, a database is a model of the business
environment that it serves. The relations within the database represent
objects in that environment. The structure of these objects can be simple
or complex, and the structure of the relationships among the relations must
mirror the structure of the objects. In this section we will describe five
common types of objects and illustrate their representation with relations.
Master this material and you will have acquired highly useful database
design skills.

**Figure 6—21**
Complex network

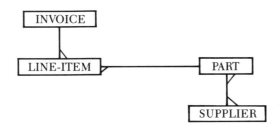

a. General structure of complex network

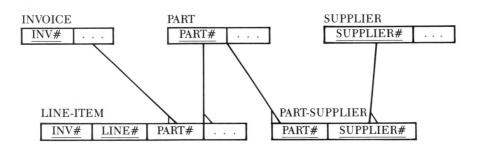

b. Relational representation of complex network

## Simple Objects

A *simple object* contains only single-valued, non-object properties. A simple object is represented by a single relation. Figure 6–22 shows two simple objects. Customer objects (Figure 6–22a) are represented by the CUSTOMER relation—CUSTOMER (Cust#, Cust-name, Amount-owed). All of the data about customers that the applications require can be stored in the fixed-length format of a single relation.

The EQUIPMENT relation (Figure 6–22b) is another example. Here, all of the required data about equipment can be stored in a single relation—EQUIPMENT (Equip#, Equip-desc, Acquisition-date, Purchase-cost).

## Composite Objects

*Composite objects* contain one or more non-object multivalued properties. They require more than one relation for their representation. The HOTEL-BILL shown in Figure 6–23a is an example of a composite object. The bill contains properties about the bill as a whole—Bill#, Arrival-date, Cus-

**Figure 6—22**
Relational represen-
tation of simple
objects

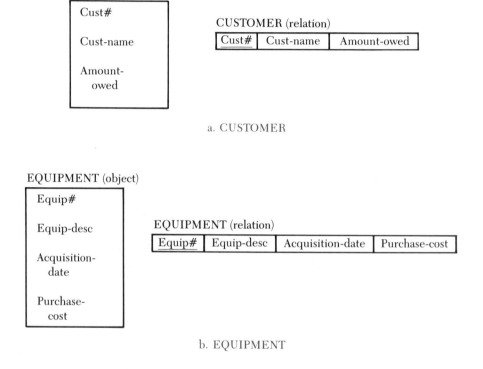

a. CUSTOMER

b. EQUIPMENT

tomer-name, and Total-due. It also contains a group of properties that are repeated for each day of the guest's stay—Charge-date, Room-charge, Food-charge, and so forth.

The multivalued attributes do not represent another object. The hotel does not view one day of a guest's stay as a separate entity. But since the bill contains a repeating group, it cannot be represented by a single relation. Relations cannot have repeating groups. Consequently, HOTEL-BILL must be represented by two relations, as shown in Figure 6–23b.

One relation, BILL, contains the nonrepeating data about the bill. The second relation, DAILY-CHARGE, contains one row for each day's charges. The example shows two bills—one for a two-day stay and one for a three-day stay. Notice that the Bill# with which each daily charge is associated is in the DAILY-CHARGE relation. Matching values of Bill# establish the relationship between BILL and DAILY-CHARGE records. Stated in other terms, Bill# in DAILY-CHARGE is a foreign key (from BILL).

The structure of the relations in Figure 6–23 is summarized in Figure 6–24. The relationship from BILL to DAILY-CHARGE is 1:$N$ and is mandatory in both directions. A bill must have at least one day's stay, and no daily charges can be incurred unless there is a guest.

In some cases the child relation of a composite object is not mandatory. For example, before a guest arrives, a bill might be stored without any daily charges. In no case, however, will the child relation of a composite object ever be allowed to exist without the parent. Thus composite objects contain a 1:$N$ relationship that can be either mandatory-to-mandatory or mandatory-to-optional (where the child is optional). Another way of expressing this fact is to say that the child relation does not represent an independent object and therefore cannot stand on its own.

To understand composite objects more fully, consider them in light of normalization theory. The attributes that pertain to the bill as a whole, such as Arrival-date, Customer-name, and Total-due, are functionally dependent on Bill#:

$$Bill\# \rightarrow Arrival\text{-}date \mid Customer\text{-}name \mid Total\text{-}due$$

The daily-charge attributes are functionally dependent on the composite key (Bill#, Charge-date):

$$(Bill\#, Charge\text{-}date) \rightarrow Room\text{-}charge \mid Phone\text{-}charge, etc.$$

Because the determinant is a composite key, this is called a composite object. The group of repeating properties is called the *composite group*.

If we tried to represent HOTEL-BILL with a single relation like HBILL (Bill#, Arrival-date, Customer-name, Total-due, Charge-date, Room-charge, Food-charge, . . . , Tax-charge), the relation would not be in domain/key normal form. The key of HBILL is (Bill#, Charge-date), but the attributes Arrival-date, Customer-name, and Total-due are functionally dependent only on Bill#. Thus there are functional dependencies that are not implied by the key. As you learned in Chapter 5, we can create domain/key normal form by splitting the relation into two relations, as shown in Figure 6–24.

Some composite objects need to be represented by more than two relations. For example, suppose there were another repeating property called Meal within a guest's daily charges. A guest might eat breakfast, lunch, and dinner at the hotel (see Figure 6–25). In this case, the Food-charge is the total of several different meal charges. A separate relation for MEAL-CHARGE is needed—MEAL-CHARGE (Bill#, Charge-date, Time, Restaurant-charge). This relation has been added to the others and the results are shown in Figure 6–26. Notice that the relationship between DAILY-CHARGE and MEAL-CHARGE is mandatory-to-optional. A guest does not need to charge a meal while staying in the hotel.

**Figure 6–23**

Composite object

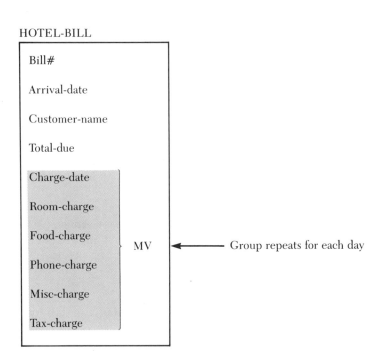

a. HOTEL-BILL object diagram

| Bill# | Arrival-date | Customer-name | Total-due |
|-------|--------------|---------------|-----------|
| 1234  | 10/27/87     | James, F.     | $224.70   |
| 5678  | 10/30/87     | Lincoln, P.   | $538.28   |

BILL

| Bill# | Charge-date | Room-charge | Food-charge | Phone-charge | Misc-charge | Tax-charge |
|-------|-------------|-------------|-------------|--------------|-------------|------------|
| 1234  | 10/27/87    | 100.00      | 0.00        | 0.00         | 0.00        | 12.35      |
| 1234  | 10/28/87    | 100.00      | 0.00        | 0.00         | 0.00        | 12.35      |
| 5678  | 10/30/87    | 90.00       | 55.30       | 10.00        | 5.00        | 11.11      |
| 5678  | 10/31/87    | 90.00       | 65.80       | 7.50         | 4.67        | 11.11      |
| 5678  | 11/01/87    | 90.00       | 72.18       | 7.50         | 7.00        | 11.11      |

DAILY-CHARGE

b. Two relations representing HOTEL-BILL

**Figure 6—24**
Relational represen-
tation of HOTEL-
BILL

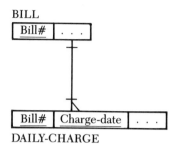

BILL

| Bill# | . . . |

| Bill# | Charge-date | . . . |

DAILY-CHARGE

**Figure 6—25**
HOTEL-BILL object
with two repeating
properties

HOTEL-BILL

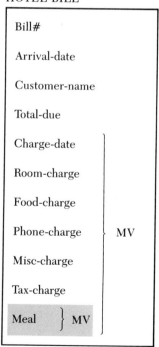

Bill#

Arrival-date

Customer-name

Total-due

Charge-date

Room-charge

Food-charge

Phone-charge        } MV

Misc-charge

Tax-charge

Meal  } MV

A composite object is represented by two or more relations. At least one of the relations (such as DAILY-CHARGE) cannot stand on its own. Each relation represents a portion of an object in the application environment.

The structure of the keys of relations representing composite objects is very significant. The key of each child relation contains the key of its parent. Consider the keys of the relations in Figure 6–26. The key of BILL is Bill#, the key of DAILY-CHARGE is (Bill#, Charge-date) and the key of MEAL-CHARGE is (Bill#, Charge-date, Time). The key of each child contains the key of its parent. This characteristic is a signal that the relations represent different aspects of the same object. When you find relations with such a nested key structure, you are probably dealing with a composite object.

## Compound Objects

A *compound object* contains at least one object property. Consequently, a compound object will be represented by at least two relations, one for each object. The significant difference between the relations that represent a compound object and those that represent a composite object is that the relations that represent a compound object stand on their own.

Consider Figure 6–27a, which shows the object diagrams for DOR-MITORY and STUDENT. Because STUDENT is an object property contained

**Figure 6–26**

Relational representation of HOTEL-BILL with two composite groups

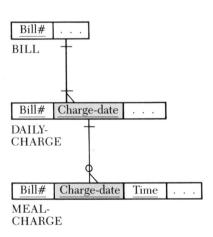

within DORMITORY, DORMITORY is a compound object. Two relations are needed to represent these objects. They are shown in Figure 6–27b.

As with the hotel bill in Figure 6–14, the relationship from DORMI-TORY to STUDENT is one-to-many. The constraints for DORMITORY are different, however, because a dormitory does not need to have any students, nor does a student need to live in a dorm. In the hotel bill example, the relationship was mandatory in both directions because two relations were being used to represent aspects of the same entity. In this case, dormitories and students happen to be independent of each other.

In general, the relationship constraints in a compound object can be any of the types we have discussed: optional-to-optional, mandatory-to-optional, optional-to-mandatory, and mandatory-to-mandatory. The requirements of the application determine the relationship constraints.

**Figure 6–27**
Compound object

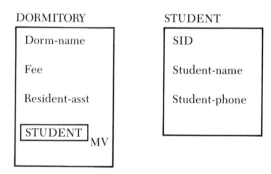

a. Object diagrams

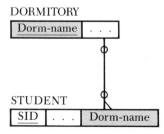

b. Relational representation of STUDENT and DORMITORY objects

Now consider the keys of the relations in Figure 6–27b. The key of DORMITORY is Dorm-name and the key of STUDENT is SID. Unlike the keys of two relations that represent a composite object—like the hotel bill—these keys have no attributes in common. They are totally separate. The key of DORMITORY represents the name of one entity and the key of STUDENT identifies a different entity. Thus, the relations represent two different, independent objects.

Another illustration of compound objects appears in Figure 6–28. In this example, we see that a book can be written by many authors, and that an author can have written many books (Figure 6–28a). Thus, each object contains the other as a multivalued object property.

**Figure 6–28**

Compound objects in an *M:N* relationship

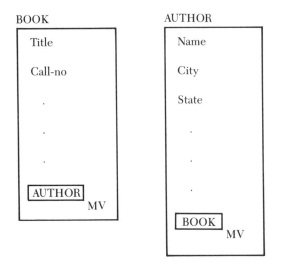

a. Object diagrams

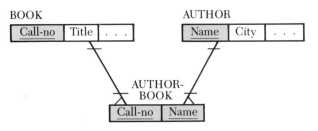

b. Relational representation

Because this is a many-to-many relationship, an intersection relation, AUTHOR-BOOK, is needed to link together records in each of the relations. The key of the intersection relation is the combination of the keys of both of its parents (Figure 6–28b). An instance of this set of relations appears in Figure 6–29. Notice that the intersection relation, AUTHOR-BOOK, contains no non-key data. This is always true of $M:N$ compound objects.

## Association Objects

Association objects are similar to $M:N$ compound objects with one notable difference: association objects contain non-key data. An *association object* is an object that documents a relationship between two (or more) other objects. Examples of association objects include the following:

- An agreement such as a contract that documents the relationship between buyer and seller.
- Transaction documentation such as a purchase order that documents the relationship between purchaser, vendor, and parts.
- An assignment such as a flight-schedule that documents the relationship between pilot and airplane.

---

**Figure 6–29**

Instance of many-to-many relationship in Figure 6–28

| Title | Call-no |
|---|---|
| Applied Statistics | QA19.42 |
| Moon Rocks | QA117.48 |
| Every Great Notion | J44.3 |
| Roads Traveled | AB553.81 |

BOOK

| Name | City | State |
|---|---|---|
| Parks | Seattle | WA |
| Witherspoon | San Francisco | CA |
| Bronte | New York | NY |

AUTHOR

| Call-no | Name |
|---|---|
| AB553.81 | Parks |
| AB553.81 | Bronte |
| QA117.48 | Witherspoon |
| QA19.42 | Witherspoon |
| J44.3 | Parks |

AUTHOR-BOOK

Intersection relation

Let us use flight-schedule as an illustration (see Figure 6–30a). Notice that the illustration presents three objects: AIRPLANE, PILOT, and SCHEDULED-FLIGHT. Both AIRPLANE and PILOT contain the object SCHEDULED-FLIGHT. Similarly, SCHEDULED-FLIGHT contains PILOT and AIRPLANE as object properties. SCHEDULED-FLIGHT also has non-object properties that indicate details about a specific flight, such as the amount of fuel needed.

Two characteristics make SCHEDULED-FLIGHT an association object: (1) SCHEDULED-FLIGHT is an independent object. Users perceive a scheduled flight as an entity in the environment. One clue is that scheduled flights are assigned flight numbers; another clue is that a SCHEDULED-FLIGHT has non-object properties, such as Fuel. SCHEDULED-FLIGHT can also enter into relationships with other objects, such as RUNWAY. (2) SCHEDULED-FLIGHT is the glue that holds together the relationship between a pilot and an airplane. It is not only an object itself, but it also documents the relationship between two other objects.

The relational representation of these objects is shown in Figure 6–30b. This structure is a simple network because the child, SCHEDULED-FLIGHT, has parents of different record types. Of particular note in this diagram is the key of the SCHEDULED-FLIGHT relation (Flight#, Date, Time). Notice that the key of this relation is *not* the composite key (Pilot#, Airplane#). Airplane# and Pilot# appear in the relation as foreign keys, but not as part of the relation's key.

Contrast SCHEDULED-FLIGHT, an association object, with the *M:N* relationship between pilots and the planes they are qualified to fly (see Figure 6–30c). In this case, QUALIFICATION does not have an independent key (the key is a composite of the foreign keys), and QUALIFICATION contains no non-key data. These facts tell us that QUALIFICATION is not an independent object; it is not regarded as an entity in the user's environment.

At first distinguishing an *M:N* relationship from an association object may seem difficult. The key to telling them apart is that an association object is an object in its own right. But an intersection relation does not represent an object; it represents only the relationship between two other objects.

The characteristics of an association object are that:

- It establishes a relationship between two other objects
- It can be an object property of each of the other objects
- It is an independent object

## Aggregation Objects

An *aggregation object* represents an entity *group*. Thus, an aggregation object is different from the objects we have discussed so far because all of the previous objects represent instances of an individual person or event. In contrast, an aggregation object represents a group of persons or things.

**Figure 6—30**
Association object

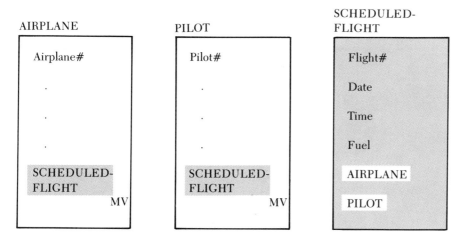

a. Object diagrams showing SCHEDULED-FLIGHT as an association object

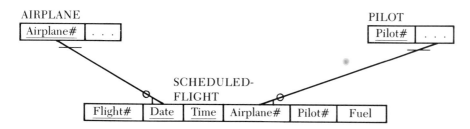

b. Relational representation

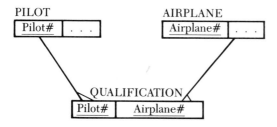

c. Intersection relation representing *M:N*
relationship—contrast with association object

**Figure 6—31**

Object diagrams of
university showing
aggregation objects

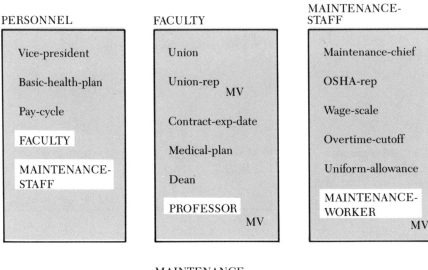

Consider the object diagrams in Figure 6–31. The three aggregation objects have been shaded: PERSONNEL, FACULTY, and MAINTENANCE-STAFF. The other two objects, PROFESSOR and MAINTENANCE-WORKER, represent individuals, not groups. Aggregation objects tell us that the user sees a group as an independent entity. For example, the faculty might be made up of individual professors, but when it comes time to negotiate a new contract, the university deals with the faculty as a whole.

The object diagram for FACULTY tells us that there are certain properties whose values all faculty members have in common—Union, Union-rep, Contract-exp-date, Medical-plan, and Dean. In other words, all faculty members belong to the same union, have the same medical plan, and so forth. Because these properties pertain to the faculty as a whole, they are part of the FACULTY object.

Similarly, MAINTENANCE-STAFF is an aggregation object that consists of several non-object properties that define the group, as well as the multivalued MAINTENANCE-WORKER object property. Finally, PERSONNEL is an aggregation object.

Structures like the one in Figure 6–31 have a property called *inheritance*. Each lower-level object inherits properties from the aggregation object(s) to which it belongs. For example, a maintenance worker inherits the OSHA representative of the group. Likewise, every professor has the same medical plan as everyone else in the group. The inheritance characteristic of aggregation objects is important for artificial intelligence and expert systems applications. We will not discuss aggregation objects further in this text.

A diagram illustrating the relationships among the objects in Figure 6–31 appears in Figure 6–32. Notice that there is a one-to-one relationship between PERSONNEL and FACULTY (there is one faculty in the university) and a one-to-one relationship between PERSONNEL and MAINTENANCE-STAFF (there is only one maintenance staff for the university). The important point here is that an aggregation object exists because the user perceives a group of individual entities as an object itself.

Figure 6–33 summarizes the five object types.

**Figure 6–32**

Relational representation of Figure 6–31

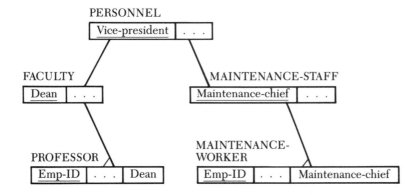

**Figure 6–33**

Summary of object
types

| | |
|---|---|
| Simple object | No object properties |
| | No repeating properties |
| Composite object | Repeating non-object property |
| Compound object | Contains object property |
| Association object | Defines relationship between two other objects |
| | May be contained within them |
| Aggregation object | Group of records treated as an entity |
| | Members inherit properties of the group |

## TRANSFORMING OBJECTS INTO RELATIONS

In this section we present guidelines for you to follow when transforming object diagrams into relations. In performing these transformations, you will produce a set of normalized relations. You should then apply normalization theory as a check. If you identify anomalies, you have made an error in transformation. The end result will be a DK/NF set of relations that can then be implemented using a DBMS.

### Transformation of Simple Objects

Figure 6–34 illustrates the transformation of a simple object into a relation. Recall that a simple object is represented by a single relation in the database. In Figure 6–34, object OBJ1 is transformed into relation R1. The property that represents the name of OBJ1 instances is OBJ1*. It is represented by the key of R1, R1* in the database.

Non-key data is represented in this and subsequent figures with ellipses (. . .).

### Transformation of Composite Objects

Composite objects are transformed by defining one relation for the object itself and another relation for each group of properties that is functionally dependent on a composite key. Figure 6–35 shows object OBJ1, which contains two composite groups, unlike previous examples that had only one. Each of these groups is represented by a relation in the database. Thus,

**Figure 6—34**
Transformation of
simple object

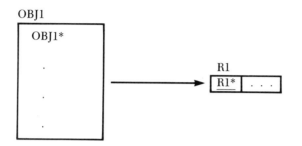

**Figure 6—35**
Transformation of
composite object

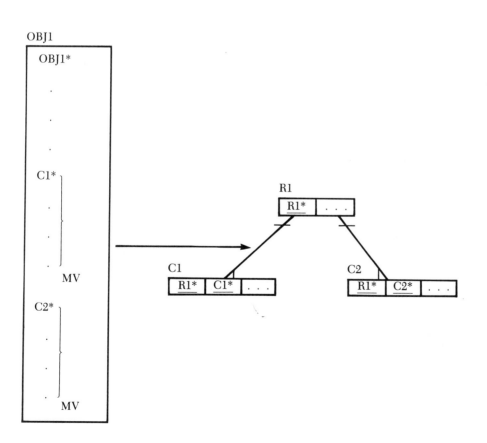

the database representation of OBJ1 is a relation R1 with key R1*, a relation C1 with key (R1*, C1*), and a relation C2 with key (R1*, C2*).

### Transformation of Compound Objects

The transformation of compound objects is somewhat more complicated than the transformation of simple and composite objects. Two objects, OBJ1 and OBJ2, can be related to one another in three ways: 1:1, 1:$N$, and $M$:$N$. When examining a set of object diagrams, it may appear that two objects can be related in as many as nine different ways (see Figure 6–36). However, relationships appearing as 0:1 and 1:0 relationships are actually 1:1 relationships, and relationships appearing as 0:$N$ and $M$:0 relationships are actually 1:$N$ relationships. Furthermore, 0:0 is no relationship at all. Consequently, we need to address only three types of compound object relationships: 1:1, 1:$N$, and $M$:$N$.

In the case of a 1:1 relationship between OBJ1 and OBJ2, we define one relation for each object, R1 and R2. Then we place the key of either relation (R1* or R2*) as a foreign key attribute in the other relation (Figure 6–37).

For a 1:$N$ relationship, the placement of the foreign key is more critical. In a 1:$N$ relationship, the key of the parent (the relation on the "one" side) is placed as a foreign key in the child relation (the relation on the "many" side of the relationship; see Figure 6–38).

Finally, to represent an $M$:$N$ relationship, we need to define one relation for each of the objects as well as an intersection relation containing pairs of keys from related records in the two original relations. The intersection relation will contain no non-key data. The name of the intersection relation is R3 and its key is the composite key (R1*, R2*). In essence, we decompose the $M$:$N$ relationship into two 1:$N$ relationships. (See Figure 6–39.)

Study Figure 6–36 and be certain you understand why the three patterns just described can be used to represent all the possible compound object relationships in that figure. (Keep in mind that a 0:0 relationship is no relationship at all.)

### Transformation of Association Objects

An association object is an object (OBJ3) that is contained in two or more other objects (OBJ1 and OBJ2) because it defines an association between them. When transforming an association object into a relation (see Figure 6–40), we must define one relation for each of the objects that are participating in the relationship—R1, R2, and R3. Each relation will have an independent—not composite—key: R1*, R2*, and R3*. The key of each of the parent relations, R1* and R2*, will appear as foreign key attributes in the relation representing the association object, R3.

Note the difference between the key of the association relation in Figure 6–40 and the key of the intersection relation in Figure 6–39. An association relation has a key and data of its own because it represents a real object in

**Figure 6—36**
Compound object relationship types

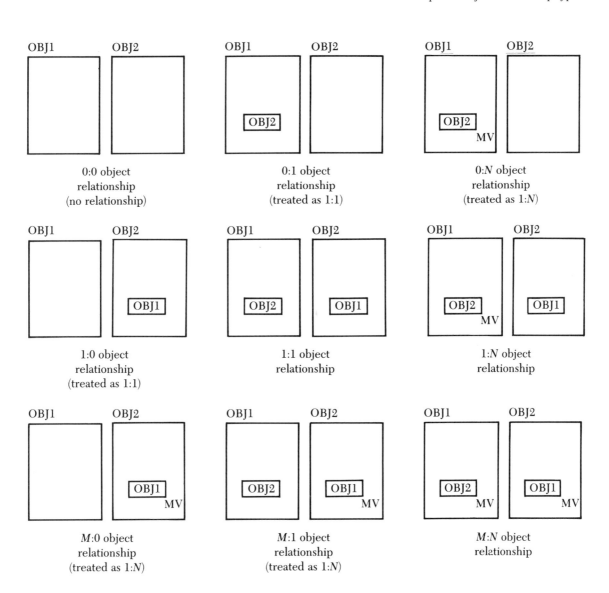

the user's work environment, while an intersection relation represents only the relationship between objects.

You now know three techniques for performing logical database design—we discussed two approaches in Chapter 5 and added another one here. First, you can perform database design *analytically*. That is, you can examine

**Figure 6—37**
Representation of 1:1
object relationship

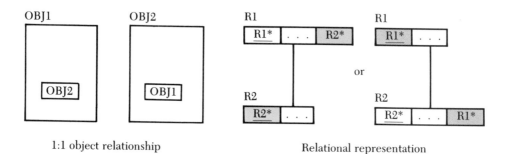

1:1 object relationship          Relational representation

**Figure 6—38**
Representation of 1:*N*
object relationship

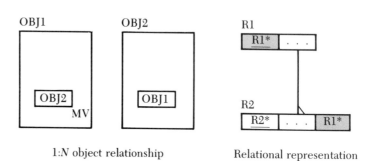

1:*N* object relationship          Relational representation

existing (or proposed) relations or files checking for domain/key normal form. Second, you can approach logical database design *synthetically.* In this case you examine the attributes and determine which ones belong together in the same relation. Finally, you can *transform object diagrams* into their relational representation, which should yield a normalized set of relations. Applying normalization theory to the result is a good way to check your design.

All of the approaches are tools you can use to get the same result. You should know all three, even though it is likely that you will use the object-oriented approach most often.

**Figure 6—39**
Representation of
*M:N* object
relationship

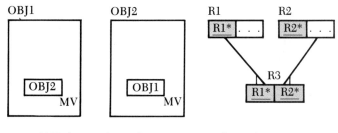

M:N object relationship      Relational representation

**Figure 6—40**
Representation of
association object

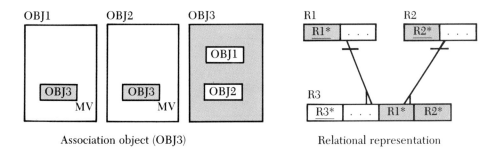

Association object (OBJ3)      Relational representation

## SAMPLE OBJECTS

To reinforce the concepts presented in this chapter, we will now consider several objects taken from actual businesses. These objects will be presented in increasing order of complexity. We will study each form and report and determine the underlying objects and their relationships. Then we will represent them using the relational model. Your goal is to learn how to produce the object structure that underlies forms and reports, and how to derive relational structures from them.

### Subscription Form

Figure 6–41a shows a magazine subscription form. There are at least two object structures that could underlie this form. If the publishers of *Fine Woodworking* consider subscriber a property of a subscription, then subscription could be a simple object, stored in the database as a single relation (Figure 6–41b). This would be appropriate if this company has only one or a few publications and is not concerned about duplicating subscriber data across their publications. (Subscriber information to a second publication

---

**Figure 6–41**
Possible representations of SUB-SCRIPTION

a. Subscription order form

b. Subscription as one object represented with a single relation would be duplicated in the object that would represent the subscription to that publication.)

But if the publisher wants to build a list of customers to use when soliciting subscriptions to other publications, then subscriber will be viewed as a separate entity. Therefore, we must define a SUBSCRIBER object and establish a relationship between SUBSCRIBER and SUBSCRIPTION. This is illustrated in Figure 6–41c. Notice that SUBSCRIBER is a compound object—it contains an object property. The 1:$N$ relationship between these objects can be represented by the relations in Figure 6–41d.

---

**Figure 6–41**

(*continued*)

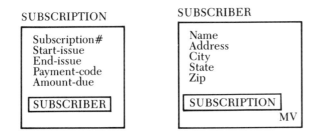

c. Subscription as two objects

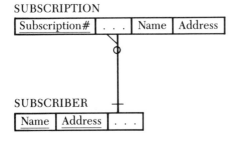

d. Relation diagram for Figure 6–41c

**Figure 6–42**

Representation of
PRODUCT

### a. Report about a product

Kellogg's®

# RICE
## KRISPIES®

**NUTRITION INFORMATION**
SERVING SIZE:  1 OZ. (28.4 g, ABOUT 1 CUP)
SERVINGS PER PACKAGE:                    13

| | CEREAL | WITH ½ CUP VITAMINS A & D SKIM MILK |
|---|---|---|
| CALORIES | 110 | 150* |
| PROTEIN | 2 g | 6g |
| CARBOHYDRATE | 25 g | 31g |
| FAT | 0 g | 0g* |
| CHOLESTEROL | 0 mg | 0mg* |
| SODIUM | 290 mg | 350mg |
| POTASSIUM | 35 mg | 240mg |

**PERCENTAGE OF U.S. RECOMMENDED
DAILY ALLOWANCES (U.S. RDA)**

| | | |
|---|---|---|
| PROTEIN | 2 | 10 |
| VITAMIN A | 25 | 30 |
| VITAMIN C | 25 | 25 |
| THIAMIN | 35 | 40 |
| RIBOFLAVIN | 35 | 45 |
| NIACIN | 35 | 35 |
| CALCIUM | ** | 15 |
| IRON | 10 | 10 |
| VITAMIN D | 10 | 25 |
| VITAMIN B₆ | 35 | 35 |
| FOLIC ACID | 35 | 35 |
| PHOSPHORUS | 4 | 15 |
| MAGNESIUM | 2 | 6 |
| ZINC | 2 | 6 |
| COPPER | 2 | 4 |

*WHOLE MILK SUPPLIES AN ADDITIONAL 30
CALORIES, 4 g FAT, AND 15 mg CHOLESTEROL.
**CONTAINS LESS THAN 2% OF THE U.S. RDA OF
THIS NUTRIENT.

**INGREDIENTS:** RICE, SUGAR, SALT,
CORN SYRUP, MALT FLAVORING,

**VITAMINS AND IRON:** VITAMIN C (SODIUM
ASCORBATE AND ASCORBIC ACID),
NIACINAMIDE, IRON, VITAMIN B₆ (PY-
RIDOXINE HYDROCHLORIDE), VITAMIN A
(PALMITATE), VITAMIN B₂ (RIBOFLAVIN),
VITAMIN B₁ (THIAMIN HYDROCHLORIDE),
FOLIC ACID, AND VITAMIN D.
TO KEEP THIS CEREAL FRESH, BHT
HAS BEEN ADDED TO THE
PACKAGING.

CEREAL-PRODUCT

Name

Calories

Protein-wt

Carbohydrate-wt

Fat-wt

Cholesterol-wt

Sodium-wt

Potassium-wt

Protein-%

Vitamin A-%

.

.

.

Copper-%

BHT-status

Ingredient ⎫
⎬ MV
⎭

### b. Object diagram

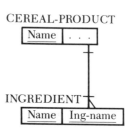

### c. Relational representation

## Product Description

Figure 6–42a shows the description of a popular packaged-goods product.
Whereas Figure 6–41a showed a generic form, Figure 6–42a shows an
instance of a product-specific report. Reports for all Kellogg's cereal products follow this format.

Figure 6–42b shows a composite object that could underlie the report. We say *could* because further investigation might reveal other objects that are not apparent from looking at only one report. The object diagram in Figure 6–42b describes cereal products with certain common properties, such as calories, carbohydrates, fats, and so forth. However, this object diagram indicates that ingredients vary with the product. For instance, some cereals contain corn, some contain wheat, some rice, and some barley. In addition, some cereals contain cane sugar, others honey, and some have both. Because of this wide variance, Ingredient is shown as a multivalued property. The relation diagram in Figure 6–42c indicates that two relations are required here—one for the product details and one for the repeating group of ingredients.

## Traffic Warning Citation

Figure 6–43a shows an instance of the traffic warning citation form used in the state of Washington. The designer of this form has given us important clues about the underlying objects of this form. Notice that portions of the form are visually divided by rounded corners, implying that different sections pertain to different objects.

Figure 6–43b is one attempt at illustrating the underlying objects of the traffic warning citation. Although it is not necessarily true, certain clues lead us to believe that driver, vehicle, and officer are independent objects. For one thing, data about each of these subjects is in a separate section on the form. But more important, each of them has its own user-defined key field—Drivers-license uniquely identifies a driver, Vehicle-license identifies every registered vehicle, and Personnel-no identifies every law officer. These fields are obviously keys. Consequently, we decided to treat those three entities as separate objects. The equivalent relation diagram appears in Figure 6–43c.

We could have incorporated *all* of the properties into one big object diagram for CORRECTION-NOTICE. Would that give us different results? Actually, the end results would probably be the same. If we were to start with one simple object diagram, we would transform it into one relation containing many attributes. When we reviewed that relation and applied the rules of normalization to it, we would discover several modification anomalies. These anomalies exist because there would be transitive dependencies in the relation, such as Number → Drivers-license → Last-name | First-name | Address. We would eliminate those anomalies by separating the relation into several relations, each of which had no anomalies. The end result would be the relation diagram in Figure 6–43c.

The traffic warning citation is an association object. It documents a relationship among other independent objects, objects that will appear in other forms and reports.

**Figure 6—43**

Representation of
traffic warning
citation

WASHINGTON STATE PATROL CORRECTION NOTICE

*a. Traffic warning citation*

## SUMMARY

During logical database design a development team produces the blueprint
for the database needed to support all application views. This is accomplished by examining the object diagrams to identify relationships among
objects, then transforming the objects into relations. There are a few basic
patterns that can be followed to make this transformation process easy.
Once a set of relations has been established, the project team needs to
review it critically by applying the rules of normalization to those relations.
When anomalies are found, the team modifies the design to eliminate them.

**Figure 6—43**
(continued)

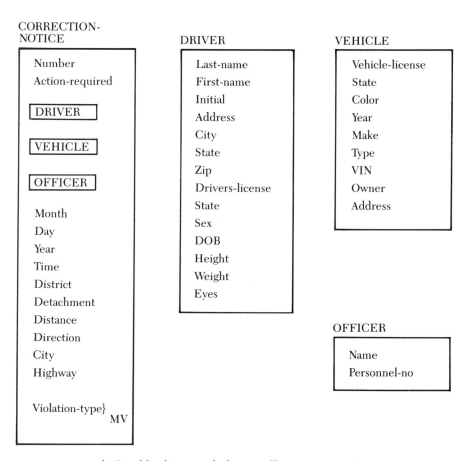

CORRECTION-
NOTICE

Number
Action-required

| DRIVER |

| VEHICLE |

| OFFICER |

Month
Day
Year
Time
District
Detachment
Distance
Direction
City
Highway

Violation-type}
      MV

DRIVER

Last-name
First-name
Initial
Address
City
State
Zip
Drivers-license
State
Sex
DOB
Height
Weight
Eyes

VEHICLE

Vehicle-license
State
Color
Year
Make
Type
VIN
Owner
Address

OFFICER

Name
Personnel-no

b. Possible objects underlying traffic warning citation

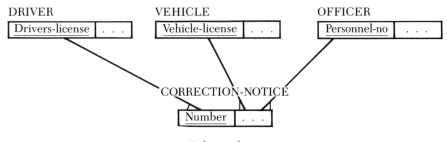

DRIVER
| Drivers-license | . . . |

VEHICLE
| Vehicle-license | . . . |

OFFICER
| Personnel-no | . . . |

CORRECTION-NOTICE
| Number | . . . |

c. Relation diagram

Even very complex record relationships can be decomposed into three simple binary relationships (a binary relationship involves only two records at a time)—one-to-one (1:1), one-to-many (1:N), and many-to-many (M:N). In each of these relationships there can be constraints concerning participation. The four possible combinations of this constraint are optional-to-optional (neither record needs to be associated with one of the other type), optional-to-mandatory (the first record must be linked to a record of the second type, but the second record does not need to be linked to a record of the first type), mandatory-to-optional (the reverse of optional-to-mandatory), and mandatory-to-mandatory (both records are required).

One-to-one relationships can be expressed by placing the key of one record in the other record. It is redundant and unnecessary to place the key of each record in the other record.

The second type of binary relationship is one-to-many (1:N), in which a single record of one type is related to many records of another type. The parent record of a 1:N relationship is the record on the "one" side. The child record is the record on the "many" side. One-to-many relationships can have optional or mandatory memberships. One-to-many relationships can be expressed by placing the key of the parent in the child record.

The third type of binary relationship is many-to-many (M:N). In an M:N relationship, a record of one type is related to many records of the second type and a record of the second type is related to many records of the first. As with the other two types of relationship, the relationship of the keys of the records in an M:N relationship will also be M:N.

Many-to-many relationships do not have a direct relational representation. To represent an M:N relationship, we create an intersection relation that contains pairs of keys from the first two relations.

Binary relationships can be combined to form three types of larger structures. A tree is a collection of record types such that each record has exactly one parent except the root, which has no parent. In a simple network, records may have multiple parents, but the parents must be of different types. In a complex network, records have multiple parents of the same type. Another way of saying this is that in a complex network, at least one of the binary relationships is M:N.

There are five different types of objects. Simple objects contain no multiple-valued properties and no object properties. Composite objects contain one or more non-object repeating properties. The group of these properties is called a composite group.

A compound object contains one or more object properties. An association object establishes a relationship between two other objects and is contained in both of them. An aggregation object is a group of other objects that is treated as an entity. Aggregation objects provide inheritance among object types.

Simple objects are represented by a single relation. The non-object properties are carried as attributes of the relation. Composite objects require two or more relations for their representation. One relation contains the nonrepeating properties, and the second contains the properties of the composite group. The key of the relation that represents the repeating properties is always a composite key. It contains the key of the object plus an identifier of the composite group within that object.

At least two relations are required to represent a compound object. Each relation has its own distinct key. There are nine different types of compound objects ranging from 0:0 to $M:N$, although the three binary relationships (1:1, 1:$N$, and $M:N$) are sufficient for representing them. The relationships of compound objects are represented by placing the key of the parent relation as a foreign key in the associated child relation.

Association objects require at least three relations for their representation. One is required for each of the objects involved. Each relation has its own key, and the relation representing the association object will contain the keys of the other two objects as foreign keys.

Aggregation objects are groups of records that are treated as an entity. Each member of the group inherits certain properties of the group. The concept of inheritance is important in artificial intelligence and expert systems applications.

## QUESTIONS **GROUP I**

**6.1** What part do object diagrams play during the logical database design phase of systems development?

**6.2** Give two examples of binary relationships other than those in this text.

**6.3** Give an example of a non-binary relationship other than the one shown in this text.

**6.4** Name the three types of binary relationships.

**6.5** Give an example of a 1:1 binary relationship other than those in this text. Illustrate your answer with a diagram similar to the one in Figure 6–4b.

**6.6** Give examples of binary relationships other than those in this text for:
   **a.** An optional-to-optional relationship
   **b.** An optional-to-mandatory relationship
   **c.** A mandatory-to-optional relationship
   **d.** A mandatory-to-mandatory relationship
   Illustrate your answer using diagrams similar to the ones in Figure 6–4c.

**6.7** Explain how keys are used to represent 1:1 relationships.

**6.8** Draw relation diagrams (like the ones in Figure 6–8a) for each of the relationships you defined in question 6.6.

**6.9** Give four examples of 1:$N$ relationships, one for each of the categories in question 6.6.

6.10   Explain how keys are used to represent 1:$N$ relationships.

6.11   Draw relation diagrams for each of the relationships you defined in question 6.9.

6.12   Give an example of an $M$:$N$ relationship.

6.13   Why can't $M$:$N$ relationships be directly represented in relations?

6.14   Show how to represent a $M$:$N$ relationship with an intersection record.

6.15   Define the terms *tree, simple network,* and *complex network.*

6.16   Give an example of a tree record structure other than one in this book.

6.17   Give an example of a simple network other than one in this book.

6.18   Give an example of a complex network other than one in this book.

6.19   Define the term *simple object* and give an example other than one in this book.

6.20   Define the term *composite object* and give an example other than one in this book. Show the composite group.

6.21   Define the term *compound object* and give an example other than one in this book.

6.22   Define the term *association object* and give an example other than one in this book.

6.23   Define the term *aggregation object* and give an example other than one in this book.

6.24   Represent your answer to question 6.19 with a relation. What is the key?

6.25   Represent your answer to question 6.20 with relations. Identify the keys.

6.26   Represent your answer to question 6.21 with relations. Identify the keys.

6.27   Represent your answer to question 6.22 with relations. Identify the keys.

6.28   Explain why 0:1 and 0:$N$ relationships have the same relational representation as 1:1 and 1:$N$ relationships, respectively.

---

**GROUP II**        QUESTIONS AND EXERCISES

6.29   Draw the relation diagram (like the ones in Figure 6–8) for Figure 6–7b. Create an instance of each of the relations that illustrates the placement of keys.

6.30   Draw the relation diagram for Figure 6–10b. Create an instance of each of the relations that illustrates the placement of keys. What is the relationship of the keys of each of the relations?

6.31   Draw the relation diagram for Figure 6–11b. Create an instance of the relations that illustrates the placement of keys.

6.32   Suppose you are working on Samantha Green's development team at Eastcoast State University. Consider the following statements describing various objects and relationships:

• Students must be enrolled in certain courses in order to use the microcomputer lab.

- Students can make appointments to use the lab by reserving a certain computer for use at a certain time.
- Each computer has a certain amount of memory and might also have special peripherals attached, such as a mouse, a speech synthesizer, or a special keyboard.

Perform the following tasks:

**a.** Draw the object diagrams for STUDENT, COURSE, COMPUTER, PERIPHERAL, and APPOINTMENT.

**b.** What type (simple, composite, compound, association, or aggregation) is each of the objects?

**c.** Transform the object diagrams into relation diagrams. Be sure to underline the key of each relation.

**d.** Identify the foreign keys (if any) in each relation.

**6.33** Modify Figures 6–42b and c to add the reports presented in Figures 6–44a and b.

---

**Figure 6—44**

Reports for exercise 6.33

FDA REPORT #6272
Date: 06/30/89
Issuer: Kellogg's Corporation
Report Title: Product Summary by Ingredient

| | |
|---|---|
| Corn | Corn Flakes |
| | Krispix |
| | Nutrigrain (Corn) |
| Corn syrup | Rice Krispies |
| | Frosted Flakes |
| | Sugar Pops |
| Malt | Rice Krispies |
| | Sugar Smacks |
| Wheat | Sugar Smacks |
| | Nutrigrain (Wheat) |

SUPPLIER LIST
Date: 6/30/89

| Ingredient | Supplier | Price |
|---|---|---|
| Corn | Wilson | 2.80 |
| | J. Perkins | 2.72 |
| | Pollack | 2.83 |
| | McKay | 2.80 |
| Wheat | Adams | 1.19 |
| | Kroner | 1.19 |
| | Schmidt | 1.22 |
| Barley | Wilson | 0.85 |
| | Pollack | 0.84 |

a. FDA report

b. Internal supplier list

**6.34** Using the album cover in Figure 6–45 as a guide, perform the following tasks:

**a.** Draw the object diagrams for the underlying objects ARTIST, ROLE, and SONG.

**b.** Identify the relationships among those objects. What types of objects are they (simple, composite, etc.)?

    **c.** Define whether each participant in a relationship is optional or mandatory.

    **d.** Transform the object diagrams into relation diagrams. What is the key of each relation? What foreign keys appear in each relation?

---

**Figure 6—45**
Album cover for
exercise 6.34

# WEST SIDE STORY
Based on a conception of Jerome Robbins

Book by ARTHUR LAURENTS
Music by LEONARD BERNSTEIN
Lyrics by STEPHEN SONDHEIM

Entire Original Production Directed
and Choreographed by JEROME ROBBINS

Originally produced on Broadway by Robert E. Griffith and Harold S. Prince
by arrangement with Roger L. Stevens
Orchestration by Leonard Bernstein with Sid Ramin and Irwin Kostal

## HIGHLIGHTS FROM THE COMPLETE RECORDING

Maria . . . . . . . . . . . . . . . . .KIRI TE KANAWA
Tony . . . . . . . . . . . . . . . . .JOSÉ CARRERAS
Anita . . . . . . . . . . . . .TATIANA TROYANOS
Riff . . . . . . . . . . . . . . . . . . .KURT OLLMANN
and **MARILYN HORNE** singing "Somewhere"

| | | | |
|---|---|---|---|
| Rosalia . . . . . . . . . .Louise Edeiken | Diesel . . . . . . . . . . . . .Marty Nelson |
| Consuela . . . . . . . . .Stella Zambalis | Baby John . . . . . .Stephen Bogardus |
| Francisca . . . . . . . .Angelina Reaux | A-rab . . . . . . . . . . . . . . .Peter Thom |
| Action . . . . . . . . . . .David Livingston | Snowboy . . . . . . . . . . . .Todd Lester |
| | Bernardo . . . . Richard Harrell | |

| | | |
|---|---|---|
| ① **Jet Song** | | [3'13] |
| (Riff, Action, Baby John, A-rab, Chorus) | | |
| ② **Something's Coming** | | [2'33] |
| (Tony) | | |
| ③ **Maria** | | [2'56] |
| (Tony) | | |
| ④ **Tonight** | | [5'27] |
| (Maria, Tony) | | |
| ⑤ **America** | | [4'47] |
| (Anita, Rosalia, Chorus) | | |
| ⑥ **Cool** | | [4'37] |
| (Riff, Chorus) | | |
| ⑦ **One Hand, One Heart** | | [5'38] |
| (Tony, Maria) | | |
| ⑧ **Tonight** (Ensemble) | | [3'40] |
| (Entire Cast) | | |
| ⑨ **I Feel Pretty** | | [3'22] |
| (Maria, Chorus) | | |
| ⑩ **Somewhere** | | [2'34] |
| (A Girl) | | |
| ⑪ **Gee, Officer Krupke** | | [4'18] |
| (Action, Snowboy, Diesel, A-rab, Baby John, Chorus) | | |
| ⑫ **A Boy Like That** | | [2'05] |
| (Anita, Maria) | | |
| ⑬ **I Have a Love** | | [3'30] |
| (Maria, Anita) | | |
| ⑭ **Taunting Scene** | | [1'21] |
| (Orchestra) | | |
| ⑮ **Finale** | | [2'40] |
| (Maria, Tony) | | |

# PART III

# USING

# A DATABASE

In this part of the text we will address two very important database topics: multi-user processing and database *application* design.

In Chapter 7, we discuss the multi-user database environment. Problems exist in the multi-user environment that do not occur on single-user database systems. Examples include coordinating concurrent processing, providing backup and recovery facilities to quickly restore the database for its many users, and deciding data ownership and processing rights and then enforcing those restrictions. All of these problems and many more are the responsibility of the office of database administration, or DBA.

Fortunately for the DBA, most DBMS products provide features that help that office in the performance of its many duties. In Chapter 7 we address not only the DBA's role in multi-user database processing but also the features DBMS products provide to help alleviate some of the problems inherent in such a system.

In Chapter 8 we consider various aspects of database application design. A database application is the collection of menus, screens, reports, and programs that users employ to process the database. To satisfy user needs, applications must be designed to be meaningful to the user and easy to use. If you design applications from the perspective of *objects* (as opposed to relations or files), then the resulting application will be easier to use. We will address such object-oriented application design techniques in Chapter 8. The concepts you learn in Chapter 8 will be useful to you whether you design database applications for mainframe computers or microcomputers. Good design principles must be used in either case.

# Multi-user Processing and Database Administration

- The Multi-user Database Environment
- Functions of the DBA
- Functions of the DBMS
- Summary

**D**atabase processing in a multi-user environment presents some challenges, both for the software engineers who design and build database management systems and later for the people who use and manage them.

DBMS software engineers must anticipate failures and build recovery routines that can quickly restore a database system to a usable state. They must allow users to access the same data concurrently, but they must provide facilities to control concurrent processing; if they do not, data integrity problems will result. They must incorporate into a DBMS the ability to let users alter the structure of the database, say to add new columns to a table or to change the rules governing column values. Perhaps most importantly, DBMS engineers must build into a DBMS a security system that affords easy access for authorized users but prevents others from accessing the data. This in itself is a difficult task.

On the managerial side, the problems of a multi-user database system are of a different nature, but they are no less challenging. Because the database is a shared resource, conflicts inevitably arise among users regarding rights to use parts of the database, responsibility for collecting and entering data, authority to modify data, and so forth. In addition, users' business needs are constantly changing, and changes may need to be made to the structure of the database—changes that help one user but might hinder another. And as new database applications are developed, coordination is needed to be sure that standards are followed and that optimum use is being made of the database. Problems dealing with the human side of the database environment fall to the office of database administration, or DBA.

In this chapter we will examine the problems inherent in multi-user database systems, and we will see how they are addressed either by DBMS routines or by the DBA.

## THE MULTI-USER DATABASE ENVIRONMENT

A *multi-user database* is a database that many users can access at the same time. These users typically employ computer terminals online to a central computer in which the database is stored. There may be a few users (for example, fifteen clerks in a billing office) or a few thousand users (for example, airline reservation clerks and travel agents using an online reservation system). We will consider the multi-user environment in the context of a company-wide database, but you should know that some multi-user databases are used only by small groups within a company whereas others are used by many people in many different companies.

Within a company, functional departments—groups of employees headed by a manager—are responsible for certain tasks. Each department is judged by how effectively and efficiently it accomplishes the tasks it is assigned. Sometimes the goals of one department conflict with those of another department.

Consider a company that offers intensive two-month training courses in automotive repair. Conflicts might occur, for example, between teachers and salespeople. The salespeople are responsible for enrolling students. Their salaries and bonuses are based on volume. The teachers are responsible for training, and they are judged by the number of students who successfully complete the course. Suppose the salespeople enroll students who do not have the necessary skills or background to complete the course. When students drop out (and demand tuition refunds), the teaching staff may appear to be doing a poor job. On the other hand, suppose the instructional staff were allowed to reject applicants whom it felt were unqualified. Probably a higher proportion of students would complete their training. But the salespeople would complain that their bonuses were being manipulated by an elitist group of teachers.

In the evolution of data processing systems, each functional department in a company typically developed its own set of files (called master files), which it periodically updated and from which it retrieved information pertinent to its own particular business needs. No department depended on another one to collect or enter its data. Rather, each department was on its own. Each department felt that it was in control of the data it needed.

Even if some departmental goals conflicted with those of another department, at least some territorial boundaries were established regarding data.

The database environment is very different from the departmental-file environment. Users collect and share data. Users seldom have absolute control over any data in the database.

Consider the automotive training program described earlier. Suppose the teaching staff depends on the sales staff to collect data about each student's educational background, reading level, and work schedule. Such data is needed to schedule the student into a class. But because the sales staff does not need the data to close a sale, it may not be careful in collecting it. And the data that salespeople do collect may be unreliable. In frustration, and to ensure it has the data it needs, the teaching staff may establish its own student master files, duplicating much of the data the sales staff collects (or is supposed to collect). As a result, the company has duplicated data in two distinct file processing systems—a poor solution.

We saw in an earlier chapter that a master-file system is not only slow, cumbersome, and redundant, but also prevents true integration of data. Data is useful to a company when it is stored in such a way that in addition to satisfying all individual departmental needs it can be used to answer corporate management questions.

## Data as a Corporate Resource

Seen in this light, a company's data is as much a resource as its personnel and its finances. In fact, data in a database needs to be managed and guarded as carefully as the company's financial assets. In recognizing that data is an organizational resource, many companies have established an office of database administration (DBA), which is to the company's data what the controller is to the company's money. Like financial resources, data is owned by the company and shared by departments in the organization. Conflicts will arise over who can access the data, who must collect the data, and who is allowed to modify and delete data. And so an unbiased individual or office—the DBA—must oversee the data, store it, guard it, and authorize access to it, keeping in mind the overall company goals as well as those of departments.

It seems only logical that data should be accorded the same recognition as money, especially now that data is widely accepted as a valuable company resource. And it also seems only logical therefore to establish companywide databases and eliminate many "private" departmental files. However, some companies encounter a great deal of resistance when developing database systems to replace existing file systems. (Imagine the resistance that might arise in the automotive repair school described earlier.) Departments using traditional file systems have control over the collection, maintenance, and processing of "their" data. Control constitutes ownership of the data and, consequently, a certain amount of power. Databases change the notion of "private" files by centrally storing shared data and allowing more than one user to access it. Some database data can be declared accessible to only one or several users. This allows for privacy even in the database. But the political power inherent in file systems is to a great extent reduced in a database system. Thus, many people still balk at the idea of relinquishing the control they have wielded over (and with) their departmental data.

To deal with such resistance, in many companies upper-level management has empowered the DBA to control the collection, maintenance, and processing of data. The DBA, on behalf of the company, grants functional rights and privileges to users to access and modify the data in order to assist the organization in meeting its goals. Companies that do not establish a strong DBA are likely to experience great difficulty when attempting to develop multi-user database systems.

In some companies, the DBA recognizes the need for *local* (or private) databases. Rather than attempt to prohibit them, the DBA officially supports local databases and consequently not only discovers their presence but also gains some control over them. For example, the DBA might establish criteria for determining when local databases are an acceptable alternative to the use of the corporate database. The DBA might specify the DBMS product or products to be used for processing local databases. Or the DBA might make some of its staff available to assist in the development of local databases and applications.

Thus, database systems do not necessarily centralize *all* of a company's data. The DBA might authorize local databases as long as there is a legitimate need for them.

## FUNCTIONS OF THE DBA

The DBA's role continues to be defined. As yet, no standards have been established for the group that holds the title. However, it is clear that the DBA must be a manager and a diplomat, and must represent the company's interests when making decisions. Whereas the DBMS addresses primarily technical problems, the DBA addresses not only technical but also managerial, psychological, sociological, and political problems in the multi-user database environment. Let us now consider some of the specific functions of the DBA. Following that we will discuss the functions of the DBMS in the multi-user environment.

The overall responsibility of the DBA is to protect the database while maximizing users' benefits. In organizations that use only small databases accessed via microcomputers, no one may actually hold the title of DBA. However, someone in the organization must perform all the functions we are about to discuss.

Although people often think of the DBA as an individual, the responsibilities of the job are often too varied to be handled by only one person.

Database administration involves highly technical knowledge (such as that needed to tune the database) as well as keen diplomatic skills (such as those needed to get several user groups to agree on data definitions or processing rights). Thus an office of database administration is usually developed. The manager of the office is often known as the *database administrator*. Consequently, the letters *DBA* refer to either the office or the manager, depending on the context. Thus, database administration might be a part-time job or it might be a full-time job for many people.

In addition to resolving conflicts among users, the DBA is called upon to perform many other functions. For example, a database requires considerable care. The design and implementation of recovery procedures, database documentation, performance evaluation, system tuning, and new feature evaluation are a few of the tasks assigned to the DBA. Ultimately, the DBA is responsible for the development, operation, and maintenance of the database system. Some of the DBA's responsibilities include the following:

- Management of database activity
- Management of the database structure
- Management of the DBMS software
- Control of concurrent processing
- Database backup and recovery
- Database security

In addition, the DBA is involved in developing new database applications, creating documentation, balancing the conflicting needs of users, measuring system performance, and many other tasks. The position of database administrator is a demanding one.

Fortunately for the DBA, the DBMS provides support and assistance for many of the functions in the foregoing list. Typical DBMS products include features that address the last three tasks. Not all DBMS products provide the same level of support in these areas, however, so the DBA must be prepared to augment a DBMS by developing programs or procedures where the DBMS is lacking.

In this section, we will examine the responsibilities of the DBA as they pertain to managing data activity, managing the database structure, and managing the DBMS software. In the last section of this chapter, we will address the functions of the DBMS as they aid the DBA in addressing concurrent processing, database security, and backup and recovery.

## Management of Data Activity

The DBA protects the data but does not own it. Rather, database data is *owned* by the users, since they provide data, retrieve it, update it, and delete it. Consequently, the DBA does not manage *data values*. Rather, the DBA manages *data activity*. The database is a shared resource, and the DBA provides standards, guidelines, control procedures, and documentation to ensure that users work in a cooperative and complementary fashion when managing the data.

**Database Standards.**    Because of the high degree of interrelated activity, database processing must be standardized processing. *Providing database standards* is one aspect of managing data activity. Every data item must have a standard name and format. Every database record must have a standard name, format, and standardized access strategies. Every database file must have a standard name and standardized relationships with other files. The DBA establishes these standards to satisfy the majority of the collective needs of all database users.

Once established, these details can be recorded in the DBMS *data dictionary.* (In fact, many details about the database and the applications can be stored in the data dictionary.) Both system developers and users can query the dictionary to determine exactly what data is being maintained, what the names and formats of data items are, and what relationships exist.

*The Data Dictionary.*    A DBMS data dictionary is an important tool for the database administrator. A data dictionary is actually a user-accessible catalog of data about the database. To understand its importance, suppose a company establishes a database consisting of 20 tables and 300 columns. Seventy-five applications are run on a regular basis. Now suppose that adhering to a new tax law requires changes in the way that employee taxes are calculated and in the formats of the data items that are used. Before modifying either data or programs, the manager of data processing needs to assess the impact of these changes in order to allocate people and testing facilities, develop user training, and so forth. The manager asks the DBA which programs reference which data items.

If a data dictionary is in place, then a simple query against it (just like a query against a database) can provide the answer to the manager's question. But if there is no record of the cross-references, then each application program needs to be studied (usually by application programmers) to determine whether it references the data items in question. Obviously, the first approach is much faster and probably much more accurate.

Data dictionaries are not new. In fact, many data processing managers developed their own long before databases became popular. Now, however, many DBMS products include an integrated data dictionary option. For example, IDMS/R, a database management system licensed by Cullinet, includes a powerful data dictionary as an option. IBM incorporates a user-accessible catalog in its DB2 relational database product. Other manufacturers offer similar options.

Some data dictionaries are *active* and some are *passive.* An active data dictionary is one whose entries are automatically modified by the software whenever changes are made to the database structure. Passive data dictionaries, in contrast, need to be separately updated when database changes are made. Otherwise they will not accurately reflect the state of the database. Active data dictionaries, which usually cost more, assure currency, but they are not available with every DBMS product. Passive data dictionaries are less expensive than active ones, but more effort is required to keep them up-to-date. Either type of data dictionary, however, greatly aids the DBA in recording and tracking data names, formats, relationships, and cross-references.

**Establishing User Processing Rights.**    A second aspect of managing data activity is the *establishment of data ownership, access, and modification rights.* Since the data is a shared resource, problems occur regarding processing rights. The DBA must consider each shared data item and, in conjunction with the users, determine access and modification rights. The DBA does this as a representative of the company, looking out for the greater company good rather than the good of one particular user group. Once processing rights have been determined, they can be identified to the DBMS, which will then enforce them via its security routines. (You will see how later in this chapter.) Thus, the problem of database security is jointly addressed by the DBA, who establishes policy, and the DBMS, which enforces that policy.

Problems can occur when two or more user groups are authorized to modify the same data. This is called the *concurrent update problem.* For example, suppose two airline ticket agents attempt to sell the last available seat on a flight to two customers at precisely the same time. If the DBMS does not delay one of them until the other is finished (enabling one passenger to get a ticket and leaving the other passenger out of luck), then it might happen that two passengers are sold the same seat. As you will learn in the next section, DBMS products are capable of preventing the concurrent update problem in various ways.

Although the DBMS prevents the concurrent update problem from occurring, the DBA is also responsible for some aspects of managing concurrency. The DBA must document the concurrent update capabilities of the DBMS and establish user procedures for problem situations. For instance, users must know how to restart a transaction if the DBMS "kills" it (killing a transaction is one method of handling the concurrent update problem). In some cases, the DBA may even restrict types of activities by user groups to certain periods of the day in order to avoid such concurrency problems, which can diminish overall system performance.

**Recovery Techniques.**    A third concern for the DBA in the management of data activity is to *develop recovery techniques and procedures.* Although, as you will learn, the DBMS performs one part of the recovery process, people play an even larger role. The DBA must anticipate failures and develop standardized procedures for handling them. Users must know what to do while the system is down and what to do first when the system is made available. The operations staff must know how to initiate a database recovery process, which backup copies of the database to use, how to schedule the rerunning of lost work (other systems are using the computer resources, too, and priorities need to be established and enforced), and so on. If a communications control program is in use (a likely situation in an online multi-user database environment), the recovery of its processing must be coordinated with database recovery. All of these problems are the responsibility of the DBA.

Finally, the DBA is responsible for *publishing and maintaining documentation* of data activity. This includes documentation about database standards, data retrieval and access rights, recovery procedures, and policy enforcement. Good documentation is especially important in this area because it is needed by diverse user groups throughout the organization. As with all documentation, keeping it current is a large and unpopular task.

Many DBMS products provide utility services to assist in the management of data activity. Some systems record the names of users and application programs that access (or are authorized to access) objects in the database. For example, the IDMS data dictionary can be queried to determine which programs can access a particular record and what actions each can take.

Figure 7–1 summarizes DBA responsibilities for the management of data activity.

## Management of the Database Structure

The creation and maintenance of the database structure—or *schemas*, as we called them in Chapter 2—are perhaps the most important responsibility of the DBA. The design of the database or databases is critical, and the DBA is involved in this activity. The DBA must ensure that database designers look at data from the user's perspective—that is, in terms of objects rather than as mere records, files, or tables. The DBA understands that if the underlying database structure is patterned after the user's point of view, the database is likely to be easy to use. If not, navigating through the database is likely to be difficult and contrived, both for application programmers

**Figure 7–1**
DBA data activity
management
responsibilities

- Provide database standards
- Establish data ownership, retrieval, and modification rights
- Create and disseminate recovery procedures
- Publish and maintain documentation

and for users of query languages. Thus, the DBA must *bring database design expertise* to development projects.

After database applications have been implemented, the DBA will *plan and implement necessary changes to the schemas.* User requirements will change, users will find better ways to accomplish their goals, database technology will change, and DBMS vendors will upgrade their products. All changes to the database structure and procedures need to be carefully managed. Once database structure is established, change is difficult. Consequently, change to the database structure is usually an evolutionary—not a revolutionary—process.

**Configuration Control.**  The DBA must periodically (and continually) monitor user activity on the database. DBMS products include features that collect and report statistics. Some of these reports may indicate, for example, which users have been active, which files and perhaps which data items have been used, and which access methods have been employed. Error rates and error types can also be captured and reported. The DBA analyzes this data to determine whether or not a *change to the database configuration* is needed to improve performance or ease the users' tasks. If so, the DBA will make the change. This might include, for example, hardware modifications, reallocation of database files to new disk locations, or the addition or deletion of database indexes.

User requests for change generally arise when a user finds a better way to accomplish a task or when a new requirement is recognized. In either case, the DBA must consider the ramifications of the change on other database system users. Any change that affects shared data cannot be made until all users' needs are considered. The DBA may decide that even though a particular change negatively affects a user, it is in the best interests of the company to make it. The DBA must carefully explain this to the user group. As you can see, DBAs must often be skillful diplomats.

Because of the size and complexity of a database and its applications, changes will sometimes have unexpected results. The DBA must be prepared to repair a database and to gather sufficient information to diagnose and correct the problem that caused the damage. The database is most vulnerable to failure after a change. Obviously, substantial changes should not be implemented when a significant proportion of the DBA staff is on vacation or busy with other projects.

**Documentation.**  The final responsibility of the DBA in the management of the database structure is *documentation.* It is extremely important to know what changes have been made, how they were made, and when they were made. A change to the database structure may cause an error that does not manifest itself for six months. Without proper documentation of the change, diagnosis of the problem is next to impossible. Dozens of job reruns may be required to identify a point where certain symptoms first occurred. For this reason, it is also important to maintain a record of test procedures and test runs made to verify a change. If standardized test procedures, test forms, and record-keeping methods are used, the recording of test results does not have to be time-consuming. Although maintaining documentation is tedious and unfulfilling, the effort pays off when disaster occurs and the documentation is the difference between solving and not solving a significant (and costly) problem.

Another reason for maintaining good documentation of changes to the database structure is to ensure that historical data can be properly employed. If, for some reason, marketing wants to analyze three-year-old sales data that has been in the archives for two years, it will be necessary to know what structure was current when the data was last active. Records that show changes to the structure can be used to answer the question. A similar situation arises when a six-month-old backup copy of data must be used to repair a damaged database. (Even though this should not occur, it sometimes does.) The backup copy can be used to reconstruct the database as it was at the time in question. Then transactions and structural changes can be applied in chronological order to bring the database up-to-date.

Figure 7–2 summarizes DBA responsibilities for the management of the database structure.

## Management of the DBMS

In addition to managing data activity and database structure, the DBA must manage the DBMS itself. The DBA should *compile and analyze statistics* about system performance and identify potential problem areas. Keep in mind that the database is serving many user groups. The DBA needs to *investigate all user complaints* about system response time, accuracy of data, ease of use, and so forth. If changes are needed, the DBA must plan and implement them.

When the vendor of the DBMS announces new product features, the DBA must consider them in light of the overall needs of the user community.

**Figure 7–2**
DBA database structure management responsibilities

- Design the schema(s)
- Provide design expertise
- Control redundancy
- Maintain configuration control of change requests
- Implement schema changes
- Maintain documentation

If the DBA decides to *incorporate new DBMS features,* users need to be notified and trained in their use. Thus, the DBA must manage and control change to both the DBMS and the database structure.

The DBA should analyze run-time statistics on database activity and performance. When a performance problem is identified, either by a report or by a user complaint, the DBA must determine whether or not a *modification to the database structure or system* is appropriate. Examples of possible structure modifications are establishing new keys, purging data, deleting keys, and establishing new relationships between objects.

Other changes to the system for which the DBA is responsible vary widely, depending on the DBMS product as well as other software and hardware in use. For example, changes to other software (such as the operating system or a communications control program) may mean that some DBMS parameters must be modified. Thus, the DBA must *tune the database system to other software* in use.

DBMS options are initially chosen when little is known about how the system will perform in the particular user environment. Consequently, operational experience and performance analysis over a period of time may indicate a change is necessary. Even if performance seems acceptable, the DBA may want to alter the options and observe the effect on performance. This process is referred to as *tuning* or *optimizing* the system.

Figure 7–3 summarizes the DBA's responsibilities for database system management.

## DBA Personnel and Placement

By now you will probably agree that the duties of the DBA are numerous and multi-faceted. The many tasks required for database administration are accomplished in different ways, depending on the size of the organization and the database. As we said before, some very small installations may not

**Figure 7–3**
DBA responsibilities
for database system
management

- Generate database system performance reports
- Investigate user performance complaints
- Evaluate and implement new features
- Modify database structure
- Tune database system to communications software and operating system
- Tune the database system

---

**Figure 7–4**
Positions in the DBA
office

- Database Administrator
- Documentation and Standards Manager
- User Representative
- Operations Representative
- DBMS Configuration Manager
- Performance Monitor

even have a person designated as the DBA, although all of the functions must be performed. In larger installations, the office of database administration often includes a staff of individuals who specialize in various aspects of the job. Figure 7–4 lists positions you may find in a typical DBA office. Not all DBA offices have one person for each position. In some cases, one person may handle two or more responsibilities. In others, notably in large organizations, two or more people may be involved in just one of these activities. The following is a summary of typical DBA staff positions.

**The Database Administrator.**    The DBA is primarily a manager and a diplomat. Although he or she should have a good foundation in data processing and the business of the organization, the DBA need not be a technical giant. The DBA needs sufficient technical background to make wise decisions but will delegate their implementation to technicians.

   The DBA must manage the staff to ensure orderly development of database projects, satisfy database users, and plan for future user requirements. The DBA must plan and budget staff, database, and computer resources. As conflicts arise among user groups, the DBA must reallocate resources to achieve maximum organizational benefits. Finally, the DBA is responsible to upper management for all database projects.

**The Documentation and Standards Manager.**    The primary responsibility of this position is to develop and maintain all database documentation and standards. The documentation and standards manager also enforces programming standards, both for new programs and for modifications to existing ones. Enforcing programming standards is accomplished in a variety of ways. For example, when program reviews are employed (and they should be), the standards manager attends them to ensure that programs meet the established standards. If this is not done on a regular basis, then spot checks can be made of new programs and program changes before they go into production. Those not adhering to published standards will remain in development until they are fixed.

In addition to the development, publication, and enforcement of standards, this individual (or group) also maintains the data dictionary, the primary source of documentation for a database and database applications. We saw earlier that the data dictionary can be useful to application programmers and other MIS personnel. Maintaining the data dictionary is an important job of the documentation and standards manager.

**The User Representative.** The user representative is also sometimes known as a user liaison. This position is growing in popularity and prestige because users are participating more and more in database design and requirements definition. The user representative reports to the DBA (not to the users), but his or her job is to bridge the gap between the users and the database group. The user liaison must know the users personally, understand the users' system requirements, and articulate those requirements to the DBA staff. The user representative also assesses the impact that system changes will have on users and helps them to understand and implement changes. Questions posed by the DBA staff to users can be handled through this channel.

In a multi-user environment, each user group is likely to be represented. If users are confident that they are being adequately represented to the DBA, their confidence in the system will be high. They are also more likely to cooperate when changes need to be made.

**The Operations Representative.** The job of the operations representative is similar to that of the user representative except that it relates to computer operations. This individual is the contact for operations planning purposes. The operations representative describes to the operations group the future needs of the database system. The operations representative has a better understanding of the hardware and the operating system than do other DBA employees. He or she works in conjunction with the performance monitor in tuning the system. For example, they would work together to determine the allocation of database files to disk units.

**The DBMS Configuration Manager.** The responsibilities of this position are to know the database system and to maintain configuration control of it. This individual focuses on the DBMS *product* rather than on specific applications. In fact, the configuration manager is often the resident expert on the DBMS in use. Because the configuration manager has great technical knowledge, he or she works with the performance monitor in tuning the database system, evaluates new DBMS features, and manages feature implementation. Both this position and the position of operations representative are technical in nature. They may even be held by the same individual.

**The Performance Monitor.** The performance monitor obtains and analyzes statistics about system performance. During the development of a new application, for example, the performance monitor measures the performance of the system, compares it to the requirements, and makes modifications where necessary. If applications respond too slowly, for instance, the performance monitor might suggest that indexes to certain files be established, that other indexes be eliminated, or that data be physically rearranged on the storage devices.

The performance monitor also investigates user complaints, probably in conjunction with the user representative. He or she works with the operations representative and the DBMS configuration manager in system tuning. This person may also be involved in new feature evaluation.

**DBA Placement.**    The organizational placement of the DBA office is a subject of considerable debate. Two principles are commonly accepted. One is that it is undesirable for the DBA to be organizationally below any group on which it imposes restrictions, constraints, or standards. For example, the DBA should not work for the programming staff. The second principle is that the DBA should not be more than one level above the organizations with which it interfaces. If it is, the DBA tends to be removed from important day-to-day activities and problems.

The DBA interfaces with and has impact on the traditional MIS groups: systems, programming, and operations. The DBA affects systems design, it imposes standards on programming, and it forces constraints on operations. Consequently, the lowest acceptable level would seem to be parallel with these three offices (Figure 7–5a). A better arrangement may be to have the DBA as a staff function reporting to the head of data processing (Figure 7–5b). Some managers say the parallel arrangement does not give the DBA sufficient power, whereas others claim the staff arrangement can give the DBA too much power and create an elitist DBA staff. The key to success is the attitude of the senior data processing officer. Either organization will work if the DBA is given recognizable lines of authority.

**Summary of the Roles of the DBA.**    As you have seen, the office of the DBA bears many responsibilities. It is ultimately responsible for the installation, management, and execution of database systems and applications. Fortunately, many of the tasks associated with multi-user database applications are performed by the DBMS. This allows the DBA to concentrate on the human side of the system—user satisfaction, system development, and so forth. This does not imply, however, that technical skills are not required.

Among other things, the DBA must know how the DBMS product works—the file structures it employs, how it builds and processes indexes, and how it navigates through the data, for example. This technical knowledge enables the DBA to achieve optimum performance and provide a system that is responsive to the users. The DBMS is powerful software. Consequently, it relieves the DBA of some of the problems of a multi-user database.

**Figure 7—5**
Two acceptable alter-
natives for DBA
placement

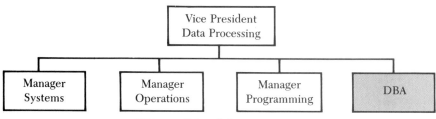

a. DBA parallel with line organizations

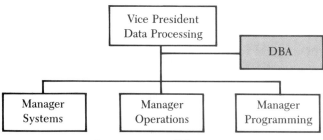

b. DBA as a staff function

## FUNCTIONS OF THE DBMS

In Chapter 2 we noted that DBMS products possess certain generic functions (Figure 7–6). The DBMS includes features that help the DBA in performing administrative functions. In this section we will address three DBMS
functions that are of particular importance to the DBA in the multi-user
environment:

- Control of concurrent processing
- Backup and recovery
- Database security

### Control of Concurrent Processing

Perhaps the most challenging problem encountered in the multi-user database environment is the control of concurrent processing. Concurrent
processing occurs because many users attempt to access the same data
resource simultaneously. Each user thinks that he or she has sole use of the

**Figure 7–6**
Functions of DBMS
products

---

- Store, retrieve, and update user data
- Store, retrieve, and update meta-data
- Enforce integrity rules and constraints
- Provide coordination and control for
  multi-user processing
- Provide facilities for backup and recovery
- Enforce security constraints

---

computer system. (Ideally, anyway. No user should be aware of others on the system.)

Each user submits work in units called *transactions*. They are also known as *atomic transactions* and *logical units of work (LUWs)*. A transaction is a series of actions to be taken on the database such that either all the actions are done successfully or the database remains unchanged. For example, a transaction to enter a customer order might include the following actions:

1. Change the customer record with the new order data
2. Change the salesperson record with the new order data
3. Insert a new order record into the database

Suppose the last step failed, perhaps because of insufficient file space. Imagine the confusion that would take place if the first two changes were applied but the third one was not. The customer might receive an invoice for an item never received, and a salesperson might receive a commission on an item never sent to the customer.

Figure 7–7 compares the results of performing these activities as a series of independent steps (Figure 7–7a) and as an atomic transaction (Figure 7–7b). Notice that when the steps are done atomically and one fails, no changes are applied to the database. Defining a series of steps as a transaction is an important aspect of concurrency control.

Concurrent processing happens when two transactions are interleaved, a normal state in the multi-user environment. In essence, the central processing unit (CPU) is able to execute only one instruction at a time. Rather than devoting all CPU time to, say, one transaction (making all the others wait for their turns), the operating system rapidly switches control among the various tasks waiting to be executed. This happens so quickly that two people seated at terminals side-by-side, using the same DBMS, may believe that their two transactions are processed simultaneously. In reality, the two transactions are interleaved. The computer performs

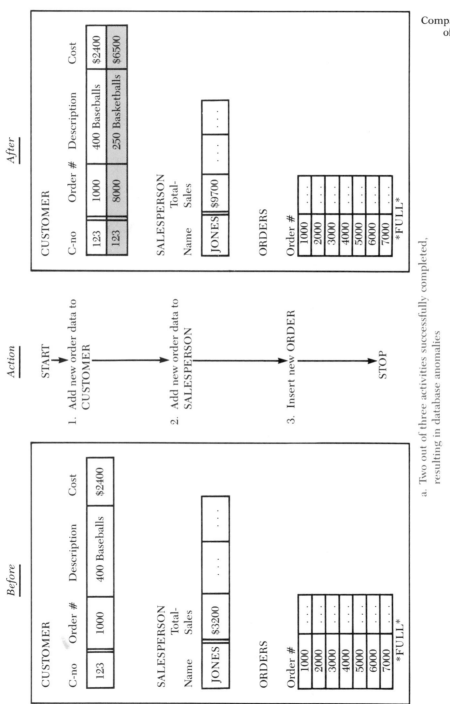

**Figure 7–7**

Comparison of results of applying serial actions versus a multiple-step transaction

**Figure 7–7**
(continued)

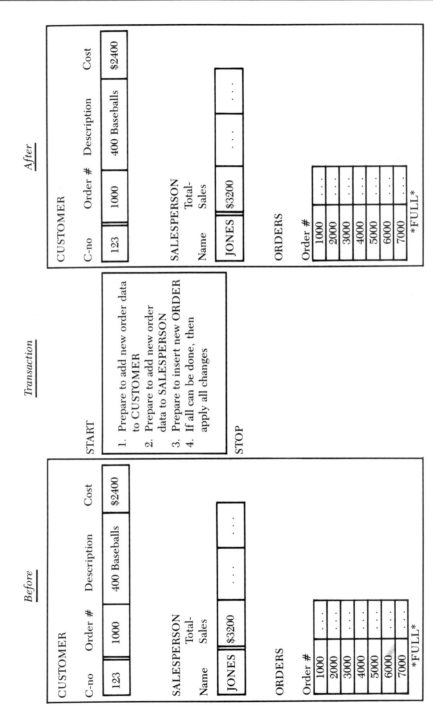

b. No change made because entire transaction not successful

**Figure 7–8**
Example of concur-
rent processing of two
users' tasks

User A

1. Read item 100
2. Change item 100
3. Write item 100

User B

1. Read item 200
2. Change item 200
3. Write item 200

Order of processing at CPU

1. Read item 100 for A
2. Read item 200 for B
3. Change item 100 for A
4. Write item 100 for A
5. Change item 200 for B
6. Write item 200 for B

instructions and task switching in billionths of a second, though, and humans cannot perceive that interleaving has taken place.

Figure 7–8 shows two concurrent transactions. User A's transaction reads item 100, changes it, and rewrites the item in the database. User B's transaction takes the same actions, but on item 200. The CPU processes user A's transaction until it encounters an I/O interrupt, a signal that control can be passed to another task. The operating system shifts control to user B. The CPU now processes user B's transaction until an interrupt occurs, at which point the operating system passes control back to A. To the users, processing appears to be simultaneous. In reality, it is interleaved, or concurrent.

When databases are distributed across two or more computer systems, simultaneous updating becomes a possibility because distributed systems, by definition, include multiple CPUs. Obviously, several CPUs can operate at one time. The control over updates in distributed databases is an exceedingly complex subject. In this chapter we will consider the fundamentals of concurrent processing on one computer. We will examine concurrent processing in more detail in Chapter 15 where we will also consider concurrency for distributed database processing.

**The Concurrent Update Problem.** The concurrent processing illustrated in Figure 7–8 poses no problems because the users are processing different data. However, suppose that both users want to process item 100. Let's say, for example, that user A wants to order five of item 100 and user B wants to order three of item 100.

**Figure 7–9**
Concurrent update
problem

|              User A              |              User B              |
| :------------------------------- | :------------------------------- |
| 1. Read item 100                 | 1. Read item 100                 |
|    (assume item count is 10)     |    (assume item count is 10)     |
| 2. Reduce count of items by 5    | 2. Reduce count of items by 3    |
| 3. Write item 100                | 3. Write item 100                |

Order of processing at CPU

1. Read item 100 (for A)
2. Read item 100 (for B)
3. Set item count to 5 (for A)
4. Write item 100 for A
5. Set item count to 7 (for B)
6. Write item 100 for B

Note: The change and write in steps 3 and 4 are lost.

Figure 7–9 illustrates the problem. User A reads the item 100 record into a user work area. According to the record, ten items are in inventory. Then user B reads the item 100 record into another user work area. Again, according to the record, ten are in inventory. Now user A takes five, decreases the count of items in its user work area to five, and rewrites the record for item 100. Then user B takes three, decreases the count in its user work area to seven, and rewrites the item 100 record. The database now shows, incorrectly, that seven of item 100 remain in inventory. To review: We started with ten in inventory, user A took five, user B took three, and the database shows that seven remain. Clearly, we have a problem.

Both users obtained current data from the database. However, when user B read the record, user A already had a copy that was about to be updated. One remedy for this concurrent update problem is to prevent multiple applications from having copies of the same record when the record is about to be changed. This approach is called *resource locking*.

**Resource Locking.**   To prevent the concurrent update problem, data that is retrieved for update must not be shared among users. (In this sense, the term *user* refers to the user of the DBMS, not necessarily the end user. Thus, a user can be either a person seated at a terminal using the DBMS query/update facility or an application program that calls the DBMS for service.)

**Figure 7–10**

Concurrent process-
ing with explicit locks

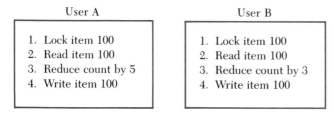

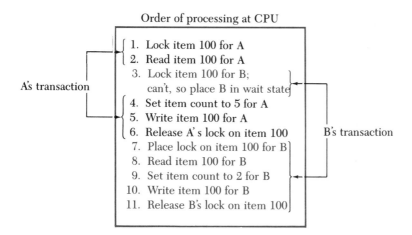

To prevent such sharing, the DBMS can place *locks* on data that is retrieved for update. Figure 7–10 shows the order of processing using a lock command. User B's transaction must wait until user A is finished with the item 100 record. Using this strategy, user B can read the item 100 record only after user A has completed the modification. In this case, the final item count stored in the database will be two, as it should be. (We started with ten, A took five, and B took three, leaving two.)

However the DBMS and application program accomplish this, they must ensure that the database suffers from no anomalies due to concurrent processing. Thus, the results of concurrently processing two transactions must be identical to the results that would have been achieved if one entire transaction were processed followed by the next one. This characteristic is referred to as *serializability.*

Serializability can be achieved by a number of different means. One way is to process the transaction, obtaining locks as needed, but not to release any lock until the end of the transaction. The rationale for this strategy, called *two-phase locking,* is discussed in Chapter 15.

The boundaries of a transaction should correspond to the definition of the object it is processing. Following the two-phase strategy, rows of each relation in the object are locked as needed. Changes are made, but the data is not committed (or rewritten) to the database until the entire object has been processed. At this point, changes are made to the actual database and all locks are released.

Consider the order entry transaction illustrated in Figure 7–7. This transaction involves the underlying object ORDER-FORM, which is constructed out of data from the CUSTOMER table, the SALESPERSON table, and the ORDER table. To ensure that the database will suffer from no anomalies due to concurrency, the order entry transaction begins by issuing all of its locks (on CUSTOMER, SALESPERSON, and ORDER) and concludes by applying all database changes and then releasing all of its locks.

Many DBMS products employ some variety of two-phase locking. One example is IBM's DB2 relational database product. The DB2 COMMIT command applies all database changes and then releases all locks. Thus, by definition, COMMIT ends a transaction. Refer to Chapter 15 for more information on this subject.

**The Deadly Embrace.**    Consider what might happen if two users want to order two items from inventory. Suppose that user A wants to order some paper and that if she can get the paper, she wants to order some pencils. Further, suppose that user B wants to order some pencils and that if he can get the pencils, he wants to order some paper. The order of processing could be as shown in Figure 7–11.

---

**Figure 7–11**
Deadlock

|  User A  |  User B  |
| --- | --- |
| 1.  Lock paper | 1.  Lock pencils |
| 2.  Take paper | 2.  Take pencils |
| 3.  Lock pencils | 3.  Lock paper |

Order of processing at CPU

1. Lock paper for user A
2. Lock pencils for user B
3. Process A's requests; write paper record
4. Process B's requests; write pencil record
5. Put A in wait state for pencils
6. Put B in wait state for paper

What has happened? Users A and B are locked in the *deadly embrace* in a condition known as *deadlock*. Each is waiting for a resource that the other person has locked. Two common ways of solving this problem are to (1) prevent deadlock from occurring or (2) allow deadlock to occur and then break it.

Deadlock can be prevented in several ways. One is to allow users to have only one lock at a time. In essence, users must lock all the resources they want at once. If user A in the illustration had locked both the paper and the pencil records at the beginning, then the deadlock would never have occurred.

The other strategy is to allow the deadlock to occur, detect it, and then break it. Unfortunately, there is only one way to break a deadlock: kill one of the transactions. If the situation in Figure 7–11 has occurred, one of the two transactions must be aborted. When that happens, the lock will be released and the other transaction can process the database unhindered. Obviously any changes the killed transaction has made to the database must be undone. We will discuss the techniques for this in the next section.

## Database Recovery

As you can see, control of concurrent processing is a very real problem in the multi-user database environment. Fortunately, DBMS products take this problem into account and are able to deal with it effectively. Users often do not even realize that concurrent processing can be a problem. However, one problem that *is* visible to the user is system failure. Procedures for periodically backing up a database, detecting when failure has occurred, restoring the database to a usable state, and reapplying all lost transactions are complex. Fortunately, DBMS products include processes that make system recovery possible.

Computer systems, database-oriented or not, can fail. When a system becomes inoperable, especially an online system, several problems must be addressed. First, from a business standpoint, business functions must continue. For example, customer orders, financial transactions, and packing lists must be completed manually. Later, when the computer is running again, the data can be entered. Second, computer center personnel must work quickly to restore the system as closely as possible to the state it was in when it crashed. Third, users must know what to do when the system becomes available again. Because some work may need to be reentered, users must know how far back they need to go.

Recovery may be exceedingly difficult. It is impossible simply to fix the problem and resume processing where it was interrupted. Even if no data is lost during a failure (which assumes that all types of memory are nonvolatile—an unrealistic assumption), the timing and scheduling of computer processing are too complex to be accurately recreated. Enormous amounts of overhead data and processing would be required for the operating system to be able to restart processing precisely where it was interrupted. It is simply not possible to roll back the clock and put all the electrons in the same configuration they were in at the time of the failure. Thus, two approaches are possible: recovery via reprocessing and recovery via rollback/rollforward.

**Recovery via Reprocessing.**   Since processing cannot be resumed at a precise point, the next best alternative is to go back to a known point and reprocess the workload from there. The simplest form of this type of recovery is to periodically make a copy of the database (called a *database save*) and to keep a record of all transactions that have been processed since the save. Then, when failure occurs, the operations staff can restore the database from the save and reprocess all transactions.

Unfortunately, this simple strategy is usually infeasible. First, reprocessing transactions takes the same amount of time as processing them in the first place. If the computer is heavily scheduled, the system may never catch up. Second, when transactions are processed concurrently, it is difficult to process them in exactly the same order as their original processing. Slight variations, such as an operator's mounting a tape more quickly, may cause one transaction to get ahead of another. Whereas customer A got the last seat on a flight during the original processing, customer B may get the last seat during reprocessing. For these reasons, reprocessing is seldom a viable form of recovery.

**Recovery via Rollback/Rollforward.**   A second approach is to save the *results* of transactions and, when failure occurs, to recover by first removing invalid changes (*rollback*) and then reapplying valid ones (*rollforward*). DBMS products perform this type of recovery in various ways. We will describe a typical approach. In general, this approach has four steps:

1. Recreate (or do not destroy) the outputs of all completed transactions
2. Abort all transactions in process at the time of the failure
3. Remove database changes generated by aborted transactions
4. Restart aborted transactions

This strategy will accurately recover the database. To be able to undo or redo database changes, a *log* must be kept of transaction results. The log contains a record of data changes in chronological order. Transactions are written to the log before they are applied to the database. If the system crashes between the time a transaction is logged and the time it is applied, then at worst there is a record of an unapplied transaction. If a transaction were applied before it was logged and the system crashed in the meantime, then it would have changed the database, but there would be no record of the change. If this happened, an unwary user might reenter an already completed transaction.

When a failure occurs, the log is used to both undo and redo transactions, as shown in Figure 7–12. To undo a transaction, the log must contain

**Figure 7–12**
Undo and redo trans-
action procedures

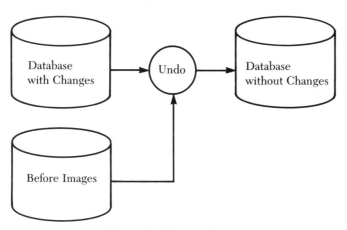

a. Removing database changes

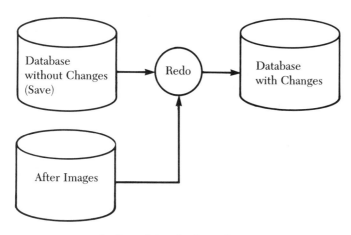

b. Reapplying database changes

a copy of every database record (or block) before it was changed. Such records are called *before images*. A transaction is undone by applying before images of all its changes to the database.

To redo a transaction, the log must contain a copy of every database record (or block) after it was changed. These records are called *after images*. A transaction is redone by applying after images of all its changes to the database. Possible data items of a transaction log are shown in Figure 7–13a.

For this sample log, each transaction has a unique name for identification purposes. Further, all images for a given transaction are linked together

**Figure 7–13**

Transaction log

| | | | |
|---|---|---|---|
| Transaction ID | Type of Operation | | |
| Reverse Pointer | Object | | |
| Forward Pointer | Before Image | | |
| Time | After Image | | |

a. Possible data-items of a log record

Relative
Record
Number

| | Transaction ID | Reverse Pointer | Forward Pointer | Time | Type of Operation | Object | Before Image | After Image |
|---|---|---|---|---|---|---|---|---|
| 1 | OT1 | 0 | 2 | 11:42 | START | | | |
| 2 | OT1 | 1 | 4 | 11:43 | MODIFY | CUST 100 | (old value) | (new value) |
| 3 | OT2 | 0 | 8 | 11:46 | START | | | |
| 4 | OT1 | 2 | 5 | 11:47 | MODIFY | SP AA | (old value) | (new value) |
| 5 | OT1 | 4 | 7 | 11:47 | INSERT | ORDER 11 | | (value) |
| 6 | CT1 | 0 | 9 | 11:48 | START | | | |
| 7 | OT1 | 5 | 0 | 11:49 | COMMIT | | | |
| 8 | OT2 | 3 | 0 | 11:50 | COMMIT | | | |
| 9 | CT1 | 6 | 10 | 11:51 | MODIFY | SP BB | (old value) | (new value) |
| 10 | CT1 | 9 | 0 | 11:51 | COMMIT | | | |

b. Log instance for three transactions

with pointers. One pointer points to the previous transaction-related record in the file (the reverse pointer), and the other points to the next transaction-related record in the file (the forward pointer). A zero in the pointer field indicates the end of the list. The DBMS Recovery Subsystem uses these pointers to rapidly locate all records for a particular transaction. Figure 7–13b shows an example of the linking of log records.

Other data items in the log are the time of the action; the type of operation (START marks the beginning of a transaction and COMMIT terminates a transaction, releasing all locks that were in place); the object acted upon, such as record type and identifier; and, finally, the before and after images.

Given a log with both before and after images, the undo and redo actions are straightforward (to describe, anyway). To undo the transaction in Figure 7–14, the recovery processor simply replaces each changed block with its before image. When all before images have been restored, the transaction is undone.

**Figure 7—14**
Example of recovery
strategy

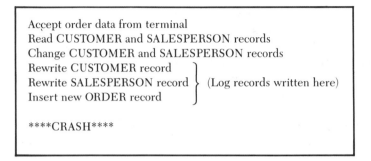

Accept order data from terminal
Read CUSTOMER and SALESPERSON records
Change CUSTOMER and SALESPERSON records
Rewrite CUSTOMER record ⎫
Rewrite SALESPERSON record ⎬ (Log records written here)
Insert new ORDER record ⎭

****CRASH****

a. ORDER transaction

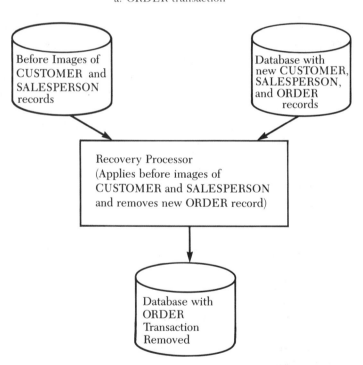

Before Images of CUSTOMER and SALESPERSON records

Database with new CUSTOMER, SALESPERSON, and ORDER records

Recovery Processor
(Applies before images of CUSTOMER and SALESPERSON and removes new ORDER record)

Database with ORDER Transaction Removed

b. Recovery processing to undo an ORDER record

To redo a transaction, the recovery processor starts with the version of the database at the time the transaction started and applies all after images. This action assumes that an earlier version of the database is available from a database save. If it is necessary to restore a database to its most recent save and then reapply all transactions, much processing time may be required. To minimize this problem, DBMS products provide a facility called *checkpoint.*

A checkpoint command provides a point of synchronization between the database and the transaction log. To perform a checkpoint, the DBMS refuses to accept any new requests, finishes processing outstanding requests, and empties its buffers. The DBMS then waits until the operating system notifies it that all outstanding write requests to the database and to the log are complete. At this point, the log and the database are synchronized. A checkpoint record is then written to the log. When the database needs to be recovered, after images only for transactions that started after the check-point need to be applied.

Checkpoints may be inexpensive operations, and it is often feasible to take three or four checkpoints per hour (or more). In this way, no more than fifteen or twenty minutes of processing will need to be recovered. Some DBMS products automatically checkpoint themselves, making human intervention unnecessary.

As you can imagine, the ability to restore the database system to a usable state is critical in most situations. (It might not be so critical in a single-user environment, however. Only one individual is inconvenienced, there is no concurrency, and the system is probably not so heavily scheduled that reprocessing large volumes of work is infeasible.) Although DBMS products include some of the recovery features we have discussed, remember that people play a vital role in backup and recovery. The DBA needs to establish procedures for computer center personnel and users to follow in the event of a system crash.

### Database Security

Now let us examine the third important function of a DBMS in the multi-user environment—the features that prevent unauthorized users from accessing the database.

Companies that develop databases are vulnerable. With a database, company data, which we have seen is a valuable resource, will be central-ized and readily accessible. DBMS products are designed to be easy for the end user to use. Unfortunately, these products are also easy for unauthor-ized users—and criminals—to use. Because they recognize the problem of unauthorized use, most DBMS vendors have incorporated security features into their products. Insofar as possible, these features allow only verifiably authorized users (people or programs) to access the data and can restrict types of processing on the data.

All of the users (and programmers) who are authorized to access a database system do not have complete access to all of the data. In fact, this is seldom the case. Some users have access to more data than other users, and some individuals have more extensive processing rights as well. For example, some users can modify or delete records, but other users cannot. In the database environment, users do not all enjoy the same privileges.

**Figure 7–15**

Sample of authoriza-
tion rules

| Subject | Entity | Action | Authorization Constraint |
|---------|--------|--------|--------------------------|
| PGM OE104J | ORDER Record | Insert | Amount less than $500,000 |
| Sally Smith | ORDER Record | Read | None |
| Payroll Dept | EMPLOYEE Record | Read | Hourly workers |
| Payroll Dept | EMPLOYEE Record | Modify | Hourly workers |
| Payroll Dept | EMPLOYEE Record | Insert | Hourly workers |
| Payroll Supv | EMPLOYEE Record | Delete | Hourly workers |
| Payroll Supv | Read Permission of EMPLOYEE Records | Grant | To payroll personnel |

In *Database Security and Integrity,* Fernandez, Summers, and Wood develop a model of database security. Their model is essentially a table of processing permissions, or *authorization rules.* As shown in Figure 7–15, the table has four columns that represent subjects, entities, actions, and authorization constraints. A row in this table indicates that the named subject has permission to take the indicated action on the listed entity, depending on the stated authorization constraints. Thus, row 1 indicates that the program OE104J is authorized to insert ORDER records as long as the amount of the order is less than $500,000.

Although this model is not used in any DBMS product, it is an effective framework for understanding security capabilities and can aid the DBA in determining processing rights and responsibilities among users.

**Subjects.** A *subject* is any identifiable user that can process the database. Examples of subjects are particular people (Sally Smith), groups of people (everyone in the Payroll Department), people operating in particular roles (a teller executing deposit transactions), application programs, and remote computers.

Determining whether or not someone who claims to be a subject really is that subject can be a problem. People can be identified by fingerprints, voice prints, and passwords, to name a few techniques. Passwords are by far the most commonly used identifiers in a computer environment. Computer equipment is identified by hardware configuration (say, the line connected to port 4) and by the presence or absence of specialized signals. Programs are usually identified by name, position in memory, or specialized protocol.

In the database environment, the subject desiring access to an entity provides his/her/its identifier (name or password, for example). For verification, the DBMS looks up the name of the subject and other data in a table and, if it is found, allows the subject access to the entity.

**Entities.** The second column of the security table in Figure 7–15 lists entities. *Entities,* as used by Fernandez, are the database units to be protected by security. (Actually, Fernandez uses the term *object*, not *entity*. We have substituted *entity* to distinguish it from the term *object* as used in this text.) Examples of entities (using relational terminology) are databases, relations, rows, attributes, views, the DBMS, programs, transactions, knowledge of status (for example, the existence or nonexistence of an attribute), and the like.

The term *granularity* is often used to refer to the size of security entities. A security system that allows access to or prevents access from the entire database as a unit has large granularity. A security system that allows access to or prevents access from a particular attribute has small granularity.

Small-granularity security systems allow close control over data. User access can be limited to the data needed to perform a specific function. On the other hand, security systems with small granularity require more overhead to administer. If a DBMS must check authorization every time a user accesses any attribute of any row, then processing will be slow and expensive.

Choosing the granularity of a security system involves making a trade-off between closely tailored security and processing efficiency. As security increases, efficiency decreases. Although the DBMS enforces the security that is put in place, the DBA is responsible for determining what security is needed in the first place. Once again we see that some aspects of a problem are best handled by the software (in this case, enforcing security), whereas others are best handled by people (in this case, determining processing rights among users).

**Actions.** The *action* column in Figure 7–15 identifies what the subject can do to the entity. Possibilities include reading, inserting, deleting, modifying, creating, destroying, and granting. Although inserting and creating may sound similar, they are actually different. Inserting means adding data to an existing structure, whereas creating means building the structure. Thus a subject can insert a row or create the structure of a table. Similarly, deleting means removing data, whereas destroying means eliminating data and structure.

The *grant* action bestows permission (such as permission to modify data) on another subject. In Figure 7–15 the last row of the table specifies that the payroll supervisor has authority to grant to payroll personnel the permission to read employee records.

Usually the DBA is given sweeping grant authority by the DBMS. When the DBMS is installed, someone needs to be identified to the system as the one to grant authority to all other individuals. This is usually the DBA. Furthermore, some DBMS products automatically assign grant authority to anyone who creates a new table. That individual, in turn, can grant permission to perform actions on the table to whomever he or she chooses. This constitutes ownership of that data.

**Authorization Constraints.** *Authorization constraints* specify limitations on permissions concerning subject, entity, and action. Several examples of authorization constraints are shown in Figure 7–15. For example, the payroll department can process EMPLOYEE records for hourly workers. If this table constituted all the authorization constraints on the database (highly unlikely), then it would be clear that the payroll department could process records *only* for hourly workers—not for supervisory or executive employees.

**Security in DBMS Products.**   No commercial DBMS provides as general a security capability as that shown in Figure 7–15. DBMS products generally offer a subset of capabilities. For example, some systems provide subject-oriented security, some provide entity-oriented security, and some provide a combination of facilities. The DBA needs to augment the DBMS in areas where it is lacking.

*Subject-oriented Security.*   With subject-oriented security, subjects are defined to the DBMS and each subject is allocated permissions. Prior to allowing a subject to perform a database action, the DBMS confirms that the subject has such authority. If the subject does not have permission, then the DBMS disallows the user request. The table in Figure 7–16 illustrates permissions that have been assigned to one user. In this case the subject is a program. The table tells us that all ORDER transactions are authorized to read CUSTOMER, SALESPERSON, and ORDER records. ORDER transactions may insert only ORDER records. They may modify all three types of records. ORDER transactions are not authorized to delete any data, nor can they grant any rights to other subjects.

*Entity-oriented Security.*   Another approach to security defines authorizations from the standpoint of database entities. In this case, each entity has

**Figure 7–16**

Subject-oriented security example: permissions granted to program processing ORDER transactions

|  |  | Entities | | |
|---|---|---|---|---|
|  |  | CUSTOMER Records | SALESPERSON Records | ORDER Records |
| Actions | Read | Y | Y | Y |
|  | Insert | N | N | Y |
|  | Modify | Y | Y | Y |
|  | Delete | N | N | N |
|  | Grant | N | N | N |

**Figure 7–17**

Entity-oriented
security example:
permissions granted
for SALESPERSON
records

Entity: SALESPERSON Record

|  |  | Subjects Who Know Password SESAME | Subjects Who Know Password ABALONE |
|---|---|---|---|
| Actions | Read | Y | Y |
|  | Insert | Y | N |
|  | Modify | Y | N |
|  | Delete | Y | N |
|  | Grant | N | N |

an authorization matrix. The matrix shows what actions can be taken by various subjects on that entity. Most often the subjects are defined by passwords. For example, in Figure 7–17, subjects who can provide the password SESAME can read, insert, modify, and delete SALESPERSON records. People who supply the password ABALONE can read SALESPERSON records but take no other action.

*Combination of Subject- and Entity-oriented Security.*   Some DBMS products provide both subject- and entity-oriented security. In this case, both subjects and entities have authorization matrices.

**Constraints via User Exits.**   Constraints on authorization rules are not generally supported by DBMS products. However, some DBMS products have an indirect way of enforcing authorization constraints. These DBMS products will exit to (call) user-written routines whenever a specified action is performed on a specified entity. The routine can then provide the logic to enforce the constraint. It should be noted that end users do not generally write such routines. They are usually developed by professional programmers.

For example, suppose no order in excess of $50,000 is to be accepted after 3:00 P.M. on a Friday or a day before a holiday. Instead, such orders are to be referred to a supervisor. In this case, the database designer specifies that whenever an ORDER record is created, a special routine is to be called. This routine will determine if the specified conditions are true. If so, the routine will disallow the insert and send a message to a supervisor.

User exits provide a great deal of flexibility. They can be employed to supplement the capabilities of a DBMS or to compensate for its deficiencies. In addition to flexibility, they offer increased control and security. But exits to user-written routines have disadvantages as well. For instance, the user organization must develop and test these routines. Such routines also add overhead to the system. And they may need to be dynamically loaded (copied into computer memory from disk storage each time they are needed) and therefore diminish system performance.

In terms of security, then, a DBMS includes facilities for identifying subjects and allowing them to access the database, for restricting the actions subjects can perform, for restricting the entities that a subject can access, and for allowing user-developed routines to be incorporated into normal processing. Thus, the *operation* of a security system is one function of the DBMS. However, as described earlier, the *administration* of a security system is a database administration function.

## SUMMARY

Database processing in the multi-user environment presents some challenges to designers of DBMS products and to the people who use those products to manage databases. Because many users share the same resources, provision must be made to resolve conflicts and to prevent one user from interfering with another's processing. Some of these problems are handled by the office of database administration and others are addressed by the DBMS.

The database administrator (DBA) is essential for success in a multi-user environment. Without a DBA, the database will be inadequately maintained and conflicting user goals will eventually lead to chaos. For all but the smallest databases the DBA responsibilities are too large for one individual, so a DBA staff must be created. Generally, technological problems are addressed by the DBMS, while human problems are addressed by the DBA.

The DBA interacts with users, data processing staff, and upper management. DBA responsibilities include management of database activity, database configuration control, development and maintenance of database applications, and management of database resources. The DBA must represent the interests of the company and avoid seeming to favor any one user group. The DBA must also be a good communicator and a skillful diplomat, especially when dealing with diverse user groups.

Finally, the DBA must have clearly established goals and well-defined authority. And the DBA must rank high enough in the organization to exercise that authority.

The database management system includes features that are essential in a multi-user environment. Although the primary functions of a DBMS are to store, retrieve, and modify data, other tasks include controlling concurrent processing, providing backup and recovery ability, and ensuring a level of database security.

Concurrent updates can be a problem if two users attempt to modify the same record at once. When this happens, anomalies can occur in the database. DBMS products solve this problem by applying locks on resources whenever the data might be changed. Locks prevent other users from accessing a record until the transaction is completed and the lock is released.

Concurrent processing can also be a problem if two users each lock resources the other one needs. The DBMS can resolve this situation, called deadlock, by terminating one of the transactions and undoing any changes it made to the database.

In the event of a system failure, the database must be restored to a usable state as quickly as possible. Any transactions in progress at the time of the crash must be reapplied, and any processing that was done manually while the system was down must be entered. Recovery can be accomplished by straightforward reprocessing or by rollback/rollforward. The latter strategy is almost always preferred. Transaction logs must be maintained in order to ensure that all lost work is reapplied. Checkpoints can be taken more frequently than database saves. Although they require some overhead, checkpoints minimize the amount of reprocessing that needs to be done in the event of a failure.

Database security means allowing only authorized subjects to perform authorized actions on specified entities, subject to any managerial constraints. Once established by the DBA, many of these access and processing rights are enforced by the DBMS. Constraints that are not enforced by the DBMS can be enforced by user-written subroutines.

---

**GROUP I**                QUESTIONS

**7.1**   Define *multi-user database*.

**7.2**   Describe a situation (other than the ones in the text) in which the goals in different user departments conflict with one another.

**7.3**   How is the database administrator analogous to the company controller?

**7.4**   Summarize the job responsibilities of the DBA.

**7.5**   What types of problems in the multi-user database environment does the DBA handle that cannot be adequately addressed by the DBMS?

**7.6**   Summarize the DBA's responsibilities for management of data activity.

**7.7**   Why is the DBA authorized to assign processing rights and responsibilities to users? Who grants that authority to the DBA?

**7.8**   Describe two situations in which database system documentation plays a major role.

**7.9**   List six positions found in a typical DBA office. Briefly describe the responsibilities of each.

**7.10**  Define *transaction*.

**7.11**  What does interleaving mean?

**7.12**  Is concurrent processing always a problem?

**7.13**  Describe the concurrent update problem.

**7.14**  What is the two-phase locking strategy and how can it be used to prevent the concurrent update problem?

**7.15**  What is deadlock?

**7.16** Describe two ways in which a DBMS can handle deadlock.

**7.17** Explain how a database can be recovered by reprocessing. Why is database recovery by reprocessing usually not feasible?

**7.18** Define *rollback* and *rollforward*.

**7.19** What are four steps for recovering a database via rollback/rollforward? What is the DBMS's role in each of these steps?

**7.20** Define *before image* and *after image*.

**7.21** Why is it usually advantageous to take frequent checkpoints of a database?

**7.22** Define *subject, entity, action,* and *authorization constraint* as they apply to database security.

**7.23** How does a DBMS implement subject-oriented security?

**7.24** How does a DBMS implement entity-oriented security?

**7.25** Explain how user exits can provide security.

---

## QUESTIONS AND EXERCISES                                **GROUP II**

**7.26** Explain this statement: A data dictionary is a database about a database.

**7.27** Interview the DBA of a local company. Determine whether a data dictionary system is in use. Is it integrated with the DBMS? If so, what are the advantages and disadvantages? If not, ask why they chose that type of data dictionary. Find out if the dictionary system is active or passive. Why was that type of data dictionary chosen?

**7.28** Interview the manager of a local small business that uses a microcomputer DBMS. Is there a DBA? If not, determine who in the company performs each of the DBA's functions. Also determine if any of the DBA's functions are not being performed. Why are they not being performed? Find out what support the DBA (or people performing the DBA's functions) receive from the DBMS (for example, run-time statistics or a data dictionary).

## CHAPTER

# 8

# Designing Database Applications

- Functions of a Database Application
- Materializing Object Views
- Application Design
- Form Design
- Report Design
- Processing Updates
- Summary

In this chapter you will learn how to design online database applications. A database can be accessed in either batch or online mode. Batch applications consist of programs that are scheduled and run by the computer operations staff. They are often written in a programming language such as COBOL or PL/I, and they closely resemble file processing programs, often processing large parts of the database at a time. They differ from file processing programs in that they call the DBMS for database I/O services. Consider, for example, a state department of motor vehicles that maintains a database of registered drivers. A batch application might be run on the last day of each month to produce renewal notices for all operators whose licenses will expire during the following month.

In contrast, a database also can be accessed *online*. Online database applications are usually run by end users. This means that the processing to be done on the database is unpredictable. For example, a bank teller (an end user) is likely to process savings account and checking account deposits and withdrawals (four distinct processes), but it is unreasonable to schedule each type of processing for a certain time of day because all are needed throughout the day. Online applications, then, require that *all* of the functions the user might need to invoke are available at all times. In this chapter you will learn how to design online database applications. You will also learn how to structure an online application so each user is able to invoke appropriate functions but can access only the data he or she needs. In addition, you will learn to design the menus, forms, and reports with which the user interfaces.

We begin by describing the purposes of a database application and then discussing the role that applications play in constructing user objects from stored data. In the next section we examine overall application design. After that we discuss the design of forms and reports, especially with respect to constructing user objects. Finally, we examine some special concerns for processing updates to database data.

This chapter provides a solid foundation in database *application design*. The concepts you learn here will be used throughout the three remaining parts of this text, which focus on the *implementation* of database applications.

## FUNCTIONS OF A DATABASE APPLICATION

An application is the user's interface with the database. Ideally, an application provides an easy-to-use interface for authorized users to make authorized requests with valid and accurate data. Ideally, an application provides informative and helpful error messages to authorized users who make unauthorized requests or mistakes, or who attempt to enter invalid data. Ideally, an application prevents unauthorized users from accessing the database. Although it often happens that these ideals cannot be fully realized in actual applications—due to limitations in DBMS products, time and budget restrictions, knowledge or abilities of the developers, or other constraints—we should try to design applications with those characteristics.

How close we come to developing *perfect* applications depends on the resources at our disposal. However, even if some of the ideals must be compromised, we still must develop *usable* applications. To be usable, a database application must serve three functions:

**1.** It prints, queries, and updates objects
**2.** It allows the user to direct and control the processing of the application
**3.** It maintains the security and integrity of the database at all times

Let us consider each of them.

### Print, Query, and Update Objects

The first function of a database application is to *print, query, and update objects*. Recall from Chapter 6 that *objects* are not stored in the database. Objects are representations of things in the user's work environment. To date, no DBMS product actually stores objects. Instead, database designers transform objects into *relations* (or sets of relations). Consequently, when a user enters a query about an object, the application must *construct* the object from data in one or several relations. For example, if a user were to enter a query about an invoice, the application, before responding to the user's request, must first construct the invoice from data in, say, two relations:

one that holds identifying data and totals for the invoice and another that contains repeating line items for the invoice. Sometimes this process is called *materializing objects*.

Printing and querying objects are easy to understand. Let's say that a user needs to see a particular invoice displayed on the computer screen. Upon receiving the query, the application constructs the object from relations and their relationships and displays it in a format that is meaningful to the user. Of course, this means that the application must have access to a predefined format for displaying the invoice, called a *form*. The form includes constants, such as screen title and column headers. It also specifies the locations of data to be displayed and the editing of the fields (such as zero suppression).

Printing usually means producing a written report, although reports can be displayed on computer screens or sent to files for later processing (for instance, copying onto microfiche).

The difficulty in developing the user interface is that users perceive their environment—and, consequently, the data stored about things in their environment—in terms of objects, but most DBMS products to date do not directly support objects. Thus, database languages manipulate relations (or files) in order to build objects. This means that in order to access a database, either (1) users must learn the database language (and at the same time learn how to navigate among relations to construct objects), or (2) someone besides the user must write applications that contain all of the behind-the-scenes object construction and that users simply activate.

In Chapter 9 you will learn the database language SQL. And you will see that for printing or querying simple objects, SQL is a relatively easy language to master, even for inexperienced users. However, for more complex requests—ones that construct objects from several relations and relationships—it is far more likely that a professional will develop an application. Then the user simply activates the application, processing forms and reports.

Updating objects is often a more complex task than printing and querying objects. When a user updates an object (inserts, modifies, or deletes one), all constraints must be enforced. For example, suppose there is a constraint that a new invoice must contain a valid customer account number. Before allowing the new invoice to be stored, some program must verify that it contains a valid customer account number. As stated in the last chapter, although the DBMS *should* enforce such constraints, in practice few do. It often falls on the *application program* to enforce domain, intra-relation, and inter-relation constraints. This means that, for example, during the processing of a transaction that adds new invoices to the database, there would need to be an exit to a programmer-written subroutine to compare the customer account number on the new invoice to the ones already stored in the database, and to reject the transaction if a matching number were not found.

Additionally, if the database is concurrently processed, updating must be controlled so that the actions of one user do not interfere with those of another. Finally, update processing must be structured so that the database can be recovered in the event of failure.

### Enable User Direction

The second characteristic of a database application is that it *allows the user to direct and control the application*. An application may include dozens of features that the user can invoke. The application must be designed so it is easy for the user to conclude (or suspend) one feature and initiate another one. Two methods are used for giving the user control over the application: *database commands* and *menus*. This is an example of a database command:

```
UPDATE CUSTOMER OBJECT WHERE Cust-num = 12345 SET Limit = 1000
```

The advantage of command-driven applications is that they are direct and to the point. The user can quickly enter a command and process the database. He or she need not fuss with menus or other structures. The disadvantage is that the user must learn and remember the commands and their syntax. The user might also need to learn how to construct objects out of relations and relationships. Command-driven applications are used in situations where a small set of commands is used frequently. Bank teller transaction processing and airline reservations are appropriate command-driven applications.

The second method for giving the user control over an application is the use of *menus*. A menu is a list of options from which the user can choose. When the user selects one option from a menu, one of two things usually happens: either another menu is presented that offers several options related to the item selected from the previous menu or an application feature is activated. Thus, menus allow users to decide which database application features they want to employ. (Menus can also be used to *control* access to application features. You will learn about designing menus and menu hierarchies later in this chapter.)

The advantage of menus is that the user does not need to memorize commands or even remember which commands are appropriate in a given context. The application guides the user by offering only appropriate options at each level. The disadvantage of menu-driven applications is that they are cumbersome for frequent operations. For this reason, it is not unusual for an application to incorporate both command-driven and menu-driven techniques, which enables the user to choose the approach appropriate for his or her skill level and familiarity with the application. Both techniques enable the user to direct application processing.

### Maintain the Security and Integrity of the Database

The third function of a database application is to *maintain at all times the security and integrity of the database*. This means that an application should allow only authorized users to perform only authorized activities using only valid data. This is far easier to state as a goal than it is to accomplish in practice. And yet, however difficult it may be to accomplish, this goal must be foremost in the minds of application developers. A company's database is too valuable an asset to allow security measures to lapse. Security and integrity protection must be designed into the application from the start.

The possibilities for security and integrity problems are endless. Users make keystroke errors, and the data they enter is sometimes incorrect. Users also try to perform operations out of sequence or to perform invalid operations. They also attempt to perform operations for which they are not authorized. An application must prevent as many unauthorized activities as possible, it must protect the database from invalid data, and it must ensure the integrity of the stored data.

Application developers employ several techniques for protecting the database. For example, passwords can be assigned to users and an authorization table like the one described in Chapter 7 can be established and enforced. Some invalid input data can be screened out by carefully designing forms. For example, if the data in a field should be no more than five characters long, the data entry screen can be designed so that no more than five characters can be entered. The application developer can take advantage of whatever DBMS features enforce integrity constraints and then augment them with external subroutines. And as mentioned earlier, menus can be designed so that, for instance, only commands appropriate to a given context can be executed in that context. This helps control activities performed on the database.

Maintaining the security and integrity of the database requires creativity. The important thing to remember is that these problems must be taken into account *during application design.* It is both dangerous and costly to wait until problems occur and then try to fix the application.

The functions of a database application are summarized in Figure 8–1.

## MATERIALIZING OBJECT VIEWS

In order to perform the three key functions, a database application must *materialize object views.* To understand this task and the challenges it presents to application developers, you need to recall how databases are designed.

**Figure 8–1**

Functions of a database application

- Print, query, and update objects
- Provide mechanisms for user to direct action
- Maintain security and integrity of database

## Object Views

First, the database designer combines various user views of an object into a composite picture of the object. Consider, for example, the SOFTWARE-PKG object at the Eastcoast State University Computer Lab. A lab attendant might say that the properties of SOFTWARE-PKG are Name, Serial-number, Hardware-requirements, and Memory-requirements. At the same time, the director of the lab might say that the properties of SOFTWARE-PKG that are important to her are Name, Serial-number, Vendor, Cost, Installation-date, and Service-contract-number. These two people have not described different objects—they have simply described their *views* of the same object. The database designer combines the object views into a single object description, listing all the properties that everyone has mentioned. Thus, the database designer constructs an object from various object views.

Following that, the database designer transforms the object descriptions into a set of relations and relationships. (You learned how to do this in Chapter 6.) The output from this step is the logical database design—a description of relations, relationships, and constraints. At this point the fundamental structure for the database has been established and the database can be implemented.

Now that the data is stored in relations (or files), users begin to access it. They query it, add and delete data, and update existing data. Only users do not (at least knowingly) process relations; they still perceive their environment (and consequently the data stored about it) in terms of objects. Thus, when a lab attendant requests data about a software package, she expects to see Name, Serial-number, Hardware-requirements, and Memory-requirements—those attributes that in her mind define a software package. Even though, say, Cost and Installation-date are also to be stored in the SOFTWARE-PKG relation, the lab attendant does not include them in her perception of a software package. Consequently, the application should not make those details accessible to the lab attendant. It should present only the data that "belongs" to her.

Although we have been saying generally that an application constructs objects from stored data, in fact, an application constructs *object views* from the stored data. An object view is simply a subset of an object used by a particular user or group of users. As such, an object view is constructed from a subset of the attributes of all the relations that make up the underlying object.

## Materialization

An application interface, such as a data entry form or a report, is the *materialization* of an object view. An object view is the user's perception of data, whereas a materialization of an object view is the physical presentation of the data in a format the user can understand. As we mentioned earlier, a screen or a report usually contains more than just data. A screen form, for example, includes, in addition to the data, borders, the current date and

**Figure 8–2**
Lab attendant's view
of APPOINTMENT
object

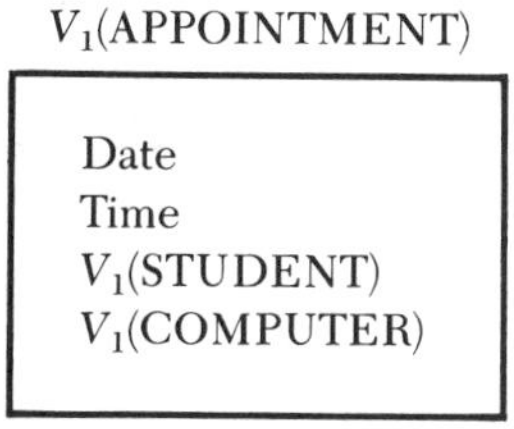

$V_1$(APPOINTMENT)

```
Date
Time
V₁(STUDENT)
V₁(COMPUTER)
```

time, and masks for numeric editing. A form (or a report), then, materializes a view of an object. It includes data the user expects to find in a format that makes the presentation of the data meaningful.

For example, consider the application at the Eastcoast State University Computer Lab. The lab attendant's view of APPOINTMENT includes Date, Time, STUDENT, and COMPUTER. (Other users' views of APPOINTMENT might be different.) We can illustrate this view with a diagram that looks like an object diagram, as shown in Figure 8–2. We call this view $V_1$(APPOINTMENT). Other views would be numbered $V_2$(APPOINTMENT), $V_3$(APPOINTMENT), and so forth.

It appears that the lab attendant's view of APPOINTMENT includes some details about students and computers, which we know from earlier discussion of this case are also objects. Actually, though, the lab attendant's view of APPOINTMENT contains as properties the lab attendant's *views* of STUDENT and COMPUTER. For example, to a lab attendant, STUDENT includes only Student-ID and Name. Other users' views of STUDENT might include the classes in which he is enrolled, the total amount of time he has spent in the lab, and his grade point average in computer-related courses. Thus, the diagram in Figure 8–2 shows $V_1$(APPOINTMENT) containing $V_1$(STUDENT) and $V_1$(COMPUTER).

This view of APPOINTMENT can be materialized in many ways. For example, the data entry form used to enter or change an appointment appears in Figure 8–3a. This form contains data in the lab attendant's view. It also contains fixed text and other items that make the form meaningful and useful.

A second materialization of $V_1$(APPOINTMENT) is shown in Figure 8–3b. This materialization is a summary report of appointments scheduled for a particular day (in this case, only those for May 2, 1989). Although the format of this report is different from that of the data entry form, it is a materialization of the same object view, namely $V_1$(APPOINTMENT). Thus, each form or report on which data from an object view appears is a materialization of that object view.

**Figure 8–3**
Materialization of V₁
(APPOINTMENT)

```
┌──────────────────────────────────────────────────┐
│              APPOINTMENT FORM                      │
│                                                    │
│   Date: ┌──────┐        Time: ┌─────────┐          │
│         │ /  / │              │         │          │
│         └──────┘              └─────────┘          │
│                                                    │
│   Student-ID: ┌─────────┐                          │
│               │         │                          │
│               └─────────┘                          │
│                                                    │
│   Computer-number: ┌─────────┐                     │
│                    │         │                     │
│                    └─────────┘                     │
│                                                    │
│                                                    │
│   Press S to save, D to delete: ┌──────┐           │
│                                 │      │           │
│                                 └──────┘           │
└──────────────────────────────────────────────────┘
```

a. Data entry form

COMPUTER LAB SCHEDULE FOR TUESDAY, MAY 02, 1989

8:00 - 8:30 am

| Unit | Student | Unit | Student |
|------|---------|------|---------|
| 162  | 490     | 167  | -       |
| 163  | 262     | 168  | -       |
| 164  | -       | 169  | -       |
| 165  | 117     | 170  | 560     |
| 166  | 344     | 171  | 241     |

8:31 - 9:00 am

| Unit | Student | Unit | Student |
|------|---------|------|---------|
| 162  | -       | 167  | -       |
| 163  | 304     | 168  | -       |
| 164  | -       | 169  | -       |
| 165  | 411     | 170  | 560     |
| 166  | 241     | 171  | -       |

b. SCHEDULED APPOINTMENTS report

To summarize, an object view is one user's perception of an object. It is a subset of the properties (maybe all of them) of the underlying object. A materialization of an object view is the presentation of the data with which a user interacts. It consists of the data in the object view plus a presentation format (including, for example, appropriate fixed text, borders, and other graphics) and constraints on data values (such as printing appointments only for May 2).

## The Role of Applications in Object Materialization

As we stated earlier, one of the tasks of an application is to materialize objects (or, more specifically, object views). This means that an application extracts the appropriate data from the database (that is, it constructs the object) and presents it in some predefined format (that is, it materializes it). If the application merely needs to display the data on a form or report, then materializing the object is the bulk of the work for the application developer. In order to accomplish this, the developer must know what data is available in this user's view (information that might be stored in the DBA's authorization table, as shown in Figure 7–15), how to construct this view from the underlying relations and relationships, and what the format of the materialization is.

However, if the application includes updates to stored data (such as adding, deleting, or modifying data), then the application also must enforce all domain constraints, intra-relation constraints, and inter-relation constraints. The materialization mechanism (such as a data entry form) must be designed to take advantage of whatever DBMS features enforce constraints, and it must be augmented with other subroutines to enforce constraints not handled by the DBMS product. In other words, the application must ensure that the structure of the *underlying object* is not violated by data changes. This is more difficult than simply materializing objects.

# APPLICATION DESIGN

Database applications may be designed in many ways. The subject has been extensively discussed in the literature. In this section, we will present an overview of an *object-oriented* method of application design. Keep in mind that we are concentrating on online user-oriented database applications. The approach taken for batch programming applications employs traditional program design methodology.

Online applications are unique in that they are user-directed, the specific features the user needs to employ are unpredictable, and only two common types of user interfaces are available, namely forms displayed on the computer screen and reports. The object-oriented approach to application design consists of four steps. They are summarized in Figure 8–4. Let's consider each of these steps.

## Step 1: Determine Applications and Scope

The first step is to determine the number of applications and the scope of each one. As described in Chapter 4, application processing will often fall naturally into groups. Because an application is the system that satisfies the needs of a particular user (or user group), we commonly include in an application all of the features appropriate for a user. In a library, for example, some users acquire books and other materials, some place materials on reserve, and others circulate books and materials by checking them in and

**Figure 8—4**

Summary of database
application design
process

---

1. Determine number of applications and application
   scope
2. For each application, design control mechanisms
   the user will employ to direct the application
3. For each menu, determine list of options
4. For each command and menu option
   a. Specify logic
   b. Design materializations
   c. Confirm that database security and integrity
      have been maintained

---

out. In this case, three applications would probably be appropriate to match
the three distinct user groups.

The scope of an application may be specified in many ways. One way
is to identify the object views the application processes as well as the actions
the user may take on the underlying objects. This work would already have
been completed during requirements definition when establishing users'
processing rights and responsibilities. Of course, for a single-user application (such as a microcomputer database system), the user's view is all-
encompassing and no processing restrictions exist. As you learned in Chapter 7, identifying and assigning processing rights is far more complex in a
multi-user database environment.

### Application Development at Eastcoast State University

For the remainder of this section, we will return to the Eastcoast State
University Computer Lab to illustrate the development of a database application. To review, this case concerns the scheduling and usage reporting of
microcomputer hardware and software for a university computer lab. The
lab contains twenty-five microcomputers of assorted capacities with various
peripherals and installed software. Additionally, some special-purpose software is available to students.

Students enrolled only in certain classes are allowed to use the lab.
Equipment is scheduled by appointment. When a student requests an
appointment, a lab attendant (a student worker) determines available times
on machines that meet the student's processing needs. The attendant then
enters student and appointment data into an appointment form displayed

on the computer screen. The student's name, ID, and class data are verified by the application that processes this form.

The Information Systems Department believed the lab was overscheduled and wanted the university to purchase more computer equipment, but it needed data to support that claim. In addition to developing database applications to schedule equipment, Samantha Green developed an application to generate reports documenting the lab's utilization.

The five objects involved in the lab's database are sketched in Figure 8–5 and the design of the database that supports these applications is shown

**Figure 8–5**

Objects processed by the Eastcoast State University Computer Lab

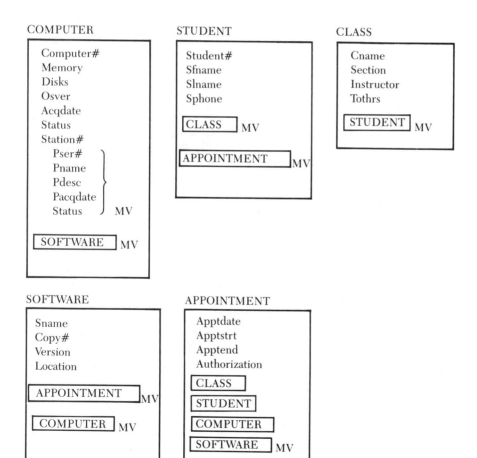

COMPUTER

- Computer#
- Memory
- Disks
- Osver
- Acqdate
- Status
- Station#
  - Pser#
  - Pname
  - Pdesc
  - Pacqdate
  - Status  MV
- SOFTWARE  MV

STUDENT

- Student#
- Sfname
- Slname
- Sphone
- CLASS  MV
- APPOINTMENT  MV

CLASS

- Cname
- Section
- Instructor
- Tothrs
- STUDENT  MV

SOFTWARE

- Sname
- Copy#
- Version
- Location
- APPOINTMENT  MV
- COMPUTER  MV

APPOINTMENT

- Apptdate
- Apptstrt
- Apptend
- Authorization
- CLASS
- STUDENT
- COMPUTER
- SOFTWARE  MV

**Figure 8–6**

Database design for
the ESU Computer
Lab's database

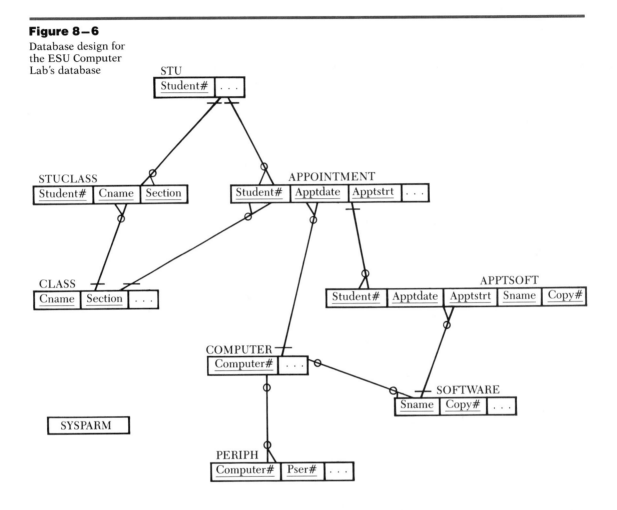

in Figure 8–6. There is a relation named for each object (STU, CLASS, COMPUTER, APPOINTMENT, and SOFTWARE). Two intersection relations (STUCLASS and APPTSOFT) represent the many-to-many compound relationships between students and classes and between software packages and appointments. The PERIPH relation stores the repeating composite data about peripheral equipment attached to each computer. And SYSPARM is a table that contains system parameters, such as the semester name and the names of lab attendants.

### Applications and Scope for the Lab Database

Objects for this application fall into three groups: those involved with resources (COMPUTER and SOFTWARE), those involved with students (STUDENT and CLASS), and the one needed for scheduling (APPOINT-

MENT). Thus, one possible alternative is to develop three database applications, one for each of these groups.

Although it would be feasible to have three applications, this approach seemed overly complicated for the lab. Recall that this is a single-user, single-micro application. All applications will be run from the same computer. It is neither possible nor necessary to segregate certain applications to certain computers. Further, all the lab attendants have the same processing privileges. In addition, because they are information systems majors, the lab attendants are sophisticated users. Thus, in this situation one application is probably more appropriate than three separate applications. In certain circumstances multiple applications might be preferable. For example, if multiple computers were being used, or if certain attendants had more processing privileges than others, or if the databases were used by additional user groups for purposes other than the ones described, then multiple applications might be necessary.

## Step 2: Design Control Mechanisms

As shown in Figure 8–4, the second step in designing an application is to determine the application control mechanisms. This means deciding whether the application is to be menu-driven, command-driven, or some combination of the two. Samantha decided to develop a menu-driven application. She arrived at this conclusion because menus are largely self-explanatory and are therefore easier to use than commands. Although menu processing is often slower than command processing, Samantha did not perceive this as a problem. Her decision was based largely on these facts:

1. Many student attendants work in the lab
2. New attendants are added to the staff several times each semester
3. The time needed to formally train attendants is rarely available
4. No pressing need for extremely fast data input exists

## Step 3: Determine Options for each Menu

Figure 8–7a shows options for the main menu and two other related menus. Figure 8–7b shows the structure, or hierarchy, of the main menu and some of the submenus.

The two primary strategies in structuring menu hierarchy are *object/action* and *action/object*. With the object/action strategy, the highest-level menu (the main menu) lists various objects that can be processed. When the user selects an object, lower-level menus lead him or her to select an action to be performed on that object. The menus in Figure 8–7 are object/action menus. Action/object menus, on the other hand, begin with a list of actions. One option might be ADD NEW DATA. After choosing an action, the user is led by lower-level menus to pick an object on which to perform the action.

In general, the object/action menus are closer to the user's perspective than are action/object menus. When people start a task, for example, they

**Figure 8—7**

Sample menus at the
ESU Computer Lab

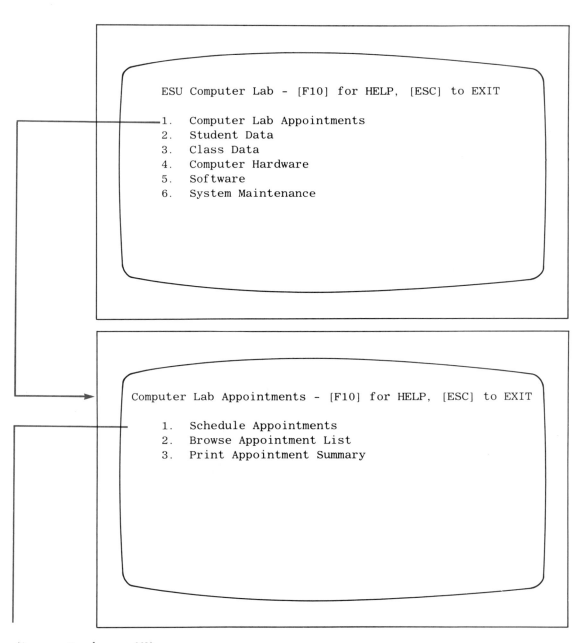

*(Arrow continued on page 269)*

**Figure 8–7**
*(continued)*

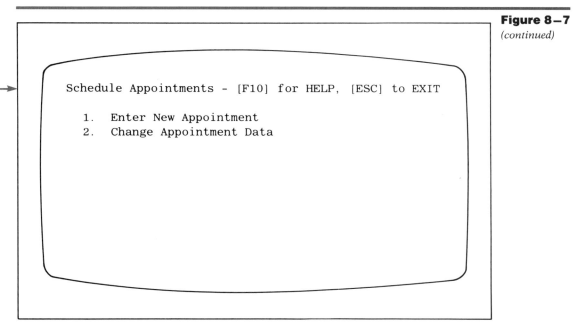

a. Appointment menus for the ESU Computer Lab's application

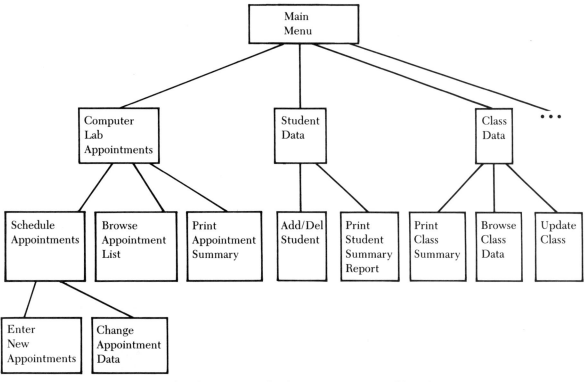

b. Hierarchy of some menus for the ESU Computer Lab's application

are more likely to think to themselves, "Now I'll process order documents. What do I want to do with them?" than they are to think, "Now I'll load some data. What data should I load?"

To illustrate the application design process, we will consider one path that might be taken if the user selects from the main menu the first option, Computer Lab Appointments (see Figure 8–7a). During the requirements phase of the project, Samantha learned that lab attendants needed to perform three appointment-related actions: schedule (or change) an appointment, browse appointments (examine them without changing them), or print an appointment summary report. Consequently, she designed a second-level menu that presents these three options.

Let's say the user selects Schedule Appointments from the second menu. The application displays a third-level menu that presents two options: Enter New Appointment and Change Appointment Data. Other paths through the menus are processed similarly. At each step, the user selects the processing options, thereby controlling the application.

Before continuing, review this application in the context of Figure 8–4. A single application is being developed for the lab. An object/action hierarchy of menus has been designed to enable users to control the application. We have considered one path through several menu levels and have reached the end of this path—that is, we have arrived at an option that does not chain to a lower-level menu. (We will forego a description of every path.) According to the application design process summarized in Figure 8–4, the next step is to specify the processing logic for this option, design materializations, and check that database security and integrity have been maintained.

### Step 4: Specify Logic, Design Materializations, Check Integrity

In some cases, the logic for an option is trivial. For instance, printing a report requires only one command, PRINT. But in other cases the logic is more complicated. For example, the logic for the option to Enter New Appointment is shown in Figure 8–8.

Two materializations need to be designed for this choice. One displays available appointments. The other is used to obtain data from the user and to display data retrieved from the database. Essentially, this computer lab appointment form is used to schedule an appointment. It is shown in Figure 8–9. To use this form, the lab attendant first enters the student ID. The application looks up the student name in the database and displays it, thereby validating the student ID. Next the attendant enters the class data (class name, section) and the application verifies that the student is enrolled in that course. Then the attendant enters the appointment date, time, and station assigned, and the application verifies the availability of the equipment at that time. If the appointment is valid, then APPOINTMENT data

**Figure 8-8**

Logic for entering a
new Appointment

```
Obtain appointment date
Display available appointments
Display LAB APPOINTMENT Form
Obtain Student#
Lookup student
Obtain Cname and Section
Validate enrollment in CLASS
Obtain appointment Apptdate, Apptstrt, Station
Verify availability
Store APPOINTMENT
Until ESC is entered
        Obtain Sname
        Lookup Sname
        Lookup Copy#
        Store APPTSOFT
```

is stored in the database. Finally, the attendant enters the names of any nonstandard software packages the student plans to use.

The last task in step 4 is to check the logic to ensure that the integrity of the database is protected. The logic of each processing option must enforce all inter-relation constraints. For the Enter New Appointment option, the program adds to the database APPOINTMENT and APPTSOFT data and makes no other changes. According to Figure 8-6, APPOINTMENT data must have STU, CLASS, and COMPUTER parents (APPTSOFT is optional). When you examine the logic in Figure 8-8, you will see that these three constraints will have been validated before an APPOINTMENT is stored.

Similarly, APPTSOFT must have APPOINTMENT and SOFTWARE parents. The APPOINTMENT data has just been stored, so the application need only verify the presence of the SOFTWARE data. This is done by looking up the software name in the database. Thus, this menu option will leave all inter-relation constraints intact. Samantha followed the same process for every processing option in the set of menus.

This discussion has illustrated the process described in Figure 8-4. Step 4 would need to be repeated until all actions of all options in the set of menus have been specified. If the application were command-oriented, then step 3 (having to do with menu design) would be omitted. For each command, the developer would need to perform step 4—that is, specify the logic, design materializations, and check database integrity.

**Figure 8–9**

Data entry form used to schedule lab appointments

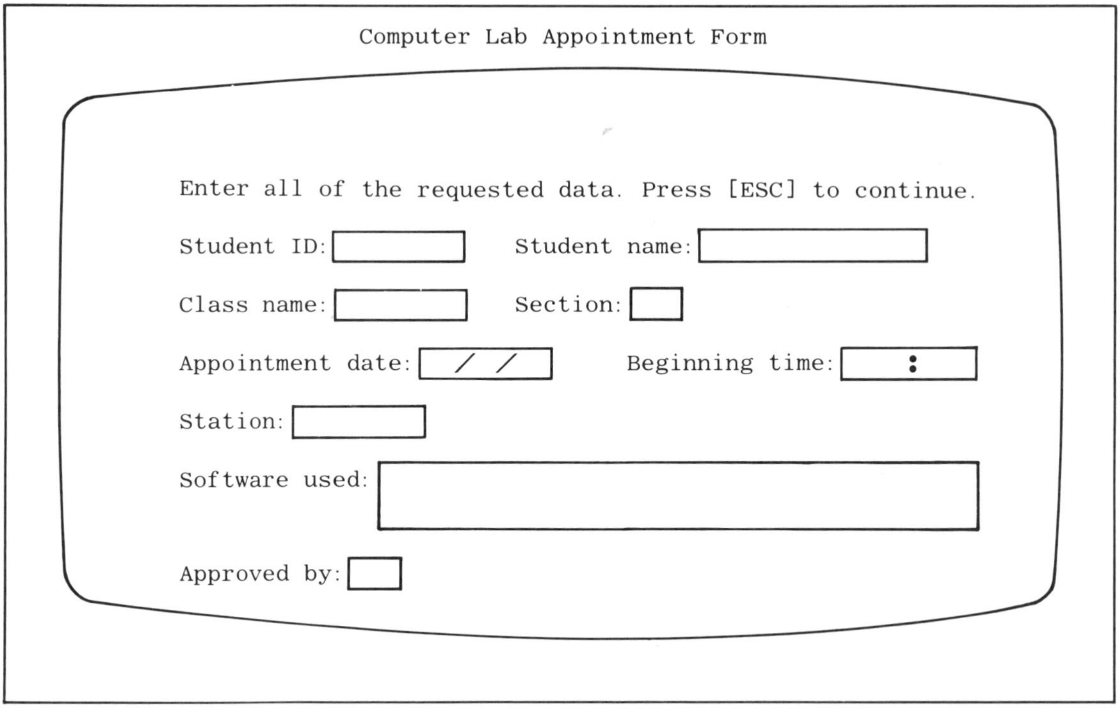

```
                    Computer Lab Appointment Form




        Enter all of the requested data. Press [ESC] to continue.

        Student ID:[        ]    Student name:[              ]

        Class name:[        ]    Section:[  ]

        Appointment date:[ / / ]    Beginning time:[   :   ]

        Station:[          ]

        Software used:[                                    ]


        Approved by:[  ]
```

## FORM DESIGN

Forms (or *screens*, or *panels*, as they are sometimes called) are the online user's primary interface with the database application. Forms are used for entering data, displaying data retrieved from the database, and updating stored data. Careful form design is critical.

Not all forms are equally useful. Some seem natural, are easy to use, and prevent data entry errors. Others seem awkward and contrived, are difficult to use, and allow the user to make errors. In this section we will discuss and illustrate several principles of form design. This is a subtopic of the general subject of user interfaces.

### Form Structure

First, to be natural and easy to use, *a form must reflect the structure of the object that it materializes.* Consider the ORDER object in Figure 8–10a. An order is sold by a SALESPERSON and placed by a CUSTOMER. The ORDER has its own data, such as Order# and Order-date. Each ORDER also includes

**Figure 8–10**
Example ORDER
object

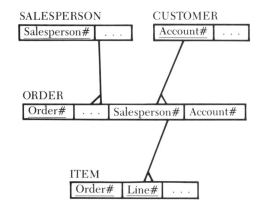

a. Object diagram for ORDER     b. Relations to represent the ORDER object

data about one or more ITEMs. The ORDER relation is the *entry point relation* of the object (see Figure 8–10b). This means that in order to materialize an order, the application begins with the ORDER relation. Given a specific order, the application then uses values of keys (such as the foreign key Salesperson#) to retrieve associated data from other relations.

You can determine which relation is the object entry point because the name of the object and the key (or at least a candidate key) of the entry point relation are the same. In this example, Order# is both the name of the ORDER object and the key of the relation ORDER.

A form that materializes ORDER should reflect the structure in Figure 8–10b. The general format of such a form is shown in Figure 8–11. In general, it is good practice to locate data that identifies the object at the beginning of the form. This means that the key of the entry point relation (and possibly other data from the entry point relation) appears first. This can serve as a title for the form and tells the user which object is being processed. Thus, the first part of the form structure in Figure 8–11 displays data about the identity of the ORDER.

Next, data about the SALESPERSON could be presented, followed by data about the CUSTOMER. After that, a section containing a variable number of ITEMs could be displayed. Finally, other ORDER-related data, such as the subtotal, tax, and order total, could be presented.

In general, all of the data from a single relation should be placed into one contiguous section of the form. Assuming the database is in domain/ key normal form (which it should be), each relation will pertain to a specific

**Figure 8–11**

Structure of form
that materializes an
order

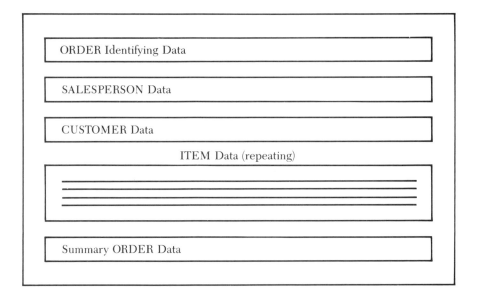

ORDER Identifying Data

SALESPERSON Data

CUSTOMER Data

ITEM Data (repeating)

Summary ORDER Data

theme (or object) and the application will be able to access all of the data for that theme in one database location. For example, SALESPERSON, CUSTOMER, and ITEM data groups are each localized on the form.

Notice, however, that this was not done for the ORDER data. Some ORDER data is located at the top of the form (the identifying data) and some at the bottom (the summary data). Such splitting is sometimes necessary to make the form useful and meaningful to the user. Splitting data like this, when done at all, usually involves only the entry point relation. As stated, a well-designed form presents identifying data (from the entry point relation) at the top of the form. But sometimes, particularly with objects that contain composite groups (like ITEM), the rest of the data for that relation cannot appear until data from other relations has been entered or displayed. Thus, in Figure 8–11, the identifying data is presented at the top, but order totals do not appear until all ITEMs have been entered or displayed.

If we were to locate all of the ORDER data in one section, then either (1) order totals would appear before ITEMs, causing the totals to be presented out of context, or (2) identifying data would be placed at the end of the form, making the form more difficult to use. Hence, in this case, a compromise is struck and the data is split.

The format in Figure 8–11 is *not* the only acceptable one. For example, SALESPERSON data and CUSTOMER data could be reversed on the form.

In a situation like this, the best strategy often is to consider the paper forms the user employs. Users find computer forms easier to use when data is presented in the same order as on paper forms. (But don't fall into the trap of replicating a poorly designed paper form on the computer.)

Although the order of SALESPERSON and CUSTOMER appears to be immaterial, the location of ITEM data with respect to SALESPERSON and CUSTOMER is probably significant. SALESPERSON and CUSTOMER data establish a context for the order and thus help to identify it. Therefore, it seems more appropriate to place them before the ITEMs. This judgment is an artistic one, however. One could argue this last point in the same sense that one could argue the best location for a handle on a clay tea pot. Still, such nuances are what make some forms easier to use than others. When in doubt, build a prototype and let the users decide.

## Data Lookup

A second principle of form design is that *users should never enter data that is already stored in the database*. For example, the user of the form in Figure 8–11 should not be expected to enter SALESPERSON or CUSTOMER data that is already present in the database. Requiring (or allowing) such duplicate data entry is an invitation for data integrity problems.

When the user enters a new ORDER, he or she should need to enter only the Salesperson# and the customer's Account#. The application should then obtain additional SALESPERSON and CUSTOMER data (such as name and address) from the database. If this data is not present in the database, then, and only then, should the user be required to enter it. Further, the user should be allowed to enter new SALESPERSON and CUSTOMER data only if he has the authority to do so. There may be important reasons for separating the authority to enter new orders from the authority to add new salespeople or customers.

This type of data retrieval is sometimes called a *lookup*. The non-key data is looked up in the database and displayed for the user. In this way users can ensure they have entered the correct key value. (The non-key data on the source document and the data obtained from the database should match.)

## Modeless Processing

Some forms are designed to facilitate *modeless processing*. This means that the application determines the mode (insert, modify, or delete) from the context. For instance, with modeless processing, the user of the form in Figure 8–11 might invoke the form and enter only an Order#. The application then searches the database for an order with that Order#. If no such order exists, the application assumes a new order is to be entered and follows its insertion logic. On the other hand, if the value of Order# *does* match an ORDER in the database, the application assumes the user wants to modify or delete that order. Consequently, the application displays the ORDER data in the form and gives the user the opportunity to change the order data or to delete the order.

Modeless processing can be convenient, but it is not appropriate for every application. Errors can occur. For example, if values of Order# are handwritten, some might be illegible. The user might misinterpret an order number and enter it incorrectly with modeless processing. What should have been order modifications could be erroneously processed as order insertions. If so, over time, the same order might be stored under several order numbers. Thus some applications require the user to indicate a specific action or select it from a menu. Then the desired application features can be activated.

The issue is one of flexibility versus control. Modeless processing is flexible, but errors can occur. Non-modeless processing is inflexible, but errors are less likely to occur.

### Pop-up Windows

It is easier for people to *recognize* than to *recollect*. For example, it is easier to select a desired salesperson's name from a list than it is to remember that person's name without prompting. Since this is true, some application forms use *pop-up windows* to present a list of options that are appropriate in a given context.

For example, suppose a user is entering an ORDER using the form in Figure 8–11 and needs to key the salesperson's number. Let's say the user knows the customer is located in Phoenix but can't remember the name (or number) of the salesperson in Phoenix. A pop-up window would be very useful here. The application could be designed so that when the user positions the cursor over the entry space for Salesperson# and presses a particular key, a list of cities and corresponding salespersons' names and numbers is presented. The user could then identify the correct salesperson and enter the data into the form. More conveniently, the user might simply choose the appropriate entry from the list displayed in the window (maybe by positioning the cursor on it) and the application would automatically copy that number into the proper space on the order form.

Unfortunately, not all DBMS products provide support for pop-up windows of this type. Often they need to be programmed into the application by means of special subroutines. Without utilities to facilitate the programming, this is a time-consuming process. Consequently, pop-up windows are not used as often as they could be.

### Cursor Movement and Pervasive Keys

Another consideration in forms design is the *action of the cursor*. The cursor should move through a form easily and naturally. Typically this means that the cursor will follow the pattern of the source data entry document. If forms are used to enter data collected by a user over the telephone (such as catalog orders), cursor movement will control the flow of the conversation. In this case, its movement should progress in a manner that the *customer* will find natural and appropriate.

Particular attention must be paid to the action of the cursor during and after an *exception condition*, or error. Suppose that while using the form in Figure 8–11 to enter an order, the user enters an invalid salesperson number. The application processing this form should move the cursor to a logical location on the form and thus help the user to respond to the error. For example, if a pop-up window containing a menu of processing options (Retry, Cancel, Browse Salespersons) is presented, then the cursor should be positioned automatically at the beginning of the list. Once the selected menu option has been processed, the cursor should automatically be positioned at the salesperson number or at the next appropriate space on the form.

The actions of special-purpose keys, such as ESC (escape), function keys (such as F1 and F2), and the like, should be *consistent* and *pervasive*. For example, if ESC is used to exit from menus, it should be used consistently for this purpose and no other (except for actions that are logically equivalent to exiting from menus).

Also, the actions of keys should pervade, or extend throughout, the entire application. For example, if ESC is used to exit from one menu, it should be used to exit from all menus. If F1 is used to delete data in one form, it should be used to delete data in all forms. If the F1 key were to serve different functions when used with different forms, then when moving from one portion of an application to another users would need to "unlearn" what they had become used to. This is not only wasteful but also frustrating and aggravating, and it causes errors.

# REPORT DESIGN

The subject of report design, even more than form design, has been discussed extensively in texts on applications development. We will not duplicate or summarize those discussions here. Rather, in this section we will discuss several concepts that relate to the notion of a report as the materialization of a database object.

## Report Structure

The principles of effective report design are similar to the principles of effective form design. In fact, you can think of a report as a "display-only" form. (Forms are used for data entry as well as for display.) As with a form, *the structure of a report should reflect the structure of the underlying object*. Thus the name of the report, or the object the report is about, indicates the entry relation into the object. As with forms, the name of the object is the same as the key of the entry point relation.

With the exception of the entry point relation, all of the data from a given relation should be located in a contiguous section of the report. Data from the entry point relation might need to be split, however, as is sometimes required with forms.

Data from relations that are parents (and grandparents, etc.) of the entry point relation is looked up and displayed. Data from relations that are children of the entry point relation often are shown as repeating groups. For example, for the ORDER object, ITEM data is listed as a repeating line after ORDER data (see Figure 8–12). For this report, ITEM data is displayed in the sequence in which it was entered. For other reports, data from child relations might be sorted. For example, the ITEM data in this report could have been sorted by Item-number. If within these repeating entries there were subgroups with the same value in the sort attribute, they might be presented on the report with control breaks. A more general report structure appears in Figure 8–13.

---

**Figure 8–12**
Sample ORDER
report

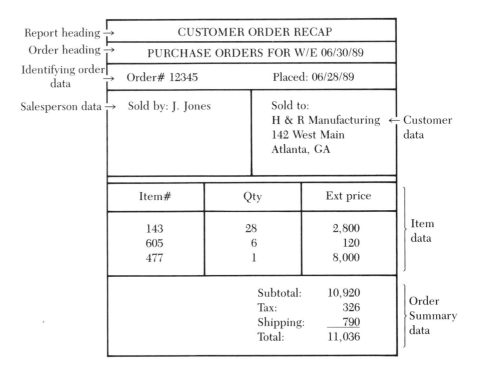

**Figure 8–13**
Structure of a report
that reflects the
structure of the
ORDER object

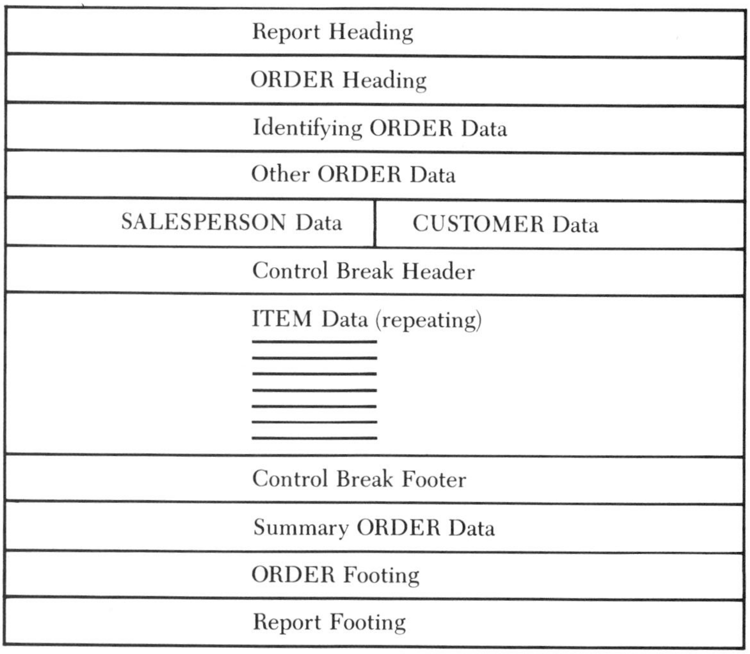

| Report Heading | |
|---|---|
| ORDER Heading | |
| Identifying ORDER Data | |
| Other ORDER Data | |
| SALESPERSON Data | CUSTOMER Data |
| Control Break Header | |
| ITEM Data (repeating) | |
| Control Break Footer | |
| Summary ORDER Data | |
| ORDER Footing | |
| Report Footing | |

## Processing of Sorted-by Clauses

The report in Figure 8–12 is about a single entity—namely, an ORDER. This report, which documents the facts about a particular order, might be used by someone in the shipping department, in customer support, or in sales. In the discussion of object diagrams in Chapter 4, we noted that when a user needs a report about objects sorted into some order, that report is not about one object. Rather, it is a report about a *collection* of objects treated as an entity (which we called an *aggregation object* in Chapter 6). A user might want data to be sorted in three different ways, which results in three different types of aggregation object. Each type is constructed differently by the application.

**Sorted by Object Key.** If the report is to be sorted by the key attribute of the entry point relation, then the aggregation object is simply a collection of those objects. Thus, an ORDER report sorted by Order# (the key attribute) is a report about the object ORDER-COLLECTION. With most DBMS products, a report about ORDER-COLLECTION is no more difficult to produce than a report about an individual ORDER.

**Sorted by Non-Key Columns of the Entry Point Relation.**   When a user needs a report sorted by a non-key column of the entry point relation, the report is about an entirely different object. For example, let's say that the ORDER relation includes an attribute called Type. Type indicates whether the ORDER has a low, medium, or high value. A report of orders sorted by Type would actually be a materialization of the object ORDER-TYPE, which contains ORDER as a multivalued object attribute. The object diagram for ORDER-TYPE appears in Figure 8–14a.

Consider another illustration. Reports often are sorted by date. Suppose ORDER contains two date columns—Order-date and Shipping-date. If the user requests a report about orders sorted by Order-date, then that report is actually a report of ORDER-DATEs, not ORDERs. ORDER-DATE, however, contains ORDER as a multivalued object property (see Figure 8–14b). Similarly, if the user requests a report about orders sorted by Shipping-date, then that report is about SHIPPING-DATE, which contains ORDER as a multivalued object property (see Figure 8–14c).

**Sorted by Attributes not in the Entry Point Relation.**   The third way in which reports can be sorted is by attributes that are foreign to the entry point relation. For example, consider a report of orders sorted by Customer-name. In this situation, the report is actually a report about CUSTOMER, not ORDER. ORDER is a multivalued object attribute within CUSTOMER. Thus, a request such as this changes the entry point relation from ORDER to CUSTOMER. This will affect the logic of the application producing the report.

Understanding which is the entry point relation may ease the task of developing the report. Proceeding as if ORDER were the entry point relation will make the report logic contrived. If ORDER is considered the entry

**Figure 8–14**
Object diagrams
allowing sorting on
various columns

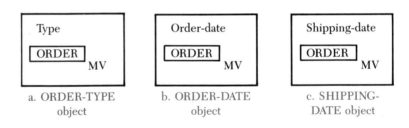

a. ORDER-TYPE
object

b. ORDER-DATE
object

c. SHIPPING-
DATE object

point, then all of the ORDERs (perhaps a million of them) need to be constructed, stored on disk, and then sorted by Customer-name. On the other hand, if CUSTOMER is considered the entry point relation, then the Customer records can be sorted (perhaps only 25,000 of them) and ORDERs (and ITEMs within ORDERs) can be quickly retrieved as child records. The second approach is much more direct and efficient.

This section has focused on report design from the standpoint of object materialization. Designing the physical appearance of the report is also important, but it does not relate to database processing. Thus we will not consider that subject here.

## PROCESSING UPDATES

When processing database updates, the application must be certain to preserve the relationships among database records. In a previous section, we said that during application development the developer had to ensure that the integrity of the database would be preserved. In this section, we will consider this topic in more depth.

Figure 8–15a illustrates the relationship between MAJOR and STUDENT relations. The policy governing this relationship is that a major (such as accounting) must have at least one student and that a student must have exactly one major. Thus, when users update either of these relations, the application program must ensure that these constraints are not violated. (We will assume in this section that such checking is not done by the DBMS.) For example, if a user attempted to delete the record for STU400 (see Figure 8–15b), the application program should disallow this request. If the request were allowed, then the Finance record would not have a child record and the mandatory constraint would be violated. Similarly, a new MAJOR, say BIOLOGY, cannot be added until there is a student who is majoring in that subject.

A record that exists inappropriately without a required parent or child is sometimes called a *fragment*. One of the functions of an application program is to prevent the creation of fragments.

The means of preventing fragments depends on the type of constraint being enforced. Figures 8–16a through 8–16d show examples of the four possible kinds of constraints. They are mandatory-to-mandatory (M-M), mandatory-to-optional (M-O), optional-to-mandatory (O-M), and optional-to-optional (O-O). These constraints are shown on one-to-many relationships, but the same four constraint types pertain to one-to-one and many-to-many relationships as well.

Figure 8–17 presents rules for preventing fragments for each of the four constraint types. Figure 8–17a pertains to actions on the parent record while Figure 8–17b pertains to actions on child records. Notice that rules govern the insertion of new records, the modification of key data, and the deletion of records.

**Figure 8–15**

Sample relationship
with mandatory-to-
mandatory constraint

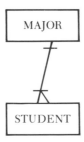

a. Sample mandatory-to-mandatory relationship

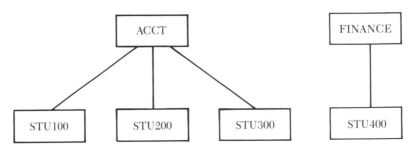

b. Sample data for the relationship in Figure 8–15a

We are concerned about changes only to key data because such changes are potentially changes in relationships. For example, in Figure 8–15b, changing the Major attribute of STU300 from ACCT to FINANCE assigns that student to the Finance Department. Thus, changes to key data can cause constraint violations, though it did not in this case. Consider the HOTEL-BILL and DAILY-CHARGE relations in Figure 8–16a. The DAILY-CHARGE relation includes the key of HOTEL-BILL (Invoice#) as part of its own key field (see the discussion of composite objects in Chapter 6). A change in a HOTEL-BILL Invoice# without a similar change in all the related DAILY-CHARGE records would invalidate the relationship between the relations.

Figure 8–17 shows rules for one-to-many relationships. The rules for one-to-one relationships are similar and will be left as an exercise (question 8.27).

**Figure 8–16**

Four types of relationship constraint

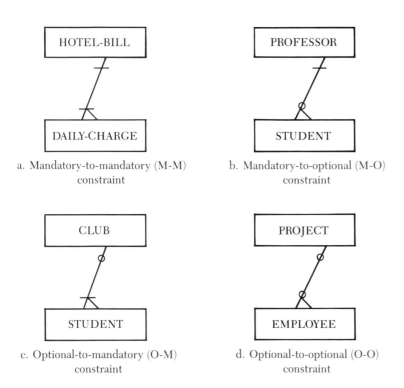

a. Mandatory-to-mandatory (M-M) constraint

b. Mandatory-to-optional (M-O) constraint

c. Optional-to-mandatory (O-M) constraint

d. Optional-to-optional (O-O) constraint

## Restrictions on Updates to Parent Records

The first row of Figure 8–17a applies to M-M constraints. A new parent record can be inserted only if at least one child record is being created at the same time. This creation could occur by inserting a new child record or by reassigning a child from a different parent (however, this later action may itself cause a constraint violation). A change to the key of a parent can be allowed in an M-M relationship only if the values in the corresponding foreign key in the child records are also changed to the new value. (It would be possible to reassign all of the children to another parent and then create at least one new child for the parent, but this is rarely done.) Thus, changing the Invoice# in Hotel-bill can be allowed as long as the Invoice# is changed in all the appropriate Daily-charge records as well. Finally, a parent of an M-M relationship can be deleted only if all of its children are also deleted or are reassigned to another parent.

The second row in Figure 8–17a defines rules for M-O constraints. A new parent can be added without restriction because parents need not have

**Figure 8—17**
Rules for preventing
fragments

Proposed Action on Parent

| Type of Rela-tionship | | *Insert* | *Modify (key)* | *Delete* |
|---|---|---|---|---|
| | M-M | Create at least one child | Change matching keys of all children | Delete all children OR Reassign all children |
| | M-O | OK | Change matching keys of all children | Delete all children OR Reassign all children |
| | O-M | Insert new child OR Appropriate child exists | Change key of at least one child OR Appropriate child exists | OK |
| | O-O | OK | OK | OK |

a. Conditions for allowing changes to parent records

Proposed Action on Child

| Type of Rela-tionship | | *Insert* | *Modify (key)* | *Delete* |
|---|---|---|---|---|
| | M-M | Parent exists OR Create parent | Parent with new value exists (or create one) AND Sibling exists | Sibling exists |
| | M-O | Parent exists OR Create parent | Parent with new value exists OR Create parent | OK |
| | O-M | OK | Sibling exists | Sibling exists |
| | O-O | OK | OK | OK |

b. Conditions for allowing changes to child records

children. Thus, for the relationship in Figure 8–16b, a new PROFESSOR record can be added without restriction. A change in the parent's key value, however, can be allowed only if the corresponding values in the child records are changed. If the key of a PROFESSOR in the relationship in Figure 8–16b is changed, then the value of Advisor in all of that professor's advisees' records must also be changed. Finally, in a relationship having an M-O constraint, the parent record can be deleted only if all children are deleted or reassigned. For the PROFESSOR-STUDENT relationship, all of the STUDENT records would most likely be reassigned.

The third row describes restrictions on O-M constraints. A parent can be inserted only if at least one child is added at the same time or if an appropriate child already exists. For the O-M relationship between CLUB and STUDENT in Figure 8–16c, a new club can be added only if an associated STUDENT record is created (either by adding a new student or by changing the value of Club in an existing STUDENT). Similarly, the key of the parent of an O-M relationship may be changed only if a child is created or if a suitable child record already exists. The Ski Club can change its name to Scuba only if at least one skier is willing to join Scuba or if a student has already enrolled in Scuba. There are no restrictions on the deletion of a parent record in an O-M relationship.

The last type of relationship constraint, O-O, is shown in Figure 8–16d. There are no restrictions on any type of update on records in an O-O relationship. Both PROJECT and EMPLOYEE records (see Figure 8–16d) can be updated at will.

## Restrictions on Updates to Child Records

The rules for preventing fragments when processing updates on child records are shown in Figure 8–17b. The rules are very similar to those in Figure 8–17a. The notable difference is that in several cases, child records can be modified or deleted as long as sibling records exist. For example, in an M-M constraint, a child record can be deleted as long as at least one sibling remains. (With an M-M constraint, the last child never leaves home!) For the M-M constraint in Figure 8–16a, a particular DAILY-CHARGE record can be deleted as long as at least one DAILY-CHARGE record for that HOTEL-BILL remains.

With the exception of considerations regarding siblings, the rules for preventing fragments when updating child records are similar to those for updating parent records. Be certain you understand each statement in Figure 8–17.

## Enforcing Constraints

As stated in Chapter 7, in the future DBMS products will enforce inter-relation constraints. Currently, however, this is seldom the case, so the task must be done by the application program.

Many of the rules set out in Figure 8–17 offer several alternatives. In these cases, the application program developer selects the option that best fits the application requirements. The point to remember is that you must consider such constraints during the design and development of application programs.

## SUMMARY

In this chapter we studied the process of database application design. A database application is the user's interface to the database system. As such, an application must perform three functions: print, query, and update objects; enable the user to control its features; and ensure that the security and integrity of the database are always maintained.

In order to serve the user, an application must materialize object views for the user. Users perceive their environment in terms of objects, although the DBMS stores data in tables or files. An object view is the collection of properties that makes up one user's perception of an object. Of course, various users perceive objects differently, hence they can have different views of the same object. When a user queries or updates an object, he is actually querying or updating his object view. Thus, before responding to a user request, the application must first construct the user's object view from data stored in one or several relations.

The presentation of an object view (such as a data entry form or a report) is called the materialization of an object. In addition to data retrieved from the database, a form or report contains fixed text, graphics, masks, and other components that make the materialization useful and meaningful to the user. A single object view can be materialized in countless ways.

Application design consists of four steps. The first step, determining applications and scope, means deciding, based on knowledge of the user's requirements, how many applications there will be and what each application will accomplish. One approach to determining this is to develop one application per user group. The scope of each application will include only the features needed by that group and will thus prevent those users from invoking features they have no need (or authority) to invoke.

In the second step the developer must decide whether the user will employ menus, database commands, or both to control the application. During the third step, options for each menu (if any) are determined. A menu option might initiate a feature (such as printing a report) or it might chain to another menu. In deciding the hierarchy of a set of menus, developers most often use the object/action approach. Thus, the highest-level menu offers the user a list of objects that might be processed, and lower-level menus enable the user to indicate the action to be taken on the selected object.

The fourth and last step of application design is to develop the programming logic for each command or menu option (except those that chain to another menu), design the forms and reports with which the user will interface, and check the logic to ensure that all constraints have been enforced.

Forms and reports should be designed to mirror the object they are materializing. Thus, knowledge of the object will help during this process. The relation whose key attribute is the same as the name of the object is called the entry point relation. Generally, data from the entry point relation appears first, followed by data from its parent relations (if any), and then followed by data from its child relations (if any). Sometimes data from the entry point relation is split on the form or report. For example, identifying information might appear at the top of a form, while summary and total information might appear at the end of the form. Such data splitting is usually necessary only for the entry point relation.

A user should never enter onto a form data that is already in the database. For example, a user should enter only a customer's account number. The application should then look up the customer's name and address and display it for the user.

Modeless processing determines what function a user wants to execute based on context. Modeless processing can be more convenient than traditional processing, but more error-prone. Consequently, in most cases users are called upon to indicate specifically what function they want to perform. This approach is more time-consuming but less inclined to errors.

Pop-up windows temporarily overlay part of a screen display. A pop-up window is like a small computer screen within the larger one. In it the application might present, say, a list or a menu. Pop-up windows are useful for displaying a limited amount of data for the user to browse, for helping the user to handle exceptional conditions, and for other situations in which the user needs to suspend, but not terminate, the current function.

The cursor guides a user through the process of entering data and responding to prompts. Moving the cursor to the next logical position on the form is a subtle but important aspect of form design. Also, the use of special keys (such as ESC or the function keys) should be consistent throughout the entire application.

Reports can be thought of as display-only forms. Hence, guidelines for report design are similar to those for form design. Reports often present data about not one object, but a group of objects, sorted into sequence on the value of some attribute. Knowing what this attribute, or sort argument, is aids the developer in writing the logic to produce the report. The sort argument can be the key of the entry point relation, a non-key attribute in the entry point relation, or an attribute not in the entry point relation. Each of these situations is handled differently.

When updating a database, an application must ensure that fragments, or records that exist inappropriately without a required parent or child, are not created. We described the rules that must be followed when updating database data. Various rules apply, depending on the type of update (insert, delete, or modify the key attribute), the type of relationship (mandatory-to-mandatory, mandatory-to-optional, optional-to-mandatory, or optional-to-optional), and the type of record (parent or child).

Current DBMS products do not enforce such inter-relation constraints. They must be enforced via programmer-written subroutines. This will probably change in future DBMS products.

**GROUP I**          QUESTIONS

**8.1**   Why is the task of updating an object more difficult for an application designer than are printing and querying an object?

**8.2**   Explain why an online database application must allow the user to direct it.

**8.3**   What means can be employed to allow the user control of an application? What are the advantages and disadvantages of each?

**8.4**   What is the difference between an object and an object view?

**8.5**   What is the relationship (if any) between an object view and relations?

**8.6**   What is the materialization of an object view?

**8.7**   What are the four steps in the object-oriented database application design process?

**8.8**   How can the separation of system features into applications be used for security and control?

**8.9**   Samantha Green decided to develop only one application for the computer lab at Eastcoast State. Describe a different scenario at that university that would make multiple applications more feasible.

**8.10**  What are the advantages and disadvantages of menu-driven and command-driven database applications? Describe a situation other than one in this text in which commands would be preferable to menus.

**8.11**  What is a hierarchy of menus? Describe approaches to developing menu hierarchies for an application.

**8.12**  How can menus be employed to control user access to database application functions?

**8.13**  Is there one materialization for each object view? Can there be more than one materialization for an object view?

8.14 Describe three functions for which forms are used.

8.15 Describe an approach toward designing a form to make its structure reflect the structure of the object view it materializes. Does this approach apply to report design?

8.16 What is an entry point relation?

8.17 If you know what object is to be materialized, how can you identify the entry point relation?

8.18 What function, if any, do prototypes serve when designing forms and reports?

8.19 What is data lookup, and how does it pertain to form design?

8.20 What is modeless processing? What are the advantages and disadvantages of modeless processing?

8.21 What is a pop-up window?

8.22 What does it mean to say that special-purpose keys should be consistent and pervasive throughout an application?

8.23 What effect do *sorted-by* clauses have on report design?

8.24 What is a fragment?

8.25 How can an application prevent fragments from being created?

---

QUESTIONS AND EXERCISES **GROUP II**

8.26 Develop a set of menus that could be used to control an application that manages a student directory. The directory includes student name, class, school-year address (dormitory name for on-campus students), and school-year telephone number. Include these features: add, modify, delete student entry; look up a particular student entry; print directory in alphabetical order on student name; print directory in alphabetical order within class; browse class entries; display students living in a particular dormitory; print off-campus student telephone directory.

8.27 Modify Figure 8–17 to describe the update rules for one-to-one relationships. Explain each entry.

8.28 Design a form that could be used to enter customer telephone orders for a direct merchant. Use the mail order form in Figure 8–18 as a guide. Keep in mind that some entries on the printed form may not be useful for computer data entry. What data might an order entry clerk *not* need to enter (that is, what data will be looked up by the application)? Will the computer form follow the same format as the mail order form? What are the major differences, if any? Why did you choose to design your form that way? Where might pop-up windows be useful?

## Figure 8—18
Direct mechant mail
order form

**ORDERED BY:** Phone( )_____ □ Day □ Night
If name or address is incorrect please print correct information.

If a peel off label is available on the back cover, please attach it here.

**GIFT ORDER or SHIP TO:** Please print-Use only if different from "Ordered by".
□ Mr.
□ Mrs.
□ Ms.
_____

_____

Street/Route                Box/Apt.

City                    State            Zip

Gift Card—From

Expedited Shipment Recipient Phone No.( )_____

| Page | Stock No. | Color | Size | Inseam | How Many | Description | Total Amount |
|------|-----------|-------|------|--------|----------|-------------|--------------|
|      |           |       |      |        |          |             |              |
|      |           |       |      |        |          |             |              |
|      |           |       |      |        |          |             |              |
|      |           |       |      |        |          |             |              |
|      |           |       |      |        |          |             |              |
|      |           |       |      |        | If you need more space, please attach a separate sheet of paper. | | |

**PAYMENT METHOD**

□ MasterCard  □ VISA     Check or Money Order (Please, no Currency)
□ American Express     AMOUNT ENCLOSED $ _____

| | | | | | | | | | | | | | |

Card Account Number

| | | — | | |

Month    Year          Customer Signature
Expiration Date Required

| | Item Total |
|---|---|
| 5% Sales Tax on Items Delivered in Maine | |
| Regular SHIPPING & HANDLING FREE within U.S. | |
| Optional FEDERAL EXPRESS (See reverse side) | |
| SPECIAL SHIPMENT or Foreign Shipment (See reverse side) | |
| **TOTAL** | |

59950

"Thank you for your order"

# PART IV

# END-USER DATABASE PROCESSING

In the end-user database environment, users initiate and run applications and enter ad hoc queries against the database without the assistance of computer professionals. Users might also design the database, build new applications, modify the database structure, and perform all database administration activities. The extent to which a user can do these things depends on several factors, including the user's expertise, the user-friendliness of the DBMS product, the scope of the system (number of users, number of applications, size of the database), the complexity of the system (for example, a computer network versus a stand-alone system), and ownership of the database. Although end-user database processing can take place on the full range of computers from micros to mainframes, microcomputers are generally more available to end-users. Consequently, they are more popular for this type of processing.

The key to end-user database processing is *the interface with the DBMS*. The user needs to feel that he can "get at" the data in the computer and manipulate the data to readily answer questions. The database language SQL provides just such a user-friendly interface. With minimal training, users can define tables, establish relationships, and make queries. (Depending on the DBMS product in which SQL is implemented, the user might also be able to easily develop his own applications.) Various implementations of SQL exist for both microcomputer and mainframe relational databases. We present SQL in Chapter 9.

As mentioned, most but not all end-user database processing is accomplished on microcomputers. Even within the microcomputer area there are distinct types of database systems, and each type has unique properties and problems. In Chapter 10 we address these distinctions. Knowing these distinctions will be useful to you if you need to develop a microcomputer database system.

Finally, in Chapter 11 we consider mainframe end-user processing. We present an overview of DB2, which is one particular implementation of the relational database language SQL. IBM developed DB2 as a user-friendly relational DBMS product for use on mainframe computers. Because DB2 is an implementation of SQL, the syntax you see in Chapter 11 may vary slightly from the syntax you will learn in Chapter 9. This is true of many languages, including, for example, COBOL and BASIC.

# Relational Processing with SQL

- Characteristics of Relational Database Applications
- Relational Data Definition
- Relational Data Manipulation
- Relational Data Manipulation Language—SQL
- Summary

**A** user has a certain natural way of perceiving things in the real (that is, business, industrial, academic) world. We saw in Chapter 3 that a user perceives the world in terms of *objects*—things that can be named, defined, talked about, even seen or touched.

In contrast, a computer "perceives" its world in terms of bits, bytes, records, and files. No special meaning is attached to these units by a computer—they are simply the stuff on which a computer operates.

The challenge for the database designer is to somehow express the user's perception of the world in terms of the computer's representation of data. Until the relational model was developed, aligning the two points of view was very difficult. In fact, the computer (actually, the computer software) was rather unswerving, and users were expected to learn how the computer "saw" things and adjust their thinking accordingly. However, the development of the relational model has done much toward reducing the user's task of learning computer database technology (see Figure 9–1).

As we saw in Chapter 5, the relational model is based on a very simple data structure, the table. Unlike some other data structures (such as linked lists), tables are familiar to most users. In fact, tables are so simple to read and understand that many users wonder why the relational model causes so much excitement. To them, storing data in tables is just common sense. But to database practitioners, using the relational model has broken down a major barrier between computer technology and the user community it serves.

Whereas other data models arose from the work of computer systems professionals, the relational model arose from the field of mathematics.

**Figure 9–1**

DBMS software
changes its orienta-
tion from the com-
puter's perspective to
the user's perspective

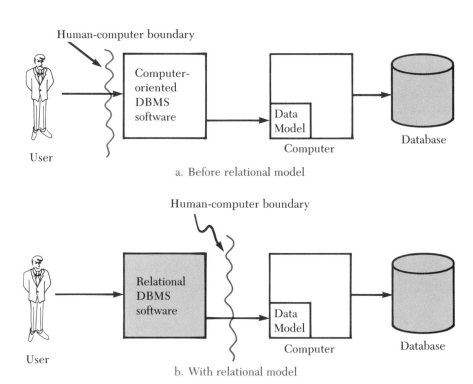

a. Before relational model

b. With relational model

What the layperson calls a *table* is a special case of what is known in mathematics as a *relation*. In mathematical terms, a relation is a structure on which certain operations can be performed. In the early 1970s, researchers determined that these operations would be useful for computer data storage and manipulation. They observed that files designed to obey certain constraints behaved like mathematical relations. Consequently, certain relational operations could be performed on them. As a result, relational theory has been employed to solve some of the problems of database processing.

A relational database, then, is a database that is perceived by the user to be a collection of tables on which certain relational operations can be performed. It does not necessarily mean that data is actually stored in physical tables, although it might be.

The relational model was first proposed by Dr. E. F. Codd in a seminal paper in 1970. Since then, this model has been the focus of extensive intellectual activity. An important series of theoretical papers has been written concerning the most appropriate way to express relations. At the same time, other papers have been written describing different techniques and languages for manipulating relational data.

Although the relational model was at first difficult to implement (performance, for example, was extremely slow), it is now used in several commercially successful DBMS products. These include, for example, SQL/DS and DB2 (licensed by IBM for the mainframe market), ORACLE (licensed by Oracle for the minicomputer market), and R:Base System V (licensed by Microrim for the microcomputer market). Other products that are not strictly relational, such as Cullinet's IDMS/R, are beginning to incorporate relational features. The trend in database products appears to be away from the traditional hierarchical and network models and toward the relational model.

In this text, we will approach the relational model in an informal and largely intuitive manner. Our objectives are to understand relational concepts from a practitioner's standpoint, to apply these concepts to database design, and to learn the database language SQL. Readers interested in more rigorous coverage of the relational model should see Date, Ullman, and the excellent series of papers that have appeared in the Association for Computing Machinery's *Transactions on Database Systems* (see Bibliography).

The first section of this chapter describes the characteristics of relational database applications. The next section presents relational data definition concepts, some of which were introduced in Chapter 5. It defines the essential terminology and shows how relationships are represented using the relational model. The remaining two sections discuss relational data manipulation. First, a survey of four types of relational data manipulation language (DML) is presented and then relational algebra is discussed. Finally, SQL (the data access language used by SQL/DS, DB2, ORACLE, and others) is described in detail. The concepts presented in this chapter will be used in Chapter 11 to implement a relational database as part of a case study.

## CHARACTERISTICS OF RELATIONAL DATABASE APPLICATIONS

What makes relational database applications different from other database applications lies not in the applications themselves but in the way the data is conceptually viewed. It is precisely because relational DBMS products treat data as if it were in simple tables that they are incredibly flexible and easy to use. Why is this so?

First, users can easily grasp the concept of storing data in tables. They can understand what key fields are, and they can see how relationships are stored within the data itself by using field values to link related rows together. This makes it possible for users to specify their own requirements when preparing a query against the database, eliminating much of the traditional dependence upon professional programmers.

Second, the structure of tables in a relational database can easily be adjusted when users' needs change. Should a user need to add a column to an existing table, for example, that task can be accomplished with some simple commands.

Third, relationships between existing rows can be quickly and easily established without having to reorganize the entire database. This flexibility makes the database more responsive to changing user needs.

Notice that the thrust of the discussion so far has been that *users* derive the benefits from a relational database. Unlike other database structures, relational databases make ad hoc queries possible. *Ad hoc* means unpredicted—and other databases are not structured to answer unpredicted questions easily. Consequently, user questions that might have been considered impossible to handle in a different database environment are answerable with a relational DBMS.

## Impact of the Relational Model

One way for a user to query a relational database is by employing a query/update language such as SQL. Because the structure of a relational database is so simple, a relatively small set of statements is needed to process it. This makes it possible for users to develop and enter their own queries against the database. (To fully appreciate this aspect of relational database processing, you must compare it to the DBMS products we will discuss in Part 5. You will then realize that for other types of databases, professional programmers are still indispensable.)

The ability to ask ad hoc questions is the basis for decision support systems (DSSs). In fact, the early focus of relational database research and application was decision support and information centers. An *information center* is a service group that has access to corporate data. Individuals within the group are skilled at retrieving information from the stored data on behalf of company managers, officers, and other decision makers. Information center personnel provide a service much like that of research librarians—they retrieve information for other people to use. Information centers might have enjoyed more success if the inexpensive microcomputer had not appeared on the scene. But the microcomputer proved to be a better alternative, interfacing directly with the mainframe computer and placing information directly into the hands of the end user, without the services of the information center. This use of microcomputers is possible primarily because of the relational database.

Decision support is certainly one of the important applications of relational databases. However, it is not the only application for which relational databases are suited. Relational DBMS products also handle companies' transaction processing. *Transaction processing* involves the continuous updating of the corporate database to keep it current. Transaction processors must often handle heavy workloads (measured in the number of transactions that must be processed each second). Although early relational products were not powerful enough to perform adequately, current products are capable of managing moderately heavy workloads.

Still another result of relational database processing is the emergence of the language SQL as a standard for information interchange between computers. Until now, transferring data from one computer to another proved difficult because each computer had its own data sublanguage. But SQL provides a standard language that can be processed on any computer. Thus, transferring data from one micro to another micro, from a mainframe to a micro, and so forth, can be accomplished via SQL. For this reason alone any student of business or computing should learn the SQL language.

So you can see that what makes a relational database different from other databases is the simple way in which data is conceptually stored. Users can readily understand the concept, master the simple query/update language needed to extract their own data, and get the information they want and need more quickly than if they had to depend on the programming staff. Decision support systems are based on the relational database. And transaction processing can be accomplished with relational databases.

Let us now consider the relational database in more depth.

## RELATIONAL DATA DEFINITION

The relational model represents data in the simple form of tables. As you will see, the importance of this model lies in the way that *relationships* are represented. First we will present data definition terminology and then we will discuss relationships.

### Terminology

A *relation* is simply a two-dimensional table that has several properties:

1. The entries in the relation are single-valued. Repeating groups and arrays are not allowed (although some relational DBMS products allow columns to contain arrays).
2. The entries in any column are all of the same kind. For example, one column may contain patient names and another patient ages. Each column has a unique name and the order of the columns is immaterial. Columns of a relation are called *attributes*.
3. No two rows in the relation are identical and the order of the rows is insignificant (see Figure 9–2).

Each row of the relation is known as a *tuple*. Each attribute has a *domain*, which is the set of values that the attribute can have.

Figure 9–2 is an *example*, or *occurrence*. The generalized format, PATIENT(Name, Age, Sex, Account-number), is called the *relation structure* and is what most people mean when they use the term *relation*. If we add

**Figure 9–2**

PATIENT relational
occurrence

|  | Col 1 (or Attribute 1) | Col 2 | Col 3 | Col 4 | Col 5 |
|---|---|---|---|---|---|
|  | Name | Age | Sex | Account Number | Physician |
| Row 1 (or Tuple 1) | Riley | 56 | F | 147 | Lee |
| Row 2 | Murphy | 17 | M | 289 | Singh |
| Row 3 | Krajewski | 25 | F | 533 | Levy |
| Row 4 | Ting | 67 | F | 681 | Spock |
| Row 5 | Dixon | 17 | M | 704 | Levy |
| Row 6 | Abel | 41 | M | 193 | Singh |

constraints on allowable data values to the relation structure, we then have
a *relational schema.*

Each tuple in a relation must be uniquely identifiable by a *key,* which
is a group of one or more attributes. In some cases, a single attribute will
suffice. The key in the PATIENT relation in Figure 9–2, for example, is
Account-number. Sometimes two or three attributes are concatenated to
form the key. And in still other cases, all of the attributes together form the
key. This can always be true because, by definition, no two rows in a relation
may be identical. However, as you saw in Chapter 5, it is preferable to have
a smaller group of attributes for the key, if it is possible.

Sometimes, two (or more) attribute groups could be used as the key.
They are both called *candidate keys.* One of them will be chosen as the *primary
key.* Figure 9–3 summarizes relational terminology.

## Expressing Relationships with the Relational Model

With the relational model, relationships are carried in the data. The fact that
patient 533 is being treated by Dr. Levy is stored in the Physician attribute
of the PATIENT relation (see Figure 9–2). If the user wants to combine
patient data with physician data, the relational model provides facilities to
do so.

**Figure 9-3**
Summary of rela-
tional terminology

| Term | Meaning |
|------|---------|
| Relation | Two-dimensional table |
| Attribute | Column in a relation; can be thought of as a field |
| Tuple | Row in a relation; can be thought of as a record |
| Domain | Set of values an attribute can have |
| Occurrence | Example of a relation showing sample attribute values |
| Relation structure | Generalized format of a relation |
| Relational schema | Relation structure plus domain constraints |
| Key | Group of one or more attributes that uniquely identifies a tuple in a relation |
| Candidate key | Group of one or more attributes that *could* uniquely identify a tuple |
| Primary key | Candidate key chosen during database design as *the* key for the relation |

In Chapter 6 we examined logical database design. After identifying the underlying objects in the user's environment, we developed object diagrams that captured not only the attributes of each object, but also the relationships of objects to one another. Once those were established, we could build a set of data structure diagrams that can then be used to establish the actual physical design of the database. If we decide to use either the hierarchical or the network database model (see Chapters 12 and 13), further modifications to the data structure diagrams are needed. However, if we choose to implement the database using the relational model, our design work is finished. The data structure diagrams (along with field definitions, domain constraints, and inter- and intra-relation constraints) lead directly to relational implementation.

We saw in Chapter 6 that objects in the user's environment can be related to one another in basically three ways: 1:1, 1:$N$, and $N$:$M$. We also saw that those three binary relationships can be used to form larger logical data structures, including trees (or hierarchies), simple networks, and complex networks. Also in that chapter we illustrated how relations can be constructed to reflect the underlying structure of the relationships we identify in a user's environment. (If necessary, review Chapter 6 before continuing.) The next section reviews how each of the three structures is repre-

**Figure 9—4**

Tree representation of
faculty data

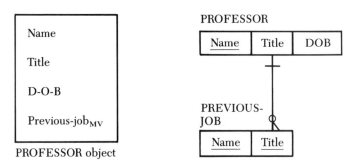

PROFESSOR object

sented with relations. Understanding this will prepare you for a discussion of relational data manipulation.

**Tree or Hierarchical Relationships.**   Figure 9–4 illustrates a two-level tree of faculty data. In this figure, the PROFESSOR object contains Name, Title, Date-of-birth (D-O-B), and from zero to many Previous-jobs. The relations that best represent the PROFESSOR object appear in the same figure. Notice that the multivalued data, Previous-job, has become a separate relation, tied back to the appropriate professor by means of the professor's name. It is necessary to do this because a relation (in this case, the PROFESSOR relation) may not contain repeating fields. Figure 9–5 further illustrates this with an instance of the PROFESSOR and PREVIOUS-JOB relations. Notice that we are representing only one object (PROFESSOR), but we need two relations to do so. This example illustrates the fact that the correspondence between objects and relations is not necessarily one-to-one.

Another example of a tree can be seen in Figure 9–6. This really is an extension of the example in Figure 9–5. We have added details about previous jobs a faculty member may have held, including the starting date, ending date, and salary during that period. Each of these details is tied back to a particular Previous-job by means of the professor's name and title. The relation structures for Figure 9–6 are

PROFESSOR(Name, Title, DOB)
PREVIOUS-JOB(Name, Title)
JOB-HISTORY(Name, Title, Start-date, End-date, Salary)

Recall that the attributes that form the primary key of a relation customarily are underlined.

Figure 9–7 shows examples of three relations that describe the PROFESSOR object. The three relations are PROFESSOR, PREVIOUS-JOB, and

| Name | Title | D-O-B |
|------|-------|-------|
| A | PROFESSOR | 6-7-42 |
| B | ASST. PROF. | 2-12-35 |
| C | ASSOC. PROF. | 8-26-49 |
| D | PROFESSOR | 10-27-32 |

a. PROFESSOR relation

| Name | Previous-job |
|------|--------------|
| A | ASSOC. PROF. |
| A | ASST. PROF. |
| A | INSTRUCTOR |
| C | ASST. PROF. |
| C | INSTRUCTOR |
| D | ASSOC. PROF. |
| D | ASST. PROF. |

b. PREVIOUS-JOB relation

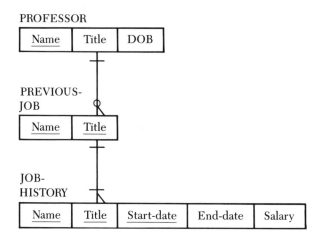

JOB-HISTORY. The relationships between rows in the JOB-HISTORY relation and the PREVIOUS-JOB relation are established by means of matching
data values in the Name and Title attributes. Similarly, as was demonstrated
previously, records in the PREVIOUS-JOB relation are associated with records in the PROFESSOR relation by means of the matching Name attributes.

**Figure 9−7**

Relational represen-
tation of Figure 9−6

| Name | Title | D-O-B |
|------|-------|-------|
| A | PROFESSOR | 6-7-42 |
| B | ASST.PROF. | 2-12-35 |
| C | ASSOC.PROF. | 8-26-49 |
| D | PROFESSOR | 10-27-32 |

a. PROFESSOR relation

| Name | Previous-job |
|------|--------------|
| A | ASSOC.PROF. |
| A | ASST.PROF. |
| A | INSTRUCTOR |
| C | ASST.PROF. |
| C | INSTRUCTOR |
| D | ASSOC.PROF. |
| D | ASST.PROF. |

b. PREVIOUS-JOB relation

| Name | Title | Start-date | Salary | End-date |
|------|-------|-----------|--------|----------|
| A | ASSOC.PROF. | SEP 90 | 30000 | |
| A | ASSOC.PROF. | SEP 89 | 29000 | SEP 90 |
| A | ASST.PROF. | SEP 88 | 28000 | SEP 89 |
| A | ASST.PROF. | SEP 87 | 26000 | SEP 88 |
| A | INSTRUCTOR | SEP 86 | 24000 | SEP 87 |
| C | ASST.PROF. | SEP 90 | 30500 | |
| C | ASST.PROF. | SEP 89 | 30000 | SEP 90 |
| C | INSTRUCTOR | SEP 88 | 26000 | SEP 89 |
| D | ASSOC.PROF. | SEP 90 | 30000 | |
| D | ASST.PROF. | SEP 89 | 29500 | SEP 90 |
| D | ASST.PROF. | SEP 88 | 29000 | SEP 89 |
| D | ASST.PROF. | SEP 87 | 27000 | SEP 88 |

c. JOB-HISTORY relation

In addition to these relation structures, we can also specify a *relational schema*. To do so, we define constraints on data values. Consider the following two examples of necessary constraints for this schema:

1. The values of Name in PREVIOUS-JOB must be a subset of the values of Name in PROFESSOR.
2. The values of Name and Title in JOB-HISTORY must be a subset of the values of Name and Title in PREVIOUS-JOB.

**Figure 9–8**

Example of a simple network

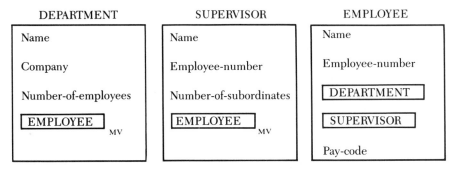

a. Object diagrams

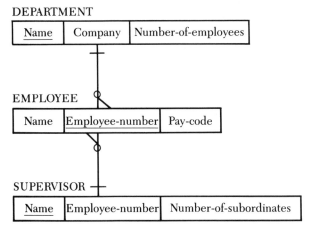

b. Relational schema

Without these constraints, we could have previous jobs and job histories that do not correspond to a professor row. More examples of constraints will be shown in Chapter 11.

**Simple Network Relationships.** Consider the DEPARTMENT, SUPERVI-SOR, and EMPLOYEE objects shown in Figure 9–8. DEPARTMENT objects have Name, Company, and Number-of-employees attributes. DEPART-MENT also contains the multivalued EMPLOYEE object. SUPERVISOR objects have Name, Employee-number, and Number-of-subordinates attributes. SUPERVISOR also contains the EMPLOYEE object and it is multivalued. Finally, EMPLOYEE objects have Name, Employee-number, DEPARTMENT,

SUPERVISOR, and Pay-code attributes. The DEPARTMENT-to-EMPLOYEE and SUPERVISOR-to-EMPLOYEE relationships are both 1:$N$. Consequently, this is an example of a simple network.

The following relation structure will represent this network:

DEPARTMENT(Name, Company, Number-of-employees)
SUPERVISOR(Name, Employee-number, Number-of-employees)
EMPLOYEE(Name, Employee-number, Department, Supervisor, Pay-code)

Observe that the attribute Name occurs in every relation. Therefore, reference to a particular Name attribute must be made by qualifying it with its relation name. Thus we refer to DEPARTMENT.Name, SUPERVISOR.Name, or EMPLOYEE.Name. Obviously, within any relation all attribute names must be unique.

Examples for these relations are shown in Figure 9–9. Again, observe that relationships among rows are carried in the values of columns. Processing these tables is done by matching data values. For example, if we want to know how many people work in the same department as Nakata, we first need to determine in which department Nakata works. So we find the EMPLOYEE row for Nakata and note that it contains the name of Nakata's department—Accounting. Next, we find the Accounting row in the DEPARTMENT table. From that row we extract the Number-of-employees column (Nemp in Figure 9–9).

**Figure 9–9**

Relational representation of Figure 9–8

| Name | Co | Nemp |
|------|-----|------|
| FINANCE | AJAX | 2 |
| ACCOUNTING | AJAX | 5 |

a. DEPARTMENT relation

| Name | Enum | Nsub |
|------|------|------|
| BAMMER | 0100 | 2 |
| RATTLEMARKER | 1001 | 1 |
| ZARTER | 1000 | 1 |

b. SUPERVISOR relation

| Name | Enum | Dept | Supv | Pcode |
|------|------|------|------|-------|
| ANDERSON | 0210 | ACCOUNTING | ZARTER | 10 |
| GLOVER | 2000 | FINANCE | RATTLEMARKER | 05 |
| JACKSON | 2001 | ACCOUNTING | BAMMER | 30 |
| NAKATA | 2101 | ACCOUNTING | BAMMER | 30 |

c. EMPLOYEE relation

Recall from Chapter 5 that when the key for one relation appears as an attribute in another relation, it is called a *foreign key*. In the previous example, the Department attribute of the EMPLOYEE relation is also the key field for the DEPARTMENT relation. Thus, within the EMPLOYEE relation, Department is a foreign key.

Foreign keys are important when defining constraints across relations. For example; the database designer may specify that a DEPARTMENT tuple cannot be deleted if the value of that tuple's Name is a foreign key in any other relation. This constraint will prevent the user from inadvertently deleting, for example, the Finance Department without doing something about Glover, who currently works in that department. Were the Finance record to be deleted from the DEPARTMENT relation while Glover's record remained unchanged, the data in the database would begin to lose its integrity. We will see more of this in Chapter 11.

**Complex Network Relationships.** Figure 9–10 shows STUDENT and CLASS objects that participate in a complex (*M:N*) relationship. Both objects contain the other as a multivalued attribute. We need three relations to represent this network: one for the STUDENT object, one for the CLASS object, and a third for the relationship between students and classes. You will recall from Chapter 5 that the STUDENT-CLASS relation is also known as an intersection relation. The relation structures are

> STUDENT(Snum, Name, Major)
> CLASS(Cname, Time, Room)
> STUDENT-CLASS(Snum, Cname)

An example of each of the relations appears in Figure 9–11. Notice that the connection between student and class is established via the STUDENT-CLASS relation. For example, to determine the names of students in a particular class, say AP150, we access the STUDENT-CLASS relation looking for the value AP150. When we find one, we obtain the corresponding student number and use it to access the student data. Using the data in Figure 9–11, we can see that student 4567 is enrolled in AP150. We use this student number to determine the name of the student, which is GLOVER.

# RELATIONAL DATA MANIPULATION

In the previous examples, we described the processing of relations in a general and intuitive manner. This is fine for learning purposes, but to process relations with a computer, we need a clear, unambiguous language for expressing what we want to do. To date, four different strategies for relational data manipulation have been proposed.

**Figure 9—10**
Illustration of a complex network

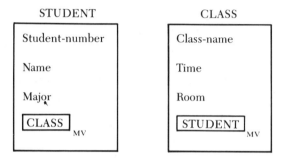

a. Object diagrams

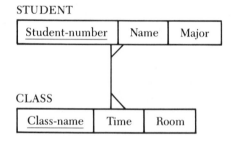

b. Relational schema

## Categories of Relational Data Manipulation Language

*Relational algebra,* one of the strategies, defines operators that work on relations (akin to the operators $+$, $-$, $\times$, and $/$ in high school algebra). Relations can be manipulated using these operators to achieve a desired result. However, relational algebra is hard to use, partly because it is procedural. That is, when using relational algebra, we must know not only *what* we want, but also *how* to get it. Although relational algebra is seldom used in industry, the underlying concepts are important because you need to understand how relations can be divided and recombined. Consequently we will discuss relational algebra later in this section.

    *Relational calculus* is a second strategy for manipulating relations. Relational calculus is nonprocedural. It is a language for expressing what we want without expressing how to get it. Recall the variable of integration in

| Snum | Name | Major |
|------|------|-------|
| 0123 | ANDERSON | ACCOUNTING |
| 4567 | GLOVER | ANTHROPOLOGY |

a. STUDENT relation

| Cname | Time | Room |
|-------|------|------|
| BA482 | MW 3 | C-150 |
| BD445 | TR 2 | C-213 |
| BA491 | TR 3 | C-141 |
| AP150 | MWF 9 | D-412 |

b. CLASS relation

| Snum | Cname |
|------|-------|
| 0123 | BA482 |
| 0123 | BD445 |
| 0123 | BA491 |
| 4567 | AP150 |
| 4567 | BD445 |

c. STUDENT-CLASS relation

calculus, a variable that ranges over an interval to be integrated. Relational calculus has a similar variable. For *tuple relational calculus*, the variable ranges over the tuples of a relation. For *domain relational calculus*, the variable ranges over the values of a domain.

Unless you are going to become a designer of relational database systems or a theoretician of relational technology, you will probably get along very well in this world without knowledge of relational calculus. Therefore, it will not be discussed in this text.

Database experts realized that although relational calculus is hard to understand and use, its nonprocedural property is highly desirable. Therefore, these people looked for other nonprocedural techniques. This led to the third and fourth categories of relational DML.

*Transform-oriented* languages are a class of nonprocedural languages that use relations to transform input data into desired outputs. These languages provide easy-to-use structures for expressing what is desired in terms of what is known. SQUARE, SEQUEL, and SEQUEL'S offspring SQL are all transform-oriented languages. As stated at the beginning of this chapter, since SQL is the basis of several popular commercial relational DBMS products, we will discuss it at some length.

The fourth category of relational DML is *graphic*. Systems based on this technology, such as IBM's QBE (Query-by-Example) and Borland's PARADOX, provide the user with a picture of the structure of a relation. The user fills in an example of what he or she wants and the system responds with actual data in that format. The four categories of relational DML are summarized in Figure 9–12.

## Sample Relations

To facilitate the discussion of relational algebra and SQL, we will use one set of examples. Six relations and their domain definitions are shown in Figure 9–13. Some brief comments about them follow. First, observe that the attribute Name is used in several relations. Thus, when we refer to a specific attribute, we will qualify it with its relation name.

The formats of the Ages and the Class-sizes domains are the same, yet the domains are different. Even though two domains have the same values, they are not the same, semantically, since they do not represent the same properties. The integer 21 in Ages represents 21 years, but the same integer 21 in Class-sizes represents the number of people in a class. Thus the value 21 represents entirely different entities.

In the following discussion, character values will be shown in single quotes. Characters not in quotes represent names. Thus, 'Room' differs from Room. 'Room' is a value, whereas Room is, say, a domain name. Concerning numeric data, numbers not in quotes refer to numeric quantities. Numbers in quotes refer to character strings. Thus, 123 is a number; '123' is a string of the characters '1', '2', and '3'.

## Relational Algebra

Although the two are conceptually similar, relational algebra is a far cry from the algebra you learned in high school. In high school algebra, variables represented numbers, and operations such as +, −, ×, and / oper-

**Figure 9—12**

Four categories of relational DML

> - Relational algebra
> - Relational calculus
> - Transform-oriented languages (such as SQL)
> - Graphic systems (such as Query-by-Example)

**Figure 9—13**
Relation and domain
definitions for exam-
ples in text

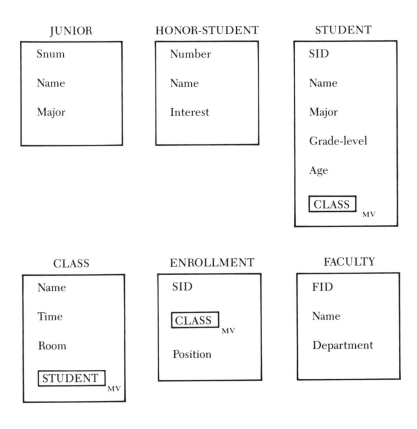

a. Object diagrams

1. JUNIOR (<u>Snum</u>, Name, Major)
2. HONOR-STUDENT (<u>Number</u>, Name, Interest)
3. STUDENT (<u>SID</u>, Name, Major, Grade-level, Age)
4. CLASS (<u>Name</u>, Time, Room)
5. ENROLLMENT (<u>Student-number</u>, Class-name, Position-number)
6. FACULTY (<u>FID</u>, Name, Department)

b. Relation definitions

**Figure 9–13**
(continued)

|   | Attribute | Domain |
|---|---|---|
| 1. | Snum | People-identifiers |
|   | JUNIOR. Name | People-names |
|   | Major | Subject-names |
| 2. | Number | People-identifiers |
|   | HONOR-STUDENT. Name | People-names |
|   | Interest | Subject-names |
| 3. | SID | People-identifiers |
|   | STUDENT. Name | People-names |
|   | Major | Subject-names |
|   | Grade-level | Classes |
|   | Age | Ages |
| 4. | CLASS. Name | Class-names |
|   | Time | Class-times |
|   | Room | Rooms |
| 5. | Student-number | People-identifiers |
|   | Class-name | Class-names |
|   | Position-number | Class-sizes |
| 6. | FID | People-identifiers |
|   | FACULTY. Name | People-names |
|   | Department | Subject-names |

c. Attribute domains

ated on numeric quantities. For *relational* algebra, however, the variables are relations and the operations manipulate relations to form new relations. For example, the operation + (or union) combines the tuples of one relation with the tuples of another relation to produce a third relation.

Although we have not stated it previously, relations are sets. The tuples of a relation can be considered elements of a set. Therefore, operations that can be performed on sets can also be performed on relations. We will first show four such set operators. Then we will discuss operators that are peculiar to relational algebra.

**Union.** The *union* of two relations is formed by combining the tuples from one relation with those of a second relation to produce a third relation.

**Figure 9-13**
*(continued)*

| Domain Name | Format |
|---|---|
| People-identifiers | Decimal (3) |
| People-names | Char (8) (unrealistic, but handy for these examples) |
| Subject-names | Char (10) |
| Classes | One of [FR, SO, JR, SN, GR] |
| Ages | Decimal from 0 to 100 |
| Class-names | Char (5) |
| Class-times | Char (5) format: DDDHH, where D is one of [M, T, W, R, F, or blank], and HH is decimal between 1 and 12 |
| Rooms | Char (5) format: BBRRR, where BB is a building code, and RRR is a room number |
| Class-sizes | Decimal from 0 to 100 |

d. Domain definitions

Duplicate tuples are eliminated. For this operation to make sense, the relations must be *union compatible*. This means that each relation must have the same number of attributes and that the attributes in corresponding columns must come from the same domain. If, for example, the third attribute of one relation comes from the Ages domain, then the third attribute of the second relation must also come from the Ages domain.

In Figure 9-13 the JUNIOR and the HONOR-STUDENT relations are union compatible. They both have three attributes and corresponding attributes come from the same domain. Snum and HONOR-STUDENT.Number come from the domain People-identifiers, JUNIOR.Name and HONOR-STUDENT.Name have the domain People-names, and Major and Interest have the domain Subject-names.

The relations JUNIOR and CLASS both have three attributes, but they are *union incompatible*. The three attributes do not have the same domain.

Figure 9-14 shows the union of two instances of the JUNIOR and HONOR-STUDENT relations. Note that the tuple [123, JONES, HISTORY], which occurs in both relations, is not duplicated in the union.

**Difference.** The *difference* of two relations is a third relation containing tuples that occur in the first relation but not in the second. The relations must be union compatible. The difference of JUNIOR and HONOR-STUDENT is shown in Figure 9-15. As with arithmetic, the order of the subtraction matters. A − B is not the same as B − A.

**Figure 9–14**
JUNIOR and
HONOR-STUDENT
relations and their
union

| Snum | Name | Major |
|------|------|-------|
| 123 | JONES | HISTORY |
| 158 | PARKS | MATH |
| 271 | SMITH | HISTORY |

a. Example JUNIOR relation

| Number | Name | Interest |
|--------|------|----------|
| 105 | ANDERSON | MANAGEMENT |
| 123 | JONES | HISTORY |

b. Example HONOR-STUDENT relation

| Snum or Number | Name | Major or Interest |
|----------------|------|-------------------|
| 123 | JONES | HISTORY |
| 158 | PARKS | MATH |
| 271 | SMITH | HISTORY |
| 105 | ANDERSON | MANAGEMENT |

c. Union of JUNIOR and HONOR-STUDENT relations

**Figure 9–15**
JUNIOR minus
HONOR-STUDENT
relation

| Snum | Name | Major |
|------|------|-------|
| 158 | PARKS | MATH |
| 271 | SMITH | HISTORY |

**Figure 9—16**
Intersection
of JUNIOR and
HONOR-STUDENT
relations

| Snum or<br>Number | Name | Major or<br>Interest |
|---|---|---|
| 123 | JONES | HISTORY |

**Intersection.**  The *intersection* of two relations is a third relation containing common tuples. Again, the relations must be union compatible. In Figure 9–16 the intersection of JUNIOR and HONOR-STUDENT is the single tuple [123, JONES, HISTORY]. This is the only tuple that occurs in both JUNIOR and HONOR-STUDENT.

**Product.**  The *product* of two relations (sometimes called the *Cartesian product*) is the concatenation of every tuple of one relation with every tuple of a second relation. The product of relation A (having *m* tuples) and relation B (having *n* tuples) has *m* times *n* tuples. The product is denoted $A \times B$ or *A* TIMES *B*. In Figure 9–17, relation STUDENT has four tuples and relation ENROLLMENT has three. STUDENT TIMES ENROLLMENT will therefore have twelve tuples. These tuples are shown in Figure 9–18. (Incidentally, the resulting relation in Figure 9–18 contains some very meaningless tuples. Other operations would need to be performed to extract some meaningful information from this relation. This is simply an illustration of the product operator.)

**Projection.**  *Projection* is an operation that selects specified attributes from a relation. The result of the projection is a new relation that has the selected attributes. In other words, projection picks columns out of a relation. For example, consider the STUDENT relation data in Figure 9–17. The projection of STUDENT on Name and Major attributes, denoted with brackets as STUDENT[Name, Major], is shown in Figure 9–19a. The projection of STUDENT on Major and Grade-level, denoted STUDENT[Major, Grade-level], appears in Figure 9–19b.

Note that although STUDENT has four tuples to begin with, the projection STUDENT[Major, Grade-level] has only three. A tuple was eliminated because after the projection was done, the tuple [HISTORY, JR] occurred twice. Because the result of projection is a relation, and because relations cannot contain duplicate tuples, the redundant tuple is eliminated.

Projection can also be used to change the order of attributes in a relation. For example, the projection STUDENT[Age, Grade-level, Major, SID] reverses the order of STUDENT attributes (see Figure 9–13 for the original

**Figure 9–17**

Examples of
STUDENT and
ENROLLMENT
relations

| SID | Name | Major | Grade-level | Age |
|-----|------|-------|-------------|-----|
| 123 | JONES | HISTORY | JR | 21 |
| 158 | PARKS | MATH | GR | 26 |
| 105 | ANDERSON | MANAGEMENT | SN | 27 |
| 271 | SMITH | HISTORY | JR | 19 |

a. STUDENT relation

| Student-number | Class-name | Position-number |
|----------------|------------|-----------------|
| 123 | H350 | 1 |
| 105 | BA490 | 3 |
| 123 | BA490 | 7 |

b. ENROLLMENT relation

order). This feature can sometimes be used to make two relations union compatible.

**Selection.**   Whereas the projection operator takes a vertical subset (columns) of a relation, the *selection* operator takes a horizontal subset (rows). Projection identifies *attributes* to be included in the new relation, but selection identifies *tuples* to be included in the new relation. Selection is denoted by specifying the relation name, followed by the keyword WHERE, followed by a condition involving attributes. Figure 9–20a shows the selection of the relation STUDENT WHERE Major = 'MATH'. Figure 9–20b shows the selection of STUDENT WHERE Age < 25.

**Join.**   The *join* operation is a combination of the product, selection, and (possibly) projection operations. The join of two relations, say A and B, operates in three steps. First, form the product of *A* times *B*. Then, do a selection to eliminate some tuples (the criteria for the selection are specified as part of the join). Then, (optionally) remove attributes with projection.

Consider the STUDENT and ENROLLMENT relations shown in Figure 9–17. Suppose we want to know the sizes of the classes for each student. To obtain this, we need to join STUDENT tuples with matching (on SID) ENROLLMENT tuples. We denote such a join as STUDENT JOIN (SID = Student-number) ENROLLMENT. The meaning of this expression is "Join

| SID | 'Name | Major | Glev | Age | Snum | Cname | Pnum |
|-----|-------|-------|------|-----|------|-------|------|
| 123 | JONES | HISTORY | JR | 21 | 123 | H350 | 1 |
| 123 | JONES | HISTORY | JR | 21 | 105 | BA490 | 3 |
| 123 | JONES | HISTORY | JR | 21 | 123 | BA490 | 7 |
| 158 | PARKS | MATH | GR | 26 | 123 | H350 | 1 |
| 158 | PARKS | MATH | GR | 26 | 105 | BA490 | 3 |
| 158 | PARKS | MATH | GR | 26 | 123 | BA490 | 7 |
| 105 | ANDERSON | MANAGEMENT | SN | 27 | 123 | H350 | 1 |
| 105 | ANDERSON | MANAGEMENT | SN | 27 | 105 | BA490 | 3 |
| 105 | ANDERSON | MANAGEMENT | SN | 27 | 123 | BA490 | 7 |
| 271 | SMITH | HISTORY | JR | 19 | 123 | H350 | 1 |
| 271 | SMITH | HISTORY | JR | 19 | 105 | BA490 | 3 |
| 271 | SMITH | HISTORY | JR | 19 | 123 | BA490 | 7 |

a STUDENT tuple to an ENROLLMENT tuple if SID of STUDENT equals Student-number of ENROLLMENT."

To form this join, we first take the product of STUDENT and ENROLL-MENT. This operation is shown in Figure 9–18. Then we SELECT those tuples from the product where SID of STUDENT equals Student-number of ENROLLMENT (only three exist). This operation leads to the relation in Figure 9–21a. Observe that two attributes are identical: SID and Student-number (Snum). One of these is redundant, so we eliminate it (in this case, we will choose Student-number) with projection. The result is the join in Figure 9–21b.

The join in Figure 9–21a is called the *equijoin* and the one in Figure 9–21b is called the *natural join*. Unless otherwise specified, when people say *join*, they mean the natural join.

In reality, forming the product of two large relations may be time-consuming. Consequently, other, more efficient methods have been devised for joining two relations. The output of these other methods is identical to the output described here.

Joining on conditions other than equality is also possible—for example, STUDENT JOIN(SID not = Student-number)ENROLLMENT, and STU-

**Figure 9–19**

Projections of
STUDENT relation

| Name | Major |
|------|-------|
| JONES | HISTORY |
| PARKS | MATH |
| ANDERSON | MANAGEMENT |
| SMITH | HISTORY |

a. STUDENT[Name, Major]

| Major | Grade-level |
|-------|-------------|
| HISTORY | JR |
| MATH | GR |
| MANAGEMENT | SN |

b. STUDENT[Major, Grade-level]

**Figure 9–20**

Examples of rela-
tional selection
operation

| SID | Name | Major | Glev | Age |
|-----|------|-------|------|-----|
| 158 | PARKS | MATH | GR | 26 |

a. STUDENT WHERE Major = 'Math'

| SID | Name | Major | Glev | Age |
|-----|------|-------|------|-----|
| 123 | JONES | HISTORY | JR | 21 |
| 271 | SMITH | HISTORY | JR | 19 |

b. STUDENT WHERE Age < 25

DENT JOIN(SID < FID)FACULTY. The latter join would result in tuples where student numbers are less than faculty numbers. Such a join may have meaning if, say, People-identifiers were assigned in chronological order. Such a join would portray pairs of students and teachers in which the student had been at the institution longer than the teacher.

There is one important limit on the conditions of a join, however. The attributes in the condition must arise from a common domain. Thus, STUDENT JOIN(Age = Class-size)ENROLLMENT is *illegal*. Even though the values of Age and Class-size are compatible, they do not arise from the same domain. Semantically, this type of join makes no sense. (Unhappily, some relational DBMS products will permit such a join.)

**Figure 9—21**

Examples of joining STUDENT and ENROLLMENT relations

| SID | Name | Major | Glev | Age | Snum | Cname | Pnum |
|-----|------|-------|------|-----|------|-------|------|
| 123 | JONES | HISTORY | JR | 21 | 123 | H350 | 1 |
| 123 | JONES | HISTORY | JR | 21 | 123 | BA490 | 7 |
| 105 | ANDERSON | MANAGEMENT | SN | 27 | 105 | BA490 | 3 |

a. Equijoin

| SID | Name | Major | Glev | Age | Cname | Pnum |
|-----|------|-------|------|-----|-------|------|
| 123 | JONES | HISTORY | JR | 21 | H350 | 1 |
| 123 | JONES | HISTORY | JR | 21 | BA490 | 7 |
| 105 | ANDERSON | MANAGEMENT | SN | 27 | BA490 | 3 |

b. Natural join

## Expressing Queries in Relational Algebra

Figure 9–22 summarizes the basic relational operations discussed. Set operations include +, −, intersection, and product. Selection picks specific tuples (rows) from a relation in accordance with conditions on attribute values. Projection picks specific attributes (columns) from a relation by attribute name. Finally, join concatenates the tuples of two relations in accordance with a condition on values of attributes.

We will now illustrate how relational operators can be used to express queries. We will use relations STUDENT, CLASS, and ENROLLMENT from Figure 9–13. Sample data is shown in Figure 9–23. The purpose of this demonstration is to illustrate the manipulation of relations. Although you will probably never use relational algebra in a commercial environment, these examples will help you understand how relations can be processed.

a. What are the names of all students?

STUDENT [Name]

This is simply the projection of the Name attribute of the STUDENT relation. The result is

| JONES |
|-------|
| PARKS |
| BAKER |
| GLASS |
| RUSSELL |
| RYE |

Observe that duplicate names have been omitted. The names JONES and BAKER actually occur twice in the relation STUDENT, but the repetitions

**Figure 9—22**

Summary of relational algebra operations

| Type | Format | Example |
|---|---|---|
| Set operations | +, −, intersection, product | STUDENT[Name] − JUNIOR[Name] |
| Selection | SELECT relation WHERE condition | SELECT CLASS WHERE Name = 'A' |
| Projection | relation[list of attributes] | STUDENT[Name, Major, Age] |
| Join | relation1 JOIN (condition) relation 2 | STUDENT JOIN (SID = Student-number) ENROLLMENT |

have been omitted because the result of a projection is a relation and relations may not have duplicate tuples.

    b. What are the student numbers of all students enrolled in a class?

        ENROLLMENT[Student-Number]

This is similar to query a, but the projection occurs on the relation ENROLLMENT. The result is

| |
|---|
| 100 |
| 150 |
| 200 |
| 300 |
| 400 |
| 450 |

Again, duplicate tuples have been omitted.

    c. What are the student numbers of all students not enrolled in a class?

        STUDENT[SID] - ENROLLMENT[Student-number]

This expression takes the difference of the projection of two relations. STUDENT[SID] has the student numbers of all students. ENROLLMENT [Student-number] has the student numbers of all students enrolled in a class. The difference is the students not enrolled in a class. The result is

    d. What are the numbers of students enrolled in the class 'BD445'?

        ENROLLMENT WHERE Class-name = 'BD445' [Student-number]

**Figure 9—23**

Example data for
relations defined in
Figure 9—13

| SID | Name | Major | Grade-level | Age |
|-----|------|-------|-------------|-----|
| 100 | JONES | HISTORY | GR | 21 |
| 150 | PARKS | ACCOUNTING | SO | 19 |
| 200 | BAKER | MATH | GR | 50 |
| 250 | GLASS | HISTORY | SN | 50 |
| 300 | BAKER | ACCOUNTING | SN | 41 |
| 350 | RUSSELL | MATH | JR | 20 |
| 400 | RYE | ACCOUNTING | FR | 18 |
| 450 | JONES | HISTORY | SN | 24 |

a. STUDENT relation

| Student-number | Class-name | Position-number |
|----------------|------------|-----------------|
| 100 | BD445 | 1 |
| 150 | BA200 | 1 |
| 200 | BD445 | 2 |
| 200 | CS250 | 1 |
| 300 | CS150 | 1 |
| 400 | BA200 | 2 |
| 400 | BF410 | 1 |
| 400 | CS250 | 2 |
| 450 | BA200 | 3 |

b. ENROLLMENT relation

| Name | Time | Room |
|------|------|------|
| BA200 | M-F9 | SC110 |
| BD445 | MWF3 | SC213 |
| BF410 | MWF8 | SC213 |
| CS150 | MWF3 | EA304 |
| CS250 | MWF12 | EB210 |

c. CLASS relation

This expression selects the appropriate tuples and then projects them onto the attribute Student-number. The result is

e. What are the names of the students enrolled in class 'BD445'?

```
STUDENT JOIN (SID = Student-number) ENROLLMENT WHERE Class-
name = 'BD445' [STUDENT.Name]
```

To answer this query, data from both STUDENT and ENROLLMENT is needed. Specifically, student names must come from STUDENT, whereas the condition "enrolled in BD445" must be checked in ENROLLMENT. Since both relations are needed, they must be joined. After STUDENT and ENROLLMENT have been joined, the select is applied, followed by a projection on student names. The result is

| JONES |
|-------|
| BAKER |

As stated previously, when two or more relations are considered, attribute names can become ambiguous. Therefore, for clarity, the relation name may be prefixed to the attribute name. Thus, in the above example, the projection is on [STUDENT.Name]. In this case, because all the attribute names are different, the prefix is optional and was added only for clarity. When attribute names are identical (for instance, a join involving STUDENT and CLASS will yield two attributes, both called Name), the prefix is required. Consider the following example.

f. What are the names and meeting times of PARKS' classes?

To answer this query, we must bring together data in all three relations. We need STUDENT data to find PARKS' student number, we need ENROLL-MENT data to learn which classes PARKS is in, and we need CLASS data to determine class meeting times. One way to respond to this query is as follows:

```
STUDENT WHERE Name = 'PARKS' JOIN (SID = Student-number)
ENROLLMENT JOIN (Class-name = Name) CLASS [CLASS.Name, Time]
```

This expression first selects PARKS' tuple and joins it to matching ENROLL-MENT tuples. Then, the result is joined to matching CLASS tuples. Finally, the projection is taken to print classes and times. The result is

| BA200 | M-F9 |
|-------|------|

We must specify CLASS.Name. Simply specifying Name is ambiguous because both STUDENT and CLASS have an attribute called Name.

Other, equivalent ways of responding to this query are also possible. One is

```
STUDENT JOIN (SID = Student-number) ENROLLMENT JOIN (Class-
name = Name) CLASS WHERE STUDENT.Name = 'PARKS' [CLASS.Name,
Time]
```

This expression differs from the first one because the select on PARKS is not done until after all of the joins have been performed. Assuming a computer performs the operations as stated, this latter expression will be much slower than the former one. Many more tuples will be joined.

Such differences are an important disadvantage of relational algebra. To the user, two equivalent queries should take the same time (and hence cost the same). Imagine the frustration if one form of a query costs 17¢ and another costs $4,356. To the unwary and unsophisticated user, the cost algorithm will appear capricious. To eliminate this situation, relational algebra expressions need to be optimized before they are processed.

## RELATIONAL DATA MANIPULATION LANGUAGE—SQL

SQL is a transform-oriented relational language. As such, SQL provides language to transform inputs into desired outputs via relations. If you work with relational DBMS products, you will likely use SQL or a related version. Consequently, we will discuss this language at some length. It is important to keep in mind that SQL is *not* a programming language like COBOL. Rather, it is a database *sublanguage*, or a data access language. It is employed to access database data and manipulate it to some extent. However, SQL statements are often embedded in programs written in traditional programming languages. Such programs then process the data.

The development of SQL began at IBM's San Jose research facilities in the mid-1970s under the name SEQUEL. Several versions of SEQUEL were released before the product was renamed SQL in 1980. Since then, IBM has continued the development of SQL, which has become a standard in the database processing industry. SQL has been implemented in various database products, including ORACLE and DB2.

This section discusses the core of the SQL language, which is akin to the core of COBOL. Keep in mind that an implementation of SQL (for example, IBM's DB2 in Chapter 11) may differ slightly from the SQL we present here.

SQL can be used interactively as a query/update language and SQL statements can be embedded in application programs. The query/update version was designed to be used by both technical and nontechnical people. In this section, we will present interactive SQL statements. Slight modifications might be needed to embed these statements in a program, as you will see in Chapter 11.

Also, SQL includes statements for data definition, data manipulation, and data control. This section discusses only the DML portions of SQL. We assume relations have already been defined. Specific DDL, DML, and control languages will be presented for the relational database product DB2 in Chapter 11.

### Terms

We have used the terms *relation, tuple,* and *attribute* when referring to the concepts of the relational model and relational designs (the outputs of the database design step). When we discuss particular implementations of relational database products and instances of relations, we will use the more familiar terms *table, row,* and *column.*

### Querying a Single Table

First, we consider SQL facilities for manipulating a single table. To follow custom, all SQL statements will be shown in capital letters. For display purposes, some SQL expressions will be indented. This is done only for clarity because, in actual practice, the position of expressions in SQL is arbitrary. Finally, to provide reference numbers for text discussion, each SQL example is numbered. These numbers are not part of SQL. They are inserted merely for discussion purposes.

**SQL Projections.**   To form a projection with SQL, we list the columns we want to see in a special format. For instance, the projection STUDENT[SID, Name, Major] is created by specifying

```
1.  SELECT      SID, NAME, MAJOR
    FROM        STUDENT
```

The keywords SELECT and FROM are always required. The columns to be obtained are listed after SELECT. The table to be used is listed after FROM. The result of this projection for the data in Figure 9–23 is

| 100 | JONES | HISTORY |
|-----|-------|---------|
| 150 | PARKS | ACCOUNTING |
| 200 | BAKER | MATH |
| 250 | GLASS | HISTORY |
| 300 | BAKER | ACCOUNTING |
| 350 | RUSSELL | MATH |
| 400 | RYE | ACCOUNTING |
| 450 | JONES | HISTORY |

Do not confuse the keyword SELECT with the relational algebra operator *selection*. SELECT is part of an SQL expression, whereas selection is the operation of obtaining rows from a table.

Consider another example:

        2.  SELECT      MAJOR
            FROM        STUDENT

The result of this operation is the following:

As you can see, duplicate rows remain. SQL does not follow the relational model convention that duplicate rows must be eliminated. This decision was made because such removal can be expensive and in many cases is not desired. If we want duplicate rows to be removed, then the qualifier UNIQUE must be specified as follows:

        3.  SELECT      UNIQUE MAJOR
            FROM        STUDENT

The result of this operation is

**SQL Selections.**    The relational algebra selection operator is specified in SQL form as follows:

    4a.  SELECT      SID, NAME, MAJOR, GRADE-LEVEL, AGE
         FROM        STUDENT
         WHERE       MAJOR = 'MATH'

The SELECT expression specifies the names of all columns of the table. FROM specifies the table to be used, and the new expression WHERE provides the conditions for the selection. The format SELECT—FROM—WHERE is the fundamental structure of SQL statements. The following is an equivalent form of query example 4a:

    4b.  SELECT      *
         FROM        STUDENT
         WHERE       MAJOR = 'MATH'

The * means that all columns of the table are to be obtained. The result of both queries is

| 200 | BAKER | MATH | GR | 50 |
|-----|-------|------|-----|-----|
| 350 | RUSSELL | MATH | JR | 20 |

We can combine selection and projection as follows:

```
5.  SELECT      NAME, AGE
    FROM        STUDENT
    WHERE       MAJOR = 'MATH'
```

The result is

| BAKER | 50 |
|-------|-----|
| RUSSELL | 20 |

Several conditions can be expressed in the WHERE clause. For example, the expression

```
6.  SELECT      NAME, AGE
    FROM        STUDENT
    WHERE       MAJOR = 'MATH'
    AND         AGE > 21
```

obtains the following:

| BAKER | 50 |
|-------|-----|

The conditions in WHERE clauses can refer to a set of values. To do this, the keyword IN or NOT IN is used. Consider the following:

```
7.  SELECT      NAME
    FROM        STUDENT
    WHERE       MAJOR IN ['MATH', 'ACCOUNTING']
```

Notice that multiple values can be placed inside the brackets. This expression means "Present the names of students who have either a math or an accounting major." The result is

| PARKS |
|-------|
| BAKER |
| BAKER |
| RUSSELL |
| RYE |

The expression

```
8.  SELECT      NAME
    FROM        STUDENT
    WHERE       MAJOR NOT IN ['MATH', 'ACCOUNTING']
```

will cause the names of students other than math and accounting majors to be presented. The result is

| JONES |
| GLASS |
| JONES |

The expression MAJOR IN means that the value of the Major column can equal *any* of the listed majors. This is equivalent to the logical OR operator you have used in your programming courses. The expression MAJOR NOT IN means the value must be different from *all* of the listed majors.

**SQL Built-in Functions.** SQL provides five built-in functions: COUNT, SUM, AVG, MAX, and MIN. COUNT and SUM sound similar but are different. Whereas COUNT computes the number of rows in a table, SUM totals numeric columns. AVG, MAX, and MIN also operate on numeric columns. AVG computes the average value, and MAX and MIN obtain the maximum and minimum values of a column in a table.

The query expression

```
9.  SELECT      COUNT (*)
    FROM        STUDENT
```

counts the number of STUDENT rows and displays this total in a table having a single row and single column as follows:

| 8 |

With the exception of GROUP BY (considered later), built-in functions cannot be intermixed with column names in the SELECT statement. Thus, SELECT NAME, COUNT(*) is not allowed.

Consider the expressions

```
10.  SELECT      COUNT (MAJOR)
     FROM        STUDENT
11.  SELECT      COUNT (UNIQUE MAJOR)
     FROM        STUDENT
```

Expression 10 counts all majors, including duplicates. Expression 11 counts only unique majors. The results are

```
10.        8
11.        3
```

The special functions can be used to request a result, as in the previous examples. And in some versions of SQL, built-in functions can be used as part of a WHERE clause. Consider the following:

```
12.  SELECT      SID, NAME
     FROM        STUDENT
     WHERE       AGE > AVG (AGE)
```

The result (the average age is 30.38) is

| 200 | BAKER |
|-----|-------|
| 250 | GLASS |
| 300 | BAKER |

Built-in functions can appear in both SELECT and WHERE clauses:

```
13.  SELECT    COUNT(*)
     FROM      STUDENT
     WHERE     AGE = MAX(AGE)
```

This operation produces the number of students who have the maximum age. The result is

| 2 |
|---|

because two rows have the age 50. (MAX obtains the maximum of the ages in the data. This is not the maximum possible age in the AGE domain, which is 100.)

**Built-in Functions and Grouping.**    To increase their utility, built-in functions can be applied to groups of rows within a table. Such groups are formed by collecting rows (logically, not physically) that have the same value of a specified column. For example, students can be grouped by major. This means one group will be formed for each value of MAJOR. For the data in Figure 9–23, a group of HISTORY majors, a group of ACCOUNTING majors, and a group of MATH majors would be produced.

The SQL keyword GROUP BY instructs the DBMS to group together rows that have the same value of a column. Consider the following:

```
14.  SELECT    MAJOR, COUNT(*)
     FROM      STUDENT
     GROUP BY  MAJOR
```

The result of this expression is

| HISTORY    | 3 |
|------------|---|
| ACCOUNTING | 3 |
| MATH       | 2 |

The rows of the STUDENT table have been logically grouped by the value of MAJOR. Then the COUNT function sums the number of rows in each group. The result is a table having two columns—the major name and the sum. Thus, for subgroups, both columns and built-in functions can be specified in the SELECT statement.

In some cases, we do not want to consider all of the groups. For example, we might form groups of students who have the same major and then wish to consider only those groups that have more than two students. In this case, we use the SQL HAVING clause to identify the subset of groups we want to consider.

Suppose we want to know the names and students' average age of all majors having more than two students. The following SQL statements will obtain this result:

```
15.  SELECT     MAJOR, AVG(AGE)
     FROM       STUDENT
     GROUP BY   MAJOR
     HAVING     COUNT(*) > 2
```

Here, groups of students having the same major are formed. Then, groups having more than two students are selected. (Other groups are ignored.) The major and the average age of these selected groups are produced. The result is

| HISTORY | 31.67 |
|---|---|
| ACCOUNTING | 26 |

For even greater generality, WHERE clauses can be added as well. Consider the following:

```
16.  SELECT     MAJOR, AVG(AGE)
     FROM       STUDENT
     WHERE      GRADE-LEVEL = 'SN'
     GROUP BY   MAJOR
     HAVING     COUNT(*) > 1
```

The results of this operation will differ depending on whether the WHERE condition is applied before or after the HAVING condition. To eliminate ambiguity, the SQL convention is that WHERE clauses are applied first. Thus, in the above operation, senior students are selected. Then groups are formed, then the groups are selected by the HAVING condition, and then the result is presented. In this case, the result is

| HISTORY | 37 |
|---|---|

## Querying Multiple Tables

In this section we extend the discussion of SQL to include operations on two or more tables. The STUDENT, CLASS, and ENROLLMENT data in Figure 9–23 will be used to illustrate SQL features.

**Retrieval Using Subquery.**   Suppose we need to know the names of students enrolled in the class BD445. If we know that students 100 and 200 are enrolled in this class, then the following will produce the correct names:

```
17.  SELECT     NAME
     FROM       STUDENT
     WHERE      SID IN[100, 200]
```

Usually, we will not know the SIDs of students in a class. We do have a facility, however, for determining those SIDs. Consider the operation

```
18.  SELECT     STUDENT-NUMBER
     FROM       ENROLLMENT
     WHERE      CLASS-NAME = 'BD445'
```

The result of this operation is

| 100 |
|-----|
| 200 |

These are the student numbers we need. Now, combining expressions 17 and 18, we obtain the following:

```
19.  SELECT     NAME
     FROM       STUDENT
     WHERE      SID IN
         SELECT     STUDENT-NUMBER
         FROM       ENROLLMENT
         WHERE      CLASS-NAME = 'BD445'
```

It may be easier for you to understand these statements if you work from the bottom and read up. The last three statements obtain the student numbers for people enrolled in BD445. The first three statements produce the names for the two students selected. The result of this query is

| JONES |
|-------|
| BAKER |

This strategy can be very useful. Realize, however, that for this operation to be semantically correct, SID and STUDENT-NUMBER must arise from the same domain.

The same strategy can be applied to three or even more tables. For example, suppose we want to know the names of the students enrolled in classes on Monday, Wednesday, and Friday at 3 o'clock (denoted MWF3 in our data). First, we need the names of classes that meet at that time:

```
20.  SELECT  .  CLASS.NAME
     FROM       CLASS
     WHERE      TIME = 'MWF3'
```

(Since we will be dealing with three different tables, we will qualify column names with table names to avoid confusion and ambiguity.) Now we obtain the identifying numbers of students in these classes by specifying

```
21.  SELECT     ENROLLMENT.STUDENT-NUMBER
     FROM       ENROLLMENT
```

```
WHERE        ENROLLMENT.CLASS-NAME  IN
    SELECT      CLASS.NAME
    FROM        CLASS
    WHERE       TIME = 'MWF3'
```

This yields

```
100
200
300
```

which are the numbers of the students in class on Monday, Wednesday, and Friday at 3 o'clock. Now, to obtain the names of those students, we specify

```
22.  SELECT      STUDENT.NAME
     FROM        STUDENT
     WHERE       STUDENT.SID IN
         SELECT      ENROLLMENT.STUDENT-NUMBER
         FROM        ENROLLMENT
         WHERE       ENROLLMENT.CLASS-NAME IN
             SELECT      CLASS.NAME
             FROM        CLASS
             WHERE       CLASS.TIME = 'MWF3'
```

The result is

```
JONES
BAKER
BAKER
```

This strategy works well as long as the desired result (the answer) comes from a single table. If, however, the result comes from two or more tables, we have a problem. For example, suppose we want to know the names of students and the names of their classes. Say we need SID, student name, and class name. In this case, the results come from two different tables (STUDENT and ENROLLMENT) and the subquery strategy will not work. We need to be able to join the tables together.

**Joining with SQL.**   To produce the names of every student's classes, we need to join the STUDENT table with the ENROLLMENT table. The following statements will do this:

```
23.  SELECT      STUDENT.SID, STUDENT.NAME, ENROLLMENT.CLASS-NAME
     FROM        STUDENT, ENROLLMENT
     WHERE       STUDENT.SID = ENROLLMENT.STUDENT-NUMBER
```

Recall that a join is the combination of a product operation, followed by a selection, followed (usually) by a projection. In expression 23, the FROM statement expresses the product of STUDENT and ENROLLMENT.

Then, the WHERE statement expresses the selection. The meaning is "Select from the product of STUDENT and ENROLLMENT those rows in which SID of STUDENT equals STUDENT-NUMBER of ENROLLMENT." Finally, after the selection, the projection of student number, name, and class name is taken. The result is

| 100 | JONES | BD445 |
|-----|-------|-------|
| 150 | PARKS | BA200 |
| 200 | BAKER | BD445 |
| 200 | BAKER | CS250 |
| 300 | BAKER | CS150 |
| 400 | RYE   | BA200 |
| 400 | RYE   | BF410 |
| 400 | RYE   | CS250 |
| 450 | JONES | BA200 |

The WHERE clause can contain qualifiers in addition to those needed for the join. For example,

```
24.  SELECT    STUDENT.SID, ENROLLMENT.CLASS-NAME
     FROM      STUDENT, ENROLLMENT
     WHERE     STUDENT.SID = ENROLLMENT.STUDENT-NUMBER
       AND   STUDENT.NAME = 'RYE'
       AND   ENROLLMENT.POSITION-NUMBER = 1
```

The additional qualifiers here are STUDENT.NAME = 'RYE' and ENROLL-MENT.POSITION-NUMBER = 1. This operation will list the student number and class name of all students named RYE who were first to enroll in a class. The result is

| 400 | BF410 |
|-----|-------|

When data is needed from more than two tables, we can follow a similar strategy. In the following example, three tables are joined:

```
25.  SELECT    STUDENT.SID, CLASS.NAME, CLASS.TIME,
               ENROLLMENT.POSITION-NUMBER
     FROM      STUDENT, ENROLLMENT, CLASS
     WHERE     STUDENT.SID = ENROLLMENT.STUDENT-NUMBER
          AND   ENROLLMENT.CLASS-NAME = CLASS.NAME
          AND   STUDENT.NAME = 'BAKER'
```

The result of this operation is

| 200 | BD445 | MWF3  | 2 |
|-----|-------|-------|---|
| 200 | CS250 | MWF12 | 1 |
| 300 | CS150 | MWF3  | 1 |

**Comparison of SQL Subquery and Join.**  Join can be used as an alternative way of expressing subqueries. For example, in expression 19, we used a subquery to determine the students enrolled in the class BD445. We can also use a join to express this query as follows:

```
26.  SELECT  STUDENT.NAME
     FROM    STUDENT, ENROLLMENT
     WHERE   STUDENT.SID = ENROLLMENT.STUDENT-NUMBER
        AND  ENROLLMENT.CLASS-NAME = 'BD445'
```

Similarly, the query "What are the names of the students in class MWF at 3?" can be expressed as

```
27.  SELECT  STUDENT.NAME
     FROM    STUDENT, ENROLLMENT, CLASS
     WHERE   STUDENT.SID = ENROLLMENT.STUDENT-NUMBER
        AND  ENROLLMENT.CLASS-NAME = CLASS.NAME
        AND  CLASS.TIME = 'MWF3'
```

Although join expressions can substitute for subquery expressions, the reverse is not true. Subqueries cannot always be substituted for joins. When using a join, the displayed columns can come from any of the joined tables, but when using a subquery, the displayed columns can come only from the table named in the FROM expression in the first SELECT.

For example, suppose we want to know the names of classes taken by undergraduates. We can express this as a subquery:

```
28.  SELECT     UNIQUE CLASS-NAME
     FROM       ENROLLMENT
     WHERE      STUDENT-NUMBER IN
         SELECT SID
         FROM   STUDENT
         WHERE  GRADE-LEVEL NOT = 'GR'
```

or as a join:

```
29.  SELECT  UNIQUE ENROLLMENT.CLASS-NAME
     FROM    ENROLLMENT, STUDENT
     WHERE   ENROLLMENT.STUDENT-NUMBER = STUDENT.SID
        AND  STUDENT.GRADE-LEVEL NOT = 'GR'
```

However, if we want to know both the names of the classes and the grade levels of the undergraduate students, then we must use a join. A subquery will not suffice because the desired results arise from two different tables. The names of the classes are stored in ENROLLMENT and the names of the students are stored in STUDENT. The following will obtain the correct answer:

```
30.  SELECT  UNIQUE ENROLLMENT.CLASS-NAME, STUDENT.GRADE-LEVEL
     FROM    ENROLLMENT, STUDENT
     WHERE   ENROLLMENT.STUDENT-NUMBER = STUDENT.SID
        AND  STUDENT.GRADE-LEVEL NOT = 'GR'
```

The result will be

| | |
|---|---|
| BA200 | SO |
| CS150 | SN |
| BA200 | FR |
| BF410 | FR |
| CS250 | FR |
| BA200 | SN |

**EXISTS and NOT EXISTS.** EXISTS and NOT EXISTS are logical operators—their value is either true or false depending on the presence or absence of rows that fit qualifying conditions. For example, suppose we want to know the student numbers of students enrolled in more than one class. The query would be

```
31. SELECT  UNIQUE  STUDENT-NUMBER
       FROM     ENROLLMENT A
       WHERE   EXISTS
          SELECT *
          FROM     ENROLLMENT B
          WHERE   A.STUDENT-NUMBER = B.STUDENT-NUMBER
                 AND A.CLASS-NAME NOT = B.CLASS-NAME
```

In this example, the query and the subquery both refer to the ENROLLMENT table. To prevent ambiguity, these two uses of ENROLLMENT have been assigned a different name. In the first FROM statement, ENROLLMENT is assigned the temporary (and arbitrary) name A. In the second FROM statement, it is assigned another temporary name, B.

The meaning of the subquery expression is "Find two rows in ENROLLMENT having the same student number, but different class names." (This means the student is taking more than one class.) If two such rows exist, then the logical value of EXISTS is true. In this case, present the student number in the answer. Otherwise, the logical value of the EXISTS is false—do not present that SID in the answer.

Another way of viewing this query is to imagine two separate and identical copies of the ENROLLMENT table. Call one copy Table A and the other copy Table B. We will compare each row in A with each row in B. First, consider the first row in A and the first row in B. In this case, since the two rows are identical, both the STUDENT-NUMBERs and the CLASS-NAMEs will be the same. Do not display the SID.

Now, consider the first row in A and the second row in B. If the STUDENT-NUMBERs are the same and the CLASS-NAMEs are different, then display the STUDENT-NUMBER. Essentially, we are comparing the first row of ENROLLMENT with the second row of ENROLLMENT. For the data in Figure 9–23, neither the STUDENT-NUMBERs nor the CLASS-NAMEs are the same.

We continue comparing the first row of A with each row of B. If the conditions are ever met, we print the STUDENT-NUMBER. When all of the row in B have been examined, we move to the second row of A. It is compared to all of the rows in B. (Actually, if we are considering the $n$th row in A, then only rows greater than $n$ need be considered in B.) The result of this query is:

| 200 |
| --- |
| 400 |

To illustrate the application of NOT EXISTS, suppose we want to know the names of students taking all classes. In SQL we express this query by selecting the names of students such that there are no classes that the student did not take. The following expresses that statement:

```
32. SELECT        STUDENT.NAME
    FROM          STUDENT
    WHERE         NOT EXISTS
        SELECT    *
        FROM      ENROLLMENT
        WHERE     NOT EXISTS
            SELECT  *
            FROM    CLASS
            WHERE   CLASS.NAME = ENROLLMENT.CLASS-NAME
            AND     ENROLLMENT.STUDENT-NUMBER = STUDENT.SID
```

This query has three parts. In the bottom part, we try to find classes the student did not take. The middle part determines if any classes were found that the student did not take. If not, then the student is taking all classes, so the student's name is displayed.

This query may be difficult to understand. If you have trouble with it, use the data in Figure 9–23 and follow the query instructions. The answer, for that data, is that no student is taking all classes. You might try to change the data so that a student does take all classes. Another approach for understanding this query is to attempt to solve it by a means other than NOT EXISTS. The problems you encounter will help you understand why NOT EXISTS is necessary.

A final example combines many SQL concepts and illustrates the power of this database sublanguage. Suppose we want to know the names of graduate students taking classes only with other graduate students. The query would be

```
33. SELECT A.NAME
    FROM    STUDENT A
    WHERE   STUDENT.GRADE-LEVEL = 'GR'
        AND NOT EXISTS
        SELECT      *
        FROM        ENROLLMENT B
        WHERE       STUDENT.SID = B.STUDENT-NUMBER
            AND     B.CLASS-NAME IN
```

```
SELECT      C. CLASS-NAME
FROM        ENROLLMENT C
WHERE       B. CLASS-NAME  =  C. CLASS-NAME
    AND     C. STUDENT-NUMBER  IN
            SELECT      D. SID
            FROM        STUDENT D
            WHERE       C. STUDENT-NUMBER  =  D. SID
                AND     D. GRADE-LEVEL  NOT  =  'GR'
```

The meaning of this query is "Present the names of students where there is no row in ENROLLMENT that matches the student with a class which is one of the classes that are matched with students who have a grade level other than graduate." The result of this query is

> JONES

The last three queries are complicated. Do not assume from this that SQL is complicated. Actually, compared to the alternatives, SQL is simple. These last three queries are difficult because we are solving queries that are logically quite complex. For most day-to-day problems, SQL queries are quite simple and straightforward.

## Changing Data

SQL has provisions for changing data in tables by inserting new rows, deleting rows, and modifying values in existing rows. SQL also has facilities for changing data structure. However, we will not consider changing data structure until we study DB2 in Chapter 11.

**Inserting Data.**     Rows can be inserted into a table one at a time or in groups. To insert a single row, we state

```
34.  INSERT INTO ENROLLMENT
     [400, 'BD445', 44]
```

Sometimes we do not know all of this data. For example, if we do not know Position-number, we could say

```
35.  INSERT INTO ENROLLMENT (STUDENT-NUMBER, CLASS-NAME)
     [400, 'BD445']
```

Position-number could then be added later. Note that this causes the value of Position-number to be *null*. A null value indicates that the value is missing—it is not the same as blanks or zeros. Unfortunately, some implementations of SQL do not discriminate between nulls and blanks or zeros. They should.

We can also copy rows in mass from one table to another. For example, suppose we want to fill the JUNIOR table that was defined in Figure 9–13.

We would then say

```
36. INSERT      INTO JUNIOR
                SELECT    SID, NAME, MAJOR
                FROM      STUDENT
                WHERE     GRADE-LEVEL = 'JR'
```

This example, and all of the techniques for identifying data developed in the previous two sections, can be used to identify rows to be moved. This feature provides quite powerful capabilities.

**Deleting Data.** As with insertion, rows can be deleted one at a time or in groups. The following example will delete the row for student number 100:

```
37. DELETE    STUDENT
              WHERE     STUDENT.SID = 100
```

Note that if student 100 is enrolled in classes, this delete will cause an integrity problem. The ENROLLMENT rows having STUDENT-NUMBER = 100 will have no corresponding STUDENT row. We addressed such integrity problems in Chapter 6.

Groups of rows can be deleted as shown in the following two examples. These examples will delete all enrollments for accounting majors as well as all accounting majors:

```
38. DELETE    ENROLLMENT
              WHERE ENROLLMENT.STUDENT-NUMBER IN
                    SELECT    STUDENT.SID
                    FROM      STUDENT
                    WHERE     STUDENT.MAJOR = 'ACCOUNTING'
39. DELETE    STUDENT
              WHERE STUDENT.MAJOR = 'ACCOUNTING'
```

The order of these two operations is important. If the order were reversed, none of the ENROLLMENT rows would be deleted because the matching STUDENT rows would have already been deleted.

**Modifying Data.** Rows can also be modified one at a time or in groups. The keyword SET is used to change a column value. After SET, the name of the column to be changed is specified, followed by the new value or way of computing the new value. Consider two examples:

```
40. UPDATE    STUDENT
    SET       POSITION-NUMBER = 44
    WHERE     SID = 400
41. UPDATE    STUDENT
    SET       POSITION-NUMBER = MAX(POSITION-NUMBER) + 1
    WHERE     SID = 400
```

In operation 41, the value of the column will be calculated using the MAX built-in function.

To illustrate mass updates, suppose the name of a course has been changed from BD445 to BD564. In this case, to prevent integrity problems, both the ENROLLMENT and the CLASS tables need to be changed. This would be accomplished as follows:

```
42.  UPDATE      ENROLLMENT
     SET         CLASS-NAME  =  'BD564'
     WHERE       CLASS-NAME  =  'BD445'
     UPDATE      CLASS
     SET         CLASS-NAME  =  'BD564'
     WHERE       CLASS-NAME  =  'BD445'
```

## SUMMARY

The relational model is unique in the way that it stores data. Storing data in simple tables makes a relational database easy for an end user to query because only a few statements need to be mastered and the concepts of data storage and relationships are easily understood. Relational databases are very flexible. They are the basis for decision support systems, but they can also be used for more mundane applications, such as transaction processing.

Relational DBMSs have given more control to users and have had some impact on traditional programming personnel. The database sublanguage SQL has become a standard for data interchange between computers. As such, it is an important topic for business and computing students to study.

The relational model represents and processes data in the form of tables called *relations*. The columns of the tables are called *attributes* and the rows are called *tuples*. The values of attributes arise from *domains*. The *degree* of a relation is the number of attributes it possesses.

With the relational model, relationships are contained in data values. Two tuples can have a relationship if they have two attributes that arise from the same domain. Trees and simple and complex networks are readily represented.

The four categories of relational data manipulation language (DML) are relational algebra, relational calculus, transform-oriented languages, and graphic-oriented systems. Relational algebra consists of a group of relational operators that can be used to manipulate relations to obtain a desired result. Relational algebra is procedural. The transform-oriented languages provide a nonprocedural capability to use relations to transform given data into wanted results. SQL is an example.

SQL constructs are simple. The SELECT, FROM, and WHERE clauses are flexible and can be used in different ways to obtain many results. Even though the constructs are simple, SQL is an exceedingly powerful language. The return for time invested to learn SQL is great.

Some aspects of SQL may seem confusing. For example, concepts such as NOT EXISTS are very sophisticated. But SQL is quite powerful with just the basic, simple facilities. In fact, most run-of-the-mill, day-to-day query requests can be expressed with a knowledge of only the SELECT, FROM, and WHERE operators.

This chapter provided an introduction to the relational model. In Chapter 11 the concepts presented here will be used to develop a relational database implementation within a case study.

---

QUESTIONS **GROUP I**

9.1 Define the terms *relation, attribute, tuple, degree,* and *domain*.

9.2 Explain the difference between a relational schemata and a relation.

9.3 Define *key* and *candidate key*.

9.4 Give an example of a hierarchical relationship among two relations. Show the DSD (like Figure 9–4), the relational schemata, and sample data.

9.5 Give an example of a hierarchical relationship among three or more relations. Show the DSD, the relational schemata, and sample data.

9.6 Give an example of a simple network relationship. Show the DSD, the relational schemata, and sample data.

9.7 Give an example of a complex network relationship. Show the DSD, the relational schemata, and sample data.

9.8 Briefly explain how relationships are represented using the relational model.

9.9 Name and briefly explain four categories of relational DML.

9.10 How does relational algebra differ from high school algebra?

9.11 Define *union compatible*. Give examples of two relations that are union compatible and two that are union incompatible.

Questions 9.12 through 9.14 refer to the following two relations:
COMPANY(Name, Number-employees, Sales)
MANUFACTURER(Name, People, Revenue)

9.12 Give an example of a union of these two relations.

9.13 Give an example of a difference of these two relations.

9.14 Give an example of an intersection of these two relations.

Questions 9.15 through 9.23 refer to the following three relations:
SALESPERSON (Name, Age, Salary)
ORDER (Number, Cust-name, Salesperson-name, Amount)
CUSTOMER (Name, City, Industry-type)
An instance of these relations is in Figure 9–24. Use the data in those tables for the following problems.

9.15 Give an example of the product of SALESPERSON and ORDER.

9.16 Show an example of
SALESPERSON[Name, Salary]
SALESPERSON[Age, Salary]
Under what conditions will SALESPERSON[Age, Salary] have fewer rows than SALESPERSON?

**Figure 9–24**

Sample data for questions 9.15 through 9.23

| Name | Age | Salary |
|--------|-----|---------|
| Abel | 63 | 120,000 |
| Baker | 38 | 42,000 |
| Jones | 26 | 36,000 |
| Murphy | 42 | 50,000 |
| Zenith | 59 | 118,000 |
| Kobad | 27 | 34,000 |

SALESPERSON

| Number | Cust-name | Salesperson-name | Amount |
|--------|-----------------------|------------------|--------|
| 100 | Abernathy Construction | Zenith | 560 |
| 200 | Abernathy Construction | Jones | 1800 |
| 300 | Manchester Lumber | Abel | 480 |
| 400 | Amalgamated Housing | Abel | 2500 |
| 500 | Abernathy Construction | Murphy | 6000 |
| 600 | Tri-City Builders | Abel | 700 |
| 700 | Manchester Lumber | Jones | 150 |

ORDER

| Name | City | Industry-type |
|------------------------|------------|---------------|
| Abernathy Construction | Willow | B |
| Manchester Lumber | Manchester | F |
| Tri-City Builders | Memphis | B |
| Amalgamated Housing | Memphis | B |

CUSTOMER

**9.17**   Show an example of a select on SALESPERSON Name, on SALESPERSON Age, on both SALESPERSON Name and Age.

**9.18**   Show an example of an equijoin and a natural join of SALESPERSON and ORDER where Name of SALESPERSON equals Salesperson-name of ORDER.

**9.19**   Show relational algebra expressions for retrieving

   **a.** The names of all salespeople

   **b.** The names of all salespeople having an ORDER row

    **c.** The names of salespeople not having an ORDER row

    **d.** The names of salespeople having an order with ABERNATHY CONSTRUCTION

    **e.** The ages of salespeople having an order with ABERNATHY CONSTRUCTION

    **f.** The city of all CUSTOMERS having an order with salesperson JONES

**9.20** Show SQL expressions for the following queries:

    **a.** The ages and salaries of all salespeople

    **b.** The ages and salaries of all salespeople (duplicates omitted)

    **c.** The names of all salespeople less than thirty years old

    **d.** The names of all salespeople having an order with ABERNATHY CONSTRUCTION

    **e.** The names of all salespeople not having an order with ABERNATHY CONSTRUCTION

**9.21** Show SQL expressions for the following queries:

    **a.** The number of orders

    **b.** The number of different customers having an order

    **c.** The number of salespeople older than the average

    **d.** The name of the oldest salesperson

    **e.** The number of orders for each salesperson

    **f.** The average size order for each salesperson

    **g.** The average size order for each salesperson, considering only orders larger than 500

**9.22** Show SQL expressions for the following queries:

    **a.** The ages of salespeople having an order with ABERNATHY CON-STRUCTION (use subquery)

    **b.** The ages of salespeople having an order with ABERNATHY CON-STRUCTION (use join)

    **c.** The ages of salespeople having an order with a customer in MEMPHIS (use subquery)

    **d.** The ages of salespeople having an order with a customer in MEMPHIS (use join)

    **e.** The industry type and ages of salespersons of all orders for companies in MEMPHIS

    **f.** The names of salespeople having two or more orders

    **g.** The names and ages of salespeople having two or more orders

    **h.** The names and ages of salespeople having an order with all customers

**9.23** Show SQL expressions for the following update operations:

    **a.** Insert a new row into CUSTOMER

    **b.** Insert a new name and age into SALESPERSON; assume salary is undetermined

    **c.** Insert rows into the table HIGH-ACHIEVER (Name, Age) where, to be included, a salesperson must have a salary of at least 100,000

    **d.** Delete customer ABERNATHY CONSTRUCTION

    **e.** Delete all orders for ABERNATHY CONSTRUCTION

f. Change the salary of salesperson JONES to 45,000

g. Give all salespeople a 10 percent pay increase

h. Assume salesperson JONES changes name to PARKS; make appropriate changes.

---

**GROUP II**          QUESTIONS AND EXERCISES

9.24   Suppose you have the task of explaining to management why relational database processing is important. Prepare a three-page report to management that discusses the significance of relational database processing. Present the major findings in this report to your class.

9.25   Obtain information on relational calculus. Show how the sample queries 1 through 33 would be processed using relational calculus.

9.26   Obtain information on SQUARE. Compare and contrast SQUARE with SQL.

9.27   Obtain information on the DBMS product Paradox. Show how queries 1 through 33 would be processed using Paradox.

9.28   Obtain information on the DBMS product INGRES. Show how queries 1 through 33 would be processed using INGRES.

9.29   Use relational algebra to express queries 1 through 34.

9.30   Obtain information about the product IDM 500. How does this product's DML differ from SQL? How does it differ from INGRES? What are the strengths of IDM 500? The weaknesses?

9.31   Obtain a copy of a micro DBMS (such as R:Base). Store the data in Figure 9–23 using this product. Process queries 1 through 33 using this DBMS.

**CHAPTER**

# Microcomputer Databases

---

- The Microcomputer Database Environment
- Classes of Microcomputer Databases
- Designing a Microcomputer Database
- Summary

---

In this chapter we will explore database processing on microcomputers. We begin with an overview of the microcomputer database environment, including profiles of typical users, the role of the user in development of the database, and the role of traditional MIS departments in corporate microcomputer database development. Next we describe three fundamental classes of microcomputer databases and discuss some of the problems inherent in each. Finally, we discuss how logical database design might be implemented using microcomputer DBMS products. The primary focus of this chapter is the microcomputer *database*. You learned the principles of database *application* development in Chapter 8. Those principles hold true for both micro and mainframe database applications and will not be discussed further in this chapter.

## THE MICROCOMPUTER DATABASE ENVIRONMENT

The advent of 16-bit microcomputers brought database processing to the masses because database processing became cost-effective and affordable. Prior to that, database technology had been of interest only to a relatively small number of mainframe computer professionals. With the micro, hundreds of thousands of people—computer professionals and lay people alike—began to use database technology to process their data. Admittedly, microcomputer databases are tiny when compared to large mainframe databases. But the principles, the development process, and the needs for administration are nonetheless the same.

### The Typical User

The typical microcomputer database user is a business or professional person who needs to keep track of something. This definition includes a wide spectrum of people. One typical user might be a seminar leader who needs to keep a mailing list of seminar participants. Another typical user is a product manager who employs a microcomputer database to keep track of product sales. A college professor might use a microcomputer database to keep track of students and their grades. A fourth user might be a personnel department consisting of several people. Within the department, one group might need to process employee benefits, another group employee wages, and another group employee insurance. Though the groups differ, they share a common employee database. Despite the differences, these typical users have something in common: they are performing database processing on microcomputers with little or no dependence on traditional computer professionals.

Microcomputer databases serve both single and multiple users, although the majority of them are for single users. Historically, microcomputer databases were developed to support a single professional's needs (and were often developed *by* that individual). After all, the database was small, the DBMS product was affordable and somewhat user-friendly, and by developing a single-user application, an individual gained control of his own information processing without needing to rely on the MIS Department. Such applications continue to be developed. But in recent years, microcomputer databases have been installed on local area networks (LANs). LANs allow a common database to be processed concurrently by several users. Although such applications are currently a small percentage of the total, they are growing in popularity. Multi-user applications are more difficult to develop and implement, and often require the skills of a professional.

### Development by End Users

Microcomputer databases and their applications are often developed by users themselves. Historically, in large corporations, users grew impatient waiting for the services of professional developers to become available. So they learned to develop their own database applications. Elsewhere, self-employed individuals or users in smaller organizations could not afford the services of a professional developer, so they learned how to do it themselves. In light of this situation, DBMS vendors—especially vendors of microcomputer products—found they could increase sales by making their products more user-friendly. In fact, the user and developer interfaces of microcomputer DBMS products were initially far superior to those of minicomputer and mainframe products.

In some cases, users successfully developed their own applications. In other cases, the complexity of the application exceeded user expertise, making user development impossible. These situations opened the door for small consulting firms (often a sole individual) to build applications on a work-for-hire basis. In the last five years, an entire industry of such consultants has arisen. Many developers specialize in particular applications, such as client billing, inventory management, or patient records management. These developers are sometimes called *value added resellers (VARs)*. This term is used because the VAR adds value to the DBMS by developing specific applications that use that product. Then the DBMS and the applications are sold as a package.

### Redefinition of the MIS Department's Role

In the early years of microcomputer database development, users did much of their own work while the traditional MIS departments continued to develop large corporate databases and company-wide applications. During that period, central control over a company's information resources began to deteriorate. Small, private databases were popping up all over, and there was seemingly no way to control the sudden decentralization of information processing. Though they largely ignored it at the start, MIS departments realized that microcomputer databases were here to stay. MIS departments now play a more prominent role in the development of microcomputer applications than they did a decade ago.

This has happened partly because MIS departments have awakened to the fact that important work is being done with microcomputer DBMS products. Though once viewed as mere toys for a handful of hackers, microcomputer DBMS products have become sophisticated, state-of-the-art information management tools, and MIS personnel have come to recognize them as such.

Another influence on the MIS Department's role in developing microcomputer databases and applications is the fact that some applications are too complex for the typical user to handle. Thus, users are beginning to appeal to the MIS Department for help.

A third factor is that some microcomputer database applications need to import data from the corporate mainframe. Consequently, the MIS Department and the user must cooperate to ensure the security and integrity of corporate data.

Today, MIS personnel are far more involved in microcomputer database development than they were a few years ago.

### The Scale of Database and Applications

Microcomputer databases tend to be considerably smaller than databases on minicomputers and mainframes. Most microcomputer databases are less than two to three million bytes, or characters. A very large microcomputer database may be ten to fifteen million bytes. Contrast this with databases on mainframes, which can range as high as a billion bytes or more.

The structure of a typical microcomputer database is simple enough to be readily comprehended and managed. Few microcomputer databases have more than ten to fifteen tables or more than fifty unique column names. Most microcomputer database applications involve fewer than ten reports and about the same number of screen forms.

The typical microcomputer database supports only one or two applications. Most are focused on solving a particular business problem, such as processing invoices, maintaining customer lists, or maintaining employee data. It is because microcomputer databases and applications are small and simple that users are often able to develop them without the aid of professional database practitioners.

### Microcomputer Database Administration

Database administration for microcomputers is both easier and more difficult than database administration for other types of database processing. Because microcomputer databases tend to be smaller than other types, there is less to administer and the task is therefore simpler. On the other hand, MIS professionals are rarely found in the typical microcomputer database environment, and users often lack the skills required to perform such administration.

Consider backup and recovery, for example. Because a microcomputer system includes less data, little concurrent processing, and generally only a single application, backup and recovery are easier—as long as someone knows how to make backups, remembers to do it, and can perform recovery when necessary. Similarly, because such systems have only one user, or at most a few, the management of data activity is simpler than in large, multi-user, multi-application database systems.

A summary of the characteristics of the microcomputer database environment appears in Figure 10–1.

## CLASSES OF MICROCOMPUTER DATABASES

Three fundamentally different kinds of microcomputer databases exist: stand-alone databases (Type I), databases whose data is imported from another computer (Type II), and databases that support concurrent processing by multiple users (Type III). See Figure 10–2 for a summary of the three types. Each type has unique properties and unique problems that must be addressed. We will consider each type and illustrate it with an example.

### Type I: Stand-Alone Microcomputer Databases

Type I microcomputer databases stand alone. They neither receive data from nor send data to other micros or terminals (Figure 10–2a). They are usually employed by one, or at most a few, users. The following example illustrates a stand-alone microcomputer database.

**Figure 10-1**

Summary of micro-
computer database
environment

Typical User
- Professional who needs to keep track of people,
  projects, resources, or other entities
- Work group that needs to process common data
- Mostly single-user systems, but multi-user systems are increasing

Development
- Historically, users did much of their own development
- VARs developed more complex and specific applications
- MIS departments are becoming more involved in development

Typical Database and Applications
- Two to three million bytes common, ten to fifteen million bytes rare
- Usually no more than fifteen tables, fifty unique columns
- Usually no more than ten reports and ten forms
- Usually supports one or two applications (though more are possible)

Administration
- Simpler than administration of mainframe systems because database is small,
  applications are few and simple
- Frequent need for user to perform administrative functions because no
  professional DBA is available

**Richard Davidson Seminars.** Richard Davidson is a clinical psychologist
who offers seminars on a variety of therapeutic techniques. Well-known
and highly regarded in his field, he uses only direct mailings to advertise
his seminars to his colleagues.

To facilitate direct mail marketing, Davidson has developed his own
microcomputer database that co tains data about his customers, seminars
they have attended, and mailing pieces he has sent to them. As shown in
Figure 10-3, the database is processed by three applications: one maintains
customer and seminar data, one produces mailing labels, and the third
produces reports and supports ad hoc queries. The menus for each of these
applications are shown in Figure 10-4.

*The Database Structure.* Davidson's applications process the CUSTOMER
and SEMINAR objects sketched in Figure 10-5a. Notice that the

**Figure 10–2**

Three types of microcomputer databases

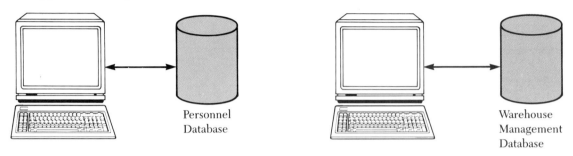

a. Type I: Stand-alone databases

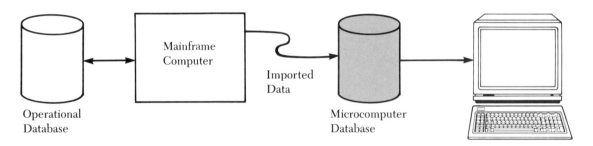

b. Type II: Data downloaded from mainframe

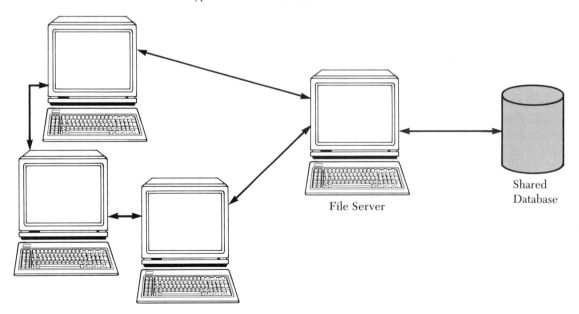

c. Type III: Multi-user database on a LAN

**Figure 10–3**
Applications used by
Richard Davidson
Seminars

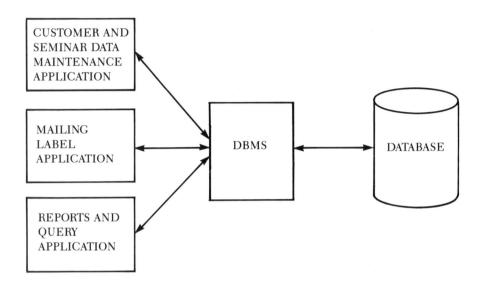

CUSTOMER object is both compound and composite (review those terms in Chapter 6, if necessary). It is compound because it contains SEMINAR as an object property. It is composite because it contains a repeating group for each mailing. The other object, SEMINAR, is compound because it contains CUSTOMER as an object property.

Figure 10–5b shows the structure of the database that supports these objects. Three relations—CUST, ENR, and MAIL—represent the CUSTOMER object. Data from two relations—SEM and ENR—is needed to represent the SEMINAR object. Observe that ENR is an intersection relation that represents the many-to-many relationship between customers and seminars.

Following the documentation that accompanied his DBMS product, Davidson was able to design this simple database. The database itself resides on his microcomputer and Davidson entered the data himself (with a little help from his clerk). Davidson or his clerk periodically updates the data. Because no concurrent processing is done, deadlock and integrity problems related to concurrency are nonexistent. Davidson needs to periodically remind himself to make a backup copy of his database and store it away from his office. With that exception, this database, like all Type I databases, is relatively easy to administer. Davidson has found no need to employ a professional database consultant to perform any development tasks.

**Figure 10–4**

Menus for Davidson Seminars' database system

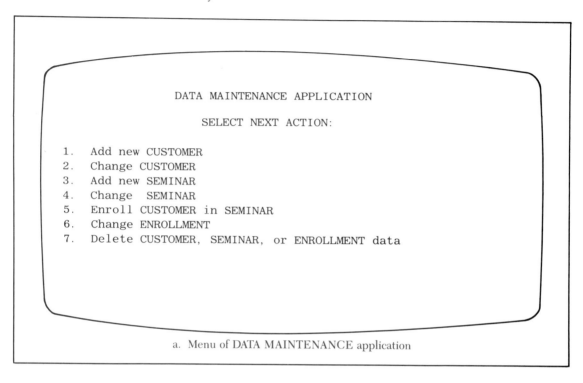

```
              DATA MAINTENANCE APPLICATION

                SELECT NEXT ACTION:

    1.   Add new CUSTOMER
    2.   Change CUSTOMER
    3.   Add new SEMINAR
    4.   Change  SEMINAR
    5.   Enroll CUSTOMER in SEMINAR
    6.   Change ENROLLMENT
    7.   Delete CUSTOMER, SEMINAR, or ENROLLMENT data
```

a. Menu of DATA MAINTENANCE application

## Type II: Databases of Imported Data

Type II microcomputer databases consist at least partly of data that is downloaded, or imported, from another computer, usually a corporate mainframe (Figure 10–2b). Once the data is stored on the microcomputer, it can be processed as if it were a Type I (stand-alone) database. Despite the similarity, problems exist in a Type II database that do not in a Type I database.

When data is transferred in bulk from one computer to another, database administration tasks change significantly, both in character and in complexity, and developers and users need to be aware of this. We will discuss these problems after presenting an example of a Type II database.

The number of Type II microcomputer databases has increased dramatically in recent years. At first, bulk data was shared between computers by transferring it on magnetic media such as diskettes. This approach was slow and cumbersome because it required the physical handling of media. This changed as microcomputers became integrated into the corporate communications network. Today many organizations have micro-to-mainframe links that allow microcomputers to communicate directly with the corporate

**Figure 10—4**
*(continued)*

```
                    MAILING LABEL APPLICATION

                    SELECT NEXT ACTION:

    1.  Print labels for all CUSTOMERS
    2.  Print labels for CUSTOMERS who have taken a given seminar
    3.  Print labels for CUSTOMERS who have not taken a given seminar
    4.  Print labels by geographic region
    5.  Print labels by professional specialty
    6.  Print other labels
```

b.  Menu of MAILING LABEL application

mainframe. In these settings, more data can be obtained faster and with greater frequency. This has resulted in an increase of Type II microcomputer databases. Let us consider an example.

**Universal Equipment.**    Universal Equipment Company manufactures and sells heavy equipment for the construction industry. Its products include bulldozers, graders, loaders, drilling rigs, and the like. Every product is assigned to a product manager in the Marketing Department who is responsible for product planning, advertising, marketing support, and development of sales support material. Each product manager is assigned a group of two or three related products.

Advertising is the product managers' largest budget item. They therefore want to be able to measure the effectiveness of ads they run. Universal's ads always contain a mail-in Request for Information card. The cards have a unique preprinted number that can be used to identify the ad that generated a particular lead. To facilitate lead tracking, the Marketing Department has developed a microcomputer database application for use by the product managers.

```
                    REPORT AND QUERY APPLICATION

                      SELECT NEXT ACTION:

       1.   Print CUSTOMER Report
       2.   Print SEMINAR History Report
       3.   Print SEMINAR Enrollment Report
       4.   Print SEMINAR Sales Report
       5.   Query the database
```

c. Menu of REPORT AND QUERY application

*The Database Structure.*    Figure 10–6a shows the objects processed by this application. AD represents an advertisement. AD-APPEARANCE is the occurrence of a particular ad in a particular publication. PRODUCT represents a particular product, such as a bulldozer. PRODUCT contains two repeating groups, one on quotas and one on sales. The groups are multivalued because sales quotas are assigned for each quarter and because product sales are recorded on a weekly basis.

This view of PRODUCT is quite simple. The complete PRODUCT object actually contains more properties, such as AD. But because the other relationships are not needed for the product managers' application, we will omit them.

The database structure that supports these objects is shown in Figure 10–6b. You should verify that this structure will adequately represent these objects before continuing.

Sales and product-lead data is transferred to the microcomputer database from the corporate mainframe by means of a micro-to-mainframe communication link. Unlike Richard Davidson's database, which contained data that Davidson himself entered, the product managers' database contains

**Figure 10–5**
Objects and relations
for Davidson Seminars'
database

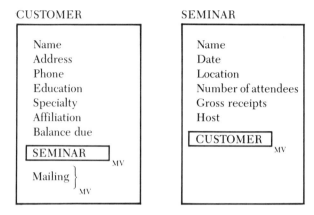

a. Objects supported by Davidson's database

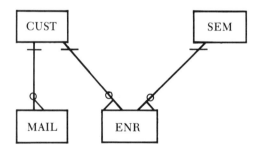

b. Relational structure to support objects in Figure 10–5a

data downloaded from the company's mainframe computer. That characteristic is what distinguishes a Type I database from a Type II database.

Every Monday the product managers run a program developed by Universal's MIS Department that updates the SALES, QUOTA, and PRODUCT-LEAD tables with data from the corporation's mainframe database. This program adds the data from the previous week to the database and also makes corrections. Product and sales data is imported for all related products to enable product managers to do comparative studies.

**Potential Problems of Type II Databases.** Importing data presents several potential problems that affect coordination, consistency, control, and com-

## Figure 10–6

Objects and relations
to support Universal
product marketing
database

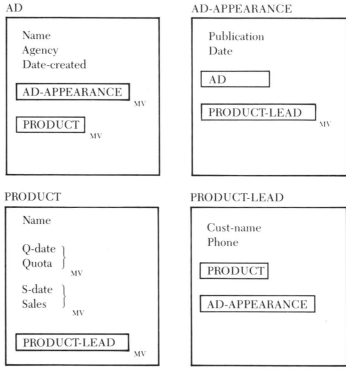

a. Objects processed by Universal product managers

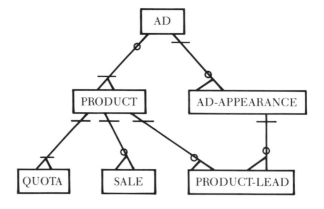

b. Relational structure to support objects in Figure 10–6a

puter crime. Let's first consider *coordination*, using the PRODUCT-LEAD and AD-APPEARANCE tables for illustration. The PRODUCT-LEAD table is updated from data on the mainframe. Leads are handled by sales personnel and are recorded on the mainframe. But the AD-APPEARANCE table is updated "locally" by product managers, based on reports prepared by the advertising manager. This situation could cause problems when an ad is run for the first time in a new issue or publication. It could happen that the ad generates leads that are recorded on the mainframe. Suppose those leads are downloaded before the product manager updates the AD-APPEARANCE table with the new ad. The program importing the data would have to reject the lead data because it violates the constraint that a PRODUCT-LEAD must have an AD-APPEARANCE parent. Thus the activities of updating and downloading must be carefully coordinated. Product managers need to insert AD-APPEARANCE data before importing data from the mainframe. Similar coordination problems can occur when updating SALES and QUOTA data.

The second potential problem of Type II databases affects *consistency*. All product managers receive downloaded SALES and QUOTA data that they are not supposed to change. But what might happen if a product manager *did* change the data? In this case, the data in that product manager's database might be inconsistent with the data in the corporate database and with the data in other product managers' databases. As a result, the reports produced by that product manager could disagree with other reports. And if several product managers update data, much inconsistent data could be generated.

Clearly, this situation calls for strict control by the DBA. The database should be designed so that data cannot be updated. If this is not possible (for example, if the microcomputer database product will not enforce such a restriction and the cost of writing programs to enforce it is considered prohibitively high), then the solution to this problem is education. Product managers need to be aware of the problems that will occur if they change data, and they need to be directed not to do so.

A third potential problem of Type II databases is *more difficult access control*. When data is transferred to several computer systems, access control becomes more difficult. At Universal, for example, SALES and QUOTA data may be sensitive. For example, the vice president of sales may not want the sales personnel to learn about upcoming sales quotas until the annual sales meeting. But if fifteen product managers have copies of this data in their databases, it can be difficult to ensure that the data will be kept confidential until the appropriate time. Further, each product manager receives SALES and QUOTA data for products other than the ones he or she manages. Product managers can be quite competitive with one another. Consequently, making this data accessible throughout the marketing department may create management problems.

The fourth potential problem of Type II databases, *increased potential for computer crime*, is closely allied to that of access control. Whereas access control involves inappropriate, but legal activity, crime involves illegal actions.

Data on the corporate mainframe can be very valuable. Universal Equipment's sales and quota data, for example, is of great interest to competitors.

When data is downloaded in bulk to one or many microcomputers, illegal copying becomes very difficult to prevent. A diskette is easily concealed. Further, employees sometimes have modems with which they access work computers from off-site locations. In such situations, the copying of data over the telephone is nearly impossible to detect or prevent.

Increased risk of computer crime is an important potential problem of Type II databases. In fact, this disadvantage alone might prohibit such a system from being developed, even though it would otherwise be an excellent solution.

The potential problems of Type II databases are summarized in Figure 10–7.

### Type III: Multi-User Microcomputer Databases

Type III microcomputer databases support the concurrent updating of a shared database (Figure 10–2c). Most Type III databases reside on a local area network, or LAN. The common database is stored on one of the LAN's

**Figure 10–7**

Summary of potential problems of Type II databases

Coordination
- Downloaded data must conform to database constraints.
- Careful timing of updates to local and downloaded data required.

Consistency
- In general, downloaded data should not be updated.
- Users need education on potential problems.
- Applications need features to prevent updating.

More Difficult Access Control
- Data may be replicated on many computers.
- Procedures to control data access are more complicated.

Increased Potential for Computer Crime
- Illegal copying is difficult to prevent.
- Diskettes and access via modem are easy to conceal.
- Risk may prevent the development of Type II applications.

**Figure 10−8**
System architecture of database processing on local area network

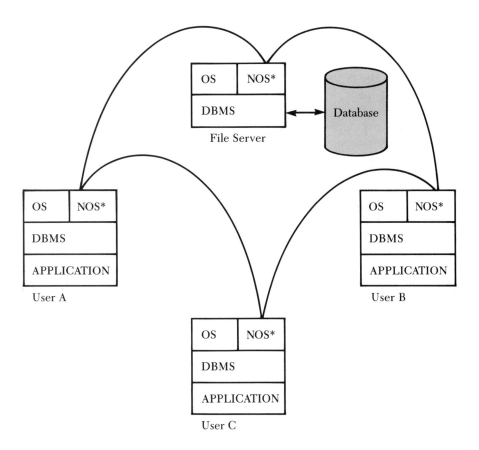

*Network Operating System

micros, called the *file server*. Microcomputers that want to process the database send requests for data actions to the file server. The general architecture of database processing on a LAN is shown in Figure 10–8.

**Legacy Systems.**   To illustrate the characteristics of a Type III database we will describe the Customer Support Department of Legacy Systems, a microcomputer software publisher. Legacy has more than thirty products and an installed base of over 50,000 customers. In addition to its software products, Legacy also sells extended customer support.

   When customers call for extended support service, the customer support personnel first request the customer's contract number. This number consists of two parts, the customer number and the license number for a particular product. This contract number must be verified against Legacy's records before service is provided.

Customer support personnel generate a record of each call. This is done to provide Legacy personnel with a record of all past contacts with all customers. (A customer may be assigned a different support representative each time she calls.) Additionally, while assisting customers, the support representatives often generate action items for departments within Legacy. For example, the representatives sometimes direct the Sales Department to ship a replacement copy of a software product to a customer.

Legacy has installed a local area network of twenty-one microcomputers in the Customer Support Department. It has also developed a database processed by two applications, the CUSTOMER SUPPORT application and the CUSTOMER PROCESSING application. The CUSTOMER SUPPORT application is used by customer support representatives while they are serving customers. The CUSTOMER PROCESSING application is used to record new licenses, to produce mailing labels for newsletters and license renewal requests, and to update customer and other data.

*The Database Structure.*   Figure 10–9a shows the four objects that need to be processed to support these applications. The CUSTOMER object contains multiple occurrences of the CALL and LICENSE objects. CALL contains CUSTOMER and multiple occurrences of the object ACTION-ITEM. ACTION-ITEM contains CALL and DEPARTMENT as well as data about the action to be taken. Finally, DEPARTMENT contains data about Legacy departments as well as multiple occurrences of ACTION-ITEM.

ACTION-ITEM is an association object establishing the relationship between CALL and DEPARTMENT. The structure of the database supporting these objects is shown in Figure 10–9b.

**Processing Rights and Responsibilities.**   Type III databases are subject to concurrent updating, so processing rights and responsibilities need to be carefully defined. Otherwise, as described in Chapter 7, inconsistent data changes can be made and, over time, the database will develop serious integrity problems.

Figure 10–10a lists the permissions granted to Legacy's customer support personnel (users of the CUSTOMER SUPPORT application), and Figure 10–10b lists the permissions granted to the administrative assistant who employs the CUSTOMER PROCESSING application. Let's look first at the CUSTOMER SUPPORT application.

Customer support representatives can read data in all of the tables and can add data to all but the DEPT table. In order to maintain data control, however, the management of the Customer Support Department decided not to allow these users to change or delete any data. Instead, when customer support representatives believe such changes are needed, they notify the manager. If the modification is approved, then the manager's administrative assistant (not a customer support representative) carries it out.

**Figure 10–9**
Legacy Systems'
database design

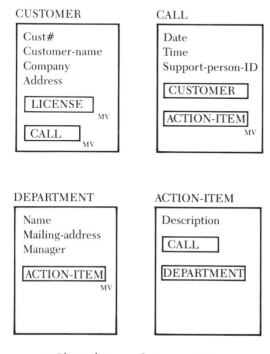

CUSTOMER

Cust#
Customer-name
Company
Address

LICENSE
MV

CALL
MV

CALL

Date
Time
Support-person-ID

CUSTOMER

ACTION-ITEM
MV

DEPARTMENT

Name
Mailing-address
Manager

ACTION-ITEM
MV

ACTION-ITEM

Description

CALL

DEPARTMENT

a. Object diagrams for Legacy Systems

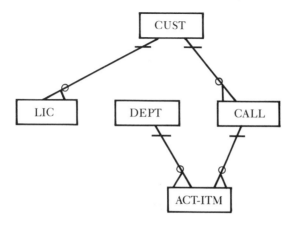

CUST

LIC    DEPT    CALL

ACT-ITM

b. Relational structure to support objects in Figure 10–9a

**Figure 10–10**

Processing rights for
Legacy Systems'
applications

Action

| Table | Read | Insert | Modify | Delete |
|-------|------|--------|--------|--------|
| CUST | Y | Y | N | N |
| LIC | Y | Y | N | N |
| CALL | Y | Y | N | N |
| ACT-ITM | Y | Y | N | N |
| DEPT | Y | N | N | N |

a. CUSTOMER SUPPORT application

Action

| Table | Read | Insert | Modify | Delete |
|-------|------|--------|--------|--------|
| CUST | Y | Y | Y | Y |
| LIC | Y | Y | Y | Y |
| CALL | Y | Y | Y | Y |
| ACT-ITM | Y | Y | Y | Y |
| DEPT | Y | Y | Y | Y |

b. CUSTOMER PROCESSING application

You may be wondering why the customer support representatives need the ability to add CUST or LIC data. Although this was not a feature of earlier versions of the system, management discovered that the support representatives often received calls from customers who had not purchased extended support. Allowing support representatives to sell such licenses over the telephone provided better customer service than did requiring the customer to contact a sales representative. Certain restrictions needed to be applied when support personnel sold a license. For example, the customer had to pay for the license with a credit card. But Legacy's management felt that this was an important service to give the customer, even though it would enable more users to update the CUST and LIC tables.

The processing rights of the CUSTOMER PROCESSING application are summarized in Figure 10–10b. The administrative assistant is the primary user of CUSTOMER PROCESSING, although the departmental manager also can employ the application. The administrative assistant is allowed to perform all categories of data changes for all tables. Certain manual procedures are enforced. For example, deletions may be made only after they have been approved by both the manager and the sales department. These reviews are necessary because some large-volume customers might be given special treatment by the sales department. Consequently, deletions should not be automatic.

**Concurrent Processing Control.**   Type III microcomputer databases are subject to all the problems of concurrent processing described in Chapter 7. The concurrent update problem can occur, so some form of record locking is required. The specific type of locking depends on the needs of the application and the DBMS product.

Legacy Systems' applications require only limited locking services. The CUSTOMER SUPPORT application, which is run concurrently by the support representatives, reads and adds data but does not make any changes or deletions. Because no changes are made, the concurrent update problem cannot occur. And because deletions are not allowed, there is no danger that a record will be removed while being accessed by a concurrent user.

The CUSTOMER PROCESSING application does make changes and deletions. Therefore it could generate concurrent update problems. Recall, however, that it has only one user, the departmental administrative assistant. Consequently, this application is run in single-user mode, which ensures that no concurrency problems are possible.

The one place where potential concurrency problems could arise is between the CUSTOMER SUPPORT and CUSTOMER PROCESSING applications. To prevent such problems, the CUSTOMER PROCESSING application locks all records before performing any changes or deletions. To reduce the negative impact of such locking on performance, the administrative assistant usually runs the CUSTOMER PROCESSING application only during periods of low workload.

**Recovery.**   Type III databases typically support groups of employees, such as departments. Therefore quick recovery from system failure is important. Unfortunately, the recovery capabilities of most microcomputer DBMS products leave much to be desired. Few microcomputer DBMS products support transaction logging, rollback, or rollforward. Instead, users are expected to reprocess their workload when failure occurs. As you learned in Chapter 7, reprocessing is slow, and the results from the reprocessed workload may differ from the results of the workload as originally processed. This situation will undoubtedly change when enough users complain loudly to microcomputer DBMS vendors. Then vendors will decide to provide better recovery features.

Legacy's DBMS suffers from limited recovery functionality. Users must perform recovery via reprocessing. Legacy decided to limit the danger of reprocessing large workloads by backing up the database every evening and before every execution of the CUSTOMER PROCESSING application.

**Figure 10–11**

Comparison of micro-
computer database
types

| Database | Distinguishing characteristics | Problems |
|---|---|---|
| Type I | Single-user stand-alone | End-user development Little prior DBA experience |
| Type II | Imports data from another source | Coordination Data consistency Access control Security |
| Type III | Multi-user | Concurrent processing Limited recovery facilities Limited locking capabilities |

In this way, when failure occurs, only a limited amount of reprocessing will need to be done. Because the Legacy database is over 15 million bytes, making frequent backups is time-consuming. However, management felt that reprocessing several days' (or weeks') work in the event of failure would both severely hinder the customer support staff and result in dissatisfied customers. Thus, management felt making frequent database backups was necessary to compensate for that weakness in the microcomputer DBMS.

Figure 10–11 summarizes the three types of microcomputer databases.

## DESIGNING A MICROCOMPUTER DATABASE

In this section we will discuss the definition of a microcomputer database. We begin with a review of the outputs of the logical design phase and then consider the definition of tables, columns, and views. Next we will discuss constraint processing and security. Notice that we are concentrating on the database itself; the techniques presented in Chapter 8 are used for application design.

### Outputs from Logical Design

The outputs from the logical design process are summarized in Figure 10–12. As described in Chapter 6, during logical design, the objects to be sup-

**Figure 10–12**

Summary of compo-
nents of logical data-
base design

```
Relations
 ● Real
 ● Views

Columns
 ● Real
 ● Virtual

Constraints
 ● Domain
        Values
        Masks
 ● Intra-relation
        Key attribute uniqueness
        Other
 ● Inter-relation

Security requirements
```

ported are identified and defined, and the relations and attributes necessary to support those objects are described. Depending on the applications, views of the database may also be defined. Furthermore, this process produces domain definitions and both intra- and inter-relation constraints. Additionally, security requirements have been specified.

These outputs are the ingredients from which the database will be produced. If they correctly reflect what the user needs, then developing a database and database applications that satisfy the user will be a straightforward process. On the other hand, if the design step is done poorly or is incomplete, then successful system development is almost impossible. This is not exactly a point of no return, but experience has shown that one more careful review of the logical design at this point is exceedingly worthwhile. As carpenters say, "Measure twice and cut once."

## Defining Tables and Columns

The definition of tables and columns is done directly from the logical design. One table is defined for each relation and one column is defined for each attribute of each relation.

How table definition is accomplished depends on the microcomputer DBMS product in use. Figure 10–13 shows two possible techniques for defining tables and columns. In Figure 10–13a, the specifications are entered all at once as a file. The file is read by the Definition Subsystem of the

**Figure 10–13**
Database definition techniques

COLUMNS
|  |  |
|---|---|
| Item# | Numeric 99999 |
| On-hand | Numeric 999 |
| Bin# | Numeric 99 |
| Desc | Text 45 |
| Units | Text 5 |
| Re-ord | Numeric 999 |
| U-price | Dollar 5.2 |
| Line# | Numeric 99 |
| Qty | Numeric 999 |
| Ext-prc | Dollar 8.2 |

TABLES

INVENTRY with Item#, On-hand, Bin#, Desc, Units, Re-ord, U-price

LINE-ITEM with Line#, Item#, Qty, Ext-prc

a. Database structure definition in text file format (input to Database Definition Subsystem)

INVENTRY

| Item# | On-hand | Bin# | Desc | Units | Re-ord | U-price |
|---|---|---|---|---|---|---|
| Numeric 99999 | Numeric 999 | Numeric 99 | Text 45 | Text 5 | Numeric 99999 | Dollar 5.2 |

b. Defining a table and columns with graphic tool

DBMS. First, column names and formats are defined. Then tables are defined as collections of columns. This illustration is generic—the terms and syntax shown here are typical of most microcomputer products that employ this technique.

Figure 10–13b shows a more graphic and more user-friendly technique for table and column definition. Using this interactive method, the developer completes a form that the DBMS Definition Subsystem "paints" on the computer screen. In this example, the upper left corner contains a space for the name of the table. Each column contains a space for the column name and, below that, the column definition. When the user enters a column name, the DBMS presents a menu of permissible data types. The developer simply selects the appropriate data type (such as Text, Numeric, or Date). A default size for that column is then displayed. The user may accept the default (such as forty-five characters for a text column or eight characters for a date) or may override it by entering the desired length.

The interactive graphic approach has a number of advantages over the text file approach. First, the graphic *looks* like a table and is therefore easier to use. Second, if the user makes an error, he or she receives immediate feedback. This is not the case with the text file, where feedback is not produced until the entire file is processed by the Definition Subsystem. Third, with the graphical approach, the developer is never given a chance to make certain errors. For example, suppose that for this DBMS, column names must be eight characters or less in length. (Note that we are specifying the length of the *name* of a column, not the length of the *data* in the column.) The space into which the developer will enter a column name is exactly eight characters wide. Consequently, the user would never be able to enter more than eight characters and could not violate this rule.

Some DBMS products support *computed* (or *virtual*) *columns*. A computed column is derived when it is needed—say, for printing on a report. It is not actually stored in the database, but the factors needed to derive it are. A common example of a virtual column is the price extension on an invoice. Price extensions are computed by multiplying the number of items ordered by the item's unit price. Because both quantity and unit price are stored in the database, it is unnecessary to store the price extension. Instead, the price extension column, say, Ext-prc, is designated a *virtual* column. This is accomplished by defining a formula in place of the column length. In this case, the formula might be Qty * Unit-prc, where Qty is the column containing the quantity ordered and Unit-prc is the column containing the unit price. Whenever it needs to be displayed or printed, the value of Ext-prc is computed by the DBMS.

## Distinguishing Column Names from Domain Names

In all microcomputer DBMS products to date (new products may correct this), confusion exists between the concepts of *column* and *domain*. Consider Figure 10–13. Observe that in both examples *column names range across the database*. For example, in Figure 10–13a, the column Item# is defined only once but appears in two tables. Once Item# has been defined for one of the tables (say, INVENTRY), then whenever the developer uses that column name again (say, within the LINE-ITEM table), the DBMS assumes the same Item# definition. Thus, the word *Item#* is serving two roles: as a column name (in both INVENTRY and LINE-ITEM) and, implicitly, as the name of a domain representing product IDs. This characteristic is typical of microcomputer DBMS products.

In some cases this dual role is an advantage. If all columns having the name Item# actually arise from a common domain, then simultaneously defining both the column name and, by default, the domain name is convenient. The DBMS vendor would probably call this a feature. If on the other hand, some uses of the word *Item#* refer to product IDs while other uses of the word *Item#* refer to a line item on an invoice, then confusion will result because both uses do not arise from the same domain. In such a case, the DBMS vendor would probably downplay the significance of this shortcoming.

Ideally, domain names range across the database but column names do not. The domain Product-numbers, for example, should have one definition for the entire database. Every column that is based on that domain should have the same semantic and physical description. On the other hand, column names should be particular to a table. The column named Number in the EMPLOYEE table should be allowed to have a different meaning than the column named Number in the PRODUCT table.

Currently, no microcomputer DBMS explicitly recognizes domains. Despite this, it is important for you to be clear in your thinking while you are defining a microcomputer database. You should distinguish between domain and column names even if the product you are using does not.

## Views

Many microcomputer DBMS products support a construct called a *view*. Unfortunately, the meaning of this term varies among products. In most cases, a view can be one (or a combination) of two things: a *subset view* or a *joined view*.

**Subset Views.**    One type of view is a subset of a table. By using subset views, sensitive data can be hidden from unauthorized users. Consider the following EMPLOYEE table from a personnel database:

EMPLOYEE (Ssn, L-name, F-name, Dept, Code, Review-date, Salary)

Suppose that not all of the users of this table need all of the data. For example, payroll clerks need all except Review-date. The personnel administrator needs L-name, F-name, Dept, Code, and Review-date, and the internal audit committee needs only Dept and Salary. To support these requirements, three views of the table (called the *base table*) can be defined, and each user or user group can be given permission to access only the appropriate one. These are the three views:

```
EMP-PAY (Ssn, L-name, F-name, Dept, Code, Salary)
EMP-REV (L-name, F-name, Dept, Code, Review-date)
DEPT-SAL (Dept, Salary)
```

Sample data for EMPLOYEE appears in Figure 10–14a. Figure 10–14b shows the data for the EMP-PAY view of EMPLOYEE. Notice that all of the rows are represented but that some of the columns are hidden. Similarly, Figures 10–14c and 10–14d illustrate the data that would appear in the EMP-REV and DEPT-SAL views of EMPLOYEE.

When a user accesses the database, he references the view he is allowed to process. He should not even be aware that the base table or other views

**Figure 10—14**
Sample data for EMPLOYEE table and three views

EMPLOYEE Table

| Ssn | L-name | F-name | Dept | Code | Review-date | Salary |
|---|---|---|---|---|---|---|
| 000-02-9876 | Jones | Pam | Acct | 3 | 1/1/88 | 53,200 |
| 001-00-9987 | Baker | Rex | Finance | 1 | 3/3/88 | 67,000 |
| 002-00-9056 | Jackson | Fred | Admin | 1 | 3/3/88 | 44,000 |
| 002-99-9898 | Smuthers | Judy | Acct | 2 | 5/1/88 | 67,900 |
| 006-99-0000 | Tang | Sue | Finance | 4 | 3/3/88 | 49,800 |
| 000-66-9999 | Adams | Diane | Acct | 1 | 4/1/88 | 53,200 |

a. EMPLOYEE data

EMP-PAY View

| Ssn | L-Name | F-name | Dept | Code | Salary |
|---|---|---|---|---|---|
| 000-02-9876 | Jones | Pam | Acct | 3 | 53,200 |
| 001-00-9987 | Baker | Rex | Finance | 1 | 67,000 |
| 002-00-9056 | Jackson | Fred | Admin | 1 | 44,000 |
| 002-99-9898 | Smuthers | Judy | Acct | 2 | 67,900 |
| 006-99-0000 | Tang | Sue | Finance | 4 | 49,800 |
| 000-66-9999 | Adams | Diane | Acct | 1 | 53,200 |

b. Data for EMP-PAY view of EMPLOYEE

EMP-REV View

| L-name | F-name | Dept | Code | Review-date |
|---|---|---|---|---|
| Jones | Pam | Acct | 3 | 1/1/88 |
| Baker | Rex | Finance | 1 | 3/3/88 |
| Jackson | Fred | Admin | 1 | 3/3/88 |
| Smuthers | Judy | Acct | 2 | 5/1/88 |
| Tang | Sue | Finance | 4 | 3/3/88 |
| Adams | Diane | Acct | 1 | 4/1/88 |

c. Data for EMP-REV view of EMPLOYEE

DEPT-SAL View

| Dept | Salary |
|---|---|
| Acct | 53,200 |
| Finance | 67,000 |
| Admin | 44,000 |
| Acct | 67,900 |
| Finance | 49,800 |
| Acct | 53,200 |

d. Data for DEPT-SAL view of EMPLOYEE

exist. The DBMS extracts from the base table the appropriate data for processing. In a properly designed system, the user is prevented from accessing data that is not in his view. (Obviously, these measures will be wasted if the EMPLOYEE table and other views are not protected by passwords or other means.)

Although views are good security devices, processing views (rather than tables) is not without problems. Notice that two of the views of the EMPLOYEE table—EMP-REV and DEPT-SAL—do not include the base table key, Ssn. Consequently, when the DBMS constructs these views by extracting specified columns from the base table, the view may contain duplicate rows. This is illustrated in Figure 10–14d, the data for DEPT-SAL. Notice that two individuals in the Accounting Department make 53,200 (verify this with the actual data in the EMPLOYEE table). Some microcomputer DBMS products—those based on strict relational theory—automatically drop duplicate rows from the view. More often, though, the user must explicitly specify that duplicates should be dropped.

The user processing a view (or the developer building DBMS applications employing views) must know whether or not duplicate rows are automatically dropped by the DBMS. This will affect the interpretation of the data. For example, let's say that the DBMS drops duplicate rows when constructing the DEPT-SAL view of EMPLOYEE. In terms of the data shown in Figure 10–14, this means that EMP-SAL will contain only one row for [ACCT, 53,200]. If the user is unaware of this, assuming incorrectly that one row exists for each employee, then she will conclude that fewer employees work for the company than actually do. Other misinterpretations can occur. For example, if the user were to compute the average salary for each department, then the calculation based on a view from which duplicate rows were dropped would be incorrect.

The views illustrated so far are subsets of table columns. Views can also be constructed from subsets of rows. For example, a view called ACCT-EMP could be defined as the rows of EMPLOYEE in which Dept equals Acct. The definition might be:

```
ACCT-EMP (Ssn, L-name, F-name, Dept, Code, Salary)
where Dept = 'Acct'
```

This view contains the key Ssn, so the potential problem of dropping duplicate rows does not exist.

Views can also be both row and column subsets. For example, suppose that Code indicates job classification and that a user needs a subset of columns only for employees with a job classification of 1. The following defines such a view of EMPLOYEE:

```
EMP-CDE1 (Ssn, L-name, F-name, Salary)
where Code = 1
```

This view contains only four of the columns of EMPLOYEE and only those rows where Code = 1. Notice that in this case the column used to qualify rows for inclusion in the view (Code) does not appear in the resulting view. However, this is not always the case.

**Updates on Subset Views.**    Updates on subset views may or may not be allowed, depending on the view, the type of update, and the DBMS product in use. Views that include the key column of the base table can be processed differently from views that do not. Consider EMP-PAY, which includes the key column, Ssn (Figure 10–14b). Because a value of Ssn uniquely identifies a row in the base table, both insertions and changes to the view data can be allowed. However, when a user inserts a row, the value of Review-date will not be entered because it is not part of the user's view. An unknown or unavailable value is called a *null value*. Some DBMS products support nulls and some do not. We will address this issue in later chapters when we examine specific DBMS products.

A deletion from EMP-PAY is possible, but probably not desirable (even if the DBMS will allow it). If deletion is allowed, the user of EMP-PAY will be deleting data in EMPLOYEE (Review-date) that she does not see. Allowing users to unknowingly delete data is a bad policy.

Neither EMP-REV nor DEPT-SAL includes the key column, Ssn. As a result, allowing users to update them is not generally a good idea and is probably prohibited by the DBMS. Why should such a restriction exist?

Consider the possible consequences if updates were allowed on views that do not include the key column of the base table. If insertions were allowed for non-key views, the key value would be null. The DBMS would have no way to verify the uniqueness of the new row. Similarly, if modifications were allowed, the DBMS would not know which row to modify. It could modify all possible rows—say, those with matching values in the other, non-key, column—but this is dangerous. For example, if the user of DEPT-SAL (Figure 10–14d) issued a command to change [ACCT, 53,200] to [ACCT, 60,000], then the DBMS could change *all* rows with those values, regardless of the value of the key. This action is dangerous, however, because the user may not even know that DEPT-SAL is a view based on EMPLOYEE and that the underlying EMPLOYEE data is being changed.

Deletions in views that do not include the key are similarly dangerous. If the user issued the command to delete all rows in DEPT-SAL with [ACCT, 40,000], then all of the qualifying rows in EMPLOYEE would be deleted. Again, the user may not even be aware of EMPLOYEE and such an action could cause havoc with the stored data. Thus, in general, updating data in views should be restricted to those views that contain the key column of the base table. Even then, updates must be made cautiously (see Figure 10–15).

**Joined Views.**    The second type of view is based on the join of two or more tables. You will recall from Chapter 9 that join is the relational operation that concatenates rows of one table to those of another, resulting in one larger table. The DEPT and EMPLOYEE base tables in Figure 10–16a have

---

**Figure 10–15**

Summary of view
processing

| | View Contains<br>Key Columns | View Does Not Contain<br>Key Columns |
|---|---|---|
| Read | Yes | Yes |
| Insert | Some columns null | Bad policy |
| Modify | Yes | Bad policy |
| Delete | Bad policy | Bad policy |

been joined to create the EMP-DEPT table in Figure 10–16b. In this case, the join is done via matching values of Name (in the DEPT table) and Dept (in the EMPLOYEE table). For this join operation to be logical, Name and Dept must arise from the same domain.

The result of a join operation is a new table, either a real one or a view. (Remember that views are treated as if they were base tables—only they are constructed by the DBMS whenever they are referenced.) A real table has a physical existence of its own; it will be stored in the database until someone removes it. If a real table is created, then it will necessarily duplicate data already stored in the base tables. This arrangement invites data integrity problems. For example, an application (or a user) might modify one of the base tables without similarly modifying the joined table, leaving them out of sync.

On the other hand, the resulting table might be a view, sometimes called a *joined view* (to distinguish it from a subset view). A joined view may contain all of the columns of the table resulting from the join operation, or it may be a subset of the join. Joined view subsets are similar to subset views of base tables.

The EMP-DEPT view in Figure 10–16b might be employed by users who need both employee and department data in the same line. A report listing all of the rows of this table, for example, would give the department data along with the employee data. Similarly, a query expressed on EMP-DEPT will generate both employee and department data.

Updates on joined views are difficult for the DBMS to carry out and are generally dangerous because of the potential for data integrity problems. In general they are prohibited by DBMS products. A better approach to updating is to develop applications that enable users to process the objects with which they are familiar (as opposed to tables). This can often be accomplished by careful forms design as discussed in Chapter 8.

With some DBMS products, both subset and joined views can be defined as part of the database structure. To the user, these views appear to be real

**Figure 10–16**
View from join of two tables

| Name | Manager | Location |
|---|---|---|
| Acct | Abernathy | C-109 |
| Finance | Crist | SV-1910 |
| Admin | Forrest | Q-990 |

DEPT

| Ssn | L-name | F-name | Dept | Code | Review-date | Salary |
|---|---|---|---|---|---|---|
| 000-02-9876 | Jones | Pam | Acct | 3 | 1/1/88 | 53,200 |
| 001-00-9987 | Baker | Rex | Finance | 1 | 3/3/88 | 67,000 |
| 002-00-9056 | Jackson | Fred | Admin | 1 | 3/3/88 | 44,000 |
| 002-99-9898 | Smuthers | Judy | Acct | 2 | 5/1/88 | 67,900 |
| 006-99-0000 | Tang | Sue | Finance | 4 | 3/3/88 | 49,800 |
| 000-66-9999 | Adams | Diane | Acct | 1 | 4/1/88 | 53,200 |

EMPLOYEE

a. Base tables

| Ssn | L-name | F-name | Dept | Code | Review-date | Salary | Manager | Location |
|---|---|---|---|---|---|---|---|---|
| 000-02-9876 | Jones | Pam | Acct | 3 | 1/1/88 | 53,200 | Abernathy | C-109 |
| 001-00-9987 | Baker | Rex | Finance | 1 | 3/3/88 | 67,000 | Crist | SV-1910 |
| 002-00-9056 | Jackson | Fred | Admin | 1 | 3/3/88 | 44,000 | Forrest | Q-990 |
| 002-99-9898 | Smuthers | Judy | Acct | 2 | 5/1/88 | 67,900 | Abernathy | C-109 |
| 006-99-0000 | Tang | Sue | Finance | 4 | 3/3/88 | 49,800 | Crist | SV-1910 |
| 000-66-9999 | Adams | Diane | Acct | 1 | 4/1/88 | 53,200 | Abernathy | C-109 |

EMP-DEPT

b. Join of DEPT and EMPLOYEE tables

tables, and in most cases, with the exception of updating data, they can be processed as if they were real tables. For security reasons, joined views, like subset views, should be protected by passwords.

## Constraints

A *constraint* is a rule about the data in the database. Microcomputer DBMS products vary in the amount of support they provide for enforcing database constraints.

Three types of constraints are expressed in the logical design. *Domain constraints* specify allowable attribute values, and possibly masks (or printing rules) for attributes. *Intra-relation constraints* specify restrictions on values within a relation. *Inter-relation constraints* specify restrictions on attribute values between relations. All three kinds of constraints need to be incorporated into the database definition to the extent the DBMS product will allow. Other external subroutines might be required to enforce constraints not handled by the DBMS.

Ideally, every constraint is defined as part of the database structure and every DBMS product enforces every constraint. It should not matter whether database changes come from a load utility program, a user-completed form on the computer screen, a transaction program, another computer, or any other source. Although no reason exists for not realizing this ideal, it is not met by current products. The needed technology and knowledge are fully developed, however, and strong constraint enforcement will undoubtedly be part of a future generation of microcomputer DBMS products.

In the meantime, developers must take advantage of whatever constraint enforcement capabilities their DBMS has and supplement the deficiencies with controls in application programs and manual procedures. Let us consider each type of constraint.

**Domain Constraints.**    A domain constraint is a statement of allowed data values. A domain constraint might also include a mask, which is the pattern used for printing or displaying data, especially numeric data. The statement of allowed values includes the data type (such as text, decimal, date, or time), the maximum length of the data, a description of the allowable range of data values, if known, or a discrete set of allowable values. Consider the following examples:

```
TEXT 24
DATE
DATE from 1/1/85 to 12/31/92
DECIMAL 5,4
TEXT IN {'freshman', 'sophomore', 'junior', 'senior'}
```

The first line indicates only the data type (TEXT) and the maximum number of characters in an entry (24). The second line specifies a date format. The default format is mmddyy. The third line defines a date field whose allowable values include only dates from 1985 through 1992. The fourth entry is for a numeric field that has five positions to the left of the decimal point and four positions to the right. The largest allowable value, therefore, is 99999.9999. Finally, the last line indicates a discrete set of four allowable values for an entry into a column arising from this domain. Many other data types and value restrictions can be defined, depending on the product. The list of examples is by no means exhaustive.

A mask is the format in which a domain value will be printed or displayed on a computer screen. You might think of a mask as a constraint on the domain's presentation. For instance, the mask for the domain for Social Security Number might be 999-99-9999, where the 9 represents a decimal digit.

Including a mask as part of the domain definition indicates that that format will be used whenever the data is presented. For columns like Social Security Number, which has a standard presentation format, this approach makes sense. In other cases, the developer might choose to define masks as part of the report or form on which the data will appear. For instance, suppose the Social Security Number is sometimes printed on a government form that has preprinted hyphens separating blank spaces for each group of digits in the number. In this case, a mask containing intervening hyphens is not appropriate. Instead, the developer would include in the report definition a more appropriate mask for Social Security Number.

Another example is an employee's paycheck total, a number that can appear on many reports and forms. In some cases, a dollar sign and commas are needed. In other cases, that punctuation is superfluous. In almost all cases, non-significant leading zeros are blank-filled. But in another case—when printed on a paycheck—leading zeros are not simply blanked out (leaving space for someone to type in a few more figures), but are replaced with a printed character, such as an asterisk. It is unlikely that a developer would define a mask as part of the domain for Paycheck-total. Rather, she would probably define a mask for each presentation of Paycheck-total.

**Domain Enforcement.**　As stated earlier, no microcomputer DBMS product explicitly recognizes domains. Instead, domains are implicitly specified within the definition of a column's data type. For example, in Figure 10–13a, Item# is defined as Numeric 99999. This statement indicates that values of Item# arise from a domain of decimal numbers from 0 to 99999. Given this definition, the DBMS will accept only numeric data in this range. Thus, some domain constraints are recognized and enforced by the DBMS.

In practice, the actual domain definition for Item# is probably more restrictive than this. Company policy may state that item numbers must have exactly five digits. Numbers less than 10000 are thus not allowed. Other constraints may exist as well. For example, the leading digit may need to be odd and the third digit may need to be either 1 or 0.

Microcomputer DBMS products provide some support for such definitions. With R:base System V, for example, the constraint that Item# must be greater than 10000 and less than 99999 can be stated as a rule that R:base will enforce. However, the constraints that the leading digit be odd and that the middle digit be 1 or 0 cannot be enforced with R:base rules. Instead, they must be enforced by an application program or a manual procedure.

No microcomputer DBMS product allows the definition of masks as part of a domain. Instead, masks are defined within reports, forms, or application programs.

Finally, be aware that we are considering only the physical definition of a domain in this discussion. The semantic definition cannot be enforced until DBMS products begin to recognize the concept of domain. Why is this important? As it stands now, DBMS products blindly allow the comparison of data from any two columns that arise from the same physical domain. For instance, it would be possible (though nonsensical) to join two tables on matching values of Area-code and IQ-score because both happen to be three-digit decimal data. This comparison is not logical. If the semantic definition of the two domains were recognized (that is, Area-code defines a telephone calling area, while IQ-score is a standardized measure of language and mathematical ability), then the DBMS product would not allow comparisons between the two domains because they describe different properties. Until such recognition becomes part of the DBMS, the DBA must be responsible for ensuring that such operations are performed only on columns that truly arise from the same domain, including both the physical and semantic components.

**Intra-relation Constraints.**   An intra-relation constraint is a constraint placed on data *within* a table. If the logical design is expressed in domain/key normal form, then the only type of intra-relation constraint that can exist is that key values must be unique. This is true because the only restrictions that are allowed are those for domains and keys. However, as you learned in Chapter 6, domain/key normal form is a design goal that is sometimes not attainable. As a result, intra-relation constraints not involving the key might need to be expressed. We will consider both types.

*Uniqueness Constraints.*   Most microcomputer DBMS products support uniqueness constraints, although many do it incompletely. To be more specific, several microcomputer DBMS products enforce column uniqueness, but not the constraint that composites (groups of columns) be unique. Other products do enforce uniqueness of composite columns.

For example, suppose we want to define a rule that the composite key (Lastname, Firstname) is unique. With some DBMS products this is not possible. With these products, it is possible to define a first rule that Lastname is unique and a second rule that Firstname is unique, and the DBMS will enforce these rules. This means, however, that only one value will be allowed for a particular Lastname and only one value will be allowed for a particular Firstname. Thus, for example, there can be only one Jones and only one Pam. Once the name [JONES, PAM] is entered in the database, [JONES, TOM] cannot be entered. The name [JACKSON, PAM] will not be allowed either.

Clearly, this is not what the user had in mind. The user wanted the combination of a particular first and last name to be unique. Unfortunately, with most microcomputer DBMS products, the uniqueness of such composite keys must be enforced by application programs or manual procedures.

*Other Intra-relation Constraints.*   As stated, domain/key normal form is a design goal. Sometimes, however, it is not possible to put relations into domain/key normal form. In that case, intra-relation constraints may exist that do not involve domain or key definitions. For example, consider the relation

```
LINE-ITEM (Inv#, Line#, Prod#, Qty, Price, Ext-Price,
Insurance)
```

and suppose that this relation has the constraint that if Ext-price is greater than 10,000, then Insurance = 50. This constraint is not implied by domains or keys, so the relation is not in DK/NF. Further, no good way exists to transform this relation into relations that are in DK/NF. Thus, we need to enforce an intra-relation constraint that does not involve key uniqueness.

To date, no microcomputer DBMS allows the definition of such constraints as part of the database structure. Constraints like this must therefore be enforced by application program or by manual procedure. The DBA is responsible for enforcing such constraints.

**Inter-relation Constraints.**   Inter-relation constraints concern the relationship of data values between or among tables. Most of these constraints involve mandatory existence across relationships, known to database practitioners as *referential integrity*. For example, students and their advisors can be represented by the relations

```
STUDENT (S#, Sname, Advisor)
FACULTY (F#, Fname, Office)
```

with this inter-relation constraint: Advisor in STUDENT must equal a value of Fname in FACULTY.

DBMS products vary in the degree to which they support referential integrity. Some allow the definition of a rule to enforce the constraint as part of the database definition. For example, the rule might be specified during the definition of the Advisor column. After indicating data type and length, the developer might indicate that the value of Advisor must be equal to any value of Fname. The rule might be stated this way:

```
Advisor EQ ANY Fname IN FACULTY
```

DBMS products that allow such rules to be defined automatically reject updates whose results would violate the constraint. Such violations could occur when a new row of STUDENT is stored, an existing row of FACULTY is deleted, or the value of Fname of an existing row of FACULTY is changed.

Enforcing constraints to ensure referential integrity is important. Suppose, for example, that Professor Jones gets married and changes his name to Page-Jones. Two modifications must be made to the database. First, the Fname in the FACULTY table must be changed from [JONES] to [PAGE-JONES]. Then all instances of Advisor in STUDENT that are equal to [JONES] must be changed to [PAGE-JONES]. Ideally, the DBMS performs both updates automatically. If it does not, then the application needs to be designed to perform both updates.

Sometimes constraints are too strict to be practical. For example, suppose that students must have advisors and professors must have advisees. The relationship between the two tables is mandatory-to-mandatory.

In this situation, it is impossible to insert a new professor whose only advisee is a new student. No matter which insertion is attempted first, it will violate the mandatory-to-mandatory constraint. The professor row cannot be inserted first because she has no advisee yet, and the student row cannot be inserted first because he has no advisor yet. A similar situation occurs when a professor (or student) row is to be deleted. Due to the mandatory constraint, the professor will have at least one advisee because the DBMS would not allow the last advisee to have been removed. Clearly we cannot delete a professor record without first assigning the student to another advisor. This would be a modification anomaly. In enforcing the mandatory-to-mandatory constraint, the DBMS will simply not allow the professor to be deleted! Notice that the last advisee cannot be deleted either. Sometimes this situation is referred to as *relationship gridlock.*

One solution to this gridlock problem is to withhold temporarily the enforcement of one of the constraints. Sometimes the DBMS has a command to toggle constraint checking on and off. If so, the toggle can be turned off, the changes made, and the toggle turned back on. Having such a toggle is not entirely beneficial, however, because constraint checking can be inadvertently or carelessly turned off. In a larger installation, it is the DBA's responsibility to determine under what conditions constraint checking can be temporarily suspended. But in the microcomputer environment, a DBA often does not exist. The user or developer needs to be aware of the dangers (and benefits) of this approach toward achieving referential integrity while avoiding gridlock.

Another technique for avoiding gridlock is to group data changes into *atomic transactions* like those described in Chapter 7. Constraint checking is deferred until the entire transaction has been processed. At that point constraints are checked, and if any have been violated, all data changes are backed out.

Still another possibility is periodically to run a utility program that scans the database tables, searching for instances in which referential integrity has not been maintained. The utility program points out where attention is required. Using that data as a guide, corrections can be made in the database data.

Obviously, microcomputer DBMS products vary widely in the support they provide for constraint checking. Consequently, the developer must know the features available in the product and establish manual procedures or application programs that will make up for the product's shortcomings in this area.

### Security

Some microcomputer DBMS products support no security, some support entity security, some support subject security, and some support both. (These terms are defined in Chapter 7.)

DBMS products that support entity security usually allow the definition of passwords on tables and views. Often, passwords can be defined that enable specific action on these entities. For example:

- The password GREEN-VALLEY enables the reading of the view HIGH-RISK-CUSTOMER.
- The password SUNNYSIDE enables the reading and updating of the CUSTOMER table.

As described in Chapter 7, the definition of passwords is typically reserved for the database administrator. In a Type I or Type II microcomputer DBMS environment, password protection may not be necessary. Introducing multi-user processing in a Type III environment, however, makes security a more crucial issue. Even if no one is officially called the DBA, someone needs to be responsible for determining processing rights and employing whatever features are provided by the DBMS product to maintain security.

DBMS products that support subject security allow the definition of user profiles. As discussed in Chapter 7, such profiles set out a table of entities that each user is permitted to access and the actions that he or she is allowed to perform on each one.

## SUMMARY

Although database principles, development, and administration requirements are the same in both mainframe and microcomputer environments, the microcomputer database environment is distinguishable in many ways. Microcomputer databases usually serve one or a few users, at most. Both the databases and the applications are often developed by users themselves, and therefore microcomputer DBMS products must be easy to use. Nonetheless, corporate MIS departments are becoming more involved as user needs outstrip user expertise.

Microcomputer databases are generally smaller than mainframe databases, often not exceeding a few million bytes (versus several billion in some mainframe databases). Also, a microcomputer database is usually processed by only one or a few applications. The size and scope of microcomputer databases and applications make database administration easier than it is on a mainframe. However, a microcomputer environment seldom includes a professional DBA to handle the administrative tasks.

Microcomputer databases can be categorized into three types: stand-alone databases, databases of data downloaded from a mainframe computer, and multi-user databases, usually installed on a local area network (LAN). Stand-alone databases present few problems because they are small, are accessed by few applications, and are used by only one or two people. Databases that get their data from another computer require special attention to coordination of activities on the microcomputer, data consistency, access control, and prevention of criminal activity. Multi-user microcomputer databases are subject to all the potential concurrent processing problems discussed in Chapter 7. Unfortunately, many microcomputer DBMS products do not yet contain the locking, recovery, or security features that are needed. In addition, the lack of an official DBA in the microcomputer database environment compounds these problems.

Database definition is accomplished by many methods, depending on the DBMS product in use. Some products employ an interactive graphic method for database definition, while others get their database definition data from a text file prepared by the developer. Regardless of the technique for entering definitions, all microcomputer DBMS products allow the developer to define tables and columns.

To define a column, the developer specifies both data type and length. Because microcomputer DBMS products do not recognize the distinction between column and domain, this definition serves both functions. However, it is important to remember that a domain definition includes a semantic part in addition to the physical part. Although many DBMS products allow operations to be performed on columns that have the same physical definition (that is, the same data type and length), such operations are not always logical and should not be permitted. This restriction will likely be incorporated into future products that recognize domains.

In addition to tables, views can also be defined. A view is a data construct that the user can manipulate like a table. However, a view is not an actual table. Rather, it is constructed by the DBMS from data in real, or base, tables whenever it is needed. A view can be a subset of a table (either a subset of columns, rows, or both), or it can be a table constructed from the join of two or more tables. Views are useful constructs because they limit a user's access to only subsets of the actual data. Views can be queried and view reports can be generated exactly the same as tables, but updates to views are generally not allowed.

Microcomputer DBMS products vary in the extent to which they enforce constraints. A constraint is a rule about database data. Domain constraints specify allowable data values. A domain constraint might also include a mask, or presentation format, of the data, but this is rare in microcomputer DBMS products. Intra-relation constraints specify restrictions on values *within* a relation. Inter-relation constraints specify restrictions on attribute values *between* relations. This last type of constraint allows the developer to establish a rule that in order to be acceptable in one table, the value of some attribute has to already exist in another table. Although ideally every constraint would be recognized and enforced by the DBMS, in practice this is not the case. Whatever constraints are not enforced by the DBMS must be enforced by programs or manual procedures.

Microcomputer DBMS products also vary in the extent to which they provide security for the database. Some allow password protection on either subjects or entities. However, security is largely maintained by programs and manual procedures in the microcomputer database environment.

## QUESTIONS

**GROUP I**

**10.1**  Why did users develop their own microcomputer databases and applications when microcomputer DBMS products first became available?

**10.2**  Do users continue to perform their own development work?

**10.3**  Describe three microcomputer database users whom you know personally.

**10.4**  What is a value added reseller (VAR)?

**10.5**  Why were traditional MIS departments not involved in the early development of microcomputer databases and applications?

**10.6**  What prompted MIS departments to become more involved?

**10.7**  Describe the principle differences between the mainframe database environment and the microcomputer database environment.

**10.8**  Why is database administration easier in the microcomputer environment than in the mainframe environment? Why is it more difficult in the microcomputer environment?

**10.9**  Describe the three types of microcomputer databases.

**10.10**  Describe an application (other than one in this text) for which a Type I database would be appropriate.

**10.11**  Describe an application (other than one in this text) for which a Type II database would be appropriate.

**10.12**  Describe a situation in which the potential for security problems would prohibit a Type II database from being implemented.

**10.13**  Describe an application (other than one in this text) for which a Type III database would be appropriate.

**10.14**  Describe the potential problems of a Type III database.

**10.15**  Explain the statement that in microcomputer DBMS products column names range across the database.

**10.16**  Why would it be better if domain names ranged across the database but column names did not?

**10.17**  What is a view?

**10.18**  How can a view be used to control access to database data?

**10.19**  Describe two types of views. Give an example of each.

**10.20**  How is a view different from a base table?

**10.21**  If a view does not contain the base table's key column, should updates be allowed? What problems might be experienced if they are?

**10.22**  What are domain constraints? Give three examples.

10.23  What is an intra-relation constraint? Give three examples, other than ones in this text.

10.24  Most microcomputer DBMS products do not support uniqueness constraints on groups of columns. Why is this a shortcoming?

10.25  What is an inter-relation constraint? Give three examples, other than ones in this text.

10.26  Describe the problem of relationship gridlock. How can it be prevented?

---

**GROUP II**          QUESTIONS AND EXERCISES

10.27  Which type of microcomputer database did Samantha Green develop for the Eastcoast State University Computer Lab? In terms of the topics presented in this chapter, what problems did she need to address?

10.28  Investigate a microcomputer database product. What technique is used for defining tables, columns, and views? Describe the constraints this product allows you to define. Can you toggle constraint checking on and off using this product?

10.29  Using a microcomputer DBMS product, define the DEPT and EMPLOYEE tables illustrated in Figure 10–16a.

   a.  Load the sample data shown in that figure.

   b.  Define the EMP-DEPT view illustrated in Figure 10–16b. Attempt to insert a record into the joined view. Does the DBMS product allow it?

   c.  Define a view of EMPLOYEE that includes Ssn, L-name, and Salary. Attempt to insert a record into that subset view. Does the DBMS product allow it?

   d.  Modify the EMPLOYEE table to include a virtual column, Bonus, equal to 5 percent of the employee's salary. Print a report listing L-name, Salary, and Bonus.

   e.  Insert this record into the EMPLOYEE table: [000–04–5555, Jones, Pam, Acct, 3, 1/1/88, 53,200]. Define a view of EMPLOYEE that includes L-name and F-name. Print a report of the data in that view. Does the name Pam Jones appear twice? What is the significance of this phenomenon?

# CHAPTER
# 11

# Relational Database Application

- Case Study: KDK Appliances
- DB2: The Product
- Relational Implementation Using DB2
- Summary

In Chapter 9 we examined the relational database model and the database access language SQL. In Chapter 10 we discussed end user database processing on microcomputers. In this chapter we will examine end user database processing on mainframe computers. We begin by considering some problems faced by a manufacturing company. We then propose a solution that requires the development of a relational database, and we define both the objects and relations needed.

Next we present an overview of the IBM relational database product called Database2 (DB2). We will examine not only the data definition and data manipulation features of DB2, but also the important features of handling concurrent processing, backup and recovery, and database security.

Finally we will present examples from the relational application developed for the company in our case study, including illustrations of interactive DB2 queries and a COBOL program that contains embedded DB2 commands.

## CASE STUDY: KDK APPLIANCES

KDK Appliances manufactures major kitchen appliances, such as refrigerators, ranges, microwave ovens, and dishwashers. The company markets its products to independent dealers, who then sell to the public. Currently, its market is primarily the northeastern United States, but it plans to develop new sales regions in the Midwest and Canada soon.

Each sales region is serviced by several salespeople. Salespeople call on dealers and explain KDK's product line, dealer training program, incentives, and local advertising programs. It is possible for one dealer to work with more than one KDK salesperson.

KDK has a large mainframe computer that handles all order processing, inventory control, personnel, and accounting functions. Stored within the mainframe are files and databases that track sales and other data to meet various reporting requirements.

In addition to the large mainframe computer, KDK has a smaller mainframe computer in its Information Center. This smaller mainframe processes extracts of operational data that are periodically downloaded (copied) from the large mainframe. No updating of data takes place in the Information Center. Rather, all updating is accomplished by the carefully controlled programs running on the large mainframe (see Figure 11–1).

Information Center personnel are systems analysts who answer users' questions by extracting data from the Information Center's database. The Information Center uses the IBM relational product Database2 (DB2) to process the relational databases. Application programs are written in COBOL.

### Problems

The Marketing Department plays a key role in the success of the company's plans to expand. The Marketing Department presently employs eight prod-

**Figure 11–1**
Relationship of
KDK's computers

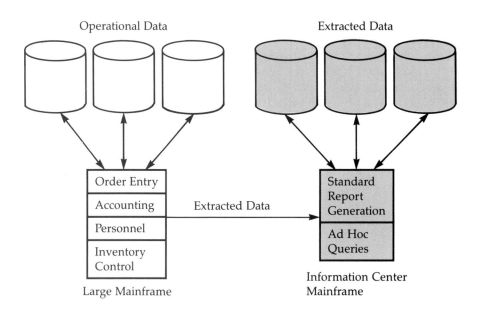

uct managers (PMs), each responsible for a particular line of products (one for refrigerators, one for ranges, and so forth). PMs, as part of their duties, develop an annual product plan for each major product (a major product being, for example, a particular refrigerator model or a specific type of microwave oven). The product plan establishes, among other things, the sales goals for the product and the budget for marketing. Marketing expenses include advertising, dealer training, salesperson training, dealer promotions, and so forth.

To make wise decisions regarding the use of marketing dollars, PMs want to access data stored in the computer. They need to know, for example, product sales by region and by salesperson. They also need to know the effect some aspect of marketing—say, advertising—has had on product sales. All the PMs know that the data they need is "in the computer." Now they want to know how to get at it.

Instant response time is not vital, because the PMs usually need quarterly, monthly, or weekly summaries of data. For example, instant access to a particular order is not important to a PM. (In contrast, consider how important response time is when performing the order entry function on KDK's large operational mainframe.)

All of the PMs are either familiar with SQL or willing to learn it. None is a programmer, though, and none has the time or the interest to learn COBOL. Typical of the questions that a PM wants answered are

- Which dealers participated in our shared advertising program this month?
- What was the total sales figure for product #45678 during March? How does that compare to sales for April?

The advertising program at KDK Appliances is interesting. KDK employs several agencies to develop advertising campaigns for various media, including newspapers (daily or weekly), periodicals (weekly or monthly), television, and radio. Much of KDK's advertising is shared with dealers. This means that in addition to the advertising copy promoting a specific KDK product, a dealer's name, address, and logo appear in the ad (see Figure 11–2). Thus, although KDK products are the central focus of the ad, a local dealer can share the benefits by sharing the cost of the ad.

Some dealers take advantage of this arrangement, whereas others do not. The share costs (percentages of the cost borne by KDK and the dealer) vary from one ad to another and from one dealer to another. Sales and marketing personnel establish the share costs for each ad.

## Overview of the Solution

After studying these problems and discussing them with several of the product managers, one of the systems analysts proposed that KDK develop a database system on the Information Center's computer, which already

**Figure 11–2**
Advertisement for a
KDK product

contains the data needed to answer most of the product managers' questions. The data would be periodically extracted from KDK's operational
mainframe computer. (The frequency depends on how up-to-date the data
needs to be. The analyst suggested that they begin downloading data once
a week. If that proves unsatisfactory, downloading can be done more or
less frequently.)

Some of the information that PMs need is highly predictable. For example, each PM needs a monthly report summarizing his or her product's

sales by region, by dealer, and by salesperson. The analyst decided to write application programs in COBOL to produce those reports. The programs will be run on a regular schedule.

In addition to the regular anticipated reports, the analyst suggested that each PM learn how to use SQL to make simple ad hoc queries against the database in the Information Center. Complex queries will be handled by Information Center personnel as needed.

## Database Security Precautions

Because the Information Center handles extracts of data for all divisions of the company, certain security precautions must be taken to protect the data and to ensure the privacy of proprietary information. First, the Information Center systems analyst must be authorized by the company's database administrator to extract sales and other data from the operational database on the large mainframe. Second, because the operational database on the large mainframe contains vast amounts of private data (such as employee salaries), only the data necessary for the assessment of product sales will be extracted.

Third, because many employees use Information Center terminals to perform queries, this database will be made available to PMs only. All other employees (except for Information Center personnel) will be prevented from using it. Fourth, PMs will be authorized to use only this database. They will have no access to databases that have been established for other user departments. The Information Center will assign each PM an identification number that will serve as a password for access to the database.

Finally, data will only be downloaded from the mainframe computer. No updates will be made to the extracted data and no data will be sent back to the large mainframe. The extracted data will be merely a snapshot of the data in the operational database, a work copy that can be destroyed when the PMs are finished with it.

## Object Definitions

To develop the proposed system, the analyst needed first to identify the objects in which the PMs were interested. To start, they examined reports, transactions, and other entities. Let us first consider the reports and identify the underlying objects needed to construct them.

**PRODUCT SALES SUMMARY Reports.** Figure 11–3 shows three examples of product sales summaries the PMs need each month. Figure 11–3a shows a sample PRODUCT SALES SUMMARY BY SALESPERSON report. It contains data about products (product number, name, description, price), salespeople (name), and sales (total units sold by each salesperson). This *suggests* the existence of PRODUCT, SALESPERSON, and SALE objects. We

**Figure 11—3**
PRODUCT SUM-
MARY reports

```
                     PRODUCT  SALES  SUMMARY  BY  SALESPERSON


Product Number:    87224

Name/Description: Mini-Mike Programmable compact microwave
                  oven
Price:            $194.99



        SALESPERSON          UNITS SOLD
        John Eberle              280
        Margaret Gosselin        200
        Hans Jensen               50
                       TOTAL     530
```

a. SALES SUMMARY BY SALESPERSON report

```
                  PRODUCT  SALES  SUMMARY  BY  DEALER


Product Number:    87224

Name/Description: Mini-Mike Programmable compact microwave
                  oven
Price:            $194.99



          DEALER                       UNITS SOLD
     Lisbon Furniture and Appliances       30
     Parks Department Store               200
     United Kitchens                       50
     Gem Appliances                       100
     Rich Appliance Co.                   100
     Sounds Terrific                       50
                           TOTAL          530
```

b. SALES SUMMARY BY DEALER report

**Figure 11-3**
*(continued)*

```
                    PRODUCT SALES SUMMARY BY REGION


Product Number:    87224

Name/Description:  Mini-Mike Programmable compact microwave
                   oven
Price:             $194.99



        REGION              UNITS  SOLD
          2                    200
          5                    330
                   TOTAL       530
```

c. SALES SUMMARY BY REGION report

will not be sure until all reports, transactions, and so forth have been examined.

The PRODUCT SALES SUMMARY BY DEALER report (Figure 11-3b) contains data about products (product number, name, description, price), dealers (name), and sales (total units sold to each dealer). Thus, in addition to the objects mentioned above, it is likely that a DEALER object will exist as well.

The third summary report, PRODUCT SALES SUMMARY BY REGION (Figure 11-3c), contains data about products (product number, name, description, price), regions (region number), and sales (total units sold in each region). Now, in addition to the potential objects already identified—PRODUCT, SALESPERSON, SALE, and DEALER—another possible object is found: REGION.

**The DEALER ACTIVITY SUMMARY Report.** Figure 11-4 shows an example of a DEALER ACTIVITY SUMMARY report. It contains data about dealers (dealer number, name, address, telephone number), sales (invoice number, date, invoice total), and advertisements (advertisement name, date, cost, and dealer's share). We have already identified both DEALER and SALE (an invoice is the record of a sale) as potential objects. The DEALER ACTIVITY SUMMARY report suggests a few more attributes of these objects, such as dealer address, telephone number, and invoice number. This report also suggests that advertisements are possible objects.

Figure 11-5 illustrates our findings so far. The potential objects are PRODUCT, SALESPERSON, SALE (or INVOICE), REGION, DEALER, and

**Figure 11—4**
DEALER ACTIVITY
SUMMARY report

```
              DEALER ACTIVITY SUMMARY


      # 6644              (617) 479-5555
      J & S Dept. Store
      75 Rock Road
      Plymouth, MA   02787
      - - - - - - - - - - - - - - - - - - - - - - - - - - - - - - - -
                    Purchases to Date
            Invoice #        Date          Total
            1013          01/02/88      15349.81
            1071          02/01/88      22467.00
            1296          03/02/88      18949.37
            1380          04/01/88      36755.29
                              TOTAL     93620.47
      - - - - - - - - - - - - - - - - - - - - - - - - - - - - - - - -
                    Advertising to Date
      Ad Name          Date       Ad Cost    Dealer's Share (%)
      Ultra          03/10/88      250.00          67
      Free Time      02/15/88      400.00          67
      St. Paddy's Sale 03/14/88    600.00          67
      Ultra          03/15/88      250.00          60
```

ADVERTISEMENT. This is by no means a complete and final list. These objects are only the beginning of our investigation. Study the object diagrams in Figure 11–5 carefully, making sure you understand them before continuing.

**The Sales Invoice Document.**   Product managers derive much information about product sales from one important document: the sales invoice. An invoice for each sale is completed by a salesperson. An *actual* invoice captures many details about the dealer, the product(s) sold, and the dollar amounts of the transaction, discounts, credits, balance due, and shipping charges. All invoice details are entered into KDK's large operational mainframe computer. Keep in mind, however, that PMs need only a *subset* of the data on an actual invoice. An invoice as viewed by a product manager is illustrated in Figure 11–6. It contains data about the invoice (number, sale date, total), salesperson (number, name), dealer (name, address), and items sold (line item number, product number, name, price, quantity sold, extended price).

It is easy to see that what we have just described as an *invoice* is an embellishment of what we have been calling a *sale*. Because the PMs are

**Figure 11—5**
Preliminary sketch of
KDK's objects

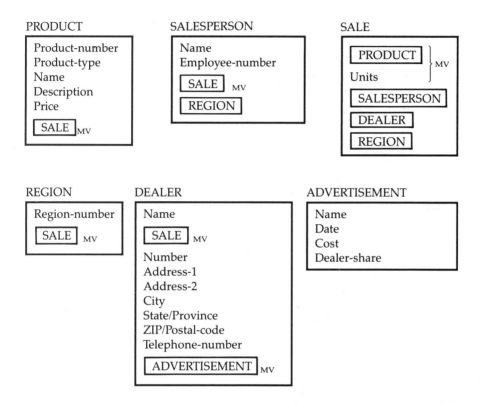

more likely to use the term *invoice* than *sale* (this was discovered by talking to the PMs), we will modify the object diagrams from Figure 11–5, replacing the SALE object with the updated INVOICE object. The results are shown in Figure 11–7.

**Advertising.** We noted earlier that KDK advertises its products to consumers in various media, such as print and television. An ad that can be run in, say, a newspaper is referred to as an *ad-copy*. Each ad-copy is given a title by the advertising agency that developed it. When a particular ad-copy is actually run in a newspaper on a certain date at a certain cost, it is referred to as an *advertisement*. Thus, an ad-copy called "Free Time" emphasizing the time-saving features of various KDK appliances might be run in several newspapers over a period of three or four months. Each instance it is run is called an advertisement.

As we noted above, each advertisement may be shared by a local appliance dealer, as long as the dealer agrees to share the cost of the ad. Because

**Figure 11—6**
PM's view of invoice

```
┌─────────────────────────────────────────────────────────────────┐
│  INVOICE 1001                                    02/01/88         │
│  SOLD TO:                         SALES REP:  #5762               │
│  Lisbon Furniture and Appliances              Paula Jasinski      │
│  692 S. Ellington Rd.                                             │
│  South Windsor, CT  06114                                        │
├─────────────────────────────────────────────────────────────────┤
│     Number   Name            Price    Qty     Cost               │
│  1  80911    Kitchen Valet   1699.99    2     3399.98            │
│  2  87755    Mity-Mike        344.99   20     6899.80            │
│  3  93861    E.Range-white    679.99   15    10199.85            │
│  4                                                               │
│  5                                                               │
│  6                                                               │
│                                 TOTAL      20499.63              │
└─────────────────────────────────────────────────────────────────┘
```

each ad-copy can target several products, and because each advertisement can be shared by a dealer, product managers need to track various aspects of advertising. After all, a very large portion of each PM's budget is devoted to advertising.

The underlying objects in the advertising portion of this system, then, are AD-COPY and ADVERTISEMENT. The object diagrams for them are illustrated in Figure 11–8. Note that this more complete definition of the ADVERTISEMENT object replaces the one seen in Figure 11–7.

**The Final Version.**   Using object diagrams like the ones we developed in Figures 11–7 and 11–8, the analyst reviewed his understanding of their problems with the PMs. This gave each of them the opportunity to correct or confirm what the analyst had done.

One point the analyst raised during this review concerned the REGION object. The analyst wanted to be sure that PMs did not need any data about a region. When the product managers concurred that they needed no additional data, the analyst decided to drop the REGION object. Thus modified, the object diagrams seemed acceptable, and the analyst proceeded with the next step, translating the object definitions into relation definitions.

## Relation Definitions

The information center analyst at KDK Appliances followed the guidelines you learned in Chapter 6 for transforming objects into relations. We will first examine the INVOICE object.

**INVOICE.**   INVOICE is a composite object because Line-item is a non-object repeating group. Thus, the INVOICE object will be represented by

**Figure 11-7**
Modified sketch of
KDK's objects, replac-
ing SALE with
INVOICE

PRODUCT

| |
|---|
| Product-number |
| Product-type |
| Name |
| Description |
| Price |
| INVOICE    MV |

SALESPERSON

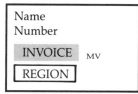

INVOICE

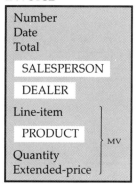

REGION

| |
|---|
| Region-number |
| INVOICE    MV |

DEALER

| |
|---|
| Name |
| Number |
| Address-1 |
| Address-2 |
| City |
| State/Province |
| ZIP/Postal-code |
| Telephone-number |
| INVOICE    MV |
| ADVERTISEMENT   MV |

ADVERTISEMENT

| |
|---|
| Ad-name |
| Date |
| Cost |
| Share-percent |

two relations. One will contain general information about an invoice. The other will contain the line items associated with the invoice. The relations have a one-to-many relationship and both relations are mandatory (see Figure 11–9). The formats of the two relations are

```
INVOICE (Number, Date, Total, Salesperson.Number, Dealer.Number)
LINE-ITEM (Invoice.Number, Line-item-number, Product.Number,
Quantity, Extended-price)
```

An example of the INVOICE and LINE-ITEM relations is shown in Figure 11–10. Notice that the key for INVOICE (Invoice.Number) is part of

**Figure 11—8**

Object diagrams for
advertising portion of
KDK database

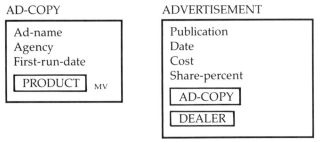

AD-COPY

| |
|---|
| Ad-name |
| Agency |
| First-run-date |
| PRODUCT  MV |

ADVERTISEMENT

| |
|---|
| Publication |
| Date |
| Cost |
| Share-percent |
| AD-COPY |
| DEALER |

**Figure 11—9**

Relationship between
INVOICE and LINE-
ITEM

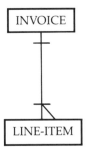

the key for LINE-ITEM. This must be done because INVOICE is a composite object.

Three foreign keys appear in the INVOICE and LINE-ITEM relations, namely Salesperson.Number, Dealer.Number, and Product.Number. These keys are needed to establish the one-to-many relationships between DEALER and INVOICE, between SALESPERSON and INVOICE, and between PRODUCT and INVOICE. Let's look at each of the objects.

**DEALER and SALESPERSON.** The DEALER object in Figure 11—7 is a compound object because it contains multivalued object properties, namely INVOICE and ADVERTISEMENT. There is a 1:$N$ relationship in both cases.

Similarly, the SALESPERSON object in Figure 11—7 is a compound object. It has a 1:$N$ relationship with INVOICE. In Figure 11—11 we have

**Figure 11—10**

Sample data in
INVOICE and LINE-
ITEM relations

| Number | Date | Salesperson. Number | Dealer. Number | Total |
|--------|------|---------------------|----------------|-------|
| 10982 | 03/12/88 | 8555 | 2425 | 38549.05 |
| 75214 | 03/12/88 | 1755 | 4528 | 60472.95 |
| 63911 | 03/15/88 | 5762 | 6178 | 12249.92 |
| 41200 | 03/18/88 | 5762 | 6644 | 147997.70 |

INVOICE relation

| Invoice-number | Line-item-number | Product-number | Quantity | Extended-price |
|----------------|------------------|----------------|----------|----------------|
| 10982 | 001 | 14365 | 50 | 14999.50 |
| 10982 | 002 | 74961 | 30 | 17999.70 |
| 10982 | 003 | 87033 | 15 | 5549.85 |
| 75214 | 001 | 87214 | 25 | 4874.75 |
| 75214 | 002 | 87224 | 100 | 25999.00 |
| 75214 | 003 | 87033 | 80 | 29599.20 |
| 63911 | 001 | 56271 | 3 | 3749.97 |
| 63911 | 002 | 80911 | 5 | 8499.95 |
| 41200 | 001 | 15965 | 200 | 129998.00 |
| 41200 | 002 | 74961 | 30 | 17999.70 |

LINE-ITEM relation

added the DEALER and SALESPERSON relations to the diagram from Figure 11–9. INVOICE is also an association object; it documents the relationship between a salesperson and a dealer. The relationships between SALESPERSON and INVOICE and between DEALER and INVOICE are mandatory-to-optional. This means that an invoice must be associated with a salesperson and a dealer, but that a salesperson or a dealer does not have to have any invoices. The relation formats are

DEALER (<u>Number</u>, Name, Address-1, Address-2, City, State/Province,
ZIP/Postal-code, Telephone)
SALESPERSON (<u>Number</u>, Name, Region)

**Figure 11–11**
Result of adding
DEALER and SALES-
PERSON relations to
Figure 11–9

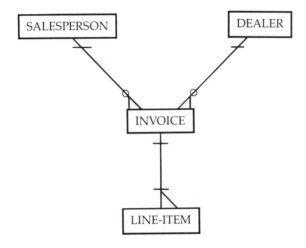

Sample data for the DEALER and SALESPERSON relations is shown in Figure 11–12. Following the guidelines established in Chapter 6, the 1:*N* relationship between DEALER and INVOICE is represented by placing the key field of DEALER (Dealer.Number) in the INVOICE relation. Similar comments hold for the relationship between SALESPERSON and INVOICE.

**PRODUCT.**   Another object in Figure 11–7 is PRODUCT. According to the object diagram, an *N*:1 relationship exists between a product and an invoice. More specifically, an *N*:1 relationship exists between a line-item and a product. A certain product—say, a dishwasher—can be found on line-items from various invoices issued to many different dealers. This can be represented relationally as shown in Figure 11–13.

The relational format for the PRODUCT relation is

PRODUCT (<u>Number</u>, Name, Description, Price)

The 1:*N* relationship between PRODUCT and LINE-ITEM has been established by placing Product.Number in the LINE-ITEM relation. Sample data for the PRODUCT relation can be found in Figure 11–14.

**ADVERTISEMENT and AD-COPY.**   Two more objects, ADVERTISEMENT and AD-COPY (see Figure 11–8), need to be transformed into relations. A dealer can share the cost of several advertisements, but any advertisement features at most one dealer. Thus, a 1:*N* relationship exists between dealer and advertisement.

**Figure 11–12**

Sample data for
SALESPERSON and
DEALER relations

| Number | Name | Region |
|--------|------|--------|
| 1043 | Ronald Hunt | 1 |
| 2711 | John Eberle | 5 |
| 8555 | Margaret Gosselin | 2 |
| 5762 | Paula Jasinski | 4 |
| 1755 | Hans Jensen | 5 |
| 6042 | Lawrence Smithers | 1 |
| 2814 | Maxine Whittier | 3 |

SALESPERSON relation

| Number | Name | Address-1 | Address-2 | City | State | ZIP | Phone |
|--------|------|-----------|-----------|------|-------|-----|-------|
| 6178 | Gem Appliances | 1005 Farmington Ave. | -0- | W. Hartford | CT | 06754 | (203) 555-4312 |
| 2425 | S. K. Lafferty | Prestige Park | Building 43 | E. Hartford | CT | 06832 | (203) 555-6789 |
| 6624 | Rich Appliance Co. | 17 Whiting Street | Suite 4143 | New Britain | CT | 06588 | (203) 555-6609 |
| 0212 | Lisbon Furniture & Appliances | 692 Ellington Road | -0- | South Windsor | CT | 06551 | (203)677-4582 |
| 9356 | Gallo's Appliance Outlet | P.O. Box 344 | 264 Park Road | W. Hartford | CT | 06431 | (203) 549-6772 |
| 4516 | United Kitchens | 114 Cummington Street | -0- | Cummington | MA | 07231 | (617) 438-0065 |
| 9101 | Parks Department Store | 21 Main Street | -0- | Worcester | MA | 07488 | (617) 756-2295 |
| 6644 | J & S Department Store | 75 Rock Road | -0- | Plymouth | MA | 02787 | (617) 555-9734 |
| 4528 | Sounds Terrific | 1433 W. Northeast Highway | Suite 5678 | Boston | MA | 07665 | (617) 885-4000 |

DEALER relation

Similarly, one ad-copy can be run several times in many newspapers. Consequently, a 1:*N* relationship exists between an ad-copy and an advertisement. Adding these relations to the ones in Figure 11–13, we arrive at the result in Figure 11–15.

The next relationship we need to incorporate is the one between PRODUCT and AD-COPY. Each product can be featured in several ads, and each ad can specify several products. Thus, we have an *N:M* relationship between PRODUCT and AD-COPY.

You will recall from Chapter 6 that many-to-many relationships are incorporated into a relational model by establishing an intersection relation

---

**Figure 11–13**

PRODUCT relation
added to diagram in
Figure 11–11

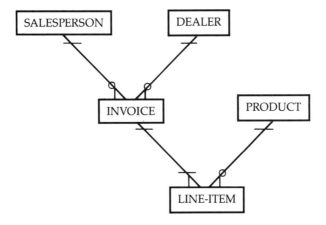

containing only keys from the two other relations. In this case, an intersection relation called PRODUCT-AD is defined. Each row contains a product number and an ad-name. The PRODUCT-AD relation is added to the ones from Figure 11–15. The result is found in Figure 11–16.

The formats for these three new relations are

```
AD-COPY (Ad-name, Agency, First-run-date)
ADVERTISEMENT (Publication, Date, Ad-name, Cost,
Share-percent, Dealer.Number)
PRODUCT-AD (Ad-name, Product.Number)
```

Sample data for the AD-COPY and ADVERTISEMENT relations appears in Figure 11–17 and for PRODUCT-AD in Figure 11–18.

### KDK Case Summary

All of the objects identified earlier can be constructed from data stored in the relations we defined. Reports summarizing product sales on various criteria (such as salesperson, region, and dealer), reports analyzing advertising, and much more can be readily extracted from the database.

The next step is to actually implement the database structure: define tables and fields, impose constraints on them, assign passwords, establish security procedures, and so forth. Following that, the analyst will test the database structure by downloading some sample data from the mainframe and making various queries. Finally, when no errors are found in testing,

**Figure 11–14**
Sample data for
PRODUCT relation

| Type/number | Name | Description | Price |
|---|---|---|---|
| 392761 | Electric range—white | Electric range | $299.99 |
| 393861 | Electric range—white | Electric range; self-clean; window | $679.99 |
| 393863 | Electric range—toast | Electric range; self-clean; window | $689.99 |
| 393867 | Electric range—avocado | Electric range; self-clean; window | $689.99 |
| 370351 | Gas range—white | Gas range; 21-inch | $279.99 |
| 370353 | Gas range—toast | Gas range; 21-inch | $289.99 |
| 374961 | Gas range—white | Gas range; 36-inch; continuous clean | $599.99 |
| 374963 | Gas range—toast | Gas range; 36-inch; continuous clean | $599.99 |
| 374976 | Gas range—avocado | Gas range; 36-inch; continuous clean | $599.99 |
| 380551 | Fifth-burner kit | Gas range 5th burner to replace griddle | $19.99 |
| 787214 | Mini-mike | Compact microwave oven | $194.99 |
| 787224 | Mini-mike | Programmable compact microwave oven | $259.99 |
| 787755 | Mity-mike | Programmable solid-state full-size microwave oven | $344.99 |
| 787033 | Mity-mike | #87755 with carousel | $369.99 |
| 415965 | Ultra wash | Electronic dishwasher | $649.99 |
| 414365 | Dishwasher | 18-inch; 2-level dishwasher | $299.99 |
| 417375 | Dishwasher—P | Dishwasher-portable | $409.99 |
| 416037 | Dishwasher—sp | Space saver dishwasher | $249.99 |
| 556681 | Porcelain-plus | Refrigerator; porcelain-on-steel; 25.8 cu ft | $1,599.99 |
| 556271 | Quiet Cold | Frost-free refrigerator; ice maker | $1,249.99 |
| 580911 | Kitchen Valet | Refrigerator; all-electronic; customized panels | $1,699.99 |
| 580922 | KDK Limited Edition | Refrigerator; frost-free; special use compartments | $2,549.99 |
| 593252 | Mini-fridge | Compact refrigerator | $99.00 |
| 593286 | Mini-fridge | Compact refrigerator/freezer | $174.99 |
| 594605 | Compact-fridge | 3.6 cu ft compact refrigerator | $219.99 |
| 594911 | Compact-fridge | #94605 with push-button defrost | $299.99 |

KDK can download sales data from the mainframe computer and begin to use the newly established database in the information center.

Some programs need to be written in COBOL and tested before they can be used to produce the product managers' reports. Inquiries can be made against the database using SQL. The relational database product used in the information center at KDK Appliances is DB2, which we will examine next.

**Figure 11–15**

Addition of AD-COPY
and ADVERTISE-
MENT relations to
those in Figure 11–13

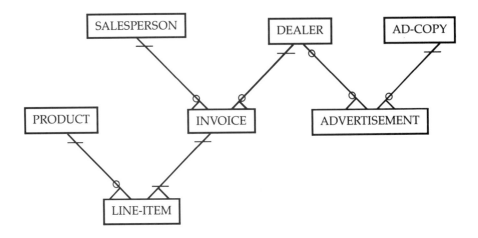

## DB2: THE PRODUCT

Database2 (DB2) is IBM's relational database management system for large mainframe computers running IBM's MVS operating system. Another popular IBM DBMS, called IMS/DB, is based on the *hierarchical* (DL/I), rather than the relational, model. IMS/DB is an older, and therefore more established, database product that was already firmly installed in many companies before the development of the relational model. To allow its customers flexibility in their choice of DBMS products, IBM designed DB2 to coexist with DL/I. Thus, DB2 allows the same application program to access both DL/I and DB2 database data. User organizations can take advantage of the newer relational product without having to abandon or convert all of their hierarchical applications. You will study DL/I in Chapter 12.

### Key Features

DB2 uses the Structured Query Language (SQL) to perform all database operations: data definition, data access, data manipulation, and authorization functions. You learned in Chapter 9 that SQL is a high-level language used for relational database processing. DB2 is one product that incorporates this flexible and powerful language.

SQL statements can be entered by a user at a computer terminal. This mode employs an interactive terminal interface called DB2I. SQL statements

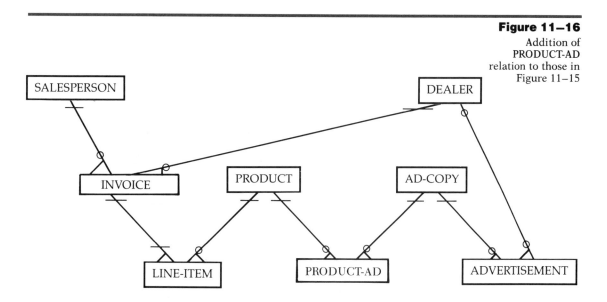

**Figure 11–16**

Addition of
PRODUCT-AD
relation to those in
Figure 11–15

can also be embedded in application programs written in assembler language, COBOL, PL/I, and FORTRAN. Later in this chapter we will present examples of both interactive commands and COBOL programs containing SQL instructions.

DB2 is well suited for the multi-user environment. It allows users to dynamically create and modify tables, views, and other database structures, to dynamically define and modify database security parameters, and to execute various database utilities online. Most functions can be performed—within certain limits—even while other users are employing the database.

Especially important in the multi-user environment is the mechanism for recovery in the event of a system failure. DB2 includes built-in features for such important services as activity logging and recovery, thus facilitating failure recovery. And because DB2 is just one of several subsystems that may be in operation at the time of a system failure, its recovery features are coordinated with those of other subsystems that may be present, such as CICS or other CCPs.

DB2 enables a person—database designer, database administrator, or end user—to define and manipulate various *constructs*.[1] Constructs include data bases, tables, views, and indexes, to name a few. In the next section, we will examine DB2 constructs and learn some SQL data definition (DDL) statements.

---

1. IBM actually uses the term *object* instead of *construct*. We have been using the term *object* to refer to things in the user's work environment. To clarify the discussion we will use the word *construct* where IBM uses *object*.

**Figure 11–17**

Sample data for AD-
COPY and ADVER-
TISEMENT relations

| Ad-name | Agency | First-run-date |
|---|---|---|
| Dishwashers | On-Target Ads | 03/10/88 |
| Free Time | Haskins | 02/15/88 |
| Microwaves | On-Target Ads | 03/12/88 |
| Presidents | Haskins | 02/03/88 |
| Ranges | On-Target Ads | 02/01/88 |
| St. Paddy's Sale | J&J Marketing | 03/12/88 |
| The Bachelor | J&J Marketing | 01/04/88 |
| The Fridge | Haskins | 02/01/88 |
| Ultra | J&J Marketing | 03/10/88 |
| Working Woman | Haskins | 03/01/88 |

AD-COPY relation

| Publ. | Date | Ad-name | Cost | Share% | Dealer.Num |
|---|---|---|---|---|---|
| Herald | 02/01/88 | Ranges | 300.00 | 25. | 6644 |
| Free Press | 02/01/88 | Ranges | 320.00 | 33. | 6178 |
| Free Press | 02/03/88 | Presidents | 450.00 | 50. | 4528 |
| Sentinel | 02/15/88 | Free Time | 400.00 | 33. | 6178 |
| Herald | 02/17/88 | Free Time | 350.00 | 50. | 6178 |
| Herald | 02/19/88 | Ranges | 300.00 | 40. | 4516 |
| Sentinel | 03/10/88 | Dishwashers | 400.00 | 50. | 9101 |
| Times | 03/10/88 | Ultra | 250.00 | 33. | 6644 |
| Courier | 03/11/88 | Ultra | 280.00 | 40. | 0212 |
| Sentinel | 03/12/88 | Working Woman | 500.00 | 40. | 9356 |
| Times | 03/14/88 | St. Paddy's Sale | 600.00 | 33. | 6644 |
| Times | 03/14/88 | The Bachelor | 550.00 | 25. | 4516 |
| Herald | 03/15/88 | Ultra | 250.00 | 40. | 6644 |

ADVERTISEMENT relation

**Figure 11–18**
Sample data for
PRODUCT-AD
relation

| Ad-name | Product-number |
|---|---|
| Dishwashers | 17375 |
| Dishwashers | 16037 |
| Dishwashers | 14365 |
| Free Time | 70351 |
| Free Time | 16037 |
| Free Time | 92761 |
| Microwaves | 87033 |
| Microwaves | 87224 |
| Microwaves | 87755 |
| Microwaves | 87214 |
| Presidents | 93286 |
| Presidents | 80551 |
| Presidents | 93861 |
| Presidents | 74961 |
| Presidents | 80922 |
| Presidents | 14365 |
| Presidents | 93252 |
| Ranges | 92761 |
| Ranges | 74961 |

| Ad-name | Product-number |
|---|---|
| Ranges | 93861 |
| Ranges | 93863 |
| Ranges | 93867 |
| Ranges | 74967 |
| Ranges | 74963 |
| Ranges | 80551 |
| St. Paddy's Sale | 15965 |
| St. Paddy's Sale | 93867 |
| St. Paddy's Sale | 94605 |
| St. Paddy's Sale | 74967 |
| The Bachelor | 15965 |
| The Bachelor | 87755 |
| The Bachelor | 93867 |
| The Fridge | 56681 |
| The Fridge | 80922 |
| Ultra | 15965 |
| Working Woman | 93867 |
| Working Woman | 87033 |
| Working Woman | 87755 |

## The DB2 Data Definition Language

In this section we will briefly describe each DB2 construct. This will help you to envision the DB2 environment. DB2 constructs include resources that application programmers (and sometimes end users) need to understand, such as tables and views, as well as resources that database designers and DBAs need to understand, such as storage groups and table spaces. We will also present SQL statements to define several objects for KDK Appliances' Information Center database.

**DB2 Constructs.** The DB2 constructs we will examine are tables, views, table spaces, indexes, index spaces, data bases, and storage groups. Although a few other DB2 constructs exist, they are not important to our discussion and therefore will not be presented.

*Tables.* Like all products based on the relational model, DB2 stores data in what the user sees as *tables* with rows and columns. You can use SQL to retrieve and change data in a table, to insert and delete rows, and to add new columns to an existing table.

*Views.* You will recall from Chapter 10 that a *view* is a virtual table. It is derived from one or several base tables and is not physically stored in the database (although table data is). Views can be accessed and manipulated much like tables, using many of the same SQL data manipulation statements used for tables. Often a user cannot tell whether he or she is processing a table or a view. Examples of a base table and a view of it are illustrated in Figure 11–19.

Database users, including application programmers and end users, need to know only about tables and views. Database designers and DBAs need

**Figure 11–19**

Example of base table and view

| Name | Salary | Hire-date | Office | Extension |
|------|--------|-----------|--------|-----------|
| Walker | 21800 | 12/85 | 321 | 246 |
| Berg | 36500 | 10/83 | 411 | ·647 |
| Dean | 42900 | 02/88 | 308 | 795 |
| Hsiu | 36500 | 09/85 | 307 | 581 |
| Cameratta | 40000 | 03/80 | 419 | 669 |

a. EMPLOYEES (base table)

| Name | Office | Extension |
|------|--------|-----------|
| Walker | 321 | 246 |
| Berg | 411 | 647 |
| Dean | 308 | 795 |
| Hsiu | 307 | 581 |
| Cameratta | 419 | 669 |

b. EMPLOYEE-DIRECTORY (view of EMPLOYEES)

to understand not only tables and views, but also physical database storage. This includes table spaces, indexes, index spaces, data bases, and storage groups.

*Table Spaces.*   A *table space* is a collection of one or more VSAM data sets, or files, used to store database data on magnetic disk. Thus, tables are stored in table spaces (see Figure 11–20). A table space can hold approximately 64 billion bytes of data, although that size is not practical.

Table spaces are DB2's recoverable units. If the database system crashes, the table spaces will be recovered, not the databases or individual tables. Perhaps you can see why huge table spaces (such as 64 billion bytes of

**Figure 11–20**
Table spaces and
tables

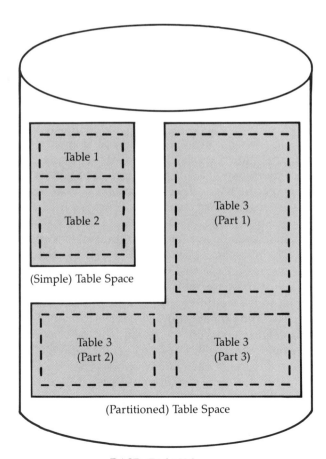

DASD (Disk) Volume

data), although theoretically possible, are in reality seldom defined. Recovery of a table space that large would be very difficult and time-consuming.

A table space can be either a *simple table space* or a *partitioned table space.* A simple table space can hold one or more tables, whereas a partitioned table space holds exactly one table.

The DBA would probably define a partitioned table space for a very large table. Each partition would then contain a part of the table based on the range of values in one or more columns. For example, each partition might contain taxpayer data based on Social Security Number. Partitions are independent of one another and can be reorganized and recovered individually.

Simple table spaces might contain several small, related tables. For example, the DBA might establish one table space for each user department and use each table space to store all tables pertinent to a particular department. Some applications require exclusive use of a table, so they issue a LOCK TABLE statement. When this happens, the entire table space is locked, preventing other tables in it from being accessed. If separate table spaces "belong" to individual user departments, it is less likely that one user will interfere with another user's processing by locking him or her out.

*Indexes.*    *Indexes* are used to reduce table access time. An index places table data in logical sequence, regardless of its physical sequence. Multiple indexes can be defined for a single table. Consider the table in Figure 11–21a. (In this example, rows are numbered to represent relative locations within the table. In practice, record addressing is far more complex, as discussed in Appendix B.) The rows might be stored in the sequence in which they appear in the figure. Now suppose that a user frequently needs to access the data by customer name. Use of the index illustrated in Figure 11–21b makes finding a specific name, and the location of that row in the CUSTOMER table, very fast because the index is arranged in alphabetical order on Name.

Similarly, suppose another user frequently accesses the table by customer number. The index in Figure 11–21c would be useful in that case. That index also ensures unique customer numbers. We will learn how later in this chapter. Of course, the table in Figure 11–21 is very small, so the effect of using an index would be insignificant. In fact, using indexes on such a small table would probably downgrade performance. Not only does index searching require time, but every addition or deletion to the CUSTOMER table would also require updates to the indexes. But if the table included, say, 800,000 records, then indexes would improve processing time.

Subject to concurrent processing restrictions, indexes can be defined at any time. An index is a physical construct, completely separate from the table to which it is related. As mentioned, DB2 automatically maintains an index once it is created. In fact, after an index has been defined for a table, DB2 decides without any direction from a user or a programmer when, if

**Figure 11—21**
Indexes on CUS-
TOMER table

| Row# | Cust# | Name | Credit-limit | ZIPcode |
|------|-------|------|--------------|---------|
| 1 | 10 | Smith | 3000 | 06413 |
| 2 | 20 | Jones | 3000 | 95060 |
| 3 | 30 | Whittaker | 2000 | 07814 |
| 4 | 40 | Murphy | 3000 | 62200 |
| 5 | 50 | Wang | 3000 | 08142 |
| 6 | 60 | Youngblood | 2000 | 62200 |
| 7 | 70 | Jones | 2000 | 95060 |

a. CUSTOMER table

| Name | Row# |
|------|------|
| Jones | 2 |
| Jones | 7 |
| Murphy | 4 |
| Smith | 1 |
| Wang | 5 |
| Whittaker | 3 |
| Youngblood | 6 |

| Cust# | Row# |
|-------|------|
| 10 | 1 |
| 20 | 2 |
| 30 | 3 |
| 40 | 4 |
| 50 | 5 |
| 60 | 6 |
| 70 | 7 |

b. INDEX on Name        c. Index on Cust#

ever, to use it. In other words, once an index has been defined, neither a user nor an application programmer actually references it.

*Index Space.* An *index space* is an area of disk storage in which DB2 stores an index (see Figure 11–22). When an index is created, DB2 automatically allocates an index space for it.

*Data Bases.* IBM uses the term *data base* (two words) to define a collection of DB2 tables and indexes and the storage areas that hold them. Of course, several DB2 data bases can exist on the same computer system. DB2 is designed to use a data base as an operational unit. This means that it can

**Figure 11—22**
DB2 indexes stored in
index spaces

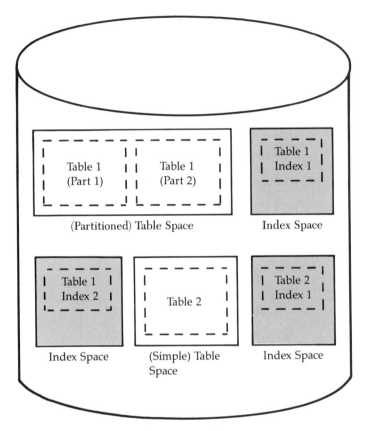

DASD (Disk) Volume

*start* a data base (make it available), *stop* a data base (make it unavailable), and assign *authorization* to use a data base (allow users to access the data).

Of course, users and application programmers do not deal directly with data bases any more than they deal with table spaces or indexes. Users and application programmers refer only to tables and views. They are shielded from needing to know anything about the underlying database structures.

*Storage Groups.*   A *storage group* is a group of disk volumes on which DB2 allocates space for user databases (see Figure 11–23). DB2 is able to manage its own data set allocation. This means that DB2 keeps track of available disk space and locates tables, indexes, and other database constructs in that space. It also releases disk space for use when it becomes available, such

**Figure 11–23**

DB2 storage groups

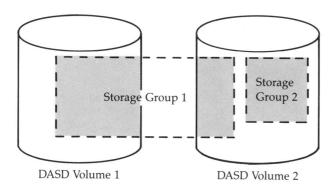

as when an index or a table is dropped. The DBA can also define, locate, and delete data sets. Sometimes this is done when the DBA is tuning, or optimizing, the database system.

**Using DB2 to Create Tables, Views, and Indexes.**   SQL data definition language (DDL) as implemented in DB2 allows us to define various DB2 constructs. In this section and the ones that follow we will illustrate SQL DDL by defining several constructs—tables, views, and indexes—for the Information Center database at KDK Appliances.

*Defining a Table.*   DB2 employs the SQL CREATE statement to define constructs. In Chapter 9 we examined only the data manipulation functions of SQL. In this chapter we will add data definition statements as well. Before defining a table, you should decide on the names of all the columns, their data types and lengths, and whether you wish to allow null values.

Allowable DB2 data types for field values are summarized in the table in Figure 11–24. A *null value* is a field value that is unknown or not applicable. A null value is different from a zero or a blank value. For example, a customer balance of zero is diff̲erent from an unknown customer balance. You can prohibit null values from specific columns when you create a table. For example, a key column should not be allowed to have null values.

Consider the SALESPERSON relation for which sample data appears in Figure 11–12. The following CREATE statement defines it:

```
CREATE TABLE SALESPERSON
      (NUMBER     CHAR(4)         NOT NULL,
       NAME       CHAR(20)        NOT NULL,
       REGION     DECIMAL (1))
```

**Figure 11—24**

Some allowable DB2
data types

| | |
|---|---|
| INTEGER | 31-bit signed binary values |
| SMALLINT | 15-bit signed binary values |
| FLOAT | Floating point values |
| DECIMAL(p,q) | Packed decimal values of $p$ (1 to 15) digits; a number of decimal places ($q$) to the right of the decimal point may be specified |
| CHAR(n) | Fixed length text data $n$ (1 to 254) characters long |
| VARCHAR(n) | Variable length text data up to $n$ (1 to 32674) characters |

This statement creates the PRODUCT relation for the sample data shown in Figure 11–14:

```
CREATE TABLE PRODUCT
    (TYPE        CHAR(1)      NOT NULL,
     NUMBER      CHAR(5)      NOT NULL,
     NAME        CHAR(25)     NOT NULL,
     DESCRIPTION CHAR(50),
     PRICE       DECIMAL(7,2) NOT NULL)
```

*Defining a View.*   The CREATE statement is also used to define a view. It includes a SELECT statement that specifies the view. The following CREATE statement defines for the PRODUCT relation a view that includes only product numbers and prices:

```
CREATE VIEW PRICELIST
     AS    SELECT NUMBER, PRICE
           FROM PRODUCT
```

Now the view, PRICELIST, can be manipulated in exactly the same way as a table. Data is retrieved from a view using the same SQL statements we use for a table. And if the view is a subset of rows or columns of a single table, it can even be used to update base table data (subject to the problems we described in Chapter 9). However, views that are the result of a join operation *cannot* be used to update table data. Let us consider another example.

This statement creates a view that contains only those rows in the PRODUCT relation for refrigerators (the Type field contains a 5):

```
CREATE VIEW REFRIGERATORS
     AS    SELECT *
           FROM PRODUCT
           WHERE TYPE = '5'
```

By specifying SELECT * we include all of the columns. By specifying WHERE TYPE = '5' we include only rows for refrigerators.

As a final example of defining a view, assume that KDK wants one particular user to have only restricted access to the DEALER and ADVERTISEMENT relations (see Figures 11–12 and 11–17). This user should be able to access only those dealers who have participated in shared advertising. We might define an appropriate joined view like this:

```
CREATE VIEW ACTIVEDEALER
     AS     SELECT DEALER.NUMBER, DEALER.NAME, TELEPHONE,
            ADVERTISEMENT.DATE, COST, SHARE-PERCENT
            FROM DEALER, ADVERTISEMENT
            WHERE DEALER.NUMBER = ADVERTISEMENT.DEALER-NUMBER
```

*Defining an Index.*    Indexes are usually defined and dropped by the DBA. As mentioned earlier, neither users nor application programmers ever reference an index. DB2 decides when to use an index and which one to use.

One reason to use an index, as described in the previous section, is to increase processing speed. Several indexes can be defined for one table, theoretically allowing rapid access on many different fields.

Another reason for defining an index on a table, however, is that an index can force the uniqueness of values of a column (or multiple columns). For example, the dealer number in KDK's DEALER relation must be unique (although dealer name, address, ZIP, and so forth do not need to be unique). The way to establish the uniqueness of the dealer number field is to issue this CREATE statement:

```
          CREATE     UNIQUE INDEX XDEALER
                     ON DEALER (DLRNUM)
```

In the next example, since UNIQUE is not specified, the resulting index might include duplicate telephone numbers. Incidentally, the index value is assumed to be ascending (ASC) unless otherwise specified (DESC):

```
          CREATE     INDEX XDLRPHONE
                     ON DEALER (PHONE DESC)
```

**Using DB2 to Change a Table.**    Often when we design a database, we are unable to anticipate *all* of the user's needs. And even if we could, user needs change over time. As a result, we sometimes need to modify our database design. Notice that we are not talking about changing the data stored in tables (that happens all the time, of course), but rather the structure of tables themselves.

DB2 offers two ways to modify table specifications: by dropping and then recreating the table, and by using the ALTER statement. The ALTER statement can be used only for adding a column to an existing table and for changing validation routines.

If you want to remove a column, change a column's data type or length, or change whether null values are allowed, then you must drop the table and recreate it. We will see how to drop a table in the next section. For now, just know that when you drop a table, you lose the table data as well as all views and indexes based on the table. You would follow these steps:

1. Define a new table with all the changes and a different name.
2. Define all indexes on the new table.
3. Copy table data from the old table to the new one.
4. Drop the old table (this loses all the views of it too).
5. Restore the original table name as a view of the new table. This allows applications that once referenced the old table to remain unchanged because the new view is processed exactly the same as the old table.
6. Define views like the ones defined for the old table. These can be exact duplicates of the old views because you can base a view on another view, just as you can base a view on a table. (Of course, if a view contains a column that has just been dropped, then the view is no longer valid.)
7. Authorize users to use the new table and views.

It should be clear that this type of database modification is done only by a DBA or someone who is authorized by the DBA.

The second option for changing a table design uses the ALTER statement. With it we can add a column to an existing table. For instance, suppose we wanted to add a salary column to the SALESPERSON relation. The following statement would accomplish this:

```
ALTER TABLE SALESPERSON
    ADD SALARY DECIMAL (7,2)
```

**Using DB2 to Delete Tables and Views.** `Periodically, the DBA needs to eliminate tables from the database. Users are rarely authorized to do this because they could inadvertently delete data they do not realize is needed by another user. In the previous section we saw how the DBA might need to delete a table in order to change its structure.

Deleting a table erases not only the table, but also all views and indexes dependent on it. Thus, dropping a table should not be done hastily.

To delete the ADVERTISEMENT table from its database, KDK's DBA would issue the following DROP statement:

```
DROP TABLE ADVERTISEMENT
```

The table and all its data would be deleted from the table space, and all indexes and views associated with it would also be erased.

The DROP statement can be used also to delete views. The DBA might authorize a user to create views and then delete them when they are no longer useful. It is unlikely that a user would be authorized to drop views that might be used by anyone else, however. That responsibility (and control) should remain with the DBA. We could delete the ACTIVE-DEALER view by issuing this statement:

```
DROP VIEW ACTIVEDEALER
```

Any applications that used that view (or views based on that view) would no longer work.

**DB2 Creation Facilities Summary.**    DB2 allows the DBA or user to define, modify, and delete various database constructs. These include tables, views, table spaces, indexes, index spaces, data bases, and storage groups. Users and application programmers are concerned only with tables and views. In addition to tables and views, the DBA and database designers also need to understand the underlying physical structures and database storage.

## DB2 Data Manipulation Language: SQL

Some differences exist in DB2 statements for the interactive user and for the application programmer. The differences exist because of differences in the user's and the programmer's environments. The interactive user wants results to be immediately displayed on a screen. The application programmer wants the DBMS to place values in columns and rows into program variables. We will address these issues in this section.

**Interactive Data Manipulation.**    Interactive DB2, or DB2I, supports all of the SQL statements described in Chapter 9. This includes ORDER BY, GROUP BY, and the built-in functions.

*Update Statements.*    The *function* of update statements is the same as described in Chapter 9. However, the *format* is slightly different. The following examples illustrate DB2I formats:

```
INSERT INTO SALESPERSON
VALUES (37721, 'Ayn Worcester',1)
```

This format is appropriate if the values for all columns in the inserted row are known. If they are not all known, then columns that are known must be identified. Null values are placed in any unnamed columns. Consider the following statement:

```
INSERT INTO PRODUCT
(TYPE, NUMBER, NAME, DESCRIPTION)
VALUES ('5','98876','Big Chill','Frost-free fridge;22.3 cu ft')
```

The result of this statement is that a row is inserted and the price column for the new Big Chill refrigerator is set to null.

The UPDATE statement is used to modify table values. In it we specify the name of the column and the new value. For example, if KDK receives notice of a dealer change of address, the following statement might be used to modify the database:

```
UPDATE DEALER
SET ADDRESS-1 = '256 East Main Street'
WHERE NUMBER = '9101'
```

As a result, the address for Parks Department Store would be changed.

We can also change several rows at a time. For instance, suppose KDK decided to merge both ranges (product type 3) and microwave ovens (product type 7) into the same product line, calling them both type 3. This change calls for replacing the type code for all microwaves to 3:

```
UPDATE PRODUCT
SET TYPE = '3'
WHERE TYPE = '7'
```

Finally, let's say that KDK applies an across-the-board price increase of 7 percent. The following instruction would modify all product prices:

```
UPDATE PRODUCT
SET PRICE = PRICE * 1.07
```

The function of the DELETE statement is to remove rows from tables. Its format is similar to the SELECT statement in that you must specify the table in which the row(s) to be deleted is found and a WHERE clause to specify the target.

To delete a particular dealer from the DEALER table, you would write

```
DELETE FROM DEALER
WHERE NUMBER = '6178'
```

To delete a group of dealers, say everyone in Massachusetts, you would use this statement:

```
DELETE FROM DEALER
WHERE STATE/PROVINCE = 'MA'
```

Finally, to delete all rows from the DEALER table, but to retain the table even though it is empty, you would enter:

```
DELETE FROM DEALER
```

Note that deleting all data from a table is not the same as dropping the table. When you DROP a table, you erase the table data, the table, and all views and indexes defined for the table.

**Accessing DB2 from COBOL Application Programs.**    DB2 application programs can be written in COBOL, PL/I, FORTRAN, and assembler language. SQL statements can be embedded in programs written in any of those languages. The examples used in this text will be embedded in COBOL programs.

As shown in Figure 11–25, all application programs that access DB2 must first be processed by the DB2 *precompiler*. The precompiler analyzes program source statements and processes those that are flagged SQL statements (you'll see how later). The precompiler inserts into the program required *table formats*, which are already written in the host language and stored on disk. It also builds for each SQL statement a *data base request module*, or DBRM, which it stores for later use. And the precompiler replaces SQL statements with host language call statements to access the DBRMs. As illustrated in Figure 11–25, the modified source code is then input to a standard language compiler for normal compilation.

The BIND process uses the DBRMs, database table definitions, available indexes, and other database data to determine the access paths for each SQL request. These it stores in the database catalog as an *application plan*, which is loaded when the first SQL call is executed.

For the DB2 precompiler to recognize statements intended for it, all SQL statements are embedded in keywords. Specifically, every SQL statement is preceded by the keywords EXEC SQL and followed by the keyword END-EXEC. In COBOL, the keyword END-EXEC is followed by a period unless the SQL statement is located in an IF statement. The general format of a DB2 SQL statement in a COBOL program is

```
EXEC SQL     statement     END-EXEC.
```

Only one statement can be included between the keywords. Multiple SQL statements require multiple EXEC SQL . . . END-EXEC statements.

DB2 SQL statements are embedded in the DATA DIVISION and the PROCEDURE DIVISION.

*SQL Statements in the DATA DIVISION.*    Two types of statements are embedded in the DATA DIVISION. The first describes data items that are used to pass *database data* between the application program and DB2. The second type describes *system data* that is shared by the application program and DB2.

*Definition of Database Data.* Figure 11–26 shows part of a COBOL program that processes the SALESPERSON table defined earlier. The DATA DIVISION includes data item definitions for all three columns of SALESPERSON. These columns have been renamed. NAME is now SALESPERSON-NAME, NUMBER is SALESPERSON-NUMBER, and REGION is SALES-REGION. The correct correspondence of names will be established in the PROCEDURE DIVISION.

**Figure 11−25**

Steps in application
program develop-
ment with DB2

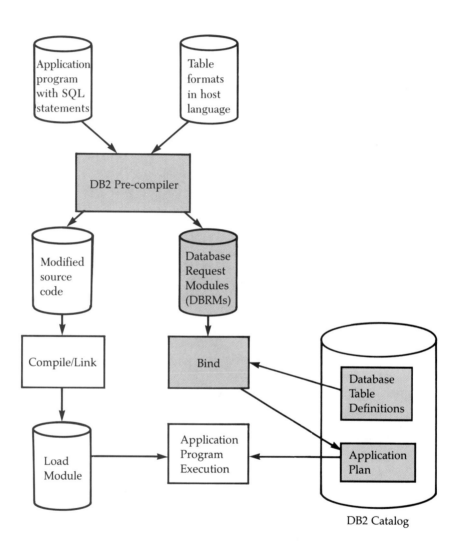

DB2 Catalog

The data types and lengths of data items do match, although COBOL
uses a different vocabulary than SQL does. For example, when we created
the table using SQL, we defined SPNUM as CHAR(4). The equivalent COBOL
definition for SALESPERSON-NUM is PICTURE X(4).

All data items that DB2 and the application program share are grouped
together. This enables the precompiler to identify them. (We show these
statements in the WORKING-STORAGE SECTION, but they could be located

**Figure 11—26**
SQL statements
embedded in COBOL
program

```
END-EXEC.

PICTURE  X(4).
PICTURE  X(20).
PICTURE  9   COMP-3.
END-EXEC.


UM.


: SALES-REGION

RSON-NUM
```

oup of data item definitions is
by the DB2 keyw… CLARE SECTION and is termi-
…th th… message E… ECTION. In Figure 11–26, the
n of S… …RSO… …e DECLARE SECTION.

…ition of … … Da… …u… …rned, the DECLARE SECTION
to de… …data it… …at … … used to transfer database data
the a… …ng p… …m an… …D… In addition to database data,
…cation … an… …e DB… … need to share system data. For
…after… … a … …nt i… …ted, DB2 sets a return code that
…whe… … … …or… …red … … …B2 and the application program

…en data … …ed in the … … …m with the DB2 SQL message
…E SQLCA (whi… …nds … … Communications Area). When
…the … …compiler processes this INCLUDE message, it inserts the data definitions seen in Figure 11–27a into the application program.

For brevity, Figure 11–27b describes only a few of the data items in
SQLCA. Knowing all of them would contribute little to your understanding
of DB2. The one data item that you need to understand is SQLCODE.

SQLCODE is set by DB2 after each SQL command is executed. If the
command is executed normally, SQLCODE is set to zero. If an unusual but
normal condition occurs, SQLCODE is set to a positive value. For example,
end of data is indicated by the value 100. If an abnormal, unexpected con-

**Figure 11—27**

DB2 Communications
Area

```
01   SQLCA.
     05   SQLCAID          PICTURE  X(8).
     05   SQLCABC          PICTURE  S9(9)  COMPUTATIONAL.
     05   SQLCODE          PICTURE  S9(9)  COMPUTATIONAL.
     05   SQLERRM
          49   SQLERRML    PICTURE  S9(4)  COMPUTATIONAL.
          49   SQLERRMC    PICTURE  X(70).
     05   SQLERRP          PICTURE  X(8).
     05   SQLERRD          OCCURS  6  TIMES
                           PICTURE  S9(9)  COMPUTATIONAL.
     05   SQLWARN.
          10   SQLWARN0    PICTURE  X(1).
          10   SQLWARN1    PICTURE  X(1).
          10   SQLWARN2    PICTURE  X(1).
          10   SQLWARN3    PICTURE  X(1).
          10   SQLWARN4    PICTURE  X(1).
          10   SQLWARN5    PICTURE  X(1).
          10   SQLWARN6    PICTURE  X(1).
          10   SQLWARN7    PICTURE  X(1).
     05   SQLEXT           PICTURE  X(8).
```

a. COBOL description of SQLCA

| Data-item | Content |
|-----------|---------|
| SQLCODE | Return code. Set by DB2 after each command. Zero indicates successful operation. Positive value indicates normal condition (such as end of data). Negative value indicates abnormal error. |
| SQLERRM | Error message. Set when SQLCODE is less than 0. |
| SQLERRP | Name of DB2 routine detecting error. Set when SQLCODE is less than 0. |
| SQLERRD | DB2 system status. |
| SQLWARN | Warning flags. Set for conditions such as data-item truncation (receiving data-item too small), null values encountered when processing SUM, AVG, MIN, or MAX, recovery from deadlock, and so forth. |

b. Content of selected SQLCA data-items

dition occurs, SQLCODE is set to a negative value. Insufficient file space is an example of an abnormal unexpected event.

*SQL Statements in the PROCEDURE DIVISION.* SQL statements in the PROCEDURE DIVISION instruct DB2 to perform some action. For example, the SELECT statement in Figure 11–26 will cause DB2 to extract from the database the name and region of salesperson 5762 and to place those values in the data items called SALESPERSON-NAME and SALES-REGION. This SQL statement is almost identical to the format followed when writing interactive SQL commands. The exception is the INTO clause that tells DB2 the name of the *host variable* (or variables) into which DB2 will place the value(s) it obtains from the database.

One problem for the DB2 precompiler is distinguishing between data names defined in the database and those defined locally within the application program. If all names are unique, then it can process the statements correctly. However, it is impossible to guarantee that the application programmer will always choose data names not already used in the database. Consequently, a colon (:) precedes the names of program variables used within any embedded SQL statement.

*Processing Multiple-Row Queries.* COBOL (as well as many other programming languages) is designed to process groups of data one record at a time. A typical COBOL program retrieves one record, processes it, retrieves the next one, processes it, and so forth, until all the records have been handled. DB2, however, processes tables. That is to say, a DB2 SELECT statement always returns a table of data. (Sometimes the table contains only one row, as in the example in Figure 11–26.) This distinction between COBOL file processing and DB2 relation processing is important for the application programmer who might be tempted to think that SQL statements correspond to simple READ and WRITE statements. They do not.

The application programmer would be better served by thinking of DB2 as a vehicle for retrieving an entire input data set, or pseudo-file, from the database. Then the data set is processed one row at a time. To do this, we define a *cursor* within the application program.

A cursor is a pointer that operates on a SELECT statement. The cursor indicates the row to be processed within the pseudo-file generated by the SELECT statement. In Figure 11–28, for example, the cursor CURRENT is defined to operate on the SELECT statement that will retrieve the names of all salespeople in region 5. In subsequent statements the program uses CURRENT to sequentially process the retrieved rows. As you can see in Figure 11–28, the logic is simply sequential file-processing logic: the cursor is opened (similar to opening a file), the first row is fetched (similar to a read), and then a loop is executed to process the rest of the data (similar to processing an entire file). Processing stops when SQLCODE is returned with a value of 100, indicating end of data. For now we will ignore other types of error processing.

The format of the FETCH statement is

```
FETCH cursor-name INTO dataname(s)
```

The datanames in the FETCH statement must match the column names identified in the SELECT statement where the cursor is defined.

More details about the programming techniques used with DB2 will appear in the example in the last section of this chapter.

**Figure 11—28**

Use of cursor to
sequentially process a
set of database
records

```
PROCEDURE DIVISION.
       .
       .
       .
     MOVE  5  TO  SALES-REGION.
     EXEC  SQL  DECLARE  CURRENT  CURSOR  FOR
           SELECT  NAME  FROM  SALESPERSON
           WHERE  REGION  =  : SALES-REGION
     END  EXEC.
       .
       .
       .
     EXEC  SQL  OPEN  CURRENT  END-EXEC.
     EXEC  SQL  FETCH  CURRENT  INTO  : SALESPERSON-NAME  END-EXEC.
     PERFORM  PROCESS-FETCH  UNTIL  SQLCODE  NOT  =  0.
     EXEC  SQL  CLOSE  CURRENT  END-EXEC.
       .
       .
       .
PROCESS-FETCH.
       (Instructions  to  process  SALESPERSON-NAME  go  here.)
     EXEC  SQL  FETCH  CURRENT  INTO  : SALESPERSON-NAME  END-EXEC.
```

## DB2 Concurrent Processing

Because DB2 allows concurrent processing, it must provide facilities to control and limit interference between users. This is done via *locks*.

Two types of locks employed by DB2 are shared locks and exclusive locks. When an application reads database data, DB2 acquires a *shared lock* on the data. A shared lock allows other applications to read the same data. However, applications that wish to modify that data need to wait until the lock has been released. This ensures that everyone has access to the most current data.

When an application needs to modify data (DB2 knows this by analyzing the SQL statements in the application), DB2 acquires an *exclusive lock* on the data. An exclusive lock prevents all other applications from accessing the data. When the application is finished with the data, the lock is released, thereby giving other applications access to the updated data. If DB2 did not acquire exclusive locks, it would be possible for a second application to use the old version of the data while it was in the process of being updated by the first application. This would compromise the integrity of the stored data.

In addition to choices about the type of lock, DB2 offers options regarding the *level*, or *size*, of a lock. The two locking units in DB2 are table spaces and pages. (Recall that a table space is an area of disk storage in which one or several base tables are stored. Table spaces are made up of *pages*, 4k-byte blocks of disk space. Pages generally contain parts of tables.) Although you might expect DB2 to apply locks to tables or even to rows within tables, this is not the case. When an exclusive lock is acquired for a table space, no application can access the data in *any* table stored in that table space.

When establishing a new database, the DBA can specify the lock level within a table space. This is done via the LOCKSIZE option of the CREATE TABLESPACE command. The format is

```
LOCKSIZE = ANY | PAGE | TABLESPACE
```

If the DBA specifies TABLESPACE, then locks (either shared or exclusive) will be applied to the entire table space in which a referenced table resides. This option improves the performance of the application, but in doing so it can seriously delay other applications needing access to something in that table space.

If the DBA selects PAGE, then locks initially are applied at the page level (DB2 may escalate to the table level if it detects poor performance). Locking at the page level results in fewer conflicts than does locking at the table space level, but more resources are required to administer it.

Finally, if the DBA specifies ANY, then DB2 selects the appropriate level, depending on the number of pages that may be required to fulfill an application's needs. If only a few pages may be referenced, then page-level locks will be applied. On the other hand, if many pages may be required, then table-space-level locks will be applied. ANY is the default value for the LOCKSIZE option. Thus, the DBA does not need to specify the LOCK-SIZE option when creating a table space. By default, DB2 can be allowed to select the proper level of locking based on the type of SQL request and the number of pages involved.

As mentioned, locks are completely transparent to end users and application programmers. All necessary locking and unlocking is performed automatically by DB2.

**COMMIT and ROLLBACK.**    All DB2 table data modifications must be either committed or discarded. When a change is committed, it is final and becomes part of the actual database data. When a commitment occurs, all page locks placed on that data are released and the updated data is made available to other applications. A commitment is automatically executed when an application terminates normally. It can also be explicitly invoked with the SQL COMMIT statement.

Sometimes DB2 table modifications need to be discarded. This occurs, for example, when an end user wants to terminate a transaction in the middle. To discard the changes, the application program issues an SQL ROLLBACK statement. This statement returns the tables to their original state (the state after the most recent COMMIT), thus eliminating any pending updates to the table. At that point, all page locks are released and other applications have access to the unchanged data.

**DB2 and the Deadly Embrace.**    When two or more applications are found locked in a deadly embrace, DB2 resolves the problem by examining the number of log records each application has written. DB2 terminates the application(s) with the fewest log records since the last commitment. The more active application is selected to continue processing.

### DB2 Backup and Recovery

DB2 stores before and after images of all database changes on a log. Changes are written to the log before they are written to the database. DB2 periodically checkpoints itself. When checkpoints occur, all changes residing in system buffers are written to the database and a checkpoint record is written to the log. Thus, at the time of a checkpoint, the log and DB2 databases are synchronized.

DB2 can recover from a system failure by first applying all before images created since the most recent checkpoint and then applying all after images of committed transactions. As a result, all committed changes can endure the crash. Transactions that were in progress at the time of the crash need to be restarted.

Databases are stored on disks and are therefore vulnerable to physical damage. Should disk damage occur, the database must be recreated from backup copies. This means the using organization must periodically save the database. In DB2, this is done via utility programs that copy table spaces, the physical storage areas that contain table data. DB2 includes an option that allows the user organization to make backup copies of only those pages in a table space that have been modified since the latest backup was done. This option can save much time because unchanged pages are not copied unnecessarily.

If disk damage occurs, DB2 recovery utilities are able to combine data from the logs and the backup copies to reconstruct the database.

### DB2 Security

DB2 provides security mechanisms to protect the database. One such mechanism is views. Another allows the DBA to assign processing capabilities to particular users.

**Views.**    Views provide data security at the field value level. Recall that a view is a subset of columns, rows, or both derived from one or more base tables. To prevent a user from accessing any data in a base table except the fields he or she needs to access, the DBA simply defines a view of the table and authorizes the user to access the view (but not the base table). We discussed how to use SQL to create a view earlier in this chapter, so the following two examples are presented without further explanation.

The user of this view of KDK's DEALER table is given access only to dealer names and telephone numbers:

```
CREATE VIEW DLRPHONES
AS SELECT NAME, TELEPHONE
FROM DEALER
```

The user of this view is given access to dealer records only in the state of Massachusetts:

```
CREATE VIEW MASSDLRS
AS SELECT *
   FROM DEALER
   WHERE STATE/PROVINCE = 'MA'
```

**DB2 Resources.**  DB2 is able to control access to various database resources, including tables, views, data bases, utility programs, the DB2 catalog, and table spaces. Because DB2 users (both end users and application programmers) access only tables and views, we will just discuss DB2's control over them. Though not shown here, system administrators and database administrators have access to all database resources.

DB2 can control access to data in tables and views. Users can be authorized to issue SELECT, INSERT, DELETE, and UPDATE statements against a table or view. Also, the columns that may be updated can be specified. The use of the ALTER command to change a table definition can also be restricted.

**Identifying Users.**  Because DB2 is used in the MVS environment, many users can access it concurrently from a variety of other subsystems, such as IMS and CICS transaction managers, TSO, and batch jobs. Although you need not understand all these subsystems, it is important to realize that each has a means of identifying authorized users. For instance, TSO terminal users have a log-on ID that identifies them, a batch job has a special parameter on the job card, and IMS users have a sign-on ID or a logical terminal name (thus the equipment, not the person, is authorized to access the system). Other systems have similar authorization IDs.

DB2 uses the connecting subsystem's ID as the identifier for the DB2 user. DB2 assigns capabilities to access certain resources to authorization IDs. Explicit authorization is accomplished by means of the SQL GRANT statement. The format is

```
GRANT capability resource-list
TO authorization-ID-list
[WITH GRANT OPTION]
```

The capabilities likely to be granted to users are the following:

- ALTER   The definition of the specified tables may be altered.
- DELETE   Rows may be deleted from the specified tables or views.
- INSERT   Rows may be inserted into the specified tables or views.
- SELECT   Rows may be selected from the specified tables or views.
- UPDATE   The values for the specified list of columns within the specified tables or views may be updated.

The resource-list for most users is simply the names of tables or views for which they will have the specified capabilities. The authorization-ID-list is the list of user IDs to whom the specified authorization is being granted. The authorization-ID-list can also be the keyword PUBLIC, which grants the authority to all users. Here are some examples that illustrate the GRANT command:

- All users are allowed to look at the DEALER table:

  ```
  GRANT SELECT ON TABLE DEALER TO PUBLIC
  ```

- An application program can insert new records into the ADVER-TISEMENT table:

  ```
  GRANT INSERT ON TABLE ADVERTISEMENT TO PROG87
  ```

- A user known by the ID TERM14 is allowed to access the view DLRPHONES:

  ```
  GRANT SELECT ON VIEW DLRPHONES TO TERM14
  ```

- Two users are allowed to change table definitions for the DEALER and SALESPERSON tables:

  ```
  GRANT ALTER ON TABLE DEALER, SALESPERSON TO USER5, USER7
  ```

- An application program is allowed to delete SALESPERSON records:

  ```
  GRANT DELETE ON TABLE SALESPERSON TO PERS000
  ```

When the DB2 database is installed, only one person is given total control over all resources. This individual is known as the system administrator (although we use the term *database administrator*), and he or she may grant authority to or revoke authority from any other individual. This is done via the GRANT statement. Of course, the resources and capabilities available to the DBA include many options besides those just shown.

The GRANT statement contains an optional clause: WITH GRANT OPTION. When used, this clause enables the grantee to give others the same capabilities over the same resources. Thus, one can pass along author-ization to others. Consider this example:

```
GRANT SELECT ON AD-COPY TO MURPHY WITH GRANT OPTION
```

This gives Murphy permission to read the AD-COPY table and allows her to authorize other users to do the same.

In addition to explicit authorization conveyed by the GRANT command, the creator of a construct is automatically given full authority WITH GRANT OPTION over that construct. This cannot be revoked unless the construct itself is deleted from the database.

If authority is revoked (by means of the REVOKE command), it has a cascading effect. This means that not only is the specified privilege revoked from the named authorization ID, but also from anyone else to whom that authorization ID granted that privilege. Suppose user A were granted authority to read a table with the GRANT option and subsequently granted that privilege to User B. When User A is transferred to another department and his authority to read the table is revoked, user B's authority stemming from the GRANT is also automatically revoked. The following illustrates the sequence of events:

1. DBA:

   GRANT SELECT ON TABLE PRODUCT TO USERA WITH GRANT OPTION
   (User A can now read the PRODUCT table.)

2. User A:

   GRANT SELECT ON TABLE PRODUCT TO USERB
   (Users A and B can now read the PRODUCT table.)

3. DBA:

   REVOKE SELECT ON TABLE PRODUCT FROM USERA
   (Neither user A nor user B can read the PRODUCT table.)

# RELATIONAL IMPLEMENTATION USING DB2

In this section we will illustrate the implementation of KDK Appliances' Information Center database using DB2. A summary of KDK's database design appears in Figures 11–29 and 11–30.

First we will create the database using interactive DB2 commands. Then we will illustrate several online queries that product managers (or Information Center personnel) might execute. Finally, we will present an application program that produces one of the standard reports needed by the PMs.

## Creating the Database Structure

Interactive DB2 statements to create the database structure presented in Figures 11–29 and 11–30 are shown in Figure 11–31. As you can see, the statements are very straightforward. Having completed the design earlier, we need only to specify the format of each table and column using DB2.

**Figure 11—29**
Summary of relations
for KDK Appliances'
Information Center
database

| | |
|---|---|
| INVOICE | (<u>Number</u>, Date, Total, Salesperson.Number, Dealer.Number) |
| LINE-ITEM | (<u>Invoice.Number</u>, <u>Line-item-number</u>, Product.Number, Quantity, Extended-price) |
| DEALER | (<u>Number</u>, Name, Address-1, Address-2, City, State/Province, ZIP/Postal-code, Telephone) |
| SALESPERSON | (<u>Number</u>, Name, Region) |
| PRODUCT | (<u>Number</u>, Name, Description, Price) |
| AD-COPY | (<u>Ad-name</u>, Agency, First-run-date) |
| ADVERTISEMENT | (<u>Publication</u>, <u>Date</u>, <u>Ad-name</u>, Cost, Share-percent, Dealer.Number) |
| PRODUCT-AD | (<u>Ad-name</u>, <u>Product.Number</u>) |

Keep in mind that this database will be used for queries only—it will be neither updated nor altered. It is a snapshot of corporate operational data, downloaded from the mainframe database for analysis by the product managers. All updates are done to the operational data in a carefully controlled environment. Therefore, other than authorizing each PM to access (SELECT) the tables, no other authority will be granted. No one needs to alter, delete, or update any of the data. And because all the PMs are given access to all the columns in all the tables, no views are necessary.

### Examples of Interactive Query

Figure 11–32 shows four sample queries of KDK's Information Center database. The first one lists the names of dealers who shared advertising with KDK during the month of March. The DB2 word DISTINCT eliminates duplicate names from the list. The name of a dealer who shared more than one ad with KDK would appear several times in the list, but we will print it only once.

This example employs the subquery technique. Recall from Chapter 9 that subqueries allow us to narrow the scope of our search through the database by qualifying one level of query with another. Read from the bottom up, the first example in Figure 11–32 begins by building a list of numbers for dealers who shared with KDK the cost of advertising during March. Then, moving up to the next SELECT statement, it extracts dealer names from the DEALER table for all the dealers whose numbers appeared in the first list. Finally, the DISTINCT option causes the DBMS to eliminate duplicate names.

**Figure 11–30**

Table descriptions for
KDK's Information
Center database

```
INVOICE
      Number                  Char (4)
      Date                    Numeric YYMMDD
      Total                   Numeric 9999.99
      Salesperson. Number     *
      Dealer. Number          *
LINE-ITEM
      Invoice. Number         *
      Line-item-number        Numeric 999 positive integer
      Product. Number         *
      Quantity                Numeric 999 positive integer
      Extended-price          Computed numeric 9(6).99
DEALER
      Number                  Char(4)
      Name                    Char(45)
      Address-1               Char(25)
      Address-2               Char(25)
      City                    Char(15)
      State/Province          Char(2)
      ZIP/Postal-code         Char(10)
      Telephone               Char(10)
SALESPERSON
      Number                  Char(4)
      Name                    Char(20)
      Region                  Numeric 9
PRODUCT
      Type                    Numeric 9
      Number                  Char(5)
      Name                    Char(25)
      Description             Char(50)
      Price                   Numeric 99999.99
AD-COPY
      Ad-name                 Char(15)
      Agency                  Char(30)
      First-run-date          Numeric YYMMDD
ADVERTISEMENT
      Publication             Char(10)
      Date                    Numeric YYMMDD
      Ad-name                 *
      Cost                    Numeric 9999.99
      Share-percent           Numeric 999.99
                              E.g., 30% is 30.00
      Dealer. Number          *
PRODUCT-AD
      Ad-name                 *
      Product. number         *
```

*Definitions for foreign keys are shown in the foreign relations.

**Figure 11–31**

Interactive DB2 statements to create tables for KDK's Information Center database

```
CREATE    TABLE     INVOICE
          (NUMBER             CHAR(4)      NOT NULL,
          DATE                DECIMAL(6)   NOT NULL,
          TOTAL               DECIMAL(7,2) NOT NULL,
          SALESPERSON-NUMBER  CHAR(4)      NOT NULL,
          DEALER-NUMBER       CHAR(4)      NOT NULL)
CREATE    TABLE     LINE-ITEM
          (INVOICE-NUMBER     CHAR(4)      NOT NULL,
          LINE-ITEM-NUMBER    DECIMAL(3)   NOT NULL,
          PRODUCT-NUMBER      CHAR(5)      NOT NULL,
          QUANTITY            DECIMAL(3)   NOT NULL,
          EXTENDED-PRICE      DECIMAL(8,2) NOT NULL)
CREATE    TABLE     DEALER
          (NUMBER             CHAR(4)      NOT NULL,
          NAME                CHAR(45)     NOT NULL,
          ADDRESS-1           CHAR(25),
          ADDRESS-2           CHAR(25),
          CITY                CHAR(15)
          STATE/PROVINCE      CHAR(10),
          ZIP/POSTAL-CODE     CHAR(10),
          TELEPHONE           CHAR(10))
CREATE    TABLE     SALESPERSON
          (NUMBER             CHAR(4)      NOT NULL,
          NAME                CHAR(20)     NOT NULL,
          REGION              DECIMAL(1)).
CREATE    TABLE     PRODUCT
          (TYPE               CHAR(1)      NOT NULL,
          NUMBER              CHAR(5)      NOT NULL,
          NAME                CHAR(25)     NOT NULL,
          DESCRIPTION         CHAR(50),
          PRICE               DECIMAL(7,2) NOT NULL)
CREATE    TABLE     AD-COPY
          (AD-NAME            CHAR(15)     NOT NULL,
          AGENCY              CHAR(30),
          FIRST-RUN-DATE      DECIMAL(6))
CREATE    TABLE     ADVERTISEMENT
          (PUBLICATION        CHAR(10)     NOT NULL,
          DATE                DECIMAL(6)   NOT NULL,
          AD-NAME             CHAR(15)     NOT NULL,
          COST                DECIMAL(6,2) NOT NULL,
          SHARE-PERCENT       DECIMAL(5,2),
          DEALER-NUMBER       CHAR(4))
CREATE    TABLE     PRODUCT-AD
          (AD-NAME            CHAR(15)     NOT NULL,
          PRODUCT-NUMBER      CHAR(5)      NOT NULL,
```

**Figure 11—32**

Sample interactive
DB2 queries against
KDK's database

1.  List the dealers who participated in shared advertising during the month of March:
    SELECT DISTINCT NAME FROM DEALER
            WHERE DEALER.NUMBER IN
            SELECT DEALER-NUMBER
                FROM ADVERTISEMENT
                WHERE ADVERTISEMENT.DATE BETWEEN 880301 AND 880331
2.  List the dealers who purchased refrigerators (product type = 5) in March:
    SELECT DISTINCT NAME FROM DEALER
            WHERE DEALER.NUMBER IN
                SELECT DEALER-NUMBER FROM INVOICE
                WHERE DATE BETWEEN 880301 AND 880331
                    AND INVOICE.NUMBER IN
                        SELECT INVOICE-NUMBER FROM LINE-ITEM
                        WHERE LINE-ITEM.PRODUCT-NUMBER IN
                            SELECT NUMBER FROM PRODUCT
                            WHERE TYPE = '5'
3.  List the products that were advertised in March:
    SELECT NUMBER, NAME, DESCRIPTION FROM PRODUCT
            WHERE PRODUCT.NUMBER IN
                SELECT DISTINCT PRODUCT-NUMBER FROM PRODUCT-AD
                WHERE PRODUCT-AD.AD-NAME = ADVERTISEMENT.AD-NAME
                    AND ADVERTISEMENT.DATE BETWEEN 880301 AND 880331
4.  Print the total sales for product #94605 for the month of March. Then print it for the month of April:
    CREATE VIEW PRODUCTSALES
            (DATE, PRODUCT, EXTENDED-PRICE)
            AS SELECT DATE, PRODUCT-NUMBER, EXTENDED-PRICE
                FROM INVOICE, LINE-ITEM
                WHERE LINE-ITEM.INVOICE-NUMBER = INVOICE.NUMBER
                    AND LINE-ITEM.PRODUCT-NUMBER = '94605'
    SELECT SUM(EXTENDED-PRICE) FROM PRODUCTSALES
            WHERE DATE BETWEEN 880301 AND 880331
    SELECT SUM(EXTENDED-PRICE) FROM PRODUCTSALES
            WHERE DATE BETWEEN 880401 AND 880430

The second example in Figure 11–32 also employs the subquery technique, only this time it is more complex. Once again we will interpret the statement by reading it from the bottom up. We begin by building a list of product numbers for refrigerators (Type = '5'). Then we build a list of invoice numbers that have line-items for any of those products. Next, we extract dealer numbers for all of those invoices occurring in March, and finally we build a list of dealer names, eliminating duplicates. This is the list of dealers who purchased refrigerators during March.

The third illustration in Figure 11–32 extracts data from several tables in order to give the user the desired results. Product names and descriptions come from the PRODUCT table. Advertisements, which are dated, are stored in the ADVERTISEMENT table. But advertisements are not directly associated with any product—they are associated with advertising copy by means of the Ad-name column. Similarly, products are not associated directly with an advertisement, but with advertising copy by means of the Ad-name column in the PRODUCT-AD table.

We begin by joining the PRODUCT-AD table and the ADVERTISEMENT table, matching on Ad-name. Then we extract unique (distinct) product numbers, and only for advertisements that ran in March. Finally we extract from the PRODUCT table the name and description for each product number we have identified.

The fourth example of a query in Figure 11–32 begins by building a view (the join of two tables) and then selecting total sales figures from the view. The view is made up of sales data for product #94605. This data is taken from the INVOICE table (date) and the LINE-ITEM table (product number, extended price). Having established this subset of the larger base tables, we can ask DB2 to calculate the two sales totals by invoking the SUM built-in function in the SELECT statement. Two SELECT statements are needed, of course, one for each month.

### Application Program Example

Figure 11–33 presents a COBOL program that prints the report shown in Figure 11–3, entitled PRODUCT SALES SUMMARY BY REGION. In this section we will examine the COBOL program, noting the placement of DB2 commands. Although this example is written in COBOL, SQL can also be embedded in PL/I, FORTRAN, and assembler language programs.

Looking at the WORKING-STORAGE SECTION of the DATA DIVISION, we find the definition of variables that will hold data values as they are retrieved by DB2 from the database. These variables are defined following the SQL message BEGIN DECLARE SECTION. Notice that each SQL statement is surrounded by the precompiler keywords EXEC SQL and END-EXEC.

Within the DECLARE SECTION we have defined a sale record, made up of six fields. Later, in the PROCEDURE DIVISION, you will see that the data for this sale record is found in four different database tables. The words END DECLARE SECTION signal the precompiler that that part of the program is complete.

The next instruction in the WORKING-STORAGE SECTION directs the precompiler to copy SQLCA into the COBOL program. Again, this is a list of parameters shared by the DBMS and the application program. The most significant field in SQLCA is SQLCODE, as described.

The remainder of the WORKING-STORAGE SECTION defines work areas and report formats to be used by the program. These are normal COBOL entries that are unaffected by the presence of DB2.

In the PROCEDURE DIVISION we find a mixture of SQL statements and ordinary COBOL instructions. The first sequence of instructions in the PROCEDURE DIVISION defines a cursor (C-1) that will be used to retrieve data from the database. The SELECT statement on which the cursor operates is lengthy, but it is easily understood. To print the report seen in Figure 11–3, we need a set of sales records containing product numbers, names and descriptions, prices, quantities sold, and regions. Those pieces of data are found in several different database tables, so in the SELECT statement we specify to DB2 the sources of the data (the four tables) and the links it needs to follow in order to retrieve that correct data

```
WHERE LINE-ITEM.INVOICE-NUMBER = INVOICE.NUMBER, etc.
```

Finally, we state that the rows (records) need to be made available to the program sorted by region number within product number.

Having established the cursor, we now have a conceptual "pseudo-file" that contains all the newly constructed sales records in the desired sequence. The rest of the program follows ordinary sequential file processing logic, testing for two control level breaks (one on region number, the other on product number).

First we open the output report file. Then we issue SQL statements to prepare the database data to be processed

```
OPEN C-1
```

We use the cursor to retrieve the first database "sale record"

```
FETCH C-1 INTO :SALE-RECORD
```

placing the data values into the fields we defined in the DECLARE SECTION above. The word SALE-RECORD is preceded by a colon (:) to help the precompiler distinguish it from words it expects to find defined in the database tables. This FETCH SQL statement effectively "reads" the first sale record from the "input file."

The next instruction sequence saves the product number and region values in work areas and writes the first set of report headers. Ready to process the first record, then, we go into a loop called PROCESS-AND-FETCH. Note that we will remain in this program loop until no more "sale records" are left in the database (UNTIL SQLCODE = 100). When that eventually happens, we close the cursor, releasing those resources to other users of this database, and terminate our program normally.

Within the main program loop, PROCESS-AND-FETCH, we find only one SQL statement. The last command in the loop is

```
FETCH C-1 INTO :SALE-RECORD
```

This instruction, like an ordinary COBOL READ, presents to the program the next sequential "record" from the database, replacing the one just

**Figure 11–33**

COBOL program to
produce PRODUCT
SALES SUMMARY
BY REGION report

```
IDENTIFICATION DIVISION.
PROGRAM-ID.  DB2-EXAMPLE.
ENVIRONMENT DIVISION.
CONFIGURATION SECTION.
SPECIAL-NAMES.
     (special names go here)
INPUT-OUTPUT SECTION.
FILE-CONTROL.
     SELECT    (SELECT statements for non-database files go here)
DATA DIVISION.
FILE SECTION.
     FD          (FDs for non-database files go here)
WORKING-STORAGE SECTION.
*
*    DECLARE VARIABLES FOR USE WITH DB2
*
     EXEC SQL  BEGIN DECLARE SECTION    END-EXEC.
01   SALE-RECORD.
     05    PRODUCT-NUMBER       PICTURE X(05).
     05    PRODUCT-NAME         PICTURE X(25).
     05    PRODUCT-DESC         PICTURE X(50).
     05    QUANTITY-SOLD        PICTURE S999        COMP-3.
     05    UNIT-PRICE           PICTURE S9(5)V99    COMP-3.
     05    SALE-REGION          PICTURE S9          COMP-3.
     EXEC SQL  END DECLARE SECTION      END-EXEC.
*    REQUEST DB2 TO COPY INTO COBOL PROGRAM
*    DEFINITIONS FOR DB2 COMMUNICATIONS AREA.
*
     EXEC SQL  INCLUDE SQLCA            END-EXEC.
*
*    DEFINE NON-DATABASE VARIABLES
*
77   PRODUCT-NUMBER HOLD      PICTURE X(5).
77   REGION-HOLD             PICTURE X.
77   SUM-UNITS-THIS-REGION   PICTURE 999         COMP-3 VALUE 0.
77   SUM-UNITS-THIS-PRODUCT  PICTURE 99999       COMP-3 VALUE 0.
01   PAGE-HEADER-1.
     05    FILLER              PICTURE X(24)   VALUE SPACES.
     05    FILLER              PICTURE X(31)
           VALUE 'PRODUCT SALES SUMMARY BY REGION'.
     05    FILLER              PICTURE X(25)   VALUE   SPACES.
01   GROUP-1.
     05    FILLER              PICTURE X(16)
           VALUE 'PRODUCT NUMBER: '.
```

**Figure 11—33**

*(continued)*

```
     05   PRODUCT-NUMBER-OUT  PICTURE X(05).
     05   FILLER              PICTURE X(59)  VALUE SPACES.
01   GROUP-2.
     05   FILLER              PICTURE X(16)
          VALUE 'DESCRIPTION:'.
     05   NAME-OUT            PICTURE X(25).
     05   FILLER              PICTURE X(39)  VALUE SPACES.
01   GROUP-3.
     05   FILLER              PICTURE X(16)  VALUE SPACES.
     05   DESCRIPTION-OUT     PICTURE X(50).
     05   FILLER              PICTURE X(14)  VALUE SPACES.
01   GROUP-4.
     05   FILLER              PICTURE X(16)
          VALUE 'PRICE:'.
     05   PRICE-OUT           PICTURE $(6).99.
     05   FILLER              PICTURE X(55)  VALUE SPACES.
01   COLUMN-HEADERS.
     05   FILLER              PICTURE X(30)  VALUE SPACES.
     05   FILLER              PICTURE X(24)
          VALUE 'REGION       UNITS SOLD'.
     05   FILLER              PICTURE X(26)  VALUE SPACES.
01   REGION-TOTAL-LINE.
     05   FILLER              PICTURE X(32)  VALUE SPACES.
     05   REGION-OUT          PICTURE X.
     05   FILLER              PICTURE X(13)  VALUE SPACES.
     05   UNITS-SOLD-OUT      PICTURE ZZ9.
     05   FILLER              PICTURE X(31)  VALUE SPACES.
01   PRODUCT-TOTAL-LINE.
     05   FILLER              PICTURE X(36)  VALUE SPACES.
     05   FILLER              PICTURE X(08).
          VALUE  'TOTAL'.
     05   TOTAL-OUT           PICTURE ZZZZ9.
     05   FILLER              PICTURE X(31)  VALUE SPACES.
PROCEDURE DIVISION.
     EXEC SQL
          DECLARE C-1 CURSOR FOR
          SELECT PRODUCT.NUMBER, PRODUCT.NAME,
               PRODUCT.DESCRIPTION, LINE-ITEM.QUANTITY,
               PRODUCT.PRICE, SALESPERSON.REGION
          FROM PRODUCT, SALESPERSON, LINE-ITEM, INVOICE
          WHERE LINE-ITEM.INVOICE-NUMBER = INVOICE.NUMBER
            AND INVOICE.SALESPERSON-NUMBER = SALESPERSON.NUMBER
            AND LINE-ITEM.PRODUCT-NUMBER = PRODUCT.NUMBER
          ORDER BY PRODUCT.NUMBER, SALESPERSON.REGION
     END-EXEC.
     OPEN OUTPUT REPORT-FILE.
     EXEC SQL   OPEN C-1        END-EXEC.
```

**Figure 11–33**

*(continued)*

```
                EXEC SQL   FETCH C-1 INTO :SALE-RECORD    END-EXEC.
                MOVE PRODUCT-NUMBER TO PRODUCT-NUMBER-HOLD.
                MOVE SALE-REGION TO REGION-HOLD.
                PERFORM ISSUE-HEADERS.
                PERFORM PROCESS-AND-FETCH UNTIL SQLCODE = 100.
                EXEC SQL   CLOSE C-1 END EXEC.
                PERFORM ISSUE-REGION-TOTAL.
                PERFORM ISSUE-PRODUCT-TOTAL.
                CLOSE REPORT-FILE.
                EXIT PROGRAM.
  *
    PROCESS-AND-FETCH.
                IF PRODUCT-NUMBER NOT EQUAL PRODUCT-NUMBER-HOLD
                THEN PERFORM ISSUE-REGION-TOTAL
                     PERFORM ISSUE-PRODUCT-TOTAL
                ELSE
                     IF REGION-NUMBER NOT EQUAL REGION-HOLD
                     THEN PERFORM ISSUE-REGION-TOTAL
                     ELSE NEXT SENTENCE.
                ADD QUANTITY-SOLD TO SUM-UNITS-THIS-REGION.
                ADD QUANTITY-SOLD TO SUM-UNITS-THIS-PRODUCT.
                EXEC SQL   FETCH C-1 INTO :SALE-RECORD    END-EXEC.
    ISSUE-REGION-TOTAL.
                MOVE SUM-UNITS-THIS-REGION TO UNITS-SOLD-OUT.
                MOVE REGION-HOLD TO REGION-OUT.
                MOVE REGION-TOTAL-LINE TO (printer record goes here).
                PERFORM WRITE-LINE.
                MOVE 0 TO SUM-UNITS-THIS-REGION.
                MOVE SALE-REGION TO REGION-HOLD.
    ISSUE-PRODUCT-TOTAL.
                MOVE SUM-UNITS-THIS-PRODUCT TO TOTAL-OUT.
                MOVE PRODUCT-TOTAL-LINE TO (printer record goes here).
                PERFORM WRITE-LINE.
                MOVE 0 TO SUM-UNITS-THIS-PRODUCT.
                MOVE PRODUCT-NUMBER TO PRODUCT-NUMBER-HOLD.
                PERFORM ISSUE-HEADERS.
    ISSUE-HEADERS.
                MOVE PAGE-HEADER-1 TO (printer record goes here).
                PERFORM WRITE-NEW-PAGE.
                MOVE PRODUCT-NUMBER TO PRODUCT-NUMBER-OUT.
                MOVE GROUP-1 TO (printer record goes here).
                PERFORM WRITE-LINE.
                MOVE PRODUCT-NAME TO NAME-OUT.
                MOVE GROUP-2 TO (printer record goes here).
                PERFORM WRITE-LINE.
                MOVE PRODUCT-DESC TO DESCRIPTION-OUT.
```

**Figure 11–33**
*(continued)*

```
    MOVE GROUP-3 TO (printer record goes here).
    PERFORM WRITE-LINE.
    MOVE UNIT-PRICE TO PRICE-OUT.
    MOVE GROUP-4 TO (printer record goes here).
    PERFORM WRITE-LINE.
    MOVE COLUMN-HEADERS TO (printer record goes here).
    PERFORM WRITE-LINE.
WRITE-NEW-PAGE.
    (instructions for printing line at top of page go here)
WRITE-LINE.
    (instructions for writing a line go here).
```

processed. As already mentioned, the loop will be executed until all appropriate data has been retrieved from the database.

The remaining COBOL paragraphs contain no SQL statements. They are used simply to format and produce the SALES SUMMARY report and would be no different if a sequential input file had been used.

You should note that because KDK Appliances' Information Center database is being used exclusively for analyzing data, no database changes are illustrated. If changes to table data were made in an application program, then either the COMMIT SQL statement would be invoked whenever a change were to be made permanent (perhaps after each valid record update) or the ROLLBACK SQL command would be invoked if the program discovered an error partway through an update. Also, a COMMIT would automatically be invoked when the program terminated. However, COMMITs are unnecessary in this sample program because it does not update the database.

## SUMMARY

This chapter began with the description of the requirements of a company that needed to analyze sales data from its operational database. The most effective and least disruptive way to do this was to download sales data from the operational database onto a smaller mainframe computer located in the company's Information Center. Then the snapshot of the operational data could be studied by product managers (PMs), giving them the timely data they needed to make decisions and to plan marketing strategies. The company, KDK Appliances, chose Database2 (DB2) as its relational database management system.

After identifying various objects that the PMs needed, we developed a relational database design. First we drew a set of object diagrams. Then we converted them into relation diagrams. With the design completed, we turned to the database management system DB2 for implementation.

DB2 is an IBM product used to process relational databases on large computers operating under MVS. DB2 uses the language SQL to define, access, and manipulate data and to grant authorizations. SQL statements can be issued interactively or they can be embedded into application programs written in COBOL, PL/I, FORTRAN, and assembler language.

DB2 allows a person to define various database constructs, such as tables, views, table spaces, indexes, index spaces, data bases, and storage groups. Users, both online end users and application programmers, refer only to tables and views. The database administrator, or someone performing other system functions, is concerned with physical database storage and organization and thus deals with other DB2 constructs as well.

Database constructs can be defined, modified, and deleted. DB2 includes SQL statements to perform all those functions.

SQL data manipulation language as implemented in DB2 includes all the relational functions we studied in Chapter 9. In addition to reading a database, we can also insert records, update stored data, and delete rows from a table. The SQL statements for these four functions are SELECT, INSERT, UPDATE, and DELETE.

When SQL statements are embedded in an application program, the entire program must first be processed by the DB2 precompiler. The precompiler finds all SQL statements (indicated in COBOL by the keywords EXEC SQL . . . END-EXEC) and translates them into equivalent host language instructions. It builds database request modules, stores them on disk, and inserts call statements into the program to access them. Thus, the application programmer needs to know little about the inner workings of the database management system. The precompiler effectively shields the programmer from it.

In order to process a multiple-row query, the application programmer needs to define a cursor, a pointer that acts on a SELECT statement. Although the SELECT statement does not actually generate a file, you can imagine that a cursor defines a pseudo-file in which DB2 will store the rows it retrieves. Then the set of retrieved rows can be processed one at a time as if in a sequential input file.

DB2 handles the potential problems of concurrent processing by using locks on portions of a database. Shared locks allow multiple concurrent accesses to the same data. But if any application needs to modify data, DB2 acquires an exclusive lock. No other application can access data that has an exclusive lock on it. When the lock is released, all applications have access to the updated data. This ensures the integrity of the data.

DB2 can lock either table spaces (which might include several tables) or pages (which contain tables or parts of tables). Locking pages causes less interference with other concurrent users but costs more to administer. Trade-offs like these are common in information processing.

DB2 logs all database changes before they are committed, or written, to the database. Database modifications that are not yet committed can be backed out by issuing the ROLLBACK command. This might be necessary if a processing error is detected or a system failure occurs. The system log enables DB2 to recover data in the event of a system crash. It applies all before images of the database since the latest checkpoint. Then it applies all after images of committed transactions (they had been logged). Any transactions that were in progress at the time of the crash need to be restarted.

DB2 security consists of granting to certain identifiable users the ability to perform certain functions on certain database resources. One way to restrict access to database table data is to define views (or subsets) of the tables and authorize users to reference them, but not the base tables. This approach protects data at the field level.

DB2 allows the database administrator to control end users' and application programmers' use of the SELECT, UPDATE, INSERT, DELETE, and ALTER commands to specified tables and views. Authorization is performed by means of the GRANT statement. When DB2 is installed, only one person is given the authority to GRANT. This privilege can be passed on to other administrators and even to users. Privileges that can be granted can also be rescinded by means of the REVOKE command. In this way, the DBA can exercise control over database access.

This chapter concluded with illustrations of KDK's Information Center database as implemented in DB2. We first established the database structure, then performed some online queries against it. We also presented a COBOL program that produces one of the many sales analysis reports needed by product managers.

---

QUESTIONS                                                                **GROUP I**

11.1   Why did KDK Appliances decide only to *download* sales data from the operational mainframe computer? What effect does that decision have on the processing privileges PMs will eventually be granted on the Information Center database?

11.2   Why does the INVOICE as defined for the Information Center database contain fewer fields than the actual invoice used for operational processing?

11.3   What is the purpose of the PRODUCT-AD relation?

11.4   Describe two modes of DB2 access.

11.5   Define each of these terms: table, view, base table. Describe their relationships to one another.

11.6   How can a view be used for database security?

11.7   Which database constructs are referenced by users and application programmers?

11.8   Explain the relationship between data base, storage group, table space, page, index space, table, and index.

**11.9**     Write DB2 SQL statements that create a table, an index, and a view. Assume the table has customer name, address, and account number. Build an index on account number. Assume the view presents unique customer names.

**11.10**    Show the DB2 statement that adds to the table a column for the customer's age.

**11.11**    Write the DB2 statement(s) that would add these records to the customer table you changed in question 11.10:
Mike Thompson, Madison, #456, 45
Paul Hand, New Haven, #722, 20
Karen Munroe, Gales Ferry, #076, 27

**11.12**    Show the DB2 statements needed to drop the table, index, and view defined in question 11.9.

**11.13**    Explain the role of the DB2 precompiler.

**11.14**    How does the precompiler know which instructions are SQL instructions and which ones belong to the host language?

**11.15**    Explain the role of a cursor in DB2 processing.

**11.16**    Explain the difference between a shared lock and an exclusive lock.

**11.17**    Why is an exclusive lock required when data is going to be modified?

**11.18**    What two lock sizes are allowed in DB2? What is the advantage of each over the other?

**11.19**    What is the purpose of the COMMIT statement? What is the purpose of the ROLLBACK statement?

**11.20**    How does DB2 handle the deadly embrace?

**11.21**    Explain how DB2 can recover from a system crash. Explain how DB2 can recover from database damage.

**11.22**    Explain the role of the GRANT statement. How can GRANT authority be given to another user?

**11.23**    Explain the role of the REVOKE statement. What is the cascade effect of the REVOKE statement?

---

**GROUP II**          QUESTIONS AND EXERCISES

**11.24**    Locate a company that is using DB2. Determine how long it has had the system, why it chose DB2, and how well it likes it. Has productivity improved as a result of using DB2? Does the company use DB2 interactively, or is it used in application programs, or both? Do users do any of their own programming using DB2? Do users develop any online inquiries using DB2? Does the company have an information center? If possible, get a copy of an application program. Explain the meaning of each embedded SQL statement. How does DB2 identify the application program as an authorized user? How often does this company back up its database? Does it copy the entire database or does it back up only pages changed since the previous backup? Has this company ever had to recover the database? What problems, if any, did it experience? Has performance ever been a problem? If so, what did the company do to improve it? Explain whether you believe that DB2 has been an effective DBMS for that company.

**11.25** Locate a company that has a relational DBMS other than DB2. Answer the questions in 11.24 for this DBMS.

**11.26** Write an application program to produce the PRODUCT SALES SUMMARY BY SALESPERSON report illustrated in Figure 11–3a.

**11.27** Write an application program to produce the DEALER ACTIVITY SUMMARY report illustrated in Figure 11–4.

# PART V

# ORGANIZATIONAL
# DATABASE PROCESSING

**O**rganizational database processing preceded the other two contexts: end-user database processing (Part 4) and distributed database processing (Part 6). The distinguishing characteristic of organizational database processing is that it is used for daily operational transaction processing. A large volume of transactions, multiple concurrent users, and multiple applications are common in such an environment.

Early DBMS products addressed the problems of organizational database processing. Although many of the design decisions made during these early years may seem primitive in retrospect, the fact remains that the early DBMS paved the way for the more sophisticated ones we enjoy today.

DBMS products geared for organizational database processing typically make efficient use of external storage and computer memory. Innovative but sometimes complex techniques are used to establish relationships among stored data, and the software employed to access and maintain them is equally complex. The products you will study in Part 5 are much too technical for the typical end user to employ. The principles on which they are based are obscure to the lay person. To the skilled database practitioner, however, these products represent the means by which large databases can be efficiently and reliably processed.

The DBMS products most widely used for organizational database processing are based on one of two data models: the hierarchical model or the network model. In Chapter 12 we present the hierarchical data model, which is the basis for IMS/DLI, an IBM DBMS. In Chapter 13 we examine the CODASYL DBTG model, the most widely implemented network data model. Then in Chapter 14 we illustrate a CODASYL DBTG implementation using IDMS/R, a DBMS product licensed by the Cullinet Corporation.

Throughout this part of the text, you will need to draw on the foundation we have already established. As you study the organizational database processing context, compare it to the end user context that you studied in Part 4. As you learn about the hierarchical and the network data models, also compare them to the relational model, noting the comparative strengths and weaknesses of each. The ability to distinguish one type of DBMS from another will be a valuable skill when designing a new information system.

# Transaction Processing and the Hierarchical Model with DL/I

* Transaction Processing
* Data Language/I
* Representation of Objects for DL/I Processing
* DL/I Data Manipulation Language
* Summary

In this chapter we will discuss transaction processing and the hierarchical data model. First we present the characteristics of transaction processing and survey its history. This discussion serves as an introduction to the organizational database processing context addressed in the next three chapters. After this overview, we will consider the hierarchical data model and one product used to process databases based on it—namely, IBM's Data Language I, or *DL/I*. We will discuss the components of DL/I and then show how these components are used to represent the various types of objects you have studied. Finally we present the DL/I data manipulation language commands and illustrate their use.

## TRANSACTION PROCESSING

Transaction processing systems can best be understood in the context of a flourishing business. Goods are purchased and sold. Clients come and go. Money is earned and spent. Time passes. At some point, somebody (perhaps an owner, a tax agent, an employee, or an auditor) asks, "What is the state of the business?" or "How much money did we make last month?" or "What were your travel expenses in 1989?" or "How much have I contributed to the stock option plan?" We could answer these questions by taking the person on a tour of the company, saying, "Here's the business, see for yourself!" Such a response would be unhelpful if not downright ludicrous. The person wants a report of the measurement of some *aspect* of the business's operation, not a tour of the entire enterprise.

To provide more realistic answers to questions like these, businesses maintain accounting and operational records. They gather names, inventory goods, count money, and so forth, and store these measurements for later reference. In some businesses, records of these measurements (or a portion of them) are stored in an *operational database.*

Such a database is, in a sense, a *model* of some aspects of the business because it represents the status of the business's components. Business, however, is dynamic, so the model must be dynamic as well. When events occur that change the business, the model must be changed. Otherwise, over time the model will bear little resemblance to the actual condition of the business.

A *transaction* is the representation of an event. The purpose of a transaction processing application is to accept transactions, modify the operational database accordingly, and produce records of the event, which are sometimes called *real outputs.* This term is used to differentiate between outputs (or changes) to the database and outputs that are produced and distributed in the business environment. An example of a real output is the confirmation of a hotel reservation. Outputs to a database can be readily changed if they are in error. But real outputs, once they have been distributed, are more difficult to change. Compensating transactions must be processed to change real outputs. The role of a transaction processing application is illustrated in Figure 12–1.

### Characteristics of Transaction Processing

Transaction processing applications differ in several ways from other applications you have studied in this text. First, transaction processing applications support basic business operations. For example, they are used to service teller lines at banks, to authorize credit card purchases, and to make hotel reservations. Thus, *fast performance* with *quick response time* is critical. A business cannot afford to make customers wait very long for the transaction processing system to respond. The turnaround time from the input of the transaction to the production of real outputs must be a few seconds or less.

Transaction processing systems must also be *reliable.* Perhaps nothing is more frustrating to employees and customers than being unable to complete a sale or other business transaction because "the computer is down." To be effective, the failure rate of a transaction processing application must be very low. Furthermore, when the system does fail, *quick and accurate recovery* is essential. Comprehensive backup and recovery, including transaction logging, rollback, and rollforward (see Chapter 7), are mandatory for most transaction processing applications.

**Figure 12–1**
Role of transaction
processing applica-
tion program

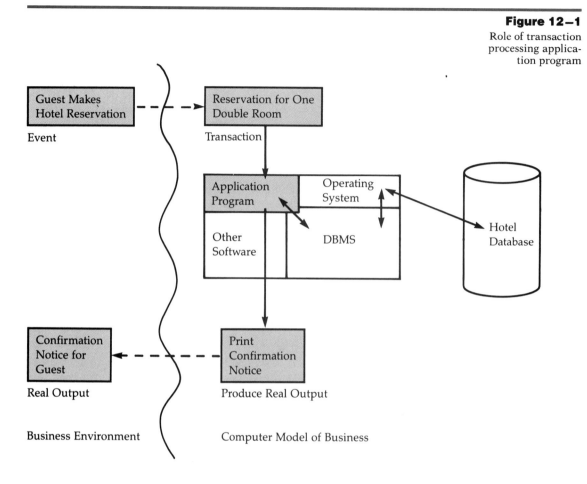

Unlike other types of database applications, *flexibility is less important* for transaction processing applications. In fact, flexibility is often undesirable. Transaction processing is standardized processing. Businesses want every transaction to be processed the same way regardless of the clerk, the customer, or the time of day. If transaction processing applications were flexible, too many opportunities for non-standard operation would exist.

Additionally, business operations change slowly. For example, commercial airlines can only rarely change the way they handle airline reservations because the social system of travel agents, customers, and employees simply cannot adapt readily to change.

Given that transaction processing supports business operations, *control* is important. For example, to prevent an employee from defrauding the company by creating bogus purchase orders and then authorizing their payment and stealing the cash, a company might distribute duties and responsibilities among several employees. In this case, one employee may have authority to issue purchase orders while another employee authorizes payments. For the sake of control, these two activities must be performed by different employees. As a further check, a transaction processing application that supports purchasing should enforce this separation of duties and authorities by allowing the purchasing agent to access only purchasing data and the payment clerk to access only payment data.

As you might guess, transaction processing applications usually have a *restricted view of the database*. For example, an order entry program need not have access to accounts payable data. When both order data and payables data are stored in the database, better control will result if the view of the order entry program is restricted to order data. Thus, with transaction processing, subsets of the database are often defined and the scope of the database available to a transaction program is restricted to a particular subset. A subset is called an *application view*, or *subschema*.

As stated, an operational database is a model of the business or organization. As such, it is a valuable asset and needs to be *protected*. Only authorized users should have access to the database, and they should be able to perform only authorized actions. Most transaction processing-oriented DBMSs provide security facilities similar to the ones discussed in Chapter 7. The DBA must ensure that applications take advantage of available security facilities and must supplement them with programs and manual procedures where necessary.

Finally, the environment of typical transaction processing applications differs substantially from that of typical microcomputer database applications. (Note, however, that microcomputers can be used for transaction processing; micros and transaction processing are not mutually exclusive.) Typical transaction processing systems operate on a mainframe or a large minicomputer. Given the importance of reliability and control, these computers often reside in a *closed and controlled environment*. Additionally, the DBMS for transaction processing usually provides extensive facilities for the support of concurrent processing and for backup and recovery. The license fee for such DBMS products is often in excess of $150,000. The characteristics of transaction processing systems are summarized in Figure 12–2.

### Databases for Transaction Processing

Database processing began with transaction processing applications. Such applications needed to relate records of one type to records of another. Stated in more familiar terms, these applications needed to process objects that were not readily represented in a file processing system. File processing was thus inadequate, and the need for support of organizational operations provided the impetus for the development of database technology.

The early years of database processing were difficult ones. In the early and mid-1960s, many efforts at data integration failed. Database engineers knew that file processing was inadequate and that some type of data modeling that facilitated the definition and processing of record relationships

**Figure 12-2**
Characteristics of
transaction process-
ing systems

- Fast performance with quick response time
- Reliable processing
- Quick and accurate recovery
- Controlled processing
- Restricted views of database for application programs
- Data protected via DBMS security mechanisms
- Equipment usually located in closed environment

was needed. But because they were the pioneers, they had to learn—and often fail—as they proceeded. The object-oriented approach you are learning about in this book is the result of many years of failure, frustration, and learning.

## Three Data Models

By the early 1970s, three different methods of modeling data were generally recognized: the hierarchical data model, the network data model, and the relational data model. The *hierarchical data model* represents data relationships using hierarchies, or trees. All data relationships must be transformed into hierarchies before they can be defined in the database. We will illustrate this model in the next sections of this chapter. As you will see, although it is possible to transform any object structure into hierarchies, the transformation is sometimes contrived. The most important and popular database product based on the hierarchical data model is *Data Language I (DL/I)*, which was developed and marketed by IBM. We will present an overview of DL/I in later sections of this chapter.

The *network data model* readily represents one-to-many relationships. Therefore it can be used to directly represent all object types we discussed in Chapter 6, except many-to-many compound objects. Such objects must be transformed into one-to-many relationships, just as we have done for the relational model in previous chapters. The most important network data model is the CODASYL DBTG (Conference on Data Systems Languages, Data Base Task Group) model. We will illustrate the use of this model in Chapters 13 and 14.

The *relational data model* is the third major data model, one that you have studied throughout this text. As you have already learned, this model was defined in 1970, but had little practical significance until relational DBMS products became available in the early 1980s. However, development of the relational model during the 1970s and 1980s has contributed much to the understanding and theory of data modeling. Furthermore, as you have seen in previous chapters, the relational model is important for database design and for the implementation of databases that are directly processed by end users.

### Predefined Relationships

Both the hierarchical and the network data models require that relationships be predefined. That is, all relationships must be anticipated and defined before implementing the database. Adding new relationships to an already-existing database is more difficult with these two models than it is using the relational model. The reason is the method used for representing relationships.

Unlike the relational model, in which relationships are established by data values, the hierarchical and network models represent relationships by means of separate *data structures*, such as indexes and linked lists (see Appendix B). These data structures must be established by the DBMS before the relationships can be represented. Consider the ramifications of this approach.

For transaction processing applications, the representation of relationships in data structures has two advantages over storing relationships within the data. First, performance is likely to be better (at least with currently available technologies). When relationships are predefined, data structures can be selected for and tuned to the workload. Most relational DBMS products cannot begin to match the performance of hierarchical and network DBMS products over a wide range of applications.

The second advantage is control. For transaction processing applications, the restriction that relationships must be predefined can be very desirable. Transaction processing needs to be standardized. Most organizations do not want users of transaction processing applications to be able to perform ad hoc processing of data. Furthermore, requirements for most transaction processing applications evolve slowly. In most cases, ample time is available to adjust the database structure as new requirements emerge. Consequently, what is generally viewed as an advantage of relational database processing is often regarded as unnecessary or undesirable for transaction processing.

### Designing Databases for Transaction Processing

The design process for databases that support transaction processing is an extension of the process described in previous chapters. As shown in Figure 12–3, we begin by defining reports, forms, and form processing logic. From these we define objects and transform our object definitions into a relational database design. If we were using a relational database, we would then develop applications and implement them as shown in Chapters 8 and 11.

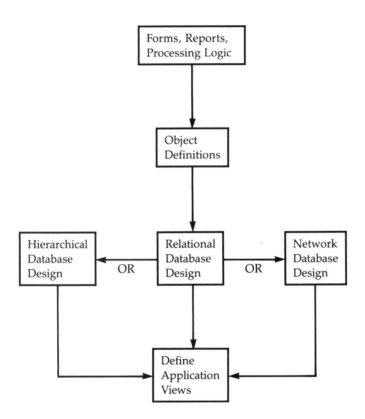

But if the database is to be organized using either the hierarchical or network data models, we must perform an additional step. We must first convert the relational design to a hierarchical or network database design. This process will be illustrated later in this chapter and in the next two chapters.

Keep in mind that although we will describe the use of the hierarchical and network data models for transaction processing, relational DBMS products can be used for transaction processing as well. In some microcomputer database applications, particularly those involving multi-user processing on LANs, relational DBMS products are used for transaction processing. Here, however, the work load is considerably less than it is in most mini- or mainframe transaction processing applications. In any case, Figure 12−3 shows that relational database design precedes implementation with any of the three models.

The last step in Figure 12−3 concerns the identification of application views. Because control and security are important for transaction processing applications, an application's view of data is often restricted to a portion of the database. In designing this view, the designer must determine the objects an application needs to access and the views of those objects. Once the views have been defined the database can be physically designed, and the database and views can be created. We will consider this topic further as we discuss the hierarchical and network data models.

## DATA LANGUAGE/I

IBM developed Data Language/I (DL/I) in the 1960s as an outgrowth of data processing needs in the aerospace industry. A joint development project was undertaken by IBM and North American Aviation. DL/I is a language for processing a database. The most popular implementation of DL/I is IMS, or Information Management System, which is IBM's primary transaction processing-oriented DBMS. Actually, IMS is both a communications processor and a database management system, so it would be more correct to say that DL/I is implemented in IMS/DB, which is the database portion of IMS. DL/I uses hierarchies (trees) to represent relationships. This means that the users' objects must be transformed into tree representations before they can be processed using DL/I.

In DL/I terms, *fields* are grouped into *segments*, and segments are the nodes of tree structures. Recall from Chapter 6 that a *tree* is a collection of segments and relationships such that each segment has at most one parent and all relationships are one-to-many from parent to child. (Throughout this discussion, we will use the DL/I term *segment* rather than *record*.) DL/I refers to a particular tree structure (a collection of related segments) as a *data base record*. (*Data base* is two words in DL/I.) A sample STUDENT data base record is sketched in Figure 12–4. The forked line notation used throughout this text is not part of DL/I notation, but it is used here for

**Figure 12–4**
STUDENT data base
record

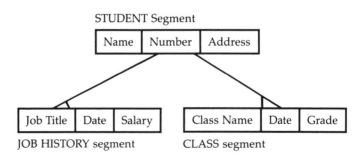

**Figure 12—5**
STUDENT data base
record occurrence

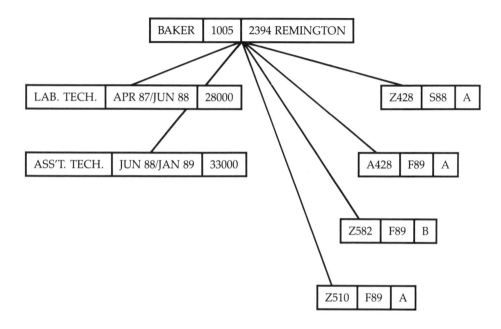

consistency. Each STUDENT segment has Name, Number, and Address fields. Also, under each STUDENT segment are a variable number of JOB HISTORY and CLASS segments. An occurrence of the STUDENT data base record is shown in Figure 12–5.

In DL/I, a *data base* is composed of data base records. These records can be occurrences of the same record type or of several different record types. For example, a DL/I data base could consist of occurrences of the STUDENT data base record in Figure 12–4 and the FACULTY data base record in Figure 12–6. The data base would comprise all occurrences of each data base record type. Figure 12–7 summarizes DL/I data structures.

Data base records are defined via a *data base description*. In the IMS implementation, a set of assembly language macro instructions indicates the structure of each data base record. (Note that this is different from the relational language SQL you studied earlier. SQL includes both data definition and data manipulation statements. DL/I is for data manipulation only.) Figure 12–8 depicts a portion of the data base description for the STUDENT data base record in Figure 12–4. The format of this description is unique to IMS.

Each segment description is headed by a SEGM macro that names the segment, shows its total length, and gives the name of the parent, if there is one. The first segment, or *root*, has no parent. Each field within a segment

**Figure 12–6**

FACULTY data base
record

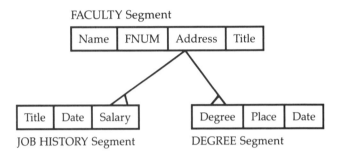

FACULTY Segment

| Name | FNUM | Address | Title |

| Title | Date | Salary |

JOB HISTORY Segment

| Degree | Place | Date |

DEGREE Segment

**Figure 12–7**

Summary of DL/I
data structures

| Data Structure | Description |
| --- | --- |
| Field | Smallest unit of data |
| Segment | Group of fields; segments must be related by hierarchical structure; each segment has a sequence field used for logical ordering |
| Data base record | Hierarchically structured group of segments |
| Data base | Collection of data base record occurrences of one or more data base record types |

is represented by a FIELD macro that indicates the field name, length, and starting position in the segment. One field within each segment is designated the *sequence field*. This field is used to order occurrences of a given segment type. The order is a logical one. It appears to the application program that segments are in order by the sequence field, but the physical ordering of segments may be different.

In Figure 12–8, the STUDENT segment is named STU and is 61 bytes long. The STU record is composed of an SNAME field in bytes 1 through 30, a NUM field in bytes 31 through 41, and an ADDR field in bytes 42 through 61. (DL/I uses uppercase letters, so all names are shown in capitals.) The sequence field for STU segments is NUM.

JOB HISTORY segments are called JOBHIST and are composed of JOB-TITLE, JDATE, and SALARY fields. CLASS segments are called CLASS and have CNAME, CDATE, and GRADE fields.

**Figure 12–8**

Data base description
for STUDENT data
base record of Figure 12–4

| | | |
|---|---|---|
| | DBD | NAME = STUDB |
| STUDENT segment description | SEGM | NAME = STU, BYTES = 61 |
| | FIELD | NAME = SNAME, BYTES = 30, START = 1 |
| | FIELD | NAME = (NUM, SEQ), BYTES = 11, START = 31 |
| | FIELD | NAME = ADDR, BYTES = 20, START = 42 |
| JOB HISTORY segment description | SEGM | NAME = JOBHIST, PARENT = STU, BYTES = 47 |
| | FIELD | NAME = JOBTITLE, BYTES = 30, START = 1 |
| | FIELD | NAME = (JDATE, SEQ), BYTES = 11, START = 31 |
| | FIELD | NAME = SALARY, BYTES = 6, START = 42 |
| CLASS segment description | SEGM | NAME = CLASS, PARENT = STU, BYTES = 10 |
| | FIELD | NAME = (CNAME, SEQ), BYTES = 5, START = 1 |
| | FIELD | NAME = CDATE, BYTES = 4, START = 6 |
| | FIELD | NAME = GRADE, BYTES = 1, START = 10 |

The data base description is assembled and can be stored in object form in a library to be called into main memory when needed. Consequently, each application programmer need not perform the time-consuming process of writing the data base description for his or her program.

## REPRESENTATION OF OBJECTS FOR DL/I PROCESSING

This section will illustrate the representation of objects using DL/I. We begin with a discussion of one method by which trees are represented in physical storage. Next we will show how a simple network can be decomposed into trees with duplication and then demonstrate how to eliminate that duplication. After that, we will present a set of objects illustrating the object types we discussed in Chapter 6 and show how to represent this set of objects so they can be processed by DL/I. Finally, we will define the DL/I terms *logical data base record* and *physical data base record* and show examples of each.

### The Physical Representation of Trees

To appreciate the way in which DL/I eliminates data duplication, you must first understand how trees are represented in physical storage. We will present the essence of one technique in this section. For more information, see Appendix B.

**Figure 12–9**

Three objects used by
university library

Figure 12–9 presents object diagrams of three objects used in a university library. TITLE contains data about a particular book title as well as two object properties, PUBLISHER and COPY. PUBLISHER contains data about a publisher and its salesperson as well as the object property TITLE. COPY contains data about a copy of a TITLE as well as a multivalued property, Due-date. This repeating property contains all of the dates on which that book copy has been due.

These three objects can be represented by the hierarchical data structure shown in Figure 12–10a. Each rectangle in Figure 12-10a is defined as a DL/I segment. Sample data for this hierarchy is shown in Figure 12–10b. Because this is a hierarchy, it can be directly represented by DL/I.

A tree like the one in Figure 12–10 can be represented in physical storage in many ways. In fact, IMS supports several different methods. One technique, illustrated in Figure 12–11, is called the *child and twin pointer* method.

Figure 12–11 assumes that each segment is stored in a separate physical record. This is unrealistic, but convenient for our purposes. In practice, many segments would be blocked into a single physical record. However, because dealing with blocking and unblocking would not contribute to your understanding of the topic at hand, we have chosen to omit it and simplify the illustration. Each record is addressed by its relative position in the file. For example, the record containing the segment for publisher P2 is located at address 12.

Each record in Figure 12–11 has three sections. One contains the key of the segment, one contains non-key data, and one contains two pointers to related segments. The first pointer is a *child pointer.* If a segment has any children, this pointer will contain the address of the record holding the first child segment. If the segment has no children, this pointer will be zero.

The second pointer is a *twin pointer.* If a segment has any siblings (segments of the same type having the same parent segment), this pointer will contain the address of the record holding the next sibling segment. If none exist, this pointer will be zero.

**Figure 12—10**
Hierarchical data
structure

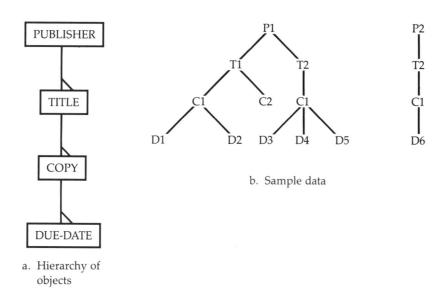

a. Hierarchy of
   objects

b. Sample data

Examine Figure 12–11 to make certain that you understand how the pointers represent the tree in Figure 12–10. For practice, follow the pointers from P1 through T2 to the due date D5.

This data structure will allow records to be inserted and deleted without reorganizing the file. The pointers are simply changed. See Appendix B for more information about this process. We will come back to this example to illustrate how duplicated data can be eliminated. But now let us consider the transformation of simple networks into trees.

## Transforming Simple Networks into Trees

Figure 12–12a shows an expansion of the library objects shown in Figure 12–9. The PUBLISHER and TITLE objects are the same. The COPY object is the same, except that a STUDENT object property has been added to it. The fourth object is STUDENT. It represents students who check out copies of titles.

The design of a database that represents these four objects is shown in Figure 12–12b. Observe that this data structure is *not* a hierarchy because COPY has two parents of different types, TITLE and STUDENT. Therefore this structure is a *simple network*.

Because this structure is not a hierarchy, it cannot be *directly* represented in DL/I. It must first be transformed into a hierarchy. Figure 12–13a shows such a transformation. Two trees have been generated, one for each

**Figure 12—11**

Child and twin
pointer representa-
tion of hierarchy in
Figure 12–10

| Record Number | Key Data | Non-key Data | Pointers Child | Pointers Twin |
|---|---|---|---|---|
| 1 | P1 | · · · | 2 | 12 |
| 2 | T1 | · · · | 4 | 3 |
| 3 | T2 | · · · | 6 | 0 |
| 4 | T1 C1 | · · · | 7 | 5 |
| 5 | T1 C2 | · · · | 0 | 0 |
| 6 | T2 C1 | · · · | 9 | 0 |
| 7 | T1 C1 D1 | · · · | 0 | 8 |
| 8 | T1 C1 D2 | · · · | 0 | 0 |
| 9 | T2 C1 D3 | · · · | 0 | 10 |
| 10 | T2 C1 D4 | · · · | 0 | 11 |
| 11 | T2 C1 D5 | · · · | 0 | 0 |
| 12 | P2 | · · · | 13 | 0 |
| 13 | T3 | · · · | 14 | 0 |
| 14 | T3 C1 | · · · | 15 | 0 |
| 15 | T3 C1 D6 | · · · | 0 | 0 |

parent of COPY. Observe that in doing this, the data of COPY and of all of its children has been duplicated. This is shown in Figure 12–13b.

In general, it is always possible to transform a simple network into trees, although some data duplication will occur. For every node that has two parents, create two trees. We will show more examples later in this chapter.

## Complex Networks

In Chapter 6 you learned that three types of data structure are based on binary record relationships: trees, simple networks, and complex networks. A relational design, however, will include only two of these types—namely, trees and simple networks. Complex networks are eliminated from relational designs because the only objects that generate them, *M:N* compound objects, are represented in a relational design as simple networks containing an intersection relation. See Chapter 6 for a review of this representation.

Thus, if you follow the process illustrated in Figure 12–3, producing the relational design before turning to DL/I, complex networks will already have been transformed into simple networks. Hence, you need to know only how to transform simple networks into trees.

**Figure 12–12**
Representation of
objects with simple
network

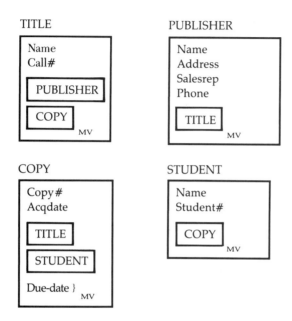

a. Four objects used by university library

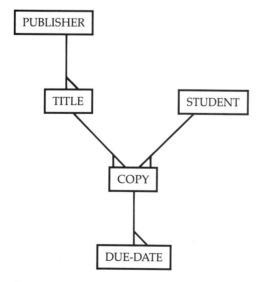

b. Simple network for objects in Figure 12-12a

**Figure 12–13**

Representing simple
network with trees

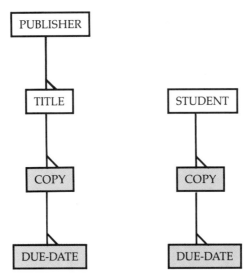

a. Two trees with duplication

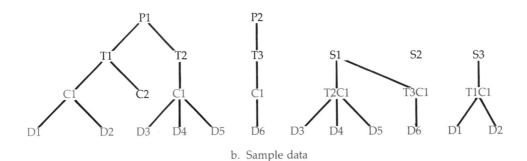

b. Sample data

### Eliminating Data Duplication

We eliminate data duplication by storing the data once and representing all subsequent references to that data by pointers. In Figure 12–14a, the PUBLISHER/TITLE/COPY/DUE-DATE tree will be stored intact, as shown in Figure 12–11. In contrast, the STUDENT/COPY/DUE-DATE tree is not stored in that form. The children segments of STUDENT contain *pointers* to data rather than data. This is illustrated in Figure 12–14b.

Figure 12–14c shows how these structures can be stored using the child and twin pointer scheme. The first fifteen records of this file are the same as in Figure 12–11. These records represent the PUBLISHER/TITLE/COPY/

**Figure 12—14**

Child and twin
pointer representa-
tion of simple
network

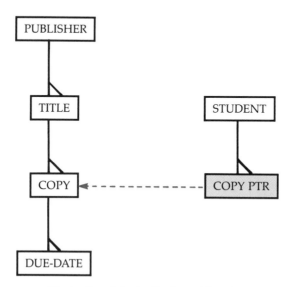

a. Eliminating data duplication with pointers

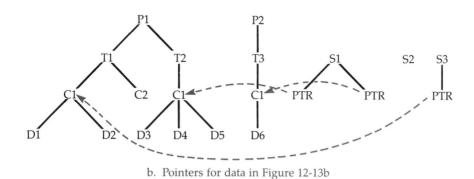

b. Pointers for data in Figure 12-13b

DUE-DATE tree. Records 16 through 21 represent the STUDENT/COPY/
DUE-DATE tree. Observe that the non-key data fields of COPY children
(such as T2 C1) have been replaced by pointers to segments containing
actual COPY data.

Using this strategy, both trees can be represented without duplicating
the COPY or DUE-DATE data. This strategy is not without risk, however.
The possibility exists that *fragments*, or children segments that become log-

**Figure 12—14**
(*continued*)

| Record Number | Key Data | Non-key Data | Pointers Child | Pointers Twin |
|---|---|---|---|---|
| 1 | P1 | · · · | 2 | 12 |
| 2 | T1 | · · · | 4 | 3 |
| 3 | T2 | · · · | 6 | 0 |
| 4 | T1 C1 | · · · | 7 | 5 |
| 5 | T1 C2 | · · · | 0 | 0 |
| 6 | T2 C1 | · · · | 9 | 0 |
| 7 | T1 C1 D1 | · · · | 0 | 8 |
| 8 | T1 C1 D2 | · · · | 0 | 0 |
| 9 | T2 C1 D3 | · · · | 0 | 10 |
| 10 | T2 C1 D4 | · · · | 0 | 11 |
| 11 | T2 C1 D5 | · · · | 0 | 0 |
| 12 | P2 | · · · | 13 | 0 |
| 13 | T3 | · · · | 14 | 0 |
| 14 | T3 C1 | · · · | 15 | 0 |
| 15 | T3 C1 D6 | · · · | 0 | 0 |
| 16 | S1 | · · · | 19 | 17 |
| 17 | S2 | · · · | 0 | 18 |
| 18 | S3 | · · · | 21 | 0 |
| 19 | T2 C1 | PTR = 6 | 0 | 20 |
| 20 | T3 C1 | PTR = 14 | 0 | 0 |
| 21 | T1 C1 | PTR = 4 | 0 | 0 |

c. Child and twin pointer representation of simple network

ically detached from a parent, will be created. For instance, suppose a STUDENT segment is linked to a COPY of a TITLE. Now suppose that the TITLE segment and its children segments (COPY and DUE-DATE) are deleted from the data base. The COPY pointer under the STUDENT segment now points to an invalid location and is therefore a fragment. Similarly, a student may not check out a book until the copy has been stored in the PUBLISHER, TITLE, COPY, DUE-DATE hierarchy.

Such dynamic constraints are unlike constraints we have encountered before. The relationship between STUDENT and COPY is optional-to-optional, but once a STUDENT segment is related to a COPY segment, that COPY segment cannot be deleted. Neither can a STUDENT segment be related to a COPY segment that has not already been entered. Such constraints are not enforced by IMS. Consequently, that task falls to the application programmer.

**Figure 12–15**
Six objects used by
university library

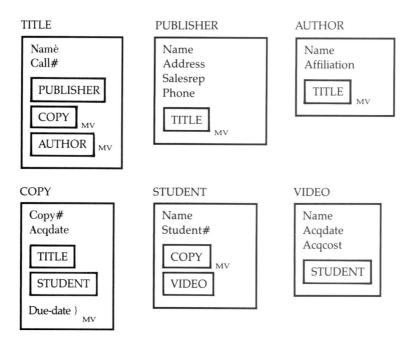

## DL/I Representation of the Library Example

To illustrate the transformation of a relational design to DL/I, consider the expanded set of library objects shown in Figure 12–15. This group contains one example of each of the object types described in Chapter 6—namely, composite objects; 1:1, 1:$N$, and $M$:$N$ compound objects; and association objects. COPY is a composite object because it contains Due-date as a multi-valued non-object property. The 1:1 compound objects are STUDENT and VIDEO (students are allowed to check out only one videocassette at a time). The 1:$N$ compound objects are PUBLISHER and TITLE. The $M$:$N$ compound objects are AUTHOR and TITLE, because an author can write many books and a book can be written by many authors. The association object is COPY, which documents the relationship between a TITLE and the STUDENT who checks it out.

A relational design for these objects is shown in Figure 12–16. One entry-point relation exists for each object. To avoid confusion, the names of the relations are slightly different from the names of the objects. In addition to these six relations, the relation DUE-DATE represents that repeating group in the COPY object, and the intersection relation TA-INT

**Figure 12–16**

Relational design for
objects in Figure
12–15

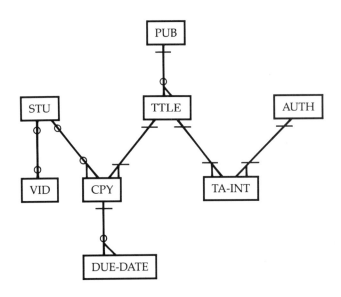

represents the *M:N* relationship between TITLE and AUTHOR. To be certain you understand this design, identify which relations are needed to construct each object.

The relational design in Figure 12–16 is not a hierarchy because two relations, CPY and TA-INT, have more than one parent. Therefore we must create two trees for each of these relations, a total of four trees. This has been done in Figure 12–17a. (Only three trees appear because the center one actually contains two trees.) Consider CPY first. Since both TTLE and STU are parents of CPY, we need to construct one tree for each of them. Thus you will see in Figure 12–17a the STU/CPY/DUE-DATE tree (part of the leftmost tree in that figure) and the PUB/TTLE/CPY/DUE-DATE tree (part of the middle tree). STU also has a child VID, which we can add under STU without problem, completing that tree.

Now consider the TA-INT relation in Figure 12–16. The purpose of TA-INT is to represent many titles for a given author and many authors for a given title. Thus, we want a tree with AUTH as parent and TTLE as child, and a tree with TTLE as parent and AUTH as child. This representation is also shown in Figure 12–17a. AUTH/TTLE/CPY/DUE-DATE is shown as a separate tree. The TTLE/AUTH relationship has been represented within the PUB/TTLE/CPY/DUE-DATE tree by adding the AUTH relation under TTLE. Thus, Figure 12–17a actually shows four trees (two for each of the

**Figure 12–17**

Representing hierar-
chies for DL/I
processing

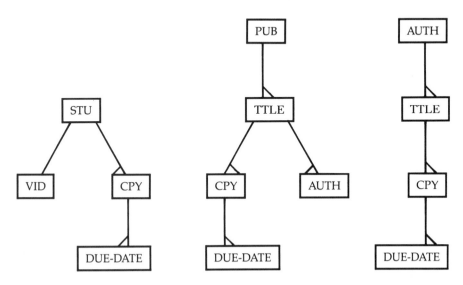

a. Logical data base records for the database in Figure 12-16

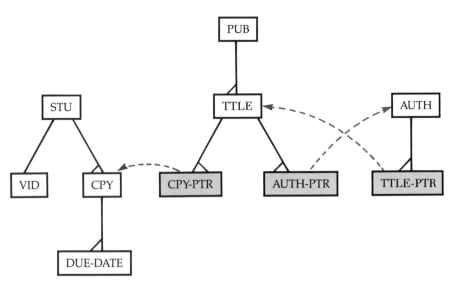

b. Physical data base records for the database in Figure 12-16

relations that have two parents), but two of the trees have been combined under the common parent TTLE.

The trees in Figure 12–17a have considerable data duplication. We eliminate that duplication with pointers, as shown in Figure 12–17b. Concerning CPY, we must choose either to put the data under TTLE and the pointers under STU or to put the pointers under TTLE and the data under STU. The choice between the two depends on the work load and the type of physical data structure used to store the trees. As a general rule, the data should be stored as part of the tree that is most frequently used. However, the particulars of this depend on specific features of IMS and are not relevant to the discussion here.

### Logical and Physical Records

DL/I divides a data base into physical and logical constructs. The terms *physical data base (PDB)* and *physical data base record (PDBR)* are used to describe the data as it exists in data storage. The terms *logical data base (LDB)* and *logical data base record (LDBR)* are used to describe the data as it appears to the application programs that process it.

LDBs differ from PDBs in either of two ways. An LDB may be a subset of a PDB, or an LDB may contain portions of two or more PDBs and represent tree structures that are not present in the PDBs.

The trees sketched in Figure 12–17a are LDBRs. They represent data as it appears to an application program. Conversely, the trees sketched in Figure 12–17b are PDBRs.

To understand LDBRs that are subsets of PDBRs, consider the PDBR STU/CPY/VID/DUE-DATE tree in Figure 12–17b. Personnel at the video checkout desk need not have access to CPY and DUE-DATE data. The application that checks out videocassettes requires only STU and VID data. To meet this need, the database developers would define an LDBR containing only STU/VID. This LDBR is a subset of the STU/CPY/VID/DUE-DATE PDBR.

All three of the LDBRs in Figure 12–17a are examples of LDBRs that contain relationships not present in the PDBRs. Consider the LDBR AUTH/TTLE/CPY/DUE-DATE. The PDBR that represents this tree is AUTH/TTLE-PTR. Clearly the LDBR is *constructed* from data in two PDBRs.

The database developer defines PDBRs and LDBRs using macro instructions similar to those shown in Figure 12–8. The specifics of these instructions are beyond the scope of this text.

### Application Views

For reasons of control, application programs are generally not allowed to access the entire database. Instead, they are given access to *views* of objects. With DL/I, a view of an object is represented by an LDBR. Thus, an application view in DL/I consists of the definition of one or more LDBRs.

Consider the university library applications. The video checkout desk needs access to STUDENT and VIDEO data. Thus, an LDBR consisting of STU/VID would be defined for application programs that support the video checkout station. The book checkout desk needs access to STUDENT and COPY data, so an LDBR consisting of STU/CPY would be defined for applications that support this function. The acquisitions desk needs access to PUBLISHER, TITLE, DUE-DATE (to determine how frequently copies are used), and COPY data, so an LDBR with only this data would be defined for programs serving that department. Similarly, LDBRs would be defined for the reference desk, the overdue fines collection clerk, and so forth.

The prevention of fragments needs to be carefully considered when defining these LDBRs and their processing. Because of the way that networks are represented, dynamic constraints can exist in addition to normal relationship constraints (M-M, M-O, and so forth). As discussed in the section on the elimination of data duplication, data that is pointed to from one PDBR must be deleted with great care. Otherwise, pointers to the addresses vacated by the deleted data will become invalid. Because IMS does not provide facilities for defining and enforcing such dynamic constraints, they must be enforced by application programs. Unfortunately, the constraints may not be apparent to programmers who see only a particular LDBR's view of the database.

Additionally, as you will see in the next section, an application program can actually delete data that is not visible in its LDBR. Because this is the case, the application programmer needs to be told which operations can be performed on data in each view. Further, with IMS, processing rights and authorities that limit allowable actions can be defined for each LDBR. As discussed in Chapter 7, these authorities need to be carefully thought out during the database design stage.

## DL/I DATA MANIPULATION LANGUAGE

DL/I processes data in segments. DL/I statements can retrieve, update, insert, and delete segments. Unlike SQL, which can be used interactively or embedded in application programs, DL/I statements *must* be embedded in application programs. DL/I is not an interactive query language. (Keep in mind that DL/I was one of the earlier database languages, used exclusively for transaction processing by information systems professionals, not by end users.)

The application programmer defines an input/output (I/O) work area that is shared by the application program and the DBMS. To insert or update a segment, the application program places new data in the work area. The DBMS takes the data from there to modify the data base. When the DBMS retrieves data from the data base, it places the data in the work area for the program to access. System status data, such as completion flags and error flags, is also placed in the work area by the DBMS so the application program can examine it.

The DL/I syntax presented in this section is general. Thus it could apply to almost any programming language. Unlike DB2, IMS does not have a pre-compiler. DL/I commands are executed by calling a DBMS subroutine from the host program. The parameters of a data base subroutine call specify the command type, search criteria, and other data. The format of data base subroutine calls depends on the host language. We will present only the DL/I commands—we will not be concerned with programming language particulars.

To illustrate the DL/I data manipulation commands, consider the LDBR in Figure 12–18. The LDBR is based on the PUB/TTLE/AUTH-PTR/CPY-PTR PDBR in Figure 12–17b.

### Get Unique (GU)

This command is used to read a particular segment into the I/O work area. For example, the statement

$$GU \quad PUB \quad (SALREP='JONES')$$

will cause the first PUB segment with the SALREP value of JONES to be placed into the I/O work area. Thus, if the occurrences in Figure 12–19 are

---

**Figure 12–18**

Sample LDBR for database in Figure 12–17b

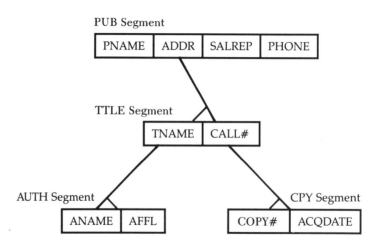

**Figure 12–19**

Two occurrences of
the LDBR in Figure 12–18

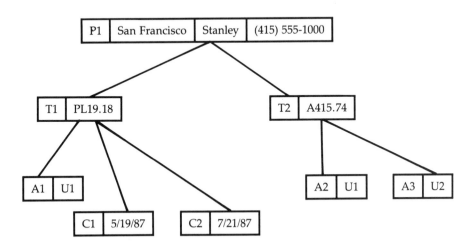

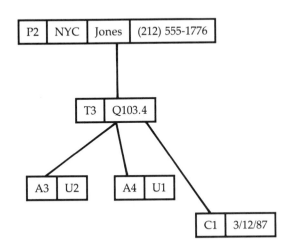

the first ones in the database, the segment P2,NYC,JONES,(212)555–1776
will be placed in the work area. The following statements will cause the
first AUTH with name A3 of TTLE T2 to be placed in the work area:

```
GU      PUB
        TTLE  (TNAME='T2')
        AUTH  (ANAME='A3')
```

If no such segment exists, the system will set an appropriate return code in the work area.

The DBMS will search for the desired segment by starting at the first occurrence of the LDBR, at the first T2 occurrence of the TTLE segment (assuming there could be more than one), and at the first A3 occurrence of the AUTH segment (again assuming there could be more than one). The order of the segments is determined by the sequence fields in each segment (see Figure 12–8). For this LDBR, assume the following sequence fields:

| Segment | Sequence Field |
|---------|---------------|
| PUB | PNAME |
| TTLE | TNAME |
| AUTH | ANAME |
| CPY | COPY# |

Thus, to find the first occurrence of AUTH A3 in TTLE T2, segments will be examined in the following order: P1 (PUB segment), T1, T2 (TTLE segments), and finally A2, A3 (AUTH segments). The segment read into the work area will be A3.

The qualifying data after the GU command is called a *segment search argument (SSA)*. In general, an SSA is the name of a segment, optionally followed by a condition. As shown, one SSA can exist for each segment in the hierarchical path for the segment to be retrieved.

### Get Next (GN)

This command is used to read the next segment. NEXT implies a current segment to start from, so it is necessary to indicate a current segment before issuing a GN command. For example, the statements

```
GU    PUB
      TTLE  (TNAME='T1')
GN    TTLE
```

will cause the first TTLE segment in the data base with TNAME field equal to T1 to be placed in the I/O work area. This establishes a current position. (Some program instructions to process that segment would probably be included following the GU command, but we have omitted them.) The GN statement reads the next TTLE segment. For the occurrence in Figure 12–19, the T1 segment will be read first, followed by the T2 segment. If a subsequent GN TTLE command is executed, the DBMS will attempt to find another TTLE segment under the current PUB segment. None exists for this occurrence, so it will search under the next PUB segment (P2) and read the T3 occurrence of TTLE. A third execution of GN TTLE will cause the system to look for the next TTLE segment. Because no more exist in the P2 occurrence of PUB, the DBMS will search the next LDBR occurrence for a TTLE segment and, if it finds one, will place it in the work area. The search will continue to the end of the data base if necessary. If no TTLE segment remains in the data base, appropriate status data will be set.

When the GN statements are executed, the system selects the next occurrence of the segment named. If no such occurrence is included under the current parent, the DBMS switches to the next parent. The application program may need to know, however, when the DBMS selects a segment from a new parent. For example, if the second GN TTLE statement is executed as discussed in the preceding paragraph, the program may need to know that a new TTLE segment has been retrieved.

To provide this information, when a segment is read, data about the path leading to the segment is placed in the work area. IMS places the *fully concatenated key* of the retrieved segment in the work area. This key is the concatenation of all sequence fields of segments leading to the segment along with the sequence field of the segment. For example, the fully concatenated key for the A4 AUTH segment is P2 T3 A4. After the second GN TTLE command is executed as described above, the system will return the key P2 T3 and the application program will be able to detect the new PUB segment by the change in PUB sequence field in the key. Now consider another example.

The commands

```
GU      PUB
        TTLE (TNAME= 'T1 ' )
GN      TTLE (CALL#> 'P ' )
```

will cause the T1 TTLE segment to be read, followed by the next TTLE segment with a call number starting with a letter beyond *P* in the collating sequence. Consequently T3 will be read next. The important point here is that sequential retrieval can be either *qualified* (with a condition after the segment name) or *unqualified* (with no condition).

Another type of sequential retrieval command requests the next segment regardless of its type. For example, the commands

```
GU      PUB
        TTLE (TNAME= 'T1 ' )
GN
```

will cause the T1 segment of TTLE to be read, followed by the A1 AUTH segment. A subsequent GN command will read the C1 CPY segment.

As an aside, this LDBR does not include DUE-DATE segments (or, as sometimes expressed in DL/I, this LDBR *is not sensitive to* DUE-DATE segments). When the GN commands are executed, no DUE-DATE data is presented to the application program. It is automatically skipped by the DBMS. IMS never presents to an application data to which the application is not sensitive.

### Get Next within Parent (GNP)

This command sequentially retrieves segments under one parent. When all segments under that parent have been read, end-of-data status is returned to the program. For example, when the commands

```
GU      PUB
        TTLE (TNAME = 'T1')
GNP     TTLE
GNP     TTLE
```

are executed, the T1 and T2 segments of P1 will be read. The second GNP command will not return data. Rather, it will cause the end-of-data status flag to be set. Contrast this with the statements

```
GU      PUB
        TTLE (TNAME = 'T1')
GN      TTLE
GN      TTLE
```

Here the second GN command will retrieve the T3 TTLE segment.

### Get Hold Commands

The three commands Get Hold Unique (GHU), Get Hold Next (GHN), and Get Hold Next within Parent (GHNP) operate exactly as the Get counterparts except that they inform the DBMS to prepare for a change or deletion of the retrieved segment. They are used in conjunction with Replace and Delete commands. When the application program replaces or deletes a segment, it must first issue one of the forms of the Get Hold commands for that segment. The DBMS will retrieve the segment and "hold" it. Then the Replace or Delete command can be issued.

### Replace (REPL)

The Replace command is used to modify data within a segment. For example, the commands

```
GHU     PUB
        TTLE (TNAME = 'T2')
        (Here the application program changes TTLE data)
REPL
```

will cause the DBMS to retrieve the T2 TTLE segment and to replace that segment with the changed data. (In this example, and in several that follow, we will show program processing in lowercase letters. The syntax of the commands to execute this logic is language-dependent and will be omitted.)

As another example, suppose it is desired to set the acquisition date of all copies of all titles to 1/1/88. The following instruction sequence will accomplish this:

```
GHU    PUB
       TTLE
       CPY
DOWHILE data remains
       Set ACQDATE ='1/1/88'
       REPL
       GHN    CPY
END-DO
```

The GHU command obtains the first CPY segment in the data base, and the GHN command obtains all subsequent ones.

Another example is to change the acquisition date to 1/1/88 only for those titles that were published by a publisher located in NYC. The programming logic for this process appears in Figure 12–20. This requires the use of both GHN and GHNP commands as follows:

```
GU    PUB (ADDR='NYC')
      (Set status-1 = 1 if data exists; 0 otherwise)
DOWHILE status-1 = 1
      GHNP TTLE
           CPY
      (Set status-2 = 1 if data exists; 0 otherwise)
      DOWHILE status-2 = 1
           (Set ACQDATE = '1/1/88')
           REPL
           GHNP    TTLE
                   CPY
           (Set status-2 = 1 if data exists; 0 otherwise)
      END-DO
      GN    PUB (ADDR='NYC')
           (Set status-1 = 1 if data exists; 0 otherwise)
END-DO
```

The GU command attempts to find the first publisher located in NYC. If one exists, the loop is executed for that publisher. The program attempts to obtain the first CPY within that publisher. If one exists, its ACQDATE is changed and it is replaced. The program attempts to read the next CPY within the current publisher parent. If one exists, it, too, is changed and replaced, and so forth. When no CPY exists within the current publisher parent, the program attempts to obtain the next publisher in NYC. If one exists, the outer loop is repeated again.

## Delete (DLET)

Delete operates in conjunction with the Get Hold commands in a manner similar to Replace. The commands

**Figure 12–20**

Logic required to
change acquisition
dates for NYC
publishers

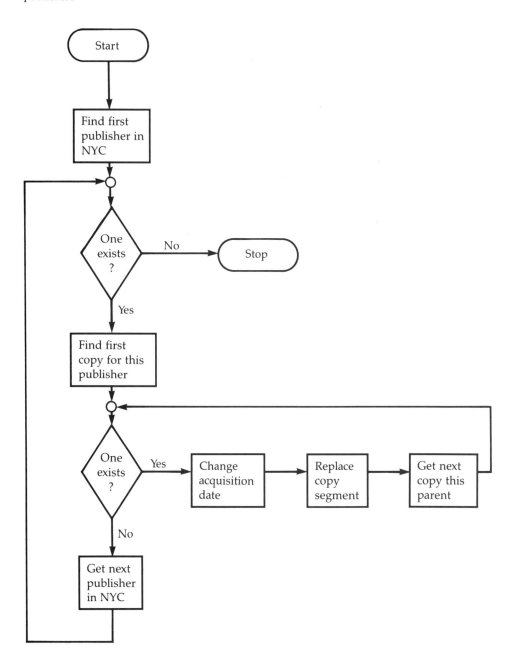

```
GHU    PUB (PNAME = 'P1')
       TTLE (TNAME = 'T1')
       AUTH (ANAME = 'A1')
DLET
```

will delete the A1 segment under T1 and P1 from the data base. When a segment is deleted, any subordinate segments are also deleted (including ones invisible to the application). Thus the commands

```
GHU    PUB (PNAME = 'P1')
       TTLE (TNAME = 'T1')
       CPY (COPY# = 1)
DLET
```

will delete not only the C1 copy segment under T1 and P1, but also all of the DUE-DATE segments under that copy. Thus, subordinate segments to which the application is not sensitive will be deleted.

Deletion of invisible data is serious and dangerous. To prevent it from happening, the database administrator, database designers, and application programmers must communicate clearly with one another. Standards need to be established and enforced. Otherwise, application programmers can unwittingly cause serious problems.

## Insert (INSRT)

Insert is used to create a new segment. For example, following instructions that placed new AUTH data in an I/O work area, the statements

```
INSRT    PUB (PNAME = 'P1')
         TTLE (TNAME = 'T2')
         AUTH
```

will insert a new AUTH segment into the data base. Because the AUTH sequence field is ANAME, the new segment will be logically inserted in order of that field. For example, if the new value of ANAME is A4, the new AUTH segment will be inserted logically as the last AUTH segment under the T2 parent.

## DL/I Data Manipulation Command Summary

Figure 12–21 summarizes the DL/I data manipulation commands. All of these commands operate on the logical structure of the data as seen by an application program. Because the physical structure of the data may be quite different from the logical structure, the DBMS must translate the logical activity into actions on the physical data structures. The application is independent of the physical structures and is freed from maintaining them.

**Figure 12—21**

Summary of DL/I data manipulation commands

| Name | Function |
|---|---|
| Get Unique (GU) | Retrieve a particular segment |
| Get Next (GN) | Retrieve the next segment |
| Get Next within Parent (GNP) | Retrieve the next segment under a particular parent |
| Get Hold Unique (GHU) Get Hold Next (GHN) Get Hold Next within Parent (GHNP) | Similar to above commands, but used to obtain a segment to be modified or deleted |
| Replace (REPL) Delete (DLET) | Used in conjunction with Get Hold commands to modify or delete a segment |
| Insert (INSRT) | Insert a new segment |

## SUMMARY

Transaction processing applications are used to update the data model of a business to keep it current. When events occur in the business environment, transactions, or records of those events, are applied to the stored data, thus keeping the company data synchronized with the status of the business.

Transaction processing applications support basic business operations. Therefore, they must possess certain characteristics to satisfy the needs of their users. Transaction processing systems must demonstrate fast response time. They must not fail often, and when they do, they must be recovered quickly and accurately. Unlike decision support applications, transaction processing applications do not need to be flexible. In fact, because business processing is standardized processing, flexibility may be undesirable. Control, however, is very important. One means of control is the use of views that restrict a database system user's access to the data.

Three data models have evolved in the last twenty years: the hierarchical data model, the network data model, and the relational data model. Early database systems were primarily transaction processing systems and were based on either the hierarchical or the network data model. Both of these models adequately support the speed and reliability requirements of transaction processing systems. However, as computer technology evolves faster computers that can handle the processing load, even the relational model is starting to be used for transaction processing.

One language that processes databases built on the hierarchical model is the IBM product DL/I. DL/I sees data in terms of segments. A segment is a group of fields. One field in the segment is designated as the sequence field and is used to logically order segments in sequence. A tree is made up of several related segments. An instance of a tree is a data base record (recall that DL/I spells *data base* as two words).

Because DL/I is based on the hierarchical model, it processes only trees in which any child segment has at most one parent. Thus, to represent networks (relationships in which a child has more than one parent), multiple trees must be created. This could result in much data duplication. DL/I eliminates data duplication through the use of pointers. Thus, data needed in two or more trees is physically stored in only one tree. All other references to that data are made by pointers to its address. DL/I uses the term *physical data base record* (or *PDBR*) to refer to physically stored data and the term *logical data base record* (or *LDBR*) to refer to application views of data, which are subsets of PDBRs.

DL/I statements to retrieve, modify, insert, and delete segments must be embedded in application programs. DL/I cannot be used interactively. DL/I data base requests are actually accomplished by issuing subroutine calls from the application program. IMS, the product in which DL/I is implemented, does not include a pre-compiler.

---

QUESTIONS                                                                     **GROUP I**

12.1   What is a transaction?

12.2   Describe the characteristics of a transaction processing application.

12.3   Why is flexibility not desirable in a transaction processing system?

12.4   What are two advantages of predefining the relationships in a hierarchical or network data model?

12.5   Define the DL/I terms *field, segment, data base record,* and *data base.*

12.6   What DL/I structure is a node on a tree?

12.7   How are DL/I data base records defined for processing by DL/I? Does DL/I include data definition language as well as data manipulation language?

12.8   What is the difference between a physical data base record and a logical data base record?

12.9   Describe the child and twin pointer method used by DL/I to link related segments to one another.

12.10  Why must simple networks be transformed into trees before they can be stored for processing by DL/I?

12.11  If you follow the database design process described in this text, why is it unnecessary to transform complex networks into trees before storing them for DL/I processing?

12.12  How does DL/I eliminate data duplication, even though logically more than one tree contains the same (duplicate) data?

12.13  What is the danger in deleting a segment that is being pointed to by another segment in the data base?

12.14  Which relations in Figure 12–16 are needed to construct each of the objects in Figure 12–15?

12.15  How can an application program delete data to which it is not sensitive?

**12.16** Consider the following organizational chart:

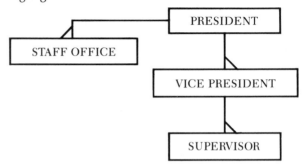

   **a.** Sketch an occurrence of this structure.

   **b.** What in this example constitutes a DL/I segment? A data base record? The data base?

**12.17** Assume each segment in question 12.16 has Name, Address, Employee-number, and Salary fields. Write a data base description similar to the one in Figure 12–8 for this data base.

**12.18** Sketch the hierarchical structure and logical pointers necessary to model the following data base records in DL/I:

a.

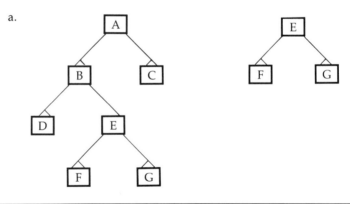

b.

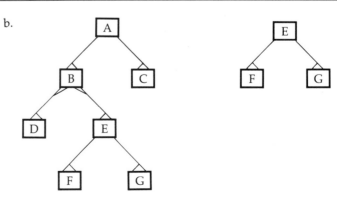

**12.19**   Assume a data base consists of three separate PDBs, as follows:

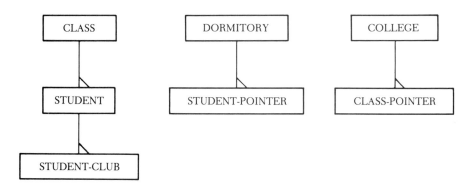

Describe the LDBR required to respond to the following requests:

**a.** Obtain the names of all students in a class taught by the College of Business.

**b.** Obtain the name of every student club that has at least one member living in Green Dormitory.

The data shown on the next page pertains to questions 12.20 through 12.24. Sequence fields are underlined.

**12.20**   Describe the results of the following retrievals:

**a.** GU    FACTORY
          PRODUCT (COST = 40)
          PART

**b.** GU    FACTORY
          WREHOUSE (NAME='W2')
          DISTRBTR

**c.** GU    FACTORY
          PRODUCT (COST = 40)
          PART (NUM-REQ = 24)
     GN   PART
     GN   PART
     GN   PART
     GN   PART

**d.** GU    FACTORY
          PRODUCT (COST = 40)
     GNP  PART
     GNP  PART

**12.21**   What will happen when the last GN PART statement is executed in question 12.20c? How will the user be able to detect this?

**12.22**   What will happen if another GNP PART statement is executed immediately after those in question 12.20d?

**12.23**   Show the DL/I statements needed to specify the following actions:

**a.** Delete the | PRT6 | 24 | segment under PRD2.

**b.** Delete all data about warehouse W3.

**c.** Delete all data about factory F1.

**d.** Delete all products costing more than $45.

12.24  Show the DL/I statements needed to perform the following modifications
and additions. In doing so, explain actions that must be performed by lan-
guage-unique commands as well:

**a.** Modify PRD2 to show a cost of $85.

**b.** Modify the cost of all products to be 10 percent greater.

**c.** Add distributor D11 to warehouse W2 and distributor D14 to warehouse W3.

**d.** Add to factory F1: PRD4, COST $105, with parts PRT2, 26 required,
and PRT4, 31 required.

**e.** Change the cost of PRD1 to $45 and add PRT6, 21 required to it.

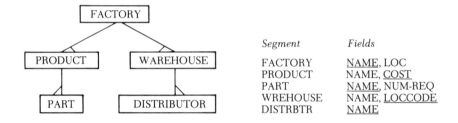

| Segment | Fields |
|---------|--------|
| FACTORY | NAME, LOC |
| PRODUCT | NAME, COST |
| PART | NAME, NUM-REQ |
| WREHOUSE | NAME, LOCCODE |
| DISTRBTR | NAME |

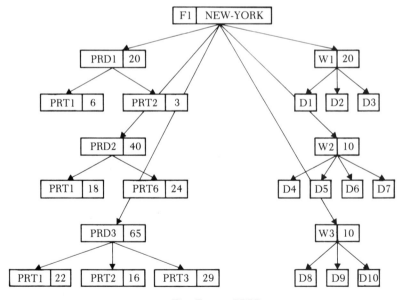

First Factory PDBR

# The Network Data Model and CODASYL DBTG

In this chapter we will introduce another data model that is frequently used to build databases to support transaction processing. The *network data model* derives its name from the fact that simple networks can be represented directly, without the transformations required for the hierarchical data model. Although several varieties of network model were once commonly used, the only one of consequence today is the CODASYL DBTG data model.

We will begin with a brief history of this model and then discuss its features and functions, starting with the data definition components. Next, we will illustrate how these components are used to represent each of the object types discussed in this text. After that, *application views*, or *subschemas*, as they are called in the DBTG model, will be presented. Finally, the DBTG data manipulation language will be discussed in the context of the library database introduced in Chapter 12.

## THE CODASYL DBTG DATA MODEL

The CODASYL DBTG data model was developed by a group known as the CODASYL (Conference on Data Systems Languages) Data Base Task Group (hence the name CODASYL DBTG). The CODASYL committee is probably best known as the group that developed the standards for COBOL. The popularity and effectiveness of COBOL is due, in large measure, to the presence of COBOL language standards. The CODASYL data model evolved over several years, and quite a few transaction processing DBMS products are based on this model. However, the CODASYL data model never enjoyed the same degree of acceptance as the COBOL specification.

Several reasons account for the failure of the DBTG model to find wide acceptance. First, as you will see, this model is complex and not very cohesive. For example, a statement in a schema definition can combine with a seemingly unrelated operation in an application program to produce spurious results. Designers and programmers must be very careful when building DBTG databases and applications. Second, the model has a decidedly COBOL flavor to it (for an example, see Figure 13–20). This similarity has been an issue in organizations where COBOL is not the language of choice. Further, the development of the CODASYL database model was heavily politicized. To avoid conflict, the committee had a tendency to include everyone's favorite idea. Reading the number and variety of options and formats of CODASYL DBTG database commands calls to mind the saying that a camel is a horse designed by committee! Finally, in fairness to this model, it originated very early in the history of database technology. Many important concepts were included in this model, but mistakes were also made. Some people believe the model was developed too soon, before the essential concepts of database technology were known and had been explored.

The history of the CODASYL model is complex. Three different versions were developed, and although the data model was twice submitted to the American National Standards Institute (ANSI) for consideration as a national standard, it was never accepted. Instead, in August 1986, the relational model and SQL were recognized as the national database standard.

The basic functions and features of the three versions of the CODASYL model are the same. Most of the commercial DBMS products based on this model are based on the earliest one, developed in 1971. Later models, in 1978 and 1981, changed some of the language and syntax (the 1971 model had inappropriately used COBOL reserved words), added features to support the definition of constraints, and made other changes. The discussion in this chapter will adhere to the 1981 model, but where it is important to know how earlier models differ from this version, concepts from the earlier models will also be presented.

Strictly speaking, only the 1971 version was called the CODASYL *DBTG* model. In subsequent versions, the *DBTG* was dropped. Common industry practice, however, refers to all versions of this model as the DBTG model, and we will follow that practice.

As you read this chapter, keep in mind that you are learning about a *model*. This model was used as the basis for the design of a number of transaction processing-oriented DBMS products. The developers of these products conformed to the model to greater and lesser degrees. You will not find a product that exactly fits the CODASYL DBTG model (of any version). However, the core features and functions of these products conform to the basic philosophy and orientation of this model.

The DBTG model (1971) introduced the terms *data definition language (DDL)* and *data manipulation language (DML)*. As you know from earlier discussions in this text, the DDL is the language used to describe the structure of the database and the DML is the language used to describe the processing of the database. Recall that DL/I, discussed in Chapter 12, does not include a DDL. Thus the CODASYL model was an improvement over the earlier database products that included only data manipulation facilities. We will consider the DDL first.

# THE CODASYL DBTG DATA DEFINITION LANGUAGE

The 1981 version of the CODASYL model provides three different types of database view. The *schema* is the complete logical view of the database. It is the entire database as viewed by the database administrator or another human. A *subschema* is a view of the database as it appears to an application program. A subschema is a subset of the database, and, in the 1978 and 1981 models, it is allowed to have records that are constructed by joining records in the schema. This is similar to a view composed of relation joins as discussed in Chapter 10. The *data structure description* is the third type of view. This description maps schema records, fields, and relationships to physical storage. It is the view of the database as it appears in physical storage. Because data structure descriptions were introduced in the second (1978) version of the model, they are not widely used. As it is unlikely that you will ever encounter them, we will omit them from our discussion.

As shown in Figure 13–1, users interact with the database via an application program (no interactive query language exists). One or more users can execute a single program. Each user has a *user working area (UWA)*. This area contains database and control data for a particular user and is similar to the IMS DL/I I/O work area described in Chapter 12. The execution of a program by one of the users is called a *run-unit*. In Figure 13–1 you will see three run-units for Application Program A. As shown in this figure, application programs view the database through a subschema. Programs may share subschemas, or each may have its own.

## CODASYL DBTG Data Definition

This section describes the basic constructs for defining databases using the CODASYL model. Database designers use these constructs to define sche-

**Figure 13—1**

CODASYL DBTG
program/data view
relationships

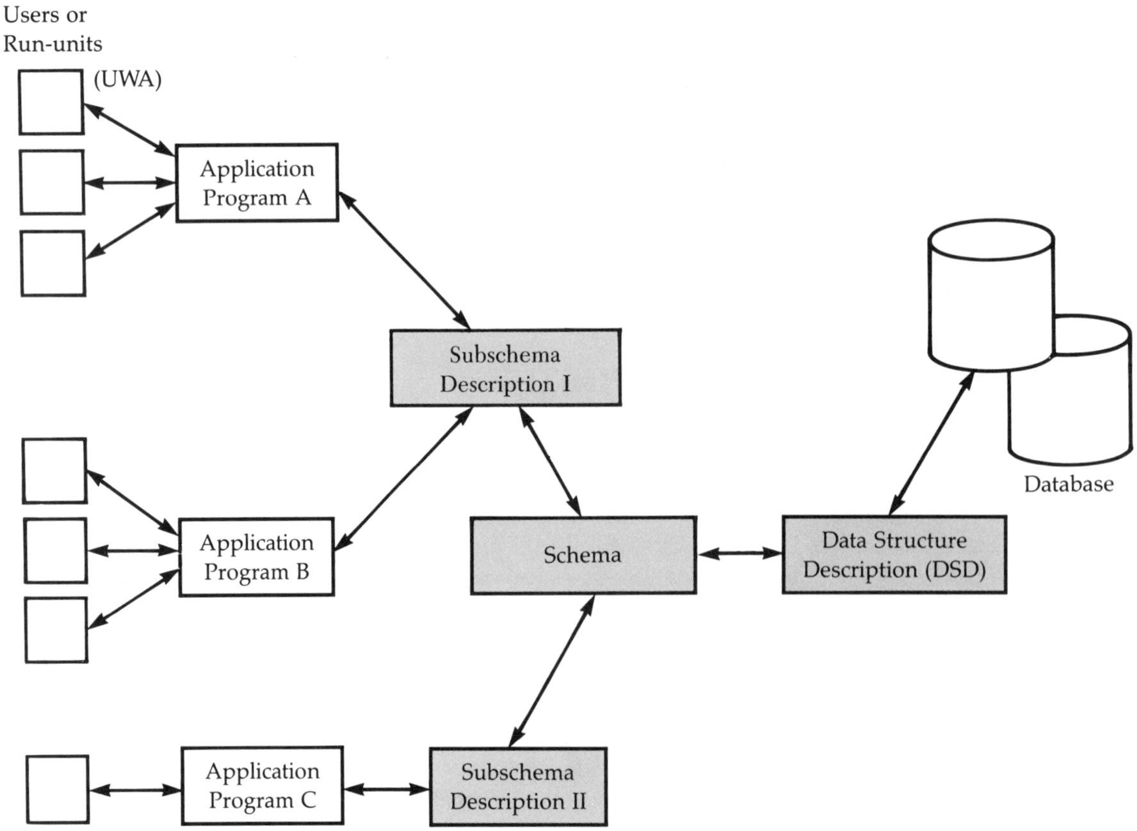

Users or
Run-units

mas and subschemas. Here and for the rest of this chapter, we will present the essence of the DDL and DML concepts and commands. This is not intended to be an exhaustive study of all options and formats. Your goal is to understand the concepts behind the CODASYL model.

**Data Definition Constructs.** The three fundamental building blocks of DBTG data definition are data-items, records, and sets.

*Data-Items.* A *data-item* is a field. It corresponds to an attribute in the relational model. Data-items have names and formats. Examples of data-items are Name, Character 25; Address, Character 40; Amount, Fixed 6.2. Although data-items arise from domains, the domain concept is not recognized by the DBTG model.

**Figure 13–2**
CODASYL DBTG
record types

a. Record composed of data-items

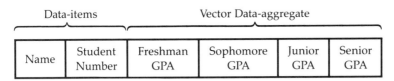

b. Record composed of data-items and a vector data-aggregate

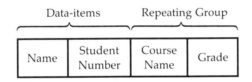

c. Record with repeating group

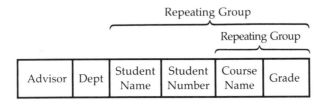

d. Record with nested repeating group

*Records.* A *record* is a collection of data-items. Figure 13–2 shows several examples of DBTG records. Figure 13–2a illustrates a simple record with no repeating data-items. Unlike the relational model, this model allows *vectors*, which are repetitions of a data-item (like GPA in Figure 13–2b), and it allows repeating groups, such as the data-items Course-name and Grade in Figure 13–2c, and the nested repeating groups in Figure 13–2d. Although such repeating groups are allowed, they are unnecessary and generally not recommended. Repeating groups were developed to represent composite objects. A better way of representing them is with two record types and a set, as shown in the next section.

**Figure 13–3**

Two occurrences of
DEPT-FAC set

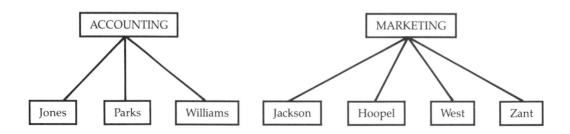

*Sets.* A *set* is a one-to-many relationship between records. Sets have *owners* and *members*. The owner of a set is the parent. In Figure 13–3, the ACCOUNTING Department is the owner of one set and the MARKETING Department is the owner of another set. Members of a set are the children in the one-to-many relationship. In Figure 13–3, JONES, PARKS, and WILLIAMS are the members of the set owned by ACCOUNTING.

Figure 13–3 shows two occurrences of a general structure. These occurrences represent instances of a one-to-many relationship between DEPARTMENT and FACULTY records. Figure 13–4 is a generalized representation of this relationship. The general structure, such as the one in Figure 13–4, is called the *set*, and examples of the structure, such as those in Figure 13–3, are called *instances*, or *occurrences*, of the set.

To define a set, we specify a set name and identify the type of record that will be the owner and the type (or types) of records that will be the members. For example, in Figure 13–5, the set STU-MAJOR has MAJOR

**Figure 13–4**

General form of
CODASYL DBTG set

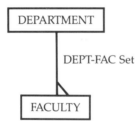

**Figure 13–5**
Example CODASYL
DBTG sets

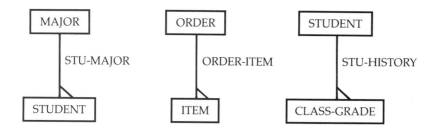

owner records and STUDENT member records. The set ORDER-ITEM has ORDER owner records and ITEM member records. The set STU-HISTORY has STUDENT owner records and CLASS-GRADE member records.

The DBTG model has specific rules regarding set definition. First, a set can have only one type of record as owner. However, one or more record types can be members. Figure 13–6a shows the set ACTIVITY. The owner record is CLUB and the member records are PROFESSOR and STUDENT. Figure 13–6b shows two instances of this set. Both PROFESSOR and STU-DENT records are members of the SKIING and BOWLING clubs.

According to the DBTG model, a member record can belong to only one instance of a particular set. Stated equivalently, a record may not have two parents in the same set. This means, in Figure 13–6, that Professor Guynes can only have the SKIING parent record. He may not have BOWL-ING as well. Furthermore, Professor Pipkin can only have the BOWLING record as parent. She may not have SKIING as well. If faculty members are allowed to belong to more than one club, a DBTG set cannot be used to represent this relationship. In fact, if faculty were allowed to belong to two clubs, this would be an instance of an *M:N* compound object. We will discuss the representation of such objects in the next section.

Although a record cannot have two owners in the *same* set, a record may have two owners if they are in *different* sets. For example, a professor may have one ACTIVITY owner and one JOB-TITLE owner. Figure 13–7 extends Figure 13–6 to allow this possibility. Dr. Guynes, for example, has both SKIING and FULL PROFESSOR records as parents.

The restrictions on set membership just described mean that a set can readily be used to represent 1:1 and 1:*N* relationships. This means that DBTG sets can directly represent composite objects, 1:1 and 1:*N* compound objects, and association objects. As stated, *M:N* compound objects cannot be represented directly with DBTG sets. The characteristics of sets are summarized in Figure 13–8.

**Figure 13—6**
Set with two member
record types and
example occurrences

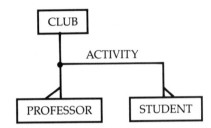

a. Set with two member record types

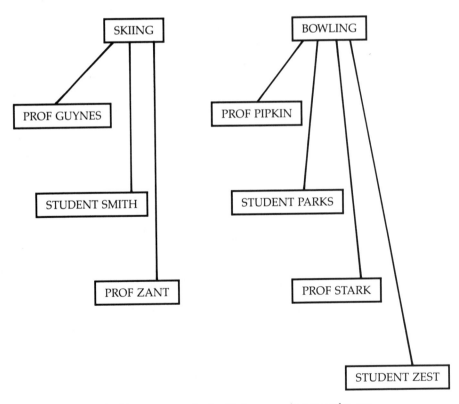

b. Occurrences of set with two member record types

**Figure 13—7**
Example of two-owner record in different sets

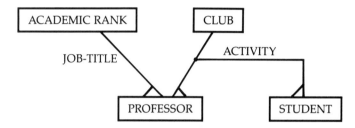

a. Record belonging to two different sets

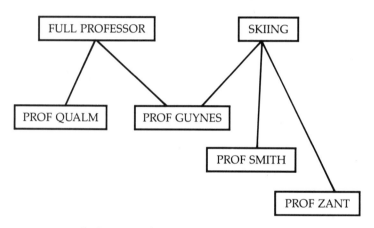

b. Instance of set structure in Figure 13-7a

*Areas.* Until 1981 the CODASYL DBTG model included a fourth data definition construct called *area* (1971), or *realm* (1978). This fourth construct referred to a collection of records and sets that could be allocated to a physical entity, such as a file, disk, or similar physical storage unit. All versions of the DBTG model were indefinite about how records or sets were to be placed into areas (alias realms). The decision regarding the use of this construct was left to DBMS product designers.

In 1981 the area (realm) construct was deleted from the CODASYL model because it was considered a physical construct and therefore inappropriate for a schema or subschema description. Consequently, we will not consider this construct further in this chapter. In the next chapter, however, this construct will reappear when we discuss IDMS/R, a product based on the 1971 DBTG model.

**Figure 13–8**

Summary of set
characteristics

---

- A set is a collection of records.
- There are an arbitrary number of sets in the database.
- Each set has one owner record type and one or more member record types.
- Each owner record occurrence defines a set occurrence.
- There are an arbitrary number of member record occurrences in one set occurrence.
- A record may be a member of more than one set.
- A record may not be a member of two occurrences of the same set.

---

## CODASYL DBTG REPRESENTATION OF OBJECTS

The representation of objects using the DBTG model is a straightforward application of the set construct. We suggest that you follow the process described in this text and summarized in Figure 12–3. First develop a relational design and then convert it to a CODASYL DBTG design.

To illustrate this conversion, we will use the six objects defined for the library in Chapter 12. For convenience, a modified Figure 12–16 showing the relational design and the six objects appears in Figure 13–9. This group of objects contains all of the object types defined in Chapter 6, and we will consider each type.

### Composite Objects

To represent a composite object in the DBTG model, we define *two records and a set*. One record type represents the object and the second represents the composite group of attributes within the object. The set represents the relationship.

Consider the COPY object in Figure 13–9. The composite group consists of the multivalued attribute DUE-DATE. The relational representation of this object is shown in Figure 13–10a and the DBTG representation is shown in Figure 13–10b. Observe that the one-to-many relationship is represented by a CODASYL DBTG set.

One important difference between the relational representation and the DBTG representation is that in the relational representation, the relationship from DUE-DATE to CPY is carried in the foreign key (Call#, Copy#). In the CODASYL representation, the relationship is not carried in the data. The foreign key (Call#, Copy#) does *not* appear in the DUE-DATE record. When a DUE-DATE record is created, the record itself is inserted into a particular instance of the HISTORY set. From that point on, the DBMS is

**Figure 13–9**

Underlying objects
and relational design
for library database

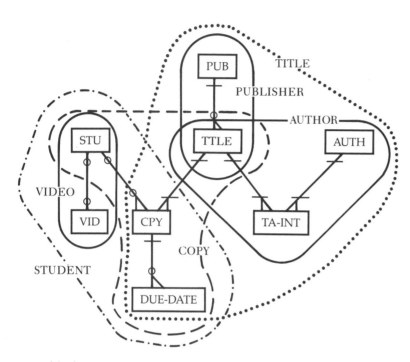

responsible for maintaining that association by means of physical location, pointers, or some other method. Unlike the relational model, the relationship is carried in *overhead data* maintained by the DBMS, and not in the data.

The set in Figure 13–10b is sometimes called an *information-bearing set* because it carries the information about which DUE-DATE records belong to which CPY records. Database practitioners disagree about the desirability of information bearing sets. On one hand, information bearing sets reduce the amount of data duplication (Call# and Copy# in this case). On the other hand, use of information bearing sets can be risky. If for some reason the overhead structure is lost or becomes suspect, it becomes impossible to determine which DUE-DATE records belong to which CPY records. Also, some people believe that burying data in overhead structures is philosophically wrong. That data, some believe, should be visible to the user rather than known only by the DBMS.

Examples can be constructed to support both positions. If the composite key is large and includes considerable duplication of data, a strong case can be made for information bearing sets. Otherwise, little harm is done by carrying the duplicate key data along, and this redundancy actually improves the reliability of the database. We will show both types in this and the next chapter.

**Figure 13–10**

Representation of
composite object

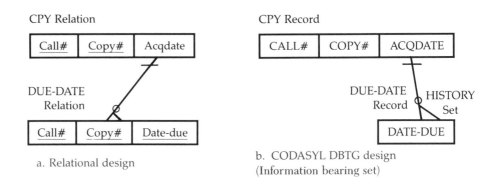

CPY Relation

| Call# | Copy# | Acqdate |
|-------|-------|---------|

DUE-DATE
  Relation

| Call# | Copy# | Date-due |
|-------|-------|----------|

a. Relational design

CPY Record

| CALL# | COPY# | ACQDATE |
|-------|-------|---------|

DUE-DATE      HISTORY
  Record          Set

| DATE-DUE |
|----------|

b. CODASYL DBTG design
(Information bearing set)

### 1:1 Compound Objects

To represent a 1:1 compound object, we define *a record for each object and a set for the relationship.* Because the relationship is 1:1, it is arbitrary which record is the parent and which is the child. In general, performance will probably be better if the record more frequently used as the entry point is the parent, but the actual answer depends on the work load, the DBMS, and the supporting data structures. As a rule, if it is more common for student data to be accessed first and video data second, then STU should be the parent. If video data is more likely to be accessed before student data, then VID should be the parent. Note that these comments pertain to the frequency with which the *relationship* is used. VID may be accessed by itself, without accessing STU, or the reverse. What matters here is identifying the record most frequently accessed first whenever the relationship is processed.

Figure 13–11 shows the relational representation of the STUDENT and VID objects (Figure 13–11a) as well as a DBTG representation (Figure 13–11b). Observe that VCHKOUT is a non-information bearing set because STUDENT# is carried as a data-item of VID.

The DBTG model provides no direct means to limit the number of child records that can belong to a set (in this case, a student is allowed only one videocassette at a time). However, we can require the STUDENT# data-item in VID to be unique, thereby limiting the number of videos per student to one.

### 1:N Compound Objects

We represent a 1:N compound object by defining *two records and a set*. Each object is stored in a record and the set represents the relationship. The

**Figure 13–11**

Representation of 1:1
compound object

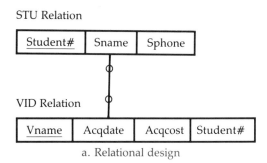

a. Relational design

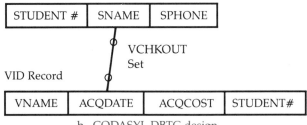

b.  CODASYL DBTG design
(Non-information bearing set)

record on the 1 side of the relationship is the parent and the record on the *N* side is the child. Stated differently, the record having the foreign key in the relational design becomes the child record of the set in the DBTG design.

Figure 13–12 shows the DBTG representation of the PUBLISHER and TITLE objects from Figure 13–9. PUB is the parent of the PUBLISHING set and TTLE is the child.

Because PNAME is included in the TTLE record, PUBLISHING is a non-information bearing set. One advantage of this arrangement is that if a report or form requires TTLE data plus the name of the publisher, including PNAME in TTLE saves DBMS processing. The appropriate PUB record need not be accessed to obtain the name. If, however, the report or form requires data besides Pname—say, Pphone—then the lookup will be necessary.

## *M:N* Compound Objects

*M:N* compound objects cannot be directly represented in the DBTG model. They must be converted to simple networks with intersection data, as is done with the relational model. Thus, we represent *M:N* compound objects

**Figure 13–12**
Representation of 1:*N*
compound object

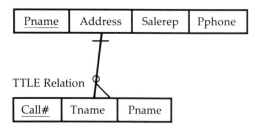

a. Relational design

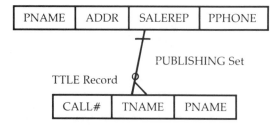

b. CODASYL DBTG design
(Non-information-bearing set)

with *three records and two sets.* Figure 13–13a shows the relational representation of the TITLE and AUTHOR objects from Figure 13–9. TA-INT has been created to represent the *M:N* relationship.

The DBTG representation of the simple network consists of three records and two sets, as shown in Figure 13–13b. One record is defined for each object and a third for the intersection data. The sets represent the *M:N* relationship. To find all authors of a given book, the program would access all TA-INT children in the T-A set and obtain the A-T parent for each. To find all titles written by a particular author, the program would access all TA-INT children of the A-T set and obtain the T-A parent for each.

The intersection record of an *M:N* object *never* contains data beyond the identities of the related records. If it did, we would call it an association object, not an *M:N* compound object.

The sets shown in Figure 13–13 are non-information bearing. If information-bearing sets were to be used here, the intersection records would have no data whatsoever, only pointers or other overhead. Nothing is wrong with that fact. It simply indicates that the function of an intersection record is to represent the relationship. If the relationship is carried in information-bearing sets, no data is needed.

## Association Objects

Figure 13–14 shows the DBTG representation of the association object COPY with its associate objects STUDENT and TITLE. To define the association object COPY, *we define one record for each object and two sets:* one for the 1:*N* relationship between COPY and TITLE and one for the 1:*N* relationship between COPY and STUDENT.

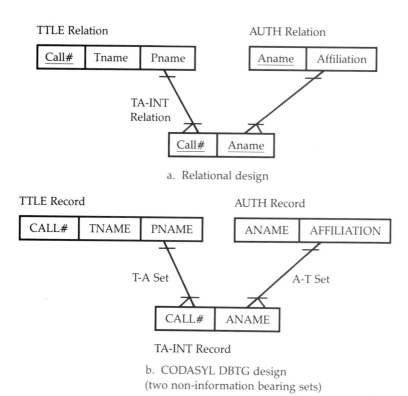

**Figure 13–13**
Representation of
*M:N* compound
object

a. Relational design

b. CODASYL DBTG design
(two non-information bearing sets)

This structure is similar to the one in Figure 13–13 except that the child record of the two sets is itself an object, seen by the user as an entity that establishes the relationship between two other objects. We would have discovered this during the requirements phase, when we found a form or report about copies. That would have told us that eventually a program would need to access the CPY record as an entry point. Conversely, the TA-INT record in Figure 13–13 is not an independent object. No program will ever access TA-INT as an entry point. Rather, TA-INT is used as a bridge between related TITLE and AUTHOR records. Stated in another way, CPY will contain data of its own, but TA-INT will not.

In this example, CHECKOUT is an information bearing set, but COLLECTION is not information bearing. The decision to structure these sets in this manner is arbitrary. Because Call# is part of the key of CPY, it is already carried in data and not by the set. But because Student# is not part

**Figure 13—14**
Representation of
association object

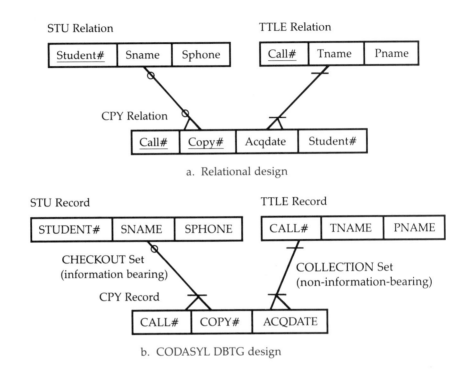

a. Relational design

b. CODASYL DBTG design

of the key, that relationship can be carried by the set. On the other hand, Student# *could* have been placed in the CPY record, making CHECKOUT a non-information-bearing set. No compelling reason supports one choice over the other—they both work. (Contrast this with the relational model, in which relationships *must* be carried in the data because information-bearing sets do not exist.)

## DBTG SET ORDERING

According to the DBTG model, member records of a set can be ordered in a variety of ways. Figure 13–15 lists the possibilities. If the set order is FIRST, when new records are placed in a set occurrence, they will be placed in the first position. Subsequently, when the set members are accessed, the new record will be the first one retrieved. This placement is logical, supported by underlying data structures. The physical placement is unknown

**Figure 13—15**
CODASYL DBTG set
member ordering
options

```
FIRST
LAST
NEXT
PRIOR
SYSTEM DEFAULT
SORTED
```

and unimportant except to the DBMS itself. If the set order is LAST, new records will be placed in the last position. In this case, set members will be ordered chronologically, by length of time in the database.

If the order is NEXT, new members will be placed in the next position after the most recently accessed member record of the set. To use this option, at least one set record must have already been accessed to establish a position. The new record is placed immediately after that most recently accessed record. If the most recently accessed record of the set were the owner, the new record would be placed at the start of the set members. If the order is PRIOR, the new record will be inserted just before the most recently accessed set record. If that record is the owner, the new record will be placed at the end of the set.

If the set is ordered by SYSTEM DEFAULT, the database designer is stating that the order is immaterial to applications. The DBMS can determine the order. Finally, set members can be SORTED on the value of a data-item they contain. In this case, the name of the data-item is identified in a separate KEY clause (as we will illustrate). Figure 13–16 shows the set ordering we will use for the library database.

As long as records belong to sets, they can be ordered within the set. For some applications, however, the entire file of records needs to be sorted, regardless of the sets to which its records might belong. To satisfy this need, the DBTG provides *system sets*.

A *system set* is a special set that has only one occurrence for each type of record. That occurrence is owned by the DBMS. To provide sequential processing, the set is defined as an ordered set based on one or more data-items in the record. Thus, if TTLE records are to be sorted by TNAME, a system set having TTLE records as members and ORDER of TNAME would be created. We have called this system set TITLE-SEQ in Figure 13–16. TTLE records can then be processed in TNAME order.

**Figure 13–16**
Set ordering for
library database

| Set Name | Order |
|---|---|
| PUBLISH | Sorted by TNAME |
| T-A | System default |
| A-T | System default |
| COLLECTION | Sorted by COPY# |
| CHECKOUT | Last |
| VCHKOUT | Last (but immaterial) |
| HISTORY | Last |
| TITLE-SEQ | Sorted by TNAME |

## SET MEMBERSHIP

The DBTG model provides a group of commands to put records into set occurrences, to take records from set occurrences, and to move records around within set occurrences. We will discuss these commands in the section on the DML. However, the allowable commands depend on the definition of *set membership*. Set membership involves two concepts: getting members into set occurrences and, once in, getting members out.

### Set Insertion Status

When we define a set in the schema, we must give it an *insertion status*, either AUTOMATIC or MANUAL. If insertion status is AUTOMATIC, whenever a member record is created, the DBMS automatically inserts the record into the set. If the insertion status is MANUAL, a member record is not put into a set occurrence until the application program executes a special command, CONNECT.

### Set Retention Status

Additionally, when a set is defined in the schema, it must be given a *retention status*. This status can be FIXED, MANDATORY, or OPTIONAL. If retention status is FIXED, once a record is placed in a set occurrence, it must remain in *that* occurrence of the set. To change its set membership, the record must be deleted from the database and recreated.

If the retention status is MANDATORY, once a record is placed in a set occurrence, it must always belong to *a* set occurrence. However, the occurrence need not be the initial one. Thus MANDATORY sets require that once

**Figure 13–17**
Set insertion and set
retention status

Retention status

| Insertion status | | FIXED | MANDATORY | OPTIONAL |
|---|---|---|---|---|
| | AUTO-MATIC | DBMS puts record in set at time of creation. Once in, it cannot be taken out. | DBMS puts record in set at time of creation. It can be moved to another occurrence with RECONNECT. | DBMS puts record in set at time of creation. It can be disconnected, reconnected, or connected. |
| | MANUAL | Application program puts record into set. Once in, it cannot be taken out. | Application program puts record into set. It can be moved to another occurrence with RECONNECT. | Application program puts record into set. It can be disconnected, reconnected, or connected. |

a record is put into a set occurrence, it must stay in *some* occurrence of the set. A special command, RECONNECT, is used to move a member record from one occurrence to another, as you will see.

Finally, if the retention status is OPTIONAL, member records can be removed, inserted, and moved from set occurrence to set occurrence *without restriction*. Figure 13–17 summarizes the interaction of set insertion and retention status.

## CONSTRAINTS

The DBTG model provides some support for domain, intra-, and inter-relation (record) constraint enforcement. The DBTG support for constraint enforcement has evolved over time within different versions of the model. We will show the capabilities of the 1981 model here. Because the DBTG model was evolving at the same time that the need for constraint enforcement was becoming apparent, constraint enforcement was not thoroughly developed.

### Domain Constraints

The DBTG model does not recognize the concept of domain. Thus, data-items are independently defined to have a particular physical appearance and particular constraints. If two or more data-items are based on the same domain, it is up to the database developer to know this and to ensure that the physical descriptions and constraints are defined in the same way.

The manner in which data-item formats are defined is rather open-ended. Various versions of the model provide a variety of data-items and formats for data-item specification. Basically, the model includes the common data formats, such as CHARACTER, FIXED, CURRENCY, DATE, TIME, and so forth. Additionally, the length of data-items and the number of places to the right of the decimal point (where appropriate) can also be specified.

In addition to format descriptions, the 1981 DBTG provides a means to limit data-item values. This is done via the CHECK statement in the schema definition. Examples of CHECK statements are

```
CHECK IS NOT EQUAL 0
CHECK IS LESS THAN 500
CHECK IS NOT NULL
```

The first two CHECK statements enforce range restrictions on allowable values. The last one ensures the existence of a value in a mandatory field, such as a key field. CHECK statements are located in the schema definition next to the data-item that they limit. Examples are shown in the next section.

### Intra-record Constraints

The DBTG model supports one type of intra-record constraint: *uniqueness*. Record instances can be defined to be unique based on one or more data-items, considered singly or as composites. For example, suppose the record type TTLE contains the data-item TNAME. (Like DL/I, the DBTG model does not support lowercase letters. Data-items will be shown in capital letters for this model.) The following statement can be inserted in the schema to ensure that duplicate titles are prohibited:

```
DUPLICATES NOT ALLOWED FOR TNAME
```

Such statements are located in the schema in the section defining the record having the constraint. Consider another example involving the record CPY, which contains the data-items CALL# and COPY#. The statement

```
DUPLICATES NOT ALLOWED FOR CALL#, COPY#
```

states that the composite (CALL#, COPY#) must be unique. Records may exist that have duplicate CALL# values (for different copies of the same book) and records may exist that have duplicate COPY# values (for copy numbers of different titles), but the combination of a particular call number with a particular copy number must be unique. Consider the difference in the preceding DUPLICATE statement for CPY and the following two statements for TTLE:

```
DUPLICATES NOT ALLOWED FOR TNAME
DUPLICATES NOT ALLOWED FOR CALL#
```

The two statements for TTLE define uniqueness for data-items independently. The single statement for CPY defines uniqueness for the composite (CALL#, COPY#). (Recall from Chapter 10 that most microcomputer DBMS products do not include this feature.)

### Inter-record Constraints

The DBTG model provides partial support for the definition of inter-record constraints, or referential integrity, through two facilities. One is via the definition of set retention status and the other is a version of the CHECK command.

Consider Figure 13–17 in light of the four types of binary record relationship constraints, namely mandatory-to-mandatory (M-M), mandatory-to-optional (M-O), optional-to-mandatory (O-M), and optional-to-optional (O-O). If the retention status of a set member is either FIXED or MANDATORY, that record will always be in a set, and hence it will always have a parent. Thus, either of these two values of retention status can be used to enforce the parent side of M-M or M-O constraints. Further, defining a set as OPTIONAL means a parent may or may not exist and thus can be used to define the parent side of O-M or O-O constraints.

Set insertion status does not facilitate the definition of inter-record constraints. In fact, some database practitioners find it to be more confusing than helpful. AUTOMATIC/FIXED and AUTOMATIC/MANDATORY definitions provide for consistent enforcement of M-x (meaning either M-M or M-O) constraints. MANUAL/FIXED and MANUAL/MANDATORY provide such enforcement once the record is placed in a set. However, MANUAL insertion status allows a child record to be stored in the database before the parent is.

Set insertion and retention status concern a child record's requirement for a parent. They do not consider a parent record's requirement for a child. Thus, these definitions do not concern the enforcement of x-M constraints. Unfortunately, such constraints must be enforced by application programs.

The 1981 model provided a version of the CHECK statement that enforces values in foreign keys. As such, it can only be used for non-information bearing sets (sets in which the key of the parent is stored as a foreign key in the child record).

For example, consider the TTLE and CPY records discussed earlier. CALL# in CPY is a foreign key from TTLE. The following CHECK statement, placed in the set definition portion of the schema, will enforce a match between the key and the foreign key:

```
CHECK IS CALL# IN TTLE = CALL# IN CPY
```

This statement, which is associated with a set—say, COLLECTION—makes sense only if CALL# is located in both records. With it, whenever a record is placed into a set occurrence, the values of CALL# must match. This is yet another way of enforcing an M-x constraint.

Perhaps you are beginning to get a feel for the inconsistent and eclectic nature of this model. Such a CHECK statement leans in the direction of inter-relation constraints in the relational model. Yet, its presence is somewhat confusing laid on top of the rest of the DBTG model. Such is the nature of emerging technology.

## A SCHEMA DEFINITION FOR THE LIBRARY DATABASE

Figure 13–18 presents a schema definition for the library database design shown in Figure 13–9. The DBTG model could be used in many ways to represent this database; Figure 13–18 is one of them. We chose options that another database designer might not have chosen. Because the DBTG model is so open-ended, several feasible definitions for the database are possible.

The schema definition has two major parts. The first concerns the definition of record structures and the second the definition of sets.

### Record Definitions

Examine the definition of the PUB record in Figure 13–18. The first statement declares that values of PNAME must be unique. Following that, the data-items are described. Notice the CHECK statement that enforces the domain constraint that PNAME may not be null.

The definition of TTLE is next. Here, two different statements declare that both TNAME and CALL# are to be unique. Because these statements are separate, they imply that value of TNAME and values of CALL# must each be unique. As stated previously, this is different from declaring that a composite group be unique. An example of composite data-item uniqueness occurs in the definition of the next record, CPY. The DUPLICATES statement in that record declares that the composite (CALL#, COPY#) must be unique.

The remaining record definitions are similar. One unusual statement appears in the definition of VID. In that record, STUDENT# is required to be unique. Because a set is defined with STU as parent and VID as child, this relationship would normally be one-to-many. The same value of STU-DENT# could appear in many different instances of VID. With the decla-

**Figure 13—18**
Library schema
definition

```
SCHEMA NAME IS LIBRARY
      RECORD NAME IS PUB
             DUPLICATES ARE NOT ALLOWED FOR PNAME
             PNAME                     TYPE IS      CHARACTER      10
                                       CHECK IS     NOT NULL
             ADDRESS                   TYPE IS      CHARACTER      25
             SALPSN                    TYPE IS      CHARACTER      20
             PPHONE                    TYPE IS      FIXED          10


      RECORD NAME IS TTLE
             DUPLICATES ARE NOT ALLOWED FOR CALL#
             DUPLICATES ARE NOT ALLOWED FOR TNAME
             CALL#                     TYPE IS      CHARACTER      8
                                       CHECK IS     NOT NULL
             TNAME                     TYPE IS      CHARACTER      50
                                       CHECK IS     NOT NULL
             PNAME                     TYPE IS      CHARACTER      10
                                       CHECK IS     NOT  NULL
      RECORD NAME IS CPY
             DUPLICATES ARE NOT ALLOWED FOR CALL#, COPY#
             CALL#                     TYPE IS      CHARACTER      8
                                       CHECK IS     NOT NULL
             COPY#                     TYPE IS      FIXED          2
                                       CHECK IS     NOT NULL
             ACQDATE                   TYPE IS      DATE


      RECORD NAME IS AUTH
             DUPLICATES ARE NOT ALLOWED FOR ANAME
             ANAME                     TYPE IS      CHARACTER      30
                                       CHECK IS     NOT NULL
             AFFILIATION               TYPE IS      CHARACTER      30


      RECORD NAME IS TA-INT
             DUPLICATES ARE NOT ALLOWED FOR CALL#, ANAME
             CALL#                     TYPE IS      CHARACTER      8
                                       CHECK IS     NOT NULL
             ANAME                     TYPE IS      CHARACTER      30
                                       CHECK IS     NOT NULL      7


      RECORD NAME IS STU
             DUPLICATES ARE NOT ALLOWED FOR STUDENT#
             STUDENT#                  TYPE IS      FIXED          10
                                       CHECK IS     NOT NULL
             SNAME                     TYPE IS      CHARACTER      30
             SPHONE                    TYPE IS      FIXED
```

**Figure 13—18**

*(continued)*

```
RECORD NAME IS VID
        DUPLICATES ARE NOT ALLOWED FOR VID#, VCOPY#
        DUPLICATES ARE NOT ALLOWED FOR STUDENT#
        VID#                      TYPE IS    FIXED        5
                                  CHECK IS   NOT NULL
        VCOPY#                    TYPE IS    FIXED        2
                                  CHECK IS   NOT NULL
        VNAME                     TYPE IS    CHARACTER   40
        STUDENT#                  TYPE IS    FIXED       10

RECORD NAME IS DUE-DATE
        DATE-DUE                  TYPE IS    DATE
                                  CHECK IS   NOT NULL

SET NAME IS PUBLISH
        OWNER IS PUB
        ORDER IS SORTED BY DEFINED KEYS
        MEMBER IS TTLE
        INSERTION IS AUTOMATIC, RETENTION IS FIXED
        KEY IS ASCENDING TNAME
        SET SELECTION IS BY VALUE OF PNAME

SET NAME IS T-A
        OWNER IS TTLE
        ORDER IS SYSTEM DEFAULT
        MEMBER IS TA-INT
        INSERTION IS AUTOMATIC, RETENTION IS FIXED
        CHECK IS CALL# IN TTLE = CALL# IN TA-INT
        SET SELECTION IS BY VALUE OF CALL#

SET NAME IS A-T
        OWNER IS AUTH
        ORDER IS SYSTEM DEFAULT
        MEMBER IS TA-INT
        INSERTION IS AUTOMATIC, RETENTION IS FIXED
        CHECK IS ANAME IN AUTH = ANAME IN TA-INT
        SET SELECTION IS BY VALUE OF ANAME

SET NAME IS COLLECTION
        OWNER IS TTLE
        ORDER IS BY DEFINED KEYS
        MEMBER IS CPY
        INSERTION IS AUTOMATIC, RETENTION IS FIXED
        KEY IS ASCENDING COPY#
        SET SELECTION IS STRUCTURAL CALL# = CALL#
```

**Figure 13—18**
*(continued)*

```
SET NAME IS CHECKOUT
        OWNER IS STU
        ORDER IS LAST
        MEMBER IS CPY
        INSERTION IS MANUAL, RETENTION IS OPTIONAL
        SET SELECTION IS BY VALUE OF STUDENT#

SET NAME IS VCHKOUT
        OWNER IS STU
        ORDER IS LAST
        MEMBER IS VID
        INSERTION IS MANUAL, RETENTION IS OPTIONAL
        SET SELECTION IS BY VALUE OF STUDENT#

SET NAME IS HISTORY
        OWNER IS CPY
        MEMBER IS DUE-DATE
        ORDER IS LAST
        INSERTION IS AUTOMATIC, RETENTION IS FIXED
        SET SELECTION IS BY VALUE OF CALL#, COPY#

SET NAME IS TITLE-SEQ
        OWNER IS SYSTEM
        ORDER IS SORTED BY DEFINED KEYS
        MEMBER IS TTLE
        INSERTION IS AUTOMATIC, RETENTION IS FIXED
        KEY IS ASCENDING TNAME
```

ration that STUDENT# be unique, however, the same STUDENT# can appear in only one VID record. Thus, this declaration turns what would normally be a one-to-many relationship into the one-to-one relationship required in the design.

## Set Definitions

One set is defined for each one-to-many relationship shown in Figure 13–9. The first set, PUBLISH, represents the relationship between PUB and TTLE. The owner record of this set is PUBLISH and the member record is TTLE. Records within the set are to be maintained in sorted order of TNAME. This is defined by two statements in the set definition. The first, ORDER IS SORTED BY DEFINED KEYS, indicates the order is to be kept by a value of one or more data-items within the member record. The particular data-item is then identified by the statement KEY IS ASCENDING TNAME. The fourth statement in the set definition specifies the set insertion and retention status. AUTOMATIC, FIXED was chosen here because every book must have a publisher and the publisher of a book cannot change.

The last statement in the set definition specifies how the DBMS is to identify a particular set occurrence when it needs one. This is necessary in several situations, as you will see when we discuss the DML. For instance, because the insertion status of TTLE is AUTOMATIC, when a new TTLE record is created, the DBMS must insert it into an instance of the PUBLISH set. The question is, which instance of that set? The SET SELECTION statement indicates how the DBMS is to identify such a set instance. This particular statement indicates the DBMS is to use the value of PNAME to identify a PUB record. The new TTLE record is to be inserted into the set occurrence owned by that PUB record.

The remaining sets are also defined in Figure 13–18. The sets T-A and A-T represent the *M:N* relationship between titles and authors. Both of these sets are non-information-bearing because they contain the keys of their parents. The order of these sets is SYSTEM DEFAULT. This means the application developers are unconcerned about the order of member records within the set. Other statements are similar to those for PUBLISH except that these sets include a CHECK clause.

Consider the set T-A. The CHECK clause in this set definition informs the DBMS to enforce the constraint that the values of CALL# in TTLE and TA-INT must match. Because the insertion status is AUTOMATIC, the retention status is FIXED, and the set selection is by value of CALL#, this CHECK clause is redundant. Unless the DBMS code is in error, it should be impossible for non-matching values of CALL# ever to occur in the same set.

Observe that the set insertion and retention status, the SET SELECTION, and the CHECK statements interact. To determine the impact of any one of these three statements, you must consider the other two. This interaction, which is used to enforce inter-record constraints, is, unfortunately, complicated and sometimes a bit mysterious. This interaction requires that not only the database designer but also the application programmer know and remember the actions of these statements. If the programmer does not understand this interaction, unanticipated results can occur.

The COLLECTION set represents the one-to-many relationship between TTLE and CPY. It is similar to the other set definitions except for the SET SELECTION statement. This SET SELECTION statement is a combination of SET SELECTION and a CHECK statement. It indicates that the DBMS is to preserve the inter-record constraint that owner and member records in this set always have the same CALL# value. When the DBMS needs a set occurrence for some reason, it is to pick the one that will enable this constraint to be maintained. Further, no data-item changes that would violate this constraint are to be allowed. This statement is equivalent to the combination of CHECK and SET SELECTION statements shown in the definitions for the sets T-A and A-T. Such a statement can be used only for non-information bearing sets.

The CHECKOUT set is similar to other sets except that its INSERTION STATUS is MANUAL and RETENTION is OPTIONAL. Records are placed into this set by application programs and can be removed without restriction. This is appropriate because copies of books can be checked out and returned dynamically. The order of this set is LAST. This means that the member records will occur in the set in chronological order. The due date for the earliest checkout will be the first record in the set.

CHECKOUT and the next set, VCHKOUT, are the only sets in this database that have MANUAL and OPTIONAL status. The other records and sets represent more permanent conditions. Authors of book titles, for example, do not change. In this database, only the allocations of students to books or videos change.

The last set is a system set. It contains all of the TTLE records in the database. The purpose of this set is to provide a logical ordering of TTLE records by TNAME.

This schema definition includes the major facilities of the 1981 DBTG DDL. It differs from earlier versions primarily in that it includes CHECK clauses and that keys and SET SELECTION statements are handled slightly differently. If you understand these statements in this schema, however, you should have little trouble understanding statements in schema definitions of DBMS products based on other versions of the DBTG model.


## SUBSCHEMA DEFINITIONS

Application programs do not access the database schema directly. Instead, they view the database via subschemas. These subschemas are basically subsets of the schema. (The 1981 model does allow the definition of virtual records via joins of actual records. We will discuss this capability under the heading "Logical Record Facility" in Chapter 14.)

Unfortunately, no accepted DBTG standard for subschema descriptions currently exists. The 1981 schema language is incompatible with the 1978 subschema language (the last date for which a subschema standard was published). In light of this situation, we will adjust the 1978 standard to the conventions of the 1981 standard as much as possible.


## SUBSCHEMAS FOR THE LIBRARY DATABASE

To illustrate the definition and use of CODASYL DBTG subschemas, we will consider two subschemas for the library database. Figure 13–19a shows the structure of the PURCHASE subschema, used by application programs

**Figure 13–19**
Sample subschema
structures

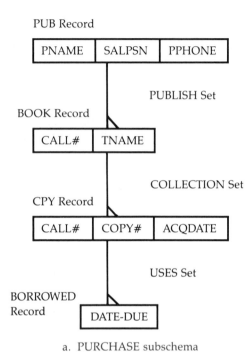

a. PURCHASE subschema

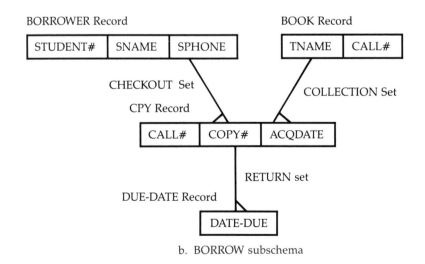

b. BORROW subschema

in the purchasing department. The second subschema, BORROW, is shown in Figure 13–19b. BORROW is used by the checkout desk when books are lent.

## The PURCHASE Subschema

The general format of a subschema description is shown in Figure 13–20. Each subschema description has three divisions. The TITLE DIVISION contains the name of the subschema, the MAPPING DIVISION contains alias descriptions, and the STRUCTURE DIVISION indicates the records, data-items, and sets in the schema that are present in the subschema.

Figure 13–21a presents a subschema description for PURCHASE. In the MAPPING DIVISION, the record TTLE is renamed BOOK and the record DUE-DATE is renamed BORROWED. Additionally, the set HISTORY is renamed USES, and the data-item DATE-DUE is renamed USE-DATE. The application program that accesses this subschema must use these aliases rather than the names in the schema description. AD is a keyword that stands for *alias definition*.

The RECORD SECTION of this subschema redefines the PUB record to omit the ADDRESS data-item. All of the data-items in BOOK, CPY, and BORROWED are to be present in the PURCHASE subschema. Finally, in the SET SECTION, the PUBLISH, COLLECTION, and USES sets are declared to be included in PURCHASE. SD is a keyword that stands for *set definition*.

## The BORROW Subschema

The subschema BORROW is defined in Figure 13–21b. The structure of the description is the same as that for PURCHASE. BORROW includes BOOK

**Figure 13–20**

Format of subschema description, 1978 specification

```
TITLE DIVISION.
(subschema name)
MAPPING DIVISION.
ALIAS SECTION.
(alternate names for records, sets, or data-items)
STRUCTURE DIVISION.
RECORD SECTION.
(records and data-items that are to appear in the subschema)
SET SECTION.
(sets to appear in the subschema)
```

**Figure 13–21**

Sample subschema
definitions for library
database

```
TITLE DIVISION.
SS PURCHASE WITHIN LIBRARY.
MAPPING DIVISION.
ALIAS SECTION.
AD     RECORD TTLE IS BOOK.
AD     RECORD DUE-DATE IS BORROWED.
AD     SET HISTORY IS USES.
AD     DATE-DUE IS USE-DATE.
STRUCTURE DIVISION.
RECORD SECTION.
01     PUB.
       05           PNAME    PIC X(10).
       05           SALPSN   PIC X(20).
       05           PHONE    PIC 9(10).
01     BOOK ALL.
01     CPY ALL.
01     BORROWED ALL.
SET SECTION.
SD     PUBLISH.
SD     COLLECTION.
SD     USES.
```

a. PURCHASE subschema definition

```
TITLE DIVISION.
SS BORROW WITHIN LIBRARY.
MAPPING DIVISION.
ALIAS SECTION.
AD     RECORD TTLE IS BOOK.
AD     RECORD STU IS BORROWER.
AD     SET HISTORY IS RETURN.
STRUCTURE DIVISION.
RECORD SECTION.
01     BOOK.
       05      TNAME    PIC X(50).
       05      CALL#    PIC X(8).
01     BORROWER ALL.
01     CPY ALL.
01     DUE-DATE ALL.
SET SECTION.
SD     COLLECTION.
SD     CHECKOUT.
SD     RETURN.
```

b. BORROW subschema description

(alias for TTLE), BORROWER (alias for STU), CPY, and DUE-DATE records. The sets included are COLLECTION, CHECKOUT, and RETURN (alias for HISTORY).

These figures present the essence of the CODASYL DBTG model's facility for subschema description. In the next chapter we will see how these concepts were implemented in an actual DBMS product. For now, we will use both the schema and subschema descriptions to illustrate the data manipulation language (DML) commands.

# THE CODASYL DBTG DATA MANIPULATION LANGUAGE

This section presents the essence of the DBTG DML. First we discuss general concepts. Then we consider single-record processing. Finally, we discuss DML processing of several records using sets.

## General DML Concepts

Most CODASYL DBTG data manipulation commands have two steps. First, a FIND command is issued to identify the record to be acted upon. The FIND command does not read or otherwise process the indicated record. It simply identifies a record for the DBMS to locate. After a record has been identified, a second DML command can be issued to perform an operation on it. Typical patterns are FIND, GET; FIND, MODIFY; and FIND, ERASE. The only DML command that does not follow this pattern is STORE. Because this command inserts a new record into the database, nothing needs to be found before it is executed.

As stated, every DBTG run-unit (a particular user connected to a particular program) has a user working area (UWA). The records in the subschema are stored in the UWA. For the PURCHASE subschema, four records are in the UWA. They are PUB, BOOK, CPY, and BORROWED. For the BORROW subschema, the records are BOOK, BORROWER, CPY, and DUE-DATE. The UWA contains other data as well. In particular, it contains *currency indicators* and *special registers.*

## Currency Indicators

Currency indicators are place markers. When the program issues a FIND command, a record is found and its identity is stored in a special variable called a *currency indicator.* Subsequently, when a GET, MODIFY, ERASE, or other command is issued, the DBMS references the currency indicator to determine which record to act on. Also, currency indicators are used as reference points for sequential processing commands, such as FIND NEXT or FIND PRIOR. We will discuss these statements later.

Several currency indicators exist. Every record type and set type in the subschema has its own currency indicator. These indicators identify the most recently processed record of a type or in a set. Also, the run-unit itself has a currency indicator that identifies the most recently processed record of any type. For the PURCHASE subschema, currency indicators exist for the PUB, BOOK, CPY, and BORROWED records, for the PUBLISH, COLLECTION, and USES sets, and for the run-unit that is processing the subschema. For the BORROW subschema, indicators exist for the BOOK, BORROWER, CPY, and DUE-DATE records, for the COLLECTION, CHECKOUT, and RETURN sets, and for the run-unit that is processing this subschema.

Initially, all of these currency indicators are null, indicating that no record has been accessed. As records are processed, the DBMS updates currency indicator values.

The currency indicators can be envisioned as variables in a table. Figure 13–22 lists the currency indicators for the BORROW subschema as it is processed. The top row shows the initial status of all the currency indicators. The indicator in the first column is the current of run-unit (the most recently processed record of any type). Indicators in other columns refer to the record and set types as listed.

The FIND command sets currency indicator values. For example, when a FIND command is executed to FIND the BORROWER record with STUDENT# equal to 150, the current of run-unit, current of BORROWER, and current of CHECKOUT are all set to point to the record for BORROWER 150 (see the second row in Figure 13–22). If a FIND command were then issued to located the CPY record with CALL# equal to R726.8.L and COPY# equal to 3, the current of run-unit, current of CPY, current of CHECKOUT, current of COLLECTION, and current of RETURN would be set to point to the CPY record having R726.8.L, COPY 3. The modified currency indicators are shown in the third row. Notice that the current of BORROWER is unaffected by the second FIND command.

### Special Registers

*Special registers* are also kept in the UWA. Unlike machine registers (which you might remember from a system architecture or assembly language course), these registers are simply data fields in which the DBMS places system information for the application program to access, such as return codes and error messages. For example, after execution of a DML command, the DBMS places a return code in a register called DB-STATUS. If the command was executed without problems, it sets DB-STATUS to zero. Other values of DB-STATUS indicate an error or an unusual situation. One common use of DB-STATUS is to signal end-of-data.

Other special registers are DB-SET-NAME, DB-DATA-NAME, and DB-RECORD-NAME. The first two are set only when an error occurs. The DBMS places the names of the record and the data-item it was processing

Resource

| Statement | RUN-UNIT | BOOK | BORROWER | CPY | DUE-DATE | COLLECTION | CHECKOUT | RETURN |
|---|---|---|---|---|---|---|---|---|
| Initial | NULL | NULL | NULL | NULL | NULL | NULL | NULL | NULL |
| FIND BORROWER with STUDENT# = 150 | BORROWER 150 | NULL | BORROWER 150 | NULL | NULL | NULL | BORROWER 150 | NULL |
| FIND CPY R726.8.L, COPY 3 | CPY R726.8.L COPY 3 | NULL | BORROWER 150 | CPY R726.8.L COPY 3 | NULL | CPY R726.8.L COPY 3 | CPY R726.8.L COPY 3 | CPY R726.8.L COPY 3 |

**Figure 13–22**

Currency indicators for the BORROW subschema

at the time of the error in these registers. DB-RECORD-NAME is set when an error occurs and also whenever a FIND or STORE command has been executed. This data is useful when the application program is processing records in a set that has members of more than one record type.

### DBTG DML for Single-Record Processing

The following examples show how FIND is used in conjunction with other commands to process the database. These commands will be shown in pseudocode form. The exact language for the product IDMS/R will be shown in the next chapter. For now, think of the DML as extensions to the COBOL (or other language) statements.

Suppose we want to *read* the BORROWER record for STUDENT# 150. The following commands will do this:

```
MOVE "150" TO STUDENT# IN BORROWER
FIND ANY BORROWER USING STUDENT#
GET BORROWER
```

The FIND command sets the current of run-unit, current of BORROWER, and current of CHECKOUT to point to the record for STUDENT #150. Then the GET command places the record into the BORROWER record area in the UWA. GET always operates on the current of run-unit record.

Suppose we want to read all CPY records for a book having the call number R726.8.L. The commands would be

```
MOVE "R726.8.L" TO CALL# IN CPY
FIND ANY CPY USING CALL#
DOWHILE DB-STATUS = 0
        GET CPY
        (process CPY data)
        FIND DUPLICATE CPY USING CALL#
END-DO
```

DB-STATUS is used here to control loop processing. This code assumes that DB-STATUS will be set to a value other than zero only at end-of-data. A more sophisticated (and appropriate) algorithm would examine the value of DB-STATUS to ensure that no other condition or error occurred. We will defer that level of detail until the next chapter.

The first FIND specifies that ANY record could qualify. The next FIND specifies DUPLICATE. This keyword means the desired record must have the same value of CALL# that the current of CPY has.

To illustrate the elimination of records, suppose we want to *delete* all CPY records of the book having the call number R726.8.L. We would use the commands

```
MOVE "R726.8.L" TO CALL# IN CPY
FIND FOR UPDATE ANY CPY USING CALL#
```

```
DOWHILE DB-STATUS = 0
            ERASE CPY
            FIND FOR UPDATE DUPLICATE CPY USING CALL#
END-DO
```

The logic is similar to that for the GET. However, the ERASE command is used in this example. Also, the words FOR UPDATE are added to the FIND command. These keywords inform the DBMS that an update is to occur. The DBMS will lock the record for the run-unit. This is similar to the DL/I GET HOLD commands described in the previous chapter.

To illustrate the *modification* of records, suppose the BORROWER with STUDENT# of 150 changes her name to WILLIS. The commands would then be

```
MOVE "150" TO STUDENT# IN BORROWER
FIND FOR UPDATE ANY BORROWER USING STUDENT#
GET BORROWER
IF DB-STATUS = 0
    THEN MOVE "WILLIS" TO SNAME IN BORROWER
        MODIFY SNAME
    ELSE do error processing
END-IF
```

In this case, the MODIFY statement indicates that only the SNAME data-item has been changed. If no data-item is listed, the DBMS is to assume that the entire record (or this subschema's view of it) has been changed.

To *create* a new record, we first build it in the UWA and then issue a STORE command. The following statements insert a BORROWER record into the database:

```
MOVE "2000" TO STUDENT# IN BORROWER
MOVE "CALBOM" TO SNAME IN BORROWER
MOVE "5258869" TO PHONE IN BORROWER
STORE BORROWER
```

After the STORE command, the new record is the current of run-unit, current of BORROWER, and current of CHECKOUT.

Although not shown, the program should examine DB-STATUS to determine if the command executed successfully. Actually, DB-STATUS should be examined after every DBMS command. In these examples, and in the following ones, we will sometimes omit this examination and subsequent error processing. This omission simplifies the discussion. Remember, however, that actual application programs need to examine DB-STATUS after every command and perform appropriate error processing when necessary.

## Processing Multiple Records with Sets

Sets are used to process records by relationship. Three commands are used to insert and remove records from sets. Several different formats of the FIND command are then used to process records within sets.

**Inserting and Removing Records from Sets.** The DBTG model provides three commands for processing set members: CONNECT, DISCONNECT, and RECONNECT. The first command places a record into a set, the second removes a record from a set, and the third changes set membership.

The allowed use of these commands depends on the set insertion and retention status. The insertion status governs the use of CONNECT, and the retention status governs the use of DISCONNECT and RECONNECT.

If the insertion status is AUTOMATIC, then CONNECT is unnecessary, at least when the record is created. (If the set retention status is OPTIONAL, then the record may be removed from its initial set assignment and later placed in a new set using CONNECT.) If the insertion status is MANUAL, then CONNECT must be used to place the record into a set.

If the retention status is FIXED, then DISCONNECT and RECONNECT are invalid. If the retention status is MANDATORY, then RECONNECT is valid but DISCONNECT is not. If the retention status is OPTIONAL, then both of these commands are valid.

The COLLECTION and CHECKOUT sets in the BORROW subschema represent the two extremes. COLLECTION is AUTOMATIC/FIXED and CHECKOUT is MANUAL/OPTIONAL. None of these commands is valid for COLLECTION. Because the insertion status is AUTOMATIC, CONNECT is unnecessary. Because the retention status is FIXED, neither DISCONNECT nor RECONNECT is valid.

On the other hand, all of these commands are necessary and valid for CHECKOUT. CONNECT must be used to place a record into CHECKOUT, and both RECONNECT and DISCONNECT may be used after that.

CONNECT places the current of the member record type into the current of the set. To illustrate its operation, suppose that student 150 wishes to check out copy 2 of the book with call number R726.8.L. The following statements will accomplish this:

```
MOVE "R726.8.L" to CALL#
MOVE "2" TO COPY#
FIND ANY CPY USING CALL#, COPY#
MOVE "150" TO STUDENT#
FIND ANY BORROWER USING STUDENT#
CONNECT CPY TO CHECKOUT
```

The first FIND command establishes copy 2 of R726.8.L as the current of CPY. The second FIND then establishes student 150 as the current of the CHECKOUT set. The copy is then placed in the set with CONNECT. Because the SET SELECTION clause is BY VALUE OF STUDENT#, the second FIND command is not actually necessary. If it were not included, the DBMS would use the value of STUDENT# to determine the set occurrence for the CONNECT command.

DISCONNECT operates similarly. The current of member record type is removed from the current of set. The following commands take copy 2 of R726.8.L from the set owned by student 150:

```
MOVE "R726.8.L" to CALL#
MOVE "2" TO COPY#
FIND ANY CPY USING CALL#, COPY#
MOVE "150" TO STUDENT#
FIND ANY BORROWER USING STUDENT#
DISCONNECT CPY FROM CHECKOUT
```

As with CONNECT, the second FIND statement is unnecessary because the SET SELECTION is BY VALUE OF STUDENT#.

RECONNECT operates by disconnecting the current of a record type from its occurrence in a set and connecting it into the current occurrence of that same set. For example, the following commands reassign copy 2 of book R726.8.L from student 150 to student 400:

```
MOVE "R726.8.L" to CALL#
MOVE "2" TO COPY#
FIND ANY CPY USING CALL#, COPY#
MOVE "400" TO STUDENT#
FIND ANY BORROWER USING STUDENT#
RECONNECT CPY TO CHECKOUT
```

The first FIND command establishes the current of CPY. The next establishes student 400 as the current of CHECKOUT. The record is then moved from student 150's set occurrence to student 400's set occurrence.

As stated, when the set insertion status is AUTOMATIC, the DBMS connects records into sets when they are created. An appropriate record must be available to serve as parent at the time the new record is created. For example, when a new CPY record is created, it will automatically be inserted into a COLLECTION set. The appropriate BOOK record must exist in the database. Consider the following:

```
MOVE "PS477.5C" TO CALL# IN CPY
MOVE "3" TO COPY# IN CPY
MOVE "11/14/87" TO ACQDATE IN CPY
STORE CPY
```

When the STORE command is executed, CPY will automatically be inserted into the COLLECTION set occurrence of which PS477.5C is the parent. If this BOOK does not exist, an error will occur.

The new CPY record is connected to the appropriate set because of the STRUCTURAL SET SELECTION statement in the definition of COLLECTION. This statement means, when necessary, to find a parent record of COLLECTION that will make the CALL# in the child record equal to the CALL# in the parent record. Because the insertion status of COLLECTION is AUTOMATIC, the DBMS must find such a parent when the STORE is executed.

Processing of a MANDATORY set is similar except that once a record is placed in a set (either MANUAL or AUTOMATIC, depending on its insertion status), only the RECONNECT command may be used. DISCONNECT is not allowed.

**Set Membership and Erase Commands.**   If a record owns a set occurrence, special considerations apply when the record is deleted. The application program can request that all children (and children of children, etc.) be erased when the record is erased, or it can be more selective.

Suppose we want to delete a BOOK record and all of the CPY and DUE-DATE records that pertain to this book. The following statements will accomplish this for the book whose call number is Q360.C33:

```
MOVE "Q360.C33" TO CALL#
FIND FOR UPDATE ANY BOOK USING CALL#
ERASE ALL BOOK
```

The keyword ALL in the ERASE command directs the DBMS to erase all CPY records (and all DUE-DATE records belonging to the set owned by CPY). If ALL is not specified in the ERASE command, the result depends on the retention status of the owned sets. If the retention status is FIXED, the erase will be successful and all owned children records will be erased as well.

If the retention status is MANDATORY, the ERASE will be disallowed. If it were allowed, the remaining child records would be fragments. Their retention status is MANDATORY and they must reside in a set. If the DBMS were to erase their parent, it would not know what to do with the fragments.

If the retention status is OPTIONAL, the ERASE will be allowed and any child records will be disconnected from the set. However, they will remain in the database.

**Using Sets for Record Retrieval.**   Once records have been placed in sets, set membership can be used to retrieve records by relationships. Or, in the terminology of this text, sets and set membership can be used to construct objects from records.

Suppose we want to process a view of the STUDENT object that contains both BORROWER and CPY records. Say we want to retrieve the call numbers of all books on loan to student 400. The following statements will do this:

```
MOVE "400" TO STUDENT#
FIND ANY BORROWER USING STUDENT#
FIND FIRST CPY WITHIN CHECKOUT
```

```
DOWHILE DB-STATUS = 0
     GET CPY
     (process CPY record to display CALL#)
     FIND NEXT CPY WITHIN CHECKOUT
END-DO
```

The first FIND command establishes the current of BORROWER as well as the current of CHECKOUT. The next FIND command sets the current of CPY to the first record in the set owned by the BORROWER with STU-DENT# of 400. The first record is then processed and the next one identified with the FIND NEXT command. In addition to FIND FIRST and FIND NEXT, this model also provides FIND LAST and FIND $n$th, where $n$ is the ordinal position of the record in the set. This last option is useful only if the set members are ordered in some manner.

Suppose we want not only the call numbers of all books on loan to student 400, but also the titles. Because titles are stored in TTLE records, we must retrieve the owner of each CPY record. Thus, we start with student 400, find a CPY record owned by that student, find the parent of that record, and then repeat the process for the next CPY record owned by that student. This can be done as follows:

```
MOVE "400" TO STUDENT#
FIND ANY BORROWER USING STUDENT#
FIND FIRST CPY WITHIN CHECKOUT
DOWHILE DB-STATUS = 0
     GET CPY
     FIND OWNER WITHIN COLLECTION
     GET TTLE
     (process CPY and TTLE records to display CALL# and
       title)
     FIND NEXT CPY WITHIN CHECKOUT
END-DO
```

The FIND OWNER statement establishes the owner of the CPY record as the current of run-unit.

## THE CODASYL DBTG MODEL AS A *MODEL*

The CODASYL DBTG model is a rich, comprehensive, and complicated model. Because of its long history and the many different versions, committees, companies, and people involved, it is inconsistent and vague. As a model, however, it is rich enough to enable the expression of database designs and application program logic for transaction processing databases and applications.

You can think of this situation as analogous to using pseudocode for specifying program logic. Pseudocode is vague in some ways, but it is entirely serviceable for the expression of program logic. Of course, when the logic is expressed in a programming language, the vagueness is replaced with statements that have one and only one interpretation to the language compiler. So it is with this model. The DBTG model can be used to express designs and logic, and, within the limits of the model, the statements can mean what you want them to mean. Once the database is implemented, however, and a particular DBMS product is used, the statements available and their function and meaning will become exact. You will see an example of this in Chapter 14, when we discuss IDMS/R, an implementation of the DBTG model.

## SUMMARY

Like the hierarchical data model, the network data model is the basis for many DBMS products that perform transaction processing. The most significant network data model is known as the CODASYL DBTG data model, named after the committee that developed it. The most significant difference between the network data model and the hierarchical data model is that simple networks can be represented directly in the network model. Thus, it was an improvement over the earlier hierarchical model.

The history of the CODASYL DBTG data model is long. Many people were involved in the model's development, and its many options and formats reflect the views of so many participants. As a result, it is a rich but not very cohesive model.

The DBTG model introduced the concept of both a data definition and a data manipulation language for DBMS products. Unlike DL/I, which includes no database definition facilities, products based on the DBTG model include both languages.

A schema is a logical view of the entire database as seen by the DBA. A subschema is a subset of the database, like a view in the relational model. It is the application program's view of the database.

All user interaction with the database is accomplished via application programs (no interactive query language requirement is included in the model). An application program can be run by one or more users. Each user has its own user work area for passing data to and from the DBMS.

The building blocks used for DBTG data definition are data-items (or fields), records (collections of data-items), and sets (a set is a one-to-many relationship between records). These building blocks can be used to represent all of the object types we have discussed in this text: composite, compound, and association. It is a straightforward step to transform a relational database definition into the equivalent DBTG database definition.

When defining DBTG sets, we specify various options, such as how members will be ordered, how members will be placed in a set occurrence (insertion status), and how, if at all, members can be removed from a set occurrence (retention status). These options allow us to enforce some database constraints. However, the DBTG model does not provide complete and comprehensive facilities for constraint enforcement.

Among the constraints the DBTG model does enforce are domain constraints (allowable values and mandatory existence), intra-record constraints (uniqueness, both of individual data-item values and of composite data-item values), and inter-record constraints (referential integrity by means of set retention status and the CHECK command).

The DBTG model also provides a data manipulation language. Generally, database accesses are accomplished in two steps. The first step is used to identify the record to be acted upon and the second step performs some operation. The DBTG FIND statement is used to identify a record. When executed, the FIND statement sets the value of one or more currency indicators.

A currency indicator is a place marker that points to the most recently identified record in a record type, set, or run-unit. Each execution of a FIND may modify one or several of these place markers. After a currency indicator is set, a subsequent instruction can access the record to which it is pointing.

Special registers are data-items in the user work area whose values are set by the DBMS to report on the status of the system. They can be accessed by the application program. Special registers are used to indicate error conditions, end-of-data, the name of the most recently processed record, and so forth.

DBTG commands are available to read, insert, modify, and delete database records. DBTG DML can be used to access and process individual database records and to process sets. The syntax shown in this chapter is generic. Exact syntax varies by DBMS product. One product based on this model, IDMS/R, will be presented in Chapter 14.

QUESTIONS                                                                **GROUP I**

**13.1**  Explain the relationship between user, run-unit, application program, subschema, schema, database, and DBMS.

**13.2**  Define the term *data-item*. How are data-items related to domains? How are domains defined using the DBTG model?

**13.3**  Define the term *record* as used in the DBTG model.

**13.4**  Define the following terms and explain their purpose: *set, owner, member, set occurrence.*

**13.5**  Give an example of a set structure. Sketch two occurrences of this set.

**13.6**  Show a DBTG representation and describe two occurrences of the following tree: School districts have schools, and schools have pupils (one record type) and teachers (another record type). Teachers have past assignments.

**13.7**  Show a DBTG representation and describe two occurrences of the following simple network: Fathers have children, and teachers teach children.

**13.8**   Show a DBTG representation and describe two occurrences of the following complex network: Children have many hobbies, and a hobby is enjoyed by many children.

**13.9**   List the DBTG currency indicators and describe situations in which each would be used.

**13.10**  Explain how most DBTG DML operations are executed in two steps.

For questions 13.11 through 13.16, provide pseudocode similar to that in the chapter. Refer to the following schema:

SALESPERSON with data-items NAME, AGE, SALARY
ORDER with data-items NUMBER, CUST-NAME, SALESPERSON-NAME, AMOUNT
CUSTOMER with data-items NAME, CITY, INDUSTRY-TYPE
SET SALE with owner SALESPERSON and member ORDER
SET PURCHASE with owner CUSTOMER and member ORDER

**13.11**  Retrieve:
   **a.** Customer with name ABC CONSTRUCTION
   **b.** Order with number 12345
   **c.** All orders for customer ABC CONSTRUCTION

**13.12**  Delete all orders for salesperson PARKS.

**13.13**  Change the industry type of ABC Construction to type J. (Assume that INDUSTRY-TYPE is a character data-item.)

**13.14**  Store a new SALESPERSON record—name is CURTIS, age is 39, salary is 65,000.

**13.15**  Change the name of customer ABC Construction to SoftSystems. Make changes to ORDER records as well, assuming the retention status of PURCHASE is
   **a.** OPTIONAL
   **b.** MANDATORY
   **c.** FIXED

**13.16**  Assuming that both SALE and PURCHASE are MANUAL, OPTIONAL sets,
   **a.** Create an ORDER record and place it in the correct set occurrences of PURCHASE and SALE.
   **b.** Change the name of a customer in an ORDER record and RECONNECT it to the correct occurrence. (Assume that the record is already in an occurrence.)
   **c.** Remove all ORDERs for customer JONES from sets to which they belong.

---

**GROUP II**     QUESTIONS AND EXERCISES

**13.17**  Research the history of the DBTG model. Summarize the changes in the DBTG model over the last ten years. Do you think the model has been improved or damaged by its development? Why or why not? Why was the DBTG model rejected as a national standard and passed over in favor of the relational model?

**13.18** Modify Figure 13–10b to make it a non-information bearing set. Modify Figures 13–11b, 13–12b, and 13–13b to make all sets information bearing ones. Modify Figure 13–14b to make CHECKOUT a non-information bearing set and COLLECTION an information bearing set. Are any of these reversals impossible to carry out? Why?

**13.19** Compare and contrast the DBTG model with the relational model. Which model is easier to understand? Which do you think would be easier to use? For what applications would the DBTG model be preferred to the relational model? For what applications would the relational model be preferred to the DBTG model?

**13.20** Locate in your community a company that uses a CODASYL DBTG DBMS. Interview personnel and determine how schemas and subschemas are designed. If possible, obtain a copy of a schema, subschema, and application program. Compare these to the concepts described in this chapter.

# CODASYL DBTG Implementation with IDMS/R

---

- What Is a CODASYL DBTG DBMS?
- IDMS/R Database Definition and Access
- IDMS/R Physical Storage
- IDMS/R Data Definition
- IDMS/R Data Manipulation Facilities
- IDMS/R Concurrent Processing and Recovery
- IDMS/R Security
- An Example of IDMS/R Use
- Summary

---

In this chapter we will illustrate the implementation of a transaction processing-oriented database using a DBMS based on the CODASYL DBTG model. First we will describe what constitutes a DBTG DBMS product, and then we will illustrate DBTG implementation using IDMS/R, the most successful DBTG DBMS product.

IDMS/R is licensed by the Cullinet Corporation. Ironically, the *R* in IDMS/R stands for *relational*. To explain, IDMS was introduced in the early 1970s, at which time it was purely a CODASYL DBTG product. In the early 1980s, however, as some of the advantages of the relational model became apparent, Cullinet began to add relational *capabilities* to its DBTG product. At that point, the company added the *R* to the name IDMS. Some proponents of the relational model claim that this was more of a marketing move than a true change in the product. They claim that the product remains basically a DBTG product with only a relational facade. Others claim this is unfair. Regardless of this debate, Cullinet is clearly adding more and more relational capabilities to its popular DBMS product.

Happily, we need not address this issue further. For the purposes of this chapter, we are concerned with the CODASYL DBTG characteristics of

IDMS/R. You will learn how to implement a DBTG schema and subschema, and how to encode DBTG commands in COBOL. We have discussed the relational model at length in other chapters. In this chapter we will consider only the CODASYL DBTG features of IDMS/R.

## WHAT IS A CODASYL DBTG DBMS?

A number of DBMS products are based on the CODASYL DBTG model. These products vary considerably in their functions and features because several versions of the CODASYL DBTG model have existed. Still, these products are built upon a common conceptual framework.

For the purposes of this text, we will say a DBMS conforms to the DBTG model if it has the five characteristics summarized in Figure 14–1. First, the database structure is defined in a single specification called the *schema* and application program views of the database are defined in subsets of the schema called *subschemas*. Second, *relations* from the logical design are represented by *records* in the DBTG implementation and non-object attributes are represented by *data-items*. Third, relationships among records are represented by DBTG *sets*. Every one-to-many relationship in the logical design is represented by a set.

Fourth, a DBTG DBMS supports the concept of *record currency*. Records identified by key value, sequential position, or set membership become current of some class (run-unit, area, record, or set). Finally, to be a DBTG product, a DBMS must provide the commands FIND, GET, STORE, MODIFY, ERASE, CONNECT, and DISCONNECT (or their equivalents).

### CODASYL DBTG DBMS Products

As mentioned in Chapter 13, it appeared that the DBTG model would become a national database standard during the early 1970s. At that time many major hardware vendors initiated development of DBTG DBMS prod-

---

**Figure 14–1**

Five required characteristics of a DBTG DBMS

1. Schema/subschema data are defined.
2. Relations are represented by records, and attributes are represented by data-items.
3. Relationships are represented by DBTG sets.
4. DML processing uses record currency.
5. FIND, STORE, GET, MODIFY, ERASE, CONNECT, and DISCONNECT commands (or equivalents) are provided.

**Figure 14—2**
DBTG database man-
agement systems

| Vendor | DBMS Product |
|--------|--------------|
| CDC | DMS-170 |
| Cullinet | IDMS/R |
| DEC | DBMS 10, DBMS 11 |
| Honeywell | IDS II |
| Unisys | DMS II, DMS-1100 |

ucts. Today, except for IDMS/R, all major DBTG systems are provided by hardware vendors. Figure 14–2 lists some vendors and DBTG DBMS products.

The oldest of all these products is Honeywell's IDS. IDS actually predated the development of the DBTG model. In fact, many DBTG concepts originated in IDS. IDS was developed at General Electric and was later acquired by Honeywell when Honeywell bought General Electric's computer products division.

Because you studied the DBTG model in the previous chapter, you know the essential functions and features of all of these products. Therefore, as we did in Chapter 11 with DB2, we have selected one of these products, IDMS/R, to present in some detail.

## IDMS/R

IDMS/R is a large, comprehensive, and complicated family of products licensed by the Cullinet Corporation. Figure 14–3 summarizes the product set. The core consists of the IDMS/R engine (the bulk of which is the original IDMS) together with the integrated data dictionary (IDD). IDMS/R makes extensive use of this dictionary. The IDD contains not only schema and subschema descriptions, but also descriptions of users, programs, systems, reports, forms, relational views, security constraints, and the like. The IDD is itself an IDMS database and can be processed by the IDMS/R query languages and other facilities.

The presence of the IDD greatly facilitates database administration and enables other products in the family to benefit from one another. For example, a column heading defined for a data-item in one report can be used without redefinition for the same data-item in other reports. This not only improves report preparation productivity, but also increases application consistency.

As shown in Figure 14–3, several product categories employ the core engine and IDD. Cullinet provides a variety of products in each of these

**Figure 14–3**

IDMS/R product
family

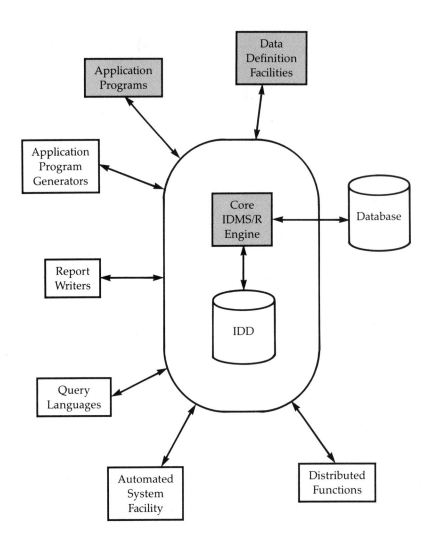

categories. *Data definition facilities* are a set of compilers and interactive processors that enable the database designer to specify the structure of the
database and related entities. You will see the application of several of these
compilers in the next section. *Application programs* issue DBMS requests that
are processed by the core IDMS/R product. In addition, Cullinet provides
*application program generators* that build application programs for standard
types of processing.

The product family includes several *report writers* that can be used to
construct reports without application programming. Additionally, Cullinet

provides both structured and natural language *query languages*. (Such languages are not part of the DBTG model. They were added by Cullinet.) The *automated system facility* (ASF) is a menu-driven system generator that can construct not only application programs but also schema, subschema, and view definitions. The ASF can be used by nonprogrammers to construct simple databases and applications and by programmers to build prototypes and the fundamental structures of more complicated applications.

Finally, Cullinet provides a number of products to facilitate *distributed database processing*. Some of these products support distribution to Type II microcomputer databases (see Chapter 10), whereas others facilitate the sharing of data among different databases on the same computer as well as between mini- and mainframe computers.

In this chapter, we will address only the components of this product family that will help you learn about processing CODASYL DBTG databases. This means that we will consider the core engine, the data definition, and the application program components of Figure 14–3.

## IDMS/R DATABASE DEFINITION AND ACCESS

Defining an IDMS/R database and preparing application programs is a five-step process, as illustrated in Figure 14–4. First, a data dictionary database that will describe the users' database must be defined. Cullinet provides a set of interactive tools, called IDD Utilities, for this purpose. Definitions of users, programs, security constraints, and other system features can be stored in the data dictionary at this time (or at any later time as well).

A data dictionary can describe more than one database. For example, the Data Administration Department might maintain one data dictionary for all of the corporation's centralized data. Such a data dictionary might describe several databases as well as many non-database files.

Data-items and records can be defined in either of two ways. The first way is to describe them separately from any particular database. The descriptions are stored in the IDD. Later, during schema definition, these predefined data-items and records can be copied into the schema description. The other way is to define data-items and records at the time the schema is defined. The first alternative is preferred if the data dictionary will be used for administering data for more than one database or for non-database files.

The second step shown in Figure 14–4 is to define and compile the schema. The schema contains the complete view of the database, including names of all records, data-items, and sets, as well as other descriptions discussed later in this chapter.

The third step is to compile the Device Media Control Language (DMCL) description. This description defines physical characteristics of the media used to store the database. It includes definitions of block and buffer sizes,

**Figure 14—4**
IDMS/R data defini-
tion and program
support facilities

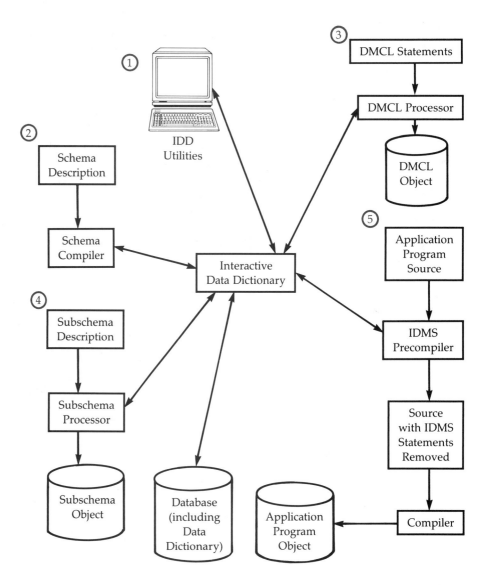

a definition of the file(s) used for journaling, and other physical file definitions. The output of the DMCL compilation is used by the operating
system when database files are opened. One or more DMCL descriptions
can be defined for each schema.

In step four of this process, subschema descriptions are compiled. For
IDMS/R, a subschema is a subset of the schema or it is a subset plus records

that are logically constructed from a subset of the schema. Schema records, data-items, and sets can be omitted from the subschema, and data-items can be reordered. The logical construction of records is basically a predefined join, as you will see. Each schema can have many subschema definitions.

The fifth and final step is to compile the application programs. As with DB2, programs using IDMS/R contain embedded DML statements that are not valid host language statements. IDMS/R statements, such as FIND or STORE, must be translated by a precompiler into valid host language statements. The IDMS/R precompiler also records in the data dictionary the operations each program performs on specific data. Because this data is tracked automatically by the data dictionary subsystem, the IDD is considered an *active* (versus *passive*) data dictionary. IDMS/R provides COBOL, PL/I, FORTRAN, and assembler precompilers.

The last section of this chapter will illustrate steps two through five of this process for the library database designed in Chapter 13. In that section you will see how databases designed for the DBTG model are implemented. Although step one, building the initial data dictionary, is a prerequisite to using IDMS/R for any database processing, it is too product-specific to be presented here.

## IDMS/R PHYSICAL STORAGE

Figure 14–5 shows IDMS/R storage structures. Each database is logically composed of one or more *areas*. Each area contains one or more *record types*. In Figure 14–6, the Example Database is composed of two areas, AREA-A

**Figure 14–5**
IDMS/R storage
structures

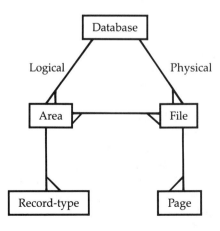

**Figure 14—6**
Example logical data-
base structure

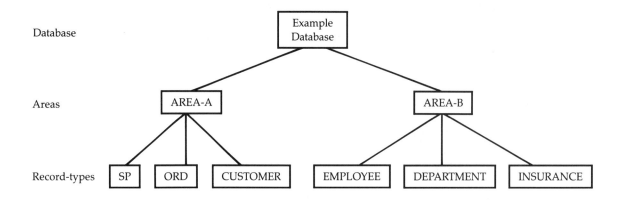

Database

Areas

Record-types

and AREA-B. AREA-A contains SP (salesperson), ORD (order), and CUS-
TOMER records, while AREA-B contains EMPLOYEE, DEPARTMENT, and
INSURANCE records.

You can envision areas as partitions of the database. IDMS/R allows
backup and recovery on an area basis. Thus the entire database need not
be saved or restored all at once. This feature saves time when backing up
and recovering large databases.

Physically, each IDMS/R database is composed of one or more *direct
access files* (see Appendix A). The relationship between areas and files is
many-to-many. A file may hold one or more areas or parts of areas, and an
area may reside on one or more files or parts of files. The particular correspondence of areas and files is determined by the database designer and
specified in the schema description, as you will see. Figure 14–7 shows one
possible correspondence of files and areas for the Example Database.

### Pages

Each file is composed of fixed-length blocks called *pages*. Pages contain
logical records and unused space. The structure of a page is shown in Figure
14–8. Pages have header and footer sections that contain DBMS overhead
data. Additionally, a *line index* is included for each logical record in the page.
The line indexes are stored in reverse order from the footer. Line index
number 1 is closest to the footer, line index number 2 is next, and so forth.
A line index contains the record ID, the location of the record in the page,
the total length of the record, and other data. The *database key (DBKEY)* of
a record is the number of the page containing the record, concatenated with
the record's line index number (counting backwards from the footer) in the

**Figure 14–7**
Area, record, and file
correspondence

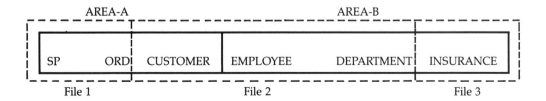

page. If the page in Figure 14–8 is numbered 2008, then the DBKEY value
for logical record C is 2008:3. Thus, every record has a unique DBKEY value.

## Set Representation

IDMS/R represents sets in two ways. One method uses *linked lists* (called
*chains* in IDMS/R documentation). For each set, a forward pointer field is
added to owner and member records. (Optionally, the designer may request
reverse pointers and owner pointers as well. For a discussion of linked lists,
see Appendix B.) Figure 14–9 shows an example of pointers for two sets
relating CUST, SP, and ORD records. CUST 100 owns ORD1 and ORD3.
CUST 200 owns ORD2. SP A owns ORD1, ORD2, and ORD3. Each ORD
record contains two pointers, one for the next sibling in the CUST-ORD set
and one for the next sibling in the SP-ORD set. A zero in the sibling pointer
indicates that no more siblings exist in the set.

**Figure 14–8**
Structure of an IDMS
page

| Header | Logical Record A | |
|---|---|---|
| Logical Record B | | Logical Record C |
| Logical Record D | | |
| Unused Space | | |
| | | D |
| C | B | A | Footer |

**Figure 14–9**

Linked lists used to
represent DBTG sets

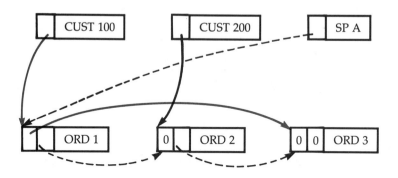

An IDMS/R pointer is a DBKEY value. For example, if ORD2's DBKEY
is 2008:1, then all pointers to ORD2 (in this example, the pointer in CUST
200 and the second sibling pointer in ORD1) would be 2008:1.

The second method of set representation is via *indexes*. With this method,
IDMS/R uses links to maintain lists of pointers to database records. In Figure
14–10, CUSTOMER records are chained to index records, which, in turn,
point to ORDER records. This sketch is simplified. Actually, IDMS/R keeps

**Figure 14–10**

Use of index to repre-
sent DBTG sets

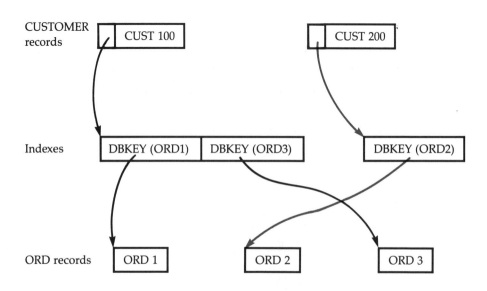

both forward and reverse links on the index records, although they are not shown in the figure.

IDMS/R uses indexes to maintain system sets as well. Consider the Library Database introduced in Chapter 12. Suppose that TTLE records are stored using CALL# as a key. This means that TTLE records can be retrieved directly by call number. Suppose, however, that users also want to retrieve TTLE records by TNAME. To satisfy this requirement, the IDMS/R database developer would define a *system set indexed on TNAME*. IDMS/R would then build a structure similar to that in Figure 14–10. The index records would contain values of TNAME in sorted order. Each index record would also contain the DBKEY of the TTLE record containing that TNAME.

# IDMS/R DATA DEFINITION

With the exception of logical records, IDMS/R data definition is fundamentally in accordance with the 1971 DBTG model. However, the discussion in Chapter 13 was based on the 1981 model, and IDMS/R differs from that model in several ways. We will first discuss those differences. Then we will describe the contents of the schema, DMCL, and subschema descriptions.

### DDL Differences from the 1981 DBTG Model

IDMS/R differs from the DBTG model in the definition and treatment of records, sets, and subschemas. We will consider each.

**Record Differences.**   With respect to record definition, the two major differences between IDMS/R and the 1981 DBTG model are that in IDMS/R (1) a record type must be assigned to an area when it is defined and (2) a location mode must be defined for each record. We will consider both.

First of all, IDMS/R supports the concept of *areas*, which is not included in the 1981 DBTG model. As mentioned earlier, an area is a group of one or more record types. Records are assigned to areas when they are defined in the schema. All records of a given type reside in a single area. Areas are mapped to particular locations in physical files by means of the schema description. The area concept was removed from the 1981 DBTG definition because the committee decided to eliminate all concepts that referred to physical constructs. The concept lived on in this implementation of the DBTG model, however. Thus, in IDMS/R, the record definition within the schema must contain the phrase

```
WITHIN AREA (area-name)
```

Second, a *location mode* must be defined for each record. This mode defines a way of allocating the record to storage and of finding it later. Three options are available: CALC, VIA, and DIRECT. (Actually a fourth option exists, but it involves the storage of non-database data that is managed by the DBMS.) A location mode of CALC (for calculation) means that a data-item (or composite) of the record will be used in an algorithm to calculate a page number. This process, called *hashing*, is explained in Appendix A. If the page is full, the record will overflow to another page and a pointer will be established to it.

The second location mode is VIA a set. With this option, the record will be stored physically close to (in this sense, "close to" means in the same page) one of its set owners. Obviously, if the record belongs to more than one set, it can be stored close to only one of its owners—otherwise data duplication would result. Thus, the VIA phrase can name only one set. If the set owner and set member are located in different areas, they will be located in the same relative position in the areas, or as close to it as possible. The advantage of this approach is that set members will have the same sequential order in their area as set owners have in theirs. Thus, when set owners are processed in sequence, set members will be processed in sequence as well. This arrangement improves performance.

The third location mode is DIRECT. With this mode, the user suggests to IDMS/R the page on which the record is to be stored. IDMS/R will place the record on that page or as close to it as possible. After the record is stored, IDMS/R will return the actual DBKEY value to the application program. The program will save this value so that it can be used to FIND the record during subsequent processing.

The DIRECT location mode gives an application program control over the physical location of data. Except in highly unusual situations, this location mode should not be used. Using it makes the application program too dependent on hardware and physical record addresses. The first two items in Figure 14–11 summarize these differences.

Figure 14–12 presents a sample IDMS/R record definition. (You will see other examples later in this chapter.) The record is named (in this case, ORD) and may be given a RECORD ID. In earlier versions of IDMS/R, the database designer *had* to assign a unique number to each record (for example, RECORD ID IS 101). With the current version, the compiler will assign these numbers if the designer specifies AUTO, as shown in the figure. After the record ID is assigned, the location mode is defined (in this case, CALC) and the record is allocated to an area (in this case, AREA-A). Finally, the data-items of the record are defined using COBOL-like notation.

**Set Differences.** IDMS/R also differs from the DBTG model in its treatment of sets. IDMS/R does not support three of the set features described in Chapter 13. First, it has no CHECK facility. IDMS/R will not ensure that specified data conditions exist among member and owner data-items. Second, it has no SET SELECTION clause. Third, it has no FIXED retention status. Only MANDATORY and OPTIONAL retention status are allowed.

IDMS/R also requires several additions to the 1981 set specification. Some examples of these are shown in Figure 14–13. First, the type of sup-

**Figure 14—11**
Features that distin-
guish IDMS/R from
1981 DBTG DDL

1. Areas supported

2. Record definitions
   - Assigned to areas
   - Location mode required:
     CALC
     VIA
     DIRECT

3. Some set constructs not supported:
   - No CHECK
   - No SET SELECTION
   - No FIXED members

**Figure 14—12**
Sample IDMS/R
schema record
definition

```
RECORD NAME IS ORD
RECORD ID IS AUTO
LOCATION MODE IS CALC USING ORD-NUM
DUPLICATES NOT ALLOWED
WITHIN AREA-A

     05    ORD-NUM       PIC 9999
     05    SP-NUM        PIC 999
     05    SP-NAME       PIC X(15)
     05    ORD-DATE      PIC 9(6)
     05    CUST-NUM      PIC 999
     .
     .
     .
     etc. for remaining data-
     item definitions
```

**Figure 14—13**
Sample IDMS/R
schema set definition

```
SET NAME IS SALES
ORDER IS SORTED
MODE IS CHAINED
OWNER IS SP
     LINKED TO PRIOR
     NEXT DBKEY POSITION IS 3
     PRIOR DBKEY POSITION IS 4
MEMBER IS ORD
     NEXT DBKEY POSITION IS 1
     PRIOR DBKEY POSITION IS 2
MANDATORY AUTOMATIC
ASCENDING KEY IS ORD-DATE
     DUPLICATES ALLOWED
```

porting data structure must be declared with one of the following two phrases:

```
MODE IS CHAINED
MODE IS INDEXED
```

If the mode is CHAINED and prior pointers are desired (that is, if the designer wants a linked list with backward pointers), the phrase LINKED TO PRIOR must also be included.

Additionally, the database designer must indicate the location of pointers in the record. In earlier versions of IDMS/R, the designer had to specify a particular position, such as NEXT DBKEY POSITION IS 3, where the 3 referred to the third pointer slot in the record. The current version does not require this. The designer can specify NEXT DBKEY POSITION IS AUTO and the schema compiler will assign the pointer position. Figure 14–13 declares specific positions so that you can understand this feature. Figure 14–14 illustrates the set pointer structure declared in Figure 14–13. Unless you have some very unusual requirements, it is better to allow the compiler to allocate pointer positions.

Observe that DBKEY positions are declared for forward pointers in both the owner and the member records. Furthermore, if PRIOR pointers are requested, the PRIOR DBKEY positions must also be declared. The remainder of the IDMS/R set definitions correspond to the discussion in Chapter 13. Set differences are also summarized in Figure 14–11.

**Subschema Differences.** Several important differences exist between IDMS/R subschemas and those defined in the 1981 DBTG model. First,

**Figure 14—14**
Instance of SALES set
from Figure 14-13

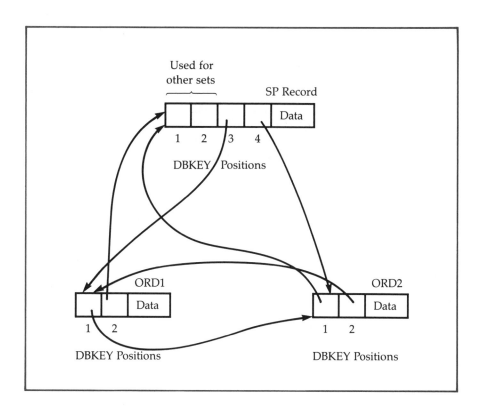

IDMS/R does not allow record, set, or data-item aliases as defined in Chapter 13. Names used in the subschema must be the same as those used in the schema. However, IDMS/R allows aliases in one special case. Records or data-items can have aliases if required to support the naming conventions of particular languages. For example, some versions of FORTRAN require data-item names to be no more than six characters in length. COBOL allows thirty-character data-names. To adapt to these language differences, a record or data-item can be given different names for use in programs written in different languages. Additional subschema differences are that areas and the DMCL must be identified in the subschema.

The biggest difference between IDMS/R subschemas and the DBTG model concerns logical records and path-groups. We will defer consideration of this topic until we present illustrations from the Library Database later in this chapter.

### Schema Definition

Figure 14–15 shows the skeleton of an IDMS/R schema description, which contains five major sections. The first section names the schema and may include comments. The second section defines files. In this case, three files are defined. Note the references to the external file names DB1, DB2, and DB3. These are the names that the operating system uses to relate files to physical devices.

The third section of the schema defines areas. The example in Figure 14–15 defines two areas. AREA-A is 500 pages long. The first 400 pages reside in relative blocks 101 through 500 of FILE1. The remaining 100 pages reside in relative blocks 101 through 200 of FILE2.

AREA-B resides on FILE2 and FILE3. The first 500 pages of AREA-B reside in relative blocks 401 through 900 of FILE2. The remaining 500 pages reside in relative blocks 1501 through 2000 of FILE3. (Unallocated blocks on the files are used for other purposes or reserved for future expansion.)

The fourth section of the schema description contains record descriptions and the fifth section contains set descriptions. A complete schema description is presented in the last section of this chapter.

**Figure 14–15**

IDMS/R schema for
Example Database

```
SCHEMA DESCRIPTION
SCHEMA NAME IS EXAMPLE
FILE DESCRIPTION
FILE NAME IS FILE1 ASSIGN TO DB1
FILE NAME IS FILE2 ASSIGN TO DB2
FILE NAME IS FILE3 ASSIGN TO DB3
AREA DESCRIPTION
AREA NAME IS AREA-A
     RANGE IS   1 THRU 500
     WITHIN FILE1 FROM 101 THRU 500
     WITHIN FILE2 FROM 101 THRU 200
AREA NAME IS AREA-B
     RANGE IS   1 THRU 1000
     WITHIN FILE2 FROM 401 THRU 900
     WITHIN FILE3 FROM 1501 THRU 2000
RECORD DESCRIPTION

     (Record descriptions like those in Figure 14-12 go here.)

SET DESCRIPTION

     (Set descriptions like those in Figure 14-13 go here.)
```

## DMCL Description

The Device Media Control Language describes sizes of file pages and the journal file. It has four sections, as shown in Figure 14–16. The first section is the DEVICE-MEDIA DESCRIPTION, which names both the DMCL module and the schema to which it corresponds. The second section defines buffers—areas of main memory used to transfer data to and from the files. The third part of the DMCL description associates areas with buffers. The area descriptions need not be repeated because the DMCL compiler will copy them from the schema.

The last section of the DMCL description names the journal files, specifies the types of devices on which journals will reside, and optionally defines archive files to which journals will be copied when they become full. Details about this section are beyond the scope of this text.

## Subschema Descriptions

An IDMS/R subschema describes the subset of the database to be included in the subschema and defines logical records and path-groups. Subschema descriptions include AREA, RECORD, and SET statements, as shown in Figure 14–17. These statements specify which constructs in the schema are to be included in the subschema.

Two options are available for defining records. First, records can be copied from the schema just as they appear there. For example, record SP in Figure 14–17 is copied in its entirety. Alternatively, a subschema record can be defined as a subset of data-items in a schema record. In this case,

---

**Figure 14–16**

Sample IDMS/R
DMCL description

```
DEVICE-MEDIA DESCRIPTION
DEVICE-MEDIA NAME IS EX-DMCL OF EXAMPLE
BUFFER SECTION
      BUFFER NAME IS BUFFPOOL
      PAGE CONTAINS 3156 CHARACTERS
      BUFFER CONTAINS 7 PAGES
AREA SECTION
      COPY AREA-A
          BUFFER IS BUFFPOOL
      COPY AREA-B
          BUFFER IS BUFFPOOL
JOURNAL SECTION
      (A description of journal files, devices,
      and the journal archive go here.)
```

**Figure 14—17**

Example of IDMS/R
subschema
description

```
SUBSCHEMA NAME IS EX-SUB OF EXAMPLE
        DMCL NAME IS EX-DMCL.

AREA NAME IS AREA-A.

RECORD NAME IS SP
        ELEMENTS ARE ALL.

RECORD NAME IS ORD
        ELEMENTS ARE
                ORD-NUM, ORD-DATE, SP-NUM.

SET NAME IS SALES.

[logical record and path-group names go here]
```

the portion to be included must be identified. As mentioned previously, all
names in the subschema must correspond to names in the schema description. However, the order of the data-items may be different. In Figure 14–17
the data-items ORD-NUM, ORD-DATE, and SP-NUM of ORD are included,
but their sequence differs from the sequence in which they were defined
in the schema record (see Figure 14–12).

Logical record and path-group statements define pseudo-records that
are logical compositions of records and sets in the subschema. The logical
record statements describe the structure of the pseudo-records, and the
path-group statements describe one or more means for accessing them. We
will illustrate this later when we implement a portion of the Library Database in IDMS/R.

**Restrictions on Subschema Design.**    STORE and ERASE commands pose
special requirements for subschema design. If a program is to issue either
STORE or ERASE commands on a record, the following information must
be included in the subschema: the record to be processed, all sets in which
the record is an automatic member, the owner records of such sets, and all
other member record types of those sets (for sets having two or more record
types as members). Additionally, for ERASE, all sets for which the record
to be deleted is an owner and all member records of those sets must be
specified.

Further, IDMS/R provides several options of ERASE, as described in
the next section. With these options, it is possible for child records, grand-

child records, and records of more distant generations to be deleted implicitly. As a general rule, IDMS/R requires that any record that can possibly be deleted indirectly via set membership must appear in the subschema along with the set that has provided the connection. This ensures that no command will remove a record that is not visible in the subschema.

## IDMS/R DATA MANIPULATION FACILITIES

IDMS/R provides basically the same DML facilities that were discussed in Chapter 13. However, the format of some commands is different, and several additional options are available because IDMS/R supports areas. First we will consider data retrieval commands and then update commands.

### Data Retrieval Commands

IDMS/R DML commands function in the two-phase mode described for the DBTG model in Chapter 13. First a record is found, establishing the current of run-unit. Then an action is taken with regard to the current record.

For example, to retrieve a record, we issue a FIND command and then a GET command. Because the FIND/GET pair is frequently used, IDMS/R combines them into a single command called OBTAIN. OBTAIN has the same parameters as FIND and acts like a FIND followed automatically by a GET. Consequently, all options and parameters defined for FIND are also available for OBTAIN.

IDMS/R supports six formats of FIND (and OBTAIN), as summarized in Figure 14–18. The first format causes a record that is current of its record type, current of a set, or current of an area to become current of run-unit. The second form of FIND is used to identify a record by its position in a set or an area. For example, the following command will identify the first ORDER record in AREA-A:

```
FIND FIRST ORD WITHIN AREA-A
```

Because IDMS/R requires all records of one type to reside in the same area, all records of a type can be sequentially processed using this form of FIND. However, the order of the records will be determined by the DBMS, and they will be in no particular *logical* order. (When records need to be processed in sequential order by data-item value, a system set is used, as discussed in Chapter 13.)

The third form of FIND identifies records by ownership. Consider the set SALES with owner SP and members ORD. If an ORD record is current of run-unit, then the command

```
FIND OWNER WITHIN SALES
```

will establish the owner of the ORD record as the current of run-unit.

**Figure 14–18**

Six formats of FIND
(and OBTAIN) recog-
nized by IDMS/R

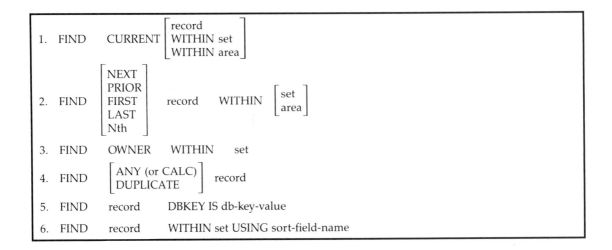

The fourth version of the FIND command identifies records based on a CALC field. To use this form of FIND, the location mode of the record must be CALC. The application program sets the value of the CALC field and then issues the FIND. For example, if the location mode of ORD is CALC USING ORD-NUM, the following commands will identify an ORD record:

```
MOVE "123" TO ORD-NUM
FIND ANY ORD
```

and then

```
FIND DUPLICATE ORD
```

The second FIND command is valid only if the schema description for ORD records includes the phrase DUPLICATES ARE ALLOWED in the location mode declaration.

The fifth mode of FIND can be used only if the application program knows a record's DBKEY. Suppose that the DBKEY for a record is stored in the variable REC-KEY. In such a case, the following FIND can be used:

```
FIND ORD DBKEY IS REC-KEY
```

This form of FIND can be used whether or not the record's location mode is DIRECT. The sole requirement is that the program obtain the record's DBKEY value. Such values can be obtained from IDMS/R in a variety of ways. However, the use of DBKEY is generally not good practice because it makes an application program dependent on physical addresses.

The last form of FIND can be used for records belonging to sorted sets. Assume that the set SALES is ordered by the data-item ORD-DATE. Then

```
MOVE "881226" TO ORD-DATE
FIND ORD WITHIN SALES USING ORD-DATE
```

will find the first ORD record in the SALES set having an ORD-DATE equal to 881226.

As mentioned, all these formats are also valid for OBTAIN. For example,

```
MOVE "881226" TO ORD-DATE
OBTAIN ORD WITHIN SALES USING ORD-DATE
```

will retrieve (FIND and GET) the first qualifying ORD record.

## Update Commands

The IDMS/R update commands are nearly identical to the DBTG update commands described in Chapter 13. Examples are shown in Figure 14-19. To STORE a record, the data-items of the record are first filled. Then the STORE command is executed. If the new record is an automatic member of any set, the currency indicators of those sets need to be established before the STORE is issued. For example, in Figure 14-19, a SALES set occurrence is established before the STORE ORD is issued.

The MODIFY command changes the values of data-items. The recommended way of changing data-items is to first fill the data-items with an OBTAIN command. Then data-item values are changed, and the MODIFY

---

**Figure 14-19**

Examples of IDMS/R
update commands

```
1.   Fill ORD data-items
     Establish SALES set occurrence.
     STORE ORD.

2.   OBTAIN ORD (using any of six forms)
     Change data-items.
     MODIFY ORD.

3.   ERASE ORD.
     ERASE ORD PERMANENT MEMBERS.
     ERASE ORD SELECTIVE MEMBERS.
     ERASE ORD ALL MEMBERS.
```

command is issued. If a CALC data-item is changed, IDMS/R might physically relocate the record in the database. In this case, the record's DBKEY value will be changed.

The IDMS/R ERASE command has four options. ERASE ORD deletes the current of run-unit record (which must be an ORD record). If, however, that record owns any sets, the ERASE command is ignored. The ERASE PERMANENT command deletes the identified record and all mandatory set members that are connected to it. Optional set members are disconnected. ERASE SELECTIVE commands delete the identified record and all mandatory set members connected to it. Optional members are also deleted if they do not belong to an occurrence of another set. Finally, the ERASE ALL command deletes the indicated record and all records that are connected to it, whether they are mandatory or optional.

IDMS/R CONNECT and DISCONNECT commands operate exactly as described in Chapter 13.

## IDMS/R CONCURRENT PROCESSING AND RECOVERY

IDMS/R provides complete facilities for control of concurrent processing and recovery. These facilities include several different forms of locking and several means of declaring transactions. The IDMS/R recovery mechanism is similar to the one described in Chapter 7.

### IDMS/R Locking Facilities

IDMS/R locking can be done at two levels of granularity. A single lock can be placed on an entire *area* or separate locks can be placed on individual *records*. An area lock is placed when the area is first opened. Record locks are placed when records are used, or at the discretion of the application program.

**Area Locks.**   Before an application program can access data, the area that contains the data must be opened. This is done by issuing a READY command. READY informs IDMS/R that the application program will be accessing data in the area and indicates whether the access will be retrieval only or retrieval and update. Additionally, depending on the parameters in the READY command, locks will be placed on the area. When an application program has completed processing of data in an area, it issues a FINISH command. At that point all locks are released.

An area can be opened for RETRIEVAL, meaning the application program will issue only FIND/GET/OBTAIN commands. Or an area can be opened for UPDATE, in which case all IDMS/R commands may be issued.

Further, when an area is readied, the application program may ask for a PROTECTED lock, an EXCLUSIVE lock, or no lock at all. A PROTECTED lock prevents other run-units from making concurrent updates of data in the area. An EXCLUSIVE lock prevents other run-units from concurrently accessing the area in any way. Neither of these is requested if the application is processing the database by itself (that is, if it is a single-user database) or if record locks are going to be used instead of area locks. Examples of READY commands are

```
READY AREA-A RETRIEVAL
READY AREA-A PROTECTED RETRIEVAL
READY AREA-A EXCLUSIVE UPDATE
```

The combinations of locks and processing intents are defined in Figure 14–20a. The consequences of issuing PROTECTED and EXCLUSIVE locks are presented in Figure 14–20b.

Area locks can cause long processing delays because an area may contain many records, and programs may lock entire areas for long periods of time. Under these conditions, record locking may be more appropriate.

**Record Locks.** If an area is readied with no locks specified, IDMS/R will provide record-level locking. Two types of record locks, analogous to the two types of area locks, are available. A *shared lock* prevents concurrent update of the record but will allow concurrent retrieval. An *exclusive lock* prevents concurrent access of any kind. Furthermore, record locks can be placed *implicitly* by IDMS/R or *explicitly* by the application program.

If the implicit lock feature is selected when IDMS/R is installed, IDMS/R will automatically place locks on records in unlocked areas. A shared lock will be placed on the current of run-unit, current of each record type, current of each set, and current of each area. Shared locks are released when currency indicators change. An exclusive lock will be placed on all modified records (STORE, MODIFY, ERASE, CONNECT, DISCONNECT). The exclusive lock will be held until a FINISH, COMMIT, or ROLLBACK command is issued (see next section).

Explicit locks are set by application programs in one of two ways. First, a lock may be obtained by issuing either a FIND or OBTAIN command with an embedded lock request. The keyword KEEP signals IDMS/R to obtain a lock. Consider these FIND statements:

```
FIND KEEP FIRST ORD WITHIN AREA-A
FIND KEEP EXCLUSIVE FIRST ORD WITHIN AREA-A
```

The first example places a shared lock on the found record, and the second example places an exclusive lock on that record.

A second way to obtain a lock on a record is to use the KEEP command. This command places a lock on a current record. Consider these examples:

```
KEEP CURRENT ORD
KEEP CURRENT WITHIN AREA-A
KEEP EXCLUSIVE CURRENT WITHIN SALES
```

**Figure 14−20**

READY command
definitions

*Lock Request*

| | | NONE | PROTECTED | EXCLUSIVE |
|---|---|---|---|---|
| *Processing* *Intent* | RETRIEVAL | No area lock. Read only. | No concurrent update. Read only. | No concurrent access. Read only. |
| | UPDATE | No area lock. Update allowed. | No concurrent update. Update allowed. | No concurrent access. Update allowed. |

a. READY command options

*Lock Status at Time of Request*

| | | NONE | PROTECTED | EXCLUSIVE |
|---|---|---|---|---|
| *Request* | RETRIEVAL/ PROTECTED | Process | Process | Wait |
| | UPDATE/ PROTECTED | Process | Wait | Wait |
| | RETRIEVAL/ EXCLUSIVE | Process | Wait | Wait |
| | UPDATE/ EXCLUSIVE | Process | Wait | Wait |

b. Processing of READY commands

The first two examples place shared locks. The first one locks current of ORD record type, and the second one locks current of an area. The third example obtains an exclusive lock on the current of SALES set.

All explicitly acquired locks are held until a FINISH, COMMIT, or ROLLBACK command is issued.

### IDMS/R Checkpoints

The term *checkpoint* has a different meaning for IDMS/R than it does for DB2. An IDMS/R checkpoint is equivalent to what we called a *transaction* in Chapter 7 and what DB2 calls a *logical unit of work* (LUW). A checkpoint is a complete, atomic, durable set of actions that is performed by a single run-unit.

A checkpoint is initiated when the READY command is issued. A checkpoint is terminated with a subsequent FINISH, COMMIT, or ROLLBACK command.

The FINISH command not only terminates the checkpoint, but also releases all locks and closes all areas from further processing. All currency indicators are set to null. The format of the FINISH command is

```
FINISH
```

COMMIT terminates the current checkpoint and initiates a new one. Once a COMMIT command has been completed successfully, all changes made to the database become permanent. They will endure system crashes.

IDMS/R COMMIT processing differs from DB2 COMMIT processing. When an IDMS/R COMMIT is executed, all changes made to the database are written to the log, and system buffers containing these changes are written to the database. After the operating system informs IDMS/R that both of these actions have been completed, a checkpoint message is written to the log. The run-unit then resumes processing. Thus, at a COMMIT point, the recovery system is guaranteed that the database and the log are synchronized.

COMMIT has two formats:

```
COMMIT
COMMIT ALL
```

The first command commits all changes to the database and releases all locks except those on current records. Currency indicators are unchanged. The second format commits all changes to the database and releases all locks, including those on current records. The currency indicators are set to null.

The ROLLBACK command aborts a checkpoint. If the journal file is kept on a disk device, all changes made in the current checkpoint are automatically removed from the database. If the journal is on tape, the area processed by the program issuing the ROLLBACK command is marked as unchangeable until the database is processed against the journal file by an IDMS/R utility. Here are the two formats of the ROLLBACK command:

```
ROLLBACK
ROLLBACK CONTINUE
```

A run-unit issuing the first command will abort the current checkpoint and will terminate. This command is equivalent to abort with FINISH. The second format rolls back the current checkpoint but allows processing to continue.

## IDMS/R Recovery

IDMS/R has two modes of recovery. One is used when the journal is maintained on tape, and another is used when the journal is on disk. We will assume in this discussion that the journal is on disk.

Recovery techniques using a disk journal are similar to those discussed in Chapter 7. IDMS/R records in the journal file the start and end of checkpoints and the before and after images of all changes in the database. The journal is used to recover from failures. The next three sections discuss recovery from unsuccessful checkpoints, system crashes, and database damage.

**Unsuccessful Checkpoint Termination.**   A run-unit can abort by executing a ROLLBACK command, by unexpectedly terminating (perhaps due to a program error), or by *timing out*. The last term requires explanation. Whenever a run-unit goes into the wait state, IDMS/R monitors the time it has been waiting. If wait time exceeds a predetermined amount (set during IDMS/R installation), the run-unit is automatically aborted. Time-out might occur when a run-unit waits too long for another run-unit to release a lock or because of a deadly embrace. Whatever the reason, a run-unit waiting too long will be aborted.

When a run-unit aborts, the before images of all changes in the current checkpoint are reapplied to the database. Assuming that implicit locks are in use, rollback will cause no problem to another run-unit because all records changed by the run-unit will have been exclusively locked. If explicit locks are used correctly, no problems will arise.

**System Crashes.**   When the system crashes, recovery is straightforward (to describe, anyway). The before images of all changes made by open checkpoints are applied to the database. Checkpoints in progress then need to be restarted. This means that when application programs are designed, they need to be made restartable at any checkpoint.

Recovery after a system crash is simpler for IDMS/R than it is for DB2. IDMS/R knows that the journal and the database are synchronized at each checkpoint. Thus every after image of a committed checkpoint is in the database, making it unnecessary to search the log for a synchronization point. (Observe the conflict in terminology!)

**Database Damage.**   When the database is damaged, it must be recovered from a previous database save. The saved copy is used to restore database files. Then all after images of checkpoints completed since the save are applied to the database. Checkpoints in progress at the time the system went down must be restarted.

IDMS/R is flexible in that the entire database can be saved (and recovered) or individual areas within the database can be saved (or recovered). However, for the operations staff, saving and recovering *portions* of the database is more complex than saving and recovering the entire database. Despite this drawback, the ability to save and recover parts of the database is a beneficial feature for large databases. Such databases need to be processed by a seasoned and well-trained operations staff.

# IDMS/R SECURITY

IDMS/R provides several types of security. All of the security features are optional, however, and the database developer or DBA must decide which to use and how to use them. We will consider IDMS/R security facilities from the standpoint of subjects, and we will use the Fernandez, Summers, and Wood security model introduced in Chapter 7. IDMS/R security features are summarized in Figure 14–21.

## User Authorization

IDMS/R provides no facility to restrict users from access to application programs or, through such programs, to the database. However, IDMS/R provides facilities to restrict the processing of schema and subschema descriptions. Users can be identified by name and specific processing permissions (display, create, modify, delete) defined for the schema and any of its subschemas. Further, permissions for unidentified users of the schema or subschema can also be established. Finally, utilities that process the integrated data dictionary have ways of identifying users and their authorizations for processing components other than schema and subschema descriptions.

Because IDMS/R provides no facility to restrict people from using application programs, such authorization must be enforced by the application program itself. For example, a table of users and their authorizations to use programs could be stored in the database. Each application could then check this table before allowing the user to proceed.

## Program Registration

In general, any program can access any subschema. If an application programmer knows the name of a subschema and can determine its contents, he or she can write a program to use the subschema.

If this freedom is considered undesirable, the database developer can invoke an optional IDMS/R feature called *program registration*. When this feature is used, no application program can access a subschema (hence, the database) unless the name of the application program has been registered in the data dictionary. Further, the name(s) of the subschema(s) that a program can access is also registered. Thus, even a registered program may only access authorized subschemas. Clearly, to ensure that this arrangement is effective, the program register in the data dictionary must itself be protected.

## Subschema Authorization

When subschemas are defined, authorization can be established regarding the actions that may be taken against entities in the database. Authorization can be defined for areas, records, and sets.

**Figure 14-21**

Security provided by
IDMS/R

| Subject | Entity | Action | Constraint |
|---------|--------|--------|------------|
| User | Schema or Subschema | ALL<br>UPDATE<br>MODIFY<br>DELETE<br>DISPLAY | YES or NO<br>YES or NO<br>YES or NO<br>YES or NO<br>YES or NO |
| User | Programs | Any | Determined by programs. |
| Programs | Subschema | Use | Can be controlled with program registration facility. |
| Subschema | Area | RETRIEVAL<br>UPDATE<br>PROTECTED | YES or NO<br>YES or NO<br>YES or NO |
| Subschema | Records | FIND(OBTAIN)<br>GET<br>STORE<br>ERASE<br>MODIFY<br>CONNECT<br>DISCONNECT<br>KEEP | YES or NO<br>YES or NO<br>YES or NO<br>YES or NO<br>YES or NO<br>YES or NO<br>YES or NO<br>YES or NO |
| Subschema | Sets | CONNECT<br>DISCONNECT<br>FIND<br>KEEP | YES or NO<br>YES or NO<br>YES or NO<br>YES or NO |
| Any | Any | Any except IDMS command. | Use database procedure. |

## Area Security

When an area is copied into the subschema, the designer can optionally state which types of READY commands the user can issue. As shown in Figure 14-21, the user of the subschema can have permission to READY the area for either retrieval or update. This permission is either YES or NO. Also, the area may be readied in the PROTECTED lock mode. This permission also is either YES or NO. None of these permissions is conditioned on the ability of the user of the subschema to supply a password or other data.

## Record Security

When a record is copied into the subschema, the developer has the option of specifying which record-oriented DML commands the user can employ. All of the commands listed in Figure 14–21 are possibilities. Again, the permission is an unconditional YES or NO.

## Set Security

When a set is copied into the subschema, the developer has the option of specifying which set-oriented DML commands can be issued by the user. FIND and KEEP refer to options of the FIND command that use set membership—for example, FIND . . . WITHIN (a set).

## Authorization by Database Procedure

IDMS/R will exit to a database procedure while processing any DML command, and the database developer has the option of implementing security measures in these procedures. The procedure might converse with the user, ask for passwords, or request other identifying data. The only restriction is that no IDMS/R command may be issued from the procedure. Consequently, security data, if any, must be stored in non-database files.

# AN EXAMPLE OF IDMS/R USE

In this section we present a sample IDMS/R implementation of the Library Database and its BORROW subschema. We will also present the part of a COBOL program that uses the BORROW subschema to check out books to students. We will use the schema and subschema defined in Chapter 13.

## The IDMS/R Schema for the Library Database

The structure of the schema for the Library Database was shown in Figure 13–9. It includes eight types of records and seven relationships. Each record is represented by a separate DBTG record and each relationship is represented by a DBTG set, as explained in Chapter 13.

As stated previously, an IDMS/R schema has five major sections. The SCHEMA statements identify the schema name, assign schema definition processing permissions, and provide other miscellaneous information to the schema compiler. The FILE statements define files that will contain portions of the database. AREA, RECORD, and SET statements define areas, records, and sets. The schema definition is concluded with a VALIDATE statement. This statement, which is not part of the five sections, is a command to the compiler to process the schema and check for errors and inconsistencies.

### The SCHEMA Statement

An IDMS/R schema for the Library Database is shown in Figure 14–22. The name of the schema is LIBRARY and it is to be assigned the next version number. The IDMS/R data dictionary and schema compiler support different versions of the same schema. This capability is especially useful as the schema evolves because changes can be made to one version and tested. If problems exist, the developers can return to a previous version. The ASSIGN phrase informs the compiler that it is to assign unique record numbers to each record starting from number 500. (Previous versions of IDMS/R required the developer to make this assignment.)

The rest of the SCHEMA statement defines a user (ABC) and gives that user ALL permissions (add, change, delete, display, etc.) for processing the schema definition. Other data dictionary users (the PUBLIC ACCESS users) may only DISPLAY the schema.

Each statement in the schema definition is preceded by the command ADD. This is a command to the schema compiler and is not considered part of the schema definition.

**FILE Statements.**    The FILE statements define two database files and a journal file. The names to be used within the schema definition for the two database files are DBEX1 and DBEX2. The external names (DDNAMEs in IBM terminology) are DBFILE1 and DBFILE2. It may seem odd to define two sets of file names. One reason for doing this is that different versions of the schema may use the same internal name throughout, but may assign that internal name to different DDNAMEs. This decoupling facilitates the administration of the external files.

In a similar fashion, the internal schema/subschema name for the journal file is JOURNAL. Its external name is EXMPJRNL.

**AREA Statements.**    The LIBRARY schema includes three areas: BOOK-DATA, STU-DATA, and VIDEO-DATA containing 1000, 500, and 100 pages respectively. BOOK-DATA is assigned to the first 1000 pages of file DBEX1. It is a STANDARD area, meaning that it is not part of a file extent. (File extent is an IBM operating system concept. If you do not know this term, do not be concerned. It has little to do with database processing.) The STU-DATA area is assigned to pages 1001 to 1500 on file DBEX1, and VIDEO-DATA is assigned to the first 100 pages of file DBEX2.

Observe how the areas have been partitioned to different physical files. Any schema that does not include video data will never use file DBEX2. Such partitioning is employed to eliminate conflict among concurrent users, to help establish effective operations procedures, and the like.

**RECORD Statements.**    Each of the eight records in the Library Database is defined with a RECORD statement. Compare these definitions with those in the design in Figure 13–18.

**Figure 14—22**
IDMS/R schema
definition

```
ADD
SCHEMA NAME IS LIBRARY VERSION IS NEXT HIGHEST
        ASSIGN RECORD IDS FROM 500
        INCLUDE USER ABC
                REGISTERED FOR ALL
        PUBLIC ACCESS IS ALLOWED FOR DISPLAY

ADD
FILE NAME IS DBEX1
        ASSIGN TO DBFILE1

ADD
FILE NAME IS DBEX2
        ASSIGN TO DBFILE2

ADD
FILE NAME IS JOURNAL
        ASSIGN TO EXMPJRNL

ADD
AREA NAME IS BOOK-DATA
        TYPE IS STANDARD
        PAGE RANGE IS 1 THRU 1000
        WITHIN FILE DBEX1 FROM 1 FOR ALL

ADD
AREA NAME IS STU-DATA
        TYPE IS STANDARD
        PAGE RANGE IS 1 THRU 500
        WITHIN FILE DBEX1 FROM 1001 FOR ALL

ADD
AREA NAME IS VIDEO-DATA
        TYPE IS STANDARD
        PAGE RANGE IS 1 THRU 100
        WITHIN FILE DBEX2 FROM 1 FOR ALL

ADD
RECORD NAME IS PUB
        RECORD ID IS AUTO
        LOCATION MODE IS CALC USING PNAME
                DUPLICATES ARE NOT ALLOWED
```

**Figure 14—22**

*(continued)*

```
          WITHIN AREA BOOK-DATA OFFSET 0 PERCENT FOR 100 PERCENT
          CALL IDMSCOMP BEFORE STORE
          CALL IDMSCOMP BEFORE MODIFY
          CALL IDMSDCOM AFTER GET

          02  PNAME
                  PICTURE IS X(10)
                  USAGE IS DISPLAY
          02  ADDRESS
                  PICTURE IS X(25)
                  USAGE IS DISPLAY
          02  SALPSN
                  PICTURE IS X(20)
                  USAGE IS DISPLAY
          02  PPHONE
                  PICTURE IS 9(10)
                  USAGE IS DISPLAY

ADD
RECORD NAME IS TTLE
          RECORD ID IS AUTO
          LOCATION MODE IS CALC USING CALL#
                  DUPLICATES ARE NOT ALLOWED
          WITHIN AREA BOOK-DATA OFFSET 0 PERCENT FOR 100 PERCENT
          CALL IDMSCOMP BEFORE STORE
          CALL IDMSCOMP BEFORE MODIFY
          CALL IDMSDCOM AFTER GET
          02  CALL#
                  PICTURE IS X(8)
                  USAGE IS DISPLAY
          02  TNAME
                  PICTURE IS X(50)
                  USAGE IS DISPLAY
          02  PNAME
                  PICTURE IS X(10)
                  USAGE IS DISPLAY

ADD
RECORD NAME IS CPY
          RECORD ID IS AUTO
          LOCATION MODE IS VIA COLLECTION SET
          WITHIN AREA BOOK-DATA OFFSET 0 PERCENT FOR 100 PERCENT
          02  CALL#
                  PICTURE IS X(8)
                  USAGE IS DISPLAY
```

**Figure 14–22**

*(continued)*

```
        02   COPY#
                 PICTURE IS 9(2)
                 USAGE IS DISPLAY
        02   ACQDATE
                 PICTURE IS 9(6)
                 USAGE IS DISPLAY

ADD
RECORD NAME IS AUTH
        RECORD ID IS AUTO
        LOCATION MODE IS CALC USING ANAME
                 DUPLICATES ARE NOT ALLOWED
        WITHIN AREA BOOK-DATA OFFSET 0 PERCENT FOR 100 PERCENT
        02   ANAME
                 PICTURE IS X(30)
                 USAGE IS DISPLAY
        02   AFFILIATION
                 PICTURE IS X(30)
                 USAGE IS DISPLAY

ADD
RECORD NAME IS TA-INT
        RECORD ID IS AUTO
        LOCATION MODE IS VIA T-A SET
        WITHIN AREA BOOK-DATA OFFSET 0 PERCENT FOR 100 PERCENT
        02   CALL#
                 PICTURE IS X(8)
                 USAGE IS DISPLAY
        02   ANAME
                 PICTURE IS X(30)
                 USAGE IS DISPLAY
ADD
RECORD NAME IS STU
        RECORD ID IS AUTO
        LOCATION MODE IS CALC USING STUDENT#
                 DUPLICATES ARE NOT ALLOWED
        WITHIN AREA STU-DATA OFFSET 0 PERCENT FOR 100 PERCENT
        CALL IDMSCOMP BEFORE STORE
        CALL IDMSCOMP BEFORE MODIFY
        CALL IDMSDCOM AFTER GET
        02   STUDENT#
                 PICTURE IS 9(10)
                 USAGE IS DISPLAY
```

**Figure 14—22**

*(continued)*

```
              02   SNAME
                      PICTURE IS X(30)
                      USAGE IS DISPLAY
              02   SPHONE
                      PICTURE IS 9(7)
                      USAGE IS DISPLAY
ADD
RECORD NAME IS VID
          RECORD ID IS AUTO
          LOCATION MODE IS CALC USING (VID#, COPY#)
                  DUPLICATES ARE NOT ALLOWED
          WITHIN AREA VIDEO-DATA OFFSET 0 PERCENT FOR 100 PERCENT
          02   VID#
                      PICTURE IS 9(5)
                      USAGE IS DISPLAY
          02   VCOPY#
                      PICTURE IS 9(2)
                      USAGE IS DISPLAY
          02   VNAME
                      PICTURE IS X(40)
                      USAGE IS DISPLAY
          02   STUDENT#
                      PICTURE IS 9(10)
                      USAGE IS DISPLAY

ADD
RECORD NAME IS DUE-DATE
          RECORD ID IS AUTO
          LOCATION MODE IS VIA HISTORY SET
          WITHIN AREA BOOK-DATA OFFSET 0 PERCENT FOR 100 PERCENT

          02   DATE-DUE
                      PICTURE IS 9(6)
                      USAGE IS DISPLAY

ADD
SET NAME IS TITLE-SEQ
          ORDER IS SORTED
          MODE IS INDEX BLOCK CONTAINS 9 KEYS
          OWNER IS SYSTEM
                  WITHIN AREA BOOK-DATA OFFSET 0 PERCENT FOR 100 PERCENT
```

**Figure 14—22**

*(continued)*

```
        MEMBER IS TTLE
                INDEX DBKEY POSITION IS AUTO
                MANDATORY, AUTOMATIC
                ASCENDING KEY IS TNAME
                        DUPLICATES ARE NOT ALLOWED

ADD
SET NAME IS CPY-SEQ
        ORDER IS SORTED
        MODE IS INDEX BLOCK CONTAINS 12 KEYS
        OWNER IS SYSTEM
                WITHIN AREA BOOK-DATA OFFSET 0 PERCENT FOR 100 PERCENT
        MEMBER IS CPY
                INDEX DBKEY POSITION IS AUTO
                OPTIONAL, AUTOMATIC
                ASCENDING KEY IS (CALL#, COPY#)
                        DUPLICATES ARE NOT ALLOWED


ADD
SET NAME IS TA-INT-SEQ
        ORDER IS SORTED
        MODE IS INDEX BLOCK CONTAINS 9 KEYS
        OWNER IS SYSTEM
                WITHIN AREA BOOK-DATA OFFSET 0 PERCENT FOR 100 PERCENT
        MEMBER IS TA-INT
                INDEX DBKEY POSITION IS AUTO
                OPTIONAL, AUTOMATIC
                ASCENDING KEY IS (CALL#, ANAME)
                        DUPLICATES ARE NOT ALLOWED


ADD
SET NAME IS VID-STU
        ORDER IS SORTED
        MODE IS INDEX BLOCK CONTAINS 6 KEYS
        OWNER IS SYSTEM
                WITHIN AREA VIDEO-DATA OFFSET 0 PERCENT FOR 100
                        PERCENT
        MEMBER IS VID
                INDEX DBKEY POSITION IS AUTO
                OPTIONAL, AUTOMATIC
                ASCENDING KEY IS (STUDENT#)
                        DUPLICATES ARE NOT ALLOWED
```

**Figure 14—22**

*(continued)*

```
ADD
SET NAME IS PUBLISH
         ORDER IS SORTED
         MODE IS CHAIN
         OWNER IS PUB
            NEXT DBKEY POSITION IS AUTO
         MEMBER IS TTLE
            NEXT DBKEY POSITION IS AUTO
            MANDATORY AUTOMATIC
         ASCENDING KEY IS TNAME
            DUPLICATES ARE NOT ALLOWED


ADD
SET NAME IS T-A
         MODE IS CHAIN
         OWNER IS TTLE
            NEXT DBKEY POSITION IS AUTO
         MEMBER IS TA-INT
            NEXT DBKEY POSITION IS AUTO
            LINKED TO OWNER
               OWNER DBKEY POSITION IS AUTO
            MANDATORY AUTOMATIC


ADD
SET NAME IS A-T
         MODE IS CHAIN
         OWNER IS AUTH
            NEXT DBKEY POSITION IS AUTO
         MEMBER IS TA-INT
            NEXT DBKEY POSITION IS AUTO
            LINKED TO OWNER
               OWNER DBKEY POSITION IS AUTO
            MANDATORY AUTOMATIC


ADD
SET NAME IS COLLECTION
         ORDER IS SORTED
         MODE IS CHAIN
         OWNER IS TTLE
            NEXT DBKEY POSITION IS AUTO
         MEMBER IS CPY
            NEXT DBKEY POSITION IS AUTO
            MANDATORY AUTOMATIC
         ASCENDING KEY IS COPY#
```

```
SET NAME IS CHECKOUT
        ORDER IS LAST
        MODE IS INDEXED BLOCK CONTAINS 12 KEYS
        OWNER IS STU
        MEMBER IS CPY
        INDEX DBKEY POSITION IS AUTO
        OPTIONAL, MANUAL

SET NAME IS VCHKOUT
        ORDER IS LAST
        MODE IS CHAIN
        OWNER IS STU
          NEXT DBKEY POSITION IS AUTO
        MEMBER IS VID
          NEXT DBKEY POSITION IS AUTO
          LINKED TO OWNER
            OWNER DBKEY POSITION IS AUTO
          OPTIONAL, MANUAL

SET NAME IS HISTORY
        ORDER IS LAST
        MODE IS INDEXED BLOCK CONTAINS 6 KEYS
        OWNER IS CPY
        MEMBER IS DUE-DATE
          INDEX DBKEY POSITION IS AUTO
        MANDATORY, AUTOMATIC
VALIDATE
```

For this schema, all RECORD IDs are to be automatically assigned by the schema compiler. (These IDs are used by the data dictionary application. They have no impact on the database itself or its applications.) As stated earlier, each record must be assigned a location mode and an area. The location mode for PUB, for example, is CALC USING PNAME, and all PUB records are to be stored in the BOOK-DATA area. The OFFSET phrase indicates that PUB records may range over the entire area. If they were to be restricted to a portion of the area, the offset would indicate this. The specifics of offsets are beyond the scope of this text.

The PUB record definition presents examples of the use of database procedures. For instance, the DBMS engine is to call the procedure IDMS-COMP before any PUB records are stored. This procedure, which is provided by Cullinet, compresses data by removing repeating characters, blanks, and so forth. It is to be called before PUB data is stored or modified. Another procedure, IDMSDCOM, is to be called after a GET command to decompress the data. Database procedures can be either prewritten by the vendor or written by the user organization.

Because IDMS/R does not support the CHECK statement, the essence of the CHECK must be implemented by some other means. Thus, for PUB, the location mode is CALC using PNAME and DUPLICATES ARE NOT ALLOWED. Because duplicates are not allowed, at most one record can have a null PNAME. Thus, in this case, the essence of the CHECK statement, PNAME IS NOT NULL, is implemented by the CALC statement.

According to the design for the TTLE record, all CALL#s and TNAMEs must be unique. The location mode of TTLE will enforce the uniqueness of CALL#. However, to enforce uniqueness for TNAME, a *system set* must be defined (see the definition of the TITLE-SEQ set). System sets are used to enforce uniqueness of other data-items as well.

The remainder of the RECORD definition defines the data-items within the record. These definitions are identical to COBOL definitions (except that they are not terminated by periods).

The location mode of CPY is VIA the COLLECTION set. This means that CPY records are to be stored in reference to the COLLECTION owner, which is TTLE. Because TTLE and CPY are in the same area, the DBMS will try to store CPY records close to their TTLE owners.

Observe that IDMS/R allows composite keys in CALC expressions. For example, the location mode of VID is CALC USING (VID#, COPY#). Because duplicates are not allowed, IDMS/R will enforce uniqueness for the composite group.

**SET Statements.**   SET statements follow the RECORD definitions. All sets except A-T and T-A have ORDER phrases. (The order for A-T and T-A is system default.) Next, the set definition includes a MODE (chain or index), an owner, and a member. Sets are assigned to areas in the owner phrase. For this schema, all DBKEY positions are to be assigned by the compiler.

For INDEX sets, the BLOCK CONTAINS expression declares how many keys are to be stored in each block. This in turn defines how many levels may be in the index. As the number of levels increases, index processing becomes slower, but the contention decreases among run-units. With fewer levels, index processing is faster, but the contention among run-units increases. Index sets require an INDEX DBKEY phrase in the MEMBER definition.

For CHAIN sets, NEXT DBKEY positions must be defined and, if desired, PRIOR and OWNER positions may be defined as well. The set T-A, for example, includes owner pointers and the OWNER DBKEY position is defined. In this schema none of the sets uses PRIOR pointers, but if they were used, DBKEY positions would need to be defined for them as well.

**The VALIDATE Statement.**   VALIDATE is the last statement in the schema definition. It tells the compiler to compile the schema and check for errors and inconsistencies. Once it is error-free, the compiled schema definition is stored in the data dictionary. This is accomplished with other data dictionary commands that we will not consider.

## DMCL Descriptions

The device media control language description for the LIBRARY schema appears in Figure 14–23. This description names buffers, specifies their lengths, and assigns them to areas. Additionally, it defines the journal files.

**Figure 14–23**
IDMS/R DMCL for
the Library Database

```
DEVICE-MEDIA DESCRIPTION.
DEVICE-MEDIA NAME IS LIBDMCL
        OF SCHEMA NAME LIBRARY.

BUFFER SECTION.
        BUFFER NAME IS BOOKBUFF
                PAGE CONTAINS 3156 CHARACTERS
                BUFFER CONTAINS 7 PAGES
        BUFFER NAME IS STUBUFF
                PAGE CONTAINS 2056 CHARACTERS
                BUFFER CONTAINS 4 PAGES

AREA SECTION.
        COPY BOOK-DATA AREA
                BUFFER IS BOOKBUFF.
        COPY STU-DATA AREA
                BUFFER IS STUBUFF.

JOURNAL SECTION.
        JOURNAL BUFFER IS LIBBUFF.
        FILE CONTAINS 3000 BLOCKS.
        FILE NAME IS LIBJRNL1
                ASSIGN TO SYSJRNL1 .
                DEVICE TYPE IS 3350.
        FILE NAME IS LIBJRNL2
                ASSIGN TO SYSJRNL2
                DEVICE TYPE IS 3350.
        ARCHIVAL JOURNAL BLOCK CONTAINS 30200 CHARACTERS.
        FILE NAME IS LIBARCH1
                ASSIGN TO ARCHJRNL.
```

### Subschema Description

A subschema contains a subset of the database plus a description of logical records and their path-groups. A subschema description consists of a NAME statement followed by the names of areas, records, and sets to be included in the subschema. The LOGICAL RECORD and PATH-GROUP statements occur at the end of the subschema definition.

Figure 14–24 shows a subschema for the Library Database. The subschema NAME statement is similar to the schema NAME statement in Figure 14–22. The version is to be the most recent, user ABC is registered for all actions against the subschema, and the general data dictionary user is allowed only to display the subschema. One difference between the subschema definition and the schema definition is that the DMCL name must be included in the subschema definition.

Next, areas, records, and sets are inserted into the subschema. In this example, the BOOK-DATA and STU-DATA areas are included. The area VID-DATA exists in the database, but it is not included in this subschema. The records TTLE, STU, CPY, and DUE-DATE are included in the subschema as well as the sets COLLECTION, CHECKOUT, and HISTORY.

The last two statements concern logical records. A *logical record* is a record that is constructed from records in the database. It is not physically stored as a record. Rather, it is materialized when needed. Logical records are not part of the DBTG model. The concept was developed by Cullinet as it added relational capabilities to IDMS. Logical records are similar to

**Figure 14–24**

BORROW subschema of the Library Database

```
ADD
SUBSCHEMA NAME IS BORROW
         OF SCHEMA LIBRARY VERSION HIGHEST
         DMCL NAME IS LIBDMCL
         INCLUDE USER ABC REGISTERED FOR ALL
         PUBLIC ACCESS IS ALLOWED FOR DISPLAY.

ADD
AREA NAME IS BOOK-DATA
         DEFAULT USAGE IS SHARED UPDATE.

ADD
AREA NAME IS STU-DATA
         DEFAULT USAGE IS SHARED UPDATE.
```

**Figure 14—24**

*(continued)*

```
ADD
RECORD NAME IS TTLE
        ELEMENTS ARE  TNAME,  CALL#.

ADD
RECORD NAME IS STU
        ELEMENTS ARE  ALL.

ADD
RECORD NAME IS CPY
        ELEMENTS ARE  ALL.

ADD
RECORD NAME IS DUE-DATE
        ELEMENTS ARE  ALL.

ADD
SET NAME IS COLLECTION.

ADD
SET NAME IS CHECKOUT.

ADD
SET NAME IS HISTORY.

ADD
LOGICAL RECORD NAME IS STU-BORROW-LR
        ELEMENTS ARE
                STU
                CPY
                DUE-DATE.

ADD
PATH-GROUP NAME IS OBTAIN STU-BORROW-LR
        SELECT FOR FIELDNAME EQ STUDENT# OF REQUEST
                OBTAIN FIRST STU
                        WHERE CALCKEY EQ STUDENT# OF REQUEST
                        ON 0000 NEXT
                        ON 0326 RETURN "NO SUCH STUDENT"
                OBTAIN EACH CPY WITHIN CHECKOUT
                        ON 0000 NEXT
                        ON 0307 RETURN "NO MORE BOOKS"
                OBTAIN FIRST DUE-DATE WITHIN HISTORY
                        ON 0000 NEXT
                        ON 0307 RETURN "NO DUE DATE"
GENERATE.
```

what we called a *joined view* in Chapter 10. Because this concept is not a part of the DBTG model, we will discuss it only briefly.

The logical record in Figure 14–24 is called STU-BORROW-LR. It consists of the actual records STU, CPY, and DUE-DATE. These three records are connected by sets and also by foreign keys. They can be combined via these connections to form a variety of constructed records. The combining and processing of the records are defined in PATH-GROUP statements.

Figure 14–24 shows one PATH-GROUP statement. Many such statements can be defined for a logical record, and each statement can have multiple paths. In this example, only one path exists, and it is to be employed when a user wants to access the copies and due dates for all books checked out by a particular student.

The logic of the path-group is: Obtain the student record having STU-DENT# equal to the STUDENT# of the request. If successful (return code of 0000), proceed with the next statement. If no such student is found (return code of 0326), return the message "NO SUCH STUDENT". Next, obtain a CPY record that is connected to STU via the CHECKOUT set. If successful, proceed with the next statement. If end-of-set is detected (return code of 0307), return the message "NO MORE BOOKS". Finally, obtain the DUE-DATE record for the CPY just found.

Once defined, this logical record constructs the essence of a table formed by joins. Figure 14–25 shows one such table. The user of this logical record can process it with DBTG DML commands. OBTAIN FIRST STU-BORROW-LR will return the first such record. OBTAIN NEXT retrieves the second one, and so forth.

Path-groups can contain update as well as OBTAIN commands, and they can become quite complicated. See the IDMS/R Logical Record Facility documentation for more information.

Note that the use of predefined path-groups is a major distinction between IDMS/R and true relational DBMS products, such as DB2. With IDMS/R, the user (in this case, the database professional developing the database and application) determines how to access and construct data. But with a truly relational product, the *DBMS* determines how to navigate through

---

**Figure 14–25**

Sample data for STU-BORROW-LR

| STUDENT# | SNAME | SPHONE | CALL# | COPY# | ACQDATE | DATE-DUE |
|----------|-------|--------|-------|-------|---------|----------|
| 123456789 | JOHNSON | 7221924 | BF1999.C2 | 2 | 870608 | 891221 |
| 123456789 | JOHNSON | 7221924 | RZ401.J3 | 3 | 840217 | 891221 |
| 123456789 | JOHNSON | 7221924 | QH81.D56 | 1 | 870608 | 891224 |

the database and extract the appropriate data. It should be clear that IDMS/
R is not a DBMS product that a layperson might employ to develop his or
her own database and applications.

## An Example of an IDMS/R Application Program

In this section we present an example of a COBOL program that processes
the Library Database. Before proceeding, you need to understand the program code that is inserted into application programs by the IDMS/R
precompiler.

**Code Inserted by the IDMS/R Precompiler.**   As with DB2, the IDMS/R
precompiler will insert code to facilitate communication between the application program and the DBMS. Figure 14–26a shows code that is inserted
into a COBOL WORKING-STORAGE SECTION. (Similar code is inserted
into programs written in other languages.) After an IDMS/R command is
executed, the application program can access this data. ERROR-STATUS
will contain a zero if the command was executed successfully.

As indicated in the last section, IDMS/R will set ERROR-STATUS to
0307 when it reaches the end of a set or area. This value will occur after
execution of sequentially oriented commands like OBTAIN NEXT. Further,
IDMS/R will set ERROR-STATUS to 0326 when it cannot find a record. This
occurs after execution of commands like OBTAIN CALC.

We will not use the other fields shown in Figure 14–26a. For your
information, DBKEY will be set to the DBKEY of the current record, and
RECORD-NAME and AREA-NAME will be set to the names of the current
record type and area. The other fields are set when an error condition
occurs.

Figure 14–26b shows code inserted into the PROCEDURE DIVISION
when the programmer issues the command COPY IDMS SUBSCHEMA-
BINDS. The purpose of this code is to connect (bind) application program
data areas to IDMS/R routines. When the BIND commands are executed,
IDMS/R determines the addresses of the records in the application program.
In this way, IDMS/R knows where to put and find data-item values.

The code presented in Figure 14–26c is inserted when the application
program issues the COPY IDMS IDMS-STATUS command. This code examines ERROR-STATUS. If ERROR-STATUS is zero, IDMS/R performs no action.
If ERROR-STATUS is not zero, various error messages are issued, a user-
written error routine (IDMS-ABORT) is called, changes are rolled back, and
IDMS/R causes the job to abort.

We could call IDMS-STATUS after each IDMS/R command is issued.
However, when an IDMS/R command might generate *normal* error messages, such as end-of-data, we will first check for the normal error condition. Because we want to conclude the program normally, if a normal error
condition is detected, we will not call IDMS-STATUS. IDMS-STATUS aborts

**Figure 14—26**

COBOL code inserted
by IDMS/R
precompiler

```
01    SUBSCHEMA-CTRL.
      03    PROGRAM-NAME          PICTURE X(8).
      03    ERROR-STATUS          PICTURE X(4).
      03    DBKEY                 PICTURE S9(9) COMPUTATIONAL
                                  SYNCHRONIZED.
      03    RECORD-NAME           PICTURE X(16).
      03    AREA-NAME             PICTURE X(16).
      03    ERROR-SET             PICTURE X(16).
      03    ERROR-RECORD          PICTURE X(16)
      03    ERROR-AREA            PICTURE X(16).

      other data
```

a. Portion of code inserted into WORKING-STORAGE SECTION

```
      MOVE 'EX-PROGRAM' TO PROGRAM-NAME
      BIND RUN-UNIT.
      BIND TTLE.
      BIND CPY.
      BIND STU.
      BIND DUE-DATE.
```

b. Code inserted by copy IDMS/R SUBSCHEMA-BINDS

```
      IDMS-STATUS    SECTION.
          IF ERROR-STATUS = 0 GO TO ISABEX.
          PERFORM IDMS-ABORT.
          DISPLAY[error messages on console].
          DISPLAY[key data-items on console].
          ROLLBACK.
          CALL 'ABORT'.
      ISABEX. EXIT.
```

c. Code inserted by copy IDMS/R IDMS-STATUS

a program any time the ERROR-STATUS is not zero. Therefore, normal errors should be ruled out before calling this routine.

**ENVIRONMENT DIVISION.**   Figure 14–27 presents a COBOL program that processes book checkouts. The first IDMS/R statements occur in the ENVIRONMENT DIVISION. Here the programmer codes messages in the IDMS-CONTROL SECTION that describe whether and how the program is operating in the communications (multi-user) environment. If the program is operating in the multi-user environment, this section names the communications control program in use and declares the interface protocols being used. These topics are outside the scope of database processing and we will not consider them here.

**DATA DIVISION.**   The precompiler inserts control and subschema data definitions in the DATA DIVISION. The precompiler searches for the phrase SCHEMA SECTION and determines the names of the subschema and schema from this section. It then adds SUBSCHEMA-CTRL (Figure 14–26a) and subschema record descriptions at the end of the WORKING-STORAGE SECTION.

For the BORROW subschema, record descriptions are inserted for TTLE, CPY, STU, and DUE-DATE records. The record descriptions inserted are the same as those declared for the records in the schema (with possible omissions and reordering as set out in the subschema). The application program refers to data-items in these records with the names declared in the schema. Thus the names CALL#, TNAME, COPY#, and so forth can be used in the application program just as though they had been declared in WORKING-STORAGE by the programmer.

**PROCEDURE DIVISION.** The PROCEDURE DIVISION processes checkout requests presented by a user at a terminal. Program code related to terminal communications or communications with the operating system is not shown. Rather, such activity is summarized in brackets and lowercase letters. The particulars of this activity depend on the communications program in use and on the nature of the communications network.

The main paragraph initializes processing. It binds the data-items, readies areas, and controls mainline execution. The program execution continues as long as the action code CO (for CheckOut) is received from the terminal. Once the code CO is not returned, the program issues the FINISH command to enable IDMS/R to complete its processing. Then STOP RUN is issued to terminate the program execution.

The processing controlled by the remainder of the program is self-evident. In summary, a value of STUDENT# is accepted from the terminal and the student record is obtained. If the student number is valid, the CHECK-OUT paragraph is performed. The program searches for overdue books. If such books are found, the user is given the chance to terminate the checkout process in the OVERDUE-PROCEDURE paragraph.

**Figure 14—27**

Sample COBOL program with IDMS/R commands

```
IDENTIFICATION DIVISION.
PROGRAM-ID.      LIB-CHECKOUT.


ENVIRONMENT DIVISION.
INPUT-OUTPUT SECTION.
FILE-CONTROL.
        SELECT [non-database file selects go here]
IDMS-CONTROL SECTION.
PROTOCOL                 MODE IS mode statement

DATA DIVISION.
SCHEMA SECTION.
DB BORROW WITHIN LIBRARY.
FILE SECTION.
COPY IDMS FILE.
[non-database file descriptions go here]
WORKING-STORAGE SECTION.
*
*       NON-DATABASE WORKING-STORAGE DESCRIPTIONS
*
77      TODAY-DATE              PIC X(6).
77      TODAY-DUE-DATE          PIC X(6).
77      ACTION-CODE             PIC X(2).
77      STU-STATUS              PIC X(2).
77      CONTINUE-CODE           PIC X(3).
*
*       DATABASE SCHEMA DESCRIPTION
*

   [IDMS/R precompiler will insert record descriptions from the
   subschema  here]
   [IDMS/R precompiler will insert SUBSCHEMA-CTRL here]

PROCEDURE DIVISION.
        COPY IDMS SUBSCHEMA-BINDS.
        READY BOOK-DATA.
        READY STU-DATA.
        PERFORM IDMS-STATUS.
        [fill TODAY-DATE and TODAY-DUE-DATE]
        [accept ACTION-CODE from terminal]
        PERFORM STU-CHECKOUT UNTIL ACTION-CODE NOT = "CO".
        FINISH.
        STOP RUN.
```

**Figure 14—27**
*(continued)*

```
STU-CHECKOUT.
        [accept STUDENT# from terminal]
        OBTAIN CALC STU.
        IF ERROR-STATUS = "0326"
                [display invalid student message on terminal]
        ELSE    IF ERROR-STATUS EQ "0000"
                        PERFORM CHECK-OUT
                ELSE PERFORM IDMS-STATUS.
        [accept ACTION-CODE from terminal]
CHECK-OUT.
        MOVE "OK" TO STU-STATUS.
        PERFORM OVERDUE-CHECK.
        IF STU-STATUS EQ "OK"
                PERFORM BOOK-CHECKOUT.

OVERDUE-CHECK.
        OBTAIN FIRST CPY WITHIN CHECKOUT.
        PERFORM OVERDUE-SEARCH UNTIL ERROR-STATUS NOT EQ "0000".
        IF ERROR-STATUS NOT EQ "0307"
                PERFORM IDMS-STATUS.
        [display check complete message on terminal]

OVERDUE-SEARCH.
        OBTAIN FIRST DUE-DATE WITHIN HISTORY.
        IF ERROR-STATUS EQ "0000"
                IF DATE-DUE LESS THAN TODAY-DATE
                        PERFORM OVERDUE-PROCEDURE
                ELSE
        ELSE IF ERROR-STATUS EQ "0307"
                [display "error - book's never been checked out"
                        on terminal]
                ELSE PERFORM IDMS-STATUS.
        OBTAIN NEXT WITHIN CHECKOUT.

OVERDUE-PROCEDURE.
        OBTAIN OWNER WITHIN COLLECTION.
        [display TNAME, CALL#, COPY#, DATE-DUE as overdue book]
        [accept CONTINUE-CODE from user]
        IF CONTINUE CODE NOT EQ "YES"
                MOVE "NO" TO STU-STATUS.
```

**Figure 14—27**

*(continued)*

```
BOOK-CHECKOUT.
        [accept CONTINUE-CODE, CALL#, COPY# from terminal]
        PERFORM BOOK-CHECKOUT-PROCEDURE UNTIL
                CONTINUE-CODE NOT EQ "YES".


BOOK-CHECKOUT-PROCEDURE.
        OBTAIN CALC CPY.
        IF ERROR-STATUS EQ "0326"
                [display "error - no such book and copy"]
        ELSE    IF ERROR-STATUS EQ "0000"
                        CONNECT CPY TO CHECKOUT
                        CALL IDMS-STATUS
                        MOVE TODAY-DUE-DATE TO DATE-DUE
                        STORE DUE-DATE
                        CALL IDMS-STATUS
                        [accept CONTINUE-CODE, CALL#, COPY#
                                from terminal]
                ELSE    CALL IDMS-STATUS.
COPY IDMS-STATUS.
*
*   IDMS PRECOMPILER WILL INSERT IDMS-STATUS HERE.   NON-ZERO ERROR-STATUS
*   CAUSES A ROLLBACK WITH ABORT.   JUST BEFORE ABORTING, HOWEVER, IDMS/R
*   WILL CALL THE USER-WRITTEN ROUTINE IDMS-ABORT.   THIS GIVES THE
*   PROGRAM ONE LAST GASP.
*
IDMS-ABORT.
        DISPLAY "ABORT USER-EXIT CALLED".
IDMS-ABORT-EXIT.
        EXIT.
```

Once overdue books have been considered, the BOOK-CHECKOUT paragraph is performed. Here the appropriate CPY record is connected to the STU record, and a new DUE-DATE record is created. The process is repeated until no more books remain to be checked out. Finally, the IDMS-STATUS and IDMS-ABORT routines are included for error processing, as described previously.

## SUMMARY

To be considered a DBTG DBMS, a DBMS product must have the five characteristics listed in Figure 14–1. Several such DBTG products exist. The one that has enjoyed the most popularity is marketed by the Cullinet Corporation. The current version is known as IDMS/R. Although IDMS/R includes some relational-like features, in this chapter we considered only the DBTG features of the product.

IDMS/R differs from the DBTG model in several ways. IDMS/R supports areas, but the DBTG model does not. IDMS/R specifies a location mode for each record type, but the DBTG model does not. IDMS/R does not support three SET features included in the DBTG model—namely, CHECK, SET SELECTION, and FIXED retention status. IDMS/R also does not support record, set, or data-item aliases, but the DBTG model does. Nonetheless, the most significant difference between IDMS/R and the DBTG model is that IDMS/R allows the definition of logical records, which are similar to tables that might result from one or several relational join operations, and the definition of path-groups. A path-group defines the means by which the DBMS will navigate through the stored data to extract the appropriate subset. This is not supported by the DBTG model. This feature also is very different from the approach taken by relational DBMS products. With a relational DBMS product, *the user never specifies how to find the appropriate data—this is always done by the system.*

IDMS/R includes compilers that are employed for defining schemas, subschemas, journal files, physical devices, and many other aspects of a database. IDMS/R supports all of the DBTG DML commands discussed in Chapter 13. It also includes facilities for controlling concurrent processing. Locking can be done at the area and record levels. The term *checkpoint* is IDMS/R's word for transaction. IDMS/R produces a journal file of before and after images.

Database security facilities are also provided. IDMS/R can control which programs can access which subschemas. Also, subschemas can define which actions can be taken with regard to areas, records, and sets. Database procedures can also be used for security.

IDMS/R statements are embedded in application programs. In this chapter you saw portions of a COBOL program that might be used in a university library to check out books to students. The IDMS/R precompiler, like other precompilers, replaces DBMS commands with host language instruction sequences. IDMS/R provides precompilers for COBOL, FORTRAN, PL/I, and assembler language programs.

---

QUESTIONS **GROUP I**

**14.1** List and describe five characteristics necessary for a DBMS to be considered a DBTG DBMS.

**14.2** List four DBTG DBMS products.

**14.3** What is a database procedure? How is it used?

**14.4** Describe the five steps of defining and using an IDMS/R database.

**14.5** Explain how the database, areas, files, pages, and records are related.

**14.6** Sketch and describe IDMS/R page layout.

**14.7**   Explain how linked lists are used to represent IDMS/R sets.

**14.8**   Explain how IDMS/R area, record, and set data definitions differ from the 1981 DBTG model.

**14.9**   Name and describe the five sections of an IDMS schema definition.

**14.10**  Explain the relationship of files and areas as defined in the schema in Figure 14–15.

**14.11**  Explain the purpose of DMCL modules.

**14.12**  Define subschema inclusion rules by which IDMS will accept a STORE command.

**14.13**  Define subschema inclusion rules by which IDMS will accept an ERASE command.

**14.14**  What is the OBTAIN command? How does it differ from a FIND command?

**14.15**  Give an example of each of the six formats of the FIND command.

**14.16**  Give an example of a STORE command. Explain what actions must be taken before the STORE is issued.

**14.17**  Give an example of an ERASE command. Explain what actions must be taken before the ERASE is issued.

**14.18**  Give an example of a MODIFY command. Explain what actions must be taken before the MODIFY is issued.

**14.19**  Describe two levels of IDMS record locking.

**14.20**  What is the difference between a PROTECTED and an EXCLUSIVE lock?

**14.21**  Give an example of READY commands to lock AREA-B for retrieval. Assume:

    **a.** Other run-units can operate concurrently without restriction.

    **b.** Other run-units can read concurrently but not update.

    **c.** No other run-unit is to access the area concurrently.

**14.22**  Explain the difference between explicit and implicit locks.

**14.23**  Under what conditions are explicit locks used? Under what conditions are implicit locks used?

**14.24**  Define the term *checkpoint* as used by IDMS/R.

**14.25**  Explain how IDMS operates to recover from each of the following. Assume that the journal is located on a direct access device.

    **a.** Unsuccessful checkpoint termination

    **b.** System crash

    **c.** Database damage

**14.26**  What facilities does IDMS/R provide to control user access?

**14.27**  What facilities does IDMS/R provide to control program access to subschemas?

**14.28**  What facilities does IDMS/R provide to control subschema activity on areas? On records? On sets?

**14.29**  Define *logical record*. Explain the meaning of the logical path for the STU-BORROW-LR logical record (see Figure 14-25).

**14.30**  Explain the functions of the code inserted by the IDMS/R precompiler as shown in Figure 14-26a.

**14.31** Explain the functions of the code inserted by the IDMS/R precompiler as shown in Figure 14-26b.

**14.32** Explain the functions of the code inserted by the IDMS/R precompiler as shown in Figure 14-26c.

**14.33** Explain the use of IDMS-STATUS in paragraphs OVERDUE-CHECK and OVERDUE-SEARCH in Figure 14-27.

---

## QUESTIONS AND EXERCISES

**14.34** Develop a subschema definition for an application program that will add library book records to the Library Database. Specify ENVIRONMENT and DATA DIVISION entries for this program.

**14.35** Locate a company using IDMS/R. Determine how long it has had the system, why IDMS/R was chosen, and how well the company likes it. If possible, obtain a copy of a schema or subschema. Explain the meaning of all entries in the schema or subschema. Also, if possible, obtain a copy of an application program. Explain the meaning of IDMS/R statements. Compare the copy of the program before precompilation with the copy afterward. How do application programs in this company do locking? Has the company ever experienced locking problems? Determine if this company is also using a purely relational DBMS. If so, find out which applications IDMS/R is used for and which applications the relational DBMS is used for.

**14.36** Locate a company that has a DBTG DBMS other than IDMS/R. Answer all the questions in 14.34 for this DBMS.

# PART VI

# DISTRIBUTED DATABASE PROCESSING

**D**istributed database processing is the third and final context we will present in this text. You have seen that the end-user context revolves around systems that enable a user to perform some or all of his or her own database manipulation. The organizational context focuses on processing centralized company data by applying large numbers of transactions to it. The distributed database processing context is the one that has emerged most recently, and it is by no means a mature discipline.

Still in its infancy, this subject is constantly evolving and will continue to change as new developments occur during the next several years. Thus, our goal in this part of the text is to present the essential concepts of distributed database processing and to describe some of the difficult issues that are yet to be resolved. This part consists of a single chapter—a fact that reflects the newness of the topic.

As you read Chapter 15, compare the problems of distributed database processing to those of centralized database processing. How are they similar? How do they differ? Solving such problems will require research and innovation. Future database systems may be very different from those in use today. Although they are new, distributed databases will undoubtedly play a very large role in the evolution of database processing.

# Fundamentals of Distributed Database Processing

* Overview of Distributed Database Processing
* Components of Distributed Database Systems
* Four Goals for a Distributed DBMS
* Systems Application Architecture
* Distributed Concurrency Control
* Failure Transparency
* Summary

**W**e conclude this textbook with a discussion of distributed database processing. This chapter will describe the characteristics and components of distributed database systems and present four processing goals for a distributed DBMS (DDBMS). Then, we will examine Systems Application Architecture (SAA), a development plan promulgated by IBM that lays interface foundations for distributed database processing. Finally, we will consider two difficult issues in distributed processing—concurrency and failure/recovery—in detail.

Before proceeding, you should be aware that the knowledge about distributed database processing continues to evolve and that this is by no means a mature discipline. As Bernstein and Goodman wrote about one aspect of distributed processing, "Distributed concurrency control, by contrast [with nondistributed], is in a state of extreme turbulence. More than 20 concurrency control algorithms have been proposed for DDBMSs, and several have been, or are being, implemented. These algorithms are usually complex, hard to understand, and difficult to prove correct (indeed, many are incorrect)."[1] Although this quotation, from two of the most prominent

---

[1]Bernstein, P.A., & Goodman, N. "Concurrency Controls in Distributed Database Systems." In *Computing Surveys*, Vol. 13, No. 2, June 1981.

researchers in the study of distributed database systems, was published in 1981, it continues to be true today.

In short, many of the problems have been identified, but few *robust* solutions are known. Further, this is an exceedingly complex subject, and research activities are splintered on different facets of the problems. Additionally, much of the work has been theoretical and important implementation issues have been ignored. For example, several of the engineers of R*, a DDBMS prototype implementation, wrote the following regarding the production of log records: "The discussions of commit protocols in the literature are very vague, if there is any mention at all, about this crucial (for correctness and performance) aspect of the protocols."[2]

At the same time, users equipped with microcomputers and local databases are increasing the pressure on the MIS Department to provide some form of distributed processing. The Type II and III microcomputer databases described in Chapter 10 are indications of this pressure. In response to this opportunity, vendors of DBMS products have begun to announce so-called DDBMS products. Unfortunately, most of these products leave unsolved many distributed database processing problems. However, in time these offerings will improve. Eventually, true distributed DDBMS products will be developed.

Your goal in reading this chapter is to understand the nature of distributed database processing, its advantages and disadvantages, special system design considerations, and the major problems that need to be overcome. Such knowledge will provide a foundation for this complicated subject, which is likely to grow and evolve tremendously during your career.

## OVERVIEW OF DISTRIBUTED DATABASE PROCESSING

*Distributed database processing* is database processing in which the execution of transactions and the retrieval and updating of data occur across two or more independent and, usually, geographically separate computers. Figure 15–1 shows a distributed database system involving four computers, or nodes.

The *distributed database management system (DDBMS)* consists of the collection of distributed transaction managers (DTMs) and database managers (DBMs) on all computers. The DDBMS in Figure 15–1 is generic. It is a collection of programs operating on different computers. These programs may all be subsystems of a single DDBMS product licensed from a single vendor. Or they may be programs from disparate sources, with some licensed from vendors and some written in-house. This figure simply illustrates the

---

[2]Mohan, C., Lindsay, B., & Obermarck, R. "Transaction Management in the R* Distributed Database Management System." In *Transactions on Database Systems*, Vol. 11, No. 4, December 1986.

**Figure 15—1**
Distributed database
architecture

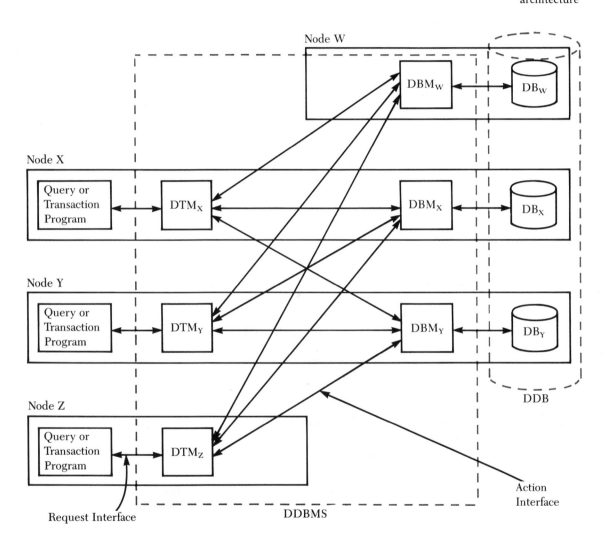

Node W

Node X

Node Y

Node Z

Request Interface

DDBMS

Action
Interface

DDB

functions that are required to accomplish distributed database processing, namely, to accept transaction requests and to process the distributed database.

A *distributed transaction manager (DTM)* is a program that receives processing requests from query or transaction programs and translates them into action commands for database managers. As you will see, an important DTM function is to coordinate and control these actions. Depending on the nature of the application and the DDBMS, the DTM may be provided as part of the DDBMS product, it may be developed in-house by the organization implementing the distributed system, or, in less sophisticated applications, some of its functions may even be performed by people.

A *database manager (DBM)* is a program that processes some portion of a distributed database (DDB). It retrieves and updates user and overhead data in accordance with action commands received from DTMs. A DBM may be a subset of a DDBMS product, or it may be a non-distributed commercial DBMS.

A *node* is a computer that executes a DTM, a DBM, or both. A *transaction node* processes a DTM, and a *database node* processes a DBM and its database.

For the example in Figure 15–1, node W is a database node running $DBM_W$ and storing $DB_W$. Node X is both a transaction and a database node with $DTM_X$, $DBM_X$, and $DB_X$. Similarly, node Y is both a transaction and a database node. Node Z is a transaction node only.

Query or transaction programs communicate with DTMs via *requests*. These requests are similar to other DBMS action requests you have already studied. Sample requests are SELECT EMPLOYEE WHERE E# EQ 123 and STORE DUE-DATE. Such requests operate on *logical constructs*. The query or application program is not referring to any particular *physical* instance of the construct. However, DTMs communicate with DBMs via actions to be executed on *specific data instances*. Thus, if a new occurrence of DUE-DATE is to be stored in $DB_X$ and $DB_Y$, then the DTM translates the logical *request* STORE DUE-DATE into two *actions*. One directs $DBM_X$ to store the new data in $DB_X$ and the second directs $DBM_Y$ to store the new data in $DB_Y$.

In principle, requests and actions could also differ in terms of their *level of abstraction*. For example, a request could be expressed in terms of an object and be translated into actions expressed in terms of composite relations or files. However, to date no such DDBMS exists.

### Advantages of Distributed Processing

Distributed processing has four primary advantages. First, it can result in *better performance* than would centralized processing. Data can be located close to the point of use so that communication time is shorter. Also, several computers operating simultaneously can yield more processing throughput than would a single computer.

Second, replicated data *increases reliability*. When a computer fails, replicated data can be obtained from other computers. The users need not depend on a sole source for their data. A third advantage is that distributed systems are more *easily scaled in size*. Additional computers can be added to the network as the number of users or size of the processing work load expands. Adding a new, smaller computer is often easier and cheaper than upgrading a single, centralized computer. Further, if the work load decreases, the size of the network can also be readily reduced.

Finally, distributed systems are more *readily tailored to the structure of the user organization*. Figure 15–2 shows the organization of a geographically distributed manufacturer. The general managers of each plant have consid-

**Figure 15–2**
Geographically dis-
tributed business

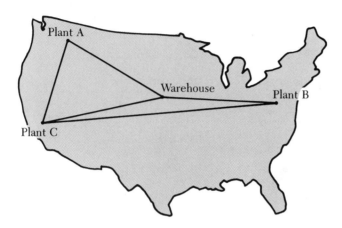

erable authority and latitude in the operation of their facilities. Having these plants depend on a single, centralized computer conflicts with the operational philosophy and policy of the company. Even in more centralized organizations, distributed processing adapts more flexibly to the structure than does centralized processing.

## Disadvantages of Distributed Processing

Oddly enough, the first two disadvantages of distributed processing correspond to the first two advantages. First, *performance can be worse* for distributed processing than for centralized processing. Depending on the nature of the work load, the network, the DDBMS, and the concurrency and failure strategies used, the advantages of local data access and multiple processors can be overwhelmed by the coordination and control tasks required. This situation is especially likely when the work load calls for a large number of concurrent updates on widely distributed replicated data (replicated data is stored on multiple databases).

Second, distributed database processing *can be less reliable* than centralized processing. Again, depending on the reliability of the processing computers, the network, the DDBMS, the transactions, and the error rates in the work load, a distributed system can be down more often than a centralized one. Both of these disadvantages indicate that distributed processing is no panacea. Although it holds the promise of better performance and greater reliability, this promise is not guaranteed.

A third disadvantage is *increased complexity,* which often translates into *high construction and maintenance expense.* Because more hardware components are involved, the required learning is greater and more interfaces can

**Figure 15–3**
Advantages and dis-
advantages of distrib-
uted database
processing

|  |  |
|---|---|
| *Advantages* | *Disadvantages* |
| Better performance | Worse performance |
| Increased reliability | Decreased reliability |
| Easily scaled in size | Increased complexity |
| Readily tailored to organization structure | Higher costs |
|  | Difficult to control |

fail. Additionally, as you will see, concurrency control and failure recovery can be exceedingly complicated and difficult to implement. Often a greater burden is placed on programmers and operations personnel. This means that more experienced (and expensive) personnel are required.

Finally, distributed database processing is *difficult to control.* A centralized computer resides in a controlled environment with closely supervised operations personnel. Processing activities can be monitored (though with difficulty). In a distributed system, processing computers often reside in the users' work areas. Physical access is frequently uncontrolled. Operations procedures are sometimes lax and performed by people who have little understanding of the importance of procedures. Finally, in the event of a disaster or catastrophe, recovery can be far more difficult to synchronize than with a centralized system. The advantages and disadvantages of distributed database processing are summarized in Figure 15–3.

## COMPONENTS OF DISTRIBUTED DATABASE SYSTEMS

As already stated, this is a confusing topic. Much of the confusion exists because many different types of processing fall under the term *distributed database processing* and can fit into the general architecture of Figure 15–1. For example, consider the system in Figure 15–4a. This system conforms to the architecture shown in Figure 15–1. In this case, each node is a mainframe computer. For this system, processing is based on the *equality of cooperating colleagues.* Each database node (W, X, and Y) has authority to insert, modify, delete, and read any data in the database it manages. (Node Z is a transaction node.) Further, the data changes are made in as close to real time as possible.

Now consider another configuration, shown in Figure 15–4b. In this case, node W is a mainframe, nodes X and Y are minicomputers, and node Z is a microcomputer. The processing rules are that only node W can modify the database. Nodes X and Y, which have copies of data on node W, are authorized for read-only access, and node Z may obtain data only from node Y. No attempt is made to keep the data current in real time. Instead, once each day, nodes X and Y are refreshed from node W (node W's data is downloaded), and once each week, node Z is refreshed from node Y.

Consider Figure 15–4c, which shows a third instance of the architecture in Figure 15–1. Here node W is a mainframe and nodes X, Y, and Z are microcomputers attached to a local area network. Node X is a gateway to the mainframe. It obtains all of the database data that X, Y, and Z need from W and stores it on its own database. Node Y, which needs frequent access to some of the data, obtains a copy of that data, but processes it on a read-only basis. When either node Y or node Z makes changes to data, it does so to the copy on X. Periodically, X refreshes W's database with data that has been changed by X, Y, and Z.

These three examples all conform to the general architecture in Figure 15–1, but they are entirely different. Each has its own set of capabilities, and each has its own set of problems. To bring order to this complexity, consider the five components of a distributed database system: hardware, the DDBMS, replicated data, procedures, and personnel.

## Hardware

As shown in Figure 15–4, processing nodes can consist of many different types of hardware. In some distributed systems (Figure 15–4a), all nodes are homogeneous. In others (Figures 15–4b and 15–4c), they are heterogeneous. Differences in processing speeds and storage capacities need to be accommodated when designing a distributed database system.

## The DDBMS

The DDBMS shown in Figure 15–1 is generic. As mentioned, the DTMs and DBMs can be subsystems of a single DDBMS product. Alternatively— and at present, more commonly—the DDBMS is a collection of programs developed in-house and products obtained from various software vendors. In many cases, DTMs are written in-house and DBMs are commercial DBMS products.

Consider the examples in Figure 15–4. For the first example, the DDBMS is a single product including both the DTMs and the DBMs. Each DTM expects to communicate only with DBMs provided by the same vendor. R*,

**Figure 15—4**

Three instances of
architecture in
Figure 15—1

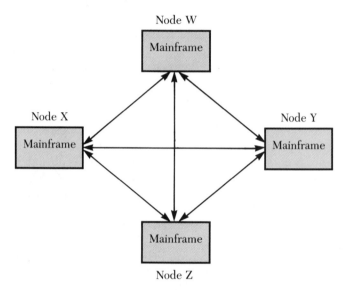

a. Distributed system of Figure 15–1
using four mainframes

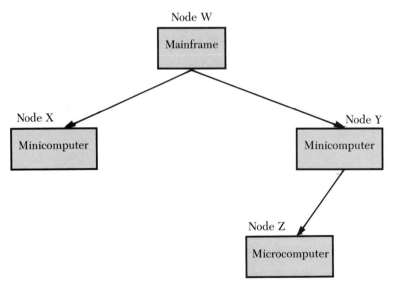

b. Distributed system of Figure 15-1
using a mainframe, two minicomputers and a microcomputer

**Figure 15–4**
(*continued*)

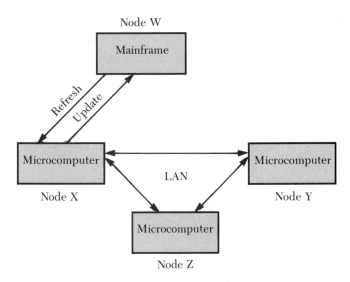

c. Distributed system of Figure 15-1 using a mainframe, LAN, and three
microcomputers

a prototype DDBMS developed by IBM, is an example of such a product.
Now consider Figure 15–4b. Here, all of the DBMs could be versions of a
commercial product like ORACLE. The DTMs, however, are not part of
ORACLE. Rather, they are in-house written application programs that access
ORACLE on a different computer and then download the database data.
Finally, in Figure 15–4c, the DBM on node W could be DB2, and the DBMs
on nodes X and Y could be R:BASE System V. An extract program provided
by the vendor of R:BASE is located on both node Y and node Z. This program obtains data from the database on node X. Thus, the DDBMS can be
either a single product or an amalgam of programs and products.

## Data Replication

The term *replication* refers to the duplication of data. A distributed database
can be non-, partially, or fully replicated. If it is non-replicated, then one
and only one copy of each data-item exists. Data-items are assigned to
particular nodes and may reside only at their assigned node. Any application needing access to the data-item must obtain it from the officially
designated node.

A partially replicated database contains some data-items that are duplicated and some that are not. A system directory indicates whether or not
a data-item is replicated and where it is stored. A fully replicated distributed

database is one in which the entire database is duplicated on two or more nodes. A node has either all of the database or none of it.

## Procedures

Distributed database systems include a multitude of procedural components. The first group of procedures concerns *processing rights*. Which nodes can do what to which data? In the simplest distributed systems, data is non-replicated and only the node that stores the data can update it. (Actually, in the very simplest system, no data is updated at all. Data is obtained from a foreign source and is only read, not modified. However, such a situation is rare.) In more complicated situations, any node can issue an update request for any data-item on its own or any other node. If the data-item is replicated, all copies are changed.

Developers of a distributed system must determine processing rights. In doing so, they must consider user requirements, capabilities of the hardware and programs, concurrency control, and other factors.

Another procedural consideration concerns *data currency*. How up-to-date must the data be? Does every node need the most current value of all the data-items it accesses? Can some databases be allowed to become out-of-date? In Figure 15–4a, all nodes have access to the most current data. But in Figures 15–4b and c, some of the nodes are processing historical—possibly outdated—data. In general, the more current the data, the more expensive the system. Because enormous numbers of processing cycles are needed to control and coordinate the system in Figure 15–4a, powerful and expensive CPUs will be required.

Closely related to the issues of processing rights and currency is the issue of *data flow*. Who updates whom? In Figure 15–4b, node W updates data on nodes X and Y, whereas in Figure 15–4c, node X updates data on node W. Such flows are determined by the requirements and the processing rights of the nodes.

Another procedural component concerns *control*. In the case of conflicting processing requests, which node resolves the conflict? In general, authoritarian control (Figures 15–4b and c) is easier to implement than schemes based on equality (Figure 15–4a).

In fact, for distributed systems like the one in Figure 15–4a, control is distributed throughout the network. No one node is in charge. Control decisions can be made by any of the nodes, depending on the control issue and the state of the system. This allows for greater flexibility but is far more complex.

## Personnel

Distributed systems vary considerably in the demands they place on people. Systems with sophisticated and powerful DDBMSs place few special demands on users. In fact, users do not even realize that they are processing distributed data. They simply access their applications and all distributed processing is taken care of by the DDBMS. Users of less sophisticated systems must become more involved. In fact, the less sophisticated the DDBMS, the greater the role people play.

Consider the system in Figure 15–4b. Users at nodes X and Y may need to invoke one or more programs to cause data to be downloaded from the mainframe. Similarly, the users at node Z may need to manually start programs to bring data down from node Y. Depending on the design of the system, the users may also bear responsibility for inspecting processing reports to determine that the correct data was transmitted and that it was error-free.

In very primitive distributed systems, the users may even bear some of the responsibilities of the DTM. For example, in some systems, users make data changes on the local database and then manually cause these changes to be made for replicated data on other nodes. In the most primitive systems, users employ the NIKE method—that is, they put on their sneakers and run from computer to computer, carrying diskettes of data changes.

## FOUR GOALS FOR A DISTRIBUTED DBMS

Traiger et al. defined four goals for a distributed DBMS.[3] These goals provide an excellent framework for a survey of the issues, problems, and solutions proposed for distributed databases.

Ideally, query facilities and transaction programs are isolated from the management of the distributed database. In this way they can realize the advantages of distributed processing without having to become involved in the particulars of the database distribution. Programmers and users can then focus on the nature and logic of the information problem they need to solve and not be forced to deal with matters that more properly belong to the DDBMS. (To simplify the discussion we will refer to query users and transaction programs simply as *transactions*.)

Specifically, transactions need database access that is transparent to data location, data replication, concurrency, and failure in the distributed database. This means that ideally, a transaction is not even aware that data is distributed. All four of these distribution issues are handled behind the scenes. We will consider each goal in turn.

### Location Transparency

Transactions need to be independent of the location of a particular data-item. If they are not, location issues greatly complicate transaction logic.

[3]Traiger, I.L., Gray, J., Galtieri, C.A., & Lindsay, B.G. "Transactions and Consistency in Distributed Database Systems." In *Transactions on Database Systems*, Vol. 7, No. 3, September 1982.

Consider the manufacturer in Figure 15–2. Suppose the data involved is not replicated, but may be stored on a computer at any facility. Now suppose the inventory manager moves three refrigerators from plant A to plant B. As a consequence, two inventory records need to be modified. If the program that processes this transaction is *not* transparent to the location of the data, it needs to consider four cases: both records at A, one at A and one at B, one at B and one at A, and both at B. Obviously, the logic of the transaction is confounded by the need to consider the data's location.

Location transparency can be provided if the distributed transaction managers are responsible for determining the location of data and issuing actions to the appropriate DBMs. This can be accomplished if DTMs have access to directories of data locations. Also, if data is moved, only the DTMs are affected. Transactions are isolated from the change in location.

### Replication Transparency

Transactions are transparent to replication if they can process without knowing how many times data is replicated, if at all. The transaction can act as if all data is stored only on a single node. With replication transparency, new duplicates can be created or existing duplicates can be eliminated without any impact on the end user's transaction or query processing.

To provide replication transparency, the transaction managers must translate transaction processing requests into actions for the database managers. Reads are straightforward. The DTM selects one of the nodes that stores the data and issues an action to read it. To facilitate the selection, the DTM may keep statistics about the time required to read data from various nodes. It selects the node with the best performance. Writing replicated data is more involved. The DTM must issue a write action for every DBM that stores a copy of that data.

This discussion assumes that every DTM has an accurate and up-to-date copy of a directory that indicates data locations. Interesting problems arise when we consider what happens when the directory must be changed to account for new copies or the elimination of copies. Clearly, coordination is critical. All directories must be installed so that no DTM thinks that data is available before it is (in the case of reads) and so that every DTM knows that data is available when it is (in the case of writes). Otherwise, a DTM may request data that is not yet available or fail to issue a write on a DBM when data has become available.

### Concurrency Transparency

Many transactions involving the distributed database can be executing at the same time, often on the same data. A DDBMS provides concurrency transparency if the results of all concurrent transactions are identical to the results that would have been obtained if the transactions had been executed one-by-one, in serial order. Stated in other terms, the results of a transaction processed concurrently with other transactions must be the same as they would have been if the transaction had been processed alone. (We called this *serializability* in Chapter 7.)

Two major strategies have been developed to provide concurrency control. One, called *distributed two-phase locking*, is an extension of the concurrency control mechanism we discussed in Chapter 7. A second method is called *timestamp ordering*. Both of these techniques have been implemented in DDBMS products. We will discuss two-phase locking in the next section.

## Failure Transparency

The fourth goal for the DDBMS is to provide failure transparency. This means that transactions are correctly processed in spite of transaction, DDBMS, network, and computer failures. Stated in terms of Chapter 7, transactions must be *atomic*. Either all of a transaction is processed or none of it is. Further, once the results of transactions have been committed, they must be permanent.

Failure transparency is the most difficult of the four goals. Part of the problem is that so many types of failure may occur. On one end of the spectrum is a node that never fails, sometimes called a *perfect node*. On the other end is a node that fails in a totally unpredictable, undetectable way. Such a node may communicate garbage over the network, it may send valid but inappropriate actions, it may be malevolent, and it may even conspire with other nodes to subvert the distributed system. Such a node is called an *insane node*, and such failures are sometimes called *Byzantine failures*. In between these extremes are *sane nodes*, which fail, but only in defined and known ways. An example of a sane node is one that is either perfect or fails to respond at all.[4]

Another reason that failure transparency is so difficult is that concurrency control is so complicated. In a sense, concurrency control problems are solved at the expense of failure recovery. It is as if a bubble of air under the carpet has been pushed from one corner only to reappear in another. Concurrency control mechanisms work as long as no failure occurs at certain times or states of the distributed database (or as long as recovery can be guaranteed to proceed in a certain manner). In the general case of partitioned (i.e., spread across several nodes), replicated databases, many theoretical and practical implementation problems still remain to be solved. We will discuss failure transparency in more detail later in this chapter.

# SYSTEMS APPLICATION ARCHITECTURE

Systems Application Architecture (SAA) is IBM's standard for programming languages, user interfaces, and communications support. Thus it differs in

---

[4]Garcia-Molina, H., Pittelli, F., & Davidson, S. "Applications of Byzantine Agreement in Database Systems." In *Transactions on Database Systems*, Vol. 11, No. 1, March 1986.

character from the distributed database technology discussed so far in this chapter. Given IBM's prominence in the industry, however, SAA is likely to become an important part of a standard interface for distributed processing, and it will likely affect any commercial DDBMS you encounter. Therefore, we will now present an overview of SAA.

### The Definition and Components of SAA

IBM sells and licenses a wide variety of hardware and software products. When IBM announced SAA in April 1987, much of this hardware was difficult to integrate. The architecture and processing concepts of the personal computer, mid-range computers such as the System/38, and mainframe computers such as the 3000 series were substantially different. IBM's customers wanted to build distributed systems, and to do so, these systems needed to be easier to connect. Responding to this need, IBM developed SAA, which is a plan and a statement of direction to integrate these systems. The plan has three components. It addresses programming languages and services, user interfaces, and communications.

### Programming Languages and Services

Versions of C, COBOL, and FORTRAN are defined for all SAA implementations. These standard versions will be implemented across all IBM computers that participate in SAA. Additionally, SAA includes an application generator that allows interactive creation of applications using a fill-in-the-blanks approach with prompting and integrated help. Finally, SAA includes a standard version of the Procedures Language, IBM's own structured programming language.

The services portion of SAA most directly affects database development. With SAA, IBM is making a commitment to implementing SQL on all the PC, System/3x, and 3000 series computers and primary operating systems. SQL will be used both as an interactive query and update language and as a means of embedding database access requests into application programs. Pre-compilers will be provided for COBOL, FORTRAN, and C. Thus, the SQL you learned in Chapters 9 and 11 will be usable on all IBM computers participating in SAA.

Additionally, SAA defines standard methods for development of interactive applications. Programmers will use standard tools to present and manipulate menus, help, data, and messages on computer screens. And standard means will be provided for transferring data to and from the user.

### User Access

SAA defines specifications for the interface between a user and the computer, including how data can appear and how the user can respond. Elements of this interface include specifications on how the machine communicates with the user and how the user can employ the facilities of the computer to respond to the machine.

SAA provides three types of user interface consistency among the various computer systems. *Physical consistency* means that IBM will provide on all its SAA computers one keyboard, with keys in the same locations, and a standard means of using a mouse. *Syntactical consistency* refers to the appearance of the user interface. SAA products will have one look. For example, command lines will be in the same screen location in all products. Finally, *semantic consistency* refers to the meaning of command words. For all SAA products, commands will have the same meaning and action. For example, RENAME will mean the same thing on all SAA products.

## Communications Support

The third component of SAA concerns intercomponent communication. A standard set of data streams is defined in SAA. Examples are the document content architecture (DCA) for text documents and the intelligent printer data stream (IPDS) for laser-type printers.

Additionally, communications processing standards are defined. These include communications management services such as the systems network architecture (SNA); session services such as the program-to-program communication protocol LU 6.2; and data link controls such as SDLC, the token-ring standard, and the packet-switch standard X.25. With these definitions, SAA hardware will become easier to integrate.

## The Implications of SAA for Distributed Database Processing

SAA will very likely affect more than just IBM products. If history is any indication of the future, SAA will become an industry standard for distributed database processing. Vendors of competitive and add-on products will adopt the SAA standard to be compatible with the industry leader.

SAA is the first step toward practical, commercial distributed processing. SAA addresses the end-user side of distributed processing, whereas the technology we will next present addresses the machine and software side. In the definition of SAA, IBM has addressed the longer lead-time side. It is far more difficult to move current users to a new interface than it is to install a new, distributed concurrency control algorithm in a DDBMS. In essence, with SAA, IBM is preparing its customer base (and because of IBM's prominence, the industry) for distributed database processing.

With both IBM and the American National Standards Institute (ANSI) endorsing SQL, the development of new applications with non-SQL facilities will begin to wane. While existing non-SQL programs and data will be around for many years (certainly into the next century), most exciting new developments will occur with SQL. All of the leading software companies either have developed or are developing SQL products.

The SQL standard provides a common base for application development products. With this base, it seems likely that vendors will develop object-oriented applications development toolkits or similar facilities. Such products will substantially increase application development productivity.

# DISTRIBUTED CONCURRENCY CONTROL

In this section and the next, we will consider some of the technical issues involved in developing DDBMS products that provide concurrency and failure transparency. These two sections contain very technical discussions. Your goal in reading them is to *understand the issues* involved in providing robust concurrency control and failure/recovery. Strive to attain knowledge from these sections that will enable you to be an informed consumer when evaluating DDBMS products. Understand the problems these products need to overcome. With this knowledge, when vendors make claims about the capabilities of their DDBMS products, you will be able to ask pertinent questions that will reveal potential limitations.

This section discusses the nature of the concurrency control problem in distributed databases and presents the essential concepts of one fundamental concurrency control method. The next section discusses failure transparency.

Distributed databases face the same concurrency problems as do any multi-user databases. The problems and their solutions are more complicated, however, because distributed database systems involve several independent computers and possibly replicated data. We begin with a discussion of the anomalies that can occur if processing is not appropriately controlled. These anomalies are the same as those described in Chapter 7 for centralized multi-user database processing. We will approach them somewhat more formally, however, to establish important terminology. The discussion in this section follows the organization set out by Bernstein and Goodman in their 1981 article cited above.

## Concurrent Processing Anomalies

Figure 15–5a illustrates the first anomaly, sometimes called the *lost update anomaly.* Suppose the transactions in this example occur in the business of the distributed manufacturer in Figure 15–2. Assume both transactions process the non-replicated data-item stored on a computer at plant A. The transactions could arise from the same DTM or from different DTMs. Both transactions reduce the quantity on hand for an item in inventory. (In these examples, we need not consider the identity of the item.)

The nomenclature $r_1(N_A)$ means a read by transaction number 1 of the value of $N$ stored at plant A. Next to that, the arrow and number indicate the value retrieved. Similarly, $w_1(N_A)$ means a write from transaction 1 of a value of $N$ to the computer at plant A. Similarly, the arrow and number indicate the value written.

**Figure 15–5**

Examples
of anomalies
due to concurrency

$T_1$ : Remove 1 unit from inventory at
plant A

$T_2$ : Remove 2 units from inventory at
plant A

|  | $N_A$ |
|---|---|
| Start | 3 |
| $r_1 (N_A) \leftarrow 3$ | 3 |
| $r_2 (N_A) \leftarrow 3$ | 3 |
| $w_1 (N_A) \rightarrow 2$ | 2 |
| $w_2 (N_A) \rightarrow 1$ | 1 |

$$3 - 1 - 2 = 1 ?$$

a. Illustration of lost update anomaly

$T_3$ : Move 4 units from warehouse (W)
to plant B

$T_4$ : Count number of units at A, B, and W

|  | $N_A$ | $N_B$ | $N_W$ |
|---|---|---|---|
| Start | 3 | 1 | 6 |
| $r_3 (N_W) \leftarrow 6$ | 3 | 1 | 6 |
| $w_3 (N_W) \rightarrow 2$ | 3 | 1 | 2 |
| $r_4 (N_W) \leftarrow 2$ | 3 | 1 | 2 |
| $r_3 (N_B) \leftarrow 1$ | 3 | 1 | 2 |
| $r_4 (N_A) \leftarrow 3$ | 3 | 1 | 2 |
| $r_4 (N_B) \leftarrow 1$ | 3 | 1 | 2 |
| $w_3 (N_B) \rightarrow 5$ | 3 | 5 | 2 |

b. Illustration of inconsistent
read anomaly

As you can see from this example, $w_1$ is lost. The write from transaction 2 overlays it. In Chapter 7, we called this the *concurrent update problem*.

A second anomaly is shown in Figure 15–5b. This anomaly, sometimes called the *inconsistent read anomaly*, occurs when one transaction reads a data-item while another one writes it. In this example, one transaction ($T_3$) is moving four units from the warehouse to plant B while another transaction ($T_4$) is counting the total number of units at plants A and B and the warehouse. Although a total of ten units exist in the three locations, $T_4$ incorrectly concludes there are only six. This occurs because $T_4$ reads $N_W$ between the time $T_3$ decrements the number from the warehouse and adds that number to the plant B inventory.

### Serial and Serial-Equivalent Executions

The situations illustrated in Figure 15–5 are anomalies because they generate incorrect and unexpected results. More specifically, they generate results different from the results that would have been produced if the transactions had been executed one at a time, or serially.

Figure 15–6 shows serial execution of $T_1$ followed by $T_2$, and $T_3$ followed by $T_4$. In both cases the results are correct and expected.

Serial transaction executions, although they ensure consistent results, prohibit concurrency. They often result in unacceptable performance. Thus, a goal of concurrency control is to allow concurrency, but in such a way that the results of the concurrent execution are the same as a serial execution.

An execution of transactions that is not serial but that generates the same results as a serial execution is said to be *equivalent to a serial execution*. Figure 15–7 shows an execution of $T_3$ and $T_4$ that is equivalent to a serial execution.

**Figure 15–6**

Examples of serial executions

| Serial Execution of $T_1$, $T_2$ | Serial Execution of $T_3$, $T_4$ |
|---|---|
| $r_1 (N_A) \leftarrow 3$ | $r_3 (N_W) \leftarrow 6$ |
| $w_1 (N_A) \rightarrow 2$ | $w_3 (N_W) \rightarrow 2$ |
| $r_2 (N_A) \leftarrow 2$ | $r_3 (N_B) \leftarrow 1$ |
| $w_2 (N_A) \rightarrow 0$ | $w_3 (N_B) \rightarrow 5$ |
| | $r_4 (N_A) \leftarrow 3$ |
| | $r_4 (N_W) \leftarrow 2$ |
| | $r_4 (N_B) \leftarrow 5$ |

**Figure 15–7**

Non-serial execution
of $T_3$, $T_4$ that is equivalent to a serial
execution

$$
\begin{aligned}
&r_3\,(N_W) \leftarrow 6 \\
&r_3\,(N_B) \leftarrow 1 \\
&r_4\,(N_A) \leftarrow 3 \\
&w_3\,(N_W) \rightarrow 2 \\
&r_4\,(N_W) \leftarrow 2 \\
&w_3\,(N_B) \rightarrow 5 \\
&r_4\,(N_B) \leftarrow 5
\end{aligned}
$$

More formally, two executions of a series of transactions are said to be equivalent if two conditions are met: (1) each read in the two executions reads data-item values produced by the same write in both executions, and (2) the final write of a data-item is the same in both executions (Bernstein & Goodman, 1981). If you examine Figure 15–7, you will find that both of these conditions are met.

These conditions make sense intuitively. They imply that the transactions receive the same inputs in both executions and that the final data-item values are the same. Observe, however, that two executions can be equivalent and not be serial. We can construct an execution equivalent to the non-serial execution in Figure 15–5a. Because it is equivalent to a non-serial execution, it too will be non-serial.

To specify conditions necessary for serial executions, we need to define another term. Two operations *conflict* if they operate on the same data-item and at least one of the operations is a write. From this it follows that two types of conflict are possible. *Read-write conflict* occurs when one operation is a read and the other is a write. *Write-write conflict* occurs when both operations are writes.

Figure 15–8 shows the inter-transaction conflicts in the transactions $T_1$ through $T_4$. For example, $r_1(N_A)$ has a read-write conflict with $w_2(N_A)$, and $w_1(N_A)$ has a write-write conflict with $w_2(N_A)$. Other conflicts are shown by the arrows. Notice that in addition to these conflicts, conflicts occur *within* transactions. Such conflicts are assumed to be managed by the transaction program and do not concern the DDBMS.

Before proceeding, we need to define several more terms. Figure 15–8 shows an *execution* of the transactions $T_1$ through $T_4$. This execution is an ordered sequence of requests to DTMs. We call an ordered sequence of requests a *schedule*. This execution is one of many possible schedules. Schedules that are equivalent to serial schedules are called *consistent schedules*. Finally, we will label requests according to the transaction that generates

**Figure 15-8**

Inter-transaction conflicts in $T_1$, $T_2$, $T_3$, $T_4$

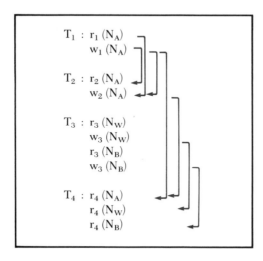

them. Thus, $REQ_i$ refers to any request that arises in the processing of $T_i$. In Figure 15-8, for example, both $r_2(N_A)$ and $w_2(N_A)$ will be referred to as $REQ_2$.

The following is a paraphrase of a fundamental theorem of serialization: Suppose we have a set of ordered transactions, $T_1$, $T_2$, ... , $T_n$. Call this ordered list T. A particular schedule, S, is a consistent schedule of T,

**Figure 15-9**

Consistent, non-serial schedule of $T_1$, $T_2$, $T_3$, $T_4$

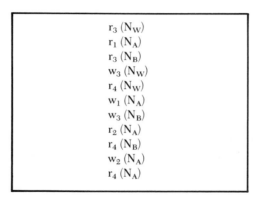

if for any two conflicting requests—say, $REQ_i$ and $REQ_j$—arising from transactions $T_i$ and $T_j$, $REQ_i$ precedes $REQ_j$ in S if and only if $T_i$ precedes $T_j$ in **T**.[5]

To understand this theorem, first realize that it is concerned only with the order of *conflicting* requests. This theorem says that for the schedule to be consistent, the order of *conflicting requests* must mirror the order of the transactions that spawn them. By implication, it also says that we need not be concerned with the order of non-conflicting requests.

Figure 15–9 shows a consistent but non-serial execution of the four transactions from Figure 15–8. Observe that the order of conflicting requests does, in fact, mirror the order of the transactions.

All of this discussion pertains to centralized processing as much as it does to distributed processing. We can focus the discussion on distributed processing by stating that the order of conflicting requests must mirror the order of the transactions *no matter where they are processed and no matter how many times they are processed*. Figure 15–10a shows a consistent, concurrent schedule of the transactions from Figure 15–8. These transactions are processed on two nodes without replication. Figure 15–10b shows a consistent concurrent schedule of these transactions where the node B data is replicated.

The discussion in the previous paragraph *implies* that all nodes agree on a single order for the transactions. In fact, *they might not*. Two nodes may each determine that their transactions should be next. As you will see, this situation creates other problems. To solve them, at times it will be necessary to abort a transaction in progress and back out its changes.

The fundamental theorem formalizes the objectives of concurrency control mechanisms. Somehow, these mechanisms must ensure that conflicting requests are processed in the order of the transactions that generate them. Before considering these mechanisms further, however, you need to understand the nature of commitment in distributed systems.

## Commitment in Distributed Systems

In Chapter 7, you learned the need for atomic processing of transactions. Either all of a transaction is committed to the database or none of it is. In centralized systems, this goal is accomplished by delaying changes to the database until the transaction is either committed or aborted.

For distributed systems, committing data changes is more complicated. Every transaction is allocated a private work space during its processing. As the transaction progresses, updates are made in the private work space, but they are not committed to the database. When the transaction finishes, if all nodes holding updates for the transaction are able to commit them to their respective databases, then the changes are made. Otherwise the transaction and all of its changes are aborted.

---

[5]Bernstein & Goodman, 1981.

**Figure 15–10**

Examples of distributed consistent schedules

| *Node Storing A & B Data* | *Node Storing W Data* |
|:---:|:---:|
| $r_1 (N_A)$ | |
| $r_3 (N_B)$ | $r_3 (N_W)$ |
| $w_3 (N_B)$ | $w_3 (N_W)$ |
| $w_1 (N_A)$ | $r_4 (N_W)$ |
| $r_2 (N_A)$ | |
| $r_4 (N_B)$ | |
| $w_2 (N_A)$ | |
| $r_4 (N_A)$ | |

a. Consistent concurrent schedule of
$T_1$, $T_2$, $T_3$, $T_4$ on two nodes

| *Node Storing A & B Data* | *Node Storing B & W Data* |
|:---:|:---:|
| $r_1 (N_A)$ | |
| $r_3 (N_B)$ | $r_3 (N_W)$ |
| $w_3 (N_B)$ | $w_3 (N_B)$ |
| $w_1 (N_A)$ | $w_3 (N_W)$ |
| $r_2 (N_A)$ | $r_4 (N_W)$ |
| $r_4 (N_B)$ | |
| $w_2 (N_A)$ | |
| $r_4 (N_A)$ | |

b. Consistent schedule with replicated data

Consider a distributed system like that shown in Figure 15–1. When a DTM issues an update request to a DBM, the DBM places the updated data in a private work space that it maintains for that transaction. (For the first such update action, it creates the private work space.) The DBM does not write the update in the database, however. If a DTM issues a read request for a data-item that the transaction has changed, the DBM provides the updated values from the private work space. This much is straightforward. However, when the transaction finishes and the DTM sends out commit actions, a complication arises.

Suppose three DBMs hold changes in behalf of a particular transaction. What if in the process of committing, one of them discovers that it cannot commit its changes? Unless something is done, only two out of three of the DBMs will update their databases. Clearly, this result is unacceptable.

To solve this problem, distributed commitment is broken into two phases. (This standard vocabulary of distributed processing includes the terms *two-phase commitment* and *two-phase locking*. They are different concepts, so be careful not to confuse them.) With two-phase commitment, the DTM that is processing the transaction issues a *pre-commit action* to all DBMs holding updated data for that transaction. This pre-commit action informs the DBMs that the transaction is finished and asks them to respond YES or NO, according to whether or not they can commit the changes they hold. If all DBMs respond YES, the DTM sends out a *commit action*. Otherwise, the DBM issues an *abort action* to all DBMs and restarts the transaction.

When a DBM receives the pre-commit action, it ensures that it can make the changes. (Depending on the form of concurrency control involved, the DBM may be unable to make the changes. Resolution of deadlock is a case in point, as you will see.) If the DBM can make the changes, it writes log records for the changes to permanent storage (storage that will survive a node failure). However, the changes are not yet written to the database. Once the DBM is certain that the log records are written, it responds YES to the DTM. Finally, when the DTM issues the commit action, the DBM actually updates the database. If the node running the DBM fails during this second phase, the changes have been recorded in the log and can be applied during recovery. We will consider recovery further. For now, you need to understand that the initial update actions issued by the DTM are provisional. They are not made permanent until after the two phases of commit.

## Concurrency Control via Distributed Two-Phase Locking

One method of enforcing the constraints of the fundamental theorem is called *distributed two-phase locking*. Using this method, DTMs are required to obtain locks before reading and writing data. Specifically, before reading a data-item, the DTM must have been granted a read lock by the DBM from which the data is read. Before updating a data-item, a DTM must have been granted a write lock from every DBM that stores that data-item.

Locks are granted with specific restrictions. A read lock may be granted as long as no other transaction holds a write lock on the data-item. A write lock may be granted as long as no other transaction has a lock of either type on the data-item. Thus, read locks may be shared with other reads but not with writes, and write locks may not be shared at all. (If a lock cannot be granted, the transaction must wait until either the lock is granted or the transaction is aborted.) Finally, once a DTM releases one lock, it may never be granted another lock. From that point it can only release locks.

The term *two-phase* arises from this last restriction. Eswaran et al. proved that the read and write locks will generate consistent schedules if and only if transactions process in two phases.[6] During the first phase, a transaction is allowed to acquire locks but it may not release any. This is called the *growing phase*. As soon as a transaction releases a lock, a point called the *locked point*, it enters the *shrinking phase*. During this second phase, it may release locks but may not acquire them.

If locks are held until the transaction terminates (by issuing an END or similar request), the growing phase lasts the entire duration of the transaction. The shrinking phase occurs after the END is issued. This processing method, described in the last section and in Chapter 7, meets the two-phase restriction. In fact, it is more restrictive than necessary to provide consistent schedules. By Eswaran's proof, processing can continue after the locked point. The only limit is that no more locks can be granted. Holding all locks until the commit point and then releasing them is thus sufficient but not necessary for the production of consistent schedules.

## Distributed Locking

For distributed databases, each DBM must include a subsystem that grants and releases locks. Furthermore, the DTMs must be programmed to incorporate the previously discussed rules. The DTM can issue a read request as soon as it obtains a single read lock. However, it must obtain write locks from all nodes that store the data-item before it issues the write commands.

To understand distributed locking, consider several examples. Suppose a replicated data-item, $A$, resides on nodes X, Y, and Z, and that transaction $T_5$ holds a read lock for $A$ on X. If another transaction, say $T_6$, wants to update $A$, it must obtain a write lock for $A$ on X, Y, and Z. The DBMs on Y and Z will issue the lock without delay. The DBM on X will not grant the lock, however, until $T_5$ finishes. Thus, read-write conflicts are avoided.

Now suppose $T_6$ holds a write lock for $A$ on X, Y, and Z. If $T_7$ wants to read $A$, it will need to obtain a read lock on one of X, Y, or Z. None of the DBMs on these nodes will grant the lock, however, until $T_6$ releases the locks. Thus, write-read conflicts are avoided.

Finally, suppose $T_8$ holds a write lock for $A$ on X, Y, and Z, and $T_9$ wants to update $A$. $T_9$ must wait until all of the write locks have been released. Then $T_9$ obtains a write lock for $A$ on X, Y, and Z. Thus, write-write conflicts are avoided.

To show that this strategy generates consistent schedules, it is also necessary to show that the order of locks remains the same as for a serial schedule. This is done in Eswaran's proof and is what gives rise to the need for the growing and shrinking phases.[7]

---

[6]Eswaran, K.P., Gray, J.N., Lorie, R.A., & Traiger, I.L. "The Notion of Consistency and Predicate Locks in a Database System." In *Communications of the ACM*, Vol. 19, No. 11, November 1976.

[7]Eswaran et al., 1976.

## Distributed Deadlock Processing

The disadvantage of controlling concurrency with locking is that deadlock can result. Figure 15–11 shows a deadlock situation among three transactions running on three nodes—A, B, and W. Each node holds a data-item, $N$, which is a count of the number of units of some inventory item at that site. $T_1$ is attempting to transfer units from A to B, $T_2$ is attempting to transfer units from B to W, and $T_3$ is attempting to transfer units from W to A.

To make the transfer, each transaction first reads the data at the two sites involved. $T_1$, for example, reads both $N_A$ and $N_B$. Before reading, it obtains a read lock on both items. When $T_1$ attempts to write $N_A$, it must obtain a write lock on it. It must wait, however, because $T_3$ holds a read lock on that data-item.

If you examine the locks carefully, you will find that $T_1$ is waiting on $T_3$, $T_3$ is waiting on $T_2$, and $T_2$ is waiting on $T_1$. This situation is diagramed in the wait-for graph in Figure 15–12. In this graph, the nodes (circles) represent transactions and the edges (lines connecting the circles) represent waits. A *deadlock* situation exists whenever a cycle, or path, goes from a node back to itself.

As with centralized processing, two fundamental strategies can be used to deal with deadlock. One is to be careful in the placement of locks and to disallow waiting that can lead to a deadlock situation. This strategy is called *deadlock prevention*. The second strategy is to place locks without restriction, but then to detect deadlock when it occurs. This strategy is called *deadlock detection*. We will consider each of these in turn.

**Deadlock Prevention.**   With deadlock prevention schemes, the lock managers in the DBMs are careful in allowing waiting to occur. When a trans-

---

**Figure 15–11**
Distributed deadlock
example

| Node A | Node B | Node W |
|--------|--------|--------|
| $r_1 (N_A)$ | $r_2 (N_B)$ | $r_3 (N_W)$ |
| $r_1 (N_B)$ | $r_2 (N_W)$ | $r_3 (N_A)$ |
| $w_1 (N_A)$-Wait | $w_2 (N_B)$-Wait | $w_3 (N_W)$-Wait |

**Figure 15–12**

Example of wait-for
graph

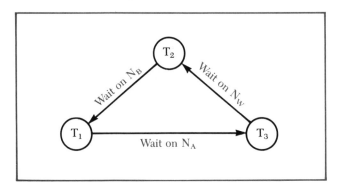

action, $T_i$, attempts to place a lock that conflicts with a lock held by a second transaction, $T_j$, the lock manager evaluates the situation and does not allow waiting if the potential for deadlock exists.

In the event of such potential, the lock manager can either deny $T_i$'s request, or it can abort $T_j$ and approve the request. If the request is denied, the strategy is called *nonpreemptive*. In this case, $T_i$ must be aborted and restarted. If $T_j$ is aborted, the strategy is called *preemptive*. In this case, $T_j$ is restarted.

Several varieties of both strategies are employed. The simplest non-preemptive strategy is not to allow waiting at all. If a transaction, $T_i$, requests a lock that conflicts with a lock held by another transaction, it is automatically aborted and restarted. This strategy simplifies lock processing but causes many restarts.

Another strategy is to assign priorities to transactions and to allow the transaction with the higher priority to have precedence. Thus, when $T_i$ requests a lock on a resource held by $T_j$, the response will be nonpreemptive if the priority of $T_i$ is less than or equal to $T_j$. It will be preemptive otherwise. As with all types of priority scheduling, there is the danger that low-priority transactions will never be allowed to complete.

Another strategy considers the *age* of transactions. Each transaction is assigned a unique birth time. When a lock conflict arises, the relative ages of the transactions determine if a transaction is allowed to wait. In *wait-die* strategy, when $T_i$ requests a lock on data held by $T_j$, $T_i$ is allowed to wait if it is younger than $T_j$. Otherwise it is aborted. This is a nonpreemptive strategy.

*Wound-wait* is a preemptive strategy. Here, when $T_i$ requests a lock on data held by $T_j$, $T_i$ is allowed to wait if $T_i$ is older than $T_j$. Otherwise $T_j$ is preempted and restarted. In both strategies, transactions keep their *original* birth time when they are restarted.

As with centralized database processing, deadlock can be prevented by having transactions request all locks in an agreed-on order. This restriction violates concurrency transparency, however, because it forces application programmers to consider concurrency issues when developing programs.

**Deadlock Detection.**   With deadlock detection strategies, waiting is allowed without restriction. All lock requests are accepted. If locks conflict, transactions are allowed to wait.

Deadlock is detected in two main ways. One involves *time-outs*. Transactions are allowed to wait a certain period of time for a resource to be freed. When the waiting time exceeds this amount, deadlock is presumed to exist, and one of the transactions involved in the lock is aborted and restarted. One problem with this strategy is that waits can result from causes other than deadlock, especially in a distributed system. Then transactions may be aborted and restarted unnecessarily.

The second approach for detecting deadlock is more precise. With it, *wait-for graphs* like the one in Figure 15–12 are constructed. The graphs are searched for cycles. If a cycle is found, a deadlock exists and one or more transactions are aborted and restarted. Data structures for representing graphs and algorithms for identifying cycles are well known.[8]

The problem with identifying cycles in a distributed database, however, is that constructing wait-for graphs requires knowledge of all locks in the distributed system. No single lock manager possesses all the needed data. Several methods exist to provide it. In one method a particular node is identified as the deadlock detector for the system. All lock managers periodically send their lock data to this *global lock manager*. This node constructs a global wait-for graph and determines if deadlocks exist. If they do, the global lock manager causes appropriate transactions to be terminated and restarted.

## Concurrency Control in R*

To date, the best-known and most successful lock processing DDBMS is R*, an experimental, but operational, prototype implementation developed by the IBM Almaden Research Center. It supports distributed partitioned databases but no redundancy. Concurrency is controlled by distributed two-phase locking. No attempt is made to prevent deadlock. Instead, deadlock is detected by algorithms on the distributed nodes.

In R*, each node is responsible for determining its own local deadlocks. There is no global deadlock detector. Instead, deadlock detection is shared among the nodes. Nodes are programmed to detect the possibility of a global deadlock and to send lock information to nodes managing transactions that may be blocked. Further, each node is responsible for processing

---

[8]Aho, A.V., Hopcroft, E., & Ullman, J.D. *The Design and Analysis of Computer Programs*, Addison-Wesley, 1975.

potential global lock data that is sent to it. Proponents of R* assert that the algorithm employed is such that only one node will detect a particular global deadlock. When detected, only local transactions are aborted.

## FAILURE TRANSPARENCY

The fourth goal for a DDBMS is to provide transparency to failure. Failures arise from a variety of sources. *Transactions* fail from erroneous data, improper procedures, or faulty programming. The *DDBMS* can fail for the same reasons. *Node hardware* can crash, and one or more links in the *network* can fail.

Clearly some failures are more serious than others. Malicious, Byzantine-type failures are beyond the scope of this book (and current technology as well). We also exclude failures in which nodes broadcast valid, but inappropriate actions. A properly formatted commit action, for example, is assumed to be valid.

Thus, in this discussion we will assume that nodes are *sane*—they either work properly or they do not work at all. Further, we will assume that the distributed system is partitioned cleanly. If node A is unable to communicate with node B, we assume that node B is unable to communicate with node A as well.

As stated previously, failure transparency should provide *atomic transactions*. Either none of a transaction should be processed or all of it should. Further, once committed, the effects of a transaction should be permanent.

In reality, such atomicity cannot be reached in all cases, even for sane failures. If too much of the network fails, or if critical portions fail at critical times, recovery with guaranteed atomicity may not be possible. The recovery manager of SDD-1, a prototype DDBMS, recognizes this fact with the definition of system *catastrophes*.[9] Catastrophes occur when too many components fail. Recovery from a catastrophe requires manual intervention and may result in a database that contains fragments of transactions.

The discussion in this section assumes that a log is kept of transaction activities so that it is possible to back out a transaction any time prior to the commit point. Also, sometimes the DDBMS must be guaranteed that a log record will survive a failure. In these cases, we will use the term *force-write*. This means that the DDBMS issues the write command and waits for the operating system to confirm that the record has been written to non-volatile storage—such as disk—before continuing.

### The Need for Directory Management

In a distributed database, each DTM maintains a directory of the location(s) of data-items. The processing of these directories is crucial, particularly in

---

[9]Hammer, M., & Shipman, D. "Reliability Mechanisms for SDD-1: A System for Distributed Databases." In *Transactions on Database Systems*, Vol. 5, No. 4, December 1980.

**Figure 15–13**
Inconsistency gener-
ated by inopportune
node failure

> $r_1 (X_A)$ - with read lock on $X_A$
> $r_2 (Y_D)$ - with read lock on $Y_D$
> A fails
> D fails
> $W_1 (Y_C)$ - with write lock on
> available copies of Y
> $W_2 (X_B)$ - with write lock on
> available copies of X
> A recovers
> D recovers
> Database is now inconsistent

a system with replication. To understand why, consider the situation shown in Figure 15–13.

This distributed replicated database has four nodes, labeled A through D. Data-item $X$ is stored on nodes A and B, and data-item $Y$ is stored on nodes C and D. Transaction 1 reads the copy of $X$ on A (first obtaining a read lock), and transaction 2 reads the copy of $Y$ on D (also with a read lock). Next, node A fails, then node D fails. Next, transaction 1 writes $Y$ on all nodes that contain $Y$. To do so, it must first obtain a write lock on those nodes. The only such node is C, given that node D has failed. Consequently, transaction 1 is able to write $Y$, even though transaction 2 has a read lock on it. Similarly, transaction 2 writes $X$ on all nodes that contain $X$. The only such node is B, given that node A has failed. Hence, transaction 2 obtains a write lock on B and writes $X$ on B, even though transaction 1 has a write lock on it.

When nodes A and D subsequently recover, the database is inconsistent. The values of $X$ differ on nodes A and B and the values of $Y$ differ on nodes C and D.

The inconsistency arose because the transaction managers were unable to detect locks held by failed nodes. The situation can be correctly processed if the directories are themselves subject to careful locking procedures. Such procedures are presented in a discussion of the *available copies algorithm* in a paper by Bernstein and Goodman.[10] This reference is also the source of this example.

---

[10]Bernstein, P.A., & Goodman, N. "An Algorithm for Concurrency Control and Recovery in Replicated Distributed Databases." In *Transactions on Database Systems*, Vol. 9, No. 4, December 1984.

A discussion of this algorithm is beyond the scope of this text. You should be aware of this type of anomaly, however, when you review DDBMS products.

### Two-Phase Commit with Acknowledgment

The discussion of two-phase commit in the last section was incomplete. Specifically, it did not consider cases in which the DTM or the DBMs failed after the pre-commit action was accepted by the DBM. A more complete discussion is summarized in Figure 15–14. In studying this example, recall that a transaction can be committed only if all DBMs involved are able to commit. A NO vote by any DBM is a veto.

**Normal Two-Phase Commit Processing.**   When the DBM receives the pre-commit action, it determines whether it can commit the transaction. If it can, it force-writes a PRE-COMMIT record on the log and sends a YES message back to the DTM. If the DBM is unable to commit the transaction,

**Figure 15–14**

Summary of two-phase commit

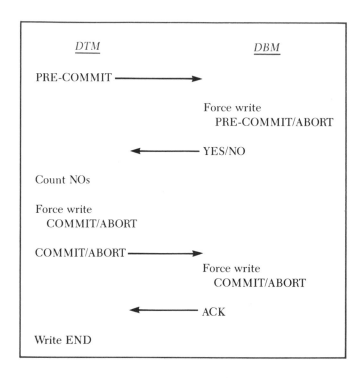

it force-writes an ABORT record on the log and sends a NO message. If it sends a NO, the DBM is guaranteed that the transaction will be aborted and it can therefore forget about that transaction.

When the DTM has received responses from all DBMs, it examines the votes. If any node responded NO, then the DTM force-writes an ABORT record in its log, aborts the transaction, and sends ABORT actions to all DBMs that voted YES. (It need not send actions to those that voted NO because they have already assumed the transaction will fail.) If all DBMs voted YES, the DTM force-writes a COMMIT record to its log and sends COMMIT actions to all DBMs.

If the DBMs receive an ABORT action, they force-write ABORT records on their logs and abort the transaction. If the DBMs receive a COMMIT action, they force-write COMMIT records on their logs and commit the transaction. In either case, the DBMs send an acknowledgment to the ABORT or COMMIT action sent by the DTM.

Once the DTM receives ACKs from all DBMs, it writes an END record in its log and forgets the transaction.

**Two-Phase Commit Processing under Failure.** Now consider what happens when either the DTM or a DBM fails at various points in this process. If a DBM fails and, during recovery, finds part of a transaction in its log with neither a PRE-COMMIT nor an ABORT record, it can ignore that transaction. The node failed in the middle of the transaction, and therefore the DTM cannot have received a YES from this node. The transaction will have been aborted. If it finds an ABORT record in its log, it can ignore the transaction for similar reasons.

If the DBM finds a PRE-COMMIT record without a COMMIT, it does not know what to do. It knows that it voted YES, but it does not know the outcome of the vote by other DBMs. Therefore, in this case, the DBM must ask the DTM for information about this transaction. Once it receives a response (either an ABORT or a COMMIT) from the DTM, it can process as under normal conditions. Finally, if the DBM finds both PRE-COMMIT and COMMIT records in the log, it knows the transaction should have been committed, and ensures it by applying after images, as described in Chapter 7.

Now consider DTM failures. If the DTM fails before sending any PRE-COMMIT actions, it aborts the transaction. It knows that all DBMs will (eventually) abort it as well, so it need take no other action. (Here, by the way, is a case of something falling through the crack between failure/recovery issues and concurrency control issues. Locks may exist on data-items on the DBMs. Those locks will stay in place until either a deadlock situation forces the DBM to abort the transaction, until the DBM fails and its recovery processor notices the incompleted transaction, or until a utility program cleans up the log. It would be better for the DTM to send ABORT actions for such a transaction during recovery so that DBMs can release their locks. Nothing in the *failure processing* algorithm, however, necessitates this.)

If the DTM finds a COMMIT record in its log with no corresponding END, it failed before all of the acknowledgments were received, and it periodically sends COMMIT actions to the DBMs that did not acknowledge. Once it receives all such acknowledgments, it writes the END to the log. If the DTM finds an ABORT record in its log with no corresponding END, it sends ABORT actions to all DBMs that have not acknowledged and writes an END to the log.

Review Figure 15–14 to make sure that you understand how this algorithm provides transaction atomicity with regard to these types of failure. In actuality, the situation is somewhat more complicated than described here, but this discussion should give you the gist of two-phase commitment. If you consider that failures can occur in the middle of failure recovery and that, especially for replicated data, directory processing needs to be considered as well, you can begin to sense how difficult failure transparency can be.[11]

### Consistency in Partitioned Networks

The final failure issue we will consider concerns distributed database processing in partitioned networks. A *partition* is a subnetwork that is created when nodes become disconnected due to node or communication line failure. Figure 15–15a shows a distributed network and Figure 15–15b shows the network broken into two partitions because of a failure of node E.

When a partition is created, if data is not replicated, the consequences, though undesired, are straightforward. A transaction can operate if all of the data it reads and writes is located on nodes in the partition in which the transaction is initiated. Otherwise, the transaction must wait until the network is recovered. For the example in Figure 15–15b, transactions initiated in partition I can run if the data they read and write is located on nodes A, B, C, or D. Transactions initiated in partition II can run if the data they read and write is located on nodes F, G, or H.

As mentioned earlier, organizations often choose to replicate data to increase reliability and performance. When data is replicated, processing during the time a partition exists must be carefully controlled, and recovery is considerably more difficult. If the network in Figure 15–15 supports order entry, and if inventory data is stored in both partitions, it would be possible to sell the same "last item" to two customers. Furthermore, once the network is recovered, the two separately processed collections of inventory data must be combined to produce a single, consistent collection.

**Correctness Versus Availability in Partitioned Networks.** A variety of anomalies can occur when processing replicated data in a partitioned net-

---

[11]Mohan, C., Lindsay, B., & Obermarck, R. "Transaction Management in the R* Distributed Database Management System." In *Transactions on Database Systems*, Vol. 11, No. 4, December 1986.

**Figure 15–15**
Sample partitions

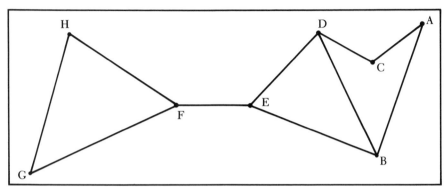

a.  Sample distributed network

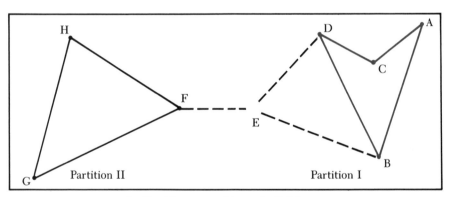

b.  Partitions caused by node E failure

work. Figure 15–16 illustrates two of them. In the first example (Figure 15–16a), nodes A and H, in different partitions, both sell diamond necklaces. They begin with the same count of four. Node A sells three necklaces while node H sells two to one customer and one to a second customer. At the point of recovery, the records in both nodes indicate that one necklace remains. In fact, a total of six necklaces were sold when only four were available. Further, at recovery, A and H have the same item count. This example shows that the recovery process must do more than ensure that data-items from separate partitions have the same value.

In the second example (Figure 15–16b), processing in two partitions violates a constraint. A customer's credit limit is $5000 and starting balance is $4500. Node A sells the customer $400 worth of goods and node H sells

**Figure 15–16**

Anomalies due to partitions

| Partition I (Node A) | Partition II (Node H) |
|---|---|
| Diamond necklace count = 4 | Diamond necklace count = 4 |
| Sell 3 diamond necklaces | Sell 2 diamond necklaces Sell 1 diamond necklace |
| Diamond necklace count = 1 | Diamond necklace count = 1 |

RECOVER

a. Update anomaly due to partition

| Partition I (Node A) | Partition II (Node H) |
|---|---|
| Cust 100 credit limit = $5000 | Cust 100 credit limit = $5000 |
| Cust 100 balance = $4500 | Cust 100 balance = $4500 |
| Sell $400 of goods to Cust 100 | Sell $300 of goods to Cust 100 |
| Cust 100 balance = $4900 | Cust 100 balance = $4800 |

RECOVER:
Recompute Cust 100 balance = $5200

b. Constraint violation due to partition

the customer $300. After recovery, the customer's balance is $5200, $200 in excess of the credit limit.

As Davidson et al. pointed out in a 1985 article, processing in partitioned networks involves a trade-off between correctness and availability.[12] Absolute correctness is easiest to provide if no processing of replicated data

---

[12]Davidson, S.B., Garcia-Molina, H., & Skeen, D. "Consistency in Partitioned Networks." In *Computing Surveys*, Vol. 17, No. 3, September 1985.

is allowed during a partition. One could argue, however, that in that case, why bother to replicate the data at all? Improved performance during non-partitions would be the only reason.

At the other extreme, availability is greatest if no restrictions are made on the processing of replicated data during partitions. For some applications, this is feasible. Given that airlines overbook flights, what difference does it make if occasionally, during partitions, the same seat is sold to different customers? Both the airlines and the passengers prefer high availability of reservations data to absolute correctness. However, the world banking system takes a different stance on this matter. Once again we come back to the need to understand system requirements.

**Strategies for Processing Partitioned Replicated Data.** Many different strategies have been proposed for the processing of replicated data in partitioned networks. Davidson et al. provides an excellent survey of many.[13] Here we will discuss one of the leading approaches.

*The Optimistic Protocol.* This strategy uses graphs (like the wait-for graphs in Figure 15–12) to keep track of dependencies among data changes. While the network is partitioned, changes are allowed without restriction (hence the name *optimistic*), and *precedence graphs* are kept that indicate which transactions have read and written which data. During recovery, the graphs of all partitions are combined and analyzed. If inconsistencies have developed, some transactions are rolled back and their changes eliminated.

Figure 15–17 shows an example of a combined precedence graph involving two partitions. The meaning of this figure is as follows: $T_{ij}$ is transaction number $j$ running in partition number $i$. The dotted arrow indicates that a transaction wrote a data-item that was read by a subsequent transaction. A solid arrow indicates that a transaction read a data-item that was later changed by another transaction. The data-items read by a transaction are above the line next to the transaction. The items written are shown below that line. Thus, $T_{11}$ read items $f$ and $g$ and wrote item $f$.

Davidson has proved that the database is consistent if and only if the precedence graph contains no cycles.[14] Because the graph in Figure 15–17 contains cycles (arrows that come back to a node), this database will be inconsistent. Actually, several inconsistencies exist here. For one, $T_{11}$ reads an old value of data-item $f$. The item had been changed by $T_{23}$, but $T_{11}$ was unaware of the change because of the partition in the network.

The strength of this strategy is its robustness. It will detect all inconsistencies, and sufficient data is available to permit correction of the database via rollback.

---

[13]Davidson et al., 1985.

[14]Davidson, S.B. "Optimism and Consistency in Partitioned Distributed Database Systems." In *Transactions on Database Systems*, Vol. 9, No. 3, September 1984.

**Figure 15–17**

Precedence graph
combined for two
partitions

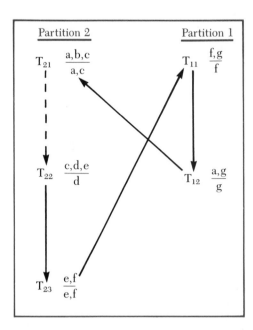

Two important disadvantages are involved, however. First, logs must be kept of all read and write activity. Although Davidson does not say so, it appears that many if not all of these log writes must be forced. This need will generate a significant performance problem.

Second, atomic transactions, once committed, cannot be rolled back. They should be permanent. But with this strategy, committed changes are not necessarily permanent. For the data in Figure 15–17, $T_{22}$ may need to be rolled back after real outputs have been generated by the transaction. Customers may have been promised diamond necklaces that cannot be delivered. The fact that the customer will later receive an apology and explanation that the necklace did not exist at the time of the sale may not be much consolation.

Even considering these disadvantages, this strategy shows promise for networks that require consistent and correct processing in spite of partitions in the network.

## SUMMARY

Distributed database processing is database processing in which the execution of transactions and the retrieval and updating of data occur across two or more independent, and usually geographically separated, computers. The distributed DBMS (DDBMS) consists of the collection of distributed transaction managers (DTMs) and database managers (DBMs) on all computers. DTMs receive processing requests from users and transaction programs, and translate them into actions for the DBMs. Coordination and control are important DTM functions. DBMs process some portion of the distributed database in accordance with action requests from the DTMs.

Advantages of distributed database processing include the potential for better performance and increased reliability. DDBMSs are more readily sized to user requirements and can be tailored to mirror organization structures. Disadvantages include the potential for worse performance and reduced reliability. Other disadvantages of DDBMSs include increased complexity, high construction and maintenance costs, and difficulty in control. The character, capabilities, and performance of distributed systems depend on the hardware used, the functionality of the DDBMS, the degree of data replication, the types of procedures, and the tasks required of the users of the system.

Four goals for a DDBMS are location transparency, replication transparency, concurrency transparency, and failure transparency. In theory, location and replication transparency are not too difficult to provide. The problems of concurrency and failure transparency are more difficult. Robust theoretical solutions are only beginning to be found. Robust practical solutions do not yet exist.

Systems Application Architecture (SAA) is IBM's blueprint for standardized programming, user, and communications interfaces. This blueprint will probably serve as the foundation for future distributed systems.

The control of concurrent processing in distributed database systems is a difficult problem. If processing is not controlled, problems such as the lost update and inconsistent read anomalies can occur. Distributed processing transactions need to be processed in such a manner that non-serial, concurrent executions of transactions have the same effect on the database as serial, non-concurrent executions would have.

Update commitment is more complicated for distributed processing than it is for non-distributed processing. The commit process must be broken into two phases. During the first phase, nodes declare the ability to commit. During the second phase, they perform actions to commit.

For both distributed and non-distributed processing, transactions must lock resources in a two-phase process. During the first phase, the growing phase, locks are acquired. As soon as the first lock is released, the growing phase is terminated and no more locks can be acquired. This is called the shrinking phase. Releasing all locks only at the end of a transaction meets this criterion, but is more restrictive than necessary.

Distributed systems perform locking using a distributed two-phase locking strategy. Distributed deadlock can occur. Therefore it must be prevented or it must be resolved by aborting one of the transactions. R* is a prototype DDBMS developed by IBM that implements distributed two-phase locking.

Failure transparency is difficult to provide. One reason is that too many types of failure exist. Limited transparency can be provided for sane node failures. Data directories must be part of the locking and recovery mechanisms for distributed failure/recovery. Two-phase commit processing must include forced writes and acknowledgment between nodes.

A network is partitioned if it is broken into two or more pieces by a failure of some type. Processing in partitioned networks can create integrity problems. Correctness and availability are trade-offs in a partitioned network. One strategy for providing integrity in partitioned networks uses precedence graphs. This strategy may at times require that committed transactions be de-committed. This is undesirable, but at present, unavoidable, at least for this type of processing.

---

**GROUP I**

QUESTIONS

15.1   Define distributed database processing.

15.2   Describe the difference between a DBMS and a DDBMS. Explain how it is possible for a DDBMS to contain DBMS products.

15.3   What is the function of a distributed transaction manager?

15.4   What is the function of a database manager?

15.5   Define *node, transaction node,* and *database node.*

15.6   Explain the difference between a request and an action.

15.7   Summarize the advantages of distributed database processing.

15.8   Summarize the disadvantages of distributed database processing.

15.9   Explain how the choice of node hardware affects the character of the distributed system. Show two alternative systems that conform to the design in Figure 15–1. Use Figure 15–4 as an example.

15.10  Explain the difference between a DTM that is provided as part of a DDBMS and a DTM that is developed in-house.

15.11  Define the terms *non-replicated database, partially replicated database, and fully replicated database.*

15.12  Explain how processing rights can vary from one distributed system to another.

15.13  How does the degree of data currency affect the design of a distributed database system?

15.14  Discuss the difference in control philosophies between the system in Figure 15–4a and 15-4b.

15.15  Explain the statement "the less sophisticated the DDBMS, the greater the role that must be taken by people."

15.16  Define and describe location transparency.

15.17  Define and describe replication transparency.

15.18  Define and describe concurrency transparency.

15.19  Define and describe failure transparency.

15.20  What is Systems Application Architecture?

15.21  Summarize SAA programming languages and services.

**15.22**  Summarize SAA user-access facilities.

**15.23**  Summarize SAA communications support.

**15.24**  What are the implications of SAA for distributed database processing?

**15.25**  Define and give an example of the lost update anomaly.

**15.26**  Define and give an example of the inconsistent read anomaly.

**15.27**  What is a serial execution? What is an execution of transactions that is equivalent to a serial execution?

**15.28**  Describe and explain the two conditions required for two executions to be equivalent.

**15.29**  Define *read-write conflict, write-read conflict,* and *write-write conflict.*

**15.30**  Define *schedule, serial schedule,* and *consistent schedule.*

**15.31**  Why is it necessary to break distributed commitment into two phases?

**15.32**  Summarize the processing of two-phase locking.

**15.33**  Give an example of a distributed deadlock.

**15.34**  What are the two primary means of dealing with distributed deadlock?

**15.35**  Explain the meaning of the wait-for graph in Figure 15–12.

**15.36**  What is a sane node?

**15.37**  Explain the processing problem depicted in Figure 15–13.

**15.38**  Explain the commit processing illustrated in Figure 15–14.

**15.39**  Define *partitioned network.*

**15.40**  Explain the problems illustrated in Figure 15–16.

**15.41**  Explain how processing in partitioned networks involves a trade-off between correctness and availability.

**15.42**  How can a precedence graph be used to determine if the processing of a partitioned database is consistent?

---

## QUESTIONS AND EXERCISES

**GROUP II**

**15.43**  Contact a corporation that has installed a distributed database system. Interview the developers and users. Map the system components into the architecture of Figure 15–1. Did the company *procure* a DDBMS or did they *assemble* the equivalent of a DDBMS from other software components? What software serves the role of the DTMs? Of the DBMs? Identify the components of the distributed system. What has the company's experience been? What problems and pitfalls have they encountered? What important factors led to successes?

**15.44**  Contact the vendor of a commercial DDBMS. What hardware does its system support? Map the architecture of the DDBMS into the scheme in Figure 15–1. What components are the DTMs? What components are the DBMs? What claims does the vendor make regarding location, replication, concurrency, and failure transparency? How does the product control concurrent processing? Does it employ two-phase locking? If not, what technique is employed? What failure/recovery mechanisms does it use? Does it employ two-phase commit? What happens when the network is partitioned? Determine the number of installations of this product and, if possible, the number of actual systems in use. What factors does the vendor believe lead to success? What problems and pitfalls are the most serious?

# File Organization

- Direct Access Storage Devices
- Direct Access Data Formats
- Basic File Organizations
- Sequential File Organization
- Summary

**C**omputer data is stored on peripherals called *secondary storage devices*. These storage devices can be divided into two broad categories: sequential and direct access. Sequential devices require that data be accessed in the sequence in which it was entered. Thus, before processing the fifth record in a sequential file, a program would first need to access the first, second, third, and fourth records. Direct access storage devices allow a program to access any record directly without accessing any preceding or succeeding records.

Sequential devices, such as tape units, keyboards, and optical readers, do not have a significant impact on database applications. They are used, for example, for obtaining instructions or for archiving database data. But the database itself, including application data, overhead data, and meta-data, is stored on direct access storage devices, typically on disk.

Despite the fact that database applications provide much greater services to the user than do file processing systems (see Chapter 2), database data is actually stored and accessed the same way as other files. The difference between a file processing system and a database application lies in the services provided by the DBMS.

In this appendix we will describe various formats used to store data on direct access storage devices. We will also examine various means of processing disk files. This background may help you better understand how a DBMS works.

## DIRECT ACCESS STORAGE DEVICES

The most common type of direct access storage device (DASD) is conventional, or hard, disk. Other types include floppy, or flexible, disks (also called diskettes), drums, and mass storage devices.

## Disk

A disk pack (Figure A–1) is mounted inside a disk unit. Data is recorded in concentric circles, or *tracks*. The number of surfaces in a disk pack as well as the number of tracks on a recording surface depend on the type of disk. For example, the IBM 3350, a disk unit used with larger IBM systems, has 16 disks per pack, 30 surfaces per pack (the top and bottom surfaces are not used), and 555 tracks per recording surface.

Data is read from or written to a disk by read/write heads. In most disk units, the heads are attached to access arms that can move to position the heads at any track on the recording surface of a disk. When the access arms are fixed in a position, data can be read from or written to one track on each recording surface. The collection of these tracks is called a *cylinder*. Note that the 3350 has 555 cylinders and that each cylinder has 30 tracks. A disk pack and read/write heads of a smaller disk unit are shown in Figure A-1.

Not all disk units have movable read/write heads. Some units, such as the Burroughs 9372, have fixed heads. Fixed-head units have one read/write head per cylinder and consequently are more expensive than movable-head units of a similar size. They may be faster, however, because no time is spent moving the read/write heads to the correct track. Some disk devices even have a combination of fixed heads on some cylinders and movable heads on others.

**Figure A–1**

Disk pack with access arms

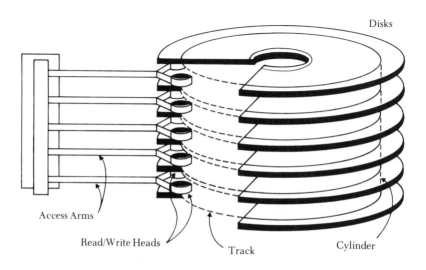

## Other Direct Access Hardware

In addition to conventional, hard disk storage units, three other types of direct access media are commonly used. One is called a *floppy disk,* or sometimes just a *floppy.* Floppies are similar to hard disk storage units, but floppies are used individually instead of in a stack. Further, this disk is flexible, hence the term *floppy* (Figure A-2).

Another commonly used direct access medium is a *drum*—a cylinder that can have data recorded on its outer surface. The tracks on a drum are circles around this surface, as shown in Figure A-3. Each track has its own read/write head, so there is no access motion and hence no delay from moving the access arms. Drums were more prevalent in the past than they are today.

A final type of DASD is actually a hybrid, or combination, of tape and disk technology. It is called a *mass storage device.* Data is stored on small rolls of magnetic tape and then moved, or *staged,* to a direct access storage device when needed. If the data has been changed during processing, then it is moved from disk back to the small rolls of tape.

**Figure A—2**
Floppy disk

**Figure A–3**
Drum (fixed read/
write heads)

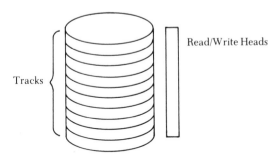

## DIRECT ACCESS DATA FORMATS

The formats of data on certain IBM DASD are described in this section. We have chosen these devices because they are typical and because they are commonly used in database applications. We are not endorsing any particular manufacturer's product.

### Key and No-Key Formats

One difference in the format of data records reflects whether the records are written with or without keys. Here, the term *key* means an identifier that is external to the record (not embedded) and which the operating system software uses to access a particular record. Embedded keys that are not used by the operating system to access records are not included in this definition of key. We will discuss them in the section "Direct File Organization" later in this appendix.

The no-key format is shown in Figure A-4. The index point is a special mark on the track that indicates the start of the track. Note that a track is a circle. Consequently, the two index points shown are actually the same point. The Gs in this figure represent gaps in the data on the track that are necessary for correct timing of activities.

To illustrate the use of these gaps, suppose the control unit of the disk is searching for the start of a track. When the index point is detected, a signal is sent from the disk to the control unit. The control unit then performs certain activities and responds with a signal to the device to read the next field (home address). While these actions occur, the disk is rotating. When the disk receives the signal to read the home address, the disk has already rotated past the index point. Consequently, there must be a gap between the home address and the index point. Other gaps are necessary for similar reasons.

**Figure A–4**
No-key data format

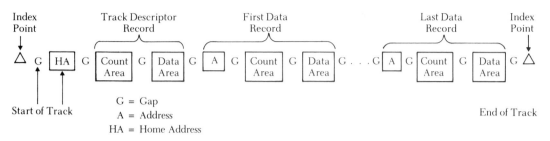

The home address area and the count and data areas of the track descriptor record indicate the address of the track (cylinder and track numbers), whether the track is operative or defective, and, if the track is defective, which alternative track has been used as a replacement. These fields normally concern the operating system, but not the DBMS or its users.

The next three areas (A, count area, and data area) constitute one data record. These areas repeat on the track for each data record. The A field is a 2-byte address marker that enables the disk drive's control unit to sense the beginning of a record.

The count area is pictured in detail in Figure A-5. The system uses the flag field to indicate the condition of the track and other information used by the control unit. The cylinder number (2 bytes), head number (2 bytes), and record number (1 byte) form the unique record identifier. KL is the key length, which is always zero for the no-key data format. DL is the length of the data area that follows. The cyclic check field is used to check for errors in reading and writing.

**Figure A–5**
Count area

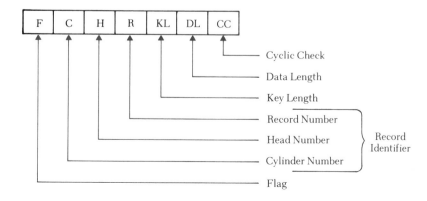

The important concept here is that the unique record identifier and the length of the data area precede each data record. The control unit knows exactly how much data to read from the count area because the area is always 11 bytes long. It refers to the DL field in the count area to obtain the length of the data area. Thus the control unit determines the length of a data area before reading it.

The data format of keyed records is very similar to that of no-key records. The only fundamental differences are that a key area precedes the data area of every data record and that the key-length field in the count area is not zero. It contains the length of the key area (Figure A-6).

### Fixed Block Architecture

A few years ago, vendors (notably IBM) developed a new disk type based on *fixed block architecture* (FBA). Disk devices using FBA do not use the record formats shown in Figures A-4 through A-6. Rather, data is stored in fixed-size containers or blocks. The IBM 3370, for example, stores data in 512-byte blocks. Data is packed into these fixed-size containers much as furniture is packed into shipping crates.

The IBM 3370 has two sets of read/write heads per disk pack. Because these heads can operate simultaneously, data can be processed much faster than devices with only one set. However, data that appears to the programmer to be stored contiguously (physically adjoining) may in fact be stored by the two sets of heads on completely separate parts of the disk. Thus, with these devices, a logically sequential file may not be physically sequential at all.

With traditional devices it is possible to access records by physical position. The cylinder, track, and record number can be used to identify a record. With FBA this is no longer possible. Instead, blocks are accessed by relative block number, and the block number is translated into a physical location by the software controlling the device.

Consequently, when data is stored on FBA devices, programs have no control over the physical location of data. This lack of control can result in inefficiencies. On the other hand, separating programs from knowledge of

---

**Figure A—6**
Key data format

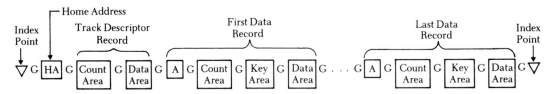

physical data locations creates device independence. Data can be moved from one device to another without any impact on programs.

### Record Blocking

As Figures A-4 through A-6 show, each data record requires a considerable amount of overhead, or information beyond the application data itself. One way to reduce this overhead is to make the physical records larger by grouping several logical records into one physical record. This process is called *record blocking*. For example, suppose the logical data records are 100 bytes long. Any number of them can be blocked together. If we group eight of them, we form a block of records 800 bytes long. Record blocking reduces the amount of overhead information per track and consequently it also potentially reduces the total amount of space for the file. It also increases the complexity of the I/O task. Either the application program or the file processing software must block records before writing them and deblock them when reading.

## BASIC FILE ORGANIZATIONS

A DBMS must interface with the operating system to perform I/O. More generally, any program, whether a DBMS or not, must do this. The portion of the operating system that does I/O is often referred to as the *data management access methods* (or just *access methods*). Figure A-7 shows the relationship of the operating system user (DBMS or application program), the access methods, and the secondary storage device on which data is stored.

Many access methods have been developed. Each assumes a particular *file organization*, and each encompasses one or more *access techniques*. Strictly speaking, the file organization is the structure of the file and the access technique is the way in which the file structure is manipulated. Commonly, however, this distinction is not made, in which case file organization describes not only structure but also access technique. We will use the latter, more common definition.

---

**Figure A—7**
Access method
interfaces

You need to understand three types of file organization: sequential, indexed sequential, and direct. Sequential file processing is used by DBMS products for producing log files and archive database copies. Indexed sequential files, as such, are not used by DBMS products. The *techniques* of indexed file processing, however, are used. No DBMS processes the database using the operating system's indexed sequential file organization. Many DBMS products, however, create their own version of indexed files. So if you learn indexed sequential file processing, you will accomplish two objectives: you will learn a type of file processing and you will learn a technique used by the DBMS itself. Finally, direct organization, or a variant closely akin to direct organization, is used by all DBMS products to organize the database itself. Therefore, learning direct organization will help you to understand how DBMS products operate.

## SEQUENTIAL FILE ORGANIZATION

Sequential file organization is the simplest of the three file organizations to be discussed. Records are written to a file in sequence. Once a sequential file is created, records can be added to the end of the file. It is not possible to insert records in the middle of the file without rewriting the file. Also, it is generally not possible to modify an existing record without rewriting the file. Records are usually read in sequence. With some systems it is possible to start this sequential reading at any record location. It is not required to start at the beginning of the file.

### Indexed Sequential File Organization

The indexed sequential file organization allows both sequential and random processing. Sequential processing can start at the beginning of the file or at any other record in the file. Random processing is accomplished by specifying the key-field value for the desired record. This record is found via indexes.

The following discussion presents the actions taken by the operating system. Application programs are not involved with the details that are described. Rather, the application program issues a command, for example, to read a particular record or to insert a new record. Finding space, updating indexes, and so forth are all done by the operating system.

Indexed sequential files are composed of three areas. The *prime area* contains records of the file. When the file is created or reorganized, all records reside in the prime area. The second area of an indexed sequential file is the *overflow area*. Records are placed in the overflow area when additions to the file cannot be fitted into the prime area. The *indexes* are located in the third area of an indexed sequential file. These indexes are used to locate a particular record for random processing.

|  | Key | Record | Key | Record | Key | Record | Key | Record |
|---|---|---|---|---|---|---|---|---|
| Track 1 | 10 | Rec 10 | 14 | Rec 14 | 18 | Rec 18 | 20 | Rec 20 |
| Track 2 | 26 | Rec 26 | 34 | Rec 34 | 41 | Rec 41 | 60 | Rec 60 |
| Track 3 | 72 | Rec 72 | 73 | Rec 73 | 74 | Rec 74 | 75 | Rec 75 |
| Track 4 | 77 | Rec 77 | 78 | Rec 78 | 79 | Rec 79 | 82 | Rec 82 |
| Track 5 | 89 | Rec 89 | 91 | Rec 91 | 93 | Rec 93 | 98 | Rec 98 |

**File Indexes.**    To understand the processing of an indexed sequential file, consider an example in which four data records fit on a track. Figure A-8 shows the first five tracks of that file. Note that each record has a unique key and that records are in order by key.

Suppose it is necessary to read record 79. One way to access this record is to sequentially read the records in the file until record 79 is found. This may be a very slow process. A faster way of finding record 79 is to use the track index (Figure A-9). The track index contains the value of the highest key on each track. To locate the track that contains record 79, it is necessary only to consult the track index and find the first track that contains a record with a key greater than or equal to 79. In this case, that is track 4. The highest key of track 3 is 75 and the highest key of track 4 is 82. Therefore,

| Track Number | Highest Key on Track |
|---|---|
| 1 | 20 |
| 2 | 60 |
| 3 | 75 |
| 4 | 82 |
| 5 | 98 |

if record 79 exists, it must be on track 4. Consequently, the next step is to sequentially read track 4 to find record 79. It is because of the combination of using an index and then reading sequentially that this access method is called *index sequential*.

Using the track index does not eliminate sequential searching. It just reduces the scope of the task. Instead of searching a large file of records, the access method is able to search a table that points toward the desired record location. Then it searches that area for the record.

If the file is long, then it may occupy many cylinders on the disk. To increase efficiency, a *cylinder index* is used in addition to the track indexes. This index shows the value of the highest key on each cylinder of the file. Thus, if the file occupies twenty cylinders, there will be twenty entries in the cylinder index. Now to find a given record, it is necessary to search the cylinder index to determine which cylinder the record is on and then to search the track index for that cylinder to determine the proper track. Finally that track is searched to find the correct record. For brevity, Figure A-10 assumes that each cylinder has only five tracks. In common practice, cylinders have more tracks, depending on the device.

If the file is very large, searching the cylinder index might be time-consuming. In this case, it might be desirable to break the cylinder into parts and create a master index on the parts of the cylinder index. For example, the cylinder index might be broken into parts having twenty entries each. The master index has the highest key in each part.

To find a particular record, it is necessary to search the master index to find the correct part of the cylinder index and then to search that part of the cylinder index to locate the cylinder on which the record resides. Following that, it is necessary to search the track index for that cylinder and then to sequentially read the track in order to find the record itself (Figure A-11).

**Indexed Sequential File Processing.**   When an indexed sequential file is created, all records are written into the prime area in sequence by key. The indexes are generated at this time. We have already seen how records can then be retrieved from the file. The process of updating a record (sometimes referred to as *update-in-place*) is similar to the retrieval process. The indexes are used to find the desired record and the new version of the record is written on top of the old one.

A deletion from the file is also straightforward. The indexes are used to find the desired record and a special mark is inserted into the record to indicate that it has been deleted. Even though the record may be physically present, subsequent attempts to read the record will result in an error. The program that performs the access must check for the special mark that indicates deletion.

Insertions to an indexed sequential file are quite troublesome because the key order of the file must be maintained. To illustrate, assume that it is necessary to insert record 55 into the file depicted in Figure A-8. The only

Cylinder Index

| Cylinder | Highest Key |
|----------|-------------|
| 1 | 98 |
| 2 | 184 |
| 3 | 278 |
| ⋮ | ⋮ |

Track Index for Cylinder 1

| Track | Highest Key |
|-------|-------------|
| 1 | 20 |
| 2 | 60 |
| 3 | 75 |
| 4 | 82 |
| 5 | 98 |

Track Index for Cylinder 2

| Track | Highest Key |
|-------|-------------|
| 1 | 107 |
| 2 | 122 |
| 3 | 148 |
| 4 | 163 |
| 5 | 184 |

Track Index for Cylinder 3

| Track | Highest Key |
|-------|-------------|
| 1 | 201 |
| 2 | 210 |
| 3 | 223 |
| 4 | 259 |
| 5 | 278 |

Assume desired record has key value 248.

1.   Search cylinder index to find correct cylinder. Cylinder 2 has highest key of 184; cylinder 3 has 278. Therefore, cylinder 3 must contain the record.

2.   Search track index for cylinder 3 to find track. Track 3 has highest key of 223; track 4 has 259. Therefore, track 4 must contain the record.

3.   Search track 4 for the desired record.

way that key sequence can be preserved is for record 55 to replace record 60 on the file. But what happens to record 60? Clearly it is undesirable to put 60 on top of 72, put 72 on top of 73, and so on, completely rewriting the remainder of the file. The answer is that record 60 is put into an overflow area and pointers are set up to ensure that record 60 can be found during subsequent processing. Doing this requires extension to the track index. If we compare Figure A-12 to Figure A-9, we see that two words have been added to each index entry. The first word holds the highest key in the overflow area for this track. The second word holds the address of the first overflow area or is null if there is none. When record 55 is inserted into the file, it replaces record 60, which is written into the overflow area, and the track index is modified accordingly. The results of these operations appear in Figure A-13. Note that a new field has been attached to record 60 in the overflow area. This field is used to point to the next record in the overflow area. In this case it is null.

**Figure A—11**
Index structure

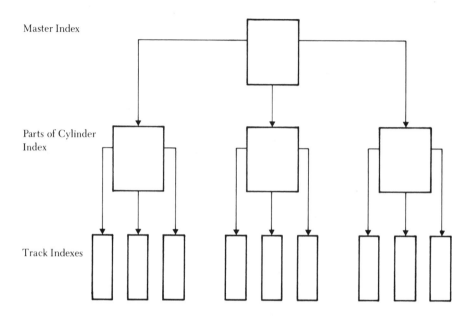

Now suppose record 24 is to be inserted into the file. A key value of 24 is greater than the last key on track 1 but less than the first key on track 2. Therefore, record 24 will be added to track 2. All records on track 2 are moved over one place and record 55 is bumped into the overflow area. The file now appears as in Figure A-14. Record 55 is the first record in the overflow area and a pointer (address) to record 60 has been added to record 55.

If record 57 were added to the file, it would be inserted into the overflow area and the address in record 55 would be modified to point to record 57 (Figure A-15). The prime area and track index would remain the same.

It should be clear from this discussion that insertions in indexed sequential files are indeed troublesome. If many insertions have been made, it usually takes a long time to find a record. At some point, processing becomes prohibitively inefficient. Then the entire file must be reorganized. Reorganizing means creating a new file with all the records in key sequence in the prime area. The operating system vendor usually supplies a reorganizing utility.

## Direct File Organization

Direct file organization is used primarily for random processing, although sequential processing is possible. (Note that the word *random* here means

| Track Number | Highest Key on Track | Highest Key in Overflow | Address of First Over-flow Record |
|---|---|---|---|
| 1 | 20 | 20 | Null |
| 2 | 60 | 60 | Null |
| 3 | 75 | 75 | Null |
| 4 | 82 | 82 | Null |
| 5 | 98 | 98 | Null |

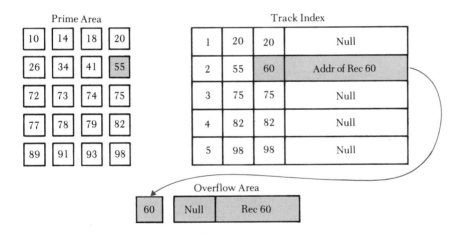

processing a specific record, usually identified by its key field. It does not mean processing records arbitrarily. The term *direct* is more appropriate, if less frequently used, to describe the manipulation of direct files.) Direct file organization differs from indexed sequential file organization in that records are in no particular order on the file. Thus sequential reading may present records in apparently nonsensical order. The programmer has greater flexibility with direct than with indexed sequential, but the programming task is more complex.

Direct organization is the fundamental organization of almost every database. DBMS products usually do their database I/O using direct orga-

**Figure A—14**

Addition of record 24

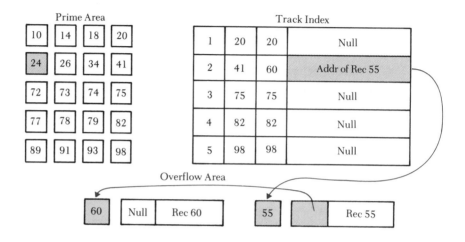

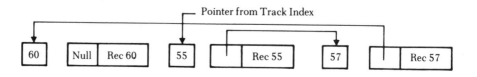

nization. Typically, when other features such as indexes are needed, the DBMS provides them on top of the operating system's direct access methods.

Records are identified in one of several ways. One method is to specify the *relative track* and *relative record number* of a desired record. Relative track means track number relative to the start of the file. Relative record number means record number relative to the start of the track. A second method of identifying a record is by *relative track* and *key*. (In this case, records must have keys.) A third method is by *relative block address*—the block number (physical record number) of the desired record relative to the start of the file. The last way is by *physical address*. This could be the actual cylinder, head, and track record number on the device, or it could be a block address and displacement within the block (FBA devices). In general, physical addresses change if the file is moved to another volume or device.

Unlike indexed sequential organization, in which each record is identified to the system by its key, direct organization does not support any

**Figure A—15**

Overflow area after
addition of record 57

particular correspondence between record content and file address. It is left to the DBMS or operating system user to establish a way of correlating records to file locations.

**Address Computation.**    Perhaps the easiest way of addressing records is to use a field or a portion of a field as a relative block address. For example, suppose an inventory file has records with part number fields. If part numbers are unique, say if they start with 1 and run consecutively in steps of 1 up to the number of parts in inventory, then the part number can be used as the relative block address of the record in the file. Unfortunately, such part numbering schemes are rare.

Another approach, sometimes referred to as a *hashing scheme*, is to perform some sort of arithmetic operation on a field of the record and to use the result as an address. For example, in a file containing student records, each record may contain a student number. If these student numbers do not start with 1 and run consecutively in increments of 1, they are not suitable for use as addresses. Addresses can be created, however, by using only the last few digits of the student number. This is sometimes referred to as the *division/remainder* method because taking the last few digits is equivalent to dividing by a number and using the remainder. For example, taking the last five digits is equivalent to dividing by 100,000 and using the remainder.

The problem with a hashing scheme is that the generated addresses may not be unique. Student records with numbers 4363570 and 8263570 will both belong at location 63570. This situation is referred to as a *collision* and the resulting addresses, 63570, are called *synonyms*.

Even though techniques for processing synonyms exist, it is always desirable to minimize them. Analysis of records may show that the last five digits are not the best ones to use. Perhaps using the second, fourth, and last three digits would lead to fewer synonyms.

Another type of hashing scheme is *folding*, in which a key is split into parts. The parts are added and the sum, or part of the sum, is used as an address. Folding can be combined with the division/remainder method. The parts of the key are added together, the sum is divided by a number, and the remainder is the calculated address. This scheme is generally effective because every character in the key participates in the hashing calculation (see Figure A-16).

A third approach for addressing a direct file is to use a cross-reference list or table. The table has keys in one column and file addresses in another (Figure A-17). To find a record, the key column is searched for a match on the desired key value. If a match is found, the address is taken from the corresponding address column. That address may be any of the four types mentioned previously. The indexes of an indexed sequential file are an extension of this concept.

A variation of this technique is often used in database systems. Consider a database of employee information that has three database record

**Figure A–16**

Hashing methods for
addressing records

| Key:    | 412483    | Key:        | 715823408         |
|---------|-----------|-------------|-------------------|
| Add:    | 412 + 483 | Add:        | 715 + 823 + 408   |
|         |           | Divide sum: | 1946/1000         |
| Address: | 895      | Address:    | 946               |

a.  Folding               b.  Folding with Division/Remainder

**Figure A–17**

Cross-reference table

|     | Address |
|-----|---------|
| Key | (Relative Block Type) |
| 123 | 1 |
| 241 | 8 |
| 618 | 6 |
| 723 | 4 |
| 1841 | 5 |
| 1981 | 2 |
| 2318 | 7 |
| 2742 | 3 |
| . | . |
| . | . |
| . | . |

types: employee SALARY, employee PERSONAL data, and employee CHILD.
Further, assume that all three types reside on the same physical file with
one database record per block. This means that relative block addresses are
also relative record addresses.

Figure A-18 shows the relationships of the SALARY, PERSONAL, and
CHILD records. To find employee information, the database system maintains a cross-reference table like that in Figure A-19. The first column has
Employee-number, the second the relative block address of the physical
record containing the SALARY record for that employee, and the third the
relative block address of the PERSONAL record.

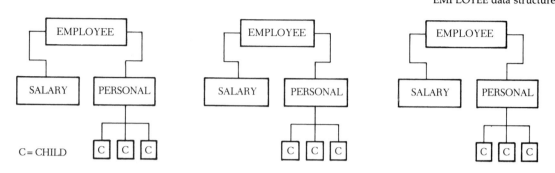

| Employee-number | SALARY Record Address | PERSONAL Record Address |
|---|---|---|
| 100 | 4 | 12 |
| 130 | 5 | 9 |
| 180 | 11 | 6 |
| 240 | 8 | 7 |
| 260 | 3 | 2 |
| 300 | 10 | 1 |

The cross-reference table for the CHILD records is within the PER-SONAL records. The first 200 bytes of each PERSONAL record contain personal data and the last 40 bytes contain space for up to ten 4-byte relative block addresses of CHILD records. One such record is shown in Figure A-20. In this example, then, part of the cross-reference table is carried with the data.

**Direct File Processing.** Because of the flexibility inherent in direct file organization, such files may be processed in many ways. A method that typifies processing using hash addressing schemes is illustrated here. Another method that does not use hash addressing is discussed in Appendix B.

**Figure A—20**

PERSONAL record

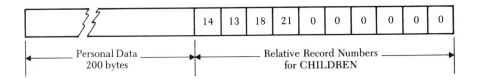

| | | 14 | 13 | 18 | 21 | 0 | 0 | 0 | 0 | 0 | 0 |

Personal Data
200 bytes

Relative Record Numbers
for CHILDREN

Consider a database of fixed-length student database records. (Fixed-length records consist of a uniform, pre-determined number of bytes. This is contrasted with *variable-length* records, which can be of different lengths.) One database record is in each block. Assume that 16,000 database records must be processed randomly by student number. The division/remainder method is used to generate relative block addresses. Finally, assume that the file is to be 80 percent full, which means that the total size of the file will occupy space sufficient for 20,000 records. The reason for having 4,000 unused record areas will soon be evident.

Assume that student numbers have six digits. One way to create a relative block address from a student number is to divide the student number by 20,000 and take the remainder. The result will range from 0 to 19,999. Because we want addresses from 1 to 20,000, we will add 1 to this remainder. This procedure will generate synonyms, so it is necessary to find a method for processing them. We establish the following rules:

1. To insert a record:
   a. If the calculated address is empty, insert the record at that address.
   b. If the calculated address is full, do not insert the record at that address. Increment the calculated address by 1. Repeat steps a and b up to ten times.
   c. If steps a and b have been repeated ten times and the record still has not been inserted, print the message FILE TOO DENSE and stop.
2. To find a record (for retrieval, updating, or deletion):
   a. Read the record at the calculated address.
   b. If this is the desired record, stop. If not, increment the calculated address by 1. Repeat steps a and b up to ten times.
   c. If steps a and b have been repeated ten times and the record has not been found, print the message RECORD NOT FOUND and stop.

These rules assume that empty or unused record areas can be identified. One way to indicate empty record areas is to insert a special mark into the first byte of each such area before any data records are loaded. The

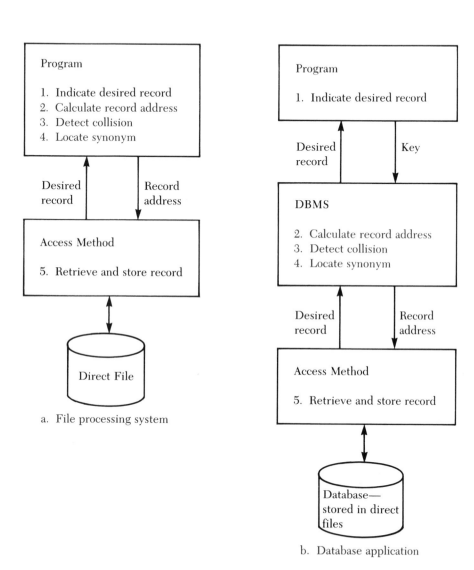

a. File processing system

b. Database application

mark must be one that cannot be confused with valid data. A bit combination that does not have a character representation may be a good choice. When a record is deleted, this special mark can be inserted into the record.

The purpose of establishing the limit of ten repetitions is to prohibit searching all the way through the file. Such searching would be extremely time-consuming. This means that the file cannot be 100 percent full because if the last empty area is at, say, 18,000, and the generated address for a record is 5, the empty record area will not be found. We accept this situation because we do not want to read from record 5 to record 18,000 to find the record.

The limit of ten is arbitrary here. We could say fifteen or twenty, but higher limits could result in slower processing. Note that if the message FILE TOO DENSE is written, it means that too many synonyms have been generated in one area. The file should be made larger and the address computation should be modified.

Actually, for this type of processing, 80 percent density is high and 60 percent might be more realistic. Note that the fewer the synonyms that exist (or the better the hashing scheme is), the more dense the file can be.

Many hashing schemes are possible. The one we used in this illustration is very simple. It could be expanded, for example, to include blocked records. When records are blocked, several data records are placed together in one physical record. Thus, several records having the same synonym can be stored in the same block. In this case, records are stored away from the calculated address only when the block becomes full. This strategy can reduce the number of extra reads. Another extension uses a hash function to generate the first location but then uses linked lists (see Appendix B) to represent alternative locations. This approach is used by several database systems, notably TOTAL and IMAGE.

As mentioned earlier, direct files are heavily used in database systems. Therefore, an understanding of direct file organization and direct file processing can be useful background for a database student. It should be noted, however, that it is the DBMS, not the application programmer, that interfaces with the access method. As illustrated in Figure A-21, if direct files are used in a file processing system, the programmer is responsible for performing the address calculation, managing collisions, locating synonyms, and, possibly, handling other related tasks. In a database system, however, the user (who can be an application programmer or an end user employing online query facilities) merely indicates which record is desired and the DBMS handles the preliminary I/O tasks. Ultimately, of course, it is the access methods of the operating system that interface with the direct files stored on disk (Figure A-7).

## SUMMARY

In this appendix you have studied the three fundamental ways in which data is stored on direct access storage devices. Each of the basic file organizations—sequential, indexed sequential, and direct—has certain advantages and disadvantages when compared with the others. If you are involved in developing a file processing system, you will need to select the appropriate file organization for that application. However, for database process-ing, direct files are currently the most widely used.

With direct file processing, different types of data records can be stored in the same file. Their locations are determined neither by arrival sequence (as in sequential files) nor by key sequence (as in indexed sequential files). Instead, an address is determined for each record based on some program-mer-defined scheme. This address might be the physical address (cylinder, head, and record number), the relative record number (the first, second, or hundredth record in the file), or some other means of locating the record in the file.

Related records, although probably physically separate from one another on the file, can be logically connected by cross-reference tables and by pointers embedded into data records themselves. Other techniques that were not discussed in this appendix can also be used to connect related records.

Although a knowledge of direct file processing is helpful background information for the database student (and in many cases for the database practitioner), you should remember that it is the DBMS, not the database user, that interfaces with the operating system in order to locate records in the database. This complex task is not the responsibility of the end user or the application programmer.

## QUESTIONS                                                                    **GROUP I**

**A.1**  Suppose an indexed sequential file has twelve unblocked fixed-length rec-ords, arranged three per track. If the key of the first record is 5, that of the second is 10, and so on in increments of 5, sketch the prime area. Sketch the track index.

**A.2**  For the file described in A.1 sketch the prime and overflow areas after each of the following actions occurs:

   **a.** Record 22 is inserted.

   **b.** Records 22 and 16 are inserted.

   **c.** Records 22, 16, and 21 are inserted.

**A.3**  If the STUDENT file considered in this appendix is 60 percent dense, how many records should the file contain?

**A.4**  How must the hashing scheme be modified for the STUDENT file if it is 60 percent dense?

**A.5**  If records A, B, and C are synonyms, which record should be closest to its calculated address? How should the input file be sorted prior to loading the file?

**A.6**  Construct a hashing scheme different from the one described in this appendix.

**A.7**  Explain how the index of an indexed sequential file can be considered an extension of cross-reference-list addressing on a direct file.

**A.8**  Describe a method for processing synonyms that is different from the one described in this appendix.

---

**GROUP II**     QUESTIONS AND EXERCISES

_____

**A.9** Write a program to create and process an indexed sequential file of student records. Assume the records have a 6-byte Student-number, which is the key, a 20-byte Name field, and a 4-byte Major field. You should load the file, dump it sequentially, and then randomly insert, delete, replace, and read records. Finally, dump the file sequentially. Be sure your program can detect efforts to insert a record that is already on the file or to delete or replace one that is not on the file.

**A.10** Write a program to create and maintain a direct file of student records. Assume the records have a 6-byte Student-number, a 20-byte Name field, and a 4-byte Major field. Create 100 empty records on the direct file and use a hash-addressing scheme on the Student-number field. The file is too dense if a record cannot be inserted in one of the three records past its calculated address. Insert, delete, read, and replace records. Be sure your program can detect efforts to insert a record that is already there or to replace or delete one that is not on the file.

**A.11** Investigate any commercial DBMS product. Determine what kind of file organization is used to store and manipulate database data. How does the file organization differ from the basic ones described in this appendix? How is it similar?

# Data Structures
# for Database Processing

---

- Flat Files
- Representing Binary Relationships
- Secondary-Key Representations
- Summary

---

The file organization methods presented in Appendix A are by themselves inadequate for database processing. Sequential files are inappropriate for storing database data. Indexed sequential files are seldom used by DBMS products because they are much too limited. Direct files are used by almost all DBMS products because of their tremendous versatility. However, even direct files, by themselves, cannot provide the services needed by database users. To provide these services, DBMS products build and maintain specialized data structures. These data structures are the topic of this appendix.

We begin by discussing flat files and some of the problems that can occur when such files need to be processed in different orders. This leads to a discussion of three data structures that address such problems: sequential lists, linked lists, and inverted lists (or indexes). We will also discuss a special form of inverted lists called a *B-tree*.

Next we illustrate how the binary relationships discussed in Chapter 6—trees, simple networks, and complex networks—are represented using various data structures. Finally, we explore how to represent and process multiple keys.

Although a thorough knowledge of data structures is not required to use most DBMS products, this kind of background is essential to database administrators and systems programmers working with DBMS products. Knowing the fundamental data structures will also help you to evaluate and compare database products.

## FLAT FILES

A *flat file* is a file that has no repeating groups. Figure B-1a shows a flat file, whereas Figure B-1b shows a file that is not flat because of the repeating field, Item. A flat file can be stored as a sequential, indexed sequential, or direct file.

Flat files have been used for many years in commercial processing. They are usually processed in some predetermined order—such as in ascending sequence on a key field.

### Processing Flat Files in Multiple Orders

Sometimes users want to process flat files in ways that are not readily supported by the file organization employed. Consider, for example, the Enrollment records in Figure B-1a. To produce student schedules, the records must be processed in Student-number sequence. But to produce class rosters, the records need to be processed in Class-number sequence.

The records, of course, can be stored in only one physical sequence. They can be in order, for example, on Student-number or on Class-number, but not on both at the same time. The traditional solution to the problem of processing records in different orders is to sort the records in student order, process the student schedules, then sort the records in class order, and produce class rosters.

For some applications, such as a batch-mode system, this solution is cumbersome but effective. But suppose both orders need to exist simulta-

---

**Figure B–1**

Examples of flat and non-flat files

Enrollment Record

| Student-number | Class-number | Semester |
|---|---|---|

Sample Data

| | | |
|---|---|---|
| 200 | 70 | 88S |
| 100 | 30 | 89F |
| 300 | 20 | 89F |
| 200 | 30 | 88S |
| 300 | 70 | 88S |
| 100 | 20 | 88S |

a. A flat file

Invoice Record

| Invoice-number | Item(s) |
|---|---|

Sample Data

| | | | | |
|---|---|---|---|---|
| 1000 | 10 | 20 | 30 | 40 |
| 1010 | 50 | | | |
| 1020 | 10 | 20 | 30 | |
| 1030 | 50 | 90 | | |

b. A non-flat file

| Student-number | Class-number | Semester |
|:---:|:---:|:---:|
| 100 | 30 | 89F |
| 100 | 20 | 88S |
| 200 | 70 | 88S |
| 200 | 30 | 88S |
| 300 | 20 | 89F |
| 300 | 70 | 88S |

a.  Sorted by Student-number

| Student-number | Class-number | Semester |
|:---:|:---:|:---:|
| 300 | 20 | 89F |
| 100 | 20 | 88S |
| 100 | 30 | 89F |
| 200 | 30 | 88S |
| 200 | 70 | 88S |
| 300 | 70 | 88S |

b.  Sorted by Class-number

neously. Suppose two concurrent users have different views of the Enrollment records. What do we do then?

One solution is to create two copies of the ENROLLMENT file and sort them as shown in Figures B-2a and B-2b. Because the data is listed in sequential order, this data structure is sometimes called a *sequential list*. Sequential lists are usually stored as sequential files. We mentioned in the introduction to this appendix that sequential files are never employed to store database data. It follows, then, that the sequential list is not a data structure used in database organization. It is not used because maintaining several orders by keeping multiple copies of the same data is usually not effective. The duplicated data creates the potential for data integrity problems (see Chapter 2).

Fortunately, other data structures allow us to process records in different orders yet do not require duplication of data. They include *linked lists* and *inverted lists*. Before we discuss these structures, we need to clarify how we will be presenting record addressing.

## A Note on Record Addressing

Usually the DBMS creates large physical records, or blocks, on its direct access files. These physical records are used as containers for logical records. Typically, each physical record has many logical records. We will assume, realistically, that each physical record is addressed by its relative record number (RRN). Thus a logical record might be assigned to physical record number 7 or 77 or 10,000. The relative record number is the logical record's physical address. If a physical record has more than one logical record, the address will also need to specify where the logical record is within the physical record. Thus the complete address for a logical record might be relative record number 77, byte location 100. This means the record begins in byte 100 of block 77.

To simplify illustrations in this text, we assume that each physical record has only one logical record. Consequently, we will not be concerned with byte offsets within blocks. This is unrealistic, but it simplifies the discussion.

## Maintaining Order with Linked Lists

Linked lists can be used to keep records in logical order that are not necessarily in physical order. To create a linked list, a field is added to each data record. The *link* field holds the address (in our illustrations, the relative record number) of the *next* record in logical sequence. For example, Figure B-3 shows the Enrollment records expanded to include a linked list. This list maintains the records in Student-number order. Notice that the link for the numerically last student in the list is zero.

Figure B-4 shows Enrollment records with two linked lists. One list maintains the Student-number order and the other list maintains the Class-number order. Two link fields have been added to the records, one for each list.

When insertions and deletions are done, linked lists have a great advantage over sequential lists. For example, to insert the Enrollment record for student 200 and class 45, both of the lists in Figure B-2 would need to be rewritten. For the linked lists in Figure B-4, however, the new record could be added to the physical end of the list. Only the values of two link

**Figure B–3**
ENROLLMENT data
in Student-number
order using a
linked list

| Relative Record Number | Student-number | Class-number | Semester | Link |
|---|---|---|---|---|
| 1 | 200 | 70 | 88S | 4 |
| 2 | 100 | 30 | 89F | 6 |
| 3 | 300 | 20 | 89F | 5 |
| 4 | 200 | 30 | 88S | 3 |
| 5 | 300 | 70 | 88S | 0 |
| 6 | 100 | 20 | 88S | 1 |

Start of list = 2

| Relative Record Number | Student-number | Class-number | Semester | Student Link | Class Link |
|---|---|---|---|---|---|
| 1 | 200 | 70 | 88S | 4 | 5 |
| 2 | 100 | 30 | 89F | 6 | 1 |
| 3 | 300 | 20 | 89F | 5 | 4 |
| 4 | 200 | 30 | 88S | 3 | 2 |
| 5 | 300 | 70 | 88S | 0 | 0 |
| 6 | 100 | 20 | 88S | 1 | 3 |

Start of student list = 2
Start of class list = 6

fields need to be changed to place the new record in the correct sequences. These changes are shown in Figure B-5.

Also, when a record is deleted from a sequential list, a gap is created. A record can be deleted from a linked list simply by changing values of the link, or *pointer*, fields. In Figure B-6, the Enrollment record for student 200, class 30 has been logically deleted. No other record points to its address, so it effectively has been removed from the chain, even though it still exists physically.

Many linked list variations exist. We can make the list into a *circular list*, or *ring*, by changing the link of the last record from zero to the address of the first record in the list. Now we can reach every item in the list starting at any item in the list. Figure B-7a shows a circular list for the Student-number order. Also, a *two-way linked list* has links in both directions. In Figure B-7b, a two-way linked list has been created for ascending and descending student order.

Records ordered using linked lists cannot be stored on a sequential file. Some type of direct access file organization is needed to permit the use of the link values. Thus either indexed sequential or direct file organization is required for linked list processing. As mentioned in Appendix A, DBMS products nearly always use direct organization.

## Maintaining Order with Inverted Lists

Logical record order can also be maintained using *inverted lists*, or, as they are sometimes called, *indexes*. An inverted list is simply a table that cross-

**Figure B–5**

ENROLLMENT data
after insertion of new
record (in two orders
using linked lists)

| Relative Record Number | Student-number | Class-number | Semester | Student Link | Class Link |
|:---:|:---:|:---:|:---:|:---:|:---:|
| 1 | 200 | 70 | 88S | 4 | 5 |
| 2 | 100 | 30 | 89F | 6 | 7 |
| 3 | 300 | 20 | 89F | 5 | 4 |
| 4 | 200 | 30 | 88S | 7 | 2 |
| 5 | 300 | 70 | 88S | 0 | 0 |
| 6 | 100 | 20 | 88S | 1 | 3 |
| 7 | 200 | 45 | 88S | 3 | 1 |

Start of student list = 2
Start of class list = 6

**Figure B–6**

ENROLLMENT data
after deletion of stu-
dent 200, class 30 (in
two orders using
linked lists)

| Relative Record Number | Student-number | Class-number | Semester | Student Link | Class Link |
|:---:|:---:|:---:|:---:|:---:|:---:|
| 1 | 200 | 70 | 88S | 7 | 5 |
| 2 | 100 | 30 | 89F | 6 | 7 |
| 3 | 300 | 20 | 89F | 5 | 2 |
| 4 | 200 | 30 | 88S | 7 | 2 |
| 5 | 300 | 70 | 88S | 0 | 0 |
| 6 | 100 | 20 | 88S | 1 | 3 |
| 7 | 200 | 45 | 88S | 3 | 1 |

Start of student list = 2
Start of class list = 6

**Figure B—7**
ENROLLMENT data
sorted by Student-
number using circu-
lar and two-way
linked lists

| Relative Record Number | Student-number | Class-number | Semester | Link |
|---|---|---|---|---|
| 1 | 200 | 70 | 88S | 4 |
| 2 | 100 | 30 | 89F | 6 |
| 3 | 300 | 20 | 89F | 5 |
| 4 | 200 | 30 | 88S | 3 |
| 5 | 300 | 70 | 88S | 2 |
| 6 | 100 | 20 | 88S | 1 |

Start of list = 2

a. Circular linked list

| Relative Record Number | Student-number | Class-number | Semester | Ascending Link | Descending Link |
|---|---|---|---|---|---|
| 1 | 200 | 70 | 88S | 4 | 6 |
| 2 | 100 | 30 | 89F | 6 | 0 |
| 3 | 300 | 20 | 89F | 5 | 4 |
| 4 | 200 | 30 | 88S | 3 | 1 |
| 5 | 300 | 70 | 88S | 0 | 3 |
| 6 | 100 | 20 | 88S | 1 | 2 |

Start of ascending list = 2
Start of descending list = 5

b. Two-way linked list

references record addresses with some field value. For example, in Figure B-8a you can see that the Enrollment records are stored in no particular order. Figure B-8b shows an inverted list on Student-number. In this list, the Student-numbers are arranged in sequence and each entry points to a corresponding record in the original data.

As you can see, the inverted list is simply an index on Student-numbers. To process ENROLLMENT sequentially on Student-number, we simply process the inverted list sequentially, obtaining ENROLLMENT data by

## Figure B–8

ENROLLMENT data and corresponding inverted lists

| Relative Record Number | Student-number | Class-number | Semester |
|:---:|:---:|:---:|:---:|
| 1 | 200 | 70 | 88S |
| 2 | 100 | 30 | 89F |
| 3 | 300 | 20 | 89F |
| 4 | 200 | 30 | 88S |
| 5 | 300 | 70 | 88S |
| 6 | 100 | 20 | 88S |

a. ENROLLMENT data

| Student-number | Relative Record Number |
|:---:|:---:|
| 100 | 2 |
| 100 | 6 |
| 200 | 1 |
| 200 | 4 |
| 300 | 3 |
| 300 | 5 |

b. Inverted list on Student-number

| Class-number | Relative Record Number |
|:---:|:---:|
| 20 | 3 |
| 20 | 6 |
| 30 | 2 |
| 30 | 4 |
| 70 | 1 |
| 70 | 5 |

c. Inverted list on Class-number

reading the records indicated by the pointers. Figure B-8c shows another inverted list for ENROLLMENT. This one maintains Class-number order.

To use an inverted list, the data to be ordered (here ENROLLMENT) must reside on an indexed sequential or direct file. The inverted lists, however, can reside on any type of file. In practice, almost all DBMS products keep both the data and the indexes on direct files.

If you compare the linked list with the inverted list, you will notice the essential difference between them. With a linked list, pointers are stored along with the data. Each record contains a link field containing a pointer to the address of the next related record. With an inverted list, pointers are stored in indexes, separate from the data. Thus the data records themselves contain no pointers. Both techniques are used by commercial DBMS products.

## *B-Trees*

A special application of the concept of inverted lists, or indexes, is called a *B-tree*. A *B*-tree is a multilevel index that allows both sequential and direct processing of data records. It also guarantees a certain level of efficiency in processing because of the way the indexes are structured.

A *B*-tree is an index that is made up of two parts—the sequence set and the index set (using IBM's VSAM terminology—VSAM file organization is based on *B*-trees). The *sequence set* is a list of pointers to every data record in the file. This list is in physical sequence, usually by primary key value. This arrangement allows sequential access to the data records. Simply process the sequence set in order, obtaining the data record to which each entry points.

The *index set* is an index pointing to groups of entries in the sequence set. This arrangement provides rapid direct access to records in the file. It is the index set that makes *B*-trees unique. An example of a *B*-tree appears in Figure B-9. An occurrence of this structure can be seen in Figure B-10.

Notice that the bottom row in Figure B-9, the sequence set, is simply a list of record pointers. It contains an entry for every record in the file (although both the data records and their addresses have been omitted for brevity). Also notice that the sequence set entries are in groups of three. The entries in each group are physically in sequence and each group chains to the next one via a linked list. This can be seen clearly in Figure B-10.

Now examine in Figure B-9 the index set above the sequence set. The top entry contains two values, 50 and 82. By following the leftmost link (to RRN2), we can access all the records whose key field values are less than or equal to 50. By following the middle pointer (to RRN3), we can access all the records whose key field values are greater than 50 and less than or equal to 82. And by following the rightmost pointer (to RRN4), we can access all the records whose key field values are greater than 82.

Similarly, at the next level, each index entry contains two values and three pointers. Each time we drop to another level, we narrow our search for a particular record. For example, if we continue to follow the leftmost pointer from the top entry, and then we follow the rightmost pointer from there, we can access all records whose key field value is greater than 32 and less than or equal to 50. We eliminated all that were greater than 50 at the first level.

*B*-trees are by definition balanced. That is to say that all the data records are the exact same distance from the top entry in the index set. This aspect of *B*-trees guarantees performance efficiency. However, the algorithms for inserting and deleting records are more complex than those for ordinary trees (which can be unbalanced) because several index entries might need to be modified when records are added or deleted to keep all records the same distance from the top index entry.

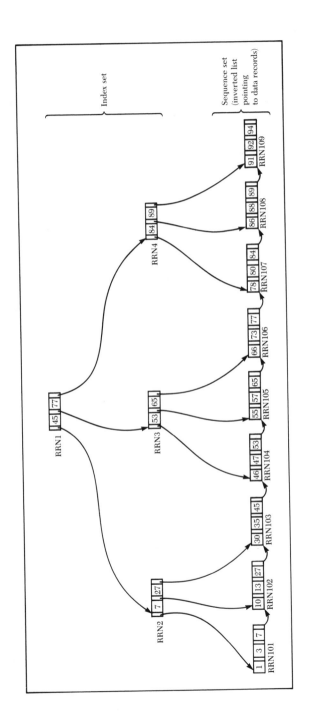

**Figure B–9**

General structure of
simple B-tree

**Figure B—10**
Occurrence of the
*B*-tree in Figure B-9

| RRN | Link1 | Value1 | Link2 | Value2 | Link3 | |
|-----|-------|--------|-------|--------|-------|---|
| 1 | 2 | 45 | 3 | 77 | 4 | |
| 2 | 101 | 7 | 102 | 27 | 103 | Index Set |
| 3 | 104 | 53 | 105 | 65 | 106 | |
| 4 | 107 | 84 | 108 | 89 | 109 | |

| | R1 | Addr1 | R2 | Addr2 | R3 | Addr3 | Link | |
|-----|----|-------|----|-------|----|-------|------|---|
| 101 | 1 | Pointer to 6 | 3 | Pointer to 8 | 7 | Pointer to 12 | 102 | |
| 102 | 10 | . . . | 13 | . . . | 27 | . . . | 103 | |
| 103 | 30 | . . . | 35 | . . . | 45 | . . . | 104 | Sequence Set |
| 104 | 46 | . . . | 47 | . . . | 53 | . . . | 105 | (Addresses of |
| 105 | 55 | . . . | 57 | . . . | 65 | . . . | 106 | data records |
| 106 | 66 | . . . | 73 | . . . | 77 | . . . | 107 | are omitted) |
| 107 | 78 | . . . | 80 | . . . | 84 | . . . | 108 | |
| 108 | 86 | . . . | 88 | . . . | 89 | . . . | 109 | |
| 109 | 91 | . . . | 92 | . . . | 94 | . . . | 0 | |

## Summary of Data Structures

Figure B-11 summarizes techniques for maintaining ordered flat files. Three supporting data structures are possible. Sequential lists can be used, but data must be duplicated to maintain several orders. Because sequential lists are not used in database processing, we will not consider them further. Both linked lists and inverted lists can be used without data duplication. *B*-trees are special forms of inverted lists.

As shown in Figure B-11, sequential lists can be stored using any of the three file organizations discussed in Appendix A. In practice, however, they are usually kept on sequential files. Additionally, while both linked and inverted lists can be stored using either indexed sequential or direct files, DBMS products almost always store them on direct files.

# REPRESENTING BINARY RELATIONSHIPS

In this section we will examine how each of the logical record relationships discussed in Chapter 6—trees, simple networks, and complex networks—can be represented using linked lists and inverted lists. First, we will review the three record relationships.

**Figure B—11**

Summary of data
structures and data
organizations used for
ordered flat files

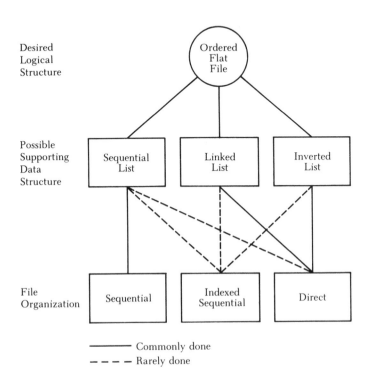

Desired
Logical
Structure

Ordered
Flat
File

Possible
Supporting
Data
Structure

Sequential
List

Linked
List

Inverted
List

File
Organization

Sequential

Indexed
Sequential

Direct

——— Commonly done
– – – – Rarely done

### Review of Record Relationships

Records can be related in three ways. A *tree* relationship has one or more
one-to-many relationships, but each child record has only one parent. The
occurrence of faculty data shown in Figure B-12 illustrates a tree. Several
1:N relationships exist, but any child record has only one parent. Figure B-13 shows a general schematic of this structure.

A *simple network* is a collection of records and the 1:N relationships
among them. The characteristic that distinguishes a simple network from
a tree is that in a simple network a child can have more than one parent as
long as the parents are different record types. The occurrence of a simple
network of students, advisors, and major fields of study in Figure B-14 is
represented schematically in Figure B-15.

A *complex network* is also a collection of records and relationships. In a
complex network, however, the relationships are many-to-many instead of
one-to-many. The relationship between students and classes is a complex

**Figure B-12**
Occurence of a faculty member record

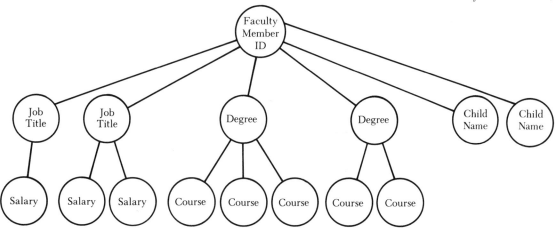

network. An occurrence of this relationship can be seen in Figure B-16. The general schematic is in Figure B-17.

We saw earlier that we can use linked lists and inverted lists to process records in orders that differ from the one in which they are physically stored. We can also use those same data structures to store and process the relationships among records.

**Figure B–13**
Schematic of faculty member tree structure

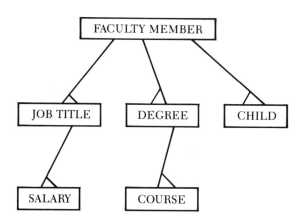

---

**Figure B—14**

Occurence of simple
network

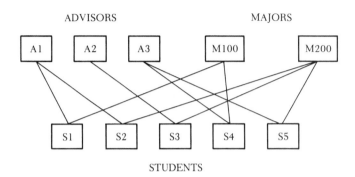

ADVISORS                    MAJORS

STUDENTS

---

**Figure B—15**

General structure of a
simple network

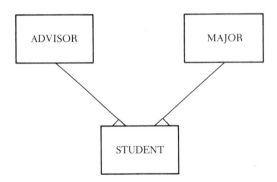

---

**Figure B—16**

Occurence of complex
network

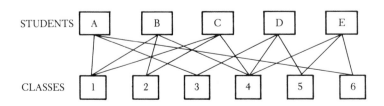

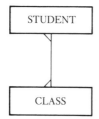

## Representing Trees

We can use sequential lists, linked lists, and inverted lists to represent trees. In using sequential lists, we duplicate much data. Consequently, DBMS products seldom use sequential lists to represent trees. Therefore we will discuss only linked lists and inverted lists.

**Linked List Representation of Trees.**    Figure B-18 shows a tree structure in which Vendor records are parents and Invoice records are children. Figure B-19 shows two occurrences of this structure. In Figure B-20, all of the Vendor and Invoice records have been written to a direct access file. VEN-DOR AA is relative record number 1 (RRN1) and VENDOR BB is relative record number 2. The Invoice records have been stored in subsequent slots as illustrated. Note that these records are not stored in any particular order, nor do they need to be.

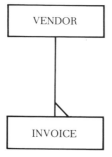

**Figure B–19**

Two occurences of
VENDOR-INVOICE
tree

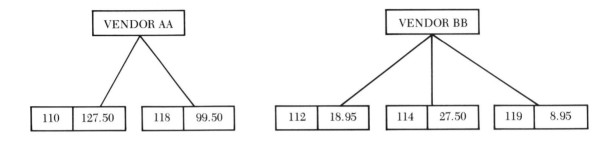

**Figure B–20**

File representation of
trees in Figure B-19

| Relative Record Number | Record Contents | |
|---|---|---|
| 1 | VENDOR AA | |
| 2 | VENDOR BB | |
| 3 | 118 | 99.50 |
| 4 | 119 | 8.95 |
| 5 | 112 | 18.95 |
| 6 | 114 | 27.50 |
| 7 | 110 | 127.50 |

Our problem is that we cannot tell from this file which invoices belong to which vendors. To solve this problem with a linked list, we will add a pointer field to every record. In this field we will store the address of some other related record. For example, we will place in VENDOR AA's link field the address of the first invoice belonging to it. This is RRN7, which is INVOICE 110. Then we will make INVOICE 110 point to the next invoice belonging to VENDOR AA, in this case RRN3. This slot holds INVOICE 118. To indicate that there are no more children in the chain, we insert a zero in the link field for RRN3.

This technique is shown in Figure B-21. If you examine the figure carefully, you will see that a similar set of links has been used to represent the relationship between VENDOR BB and its invoices.

The structure in Figure B-21 is much easier to modify than a sequential list of the tree. For example, suppose we add a new invoice—say, number 111—to VENDOR AA. To do this, we just add the record to the file and insert it into the linked list. Physically, the record can be placed anywhere.

| Relative Record Number | Record Contents | | Link Field |
|---|---|---|---|
| 1 | VENDOR AA | | 7 |
| 2 | VENDOR BB | | 5 |
| 3 | 118 | 99.50 | 0 |
| 4 | 119 | 8.95 | 0 |
| 5 | 112 | 18.95 | 6 |
| 6 | 114 | 27.50 | 4 |
| 7 | 110 | 127.50 | 3 |

But where should it be placed logically? For this example, let's assume the children are to be kept in ascending order on invoice number. In that case, we need to make INVOICE 110 point to INVOICE 111 (at RRN8), and we need to make INVOICE 111, the new invoice, point to INVOICE 118 (at RRN3). This modification is shown in Figure B-22.

Similarly, deleting an invoice is easy. If INVOICE 114 is deleted, we simply modify the pointer in the invoice that is now pointing to INVOICE 114. In this case, it is INVOICE 112 at RRN5. We will give to INVOICE 112

| Relative Record Number | Record Contents | | Link Field | |
|---|---|---|---|---|
| 1 | VENDOR AA | | 7 | |
| 2 | VENDOR BB | | 5 | |
| 3 | 118 | 99.50 | 0 | |
| 4 | 119 | 8.95 | 0 | |
| 5 | 112 | 18.95 | 6 | |
| 6 | 114 | 27.50 | 4 | |
| 7 | 110 | 127.50 | 8 | |
| 8 | 111 | 19.95 | 3 | ← Inserted Record |

**Figure B–23**

Deletion of INVOICE
114 from file in
Figure B-22

| Relative Record Number | Record Contents | | Link Field | |
|---|---|---|---|---|
| 1 | VENDOR AA | | 7 | |
| 2 | VENDOR BB | | 5 | |
| 3 | 118 | 99.50 | 0 | |
| 4 | 119 | 8.95 | 0 | |
| 5 | 112 | 18.95 | 4 | |
| 6 | 114 | 27.50 | 4 | ← Deleted Record |
| 7 | 110 | 127.50 | 8 | |
| 8 | 111 | 19.95 | 3 | |

the pointer that INVOICE 114 had before deletion. In this way, INVOICE 112 will point to INVOICE 119 (see Figure B-23). We have effectively cut one link out of the chain and welded together the ones it once connected.

**Inverted List Representation of Trees.**   A tree structure can be readily represented using inverted lists. The technique is to store each one-to-many relationship as an inverted list. These lists are then used to match parents and children.

Using the Vendor and Invoice records shown in Figure B-21, we see that VENDOR AA (in RRN1) owns INVOICEs 110 (RRN7) and 118 (RRN3). Thus RRN1 is the parent of RRN7 and RRN3. We can represent this fact with the inverted list shown in Figure B-24. The list simply associates a parent's address with the addresses of each of its children.

If the tree has several 1:N relationships, then several inverted lists will be required, one for each relationship. For the structure in Figure B-13, five inverted lists are needed.

### Representing Simple Networks

As with trees, simple networks can also be represented using linked lists and inverted lists. They can also be decomposed into trees as illustrated in Chapter 12.

**Linked List Representation of Simple Networks.**   Consider the simple network in Figure B-25. It is a simple network because all the relationships

**Figure B-24**
Inverted list repre-
sentation of
VENDOR-INVOICE
relationship

| Parent Record | Child Record |
|:---:|:---:|
| 1 | 7 |
| 1 | 3 |
| 2 | 5 |
| 2 | 6 |
| 2 | 4 |

**Figure B—25**
Simple network
structure

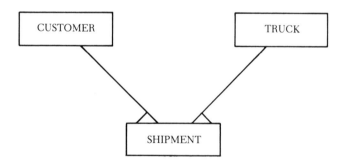

are 1:N and Shipment records have two parents of different types. Each SHIPMENT has a CUSTOMER parent and a TRUCK parent. The relationship between CUSTOMER and SHIPMENT is 1:N because a customer can have several shipments. The relationship from TRUCK to SHIPMENT is 1:N because one truck can hold many shipments. An occurrence of this network is shown in Figure B-26.

In order to represent this simple network with linked lists, we need to establish one set of pointers for each 1:N relationship. In this example, that means there will be one set of pointers to connect CUSTOMERs with their SHIPMENTS and another set of pointers to connect TRUCKS with their SHIPMENTS. Thus a Customer record will contain one pointer (to the first SHIPMENT it owns), a Truck record will contain one pointer (to the first SHIPMENT it owns), and a Shipment record will have two pointers, one

**Figure B–26**

Occurence of simple
network in
Figure B-25

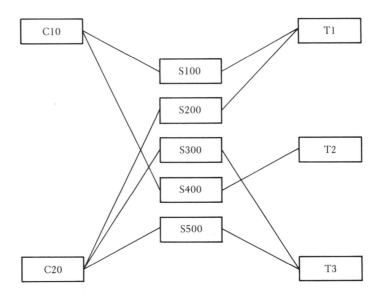

for the next SHIPMENT owned by the same CUSTOMER and one for the
next SHIPMENT owned by the same TRUCK. This scheme is illustrated in
Figure B-27.

**Inverted List Representation of Simple Networks.**   A simple network has
at least two 1:$N$ relationships. Each relationship can be represented using
an inverted list, as illustrated in our discussion of trees.

For example, consider the simple network shown in Figure B-25. This
network has two 1:$N$ relationships, one between TRUCK and SHIPMENT
and one between CUSTOMER and SHIPMENT. We can store each of these
relationships in an inverted list. Figure B-28 shows the two inverted lists
needed to represent the example in Figure B-26. Records are loaded into
the same positions as in Figure B-27.

## Representing Complex Networks

Complex networks can be physically represented in a variety of ways. One
way is to decompose them into trees or simple networks and then to represent these simpler structures using one of the techniques we just described.
Another way is to represent them directly using inverted lists. Linked lists
are not used by any DBMS product to directly represent complex networks.

| Relative Record Number | Record Contents | Link Fields | |
|---|---|---|---|
| 1 | C10 | 6 | |
| 2 | C20 | 7 | |
| 3 | T1 | | 6 |
| 4 | T2 | | 9 |
| 5 | T3 | | 8 |
| 6 | S100 | 9 | 7 |
| 7 | S200 | 8 | 0 |
| 8 | S300 | 10 | 10 |
| 9 | S400 | 0 | 0 |
| 10 | S500 | 0 | 0 |

CUSTOMER Links          TRUCK Links

In practice, complex networks are nearly always decomposed into simpler structures. Therefore we will consider only representations using decomposition.

**Decomposition into Simple Networks.**  A common approach to representing complex networks is to reduce them to simple networks and then to represent the simple networks with linked lists or inverted lists, as discussed in the previous section. Note, however, that a complex network involves a relationship between two records, whereas a simple network involves relationships among three records. Thus, to decompose a complex network into a simple one, we need to create a third record type.

The record that is created when a complex network is decomposed into a simple one is called an *intersection record*. Consider the student-class complex network. An intersection record will contain a unique key from a Student record and a unique key from a corresponding Class record. It will contain no other application data, although it might contain link fields.

The general structure of this relationship is shown in Figure B-29. Assuming the record names are unique (such as S1, S2, C1, and so forth),

**Figure B–28**

Representation of
simple network with
inverted lists

| Customer Record | Shipment Record |
|:---:|:---:|
| 1 | 6 |
| 1 | 9 |
| 2 | 7 |
| 2 | 8 |
| 2 | 10 |

| Truck Record | Shipment Record |
|:---:|:---:|
| 3 | 6 |
| 3 | 7 |
| 4 | 9 |
| 5 | 8 |
| 5 | 10 |

**Figure B–29**

Decomposition of
complex network to
simple network

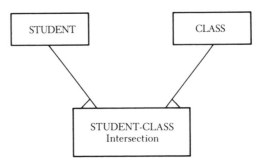

an instance of the STUDENT-CLASS relationship is illustrated in Figure B-30.

Notice that the relationship from STUDENT to intersection record is 1:$N$ and that the relationship from CLASS to intersection record is also 1:$N$. Thus we have created a simple network that can now be represented with the linked list or inverted list techniques shown previously. A file of this occurrence using the linked list technique is shown in Figure B-31.

### Summary of Relationship Representations

Figure B-32 summarizes the representations of record relationships. Trees can be represented using sequential lists (although we did not discuss this

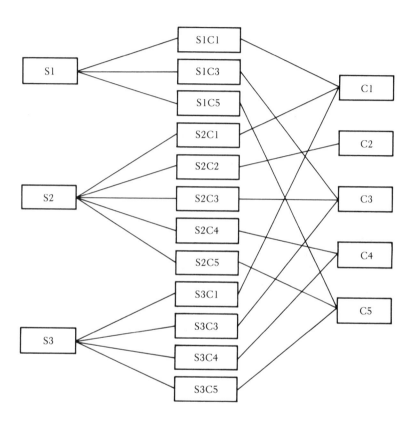

approach), linked lists, and inverted lists. Sequential lists are seldom used in DBMS products. A simple network can be decomposed into trees and then represented, or it can be represented directly using either linked or inverted lists. Finally, a complex network can be decomposed into a tree or a simple network (using intersection records), or it can be represented directly using inverted lists.

## SECONDARY-KEY REPRESENTATIONS

In many cases the word *key* indicates a field (or fields) whose value uniquely identifies a record. This is usually called the *primary key*. Sometimes, however, applications need to access and process records by a *secondary key*—one that is different from the primary key. Secondary keys might be unique

**Figure B—31**

Occurence of network
in Figure B-30

| Relative Record Number | Record Contents | Link Fields | |
|:---:|:---|:---:|:---:|
| 1 | S1 | 9 | |
| 2 | S2 | 12 | |
| 3 | S3 | 17 | |
| 4 | C1 | | 9 |
| 5 | C2 | | 13 |
| 6 | C3 | | 10 |
| 7 | C4 | | 15 |
| 8 | C5 | | 11 |
| 9 | S1C1 | 10 | 12 |
| 10 | S1C3 | 11 | 14 |
| 11 | S1C5 | 0 | 16 |
| 12 | S2C1 | 13 | 17 |
| 13 | S2C2 | 14 | 0 |
| 14 | S2C3 | 15 | 18 |
| 15 | S2C4 | 16 | 19 |
| 16 | S2C5 | 0 | 20 |
| 17 | S3C1 | 18 | 0 |
| 18 | S3C3 | 19 | 0 |
| 19 | S3C4 | 20 | 0 |
| 20 | S3C5 | 0 | 0 |

STUDENT
Links

CLASS
Links

**Figure B—32**

Record relationships,
data structures, and
file organizations

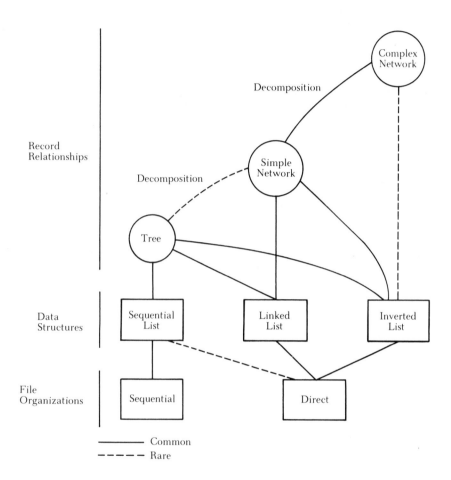

(such as a professor's name), or they might be nonunique (such as a customer's ZIP Code. In this section we will use the term *set* to refer to all records having the same value of a non-unique secondary key. For example, there is a set of records having ZIP Code 98040.

In Appendix A we discussed using keys to associate records with particular file locations. For example, we might apply a hashing algorithm to a key in order to generate a relative record address. Clearly only one record key can be used for this purpose. The key used for this is the primary key. Secondary keys can be used to identify records, but they must reference the physical location determined by the primary key.

Some DBMS products do not use key values to determine record locations at all. Instead, the DBMS assigns records to locations in accordance with available space and other considerations known only to the DBMS. For these systems there are no primary keys. Every key is considered a secondary key and is processed using one of the techniques in this section.

Both linked and inverted lists are used to represent secondary keys. As you will see, linked lists are practical only for non-unique keys. Inverted lists, however, can be used for both unique and non-unique key representations. We will discuss the linked list representation first.

### Linked List Representation of Secondary Keys

Consider an example of Customer records as shown in Figure B-33. The primary key is Account-number and the secondary key is Credit-limit. Possible Credit-limit values are 500, 700, and 1000. Thus there will be a set of records for the limit of 500, a set for 700, and a set for 1000.

To represent this key using linked lists, we will add a link field to the Customer records. Inside this link field we will create a linked list for each set of records. Figure B-34 shows a database of eleven customers. For brevity, only Account-number and Credit-limit are shown. A link field has been attached to the records. Assume that one database record occupies one physical record on a direct file using relative record addressing.

Three pointers need to be established so we know where to begin each linked list. These pointers are called *heads* and are stored separate from the data. The head of the 500 linked list is RRN1. Record 1 links to record 2, which in turn links to record 7. Record 7 has a zero in the link position, indicating that it is the end of the list. Consequently, the 500 credit limit set consists of records 1, 2, and 7. Similarly, the 700 set contains records 3, 5, and 10, and the 1000 set contains relative records 4, 6, 8, 9, and 11.

To answer a query such as "How many accounts in the 1000 set have a balance in excess of 900?" the 1000 set linked list can be used. In this way, only records in the 1000 set need to be read from the file and examined. The advantage of this approach is not readily apparent in this small example. Suppose, however, that 100,000 Customer records exist and that only 100 of them are in the 1000 set. Without a linked list, all 100,000 records would have to be examined. With the linked list, only 100 records need to

---

**Figure B—33**
Customer record

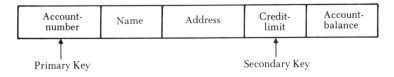

Primary Key          Secondary Key

**Figure B—34**
Representing Credit-
limit secondary key
using linked list

| Relative Record Number | Link | Account- Number | Credit- Limit | Other Data |
|---|---|---|---|---|
| 1 | 2 | 101 | 500 | |
| 2 | 7 | 301 | 500 | |
| 3 | 5 | 203 | 700 | |
| 4 | 6 | 004 | 1000 | |
| 5 | 10 | 204 | 700 | |
| 6 | 8 | 905 | 1000 | |
| 7 | 0 | 705 | 500 | |
| 8 | 9 | 207 | 1000 | |
| 9 | 11 | 309 | 1000 | |
| 10 | 0 | 409 | 700 | |
| 11 | 0 | 210 | 1000 | |

HEAD-500 = 1
HEAD-700 = 3
HEAD-1000 = 4

be examined, namely the ones in the 1000 set. Using the linked list saves having to do 99,900 reads.

**Disadvantages of Linked Lists for Secondary-Key Representations.** Linked lists are not an effective technique for every secondary-key application. In particular, if the records are processed nonsequentially in a set, linked lists are inefficient. For example, if it is often necessary to find the 10th or 120th or $n$th record in the 500 Credit-limit set, processing will be slow. Linked lists are inefficient for direct access.

Also, if the application requires that secondary keys be created or destroyed dynamically, the linked list approach is undesirable. Whenever a new key is created, a link field must be added to every record. This often requires reorganization of the database—a time-consuming and expensive process.

Finally, if the secondary keys are unique, each list has a length of one and a separate linked list exists for every record in the database. For example, suppose the Customer records contain another unique field—say, Social Security Number. If we attempt to represent this unique secondary key using a linked list, every Social Security Number will be a separate linked list. Further, each linked list will have just one item in it—the single record having the indicated Social Security Number. Since this situation is unworkable, linked lists cannot be used for unique keys.

## Inverted List Representation of Secondary Keys

A second technique for representing secondary keys uses an inverted list. One inverted list is established for each secondary key. The approach varies depending on whether key values are unique or non-unique.

**Unique Secondary Keys.**   Suppose the Customer records in Figure B-33 contain Social Security Number (SSN) as well as the fields shown. To provide key access to the Customer records using SSN, we simply build an inverted list on the SSN field. Sample CUSTOMER data is shown in Figure B-35a and a corresponding inverted list is illustrated in Figure B-35b. This inverted list uses relative record numbers as addresses. It would be possible to use Account-numbers instead, in which case the DBMS would locate the desired SSN in the inverted list, obtain the matching Account-number, and then hash to the record itself.

**Figure B—35**

Representing unique
secondary key with
inverted lists

| Relative Record Number | Account-number | Credit-limit | Social Security Number (SSN) |
|---|---|---|---|
| 1 | 101 | 500 | 000-01-0001 |
| 2 | 301 | 500 | 000-01-0005 |
| 3 | 203 | 700 | 000-01-0009 |
| 4 | 004 | 1000 | 000-01-0003 |

a.  Sample CUSTOMER data (with SSN)

| SSN | Relative Record Number |
|---|---|
| 000-01-0001 | 1 |
| 000-01-0003 | 4 |
| 000-01-0005 | 2 |
| 000-01-0009 | 3 |

b.  Inverted list for SSN secondary key

**Figure B—36**
Inverted list for
Credit-limit key in
Figure B—33

Account-number

| Credit-limit | | | | | |
|---|---|---|---|---|---|
| 500 | 101 | 301 | 705 | | |
| 700 | 203 | 204 | 409 | | |
| 1000 | 004 | 905 | 207 | 309 | 210 |

**Non-unique Secondary Keys.**    Inverted lists can also be used to represent non-unique secondary keys. However, because each set of related records can contain an unknown number of members, the entries in the inverted list are of variable length. For example, Figure B-36 shows the inverted list for the Credit-limit sets for the CUSTOMER data. The 500 set and the 700 set each have three members, so there are three account numbers in each entry. The 1000 set has five members, so there are five account numbers in that entry.

In reality, representing and processing non-unique secondary keys are complex tasks. Several different schemes are used by commercial DBMS products. One typical method uses a values table and an occurrence table. Each values table entry consists of two fields. The first field has a key value. For the Credit-limit key the values are 500, 700, and 1000. The second field of the values table entry is a pointer into the occurrence table.

**Figure B—37**
Values and occur-
rence tables for
Credit-limit key in
Figure B—33

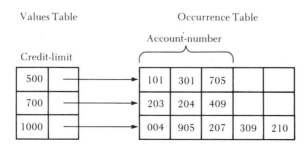

Values Table                          Occurrence Table

The occurrence table contains record addresses. Addresses of records having a common value in the secondary-key field appear together in the table. Figure B-37 shows the values and occurrence tables for the Credit-limit key.

To locate records having a given value of the secondary key, the values table is searched for the desired value. Once the given key value is located in the values table, the pointer is followed to the occurrence table to obtain the addresses of records having that key value. These addresses are used to obtain the desired records.

When a new record is inserted into the file, the DBMS must process each secondary-key field. For non-unique keys, it must ensure that the new record key value is in the values table. If so, it adds the new record address to the appropriate entry in the occurrences table. If not, it must insert new entries in the values and occurrence tables.

When a record is deleted, its address must be removed from the occurrence table. If no addresses remain in the occurrence table entry, the corresponding values table entry must also be deleted.

When the secondary-key field of a record is modified, the record address must be removed from one occurrence table entry and inserted in another. If the modification is a new value for the key, an entry must be added to the values table.

**Advantages and Disadvantages of the Inverted List Approach.**     The inverted list approach to representing secondary keys overcomes objections stated for the linked list approach. Direct processing of sets is possible. For example, the third record in a set can be retrieved without processing the first or second ones. Also, it is possible to dynamically create and delete secondary keys. No changes are made to the records themselves; the DBMS just creates additional inverted lists. Finally, unique keys can be processed efficiently.

The disadvantages of the inverted list approach are that it requires more file space because the tables use more overhead than pointers and that the DBMS programming task is more complex. Note that the *application programming* task is not necessarily any more or less difficult, but it is more complex to write DBMS software that processes inverted lists than it is to write software that processes linked lists. Finally, modifications are usually processed more slowly because I/O is required to access and maintain the values in the occurrence tables.

## SUMMARY

In this appendix we surveyed data structures used for database processing. A flat file is a file that contains no repeating groups. Flat files can be ordered using sequential lists (physically placing the records in the sequence in which they will be processed), linked lists (attaching to each data record a pointer to another logically related record), and inverted lists (building a table, separate from the data records, containing pointers to related records). B-trees are special forms of inverted lists.

Sequential lists, linked lists, and inverted lists, or indexes, are fundamental data structures. (Sequential lists, however, are seldom used in database processing.) These data structures can be used to represent record relationships as well as secondary keys.

The three basic record relationships—trees, simple networks, and complex networks—can be represented using linked lists and inverted lists. Simple networks can be decomposed into trees and then represented. Complex networks can be decomposed into simple networks containing an intersection record and then represented.

Secondary keys are used for accessing the data on some field besides the primary key. Secondary keys can be unique or non-unique. Non-unique secondary keys can be represented with both linked lists and inverted lists. Unique secondary keys can be represented only with inverted lists.

## QUESTIONS                                                **GROUP I**

**B.1**   Define a flat file. Give an example of a flat file (other than one in this text) and an example of a file that is not flat.

**B.2**   Show how sequential lists can be used to maintain the file from question B.1 in two different orders simultaneously.

**B.3**   Show how linked lists can be used to maintain the file from question B.1 in two different orders simultaneously.

**B.4**   Show how inverted lists can be used to maintain the file from question B.1 in two different orders simultaneously.

**B.5**   Define a tree and give a sample structure.

**B.6**   Give an occurrence of the tree from question B.5.

**B.7**   Represent the occurrence from question B.6 using linked lists.

**B.8**   Represent the occurrence from question B.6 using inverted lists.

**B.9**   Define a simple network and give a sample structure.

**B.10**   Give an occurrence of the simple network from question B.9.

**B.11**   Represent the occurrence from question B.10 using linked lists.

**B.12**   Represent the occurrence from question B.10 using inverted lists.

**B.13**   Define a complex network and give a sample structure.

**B.14**   Give an occurrence of the complex network from question B.13.

**B.15**   Decompose the complex network from question B.14 into a simple network and represent an occurrence of it using inverted lists.

**B.16**   Explain the difference between primary and secondary keys.

**B.17**   Explain the difference between unique and non-unique keys.

**B.18**   Define a file containing a unique secondary key. Represent an occurrence of that file using an inverted list on the secondary key.

**B.19** Define a non-unique secondary key for the file in question B.18. Represent an occurrence of that file using a linked list on the secondary key.

**B.20** Perform the same task as in question B.19, but use an inverted list to represent the secondary key.

---

**GROUP II** QUESTIONS

**B.21** Using the linked list structure in Figure B-4, develop an algorithm to produce a report listing the IDs of students enrolled in each class.

**B.22** Develop an algorithm to insert records into the structure in Figure B-4. The resulting structure should resemble the one in Figure B-5.

**B.23** Using the inverted list structure shown in Figures B-8a, b, and c, develop an algorithm to produce a report listing the IDs of students enrolled in each class.

**B.24** Develop an algorithm to insert a record into the structure in Figure B-8a, being sure to modify both of the associated inverted lists in Figures B-8b and c.

**B.25** Develop an algorithm to delete a record from the structure in Figure B-34, which shows a secondary key represented with a linked list. If all records for one of the Credit-limit categories (say, 1000) is deleted, should the associated head pointer also be deleted? Why or why not?

**B.26** Develop an algorithm to insert a record into the structure shown in Figure B-34. Suppose the new record has a credit-limit value that differs from the ones already established. Should the record be inserted and a new linked list established? Or should the record be rejected? Who should make that decision?

# Glossary

**Aggregation object.** An object that represents groups of objects and provides inheritance.

**AI.** *Artificial Intelligence.*

**Anomaly.** Undesirable consequence of a database modification.

**Application.** A business computer system that processes a portion of a database to meet a user's information needs. Consists of menus, forms, reports, and programs.

**Application meta-data.** Data about report and screen formats used by a particular application. *Contrast with* **Meta-data.**

**Association object.** An object that documents the relationship between at least two other objects. An association object is an independent entity, and its key is usually not a composite. *Compare to* **Intersection relation.**

**Atomic transaction.** *See* **Transaction.**

**Attribute.** A column in a relation.

**Base table.** The table from which views are derived.

**Binary relationship.** A relationship between two entities, usually in the context of relations.

**Call.** A programming language statement that passes temporary control to an external subroutine. The specific command used depends on the language. Examples include CALL, GOSUB, and BAL.

**Candidate key.** An attribute or attribute group that could be used as the key of a relation. *See also* **Primary key.**

**Cartesian product.** *See* **Product.**

**CCP.** Communications Control Program.

**Chain.** To display a submenu in response to the selection of an option on a higher-level menu.

**Checkpoint.** The point of synchronization between a database and a transaction log.

**COBOL.** *Common Business-Oriented Language.* The most widely used programming language for business applications.

**CODASYL.** *Conference on Data Systems Languages.* The committee that developed standards for COBOL and the network data model known as the DBTG model.

**Commit.** To make database modifications permanent so that they will survive system failures.

**Common database.** A database shared by multiple applications.

**Complex network.** A collection of record types in which at least one relationship is many-to-many (*M:N*).

**Concurrent processing.** The interleaving of execution of at least two programs.

**Constraint.** Any rule on static values of attributes whose truth can be evaluated.

**CPU.** *Central Processing Unit.* The logic and internal memory portion of a computer.

**Currency indicator.** In the CODASYL DBTG model, a variable in which the identity of the most recently accessed record of a certain type is stored. Currency indicators exist for run-unit, set, and record type.

**Cursor.** The symbol displayed on a computer screen indicating the position into which the next entry will be made. The cursor usually appears as a blinking box or underscore.

**Data Administration Subsystem.** A collection of DBMS system utility programs that perform database maintenance functions, such as archiving, purging, and reorganizing.

**Data dictionary.** A user-accessible catalog of data about a database. An *active data dictionary* is one whose entries are updated automatically whenever changes are made to the database structure. A *passive data dictionary* is one whose entries need to be manually updated whenever database structure changes are made.

**Data Dictionary Subsystem.** A DBMS subsystem that provides query and report functions on the database meta-data. Used primarily but not exclusively by the DBA.

**Data model.** A language describing the structure and processing of a database. *See* **Hierarchical data model, Network data model,** and **Relational data model.**

**Database.** A self-describing collection of integrated records.

**Database administrator.** The individual or group responsible for the development, operation, and maintenance of a database.

**Dataflow diagram.** A chart used by systems analysts to illustrate business functions and their data interfaces. Sometimes called a *bubble chart.*

**DB2.** *Data Base 2.* A relational DBMS developed by IBM for mainframe computers.

**DBA.** *Database administrator.*

**DBKEY.** *Database key.* In IDMS/R, the physical address of a database record. Consists of the number of the page containing the record, concatenated with the record's line index number.

**DBM.** *Database Manager.* In a DDBMS, software that processes some portion of a distributed database in accordance with action requests from DTMs.

**DBMS.** *Database Management System.* A program or collection of programs used to establish, maintain, and process a database.

**DBMS Engine.** A DBMS subsystem that receives logical I/O requests from other subsystems and translates them into physical I/O requests that it issues to the operating system.

**DBTG.** *Data Base Task Group.* A subcommittee of CODASYL that developed the network data model known as the DBTG model.

**DDBMS.** *Distributed DBMS.* The collection of DTMs and DBMs on all computers that process a distributed database.

**DDL.** *Data Definition Language.* The portion of a data model pertaining to the definition of database structure.

**Deadlock.** A condition that can occur during concurrent processing in which each of two (or more) programs is waiting to access data the other one has locked. Also called the *deadly embrace.*

**Deadly embrace.** *See* **Deadlock.**

**Definition Tools Subsystem.** A DBMS subsystem consisting of tools and utilities for defining and changing the database structure.

**Determinant.** A group of one or more attributes upon which at least one other attribute is functionally dependent. In the functional dependency $(X,Y) \rightarrow Z$ the determinant is $(X, Y)$.

**Difference.** The relational operation performed on two relations, A and B, producing relation C such that C contains tuples that occur in relation A but not in relation B.

**Distributed database system.** An information system in which the execution of transactions and the retrieval and updating of data occurs across two or more independent (and usually geographically separated) computers.

**DL/I.** *Data Language I.* Language developed by IBM to access hierarchical databases.

**DMCL.** *Device Media Control Language.* In IDMS/R, language used to define the physical characteristics of the media used to store a database.

**DML.** *Data Manipulation Language.* The portion of a data model pertaining to the modification of data.

**Domain.** The set of all possible values a variable can have. Includes a physical description (such as length and data type) and a semantic description (describing the function or purpose of the variable).

**Download.** To copy database data from one computer to another. Also called *importing data.*

**DSS.** *Decision Support System.* An information system used to answer ad hoc queries. Often includes a relational database.

**DTM.** *Distributed Transaction Manager.* In a DDBMS, software that receives processing requests from transactions and translates them into DBM action requests.

**Entity.** A class of things that exist in the user's business environment.

**Entity instance.** An occurrence of an entity, for example, a particular customer, invoice, or stock item.

**Entity-relationship diagram.** A diagram used in database design that illustrates business entities and associations among them. Also called *E-R diagram.*

**Entry-point relation.** The first table referenced by an application when it is processing an object that contains multiple tables.

**Equijoin.** The join of relations A and B such that the result, C, contains duplicate attributes. *See also* **Join** and **Natural join.**

**E-R diagram.** *See* **Entity-relationship diagram.**

**File processing system.** A computer system in which data is stored in separate, non-integrated files.

**File server.** In a Local Area Network (LAN), the microcomputer on which the common database is stored.

**Foreign key.** An attribute that is a key of a different relation.

**Form.** A computer screen in which data is both displayed and entered. Also called *data entry form* or *panel*.

**Forms generator.** That portion of the Application Development Subsystem that enables a user to define a data entry form or a screen display format.

**Fragment.** A database record that exists inappropriately without a required parent or child record.

**Functional dependency.** Relationship between attributes X and Y such that, given the value of X, one can determine the value of Y. Written as $X \rightarrow Y$.

**Granularity.** A term used to describe the relative scope of database resources that can be locked. Locking an entire database is *large granularity*; locking data items is *small granularity*.

**Hierarchy.** *See* **Tree.**

**Hierarchical data model.** A data model that represents all data relationships using hierarchies, or trees.

**IDMS** and **IDMS/R.** Database management systems licensed by the Cullinet Corporation. Based on the CODASYL DBTG model.

**Import.** *See* **Download.**

**IMS.** *Information Management System.* A transaction processing-oriented communications processor and DBMS developed by IBM. Uses DL/I as database access language.

**Information-bearing set.** In the CODASYL DBTG model, a set in which the relationship is carried only in overhead data structures, not in foreign keys.

**Inter-relation constraint.** The rule that requires the value of an attribute in a row of one relation to match the value of an attribute found in another relation.

**Intersection.** The relational operation performed on two relations, A and B, producing relation C such that C contains only tuples found in both A and B.

**Intersection relation.** A relation that represents a many-to-many relationship between two other relations. An intersection relation contains only two attributes, namely the keys of the two associated relations. It never contains any non-key data. *Compare to* **Association object.**

**Intra-relation constraint.** A rule governing the value of attributes within a relation.

**I/O.** *Input/Output.*

**Join.** The relational operation performed on two relations, A and B, producing relation C such that C contains the product of A and B, minus duplicate tuples and, optionally, minus duplicate attributes. *See also* **Natural join** and **Equijoin.**

**Key.** A group of one or more attributes that uniquely identifies a row (or tuple or record).

**LAN.** *Local Area Network.* A collection of geographically close microcomputers that communicate. Usually located within a mile of each other.

**Log.** A record of all database changes.

**Logical Unit of Work.** *See* **Transaction.**

**Lock.** A DBMS command used in concurrent database processing to prevent anomalies due to concurrent updating. When data is locked by a program, other programs are limited in their access to the data.

**LUW.** *Logical Unit of Work.* IBM DB2 term for *transaction.*

**Mask.** A restriction placed on the contents or presentation format of a variable.

**Materialization.** The physical presentation of data in the form of a screen or report.

**Menu.** A list·of application options displayed on the computer screen from which the user can select.

**Meta-data.** Data about the structure of a database that is stored in the data dictionary. *Compare to* **Application meta-data.**

**MIS Department.** *Management Information Systems Department.* The generic name for the computer or information systems department in a company.

**Modem.** *Modulator-demodulator.* A device used for computer-to-computer telecommunications.

**Multivalued dependency.** A functional dependency that exists when at least one attribute in a relation with at least three attributes is multivalued and two attributes are functionally dependent only on the other one. Thus a multivalued dependency exists in relation $R(A,B,C)$ if $A \rightarrow\rightarrow B$, and/or $A \rightarrow\rightarrow C$, and $B \leftarrow/\rightarrow C$.

**Natural join.** A join of relations A and B such that the result C contains no duplicate tuples and no duplicate attributes. *See also* **Join** and **Equijoin.**

**Natural language interface.** A DBMS interface that enables users to enter queries in standard natural-language sentences such as English or Japanese.

**Network data model.** A data model in which all relationships are one-to-many and a child can have multiple parents as long as they are different record types.

**Node. 1.** An entity in a tree. **2.** A computer in a distributed database system.

**Normal form.** A rule or set of rules governing the structure of a relation in order to eliminate certain modification anomalies. These normal forms have been defined: first, second, third, Boyce-Codd, fourth, fifth, and domain-key.

**Normalization.** The process by which attributes are grouped together to form a well-structured relation.

**Null.** An unknown or unavailable attribute value.

**Object.** A named collection of properties that sufficiently describes an entity in the user's work environment.

**Object diagram.** An illustration used to document an object, its properties, and its association(s) with other objects.

**Object instance.** The representation of one particular entity.

**Object view.** The portion of an object that is visible to a particular application.

**Panel.** *See* **Form.**

**Partition.** In a distributed database, that portion of a network that is separated from the rest of the network by a failure.

**PL/I.** *Programming Language I.* A programming language used in both business and scientific applications.

**Pointer.** A link or address in one data unit (such as a segment or a record) to a related data unit.

**Precompiler.** A program that translates database commands embedded in a program into appropriate host-language instructions.

**Primary key.** An attribute or attribute group chosen as the key of a relation. *Compare to* **Candidate key.**

**Processing Interface Subsystem.** A DBMS subsystem that enables users and programs to access the database via the DBMS Engine. Includes interactive query languages, programming language interfaces, and DBMS product-specific programming languages.

**Product.** A relational operation performed on two relations, A and B, producing relation C such that C contains the concatenation of every tuple in A with every tuple in B.

**Projection.** The relational operation performed on relation A, producing relation B such that B contains only selected attributes of A.

**Property.** A characteristic of an object.

**Prototypes.** A quickly developed mock-up of something real, such as a set of menus, a data entry form, or a report. A working model.

**QBE.** *Query by Example.* A graphic database interface developed by IBM.

**R\*.** A prototype DDBMS developed by IBM.

**Real output.** Output produced by an information system for a system client.

**Referential integrity.** The condition of a database in which all inter-relation constraints are satisfied.

**Relation.** A two-dimensional table containing single-valued entries and no duplicate rows.

**Relational database.** A database structured in accordance with the relational data model.

**Relational data model.** A data model in which (1) data is stored in tables and (2) associations between tables are represented within the table data, not in overhead data structures.

**Relational schema.** A relation structure plus a definition of inter-relation constraints.

**Relationship.** An association between two entities.

**Report.** An extraction of data from a database. Report data can be printed, displayed on a computer screen, or stored on some other medium. *Compare to* **Form.**

**Run-unit.** In the CODASYL DBTG model, the execution of a program by one user.

**SAA.** *Systems Application Architecture.* An IBM plan for standardized programming, user, and communications interfaces.

**Schema.** A complete and logical view of a database.

**Screen.** *See* **Form.**

**Selection.** The relational operation performed on relation A, producing relation B such that B contains only selected rows of A.

**Set.** In the CODASYL DBTG model, a one-to-many relationship between records. The parent of the relationship is called the set *owner,* and the children are called set *members.*

**Simple network.** A collection of record types such that a child record has two or more parent records and the parents are different types.

**SQL.** *Structured Query Language.* A relational database access language developed by IBM. SQL became the ANSI database standard in 1986.

**Subschema.** A subset of a database processed by one or more applications. Also called *application view.*

**Transaction. 1.** A series of actions to be taken on a database such that either all the actions are successfully performed or the database remains unchanged. Also called *atomic transaction* and *LUW.* **2.** The record of an event that occurs in the business world.

**Tree.** A collection of record types such that each record has exactly one parent, except the root, which has no parent.

**Tuple.** A row in a relation.

**Union.** The relational operation performed on two relations, A and B, producing relation C such that C contains all the tuples of A and B minus any duplicates.

**VAR.** *Value Added Reseller.* A person or group who develops an application based on some DBMS product and then markets the package.

**View.** The subset of a database that can be accessed by an application. *See* **Subschema.**

**WYSIWYG.** *What You See Is What You Get.* A term used in reference to prototype, form, and report generators that produce an exact model of the final product.

# Bibliography

Aho, A.V., Hopcroft, E., & Ullman, J.D. *The Design and Analysis of Computer Programs.* Addison-Wesley, 1975.

ANSI X3H2. *Proposed American National Standard for a Data Definition Language for Network Structured Databases.* American National Standards Institute, 1981.

ANSI X3H2. *Overview of DBCS/Programming Language Interface.* American National Standards Institute, 1982.

Astrahan, M.M., et al. "System R: Relational Approach to Database Management." In *Transactions on Database Systems,* Vol. 1, No. 2, June 1976.

Astrahan, M.M., et al. "System R: A Relational Database Management System." In *Computer,* Vol. 12, No. 5, May 1979.

Astrahan, M.M., et al. "A History and Evaluation of System R," *IBM Research Report* RJ2843, June 1980.

Atre, S. *Data Base: Structured Techniques for Design, Performance, and Management.* John Wiley, 1980.

Bernstein, P.A., & Goodman, N. "Concurrency Control in Distributed Database Systems." In *Computing Surveys,* Vol. 13, No. 2, June 1981.

Bernstein, P.A., & Goodman, N. "An Algorithm for Concurrency Control and Recovery in Replicated Distributed Databases." In *Transactions on Database Systems,* Vol. 9, No. 4, December 1984.

Bernstein, P.A., Rothnie, J.B., & Shipman, D.W. *Distributed Data Base Management.* IEEE Catalog No. EHO 141-2, 1978.

Blasgen, M.W., et al. "System R: An Architectural Overview." In *IBM Systems Journal,* Vol. 20, No. 1, January 1981.

Boehm, B.W. *Software Engineering Economics.* Prentice-Hall, 1981.

Bohl, M. *Introduction to IBM Direct Access Storage Devices.* Science Research Associates, 1981.

Boyce, R.F., et al. "Specifying Queries as Relational Expressions: SQUARE." In *Communications of the ACM,* Vol. 18, No. 11, November 1975.

Bray, O.H. *Distributed Database Management Systems.* Lexington Books, 1982.

Britton-Lee Corporation. *IDM 500.* Britton-Lee, 1982.

Browning, D. "Data Managers and LANs." In *PC Tech Journal,* Vol. 5, No. 5, May 1987.

Cardenas, A.F. *Data Base Management Systems.* Allyn & Bacon, 1979.

Chamberlin, D.D., et al. "SEQUEL 2: A Unified Approach to Data Definition, Manipulation, and Control." In *IBM Journal of Research and Development*, Vol. 20, No. 6, November 1976.

Chen, P. "The Entity-Relationship Model: Toward a Unified View of Data." In *ACM Transactions on Database Systems*, Vol. 1., No. 1, March 1976.

Chen, P. *The Entity-Relationship Approach to Logical Data Base Design.* QED Information Sciences, Data Base Monograph Series, No. 6, 1977.

Chen, P. *Entity-Relationship Approach to Information Modeling.* E-R Institute, 1981.

Chorfas, D.N. *Databases for Networks and Minicomputers.* Petrocelli, 1982.

Chu, W.W., & Chen, P.P. *Centralized and Distributed Data Base Systems.* IEEE Catalog No. EHO 154-5, 1979.

CINCOM Systems Incorporated. *TOTAL Reference Manual.* CINCOM Systems, 1982.

CODASYL. *Data Base Task Group Report, 1971.* Association for Computing Machinery, 1975.

CODASYL COBOL Committee. *COBOL Journal of Development,* 1978.

CODASYL Data Base Administrators Working Group. *Data Structure Definition,* 1978.

CODASYL Data Description Language Committee. *DDL Journal of Development,* 1978.

Codd, E.F. "A Relational Model of Data for Large Shared Databanks." In *Communications of the ACM*, Vol. 13, No. 6, June 1970.

Codd, E.F. "Extending the Relational Model to Capture More Meaning." In *Transaction on Database Systems*, Vol. 4, No. 4, December 1979.

Codd, E.F. "Relational Database: A Practical Foundation for Productivity." In *Communications of the ACM*, Vol. 25, No. 2, February 1982.

Cortada, J.W. *EDP Costs and Charges.* Prentice-Hall, 1980.

Cullinet Corporation. *IDMS/R COBOL Programmer's Reference Manual.* Cullinet Corp., 1986.

Cullinet Corporation. *IDMS/R Logical Record Facility.* Cullinet Corp., 1986.

Cullinet Corporation. *IDMS/R Systems Overview.* Cullinet Corp., 1986.

Date, C.J. *An Introduction to Database Systems*, Third Edition. Addison-Wesley, 1981.

Davidson, S.B. "Optimism and Consistency in Partitioned Distributed Database Systems." In *Transactions on Database Systems*, Vol. 9, No. 3, September 1984.

Davidson, S.B., Garcia-Molina, H., & Skeen, D. "Consistency in Partitioned Networks." In *Computing Surveys*, Vol. 17, No. 3, September 1985.

DeMarco, T. *Structured Analysis and System Specification.* Yourdon Press, 1978.

Dolan, K. *Business Computer Systems Design.* Mitchell, 1983.

Ellzey, R.S. *Data Structures for Computer Information Systems.* Science Research Associates, 1982.

Elson, M. *Data Structures.* Science Research Associates, 1975.

Eswaran, K.P., Gray, J.N., Lorie, R.A., & Traiger, I.L. "The Notion of Consistency and Predicate Locks in a Database System." In *Communications of the ACM*, Vol. 19, No. 11, November 1976.

Ewing, J.J. "An Object-Oriented Operating System Interface." In *Conference Proceedings from the Object-Oriented Programming Systems, Languages and Applications, ACM SIGPLAN*, Vol. 21, No. 11, November 1986.

Fagin, R. "Multivalued Dependencies and a New Normal Form for Relational Databases." In *Transactions on Database Systems*, Vol. 2, No. 3, September 1977.

Fagin, R. "A Normal Form for Relational Databases that Is Based on Domains and Keys." In *Transactions on Database Systems*, Vol. 6, No. 3, September 1981.

Fernandez, E.B., Summers, R.C., & Wood, C. *Database Security and Integrity*. Addison-Wesley, 1981.

Flavin, M. *Fundamental Concepts of Information Modeling*. Yourdon Press, 1981.

Freedman, D.P., & Weinberg, G.M. *Walkthroughs, Inspections, and Technical Reviews* (3rd Ed.). Little, Brown, 1982.

Garcia-Molina, H., Pittelli, F., & Davidson, S. "Applications of Byzantine Agreement in Database Systems." In *Transactions on Database Systems*, Vol. 11, No. 1, March 1986.

Gray, J., et al. "The Recovery Manager of the System R Database Manager." In *Computing Surveys*, Vol. 13, No. 2, June 1981.

Hammer, M., & McLeod, D. "Database Description with SDM: A Semantic Database Model." In *Transactions on Database Systems*, Vol. 6, No. 3, September 1981.

Hammer, M., & Shipman, D. "Reliability Mechanisms for SDD-1: A System for Distributed Databases." In *Transactions on Database Systems*, Vol. 5, No. 4, December 1980.

Hawryszkiewycz, I.T. *Database Analysis and Design*. Science Research Associates, 1984.

Herlihy, M. "Dynamic Quorum Adjustment for Partitioned Data." In *Transactions on Database Systems*, Vol. 12, No. 2, June 1987.

Hubbard, G.U. *Computer-Assisted Data Base Design*. Van Nostrand Reinhold, 1981.

IBM Corporation. *SQL/Data System General Information*. IBM Document GH24-5012-0, 1981.

IBM Corporation. *SQL/Data System Planning and Administration*. IBM Document SH24-5014-1, 1982.

IBM Corporation. *SQL/Data System Application Programming*. IBM Document SH24-5018-1, 1982.

IBM Corporation. *System/38 Control Program Facility Concepts*. IBM Publication Number GC21-7729, 1982.

IBM Corporation. *System/38 Installation Manual-Conversion Planning*. IBM Publication Number GC21-7732, 1982.

IBM Corporation. *IBM Database 2 Relational Concepts*. IBM Document GG24-1581, 1983.

IBM Corporation. *IBM Database 2 Concepts and Facilities Guide*. IBM Document GG24-1582, 1983.

IBM Corporation. *IBM Database 2 SQL Usage Guide.* IBM Document GG24-1583, 1983.

IBM Corporation. *IBM Database 2 V1 R2 Release Guide.* IBM Document GG24-1702-0, 1986.

Inmon, W.H. *Effective Data Base Design.* Prentice-Hall, 1981.

Jackson, M.A. *Principles of Program Design.* Academic Press, 1975.

Johnson, L.F., & Cooper, R.H. *File Techniques for Data Base Organization in COBOL.* Prentice-Hall, 1981.

Kapp, D., & Leben, J.F. *IMS Programming Techniques.* Van Nostrand Reinhold, 1978.

Kim, W. "On Optimizing an SQL-Like Nested Query." In *Transactions on Database Systems,* Vol. 7, No. 3, September 1982.

Knuth, D.E. *The Art of Computer Programming: Fundamental Algorithms.* Addison-Wesley, 1968.

Knuth, D.E. *The Art of Computer Programming: Sorting and Searching.* Addison-Wesley, 1973.

Kroenke, D.M. "Developing Object-Oriented Database Applications on Microcomputers." In *Proceedings of the Second International Conference on Computers and Applications,* Beijing, June 1987.

Lamport, L. "Time, Clocks, and the Ordering of Events in a Distributed System." In *Communications of the ACM,* Vol. 21, No. 7, July 1978.

Litwin, W., & Abdellatif, A. "Multidatabase Interoperability." In *Computer,* Vol. 19, No. 12, December 1986.

Lum, V.Y., Yuen, P.S.T., & Dodd, M. "Key to Address Transform Techniques: A Fundamental Performance Study on Large Existing Formatted Files." In *Communications of the ACM,* Vol. 14, No. 4, April 1971.

Lyon, J.K. *The Database Administrator.* John Wiley, 1976.

Maier, D., Stein, J., Otis, A., & Purdy, A. "Development of an Object-Oriented DBMS." In *Conference Proceedings from the Object-Oriented Programming Systems, Languages and Applications, ACM SIGPLAN,* Vol. 21, No. 11, November 1986.

Martin, J. *Computer Data-Base Organization.* Prentice-Hall, 1975.

Microrim Corporation. *R:BASE System V User's Manual.* Microrim Corp., 1986.

Mohan, C., Lindsay, B., & Obermarck, R. "Transaction Management in the R* Distributed Database Management System." In *Transactions on Database Systems,* Vol. 11, No. 4, December 1986.

Nolan, R.L. *Managing the Data Resource Function.* West Publishing, 1974.

Oracle Corporation. *ORACLE.* Oracle Corp., 1987.

Orenstein, J.A. "Spatial Query Processing in an Object-Oriented Database System." In *ACM SIGMOD International Conference on Management of Data, 1986,* Vol. 15, No. 2, June 1986.

Orr, K.T. *Structured Systems Development.* Yourdon Press, 1977.

Orr, K.T. *Structured Requirements Definition.* Ken Orr & Associates, 1981.

Page-Jones, M. *The Practical Guide to Structured Systems Design.* Yourdon Press, 1980.

Palmer, I. *Data Base Systems: A Practical Reference.* QED Information Sciences, 1975.

Peters, L.J. *Software Design: Methods and Techniques.* Yourdon Press, 1981.

Putnam, L.H. *Software Cost Estimating and Life-Cycle Control: Getting the Software Numbers.* IEEE Catalog No. EHO 165-1, 1980.

Reisner, P. "Human Factor Studies of Database Query Languages: A Survey and Assessment." In *Computing Surveys,* Vol. 13, No. 1, March 1981.

Schaeffer, H. *Data Center Operations.* Prentice-Hall, 1981.

Skarra, A.H., & Zdonik, S.B. "The Management of Changing Types in an Object-Oriented Database." In *Conference Proceedings from the Object-Oriented Programming Systems, Languages and Applications,* ACM SIGPLAN, Vol. 21, No. 11, November 1986.

Stonebreaker, M.R., et al. "The Design and Implementation of INGRES." In *Transactions on Database Systems,* Vol. 1, No. 3, September 1976.

Traiger, I.L., Gray, J., Galtieri, C.A., & Lindsay, B.G. "Transactions and Consistency in Distributed Database Systems." In *Transactions on Database Systems,* Vol. 7, No. 3, September 1982.

Tsichritzis, D.C., & Lochovsky, F.H. *Data Models.* Prentice-Hall, 1982.

Tufts, R.J. Private correspondence, April 1982.

Ullman, J.D. *Principles of Database Systems.* Computer Science Press, 1980.

Vetter, M., & Maddison, R.N. *Database Design Methodology.* Prentice-Hall International, 1981.

Warnier, J.D. *Logical Construction of Systems.* Van Nostrand Reinhold, 1981.

Weinberg, V. *Structured Analysis.* Yourdon Press, 1978.

Welty, C., & Stemple, D.W. "Human Factors Comparison of a Procedural and a Nonprocedural Query Language." In *Transactions on Database Systems,* Vol. 6, No. 4, December 1981.

Wiederhold, G., "Views, Objects, and Databases." In *Computer,* Vol. 19, No. 12, December 1986.

Woelk, D., Kim, W., & Luther, W. "An Object-Oriented Approach to Multi-Media Databases." In *ACM SIGMOD International Conference on Management of Data, 1986,* Vol. 15, No. 2, June 1986.

Yourdon, E., & Constantine, L.L. *Structured Design.* Prentice-Hall, 1979.

Zaniolo, C., & Melkanoff, M.A. "A Formal Approach to the Definition and the Design of Conceptual Schemata for Database Systems." In *Transactions on Database Systems,* Vol. 7, No. 1, March 1982.

Zloof, M.M. "Query by Example." In *Proceedings of the National Computer Conference,* AFIPS, Vol. 44, May 1975.

# Index